A Textbook of Social Psychology

Brief Edition

J.E. Alcock
Glendon College, York University

D.W. Carment
McMaster University

S.W. Sadava
Brock University

J.E. Collins
Sheridan College

J.M. Green
Sheridan College

Prentice Hall Allyn and Bacon Canada
Scarborough, Ontario

Canadian Cataloguing in Publication Data

Main entry under title:
  A textbook of social psychology

Brief ed. of 3rd ed.

ISBN 0-13-262684-5

1. Social psychology. I. Alcock, James E.

HM251.A55 1996   302   C96-931016-1

 © 1997 Prentice-Hall Canada Inc., Scarborough, Ontario
A Division of Simon & Schuster/A Viacom Company

Prentice-Hall, Inc., Englewood Cliffs, New Jersey
Prentice-Hall International (UK) Limited, London
Prentice-Hall of Australia, Pty. Limited, Sydney
Prentice-Hall Hispanoamericana, S.A., Mexico City
Prentice-Hall of India Private Limited, New Delhi
Prentice-Hall of Japan, Inc., Tokyo
Simon & Schuster Asia Private Limited, Singapore
Editora Prentice-Hall do Brasil, Ltda., Rio de Janeiro

ISBN 0-13-262684-5

Acquisitions Editor: Rebecca Bersagel
Developmental Editor: Lisa Berland
Copy Editor: Karen Alliston
Production Editor: Amber Wallace
Production Coordinator: Deborah Starks
Permissions/Photo Research: Karen Taylor/Alene McNeill
Cover and Text Design: Petra Phillips
Cover Image: Sheila King
Page Layout: Bookman Typesetting Co.

1 2 3 4 5   CC   00 99 98 97 96

Printed and bound in USA

We welcome readers' comments, which can be sent by e-mail to
  collegeinfo_pubcanada@prenhall.com

TABLE OF CONTENTS

■ CHAPTER 5: SOCIAL INFLUENCE

■ CHAPTER 6: PREJUDICE, DISCRIMINATION, AND SEXISM

PREFACE

APPROACH TAKEN AND CRITERIA USED

Two new names (the college team) have been added to the familiar three who have provided Canadian university students with a solid introduction to social psychology since 1987 through three editions. Response to the original text tells us that its strength is in the depth and breadth of its coverage and the analysis of Canadian social issues and problems.

Social psychology is one of the most useful fields in psychology because it provides a variety of perspectives from which to view people and the way in which they interact and relate to each other. It speaks to our curiosity about our social behaviour with credible information based on research findings. In Canadian community colleges, we find that many of the questions students have about the way people understand and relate to others are the topics social psychologists typically address. In addition, many college programs emphasize the importance of interpersonal skills. Social psychology provides an interesting knowledge base from which to view and enhance these skills.

In addressing these interests and needs of college students, we are pleased to present the first Canadian social psychology textbook written by Canadian college and university professors for Canadian students. This text is smaller and shorter than the university text. However, every effort has been made to maintain the integrity of the original work. There is one less chapter, a change accomplished by combining material into one chapter that had been discussed previously in two. We resisted the idea of combining the three applied chapters, as we believe the topics merit individual attention.

This college edition is designed for one-semester social psychology courses in Canadian community colleges. In it, research, theory, and application are integrated in a format that college students will find comprehensible, interesting, and challenging. Both writing style and content are designed to be easily understood with a minimal background in psychology. We hope this edition will provide college students, as the original text has university students, with a solid and stimulating introduction to social psychology. As with the original text, research is international in scope, and examples are drawn largely from the Canadian experience—for example, bilingualism, justice, and health issues.

ACKNOWLEDGMENTS

This text is the result of a truly collaborative effort. The order of the authors' names is alphabetical with the senior authors who wrote the longer edition appearing first.

We are indebted to our developmental editors Lisa Berland and Karen Sacks whose vision of excellence, from start to finish, kept us moving forward. A special acknowledgment is due to Karen Alliston who edited the text with such thoroughness and tact. We wish to express particular gratitude to Amber Wallace and Valerie Adams, production editors, for putting it all together with such style. Our appreciation is also extended to Karen Taylor and Alene McNeill who helped out at a crucial moment and to Petra Phillips, the designer, for the wonderful visual presentation. We are delighted that Sheila King has produced such a beautiful piece of artwork for the cover. Of course, none of this would have been possible if Charmaine Sherlock had not approached us or without the efforts of our acquisitions editors, Marjorie Munroe who believed the book should be written and began the process, and Rebecca Bersagel who saw us through to the end. Thank you.

We would also like to express our appreciation to the reviewers who offered so many helpful suggestions: Gary Bonczak, Sir Sandford Fleming College; Jacquie Bowery, Confederation College; Rosalie Hawrylko, Capilano College; Pepi Lucas, Centennial College; Beverly McLeod, Mount Royal College; Sara Pawson, Kwantlen College.

FEATURES

- Chapters on contemporary social issues, such as those relating to law, the environment, and health. These make the text especially adaptable to a variety of different college programs. For example, the chapter on health and illness is particularly useful for students in health care programs, while the chapter on justice is especially relevant for those in law and security programs. Teachers who happen to teach social psychology in several programs during a semester can select the most appropriate chapters while using the same textbook for all programs.

- Examples drawn from significant Canadian political, historical, and social events. These examples illustrate concepts and facilitate their application to everyday life. Many of the chapters begin with vignettes that pique curiosity about the topics covered.

- Marginal definitions of terms and focus questions at the point where concepts are introduced in the text. These help students to check their understanding of concepts. Teachers can easily direct students to these highly visible explanations and questions.

- Chapter summaries of key points at the end of every chapter. These summaries provide a quick review and also help students identify topics that need more study.

- Definitions of key terms at the end of the book.

- Self-diagnostics integrated within the test at the ends of sections and chapters so that students can monitor their ongoing comprehension. Answers to questions are provided. Students do not need to spend money for a separate study guide.

- Photographs, figures, and tables, which clearly illustrate the text, are integrated with the text.

- Text boxes, which illustrate topics or introduce related topics or applications, are included in every chapter.

- References to video clips of relevance to the text are provided to enhance use of the CBC video supplement available to instructors.

- Suggestions for further reading are found at the end of every chapter. Each suggestion includes a brief description indicating how the suggested material relates to topics in the chapter.

- A brief section at the end of every chapter, entitled "Issues and Activities," which includes thought-provoking questions on controversial issues and activities for students.

- NFB video to accompany text discussion in Chapter 6.

ORGANIZATION

The text is divided into four main sections. These sections are organized around the following themes: (1) an introduction to social psychology; (2) social thinking and social influence; (3) social relations and interactions with others; and (4) contemporary social issues.

The introduction (Chapter 1) discusses what social psychology is and what it is not, as well as its relation to other disciplines. This section also includes an overview of research strategies used in social psychology, including a consideration of the usefulness of the scientific method for understanding human social behaviour and the ethical concerns involved in conducting social psychological research. Chapter 1 focuses on topics and issues that will help students understand the rest of the book.

The second section includes Chapters 2 to 5. This section begins with a consideration of how we view ourselves and the social world around us, and of how we communicate with others. These are topics of fundamental interest to college students. Included in Chapter 3 is a section on bilingualism, which is of particular relevance to Canadian students. The section concludes with a discussion of how we form and change our attitudes, and influence the attitudes and behaviours of others.

In the third section, the chapters focus on a variety of topics concerned with our relations and interactions with others. It includes positive elements such as prosocial behaviour, and interpersonal attraction and interpersonal relations, as well as negative elements such as prejudice and discrimination, and aggression and violence. In this section we explore the application of social psychological principles to the richness and complexity of human experience. The chapters in this section may be covered in any order.

Finally, there are three applied chapters on areas of contemporary social concern: justice, the physical environment, and health and illness. While these chapters may have particular relevance to specific college programs, the topics are covered in a manner designed to make them generally appealing. All or parts of these chapters may be covered in any order according to the interests of students or requirements of particular programs.

SUPPLEMENTS

- Instructor's Manual, including suggestions for teaching and resources to be used.
- Test Item File, including multiple-choice, short answer, and essay questions.
- Video clips from recent CBC programs.
- NFB video to accompany text discussion in Chapter 6.

PICTURE/VISUAL CREDITS

CARTOON CREDITS

A Textbook of Social Psychology

Brief Edition

INTRODUCING SOCIAL PSYCHOLOGY

We cannot live only for ourselves. A thousand fibers connect us with our fellow men . . .

Herman Melville

Esau asked, "What was the meaning of all the company that I have met?"

■ LEARNING OUTCOMES

1. Knowledge about how social psychology is similar to and different from other disciplines.

2. An understanding of the basic nature of scientific inquiry.

3. Knowledge about the principal methods of research in social psychology and their strengths and weaknesses.

4. An appreciation for the ethical issues that can arise in social psychological research.

5. Knowledge about different perspectives in social psychology.

6. An appreciation for the usefulness of the scientific method for addressing human problems as demonstrated by examples from applied social psychology.

■ FOR REFLECTION

• Can social psychology be a science?

• What is a good experiment?

• Is it ethical to deceive subjects during an experiment or to cause them distress?

■ CHAPTER OUTLINE

"Absence makes the heart grow fonder"; "Out of sight, out of mind"; "Dress for success"; "Power corrupts—absolute power corrupts absolutely"; "First impressions last"; "Opposites attract"; "Actions speak louder than words."

All of these familiar expressions contain common sense ideas about social behaviour, and constitute our "naive psychology" which has grown out of generations of experience. Think about testing them critically. Which is right: "Out of sight out of mind" or "Absence makes the heart grow fonder"? Can we find historical evidence, or could we demonstrate in group experiments, that leaders who have greater personal power tend to act in a corrupt way? If we were to control for other influences, would people who dress in a certain way meet with measurably greater success? Social psychology begins with the "stuff" of common experience and applies the methods of science to build valid and verifiable explanations or **theories** of social behaviour (see Box 1-1).

theory *A set of statements and assumptions that link concepts and hypotheses to observations.*

What do social psychologists study?

WHAT SOCIAL PSYCHOLOGY IS AND WHAT IT IS NOT

Social psychology is the discipline that sets out to understand how the thoughts, feelings, and behaviours of individuals are influenced by the actual, imagined, or implied presence of others (Allport, 1935). What does this definition tell us about social psychology? First, social psychologists study not only actual, observable behaviour, but also what can be inferred about the inner lives of people: how they feel; their attitudes, opinions, and ideologies; how they form impressions and try to make sense of their world. Second, human experience is understood in terms of the influence of other people. Obviously social influence is not the only kind; we may be affected by our physical health, physical aspects of weather, what we have learned, our brain and nervous system processes, psychotic and drug states, hormones, or what we have eaten. However, social psychologists focus on the vital role of social influences and social relationships. Finally, the definition tells us that people are influenced by other people even if they are not immediately present. We are aware of belonging to certain family, occupational, and cultural groups. We are aware of liking, loving, or feeling responsible for certain people in our lives. And we are profoundly influenced by these groups in our thoughts and actions.

To better appreciate the range of phenomena studied by social psychologists, let us consider the following examples:

(1) Concern is often expressed about the level of violence in hockey, from the "peewee" league to the National Hockey League. Human **aggression** is an area of substantial research in social psychology.

(2) In a highly competitive economic situation, a job interview can be decisive. Social psychologists have studied **how first impressions are formed** and how people act to influence or **manage the impression** others have of them.

(3) Amnesty International has documented the physical torture routinely used in many countries. For the most part, those who practise torture are not unusually sadistic by nature but simply **obedient** to the instructions of authority. A series of important experiments has been conducted on **obedience to authority**.

Social psychologists study not only actual, observable behaviour, but also what can be inferred about the inner lives of people: how they feel, their attitudes, opinions, and ideologies.

(4) A large proportion of all marriages in North America will eventually end in divorce. **Social attraction** and the evolution of **intimate relationships** are areas of current, intensive research.

(5) While Québécois entrepreneurs move into the North American, English-speaking business milieu, English Canadian parents in unprecedented numbers enrol their children in French immersion programs. There has been extensive research on the social aspects of **bilingualism**.

BOX 1-1

FROM COMMON SENSE TO RESEARCH HYPOTHESIS

Consider another old saying: Familiarity breeds contempt. That is, the more familiar we become with people or things, the less attractive they become to us. Even when two people are familiar enough to marry, we know that the honeymoon will eventually end and that it will be difficult, if not impossible, to recapture the magic of that early stage.

The saying also seems to hold true of objects and places: we often feel bored, with an "itch to travel" or for a "change of scenery."

And yet, there are many events in our experience which do not demonstrate that "familiarity breeds contempt." Consider the following:

(1) Students tend to feel rather uncomfortable in class in the first days of the new school year, particularly if they don't know many other students. As the course goes on, they feel more and more comfortable and positive about the experience, even though they may not have interacted with many classmates. The people, the professors, the lecture room all seem familiar now. The same experience often occurs with people who commute daily to work by bus or train, immersed in their newspapers or daydreams but comfortable with the "familiar strangers" beside them, as Stanley Milgram has called them.

(2) The Eiffel Tower is one of the best known and loved physical landmarks. When it was first built in 1889 for the World Fair, it was almost universally detested by the citizens of Paris who felt that France had lost its position as a cultural leader (Harrison, 1977). Similar reactions first greeted the construction of Toronto's distinctive City Hall. Eventually, residents of both cities developed a strong sense of pride in these monuments as symbols of their civic identity.

(3) In recent years, many radio stations have switched from a "Top Twenty" format, in which new music is aired, to a format in which only familiar and popular music from the present and recent past is played.

(4) Another familiar common-sense expression assures us that "there's no place like home."

The once-controversial Toronto City Hall.

Certainly no place is as familiar as home.

How can we subject the principle that "familiarity breeds contempt" to experimental test? Zajonc (1968a) conducted a series of controlled experiments in which he varied the number of times different groups of subjects were exposed to certain stimuli. In one such experiment, subjects were shown a series of photographs from a university yearbook. Some of the faces were repeatedly shown, as often as 25 times, while others were shown only once or twice.

Subjects were considerably more favourable to the faces seen more frequently. On a scale of 1–4, subjects rated photographs seen once as 2.8 and those seen 25 times as 3.7. In other experiments by Zajonc, the same was found to be true for other stimuli, including Chinese alphabet characters, foreign words, and the frequency with which names of cities, flowers, trees, and vegetables occur naturally in speech.

In later chapters, consideration will be given to more of the research on this "mere exposure effect," when and why it occurs, what it means, and what other factors influence our like or dislike of someone or something.

(6) From 1989 until 1992, Canadian political leaders debated and squabbled over the implementation of the Meech Lake Accord. When the Accord died, they debated and squabbled some more until they reached agreement in the form of the Charlottetown Accord. These circumstances reflect **conflict** and **negotiation**, which have been researched extensively by social psychologists.

(7) In the 1992 referendum campaign, Canadians were bombarded by information aimed at convincing them to vote for, or vote against, the provisions of the Charlottetown Accord. **Persuasion** and **attitude change**, phenomena studied by social psychologists, had much to do with the historical event.

(8) In the 1995 Quebec referendum campaign, Canadians became more aware of the differences in self-perception and attitudes of those who favoured the NO versus those who favoured the YES campaigns. **Self-perception** and the **perception of others and of events in the social world** are areas of intensive research.

(9) Society has become more concerned with the protection and rehabilitation of the victims of sexual and other crimes. Research on **social cognition** has shed light on their experience and how they might best be helped.

(10) **Prejudice**, a continuing problem in human societies, has also endured as a topic of research in social psychology.

(11) Many trials are decided by the credibility of a key witness. Social psychologists have studied **eye witness testimony** and other aspects of the legal system.

(12) Why people differ in the extent to which they engage in health behaviour and comply with recommendations from health professionals is also of interest to social psychological researchers.

As you can see, social psychologists study a wide range of social phenomena. To clarify what social psychology is and what it is not, let us compare it with other areas of psychology and with other disciplines. Social psychology shares with other areas of psychology a **focus on the individual**. In particular, there is considerable overlap in the interests of social psychology and the study of personality. However, the study of personality is directed towards individual differences in the way people think, feel, or act, and above all emphasizes factors operating within individuals. Social psychology, by contrast, looks at the situational factors that cause people in general to behave in certain ways. Thus, for example, while personality psychologists study the characteristics of those people who tend to behave aggressively, social psychologists also investigate situations in which people are likely to behave aggressively. Of course, behaviour is determined by both person and environment, and students of social psychology must understand both types of influences.

Social psychology also shares many areas of interest with other social sciences, especially sociology (the study of society and social institutions) and anthropology (the study of human culture). Major differences are found in each discipline's **basic unit of analysis and level of explanation**. The usual focus of study in these other social sciences is the large group, institution, or custom (e.g. the school, social class structure). The rate or typical pattern of behaviour is also of concern. By contrast, social psychology focuses on the individual, or at most, a small group. Sociologists and anthropologists generally explain phenomena in terms of such external characteristics as class mobility, customs of parental discipline, and the distribution of power in society. Social psychologists generally **explain the behaviour of individuals in terms of specific sit-**

How is social psychology similar to and different from other related disciplines?

uations as well as **psychological processes** such as attitudes, emotional states, or perception of cause and effect.

Both psychology and sociology have subdisciplines called "social psychology," which have subject areas in common but differ in research methods, theories, and theoretical orientation. Psychological social psychologists frequently do laboratory experiments, while sociological social psychologists often rely on participant observation, in which the researcher actually joins the institution or group and describes it from the inside. And while most social psychologists in sociology work within the framework of **symbolic interactionism** (how people come to attach meaning to experience through interaction with other persons), within the field of psychology, social psychologists study the cognitive processes within individuals by which they try to make sense of their world.

SELF-TEST QUESTIONS

SELF ? TEST

1. Social psychology is concerned with

a) individual differences in the way people think, feel, or act

b) situational factors that cause people in general to behave in certain ways

c) the study of large groups, institutions, or customs

d) explaining behaviour in terms of external characteristics such as class mobility and the distribution of power in society

2. The idea that we need to look at factors within the individual in order to understand behaviour is characteristic of

a) the cognitive perspective

b) behaviourism

c) social modelling theory

d) reinforcement theory

3. The behaviourist perspective in social psychology emphasizes

a) the importance of how individuals perceive their environment

b) the small group approach to understanding behaviour

c) that our beliefs, feelings, and behaviour are influenced by external reinforcement

d) the importance of individual differences

RESEARCH METHODS IN SOCIAL PSYCHOLOGY

For most people "science" describes specific fields of study (physics, geology, biology), impressive laboratory technology, and precise measurement. It may seem surprising that a field such as social psychology can be "scientific." How can the study of violence, helping, leadership, bilingual communication, impression formation, and attitudes be "scientific" in the sense that research into the mysteries of the atom, origins of rocks, or the human cell is scientific? Yet the scientific method is arguably even more important in a field where it is difficult to quantify data, because it is in such areas of study that the vulnerability to fuzzy

model *A mini-theory or set of propositions and assumptions about a specific phenomenon.*

behaviourism *A theoretical orientation based on the premise that all behaviour is governed by external reinforcement.*

What purposes do theories serve in social psychology?

social learning theory *The view that learning can occur as a result of watching other people and the consequences of their behaviours.*

cognitive perspective *Psychological perspective that focuses on how we process, store, and retrieve information.*

independent variable *A condition in an experiment that is manipulated by the experimenter.*

experimental group *Group that receives the treatment variable.*

control group *Group in an experiment which does not receive the treatment variable and whose behaviour serves as a basis for comparison.*

extraneous variable *A factor not included in the design of the study, and which influences the study's outcome.*

dependent variable *A measured outcome in an experiment.*

and erroneous thinking is greatest. However, it is not nearly so straightforward to apply the scientific method to social behaviour as it is to apply it to the realm of inanimate objects or biological processes. In this section, after a brief description of the nature and role of theory in social psychology, we will survey the research strategies used by social psychologists.

THEORY IN SOCIAL PSYCHOLOGY

Because social psychology is a comparatively young discipline and because human social behaviour is so complex, no single or grand theory has yet emerged. Indeed, so much of what we loosely refer to as "theory" in social psychology is not really theory in the sense that the term is used in the natural sciences. Our **theories** are more like **models**, usually built upon a loosely related set of assumptions. As we will see in subsequent chapters, various mini-theories or models have been developed to account for specific phenomena, such as leadership or aggressive behaviour.

While social psychologists have developed theories from a variety of viewpoints, two major perspectives have dominated: behaviourist and cognitive. The **behaviourist** perspective has led social psychologists to search for environmental or situational factors that influence behaviour. For example, researchers working within this perspective have explained the influence of film and television on aggression in terms of **social learning theory**, which states that we can learn by watching how other people act and by observing the consequences of their behaviours. By contrast, psychologists working within the **cognitive perspective** focus on the role of internal cognitive processes in behaviour. For example, they have developed attribution theories that are concerned with how people explain the reasons for behaviour in everyday life.

As in other areas of psychology, theories in social psychology are used to generate ideas for research and to provide a framework for organizing related research findings. We will turn now to an overview of the research strategies commonly used by social psychologists.

THE EXPERIMENTAL METHOD

When researchers are interested in drawing causal inferences about how variables influence one another, they use experimental designs because these afford the greatest opportunity for control. (See Box 1-2 for an illustration of the importance of control.) Using the experimental method, the researcher deliberately assigns subjects randomly to two (or more) groups and applies a treatment variable (**independent variable**) to one group (**experimental group**) but not the other (**control group**). Care is taken to exclude other factors (**extraneous variables**) that might interfere with the outcome. Then the researcher measures the effect of the treatment by comparing the performance of the two groups on some behavioural variable of interest (**dependent variable**). For example, suppose the researcher is interested in the effects of sleep deprivation on aggression. Subjects in one group might be asked to go without sleep for 24 hours, while subjects in the other would be allowed their usual amount of sleep. In this case, the amount of sleep deprivation is the independent variable manipulated by the researcher. The group asked to go without sleep for 24 hours is the experimental group. The group allowed the usual amount of sleep is the control group. Subsequently, the subjects could be assessed for the amount of aggression displayed. This measure is the dependent variable. If those who went without sleep were generally found to be more aggressive than those in the other group, the researcher could conclude that lack of sleep caused the greater aggressiveness, since the two groups of subjects were otherwise treated the same.

In this experiment, if the subjects who were required to go without sleep drank a lot of coffee to stay awake, their caffeine consumption could possibly be responsible for any effects observed. In that case, caffeine consumption would be an extraneous variable. Of course, it is important to make sure at the beginning of the experiment that one group is not more aggressive than the other. Random assignment of subjects (discussed below) is one way to ensure that groups start out equal.

Social psychologists use different types of experiments, depending on the nature of the phenomena they are interested in investigating. In the pages that follow, three different types of experiments are discussed: laboratory experiments, field experiments, and quasi-experiments. We will see some of the advantages and disadvantages of each of these types.

How are cause-effect relationships investigated by the experimental method?

THE LABORATORY EXPERIMENT

Most social psychological experiments are conducted in a laboratory setting. Apart from the obvious convenience, there are compelling reasons to bring behaviour into the laboratory for careful scrutiny. First, it is very difficult to carry out experiments in a natural setting for it is not always possible to eliminate extraneous variables, and sometimes it is difficult even to foresee what the potential sources of such variables might be. For example, in the experiment on aggression described above, eliminating all the factors other than sleep deprivation which might influence aggression would be extremely difficult in a natural setting. Second, since social behaviour is complex, it is usually necessary to reduce it to its component parts and study each of them in turn in order to understand the ways in which several variables interact to determine behaviour.

However, there are several drawbacks to the laboratory experiment. Although the experiment seems straightforward enough, it is actually complex. There are a number of considerations that must be taken into account in order to ensure that the results are not misleading. Some of the major concerns include the procedure used to assign subjects to experimental conditions, the possibility of un-

BOX 1-2

THE IMPORTANCE OF CONTROLS

Control groups are essential to the evaluation of causal relationships, as this anecdote about the assessment of surgical procedures, recounted by a physician, makes clear: "One day when I was a junior medical student, a very important Boston surgeon visited the school and delivered a great treatise on a large number of patients who had undergone successful operations for vascular reconstruction. At the end of the lecture, a young student at the back of the room timidly asked, 'Do you have any controls?' Well, the great surgeon drew himself up to his full height, hit the desk, and said, 'Do you mean did I not operate on half of the patients?' The hall grew very quiet then. The voice at the back of the room very hesitantly replied, 'Yes, that's what I had in mind.' Then the visitor's fist really came down as he thundered, 'Of course not. That would have doomed half of them to their death.' God, it was quiet then, and one could scarcely hear the small voice ask, 'Which half?'" (Peacock, 1972)

randomization
Assignment of subjects by chance to various experimental conditions.

wanted experimenter or subject effects, and whether the experiment has realism and validity.

(1) *Randomization.* Usually, experimenters assign subjects to groups, using a **randomization** procedure such as a random numbers table or rolls of dice. This is done to minimize the individual differences that might otherwise influence results, making evaluation of the independent variable impossible. Most of the time, this is a satisfactory method. The problem is that experimenters are not always aware of those times when it is not satisfactory. In addition to randomly assigning subjects, researchers use statistical procedures to evaluate data which take into account the possibility that differences observed could have arisen by chance at the time of the assignment into groups.

(2) *Experimenter and subject effects.* Although both experimenters and subjects may be well-intentioned, they may unwittingly engage in behaviours that bias results. Experimenters may unintentionally provide cues indicating behaviours expected in relation to the hypothesis. Cues that give subjects ideas, correct or incorrect, about the hypothesis under investigation are called demand characteristics. The helpful or compliant subject may respond in a manner which supports the perceived hypothesis (Adair, 1973). To avoid this situation, blind and double-blind techniques may be used. When the subjects are unaware of which group they belong to (they are **blind**), they cannot act to support the experimenter's hypothesis even though they know what it is. When the experimenter who interacts with subjects is also unaware of the subjects' group (the **double-blind** situation), then he or she cannot react to subjects differently, based on whether they are in the experimental or control group.

blind technique
Experimental strategy in which subjects are unaware of the group to which they belong.

double-blind *A control in research whereby neither the subject nor the experimenter who interacts with the subject knows to which condition the subject has been assigned.*

(3) *Realism and validity.* Much concern has been expressed over the narrowness and lack of realism in many social psychological experiments. Perhaps, the criticism goes, the behaviour has little to do with what occurs in the "real world." In a study of aggressiveness, if a subject really believes he or she is causing pain to another subject (**experimental realism**), then the results of such a study should generalize to other situations where people have a similar belief, quite apart from how contrived the experimental situation is. **External validity** refers to the degree to which the behaviour observed in the laboratory corresponds to "real" behaviour in the outside world. For example, subjects in an experiment may comply with instructions that they think will result in causing pain to others simply because they were asked to do so. In the real world people sometimes justify the harm they do to others in terms of obeying orders. When external validity is high, researchers can generalize from the laboratory situation to life outside the laboratory. However, it is important to remember that research findings do not necessarily apply beyond the culture or subculture from which the subjects were drawn.

experimental realism
Extent to which the situation encountered in an experiment involves subjects in such a way that they react naturally.

external validity *Degree to which findings from a laboratory can be generalized in order to predict how the subject would act in the real world.*

THE FIELD EXPERIMENT

field experiment
Experiment conducted in a natural setting in which subjects do not know that they are participating in an experiment.

One way to increase external validity is through the **field experiment**, an experiment run not in the laboratory but the "real world." As in a laboratory experiment, two or more groups of subjects are formed (one of which is a control group), and the experimenter manipulates an independent variable. The main difference between a laboratory and a field experiment is that subjects in a field experiment have no idea that research is being conducted or that their behaviour is being monitored. The subjects are those who happen to be in a given location at that moment. An example of a field experiment is provided by Doob and Gross (1968). They studied whether frustration leads to aggression in a naturalistic setting. They examined what happened when a driver (a confederate) stalled at a traffic light, using horn honking as a measure of aggression. Social status of the driver was a second independent variable, which they manipulated by having the confederate drive a high or low status car. They found, as expected, that drivers behaved more aggressively (honked more) towards low status drivers.

Despite the obvious advantages of the field experiment with regard to external validity, it has one important shortcoming: the field situation makes it more difficult to control or eliminate extraneous variables. Whether this "trade-off" between extraneous variables and external validity is worthwhile must be evaluated carefully in advance of each situation.

THE QUASI-EXPERIMENT

Sometimes events in the real world provide the opportunity to study the effects of naturally occurring changes in some social psychological variables of interest. For example, if a researcher were interested in studying whether spot check programs are associated with reduced drinking, he or she could compare the amount of drinking in a community before and after the institution of such a program. There are several designs used in **quasi-experiments**. The example just described has a single group pre-test/post-test design. The major advantage of a quasi-experiment is that it allows the researcher to study the effects of powerful manipulations that the researcher cannot produce. Its major disadvantage is that, strictly speaking, conclusions about cause and effect are not possible.

NON-EXPERIMENTAL METHODS

Non-experimental methods involve data collection without the manipulation of an independent variable. For example, simply observing people in a natural setting can provide a great deal of information about behaviour. The difference between casual observation by a lay person and observation by a social psychological researcher is that while the lay person depends on his or her direct experience, the social psychologist relies upon systematic observation, usually under conditions that allow for the control of variables which might otherwise interfere with such observation. There are a number of different non-empirical research methods that may be employed, including the archival, case study, survey method, and field study approaches. These strategies are described briefly in the following paragraphs.

THE ARCHIVAL APPROACH

Sometimes it is convenient for researchers to use data that has already been collected for other purposes. For example, with respect to the impact of spot check programs on drinking patterns, we might start an investigation by examining existing data from countries where there are year-round spot checks for impaired driving. We could then compare their per capita rate of alcohol consumption to that in countries not using spot checks to see if these rates support the hypothesis that police roadside checks lead to less alcohol use.

The **archival approach** has several important advantages. It allows researchers to study large populations over an expanse of time and events that could not be studied by other means. It eliminates the time, effort, and expense of data collection. However, a disadvantage of this strategy is that the researcher's choice

quasi-experiment A field study of the effects of some naturally occurring event or change.

What is the main difference between experimental and non-experimental methods?

What are the main non-experimental methods? How do researchers describe behaviour using these methods?

archival approach Research strategy that uses data already collected for other purposes.

of variables is limited by whatever data has been published. In addition, the researcher cannot draw conclusions about whether there is a causal relationship between variables.

CASE STUDIES

case study In-depth analysis and investigation of a single case.

The **case study** is an in-depth investigation and analysis of a single instance of a phenomenon of interest. Such a study, which might focus on a single individual, group of people, or specific event, is often the only way of studying a phenomenon which is rare and which cannot be duplicated in the laboratory. For example, in an examination of the effects of spot checks on alcohol consumption, the case study approach might involve in-depth interviews with people who have been convicted of impaired driving in the past, examining in detail the importance they give such checks as an influence on their drinking behaviour.

The major advantage of the case study approach is that it allows for intensive investigation of a phenomenon in a specific instance and lets us follow the development of the phenomenon over time. Case studies are often excellent starting points for research in that they can generate hypotheses which can then be explored in more detail by other means.

On the other hand, case studies have drawbacks. The case we study may not be a typical one. The people's accounts may be inaccurate or distorted; their memory may be biased. They may provide the information that they think the researcher wants to hear or that they consider appropriate for some other reason. Like other non-experimental methods, case studies do not allow for conclusions about cause and effect.

SURVEY METHOD

survey Technique for collecting data by questioning a representative random sample of people.

This method involves going out and asking questions about the phenomenon of interest. The structured interview is one of a variety of survey techniques. Using a series of questions that have been carefully chosen and listed in a specific order, the interviewer poses each question to the respondent and records the answer. Another survey technique is the questionnaire, in which the respondent is asked to give written responses to a set of printed questions. An advantage of the questionnaire is that it does not require the time and effort that must go into interviews. A large amount of data can be gathered quickly and inexpensively. The survey method is especially useful for collecting data from a large number of people and is often the only way of obtaining data about thoughts, feelings, and private behaviour not open to direct observation. (The CBC video shows the steps involved in conducting election polls.) However, like other methods discussed in this section, the survey provides information about interrelationships among variables of interest and cannot directly establish whether or not one variable causes another. (See the cartoon for problems associated with conducting surveys.)

FIELD STUDY

field study Direct observation of people in a natural setting.

The **field study** involves direct observation of the spontaneous behaviour of a group of people in a natural setting; for example, the systematic observation of people attending New Year's Eve parties. Data may be recorded by means of audiotape or videotape, or by manually recording various behaviours by shorthand (and so "coding" the behaviours of interest). A field study can take one of two forms: either the observer remains aloof and simply observes, or he or

"And four per cent of the respondents had handwriting so bad we have no idea what they thought."

she becomes a participant observer, mixing with the group in as unobtrusive a way as possible. **Participant observation** is the traditional approach of the anthropologist who lives among the people he or she wishes to study, usually for periods of a year or more.

However, we are never sure just how typical the situation is that we are studying. The researcher's behaviour can influence the behaviours observed. And working in close proximity with people of interest, often over a considerable period of time, makes it difficult to remain unbiased.

In summary, non-experimental methods are useful for gathering information about what goes on in real-life situations. However, such information, while useful for generating hypotheses for further research, can offer a biased picture of reality. The most serious shortcoming of non-experimental methods is the inability to demonstrate causal relationships among variables of interest.

CORRELATIONAL APPROACH

Sometimes researchers are interested in behaviours which for ethical reasons they would not want to manipulate. For example, a researcher might be interested in whether watching many television programs containing violent and aggressive themes causes children to act aggressively and to grow up to become aggressive adults. In this case, we would not want to subject youngsters to an experience that we expect will lead to undesirable behaviour. Nor would we want to wait for children to grow up in order to finally test whether such TV viewing causes aggressive behaviour. **Correlational research** allows us to investigate whether variables of interest (in this case TV viewing of violence and aggressive behaviour) are related. Note also that correlational studies focus on behavioural stabilities while experimental studies, by their very nature, focus on behavioural change. Powerful statistical techniques are emerging for analysis of correlational data that allow causal inferences to be drawn, though not with the clarity obtained in experimental settings.

participant observation *Study in which observations are made by a researcher who mixes in unobtrusively with the group being studied.*

How does correlational research differ from experimental and descriptive research?

correlation *Extent to which scores on one measure are predictable by scores on another measure.*

13

CROSS-CULTURAL RESEARCH

Social psychology has been justifiably criticized for biased sampling in research. University students are the most available and, therefore, typical subjects in social psychological experiments. And because most social psychology research

has been conducted in the United States, it follows that most experiments have been carried out on U.S. college students. Yet there is no particular reason to assume that such subjects are representative of people in general everywhere. The findings of any experiment are much more convincing if they can be replicated with diverse populations.

Thus the case can be made for **cross-cultural research** in which social psychological experiments are carried out in a number of different cultures (Triandis and Brislin, 1980; Kagitçibasi and Berry, 1989; Berry, Poortinga, Segall and Dasen, 1992). Such studies often involve close collaboration among social psychologists of many nations.

Cross-cultural research is difficult to do for a number of reasons. Replicating a study designed for one culture in another culture can be exceptionally challenging. Research methods may be difficult to adapt. Verbal instructions, interviews, or questionnaires must be translated into other languages, and the translations must be accurate and equivalent in the nuances of meaning. Content that is appropriate for one culture may not be suitable for another. Situations may also have different meanings in different cultures, confounding the experimental results.

In spite of these and other problems, cooperative research across cultures is valuable, particularly in showing us how far our theories can be generalized. Berry (1978) argues for the development of many distinctive, local social psychologies, each studying problems as defined by that particular culture. Taken collectively, they may furnish the basis for the development of a truly universal social psychology.

Most research in social psychology has been conducted with university undergraduates. What implications does this have for external validity?

Why is cross-cultural research valuable? Why is it difficult to do?

SELF-TEST QUESTIONS

4. **An experimenter studied helping behaviour in rural and urban populations. Helping behaviour was the**
   a) independent variable
   b) operational definition

c) *extraneous variable*

d) *dependent variable*

5. Which of these methods might allow the researcher to draw causal inferences?

a) *field studies*

b) *archival method*

c) *case studies*

d) *experimental method*

6. In which of the following situations would a quasi-experiment be most appropriate?

a) *when a large population is studied over a long time*

b) *when a phenomenon is studied in depth*

c) *when a naturally occurring phenomenon is used as the independent variable*

d) *when control is necessary over extraneous variables*

7. If two variables decrease in a more or less regular fashion (e.g. a decrease in temperature and a decrease in the eating of ice cream), they are

a) *positively correlated*

b) *statistically significant*

c) *causally related*

d) *negatively correlated*

8. Extraneous variables refer to

a) *variables that the experimenter chooses to discard*

b) *variables that the experimenter did not consider which may have had an influence on the experiment*

c) *dependent variables that are measured*

d) *independent variables that are manipulated*

ETHICAL CONSIDERATIONS IN RESEARCH

As we have seen, the researcher who carries out a psychology experiment is in a position of some authority over the subject. This authority, especially if accompanied by a difference of status conferred by age or academic position, creates a relationship of trust. The subjects have the right to assume that the experimenter will not harm or exploit them. It is the researcher's responsibility to conduct research in an ethically responsible manner so that participants in the research do not suffer in any way as a result.

Sometimes ethical problems arise not because of what is done to subjects, but because of what is *not* done. This occurs most often in medical research: do researchers have the right to assign disease sufferers to a control group if they are

Why are codes of ethics necessary when doing research?

studying a drug that could halt the progress of a deadly disease such as AIDS? If research proves the drug useful, some of those in the control group who were denied the treatment may indeed have died as a result. On the other hand, without controlled studies, how can we determine if a treatment is effective and without serious risks?

While such a dilemma rarely arises in social psychological research, it does occur from time to time. For example, Langer and Rodin (1976) compared an experimental and a control group of elderly residents in a nursing home and found that those in the experimental group (who were encouraged to take part in decision-making and thus live somewhat more independently) showed considerable improvement in alertness, activity, and general well-being. While 93 percent of those in the experimental group showed overall improvement, 71 percent of the control group were judged to have become more debilitated over the period of the study. A subsequent study (Rodin and Langer, 1977) showed that during the 18-month period that followed the intervention, 15 percent of the subjects in the responsibility-induced group died, compared with 30 percent of those in the comparison condition.

Without the research, the importance of participation in decision-making would not be evident, yet in retrospect, we may regret that those in the control condition became more debilitated or even died, when they might have benefited from being in the experimental condition.

Professional codes of ethics for people in the medical profession go back at least 2500 years to the Hippocratic Oath, a version of which is still imposed upon graduating physicians today. It requires physicians to be responsible to their art and to their colleagues on the one hand, and to protect the interests of their patients on the other. The latter aspect of the oath involves two famous principles: that the physician should do no harm, and that confidentiality must be observed.

Psychologists have developed their own codes of ethics, both to govern the application of psychology, as in clinical psychology, and the use of subjects, both human and animal, in research. These codes involve concern for the welfare of society, respect for science and psychology and, of course, the welfare of the subject or client. The American Psychological Association (1992) has drawn up a set of principles directly aimed at the conduct of research involving human subjects. The code of ethics of the Canadian Psychological Association, which is general enough to apply to research as well as applied practice, is built around four primary ethical principles (Sinclair, Poizner, Gilmour-Barrett and Randall, 1987): respect for the dignity of the person, responsibility to society, integrity in relationships, and responsible caring. Although the fourth principle may be pertinent to applied psychology, all of them have something to say about how we should treat people who come under our influence, whether as clients, patients, or subjects in an experiment.

All research methods involving human subjects give rise to ethical concerns. Although the laboratory experiment is often cited when research ethics are discussed, the use of unobtrusive measures in the world outside the laboratory also produces many ethical problems (Wiesenthal, 1974). Among the ethical concerns that researchers have to cope with, protection from harm, the right to privacy, the practice of deception, and the need for informed consent and debriefing have received the most attention. These are discussed in the following section.

THE RIGHTS OF SUBJECTS

PROTECTION FROM HARM

It is obvious that the researcher is responsible for protecting subjects from physical harm. However, suppose that the researcher is running a field experiment to observe the influence of the apparent **status** of a confederate, as indicated by the way he or she is dressed, on the extent to which pedestrians copy the confederate's action and cross a street against a red light. If a subject in such a field experiment were to be struck by a car as a result, is the researcher guilty of failing to protect the subject from harm? And might not a subject be put at risk during *future* jaywalking, which might occur because of such modelling behaviour?

status The position that a person holds to which we attach a high or low ranking.

While ethics committees are unlikely to approve research that poses any such physical danger to the subject, it is often more difficult to assess in advance the possibility of emotional harm. Situations that most people would find benign could conceivably produce much distress for certain vulnerable individuals. If you participated in experiment that led you to believe you were in a real emergency situation, and you acted only to save yourself, would this knowledge be emotionally harmful? Some subjects might benefit from the experience, striving in the future to think more about helping others, while other subjects might conceivably suffer long-term loss of **self-esteem**. Although, as will be discussed later, appropriate debriefing procedures should prevent any enduring emotional damage, the researcher must still be sensitive to the possibility of such harm, and not simply assume that debriefing will take care of everything.

self-esteem A feeling of self-worth.

RIGHT TO PRIVACY

We take for granted in our society that, except under unusual circumstances sanctioned by some legal authority, other people have no right to pry into our affairs without our knowledge or permission. In case-study research or survey studies this does not usually pose a problem, since the participants know what information is being requested. Threats to the right to privacy arise primarily in research in which deception is used and subjects do not know what aspect of their behaviour is being studied, and in field studies and field experiments in which subjects do not even know they are subjects.

As you become more familiar with social psychological research, you will encounter experiments that have involved invasion of privacy, e.g., asking intimate questions or even observing people at urinals. Yet before concluding that such research should never be undertaken, consider the degree to which subjects are exposed to potential stress, loss of self-esteem, etc., compared with the potential benefits, for example, new knowledge about human behaviour, that the research may provide. Such evaluations are often difficult to perform, and that is why codes of ethics and ethics committees are so important.

Anther aspect of the right to privacy issue is **confidentiality**. Whether subjects consent to allow their privacy to be invaded or not, one must maintain the confidentiality of subjects' responses, unless explicit permission to the contrary has been obtained. Very few people would appreciate seeing their names published alongside their data; and, in general, individual subjects' data are not of specific interest and are not identified in research reports. Yet data records must be stored somewhere, and the ethical researcher needs to ensure that such confidentiality is safeguarded, whether at the stage of data analysis, data reporting, or data storage.

confidentiality Protecting the identity of a research subject.

A number of years ago, a prominent citizen left his own city in southern Ontario to seek psychiatric counselling in a medical centre in another city. As part of a research project, he allowed the sessions to be videotaped for later analysis. A few years later, a member of the psychology department at the same university contacted the psychiatry department and asked for any film materials that might be used in an introductory lecture on abnormal psychology. A few weeks later, several thousand students were shown a videotape of one of this man's therapy sessions! Obviously, an error was made, which demonstrates the great potential for harm that exists if care is not taken to ensure confidentiality.

There is another aspect of confidentiality that bears consideration. Suppose a researcher has all participants in a study complete some measure of emotional adjustment. What should be done if it is discovered that a participant has a strong degree of maladjustment for which psychotherapy might be recommended? Such a circumstance places the researcher in an ethical dilemma if the evidence suggests that the participant is so emotionally troubled as to pose some danger to himself or others. On the one hand, it is not ethical to inform the subject (or someone else) of his or her problems, since by agreeing to participate in the experiment the subject did not contract to learn of such problems, real or otherwise. On the other hand, if the information available indicates that the subject or other people are at some risk, then there is also an ethical obligation to avoid harm to the participant or to others (American Psychological Association, 1992). The researcher would have to weigh carefully the right of confidentiality against the potential risks to the participant or others brought about by maintaining confidentiality. In practice, the data emerging from psychological tests are unlikely to demonstrate such powerful evidence of potential risk. Therefore, confidentiality would win out, and nothing would be said to the subject or to anyone else about the subject's test results. The wise researcher, however, would seek informed consent in advance, warning of disclosure in the event of any indications that the participant or others are at risk.

In recent discussions, the Ontario College of Physicians and Surgeons has proposed that confidentiality does not need to be maintained in cases where a patient threatens someone's security. In these cases a report may be made to the police. Doctors would notify police "if the threat is directed at a person [or a group of people], there is a specific plan that is concrete and 'do-able', and the method for carrying out the threat is available to the person."

This proposal is to be worked out over the next two years. Concern has been expressed about whether patients will be as open if they know their discussions are no longer confidential (*The Globe and Mail,* June 11, 1996).

Finally, suppose that during the unobtrusive observation of customers in a store the researcher observes someone committing a crime. Can the psychologist be expected to refuse to give testimony in a court of law on the grounds that he or she must provide confidentiality to the subjects? As Wiesenthal (1974) points out, psychologists have no privilege in this regard and would be required to testify. Thus, even the use of unobtrusive measures can produce ethical problems with regard to confidentiality.

INFORMED CONSENT

As mentioned earlier, every empirical approach is vulnerable to ethical compromise. The laboratory experiment has its own special ethical problems brought

What are some of the concerns that the issue of confidentiality must deal with?

about by the common use of deception. It is difficult to observe subjects' natural reactions in a situation when they are aware of being observed; one of the appeals of field experiments is that subjects act naturally since they do not know that they are subjects. However, if the experimenter is clever, it is often possible to disguise the real aim of the laboratory experiment so that subjects react almost as though they were in a real-life situation (Elms, 1982).

The use of deception was not all that common prior to 1960, but its use mushroomed during the 1960s and continues to increase (Adair, Dushenko and Lindsay, 1985). Between one-half and three-quarters of published social psychological research reports involve some element of deception (Gross and Fleming, 1982; Christensen, 1988).

The issue of deception became a major controversy with the publication of Milgram's (1963) study of obedience (see Chapter 5), in which subjects were told they were participating in a study of learning that involved their administration of progressively stronger electric shocks to a "learner." Milgram was heavily criticized (e.g., Baumrind, 1964) for the way in which his subjects were exposed to potentially disturbing emotional reactions upon learning the true nature of the experiment and evaluating their own behaviour in that context. Milgram (1964) countered that the debriefing of the subjects had prevented any emotional damage to them, since they learned that no one had actually been hurt and that their behaviour had been reasonable given the circumstances. Psychiatric interviews of the subjects one year after the experiment seemed to indicate that they had experienced no enduring effects.

It is important to understand that social psychological knowledge is much richer because of the Milgram research; it has brought about an understanding of human compliance with authority that was formerly inconceivable. Yet the ethical dilemma remains; is it, in principle, ever acceptable to deceive subjects, to decide for them what level of emotional stress is tolerable? If we rule out deception, we make much social psychological research all but impossible. Do we stop our research? In so doing, may we not one day be judged guilty of a greater sin, that of failing to use the powerful methodology of science to understand human social behaviour so that we can learn to reduce aggression, diminish prejudice, and enhance quality of life?

Obtaining **informed consent** is one way of safeguarding the rights of subjects: if subjects are told as fully as possible what will happen to them in the experiment (without destroying the effectiveness of the experimental manipulation), then they can freely choose whether or not to participate. Such informed consent will also help curb resentment towards whatever deception is practised, for if subjects are told that it is impossible to describe the experiment in full detail without influencing their behaviour in it, they are likely to accept the necessity for deception when they eventually learn they were deceived.

On the other hand, perhaps psychologists worry too much about the effects of deception. No one has yet shown any long-term negative consequences resulting from deception in a social psychological experiment (Elms, 1982). Empirical studies of the reaction of participants to experiments using deception indicate that they do not appear to share the negative view of deception held by some psychologists. Rather, they are more likely to view the deception as a necessary withholding of information or a necessary misrepresentation (Christensen, 1988; Smith, 1983).

Does informed consent guarantee that no deception will be used?

informed consent
Providing enough information for a subject to make an informed decision about participation in an experiment.

debriefing Explaining to the subject what the experiment was about.

dehoaxing Explaining, when the experiment is over, what deception was used and why.

desensitization After research, helping the subject to understand and resolve changes in behaviour or attitudes.

How is debriefing done?

role play A research method whereby subjects act out roles as they believe others would.

DEBRIEFING

Debriefing is used to protect subjects against any long-term harm fostered by deception. Most social psychologists go to great lengths to debrief their subjects following an experiment. Debriefing involves both **dehoaxing** and **desensitization** (Holmes, 1976), as well as undoing any possible effects of the experimental manipulation on the subject.

Dehoaxing involves informing subjects that they have been deceived and explaining the purpose of the experiment. Desensitization is intended to help the subjects accept the new information they have about themselves and put it into context, and respond to any questions and anxieties that might arise. Undoing the effects of the experimental manipulation includes such actions as ensuring that subjects who have been misinformed about real-life events leave the experiment with accurate information. This form of debriefing goes beyond dehoaxing, for there is a need to do more than inform the subject about the deception and the misinformation; the researcher should ensure that this new information really does mitigate the effects of the experiment on the subject. Undoing the effects of the manipulation is especially important in pornography research in which subjects are shown pornographic materials, sometimes over repeated intervals. If, as some researchers indicate, such exposure leads some male subjects to become more accepting of myths about rape (e.g., "rape victims usually enjoy being raped"), particular care must be taken to undo this effect. (It may be debated whether debriefing, which by its very nature is an intellectual exercise, *can* undo this effect.) Some researchers in this area have worked to establish satisfactory ethical procedures to guide the actual practices involved in debriefing, and have even presented evidence suggesting that careful and appropriate debriefing can actually lead to a lower rate of acceptance of rape myths than existed prior to the experiment (Check and Malamuth, 1984, 1990).

While debriefing is considered to be a necessary part of any experiment in social psychology, it should be noted that in the case of highly stressful situations, debriefing may sometimes not only fail to undo whatever damage has been done, but may even make matters *worse*. For example, subjects who follow orders in an experiment on obedience may not perceive their actions as "blind obedience" until so informed in the debriefing. Moreover, it may not be desirable for subjects to witness role models (university professors or their assistants) in the act of lying. The fact is that the major advantage of debriefing in such instances may be in reducing the experimenter's guilt rather than in helping the subject (Campbell, 1969a). It is also important to remember that deception and debriefing are two separate issues (Jung, 1982). Successful debriefing does not by itself overcome the moral problem of deceiving, when it exists.

ALTERNATIVES TO DECEPTION

What if we were to try to conduct experiments without using deception at all? Kelman (1967) has advocated an approach in which subjects **role play**. Instead of being deceived about the nature of the research, subjects are given a description of a situation by the experimenter and then asked to behave as they think other people would in such a situation. However, as you can imagine, role-playing studies have not proven very useful to psychologists, for all they tell us is how the subjects *think* others would act in that situation; the researcher's intuition, informed by a thorough knowledge of the scientific literature, would in all likelihood provide a better guide.

A related and somewhat more useful technique is that of **simulation.** Again, no deception is employed and the subjects are informed of the situation in which they find themselves. In this case, however, the subjects act and react to each other and to the situation rather than simply playing a role corresponding to how they think others would act. Although simulations can evoke powerful emotional responses they pose several problems. First, although outright deception is not involved, there is another serious ethical question: if the researcher can foresee that the subjects may experience discomfort, is it ethical to expose them to that discomfort even if they are warned in advance? Moreover, what use can be made of the results? Can we be certain that the observed outcome was truly an indication of how people in general would react in such situations, and not that it was merely idiosyncratic? We may be able to generalize from our results less than we think, despite the apparent realism.

simulation A research method whereby subjects react to situations as they expect others would.

As you can see, role playing and simulation cannot eliminate the need for deception in social psychological research. While informed consent and debriefing can help avoid the more serious negative effects, there is no general solution to the problem of deception, except to say that the experimenter must take all reasonable precautions to ensure that the negative consequences of the deception are likely to be minimal, and that even this risk is justified by the importance of what might be learned from the experiment. Canadian universities and granting agencies require that experiments involving human subjects first be cleared by an ethics committee whose task it is to protect subjects from undue exploitation, unnecessary deception, or potential harm. Ethics committees, which evaluate the work of peers, are usually more objective in making judgments than individual researchers eager to verify their hypotheses.

SELF-TEST QUESTIONS

9. At least _____ percent of social psychological research involves some element of deception.

a) 20

b) 50

c) 15

d) 85

10. Informed consent means that

a) there is absolutely no deception involved in an experiment

b) subjects are asked to help design the experiment

c) information that might influence behaviour is held back, and everything else is explained

d) researchers may use any amount of deception that they wish without regard for the effects on subjects

11. After an experiment has been completed, _____ is used to explain the true purpose of the research.

a) dehoaxing

b) desensitization

c) informed consent

d) manipulation

PERSPECTIVES ON SOCIAL PSYCHOLOGY

CANADIAN

It is generally accepted that psychology as an academic discipline began in Leipzig in 1879 with the establishment of Wilhelm Wundt's laboratory. However, psychology courses had been taught long before that. The first course in psychology taught in a Canadian university was given in 1843 by a philosophy professor at the University of Toronto (Myers, 1965). The first chair of psychology in Canada was established at Dalhousie University in 1866 (actually the "Chair of Psychology and Metaphysics") (Page and Clark, 1982). The first psychology laboratory in Canada was set up by James Baldwin at the University of Toronto in 1890 (he subsequently founded the psychological laboratories at Princeton and Johns Hopkins) (Myers, 1965). It was not until 1929, however, that graduate psychology programs were established in Canada, at McGill and Toronto (Wright, 1969).

Not long after psychology began to be recognized as a separate discipline, social psychology took root in Canadian universities at about the same time that it did in the United States (Gardner and Kalin, 1981). A course in social psychology was introduced at McGill University in 1913 (Ferguson, 1982), the University of Saskatchewan in 1919 (McMurray, 1982), the University of Manitoba in 1923 (Wright, 1982), the University of Toronto during the 1920s (Wright, 1990), the University of Alberta in 1933 (Nelson, 1982) and Queen's University (Inglis, 1982) and the University of Western Ontario (Wright, 1990) during the 1930s. Social psychology in Canada is older than most Canadian universities!

Most Canadian social psychological research differs little from research conducted in the United States (Rule and Wells, 1981). Nonetheless, there have been continuing efforts to tailor the development of social psychology in Canada to serve the Canadian context. This trend has led, for example, to the development of research groups focusing on language and bilingualism and on multiculturalism. Canadian researchers have become world leaders in these domains.

This book came into being in part because of the authors' concern that social psychology, as carried out in the United States and discussed in the textbooks from that country, may not accurately describe social behaviour in Canada. For instance, the United States has stressed a "melting pot" concept of society, while Canada places emphasis on a "cultural mosaic." This difference may well have important consequences for some social psychological phenomena.

Teaching social psychology using textbooks rooted in the social and cultural context of another nation is problematic (Alcock, 1978; Berry, 1978a, 1978b;

In what areas of research does Canadian social psychology excel?

Kalin and Gardner, 1981; Sadava, 1978a, 1978b). First, what we learn from U.S. texts about such topics as racial prejudice, aggression, and the social psychology of justice and law may actually be erroneous when applied to the Canadian context. Second, such learning carries the risk of influencing Canadian social behaviour to become more American. If people believe that murder rates are going up, for example, they may become more fearful, and feel a greater need to arm themselves, bringing about a greater likelihood of lethal aggression. Finally, while U.S. textbooks generally do an excellent job of sensitizing students to social issues in that country, Canadian students may not react in the same way. For example, while prejudice continues to be a problem in Canada, Canadian students using a U.S. book can escape the challenge to their social conscience that their U.S. counterparts must face when reading about racial prejudice in their own country.

This textbook considers that social psychology has both a national and an international flavour. By studying social psychology within the Canadian context, and by bringing together the best in Canadian, American, European, and other research, both the culture-specific and universal aspects of social psychology are addressed.

INTERNATIONAL

Despite its European roots, throughout most of its history social psychology has been dominated by researchers from the United States. Indeed, one can view the U.S. as the first of three "worlds" in which psychologists carry out research and practice (Moghaddam, 1987; 1990), since it is the major producer of psychological knowledge. The second world is made up of the other industrialized nations, including Canada, Great Britain, Australia, France, and Russia. In some ways the second world is as productive as the first world, but its influence is greatest among its own constituents and upon the third world. The third world comprises the developing nations, such as India, Nigeria, and Cuba. While the first world (the U.S.) exports its knowledge to the second and third worlds, it is little influenced by the psychology of the other two worlds. The third world is primarily an importer of psychological knowledge, and is limited by lack of resources in its ability to generate such knowledge.

Psychologists in all three "worlds" are becoming more sensitive to the relevance and appropriateness of first- and second-world psychology for societies of the third world (Moghaddam, 1987).

There are a growing number of collaborative studies in which social psychological experiments are carried out in a number of different cultures. The "second-world" social psychology that has developed in Europe is also fairly distinctive. Beginning in the late 1960s, European social psychologists, led by such people as Serge Moscovici in France and Henry Tajfel in Great Britain, worked to develop a social psychology that would differ from the discipline of the U.S., which was viewed as too steeped in the individualistic value system of that country (Moghaddam, 1987). European social psychology has succeeded in developing its own unique areas of interest and expertise. It places much more emphasis than does U.S. social psychology on the study of intergroup relations and research into such topics as minority group influence, social control, conformity, and the social psychological aspects of political economy and ideology (Taylor and Moghaddam, 1987). And few U.S. social psychologists ever publish in, or read, the leading European English-language social psychology journals. This is not the case for Canadian social psychologists, who are really part of the second world (Jaspers, 1980). In this textbook, the reader will find considerable discussion of European research.

APPLIED SOCIAL PSYCHOLOGY

From its inception social psychology has been vitally concerned with the problems of people and society. In its formative years, social psychologists worked to understand such phenomena as the economic depression, labour/management conflicts, racial prejudice, and the rise of fascism in the 1930s (Fisher, 1982). Social psychologists applied their skills to the war effort during the Second World War: for example, the University of Toronto's David Ketchum employed his social psychological knowledge at the War Information Board in Ottawa (Wright, 1990). In recent years, the range of real-life problems has broadened considerably (see Table 1-1 for examples).

Can all this research actually have practical benefits for people and societies? Public policy in Canada has been influenced significantly by work in a number of areas (Rule and Adair, 1984). As mentioned earlier, as a result of pioneering research originating with Wallace Lambert's group in Montreal, an internationally recognized model of successful bilingual education has been developed which combines language training with cultural integration (Gardner and Desrochers, 1981). Research on the adaptation of northern native peoples to cultural and

TABLE 1-1 **Some recent topics discussed in the Journal of Social Issues**

Topic	*Issue*
Teenage parenting: Social determinants and consequences	1980, 36(1)
Energy conservation	1981, 37(2)
Sexual harassment on the job	1982, 38(4)
Images of nuclear war	1983, 39(1)
Criminal victimization	1984, 40(1)
Social support	1985, 41(1)
Media violence and antisocial behaviour	1986, 42(3)
Deterrence theory and international conflict	1987, 43(4)
Psychological effects of unemployment	1988, 44(4)
Managing the environment	1989, 45(1)
Moral exclusion and injustice	1990, 46(1)
Perceived control in vulnerable populations	1991, 47(4)
Psychological perspectives on abortion and its alternatives	1992, 48(3)
New medical technologies	1993, 49(2)
Environmental policy and justice	1994, 50(3)
Dynamics of sexual harassment	1995, 51(1)

economic changes, such as the James Bay hydroelectric project, has provided information that cannot be ignored by governments or by native groups in future policy decisions (Berry, Wintrob, Sindell and Mawhinney, 1982). Other research has contributed to Canada's multiculturalism policy, which encourages various ethnic groups to maintain their cultural heritages while being integrated into the Canadian "mainstream" (Kalin and Berry, 1979). Recommendations for changes in our legal system by a parliamentary law reform commission were influenced by research concerning the reliability of eyewitness testimony, the unanimity rule in jury decisions, and the assessment of defendants' "fitness" for trial. Research concerning the impact of TV advertising directed at young children led to a legislated ban on such "targeted" advertising in Quebec and some voluntary restraints in the rest of Canada (Goldberg, 1982).

Social psychology has evolved as a discipline in which there is constant feedback between laboratory-based research and real-life problems. In many cases, theories developed through "pure research" have been applied to social issues; for example, attribution theory has been applied in understanding the experience of being physically ill, marital conflicts, and addiction to cigarette smoking. On the other hand, some research begins at the level of real-life problems (Fisher, 1982).

Lewin (1948) has described this work as *action research*, in which the researcher obtains data about a problem or organization, feeds these data into the relevant system in order to influence change, measures the changes, and then repeats the process. Note that this model implies that the social psychologist thus becomes an agent of change, a skilled advocate of policies, as well as a theoretician and researcher.

SELF-TEST QUESTIONS

12. Studies in language and multiculturalism are prominent in the research of
a) Canada
b) the United States
c) Great Britain
d) Germany

13. Canada is considered part of the second world in terms of psychological research. _____ nations also make up this group.
a) Asian
b) European
c) African
d) South American

14. Research undertaken for the sake of knowledge only is known as _____ research.
a) applied
b) mainstream

c) pure

d) action

SUMMARY

(1) Social psychology scientifically studies the thoughts, feelings, and behaviours of people, focusing particularly on the role of social influences.

(2) The scientific method consists of formulating hypotheses, testing them through systematic observation, and building theories from these findings.

(3) In social psychology both experimental and non-experimental methods of research are used. All methods have both advantages and disadvantages.

(4) Non-experimental research methods include the archival method, case studies, survey interviews or questionnaires, and field studies.

(5) Correlational research involves studying the extent to which several variables or characteristics are related.

(6) In experimental research, subjects are assigned randomly to experimental and control groups so that we assume they are identical groups before the experiment begins. An independent variable is manipulated so that its effects can be observed by comparison between groups. Other confounding variables that may influence the results are controlled. Experimental research methods include laboratory experiments, field experiments, and quasi-experiments.

(7) Ethical concerns in social psychological research include: protection from harm, the right to privacy, the use of deception in experiments, the need for debriefing, and informed consent.

(8) Canadian social psychology examines issues such as bilingualism and multiculturalism from a uniquely Canadian perspective.

(9) Canadian experience in issues such as prejudice, aggression, and the justice system differs from the experience in the U.S.

(10) It is important to draw on international research from Europe as well as the U.S.

FOR REVIEW

Social psychology shares with other areas of psychology a focus on the _____(1). Theories in social psychology have been dominated by the _____ and _____(2) perspectives.

Research in social psychology involves the use of a number of different methods. Survey research usually involves _____(3) measures. _____(4) research uses data already collected for some other reason. _____(5) studies allow researchers to investigate whether the variables of interest are related. When researchers compare sample means of scores from experimental and control groups, they want to know whether any difference between them was likely to have been caused by chance or by the _____(6) variable. The best way to ensure that subjects in various experimental conditions are undifferentiated before an experiment begins is by the _____(7) assignment of subjects to experimental and control groups. Double-blind experimental designs are useful in avoiding both _____(8) effects. The field experiment involves a trade-off of greater external validity for less control of _____(9) variables. The major advantage of a _____(10) is that researchers can study the effects of a major event that could not be produced in the laboratory. Although _____(11) research is difficult to do, it is valuable particularly in showing how far theories can be generalized.

There are four ethical principles that must be considered when doing research. They are _____(12). In order to maintain _____(13) it is important to be sure that people cannot be identified with their specific data. Therefore, good data storage is essential. It is very difficult to avoid some _____(14) in research. In order to protect the rights of subjects, researchers obtain _____(15). This means that subjects will be told as much as possible without providing information that might influence their behaviour during the study. After the research is complete, debriefing is used. It has two components. _____(16) explains the real purpose of the experiment, including any deception that was used. _____(17) deals with any concern or anxiety that the subjects might have about the research and their participation in it.

Two areas of research in which Canadian psychologists have played a prominent role are _____ and _____(18). Studies in these areas demonstrate how public policy has been influenced by research. We refer to this type of research as _____(19). This differs from _____(20), which is done to increase knowledge and may not have any real-world application.

ISSUES AND ACTIVITIES

(1) Make a chart or table to summarize information about the research strategies described in this chapter. For each type of research indicate suitable uses, advantages, and disadvantages.

(2) Academic journals are essential for keeping the knowledge base of a discipline current. Look for and compile a list of 15 social psychology journal articles written no earlier than 1990. Five of the articles should be Canadian, five American, and five European. Can you observe any differences in the issues of interest to researchers working in Canada, the U.S., and Europe? (Hint: The *Annual Review of Psychology*, 1996, *47*, is a good place to start for Canadian material. Any *Annual Review* chapter, as well as any article cited in an *Annual Review* chapter, may be purchased from the Annual Reviews Preprints and Reprints service, 1-800-347-8007; 415-259-5017; email: arpr@class.org)

(3) View the video segment on election polls and discuss the following:

a) Describe the four basic steps used when conducting polls.

b) Discuss the questions people need to ask in order to critically evaluate polls.

• FURTHER READING

AGNEW, N.M. and PYKE, S.W. (1982). *The science game*. Third Edition. Englewood Cliffs, NJ: Prentice-Hall. Excellent discussion of the nature of science and its methods, as well as the "culture" of science.

ALLPORT, G.W. (1968). The historical background of modern social psychology. In G. Lindzey and E. Aronson (Eds.), *The handbook of social psychology*

(Vol. I, pp. 1–80). Reading, MA: Addison-Wesley. In-depth discussion of the roots of modern psychological theory and methods.

EARN, B. and TOWSON, S. (Eds.) (1990). *Social psychology: Readings for the Canadian context.* Peterborough, Ontario: Broadview Press. A collection of research papers representative of social psychological research in Canada and elsewhere, along with interviews with a number of prominent social psychologists working in Canada.

JUNG, J. (1982). *The experimenter's challenge.* New York: Macmillan. Thorough discussion of the ethical dilemmas that face researchers using human subjects. Also includes a complete introduction to research method and design in psychology.

MILLER, A.G. (1986). *The obedience experiments.* New York: Praeger. Assessment of the enduring impact of the Milgram studies, and an examination of the ethical issues they raise.

SHARPE, D., ADAIR, J.G. and ROESE, N.J. (1992). "Twenty years of deception in research: A decline in subjects' trust?" *Personality and social psychology bulletin, 18,* 585–590. A report of research into subjects' views of deception in social psychological research.

SUGGESTED WEBLINKS

Canadian Psychology (table of contents; abstracts of articles in journal)
> http://www.cycor.ca/Psych/Psynopsis/scholar.html

Current Research in Social Psychology (Journal)
> http://www.uiowa.edu/~grpproc/crisp.html

Links to Psychology Departments of Canadian universities
> http://www.uwinnipeg.ca/~baldwin/canpsydp.html

Statistics Canada
> http://www.statcan.ca

Style guide for writing in psychology
> http://www.lib.uwaterloo.ca/discipline/psyc/APA_style.txt

Research Methods

American Psychological Society: Psychological experiments on the Net. Includes some ongoing social psychological studies being conducted via the Internet.
> http://psych.hanover.edu/APS/exponnet.html

Canadian Psychological Association Code of Ethics
> http://www.uwinnipeg.ca/~clark/research/cpaethics.html

Twenty science attitudes
> http://vanbc.wimsey.com/~ted/bcs/ratenq/Re3.3-Attitude.html

ANSWERS TO SELF-TEST QUESTIONS

1. b; 2. a; 3. c; 4. d; 5. d; 6. c; 7. a; 8. b; 9. b; 10. c; 11. a; 12. a; 13. b; 14. c.

ANSWERS TO FOR REVIEW

1. individual; 2. behavioural, cognitive; 3. self-report; 4. Archival; 5. Correlational; 6. independent; 7. random; 8. experimenter and subject; 9.

extraneous; 10. quasi-experiment; 11. cross-cultural; 12. respect for dignity of the person, responsibility for society, integrity in relationships, responsible caring; 13. confidentiality; 14. deception; 15. informed consent; 16. dehoaxing; 17. Desensitization; 18. bilingualism, biculturalism; 19. applied research; 20. pure research.

SOCIAL PERCEPTION AND COGNITION

We do not see things as they are,
We see them as we are.

The Talmud

Yon Cassius has a lean and hungry look
He thinks too much; such men are dangerous
Would he were fatter

William Shakespeare (Julius Caesar)

■ LEARNING OUTCOMES

1. An understanding of how we perceive ourselves and other people.

2. An understanding of how we make judgments about the causes of events and people's actions.

3. Knowledge about the unconscious biases that affect how we perceive people and how we understand their behaviour.

4. An appreciation for how and why we tend to think in terms of categories, and for how automatic thinking influences our memory and interpretation of the world.

5. An understanding of how we unconsciously use certain biases or assumptions as "cognitive shortcuts" in order to arrive at decisions and judgments.

■ FOR REFLECTION

• What are the effects of the way we perceive ourselves?

• How do we form first impressions of people? Are they accurate?

• How do we influence the image that others have of us?

• Are there differences in how we make sense of our physical world and our social world?

■ CHAPTER OUTLINE

On October 30, 1995, Canada reached a turning point in its history. In the Quebec referendum on sovereignty, the NO side won a narrow victory with 50.6 percent of the votes compared to 49.4 percent for the YES side. At the centre of this division are differences in the ways Quebeckers identify themselves and in their visions of Quebec and Canada. During the campaign, these differences became critically apparent.

    Many Quebeckers on the YES side see themselves as a distinct francophone people who have been ignored and unfairly treated in a Canada generally indifferent to their concerns. Their vision of the best future, even after the referendum, is of a sovereign country in North America, characterized by a distinct culture and the French language. Their view of Canada, as indicated in the Sovereign Manifesto, is that it is too large and too divided to work efficiently. They consider the goal of the federal government to be the gradual persuasion of Quebeckers that there is no such thing as a Quebec identity or culture, but only a Canadian culture. This Canadian culture is multicultural and expresses itself in a variety of languages, one of which is French.

By contrast, many Quebeckers on the NO side perceive themselves as Quebeckers and Canadians, with a history shared with other Canadians. As Prime Minister Chrétien said in his last bid for unity, "Canada without Quebec is no more Canada and Quebec without Canada is no more Quebec." For many Quebeckers on the NO side, the future is brighter as a Canadian province than as a separate nation faced with economic and political uncertainty. For them, the goal of the federal government must be a renewed federalism designed to serve the needs of all Canadians.

Social psychology provides considerable insight into the way people perceive themselves and others, as well as events in the social world. In this chapter we will see that our social perception and cognition is rich and complex. We begin with a discussion of self-perception followed by how we form impressions of other people. The discussion then turns to the study of attributions, the processes by which we perceive causality in our social world. Finally we examine the processes by which we construct our broader view of the social world.

PERCEIVING OURSELVES

The self is our most important construct. For example, in spite of a room being noisy we nevertheless hear someone across the room mention our name (Moray, 1959). Also, we remember self-relevant information better than other information (Rogers, Kuiper and Kirker, 1977). Oliver Sacks (1985) describes a patient, William Thompson, who is absolutely devastated because he has no sense of self. Thompson, who cannot remember anything from one minute to the next, is forced into a "veritable delirium of identity-making and seeking" (Sacks, p. 110) by the mere presence of others.

The self is a multi-faceted construct. It consists of beliefs and feelings as well as related behaviours. The primary affective component is self-esteem. Cognitive components include schemata, and other representations of identity (Goffman, 1959; Markus and Nurius, 1986; Markus and Wurf, 1987). Affective and cognitive self-aspects influence and are influenced by behaviour.

SELF-CONCEPT
SELF-SCHEMATA

self-schemata Cognitive representations of information and beliefs about the self, which are acquired through experience.

Schemata are cognitive representations of information acquired through experience. Much of the information we have about the self is represented in **self-schemata**. They influence our attention in social contexts and provide frameworks for organizing and remembering self-related information (Markus, 1977). We more efficiently process information that is consistent with our own schemata. Research has demonstrated that subjects respond more quickly to schema-consistent information for a variety of dimensions, such as independence/dependence (Markus, 1977), weight (Markus, Hamill and Sentis, 1987), and gender (Bem,

1981). By contrast, we usually ignore information that is irrelevant unless we have a good reason for choosing to exert the extra effort needed to understand and remember it (Fiske and Taylor, 1984). Other research suggests that the self-schemata of men and women differ: in men they are based on unique abilities and independence; in women they are based on interdependence and connectedness with others (Josephs, Markus and Tafarodi, 1992).

Self-schemata are different from other schemata in a number of important ways. Self-schemata are usually larger and more complex. They contain much more information, including some with strong emotional overtones. The relationships among the components involve complex networks. Self-schemata are also activated more frequently than other schemata (Markus and Sentis, 1982).

IDENTITIES AND ROLES

As well as self-schemata we have **role schemata**, which help to define our positions in society (Fiske and Taylor, 1984, 1991). Information about characteristics such as occupation, sex, and age is used to identify the roles we assume. Norms about appropriate behaviours help us to portray these roles. For example, we have expectations about how grandmothers, teachers, firefighters, students, politicians, and others in society typically behave. Consider how a role schema may influence self-concept in the case of a police officer like the one in the photo.

We identify ourselves in terms of the roles we portray, the activities in which we characteristically engage, and the nature of our relationships with others. We may be students, store clerks, skiers, basketball players, sons, daughters, aunts or uncles. The characteristics of our roles and identities constitute an intricate web of information. They contribute to what Linville (1985) calls **self-complexity**. According to Linville, individuals who have rich and varied images of themselves are high in self-complexity. By contrast, individuals who have limited roles and few self-images are characteristically low in self-complexity.

How do we organize and remember information about the self?

How might a police officer's role schema affect self-concept?

role schemata *Cognitive representations which help to define our positions in society.*

self-complexity *Degree of richness and variety in individuals' images about themselves.*

POSSIBLE SELVES

Not only does the self contain information about what we are like currently, but it also includes information about other unrealized selves. For example, we have a self-construct for the self we think we ought to be and another one for the self we think significant others would like us to be. You may think you should be gregarious and easy-going. By contrast, your parents may think you should be less concerned with socializing and more reflective and studious. We also have two ideal selves, one based on our own ideals and the other based on the ideals of others (Higgins, 1987, 1989). Your ideal may be to become a popular entertainer, whereas your best friend may think you would make a good music teacher.

In addition to these ideal and ought selves, we have possible selves which represent our ideas of what we might become, including both desirable and undesirable selves (Markus and Nurius, 1986). One desirable possible self may be a successful businesswoman. This cognitive representation may inspire and motivate. On the other hand, an undesirable self may be an unemployed self. This view may cause fear, dread, and dejection.

In summary, we have many different constructs about the self. We have self-schemata, role schemata, identities, and potential as well as actual selves. All these constructs represent the beliefs or ideas we have about ourselves.

SELF-ESTEEM

self-esteem Evaluations of the self.

While self-concept represents knowledge and beliefs, **self-esteem** is concerned with feelings towards the self. Whether we feel good about ourselves depends on how we evaluate ourselves in comparison to both internal and external standards. Our self-esteem is also affected by the need to think well of ourselves. We will briefly examine each of these influences and their consequences for everyday life.

What influences how we evaluate ourselves?

DISCREPANCY THEORY

The notion of possible selves (Higgins, 1989) has interesting implications for our level of self-esteem and related emotional well-being. According to discrepancy theory, possible selves provide a set of internal standards (self-guides) for how we could or ought to be. The differences between these internal standards and how we actually are determine our overall self-esteem. Failure to match our aspirations (discrepancy between actual and ideal selves) or our obligations (discrepancy between actual and ought selves) produces low self-esteem and negative emotions. For example, failure to live up to your ideal of a popular and clever student may lead to disappointment. Table 2-1 shows Higgins' possible selves and the specific emotions associated with discrepancies between the actual self and each of these possible selves.

TABLE 2-1 **Negative discrepancies between the actual self and alternate views of the self**

Type of discrepancy	Associated emotions
actual self vs. own ought self	guilt, self-criticism, anxiety (e.g. guilty feelings when you cheat on a test)
actual self vs. other ought self	fear, shame, anxiety (e.g. fear of what will happen when your teacher finds out you cheated)
actual self vs. own ideal self	sadness, depression (e.g. disappointment because you failed to live up to your ideal of being a clever and popular student)
actual self vs. another's ideal self	rejection, depression (e.g. sadness experienced because you did not become a doctor and your mother always wanted you to be one)

SOCIAL COMPARISON THEORY

Festinger first drew attention to the importance of **social comparison** in interpreting our actions and feelings in an influential paper in 1954. In his view people have a need for self-knowledge to accurately evaluate their actions and opinions. In the absence of objective standards people evaluate themselves through comparisons with others, especially others to whom they are similar. More recently, psychologists have proposed additional goals of social comparison: **self-enhancement** (Wills, 1981) and self-improvement (Wood, 1989). In self-enhancement social comparison serves the desire to feel positive about oneself and one's abilities. Downward social comparison offers a means to improve self-esteem: people feel better when they can compare themselves with someone who is disadvantaged or less capable. By contrast, upward social comparison offers a means to self-improvement through comparing oneself to another individual who is more capable or successful.

SELF-SERVING BIAS

Protecting one's ego and self-esteem is a powerful need in daily life. To meet this need people frequently use the **self-serving bias.** Since success and failure have implications for self-esteem, people tend to attribute their own success to internal factors and their failure to external factors. For example, in one study, students receiving good grades in an examination attributed those grades to ability or effort, but those attaining mediocre grades tended to attribute those results to task difficulty or just bad luck (Bernstein, Stephan and Davis, 1979). Attributions in which people take credit for success but deny responsibility for failures are most likely to occur when the person has chosen to engage in the activity, is highly involved in it, and when performance and its results are public rather than private (Bradley, 1978). Incidentally, this bias is not limited to Western countries; people in Japan, Latin America, and the former Yugoslavia are also more likely to attribute success rather than failure to their own ability (Chandler, Shama, Wolf and Planchard, 1981).

In situations where other needs (e.g. the need for achievement) predominate over the need to defend self-esteem, we do not use the self-serving bias. Consider a field experiment by Taylor and Reiss (1989), in which success and failure were manipulated experimentally in a realistic setting. The subjects were competitive skiers who participated in a giant slalom race. Each competitor had two runs that were timed electronically, and the times were announced after each run. For half of the racers, the "success group," 0.7 seconds were subtracted from their real times before the announcement, while in the "failure group," 0.7 seconds were added to their times. Subsequent questioning showed that those in each group perceived their performance as a success or failure as expected, and that none suspected the times had been rigged. Then subjects filled out questionnaires that assessed their attributions for performance. The results in this case show some deviation from a self-serving bias. That is, while subjects tended to attribute success to internal facilitating factors (such as strong effort or high ability), they also tended to attribute failure to internal debilitating factors, such as lack of effort. Thus in certain situations, such as those in which self-improvement is an important goal, our attributions are quite logical in that we attribute our successes to factors that facilitate our success and failure to debilitating factors, even if our self-esteem may be involved.

The explanation for the self-serving bias is more complicated than one would expect. An obvious hypothesis is that since success and failure are so important

social comparison
People's tendency to evaluate themselves in relation to other people, especially when a situation is ambiguous or uncertain.

self-enhancement
Comparison to others which contributes to good feelings about oneself.

self-serving bias
Attributions that are motivated by a desire to protect or enhance one's self-esteem.

to how we evaluate ourselves, we deliberately make internal attributions for success and external ones for failure. Internal attributions for failure would lower our self-esteem and would thus be difficult to accept emotionally. Some degree of a self-serving bias may actually contribute to people's comfort and happiness by protecting their self-esteem (Taylor and Brown, 1988). Yet, when people are depressed, they tend to be relatively accurate in judging the extent to which they are personally responsible for their success and failure (Sweeney, Anderson and Bailey, 1986; Alloy and Abramson, 1979). Other research has shown that the bias is an unconscious defensive process. Even when subjects believed a machine would reveal their true feelings, they responded in a self-serving manner, attributing success to themselves and failure to external factors (Reiss, Rosenfeld, Melburg and Tedeschi, 1981). Thus the self-serving bias is an example of automatic responding; that is, responding without thinking.

SELF-PRESENTATION AND SELF-EXPRESSION

self-presentation
Behaviour intended to create a desirable impression.

Most of us want to be liked and approved by others. Our effort to create a favourable impression is called **self-presentation**. Fiske and Taylor (1991) discuss a number of ways to create a positive impression. One strategy is **behavioural matching**, in which the person matches his or her behaviour to that of the individual whose approval is sought. Another technique of impression management is **conforming to situational norms**. For example, at a funeral, wearing dark clothes and expressing condolences is appropriate in many cultures. In the absence of situational norms or standards of appropriate behaviour, people usually attempt to convey a positive image and to make their good points obvious in the interest of **self-promotion**. People may also attempt to create a favourable impression through **ingratiation**, by flattering others.

It is important to note that there are many occasions when self-expression predominates over creating a favourable impression. Indeed, Snyder and Gangestad (1982) found that people prefer social situations that allow them to act in a manner consistent with their self-concept. Swann and Read (1981) found that, when people think others have misconceptions about them, they are particularly motivated to act in a manner that confirms their self-concept.

When we interact with others as we go about our daily lives, we take all the various aspects of the self with us. Who we are and how we feel about ourselves influences how we perceive other people and interpret events. We will turn now to our perception of others, followed by our view of the social world.

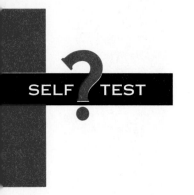

F•O•C•U•S

What influences whether we engage in impression management or self-expression?

SELF ? TEST

SELF-TEST QUESTIONS

1. Schemas have important effects on
a) what we will pay attention to
b) memory
c) how we interpret events
d) all of the above
e) both a and c

2. If you perceive yourself as friendly, intelligent, and a future corporation president, this is part of your

a) *role schema*

b) *event schema*

c) *self schema*

d) *prototype*

e) *stereotype*

3. In the experiment by Taylor and Reiss (1989), in which success and failure of skiers was manipulated, subjects tended to attribute

a) *success to internal factors and failure to external factors*

b) *both success and failure to internal factors*

c) *both success and failure to external factors*

d) *success to external factors and failure to internal factors*

4. Attributions in which people take credit for success but deny responsibility for failures are most likely to occur when

a) *the person has chosen to engage in the activity*

b) *the person is highly involved in the activity*

c) *performance and its results are public rather than private*

d) *all of the above*

PERCEIVING OTHERS

You meet, smile, converse. You find this person pleasant, interesting, intelligent, and considerate. How did you so quickly arrive at this very favourable impression? How we process and combine pieces of information about another person in order to construct a first impression, and the impact of such impressions, are of continuing interest to researchers. We turn now to a discussion of the nature of impression formation and to the kinds of thinking processes involved.

FORMING IMPRESSIONS

One of the first experiments on this topic was conducted by Asch (1946). To one group of students he read a list of personal traits: "intelligent, skillful, industrious, warm, determined, practical, cautious." To a second group he read the same list except that "cold" was substituted for "warm." All the subjects then wrote a brief paragraph describing the type of person to whom the traits applied. They were also given a new list of adjectives and asked to check those that applied to the person they had just described. When the responses were examined, the descriptions obtained from the two groups were strikingly different. The "warm" trait generated impressions of a person who was more popular, wise, humorous, and imaginative. Asch also found that by substituting "polite" and "blunt" for "warm" and "cold," not all characteristics had the same effect. He called traits such as "warm" and "cold" **central traits** because they seemed to be related to a wide range of other traits. **Peripheral traits** such as "polite" and "blunt" did not have such a broad impact.

How do we form first impressions of other people?

37

Kelley (1950) demonstrated that the effect was not confined to the laboratory when he had a "guest lecturer" give a talk to various psychology classes. In half of these classes the introduction included the adjective "warm," and in the other half, the adjective "cold." The actual introduction went as follows: "Mr. _____ is a graduate student in the Department of Economics and Social Science at M.I.T. He has three semesters of teaching experience in psychology at another college. This is his first semester teaching EC-70. He is 26 years old, a veteran, and married. People who know him consider him to be a rather cold (or a very warm) person, industrious, critical, practical, and determined." In all cases the content and delivery of the lecture was the same. Afterwards the students were asked to give their impressions of the lecturer. The results showed that the students given the "cold" cue rated the lecturer as more unsociable, self-centred, unpopular, formal, irritable, humourless, and ruthless. These data clearly support those originally obtained by Asch. In addition, Kelley found that students in the "warm" condition were more likely to ask the speaker questions and to interact with him, indicating that behaviour, as well as perception, was affected.

Asch argued that these results indicate that impressions of others are "dynamic wholes" rather than the sum of a number of separate components. This view was challenged by Wishner (1960). He demonstrated that some traits are central while others are peripheral, depending on the context. A trait would be central if the characteristics to be subsequently judged were related to it, but would be peripheral if they were unrelated.

Another view is that impression formation is similar to doing algebra. Information about another person is usually acquired sequentially. Let us assume that each of us has a "mental rating scale" that we apply to the various things we learn about others. For the purposes of illustration, our evaluations can range from +3 (very positive) to –3 (very negative). Thus, for example, on the characteristic of sincerity we might rate a person as very sincere (+3), somewhat sincere (+1), or rather insincere (–2). Similarly, we may evaluate a person as extremely intelligent (+3), average in intelligence (+1 or 0), or utterly stupid (–3). We might then put this information together by adding or by calculating a "running average." Anderson (1978) proposed that we use a weighted average. In his view, information should not only be evaluated but should be judged as to its importance. See Table 2-2 for models of impression formation.

Cognitive psychologists have shown that we use a variety of mental representations and strategies in person perception. Together these enable us to efficiently process verbal information as well as other details about physical appearance and behaviour. Categorical thinking involving prototypes, stereotypes, and schemata plays an important role.

TABLE 2-2 Models for forming impressions of people

Additive model	*Averaging model*	*Weighted averaging model*
Intelligent: + 3	Intelligent: + 3	Intelligent: + 3 × W_1
Sincere: + 1	Sincere: + 1	Sincere: + 1 × W_2
↓	↓	↓
overall impression: + 4	overall impression: + 2	overall impression: depends on values for W_1 and W_2

CATEGORICAL THINKING

PROTOTYPES

Cantor and Mischel (1979) suggest that we often use **prototypes**, representations or mental images of a typical example of a category. For example, you may picture a dog as a prototype of the category mammals. It has four legs, fur, and lives on land. If you were to see an unfamiliar animal in the zoo, you would decide whether it was a mammal by comparing it with a dog (which might give you trouble when it comes to whales). Similarly you may have a prototype for a grandparent: someone who is silver-haired, smiling, wrinkled, and loves babies. When we use prototypes to identify the animals or people we encounter, they influence what we notice and later remember about them. The extent to which the animal or person in question resembles the prototype, and the extent to which we allow for variations, will determine how quickly the animal or person is identified with the appropriate category.

Brewer, Dull and Lui (1981) demonstrated that prototypes facilitate processing and memory for relevant information, whether that information is consistent or inconsistent with the prototype. They presented subjects with photos and verbal labels of people in certain categories (e.g. respected elder statesman, sweet grandmother). Then they provided more information about the person. This information was processed more rapidly and included more frequently in the subject's impression of the person when it was consistent with the prototype (e.g. "kindly" for grandmother) than when it was inconsistent (e.g. "aggressive" for grandmother). They also found that information that was not part of the prototype, but not inconsistent with old age (e.g. "hard of hearing"), tended to be forgotten. Conversely, information that was not part of the prototype and was inconsistent with old age (e.g. "runs ten kilometres a day") was remembered by most subjects.

STEREOTYPES

A particular kind of prototype for which a "consensus exists among members of a group regarding the attributes of another" (Taylor, 1981, p. 155) is a **stereotype**. For example, Gardner et al. (1988) have found that English Canadians view French Canadians as proud, talkative, and excitable. Over the years, the stereotype regarding smokers has shifted from one of sophistication to one of less self-control and less consideration for others (Dermer and Jacobsen, 1986). Since stereotypes are intrinsic to prejudice, and fulfill needs related to this problem, a full discussion of them will be presented in that context (see Chapter 6). However, it is important to understand that stereotypes enable us to organize our thoughts about people, reducing complexity to manageable proportions where we might otherwise suffer from information overload. They help to guide our own behaviour and to interpret the behaviour of people from other groups. While the content of the stereotype may or may not be accurate, its existence helps us to make sense of the social world.

SOCIAL SCHEMATA

At a more complex level are **social schemata**. As discussed above in the section on self-perception, schemata are cognitive structures that encompass interconnected beliefs, information, and examples. For example, we have a schema of a "young executive" who wears designer clothes, eats gourmet foods (but never to excess), drinks bottled water or fine wine, is very conscious of health and phys-

prototype Representation or mental image of the most typical or best example of a category.

How does categorical thinking influence our perception of other people?

stereotype A kind of prototype, consisting of rigid beliefs, for which consensus exists among members of a group.

social schemata Cognitive representations about persons or social categories, which help us to organize and remember relevant information.

ical appearance, is very ambitious and career-oriented, and advances on the "fast track" by "networking" and faxing memos from a BMW. The schema may also include exclusionary features, which indicate who cannot belong to the category. Exclusionary features that indicate someone is not a "young executive" include having a large family, eating beef stew, driving a Volkswagen, and being overweight. As Anderson, Lepper and Ross (1980) demonstrated, we all have a schema for the "working man." This schema is illustrated by the accompanying photograph.

We also have **person schemata** for specific people, such as a famous movie star, a particular politician, a parent, a professor. For example, we may have a schema of the current prime minister as being honest, hard-working, concerned with people in distress, wanting to conciliate and resolve conflicts between people, groups, and regions. What makes this a schema, rather than simply a collection of characteristics, is that we see all the information logically fitting together into an overall impression of the prime minister.

We have several other types of schemata for people, including those for types of persons. For example, we have a schema for people who are "extroverts," which includes such characteristics as being sociable, outgoing, lively, and impulsive. As mentioned earlier, we have schemata for social roles. For example, we have a schema for the role of teacher which includes our knowledge about what teachers are supposed to do and not do. Role schemata are generally restricted to role-relevant situations.

Everyone has a schema for a "working man."

person schemata
Schemata for specific individuals.

heuristics *Cognitive shortcuts used to simplify judgment or decision making.*

representativeness heuristic *Shortcut used to judge category membership by comparing an example to typical members of a category.*

Social schemata help us to organize and simplify a lot of information that we have received. They help us to interpret new information more rapidly, and influence what will be encoded and remembered.

HEURISTICS

Another way we simplify processing in perceiving others is through the use of **heuristics**, cognitive shortcuts based on implicit rules of thumb. We must often make complex judgments under conditions where it would be unrealistic to try to be thorough.

REPRESENTATIVENESS HEURISTIC

In trying to make a quick judgment about a person we may simply estimate the extent to which the individual is like the typical member (prototype) of a social category. Consider the following description: Steve is "very shy and withdrawn, invariably helpful but has little interest in people or in the world of reality. A meek and tidy soul, he has a need for order and structure and a passion for detail" (Tversky and Kahneman, 1974). Would you guess that Steve is a farmer, trapeze artist, librarian, or surgeon? The representativeness heuristic provides us with a quick and easy solution. We simply estimate the extent to which Steve is similar to or representative of the typical person (prototype) in each occupation, and likely conclude that Steve is a librarian.

The research shows that we often ignore relevant statistical information that would help us to make a more informed judgment. Regarding Steve's occupation, **base-rate information** indicates that there are more farmers than librarians, making it more likely that Steve is a farmer than a librarian. Hamill, Wilson and Nisbett (1980) conducted a study that provided a rather dramatic social demonstration of the use of the representativeness heuristic instead of base-rate information. Subjects saw a videotape in which a psychologist was ostensibly interviewing a prison guard. For half the subjects, the guard expressed very negative, even brutal, attitudes towards prisoners (i.e. they're all losers who should be kept locked up). The other half saw a guard expressing more optimistic, humane attitudes towards prisoners and their rehabilitation. Some of each group were told that this guard was quite "typical" of prison guards, others that the guard was quite "atypical" (humane or inhumane), and others were given no base-rate information about how typical or representative this person was of prison guards. Subjects then answered a questionnaire about their attitude towards prison guards in general. Those who had viewed an interview with a humane guard expressed significantly more positive attitudes towards this group, regardless of whether the person was represented as typical or atypical. That is, people tended to infer about a group from a particular example and ignore base-rate information.

THE FALSE CONSENSUS EFFECT

A useful rule of thumb is to simply extrapolate from our own reactions in order to infer what others' attitudes or behaviour choices would be. For example, in an experiment, students were asked to walk around campus for thirty minutes wearing a large sandwich board carrying the message "Eat at Joe's." Some agreed, and some refused, but both groups later estimated that over two-thirds of the other students on campus would have made the same decision as they did (Ross, Greene and House, 1977). Other studies have shown that subjects overestimate the extent to which others have the same smoking habits and hold the same political attitudes as they do (Sherman, Chassin, Presson and Agostinelli, 1984; Fields and Schuman, 1976). However, there are limits to this heuristic. We may want to see ourselves as unique in possessing certain positive attributes, and would thus underestimate the number of people who share these desirable attributes (Campbell, 1986).

ILLUSORY CORRELATIONS

Another influence on our perceptions of others is our tendency to perceive a relationship where little or none actually exists. This type of perception is an **illusory correlation.** One source of illusory correlations is associating items according to our prior expectation. For example, consider the stereotypical view that college students in computer programs are unemotional and analytical thinkers. When we learn that a new acquaintance is a computer student we may assume

What are the advantages and disadvantages of the cognitive shortcuts we use in perceiving others?

base-rate information
Information about the frequency with which some characteristic or event occurs in a group.

false consensus effect
Tendency to overestimate the extent to which others agree with our opinions.

illusory correlation
Perception of a relationship where little or none exists.

that she is unemotional and analytical, although such may not be the case. Another source of illusory correlations is the association of groups because of a particularly distinctive shared characteristic. Features that are unusual stand out and are more readily recalled than less salient features. This topic will be discussed further in Chapter 6.

SELF **TEST**

SELF-TEST QUESTIONS

5. Research has shown that people who are told that someone is warm, as opposed to cold, will

a) react more favourably to them in every situation

b) make more favourable ratings of that person on other traits

c) make favourable judgments only in interpersonal situations

d) make more favourable judgments only in intimate situations

6. If you visualize a character in a well-known soap opera as a typical representation of the category physicians, you use a

a) stereotype

b) schema

c) prototype

d) illusory correlation

7. Which heuristic would cause someone to think of nursery school teachers as invariably female, even if told that 50 percent of the nursery school teachers in a centre were males?

a) representativeness

b) false consensus

c) availability

d) simulation

8. Stereotypes are a subcategory of

a) prototypes

b) self schemata

c) social schemata

d) role schemata

ATTRIBUTIONS OF CAUSALITY

causal attributions
People's explanations for the causes of behaviour or events.

As we attempt to figure out what people are like, we often try to determine why they behave the way they do. We make **causal attributions** that go beyond our first impressions, using many kinds of information. We also try to account for the way events in the social world turn out. Psychologists have developed several models that specify the types of information we use and describe how we use it to explain the causes of behaviour and events. We will now turn to a brief examination of two of these models: Kelley's covariation model and Weiner's theory of achievement attribution.

How do we explain the reasons for behaviour?

ATTRIBUTION THEORIES

COVARIATION MODEL (KELLEY, 1972B)

Kelley is particularly concerned with social interactions in which events may be caused by the **actor** (the person performing the behaviour), the **entity** (the person to whom the behaviour is directed), or the **situation** (the social context in which the behaviour occurs). He argues that people behave as "naive scientists" in the sense that we sift through various events, past and present, attempting to eliminate alternative possible causes in order to arrive at a best guess or hypothesis about the real cause.

Let's consider an example: Mike greets Anne very affectionately when she arrives. You may wonder, "Why did Mike behave in that way?" You may attribute his behaviour to the actor (Mike is an affectionate person), to the entity (Anne is very lovable), or to the situation (a reunion of close friends). The perceiver evaluates the available evidence:

(1) **Distinctiveness of the entity.** Does the actor respond distinctively, that is, in a special way? Does Mike show the same affection to everyone or only to Anne? If the latter is true (high distinctiveness), an entity attribution is appropriate.

(2) **Consensus across actors.** Do others act in the same way towards the entity? If everyone is affectionate towards Anne (high consensus), we would attribute Mike's behaviour to the entity (Anne) or the situation. If, on the other hand, only Mike acted in this way (low consensus), an attribution to the actor is likely.

(3) **Consistency.** Does the actor behave in this way to the entity across situations? Is Mike always affectionate towards Anne? If consistency is high, we would attribute his behaviour to the actor or the entity. If consistency is low, however, we would make a situational attribution.

Of course, wherever possible, we would use all three sources of information together. For example, knowing only that Mike's behaviour is consistent would tell us that it was caused by the actor or entity. But, knowing that consistency is high and that consensus and distinctiveness are also high (Mike is affectionate to Anne and only to Anne, and so is everyone else) would lead to a confident entity attribution: Anne really is lovable. However, if consistency is high but consensus and distinctiveness are low (Mike is always affectionate to Anne but others are not, and Mike is also affectionate to Ruth, Mary, John, and Peter), we would attribute the action to the actor: Mike is really a very affectionate person. See Figure 2-1 for a summary.

THEORY OF ACHIEVEMENT ATTRIBUTIONS (WEINER, 1974, 1980)

In Weiner's view, we evaluate much of our social experience in terms of success and failure. In some cases it is defined in concrete ways: passing an examination, or getting a job. At other times success or failure is experienced in more subtle ways: having a child who is admired, or being "lucky at love." Weiner suggests that achievement attributions involve a two-step process. First, we decide whether the success or failure was caused by something about the person (internal) or the situation (external). Then we must decide whether the internal or external cause was stable or unstable in nature. When a cause is stable, we expect the same outcome to occur again and again. In the later version of the model (1980), Weiner added a third dimension: whether the occurrence was controllable by the actor. Thus we can choose among eight types of explanations for success or failure. In Figure 2-2 we outline one example based on a student's final grade in psychology.

FIGURE 2-1 **How we attribute social behaviour to internal or external causes**

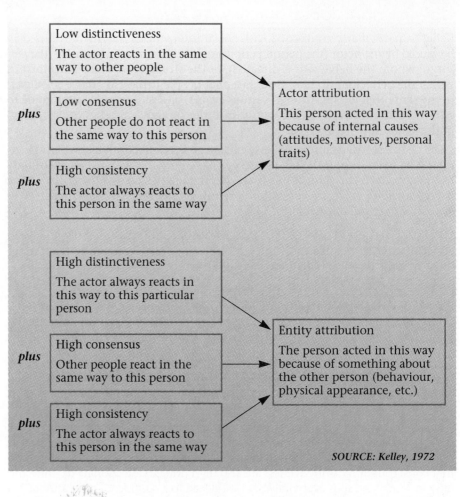

Low distinctiveness

The actor reacts in the same way to other people

plus

Low consensus

Other people do not react in the same way to this person

plus

High consistency

The actor always reacts to this person in the same way

Actor attribution

This person acted in this way because of internal causes (attitudes, motives, personal traits)

High distinctiveness

The actor always reacts in this way to this particular person

plus

High consensus

Other people react in the same way to this person

plus

High consistency

The actor always reacts to this person in the same way

Entity attribution

The person acted in this way because of something about the other person (behaviour, physical appearance, etc.)

SOURCE: Kelley, 1972

An interesting test of Weiner's model has been its application to data from the sports pages (Lau and Russell, 1980). Content analyses were performed with reports of games in which causal explanations for winning and losing were recorded. In general, unexpected outcomes ("upsets") generated a greater number of attributions. With "upsets" there seemed to be more to explain or justify. A self-serving bias was also evident. Winning was generally attributed to internal factors: "We all had a great day; everyone gave 150 percent." Losing was attributed to unstable external factors: "It just wasn't our day." While some studies have not fully replicated these findings (Marks, Mutrie, Brooks and Harris, 1984), other research indicates that winners tend to make attributions to more stable and controllable causes than do losers (Grove, Hanrahan and McInman, 1991).

Attributions about failure are very important. When we consciously supplant one explanation for another with the goal of influencing others, we're making an excuse. Thus, for example, if we fail an exam, we may attribute the failure to a headache or the unfairness of the instructor. Such excuses serve to protect our self-esteem, to prevent or lessen the anger of someone else (one's parents?), and to maintain positive expectations about the future. Since the excuse is an unstable external attribution, we expect that the situation will not happen again (Weiner, Figueroa-Muñoz and Kakihara, 1991).

FIGURE 2-2 Attributions about achievement: A final grade in social
psychology

	Stable		Unstable	
	Internal	External	Internal	External
Controllable	typical effort	professor dislikes student	unusual effort	unusual disruption by other student
Not controllable	lack of ability	task difficulty	mood	luck

SOURCE: Weiner, 1979

ATTRIBUTIONAL BIASES

So far we have seen that these attribution theories are models of essentially conscious and rational processes. However, as we have already seen, human beings sometimes fall short of this ideal of rationality. See Box 2-1 for the application of attribution theory to the problem of insomnia. Consider the part rationality played in the experimental outcomes reported.

Biases can have a pronounced effect on the process of attribution. We will examine two of these biases: the fundamental attribution error and the actor versus observer bias.

FUNDAMENTAL ATTRIBUTION ERROR (ROSS, 1977)

In explaining why people do what they do, we tend to make dispositional attributions (assign cause to personality characteristics of the actor) and to underestimate the power of the situation. This tendency to exaggerate the importance of personal factors and to underestimate the influence of other people and other aspects of the situation is called the **fundamental attribution error** because it is so pervasive. For example, we tend to attribute what people write or say to their "true beliefs" even when we are told that the person was instructed to argue a certain position (Jones and Harris, 1967). If we meet someone who is abrupt and rude to us, we tend to attribute this to a personal characteristic of rudeness, despite the fact that there may have been external causes, such as family problems, unreasonable professors, illness, or lateness for an important appointment.

The fundamental attribution error explains why readers of this textbook may be surprised by the results of much of the research described. Studies will demonstrate the power of the situation in causing people to conform, to do what they have been told to do by authority, to help or harm someone, or to act in ways contrary to their own attitudes. These studies challenge our assumption that our actions flow from our own beliefs, values, and moral character.

ACTOR VERSUS OBSERVER BIAS

People generally tend to attribute the actions of others to stable personality characteristics, but see their own behaviour as more strongly influenced by situational factors. This does not contradict what we have just described. In addi-

How do biases influence the attributions we make?

fundamental attribution error Tendency to exaggerate the importance of personal factors and underestimate the influence of the situation.

actor versus observer bias Tendency to attribute the actions of others to personality characteristics, but to see the situation as more influential on one's own behaviour.

BOX 2-1
ATTRIBUTIONS IN THE CLINIC: A CASE OF INSOMNIA

Attribution theory has been applied a number of ways to alleviate clinical problems. For example, people with insomnia go to bed with the expectation that they will have trouble getting to sleep. Hence, they experience restlessness, irritability, or anxiety, perhaps even confusing thoughts and an accelerated heart rate. These symptoms, of course, make it more difficult for them to fall asleep. While they began with the one problem—insomnia—they now face the additional problem of worrying about insomnia, and attributing it to "something wrong with me." In short, thinking about the problem exacerbates the problem.

Storms and Nisbett (1970) recruited subjects who reported having difficulty falling asleep. Two groups of them were given a placebo "medication" to take before bedtime while a control group received no pills. One medication group was told that the pills would reduce arousal, making them feel relaxed, while the others were told that they would increase arousal. The results showed that those who were told that the pills would decrease arousal fell asleep an average of fifteen minutes later than before, while those who expected the pills to increase arousal fell asleep twelve minutes faster. Those subjects who believed that the pills caused their aroused state were no longer attributing this problem to "something wrong with me," and had broken the exacerbation cycle. Worrying about insomnia no longer kept them awake.

We might question the ethics of using such deception with patients. A patient who suffers from insomnia might wonder why a stimulant drug would be prescribed. Indeed, attempts to replicate the study have not been successful (Bootzin, Herman and Nicassio, 1976). Other approaches assist people in making truthful and non-exacerbating attributions about their problems. Indeed, another group of insomniacs was informed that the problem might be caused by a relatively high base-line level of physiological arousal. Not having to worry about what was keeping them awake, they had less difficulty in falling asleep (Lowery, Denney and Storms, 1979).

tion to making the fundamental attribution error, we also are more likely to attribute our own behaviour rather than the behaviour of others to situational causes (Watson, 1982).

For example, consider a study in which male students were asked to write paragraphs explaining why they had chosen their girlfriends and university majors, and why their best friends had chosen their own girlfriends and majors (Nisbett, Caputo, Legant and Marecek, 1973). Responses were coded for causal attributions. Subjects tended to attribute their own decisions to external reasons (e.g. "I decided to major in psychology because it was interesting"), but attributed their friends' decisions to dispositions (e.g. "He's going out with her because he's insecure").

Why do the attributions of actors and observers differ in this manner? One reason is that they have different perspectives from which to view the event. The actors' behaviour captures the attention of observers. By contrast, actors usually cannot directly observe themselves, and are more aware of the situation than they are of themselves. However, when actors are shown a videotape replay of themselves in a conversation, they tend to attribute their actions more to their own characteristics (Storms, 1973). Also, actors and observers have access to different information. Actors know how they have acted in different situations and therefore would be better able to judge how various situations influence their behaviour.

This bias is not an invariant law. When we can clearly identify external causes for a behaviour, we make external attributions as actors and observers alike

(Monson and Hesley, 1982). For example, we would readily attribute the fear of people in a devastating earthquake to the situation. On the other hand, if we know someone well and like or identify with that person, we tend to see the world more as they do. Under these conditions, even as observers, we use more situational attributions (Regan and Totten, 1975). Finally, the effects of one bias may overcome the effects of another. For example, we often give ourselves the benefit of the doubt or take credit for successes (internal attributions).

SELF-TEST QUESTIONS

9. Attribution is concerned with

a) the formation of person prototypes

b) how people assign causes to events

c) ascribing one's positive characteristics to learning

d) the difference between actor's and observer's ideas about the cause of an event

10. Which of the following is an internal attribution?

a) the weather

b) good luck

c) peer group pressure

d) mood

11. If Simon rarely laughs at any movie but laughs at this one, and so does everyone else in the theatre, we would conclude (according to the covariation model) that

a) Simon is one funny guy

b) the movie is not likely very funny

c) the movie is very funny

d) Simon and his friends all have a great sense of humour

12. Which of the following represents the fundamental attribution error?

a) you attribute your own behaviour at a party to the situation

b) you attribute the behaviour of someone else at a party to their strange personality characteristics

c) you attribute success to yourself and failure to bad luck

d) you attribute your failure in an exam to the unfairness of the exam

PERCEIVING EVENTS IN THE SOCIAL WORLD

Our perception and interpretation of events in the social world are facilitated by mental representations of our knowledge of the social world and by thinking strategies that help us to deal with its richness and complexity. In this section we will focus on the schemata we use to represent familiar events (scripts) and on the heuristics we apply to help us organize our perceptions.

script *A type of schema that represents routine events.*

F·O·C·U·S

How do scripts influence our perception and memory of events?

SCRIPTS

With experience in social situations, we develop expectations about the sequence of events and the roles people play in these situations. The type of schema that represents routine events is called a **script**. For example, we have a script about what happens when a group of friends goes to a hockey game. It begins with purchasing the ticket, presenting it to a ticket taker, and finding our seats. We may buy a program and begin identifying players as they warm up. We stand for the national anthem, then sit and shout encouragement during the opening face-off. Purchasing snacks and liquid refreshments between periods is usually part of the ritual. We have standard reactions to a goal by our team, to a goal by their team, to a fight, and we know when and how to express disapproval of actions by the referee or opposition. All of these events "fit" as part of what happens when we go to a hockey game. Such scripts enable us to experience events as predictable, understandable, and comfortable.

Although many of our scripts pertain to events we have experienced personally and frequently, we also have scripts for events that are familiar to us because of our reading or observation of other people. We may have scripts for events in other countries that we have not yet visited and for events that exist only in our imagination. Many of our ideas are developed and altered through communication with others. Some of our scripts contain shared meanings and symbols that are common to a group to which we belong or to our culture. For example, our script for a hockey game has evolved in our culture and is shared by its members today. Our hockey game script may be quite different from one held by Russians or Swedes.

As well as helping us to develop expectations for events and to organize our behaviour in social situations, scripts also influence our memory of these situations. Bower, Black and Turner (1979) studied the influence of scripts on recall. They developed scripts for commonly experienced events such as shopping for groceries or visiting a doctor. Subjects read stories about these situations that did not conform in every detail to the appropriate script. In examining the subjects' memory of the content of the stories, Bower et al. found that they inserted information that had not been in the stories but was consistent with the script.

Ross and Conway (1986) demonstrated that memory of past events can be influenced by our expectations of what should have happened. Subjects enrolled in an extravagantly advertised study skills program. After an initial questionnaire in which they evaluated their own study skills before entering the program, subjects were assigned randomly to the program or to a waiting list. After the program was completed, all subjects were re-interviewed. A follow-up showed that the program had no significant effect on their grades. However, subjects believed that they had improved. When asked to recall how they had rated their skills previously, subjects who completed the program recalled "before" as worse than it had seemed to them at the time. These subjects applied a script that included expectations for self-improvement, distorting their memory of the past. Like stereotypes, prototypes, and other schemata for types of people and roles, scripts influence our attention, encoding, and memory of information (Fiske and Taylor, 1991).

HEURISTICS

AVAILABILITY HEURISTIC

One of the most important cognitive "rules" discovered by Tversky and Kahneman (1974) is deceptively simple: if something comes readily to mind, we tend to assume that it's likely true and we use it. The **availability heuristic** can be demonstrated by means of the following question: Which is more common, words that begin with the letter "k" or those that have "k" as the third letter? In fact, in the English language there are more than twice as many words with "k" as the third letter (e.g. awkward, bake) as there are with "k" as the first letter (e.g. king, know). However, most people incorrectly estimate that more words begin with that letter, probably because it is easier to think of such examples (Tversky and Kahneman, 1982).

A simple experiment illustrates the phenomenon. Subjects were presented with evidence concerning a trial for driving while intoxicated (Carroll, 1978). While the evidence was equally strong in both cases, one group of subjects was told that the defendant had staggered and fallen against a table at a party. The other group was told that when he fell against a table, he knocked over a bowl of bright green guacamole onto a white carpet. Forty-eight hours later, the subjects who had read the second description judged the defendant as more probably guilty of drunk driving. Thus availability was enhanced by vividness of the information.

The availability heuristic can also be seen at work in our tendency to be influenced by extreme examples. This is illustrated in a study (Rothbart, Fulero, Jensen, Howard and Birrell, 1978) in which subjects read fifty statements about actions by hypothetical strangers. While forty of the statements were innocuous, ten described crimes. For one group of subjects, the crimes were fairly mild and non-violent (e.g. petty vandalism, shoplifting). For a second group of subjects, the crimes were serious and violent (e.g. murder, rape). Later, subjects in both groups were asked to estimate the frequency of crime. This estimate was much higher for subjects in the second group than for those in the first. Since extreme cases bias our inferences about the frequency of an event, it is not surprising that television may distort our perception of reality with its focus on crime, scandal, violence, and other bad news.

SIMULATION HEURISTIC

We have seen how our expectations and the availability of information influence our social perception. Our response to events is also influenced by our ideas about what outcomes might have occurred. In such situations we use the **simulation heuristic**. A study by Kahneman and Tversky (1982) provides a good example of this phenomenon. Subjects were given two different scenarios about men who missed their flights because of late arrival at the airport, and were asked to judge which of the two men would be more upset. They were told that Mr. Crane and Mr. Tees were scheduled to leave the same airport at the same time but on different flights. Both were caught in the same traffic jam on their way to the airport, and both arrived thirty minutes after the scheduled departures of their flights. Mr. Crane was told that his flight left on time, while Mr. Tees was told that his flight had been delayed and had just left five minutes ago. Most people respond that Mr. Tees would be more upset. They imagine that Mr. Tees could have made his flight, if it were not for some minor mishap on the way to the airport. However, it is inconceivable that Mr. Crane could have made it on time since he arrived so much later than the actual departure time. The simulation heuristic enables us to imagine "if only" conditions, which explains much about our reactions to near misses, second-guessing, and other frustrations.

ILLUSION OF CONTROL

In our efforts to efficiently process social information we construct a view in which the world is perceived as simpler and more predictable than it really

availability heuristic
Strategy of making judgments in terms of readily accessible and easily remembered information.

How do heuristics help and hinder us in our perception of a complex social world?

simulation heuristic
Tendency to use "if only" conditions in responding to near misses and other frustrations.

illusion of control
Exaggerated belief in our own capacity to determine what happens to us in life.

just world phenomenon
Illusory belief that the world is just and that people get what they deserve (that good things happen to good people and bad things happen to bad people). This belief often leads to blaming the victim.

is. We also tend to perceive events as being more controllable. Langer (1975) suggests that we cling to an **illusion of control**, an exaggerated belief in our own capacity to determine what happens to us in life. This tendency was demonstrated in an experiment by Wortman (1975). Subjects were presented with two coloured marbles in a can, each representing a different prize. Some were told which marble represented the desirable prize, while others were not. Then subjects either chose a marble or were given one, without being allowed to see which was which. Subjects had no control over the outcome in either condition. However, they attributed more responsibility to themselves when they picked their marble without looking at it than when it was selected for them.

Lerner (1977) suggests an important implication of the illusion of control. People may have an illusory belief in a **just world** in which good outcomes are believed to happen to good people and bad outcomes to bad people. In such a world people get what they deserve and deserve what they get. For example, when you read about an automobile accident in which the driver was killed, your anxiety level about driving may increase. However, when you find that the driver was not wearing a seatbelt, your anxiety decreases because you always wear one. Indirectly, you have blamed the victim in order to reduce your own anxiety. In several laboratory experiments, Lerner found that after seeing someone picked at random and ostensibly subjected to electric shocks, subjects who observed the event tended to see the victims as somehow deserving of their predicament.

In this world view, victims do not exist. Poverty, oppression, tragedy, and injustice all happen because they're deserved. These beliefs may be useful to justify unjust practices. For example, in a comparative study of both children and university students, scores on a scale of just world beliefs were higher among white South Africans than white British subjects, even though the South Africans came from the relatively more liberal English-speaking population (Furnham, 1985). Two other examples provide further illustration. First, some have blamed the six million Jewish victims of the Holocaust for their fate, ignoring both the overwhelming and brutal Nazi force directed against them and the heroic revolts in the ghettos and concentration camps (Davidowicz, 1975). Second, there is a persistent tendency, somewhat greater among men, to attribute responsibility for a rape to the victim. This tendency is due to the false perception that the victim was somehow "asking for it" (Burt, 1980).

Although it is important for people to understand and make sense of people, events, and situations in their lives, we rarely attempt to do this in an optimal manner. Of course, the best way to understand anything is to gather as much information as possible and think about it logically and carefully. However, because there is simply too much information to process and too little time in which to do it, we often cope with this state of affairs by taking cognitive shortcuts. After all, we must figure out what is happening, decide what to do, and then act. We cannot take the time and effort to do what we would logically need to do in order to "understand" the world. Instead, we apply schemata to filter and interpret information, quickly form an impression of someone, apply some quick decision rules to arrive at explanations for their actions, and then act. We are subject to an impressive array of biases, a few of which we have discussed in this chapter. And yet, we are right enough, often enough, to function rather well in our social lives.

SELF-TEST QUESTIONS

13. A schema for playing baseball (the rules, customs, manner of dressing, batting, and speaking, etc.) is called a

a) role schema

b) social schema

c) script

d) prototype

14. We tend to value a lottery ticket more when we can choose the numbers. This shows the effects of

a) attribution of success and failure

b) self-serving bias

c) scripts

d) illusion of control

15. According to the textbook, the illusion of control leads logically to

a) self-serving bias

b) belief in a just world

c) fundamental attribution error

d) tendency to make situational attributions

16. Tversky and Kahneman (1974) found that we often ignore _____ information in favour of the _____ heuristic.

a) base rate, representativeness

b) objective, availability

c) base rate, availability

d) objective, representativeness

SUMMARY

(1) Self-perception involves cognitive (self-concept), affective (self-esteem), and behavioural components. Cognitive representations of the thoughts and beliefs we have about the self include self-schemata, role-schemata, potential selves, and other representations of identity. Self-esteem is concerned with evaluations of the self as well as strategies people use to maintain positive feelings and ward off threats to a sense of personal worth. The behavioural component involves both self-expression and impression management (self-presentation).

(2) In developing impressions of others we may simply add traits together or average them to arrive at an overall impression.

(3) In making causal attributions, Kelley suggests that we function as "naive scientists." We focus on information about consistency across situations, distinctiveness of the person's behaviour, and consensus among individuals in their behaviour towards the individual of interest.

(4) Weiner's achievement attribution model focuses on whether a result is perceived to have been caused by something internal or external, stable or unstable, and controllable or uncontrollable.

(5) Attributions are influenced by certain biases. We overestimate dispositional causes of behaviour (the fundamental attribution error), attribute our own behaviour to situations to a greater extent than the actions of others (actor versus observer bias), and we use self-serving attributions (self-serving bias).

(6) We tend to believe that we control our environment, and that the world is fundamentally "just"; thus we blame victims for their fate.

(7) Our thinking about people and events in the social world is organized into schemata, complex integrations of information and examples of people, roles, and events. Types of schemata include prototypes (best exemplars of categories) and stereotypes (rigid generalizations about the attributes of a particular group of people).

(8) We tend to apply certain "rules" (heuristics) as cognitive shortcuts. We often ignore information about base rates, exaggerate relationships between events (illusory correlation), and use typical examples (representativeness heuristic) to make judgments. We overemphasize extreme cues, and use what readily comes to mind (availability heuristic). We also overestimate the extent to which others believe and act as we do (false consensus effect).

FOR REVIEW

Much of our beliefs and information about the self is represented in cognitive frameworks called _____(1). We have representations for the actual self and for other unrealized selves. The schemata we use to help define our positions or roles in society are called _____(2).

Self-esteem is concerned with feelings about and _____(3) of the self. According to discrepancy theory, our level of self-esteem and related emotional well-being is influenced by our awareness of the differences between the actual self and _____(4). To protect one's ego and self-esteem people frequently take credit for their successes and attribute their failures to external factors. This tendency is called the _____(5). Social comparison serves the desire to feel positive about oneself and one's abilities in _____(6). Most of us want to be liked and approved. Our effort to create a favourable impression is called _____(7).

According to Asch, the impressions we form of others are _____(8). Another view of impression formation is that we put together sequentially acquired information as if we were doing some _____(9). In forming ideas about categories of people or objects, we are often influenced by a _____(10) of that category. A particular kind of prototype, consisting of rigid beliefs about the attributes of a group, is called a _____(11). When we make a quick judgment about a person based on whatever information first comes to mind, we are using the _____(12) heuristic. When we evaluate an individual by estimating the extent to which that person is like a prototype, we are using the _____(13) heuristic.

There are several theories about the attributions we make to account for behaviour. According to Kelley's covariation model, we evaluate behaviour in terms of distinctiveness, consistency, and _____(14). Weiner's model of attributions about achievement suggests that we must decide whether it was controllable or not, stable or unstable, and _____(15). We tend to make _____(16) attributions about our own actions, and _____(17) attributions about the actions of others. People tend to blame a victim for his or her fate because of their belief in a _____(18).

With experience in social situations, we develop expectations about the sequence of events and roles people play in these situations. The type of schema

FOR REVIEW

that represents a routine event is a _____(19). Like other types of schemata, scripts influence our attention, encoding, and _____(20) for information.

ISSUES AND ACTIVITIES

1. Apply the concepts in this chapter in a discussion of the 1995 referendum on Quebec sovereignty.

2. Develop a script for a routine event, such as a first date or going to the dentist. Ask 20 to 30 people to describe the roles and sequence of activities that characterize your chosen event. Use the information given most frequently to develop your script.

3. In this chapter we have seen that we use a number of cognitive shortcuts and that our thinking is often biased and not logical. Discuss specific examples that demonstrate how these characteristics of our social perception and cognition both help us and harm us.

4. Carry out an attribution study of smoking (smokers vs non-smokers vs ex-smokers). Devise a brief questionnaire to assess why people smoke (e.g. a powerful habit, pleasure, social pressure). Is there an actor vs observer bias? Do non-smokers or ex-smokers make different attributions about smoking than do smokers?

• FURTHER READING

FISKE, S.T. and TAYLOR, S.E. (1991). *Social cognition,* Second Edition. New York: McGraw-Hill. An excellent general introduction to various topics in social cognition.

ROSS, L. and NISBETT, R.E. (1991). *The person and the situation: Perspectives of social psychology*. New York: McGraw-Hill. This book has interesting chapters on the power of the situation and on construing the social world.

SUGGESTED WEBLINKS

Journal of Personality and Social Psychology (Table of Contents)
    http://www.apa.org/journals/psp.html

Social and Personality Section, Canadian Psychological Association
    http://www.uwinnipeg.ca/~baldwin/14index.html

Social Cognition Paper Archives
    http://www.psych.purdue.edu/faculty/esmith/www/scarch.html

ANSWERS TO SELF-TEST QUESTIONS

1. d; 2. c; 3. b; 4. d; 5. b; 6. c; 7. a; 8. a; 9. b; 10. d; 11. c; 12. b; 13. c; 14. b; 15. d; 16. a.

ANSWERS TO FOR REVIEW

1. self-schemata; 2. role schemata; 3. evaluations; 4. alternate views of the self; 5. self-serving bias; 6. self-enhancement; 7. self-presentation; 8. dynamic wholes; 9. cognitive algebra; 10. prototype; 11. stereotype; 12. availability; 13. representativeness; 14. consensus; 15. internal or external; 16 situational; 17. dispositional; 18. just world; 19. script; 20. memory.

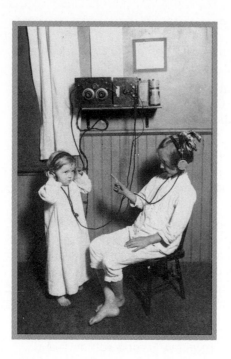

COMMUNICATION

If one knows his neighbour's tongue, he possesses the key of his house.
Abbé Arthur Maheux

What do you mean we don't communicate? Just yesterday I faxed you a reply to the recorded message you left on my answering machine.
Wall Street Journal

■ LEARNING OUTCOMES

1. An appreciation for the role of non-verbal behaviour in human communication.

2. An understanding of how verbal and non-verbal behaviour combine to provide a double-coded communication system.

3. An awareness of how speech style influences impression formation and marks group boundaries.

4. Knowledge about the nature of second language acquisition and its social psychological consequences.

■ FOR REFLECTION

• How can we communicate without using words?

- What is involved in having a conversation?
- How does the way we speak depend on our relationship to the listener?
- Is there more to becoming bilingual than learning grammar and vocabulary?

■ CHAPTER OUTLINE

Non-Verbal Communication

    Functions

    Kinesics: Facial Expression and Eye Contact

    Kinesics: Body Language

    Haptics: Touch Communication

    Paralanguage

Coordination of Verbal and Non-Verbal Communication

Verbal Communication

    Spoken Language and Written Language

    Functions

    Language and Gender

Language and Social Interaction

    Speech Acts

    Speech Style and Accommodation

    Standard and Non-Standard Speech

    Language and Group Identity

    Communication between Bilinguals

Second Language Learning

    Myths about Second Language Learning

    Immersion Programs in Schools

    Who Succeeds in Second Language Learning?

Summary

For Review

Issues and Activities

Further Reading

Suggested WebLinks

Answers to Self-Test Questions

Answers to For Review

Communication is the essence of social interaction. Whether by words, facial expressions, or gestures, whether through direct contact, telephone conversations, or the printed page, humans inform each other of their thoughts and feelings, their wishes and ideals, their intentions and needs. They threaten, command, reward, tease, and entertain each other. They teach, exchange points of view, and coordinate their activities. They communicate non-verbally by means of gestures, facial expressions, body position, and non-linguistic sounds (sighs, laughs, grunts, and so on), and they communicate verbally through language. Indeed, it is difficult to imagine being in the presence of another person without continually communicating in one way or another.

While non-verbal communication provides a powerful means of sending information, it is language that distinctly characterizes human communication. It is impossible to do justice to the study of human social activity without examining verbal activity, for virtually every utterance a person makes in the presence of others demands a response. How the listener responds often reflects various aspects of the interaction, such as the status levels of speaker and listener, and the emotional relationship between them. Language itself plays a role in shaping these interactions between individuals. In addition, language is used to define group identities and to mark boundaries between groups.

Unfortunately, sometimes people miscommunicate, leading speakers to believe that they understand each other when in fact they do not. Exchanging words is easy; true communication of ideas and feelings is not always so. Miscommunication can lead to problems and conflicts (see Chapter 11) among individuals, groups, and even nations. As we shall see, miscommunication is most likely to occur when the communicators are of different genders (Tannen, 1990), different cultural or linguistic backgrounds, or even when one of the communicators is in a mood state such as depression (McCann and Lalonde, 1993).

Given the importance of language in social interaction, it is surprising that until recently social psychologists have largely neglected the study of language. In Canada, of course, linguistic factors have always played an important role in our social and political lives. Moreover, Montreal is one of the world's natural living laboratories for the study of social psychological aspects of language and bilingualism. It is the second largest French-speaking city in the world, and has an English-speaking population that is larger than all but a few other Canadian cities. It is also noteworthy that Canada is a world leader in telecommunications research. Electronic communication raises all sorts of important social psychological questions: "How does using the telephone affect understanding?" "How do leaders emerge in video conferencing networks?" Social psychologists in Canada have made important contributions to research in these areas (Gardner and Desrochers, 1981; Johnston and Strickland, 1985).

This chapter begins with the examination of non-verbal methods of communication. Next, language is discussed, with a particular emphasis on its social aspects. Finally, the role of language in intergroup relations is explored, as well as the social psychological aspects of bilingualism.

NON-VERBAL COMMUNICATION

A raise of the eyebrows, a pucker of the lips, or a clenching of the fist can often communicate more about how we feel than could a dozen words. Yet communication researchers showed little interest in the importance of body movements, gestures, and facial expressions until the 1960s. Since that time, however, interest in non-verbal behaviour has mushroomed, leading to a whole new field of psychological research (Rimé, 1983).

It is now known that verbal and non-verbal communication are intimately related and generally represent different aspects of a common process in the brain rather than two separate processes. Although we sometimes use non-verbal gestures deliberately to communicate, much of our non-verbal behaviour occurs without our intent or awareness. We have all observed people making various gestures while they talk on the telephone, especially when they are excited about something. The gestures are obviously not intended to communicate anything. Research suggests that non-verbal behaviour is a fundamental part of the process of translating thoughts into words (Rimé, 1983). Accordingly, our non-verbal and verbal responses should be highly correlated, unless we make a deliberate attempt to hide what we are thinking or feeling.

***Is non-verbal commu-
nication deliberate?***

FUNCTIONS

Non-verbal behaviours have a variety of functions. (1) They help to regulate spoken language, for example, by coordinating turn-taking in conversation. (2) They can provide information: we use them to express our feelings, and we interpret non-verbal behaviours in order to understand the feelings of others. For example, they can indicate whether someone is interested in or attracted to us. An utterance said with a smile will be interpreted quite differently than one said with a frown. (3) They can be used to express intimacy, such as when two lovers gaze intently into each others' eyes. (4) They can be used to establish dominance or to promote social control. We threaten others with non-verbal signals or ingratiate ourselves by smiling. (5) They can be used to help reach goals. We draw another person's attention to something we want by pointing to it.

Within a particular culture or society, everyone understands the meaning of various facial expressions and gestures. Otherwise, they would be of little use in communication. For the most part we learn to use and to react to non-verbal communication through interaction with others. As children, we imitate the motions and gestures of older people and grow to be sensitive to various non-verbal cues. Often we are unaware of the specific cues that gave us a particular impression about someone. And we're often also unaware of the non-verbal signals we give. However, we are aware that specific gestures are appropriate in some situations but not in others. **Social norms** govern the use of non-verbal communication. For instance, you would not roll your eyes towards the ceiling while listening to a professor criticize your essay plan, because such an act would be disrespectful. However, if the same professor asked you about how you were enjoying your part-time job, the same eyeroll could be employed quite appropriately.

***What are the functions
and types of non-verbal
communication?***

social norms Shared beliefs about which behaviours are acceptable and not acceptable for group membership.

Non-verbal behaviour falls into a number of different categories, including the following: kinesics, physical appearance, paralanguage, proxemics, and haptics (Burgoon, Buller and Woodall, 1989). Kinesics refers to all bodily movements except those that involve contact with someone else. This is the "body language" of popular literature. Physical appearance, of course, refers to the natural aspects of our body as well as decorations: the way we style our hair, wear clothes, and our natural beauty or lack of it. Paralanguage refers to all non-verbal aspects of speech itself: pitch, loudness, sighs, laughs, silences, grunts, coughs, and groans. Haptics refers to the perception and use of touch as communication, while proxemics refers to the perception, use, and structuring of space as communication.

In the sections that follow, we shall focus on (1) kinesics, discussing facial expression and eye contact, and body position and gestures ("body language"); (2) haptics; and (3) paralanguage. Proxemics will be discussed in the context of social psychology and the environment in Chapter 14.

BOX 3-1

NON-VERBAL BEHAVIOUR AND THE BALLET

Music can be written down precisely. So can dialogue, at least as far as the words are concerned, although the director of a play decides how the words are said and how the actors move about the stage. But how does one record on paper the many and intricate movements needed for a ballet production? The ballet is all non-verbal behaviour.

FIGURE 3-1 **Labanotation, 1953 (opening dance from Balanchine's version of Swan Lake)**

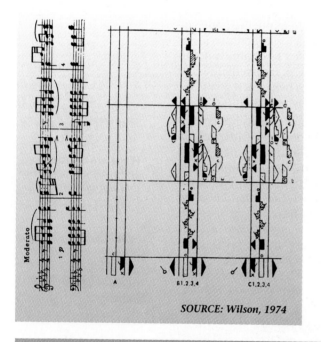

SOURCE: Wilson, 1974

FIGURE 3-2 **Benesh system, 1955 (from The Lady and the Fool)**

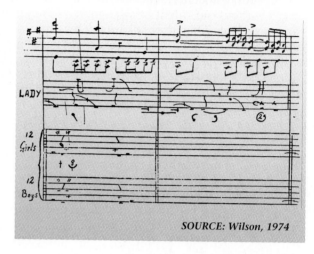

SOURCE: Wilson, 1974

Over the years, various attempts have been made to develop a uniform coding system for recording the movements, the earliest being that of Guglielmo Ebreo of Pesaro in 1463. Of many systems in use today, two systems of notation have become predominant. The first, which appeared in 1953, is referred to as *Labanotation*, named after its inventor, Rudolf von Laban. This system (see Figure 3-1) uses three vertical lines and symbols to indicate the dancer's position and movements. It allows for the recording of any human movement (Wilson, 1974). The second system is the *Benesh system*, a simple notational movement copyrighted by Joan Benesh and the Royal Ballet and School in 1955. It involves the use of symbols superimposed on a music stave (see Figure 3-2).

kinesics *Body language; all the bodily movements that convey information during a conversation except those involving contact with someone else.*

facial display *A pattern of expressions that communicates information, particularly about the emotional state of the individual.*

KINESICS: FACIAL EXPRESSION AND EYE CONTACT

Facial expression plays a major role in communication. In fact, when there appears to be a contradiction between the meaning of spoken words and facial expression, people consider facial expression to indicate the meaning more accurately (Bugental, Kaswan and Love, 1970; Mehrabian, 1968).

ARE FACIAL DISPLAYS OF EMOTION UNIVERSAL?

Charles Darwin suggested in 1872 that human emotional expression developed from that of animals. He pointed out similarities between facial expressions in people and in animals, between children and adults, and between sighted and blind people. In Darwin's view emotional expressions are innate and universal, and serve an important communicative function. For example, an angry expression warns others and therefore helps prevent physical fights that could be life threatening.

Since Darwin first wrote his book, *The Expression of the Emotions in Man and Animals*, a number of psychologists have been interested in the similarity of emotional expression across cultures. Some famous research on this topic was conducted by Ekman and Friesen (1971). They showed people in Japan, the United States, Borneo, New Guinea, and South America photographs of emotional displays and asked them to identify them by choosing the best label from a set of six words. They found high agreement among people in these different countries in the labels chosen for the various photographs. People living in a remote part of New Guinea, who were still living in a "Stone Age" culture isolated from contact with outsiders, were given a modified version of the task in which they matched the photographs to stories. Even the interpretations of these isolated people showed high agreement with results from other countries. In a more recent study conducted in ten countries, including Sumatra, Hong Kong, Turkey, Germany, and the United States, Ekman, Friesen et al. (1987) asked subjects to rate photographs in terms of which of six basic emotions were being displayed. Once again there was high agreement across various cultures about which emotion was most evident. (See Table 3-1.)

SOCIAL NORMS AND FACIAL EXPRESSIONS

While there are universals in facial expressions, social norms within a given culture dictate the use of facial displays to express emotions. For example, while it is appropriate to smile and laugh at a party, it is not appropriate to do so at a funeral. In some cultures the display of emotions is encouraged; in others it is frowned upon. People in Japan are taught to control their facial displays especially with regard to negative emotion, and to use laughter or smiling to conceal anger or grief (Argyle, 1975).

TABLE 3-1 **Single-emotion judgment task: Percentage of subjects within each culture who chose predicted emotion**

Nation	Happiness	Surprise	Sadness	Fear	Disgust	Anger
Estonia	90	94	86	91	71	67
Germany	93	87	83	86	61	71
Greece	93	91	80	74	77	77
Hong Kong	92	91	91	84	65	73
Italy	97	92	81	82	89	72
Japan	90	94	87	65	60	67
Scotland	98	88	86	86	79	84
Sumatra	69	78	91	70	70	70
Turkey	87	90	76	76	74	79
United States	95	92	92	84	86	81

SOURCE: Ekman et al., 1987

**What is the evidence
both for and against
the universality of
facial displays of emo-
tion? Why is this an
important issue in non-
verbal communication?**

**How is eye contact
used in non-verbal
communication?**

In an intercultural study of reading emotional expressions, Argyle (1975) showed Italian, Japanese, and English subjects photographs of facial displays from performers in the three countries. He found that Italian and English subjects judged emotions of their own group and the other group well. However, they had difficulty judging Japanese expressions. Japanese subjects could interpret Japanese expressions better than the English or Italian subjects could. However, even the Japanese subjects found the Italian and English facial expressions easier to interpret than Japanese ones. (See Table 3-2.)

Cultural distinctiveness in facial displays can lead to serious misperceptions. During World War II, Allied propaganda leaflets and posters showed a picture of a grinning Japanese soldier plunging his bayonet into an Allied soldier. While the expression on his face conveyed "sadistic glee" to Western eyes, to the Japanese, this same expression indicated grim determination rather than pleasure.

EYE CONTACT

The importance of eye contact in non-verbal communication is evident shortly after birth. Within a few days of birth, the infant will make eye contact with the caregiver. The distance at which the infant focuses most easily turns out to be the distance between infant and mother during breastfeeding (Burgoon, Buller and Woodall, 1989). Not only does the infant make eye contact, the gaze of others is arousing to infants, just as it is to primates, horses, dogs, and cats.

Because of its importance in non-verbal communication, it is worth considering the various ways in which eye contact can be used. Kleinke (1986) suggested that eye contact can serve all the purposes of non-verbal communication. It can provide information; for instance, when one person wishes to initiate interaction with another, he or she may look directly at the other's eyes. If the person looks back it means that he or she is also willing to engage in interaction. Conversely, by avoiding eye contact an individual can avoid interaction (Argyle, 1971). In conversations, gazing is important in regulating turn taking. Gaze can also be used to regulate other aspects of a social interaction. It can threaten, punish, or show dominance. In general, within a particular society, visual behaviour is very important in establishing and maintaining dominance (Ellyson and Dovidio, 1985). Gazing increases as the attraction between two people increases, although a high degree of eye contact does not always indicate affection (Patterson, 1982). "Making eyes" at someone is a means of indicating sexual or affectional interest.

TABLE 3-2 **Percentage of respondents who correctly judged facial
expression of emotion**

	Performers		
Judges	*English*	*Italian*	*Japanese*
English	63	58	38
Italian	53	62	28
Japanese	57	58	45

SOURCE: Argyle, 1975

Although we may not be aware of it, the way we look at others can reflect our perception of our relative social power (Dovidio and Ellyson, 1985). This effect is particularly evident in male-female interactions. In one study (Dovidio, Ellyson, Keating, Heltman, and Brown, 1988), male and female subjects were paired and then offered three topics of discussion. The male was expert on one topic, the female on another, and they possessed an equal level of expertise on the third topic. During their conversation, the amount of time each one spent looking at the other while talking or listening was recorded. The results indicated that when women were in positions of high expertise, they were likely to display their power non-verbally. That is, they looked at their partner as much while speaking as while listening. Both males and females low in expertise looked more often while listening than while speaking. Most interestingly, when there was no difference in expertise, women reacted as if they were low in expertise, and men reacted as if they were high in expertise. These findings suggest that women may unknowingly signal that they are of lower power to males of equal power. This behaviour would reinforce the traditional status difference between men and women.

The thrill of victory.

KINESICS: BODY LANGUAGE

One need only observe a mime artist to recognize the power of the eyes and face in communicating feelings and thoughts. But the mime communicates through the use of the whole body. There are a number of popular books that promise to teach readers how to understand and exploit "body language." These books should be approached cautiously because many of them do not back up their claims with any research evidence. There is evidence which demonstrates that certain postures are often perceived by others as reflecting specific feelings. For example, leaning towards another person is generally interpreted to mean that one is taking a positive stance and is ready to pay attention to that person. Other examples appear in Figure 3-3.

GESTURES

Gestures, another form of "body language," vary in meaning and amount from society to society and from culture to culture. For instance, the thumb-up sign means OK in many Western countries, whereas in Northwest Spain it means "Long live the Basques!" and in Japan it may mean a male companion or the number 5. A sideways nod of the head means "no" in Canada, but "yes" in India. In Turkey, "no" is signalled by rolling the eyes upward (Rubin, 1976). Drawing one's finger across one's throat means "I've had it" in Canada; in Swaziland it means "I love you." These cross-cultural differences in the meaning of some gestures can lead to serious communication difficulty. For example, a missionary girl's attempt to shake hands with an African chieftain created problems when he interpreted the gesture as an attempt to throw him to the ground (Argyle, 1975).

Greeting someone by kissing on both cheeks is commonplace in many countries. However, such behaviour may make anglophones feel uncomfortable.

How does cultural variation in gestures affect the communication process?

FIGURE 3-3 Body language interpreted

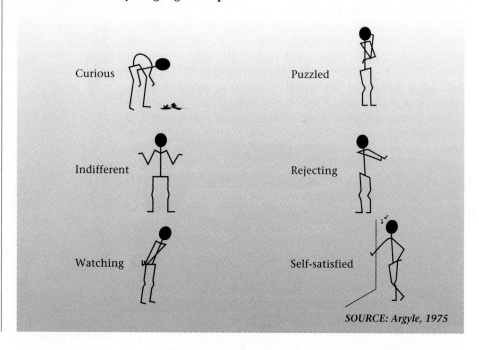

Curious

Puzzled

Indifferent

Rejecting

Watching

Self-satisfied

SOURCE: Argyle, 1975

BOX 3-2
LANGUAGE WITHOUT WORDS

In 1904 Wilhelm van Osten, a retired Berlin schoolteacher, claimed that he had found a way of teaching animals to think, "talk," and even do arithmetic. His only subject had been a horse, Clever Hans. By teaching Hans to associate a number with each letter of the alphabet (which he did by means of a blackboard!), the horse was able to tap out messages with his right front hoof. He also communicated by means of head movements, a nod indicating "yes," a side-to-side movement meaning "no." Hans could apparently combine letters into words and words into sentences, count up to 100, count objects or people, solve arithmetic questions, tell the time, and read German. He could select from a series of written words any word that someone spoke to him by pointing at it with his nose. He could answer questions such as "If the eighth day of the month comes on Tuesday, what is the date of the following Friday?" Indeed, the horse seemed to have telepathic abilities, for he could answer questions that someone was only thinking about.

Psychologist Oskar Pfungst (1911) set about systematically to study Hans' remarkable talent. He found that the presence of the horse's trainer was not necessary, thus ruling out the use of a secret cueing system. However, Pfungst discovered that Hans had to be able to see the questioner in order to respond correctly, and that if the questioner did not know the answer to his or her own question, Hans was unable to give a correct answer. After much perseverance, he determined that Hans had discovered regularities in human nonverbal behaviour: questioners were involuntarily giving cues to Hans that directed him to the correct answer. As Hans tapped out his answers, the questioner would make a slight and involuntary upward movement of the head when the correct number of taps was given, at which point Hans would stop. There were other involuntary cues as well, and Pfungst concluded that van Osten, unaware of the basis of Hans' "ability," had consistently and unwittingly reinforced the horse's responses to subtle cues while he was in the process of "educating" him. The horse was so sensitive to van Osten's movements that he was able to respond to movements of the trainer's head measuring only one fifth of a millimetre!

Francophones gesture more than anglophones. In an interesting experiment Lacroix and Rioux (1978) presented both anglophone and francophone "judges" with videotapes of bilingual people (shown from the neck down) speaking at one time in French and at another time in English. Non-verbal behaviour did not vary according to the language being spoken. However, it did vary substantially according to whether the speaker's first language was English or French. Francophones gestured more than anglophones regardless of which language they spoke.

HAPTICS: TOUCH COMMUNICATION

Where and when one person touches another person is a powerful communication agent. The interpretation of touch reflects both the social context and the relationship between the two individuals. The significance of a man touching a woman differs according to whether that woman is his wife, an acquaintance, a stranger, or a patient (Argyle, 1975). A slap on the back can mean one thing if a person has just scored a goal in hockey, but quite another if the person has just done something wrong.

Touches can be organized into a number of different categories. Jones and Yarbrough (1985) analyzed 1500 naturally occurring bodily contacts between people and concluded that touches can be organized into five categories: positive affect (showing appreciation or affection), playful, control (gaining attention or compliance), ritualistic (marking greetings or departures), and task-related (e.g. touching in a physician-patient relationship). Two other categories are negative affect (e.g. gently pushing away someone's annoying hand) and aggressive touches (e.g. kicks, punches) (Burgoon, Buller and Woodall, 1989).

The amount of touching varies considerably from culture to culture. In India, two men engaged in conversation often hold hands. To do that in Canada would lead to a serious misunderstanding, for we have rather strict rules for men about touching people of the same gender. People in Latin America, Greece, Turkey, and Arab countries tend to touch each other a great deal, while relatively little touching occurs among North Americans, Northern Europeans, and Asians (Argyle, 1975). Misunderstanding typically occurs when people from a "contact culture" visit a "non-contact" culture.

Within a given culture there are also differences with respect to where a person touches another person. In North America the degree of bodily contact depends very much on age, the relationship between the individuals (Argyle, 1975), and gender. Men have been observed to touch women more often than women touch men, and people are much more likely to touch people of the opposite sex than those of the same sex, except for older adults (Henley, 1973; Hall and Veccia, 1990). Women generally enjoy being touched more than men do, except that men enjoy being touched by a stranger of the opposite sex whereas women do not (Heslin, 1978). Heslin also found that men are more likely than women to read sexual connotations into touches. Thus, a woman who uses a lot of touches to express herself while talking to a man may inadvertently be taken as suggesting a sexual interest in him (Heslin and Alper, 1983). As Figure 3-4 illustrates, both sexes reported touches by someone of the same

haptics *Perception and use of touch in communication.*

What are some different types of touch communication? How is touch communication regulated?

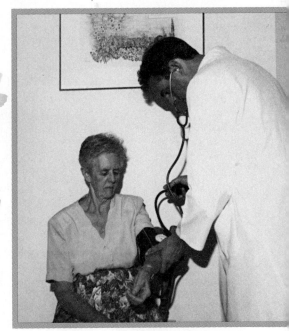

The touching involved in the physician-patient relationship is task-related.

FIGURE 3-4 Perceived pleasantness of touch from same-sex and opposite-sex strangers and close friends for males and females (on a 10-point scale)

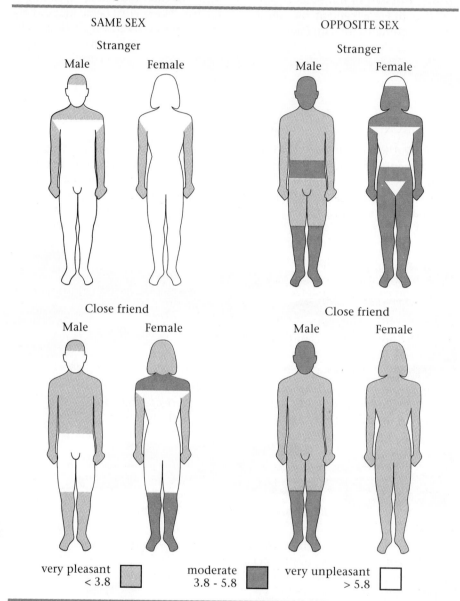

SOURCE: Burgoon, Buller and Woodall, 1989

sex as being more or less unpleasant and touches by an opposite-sex close friend as pleasant.

PARALANGUAGE

paralanguage Non-verbal aspects of speech that convey information.

We can say exactly the same words in different ways and communicate different messages. For example, saying "You pig!" to a friend dipping into a box of chocolates can communicate either friendly teasing or criticism, depending on how it is said. Volume, stress, pitch, tone of voice, pauses, and even non-linguistic sounds such as grunts or sighs are paralinguistic elements that help to convey the meaning of a message. Certain patterns of these elements may communicate specific emotions. For instance, aggression or dominance tends to be signalled by a low pitch, while happiness and friendliness usually involve a higher pitch (Frick, 1985).

SELF-TEST QUESTIONS

1. Cross-cultural studies of facial expression indicate that

a) it is usually easier to judge the expressions of people from a culture other than one's own

b) the lack of cross-cultural variability makes all cultures equally easy to judge

c) it is usually easier to judge the expressions from one's own culture

d) facial expression lacks meaning

2. The term paralanguage refers to

a) the communication of pre-linguistic societies

b) misleading communication

c) the non-verbal aspects of speech

d) the development of patterns of communication

3. Which of the following information can be communicated by eye contact?

a) degree of liking

b) strength of emotion

c) social power

d) all of the above

4. Gestures

a) show great similarity from culture to culture

b) are produced more by people who have difficulty expressing emotions

c) are culture specific

d) are used only to provide information that cannot be provided verbally

COORDINATION OF VERBAL AND NON-VERBAL COMMUNICATION

As has already been said, both verbal and non-verbal signals are involved in virtually every communication. Research suggests that often the total impact of a message is determined in only a small way by what is said; how it is said is more important and facial expressions are more important still, especially when emotion is involved. Perhaps this explains why foreign films dubbed into English often seem rather "flat." The message communicated by the dubbing may not correspond to the message conveyed by the actors' faces (Vander Zanden, 1977). Normally, of course, we expect considerable consistency between verbal and non-verbal elements of communication. If someone is smiling when discussing

How do verbal and non-verbal communication complement each other?

his bad fortune, or if someone appears depressed while talking about how happy she feels, we become confused or start to worry about the speaker's emotional condition.

One area in which non-verbal and verbal communication clearly complement each other is in **conversational control**. While words make up the content of our conversation, non-verbal signals regulate the form of conversation. Without such regulation, conversations would turn into traffic jams. The signals people use in conversational control are subtle and not explicit. We know what to do in a conversation without being able to specify the rules. In every linguistic group, there are norms that cover not only who speaks next, but virtually every aspect of the conversation from beginning to end.

According to Grice (1975), a conversation is a cooperative venture to which both parties contribute until an agreed-upon conclusion. Grice argued that we use four basic rules or maxims pertaining to our expectations of conversations. First, we expect speakers to be informative, but not to give more information than the topic warrants. Second, we expect speakers to be relevant; that is, to say what is related to the aims of the conversation. In addition, we expect speakers to be truthful and to speak in a concise and orderly manner. When these maxims are not followed, we indicate our displeasure or frustration verbally or non-verbally to our conversational partner.

Another set of norms for conversations relates to the organization of turn taking. We begin conversations by using a limited set of openers (Schegloff, 1972). We may address the other person by name or use some stereotypical comment such as "Hi!" or "How may I help you?" Three simple rules determine turn taking (Sacks, Schegloff, and Jefferson, 1974). First, the current speaker is in charge of selecting who speaks next. The choice may be signalled by both verbal (e.g. a question directed to another person) and non-verbal (e.g. eye contact with the chosen speaker) behaviours. Second, if the first rule is not used, then anyone can jump into the conversation. When we want to speak, we look for non-verbal cues that signal the end of a turn. Paralinguistic cues include such features as a long pause or a drop in pitch or loudness. The cessation of gesturing also serves as a non-verbal cue for turn-yielding. Third, if no one jumps into the conversation, the current speaker may continue. A conversational closing is preceded by a pre-closing statement. Participants may also signal that closing is desirable by non-verbal behaviours such as shifting weight or looking at a watch. Like conversational openings, closings often involve stereotypical statements and gestures such as the usual terminal exchange, "Goodbye," and a wave of the hand.

SELF-TEST QUESTIONS

5. When there is a contradiction between what is said and what is conveyed by facial expression

a) what is said takes precedence over any facial expression

b) facial expression is given more importance by the listener only when emotions are being discussed

c) the listener generally asks for more information

d) facial expression is usually taken to be a better indicator of meaning than speech

6. Non-verbal communication has persisted in spite of our development of verbal language because

a) it is sometimes easier to use than speech for communicating some things

b) it is easier to control than speech

c) it lacks the subtlety of speech for emotional expression

d) it takes less concentration to produce

7. According to Grice, we expect speakers to be

a) informative

b) relevant

c) truthful

d) all of the above

8. Which of the following is a turn-yielding signal in a conversation?

a) a long pause

b) looking directly at the interviewer

c) cessation of gesturing

d) all of the above

VERBAL COMMUNICATION

SPOKEN LANGUAGE AND WRITTEN LANGUAGE

It is thought that language ability evolved in primitive humans because the ability to communicate in a precise way had survival value. While non-verbal behaviour is often a better guide to the speaker's feelings and intentions, it does not go very far in helping two people coordinate their attempts to build a bridge or defend a village.

All spoken language is based on a phonetic system in which short, meaningless sounds called **phonemes** are combined into units of meaning called **morphemes**. By using a relatively small number of these sounds (up to 45, depending on the language), and by combining them two, three, or four at a time, different human languages have generated as many as 100 000 morphemes (Argyle, 1969). It was quite a step for our ancestors to go from speech to writing, and initially a different symbol was used for each word (e.g. a hieroglyphic). Such a system necessitated a very large number of symbols. The Chinese developed a set of 10 000 characters, each one representing a different syllable in the language. These characters are still in use today. In order to read a newspaper, it is necessary to know several thousand characters. In most languages, a few symbols representing the spoken phonetic code, rather than syllables or words, eventually came to be used in place of thousands of symbols.

FUNCTIONS

Language serves as a means of precise communication, not only in the present but across the generations. It allows a social group to pass its beliefs, knowledge, and values from one generation to the next. The words of Plato, Shakespeare, Churchill, or Gandhi can inspire each new generation as much as they did when they were first uttered. Without language, modern culture as we know it could

What functions does written language serve that spoken language cannot?

phonemes short, meaningless sounds that are combined into morphemes.

morpheme Smallest unit of meaning in language.

never have developed. Just as written language made ideas available across time, so the printing press made knowledge available to all classes or groups of people. Not only does language serve as a vehicle for the transmission of ideas, but the form that language takes can itself reflect certain beliefs and values.

LANGUAGE AND GENDER

Most people believe that men and women have typical and distinctive styles of speaking (Haas, 1979). Research evidence indicates that men are more likely to talk about sports, business, and politics, whereas women are more likely to talk about family and home. Men tend to be more direct and assertive in making a request. Men tend to use more slang, profanity, and puns. They are likely to use words and expressions about time, space, and quantity, and hostility and destructiveness. Women, on the other hand, refer more to emotional states. The common belief that women talk more than men is not supported by research findings. Although little girls tend to talk more than little boys, adult women talk less than men, especially in the presence of men. Some studies have shown that women often address men in a powerless speech style (e.g. using tentative remarks, and intonations that involve a rising pattern at the end of a statement). However, these differences have not been consistently borne out by research (Wiemann and Giles, 1988). One study found that when a woman was in conversation with a man, she was actually more influential when she spoke in a tentative way than when she was assertive, although the opposite was true when she was in conversation with a woman. Language had no effect on how influential men were, either with women or men (Carli, 1990). How conversational styles of men and women differ is shown in the CBC video *Talking 9 to 5*.

An important aspect of the transmission of values through language is the way that the English language has both reflected and reinforced the historical cultural view of masculine superiority and male domination (Smith, 1985). Until recently we would say "his" instead of "his or her," and we would speak of "mankind," "workmen's compensation boards," and so on, as though women were not important. Many nouns, (e.g. author, professor, doctor, and minister) evoke the image of a man more readily than a woman. The usual order of words in which the word referring to the male occurs first (husband and wife, son and daughter, host and hostess) also may imply that men are more important than women. Expressions like "Bill's widow" suggest ownership. We often refer to a woman whose husband has died in this manner, but we seldom refer to a man whose wife has died in a similar fashion (e.g. "Eleanor's widower"). The policy of insisting on non-sexist language is becoming increasingly common in Canadian society as a result of growing concern about human rights.

How is gender related to speech style and to the transmission of values?

SELF-TEST QUESTIONS

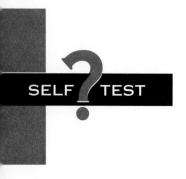

SELF TEST

9. **The short meaningless sounds that form the basis of a language system are**
a) phonemes
b) morphemes
c) hieroglyphics
d) grunts

10. Research on language and gender

a) has found that men tend to be more direct and assertive in making a request than women

b) has consistently found that women address men in a powerless speech style

c) has found that there are no longer differences in language use related to gender

d) has consistently found that women talk more than men

LANGUAGE AND SOCIAL INTERACTION

SPEECH ACTS

When we speak to another person, our goal is not just to express our thoughts but to affect the other person or to enter into some kind of social interaction. Searle (1969, 1975) pointed out that we can classify utterances according to the speaker's intention or goal. For example, we may convey thanks, give an order, or make a commitment. According to Searle, our words and intentions together comprise speech acts. **Speech act theory** distinguishes between direct speech acts and indirect speech acts. In direct speech acts the meaning of the sentence is consistent with the speaker's meaning or intention. In indirect speech acts such consistency is lacking.

The social interaction between individuals, as well as considerations of their status, influences the choice of speech acts. The speaker's intention is the same whether she says "Open the window" or "It's very warm, isn't it?" It is appropriate for a teacher to say "Open the window" to a pupil because of the classroom situation and the status difference between the teacher and pupil. However, it is not appropriate to say this to one's host at dinner. In this situation, adults consider status and the impositions created by the request (Gibbs, 1986). Accordingly, one might say "It's very warm, isn't it?" in hopes that the host will find it convenient to open the window.

Through the use of indirect speech acts we can avoid direct challenges to authority or "high-status" individuals. While it might be appropriate to say "That doesn't make sense" to a peer, a student is more likely to say "I'm not sure that I follow you" to a professor. By doing so, an unpleasant situation may be avoided.

Indirect speech acts also help us to save face (Holtgraves, 1986). For example, if Martha wears a dress to work that she worries may be viewed in a negative way by her co-workers, instead of asking, "Do you like my new dress?" she might say, "I bought a new dress" and point to herself. Instead of commenting that the dress is ugly, which would be a threat to Martha's self-esteem, a co-worker could respond by saying, "Well, it certainly is different. Where did you get it?" By her indirect response she has saved face while conveying her negative opinion.

SPEECH STYLE AND ACCOMMODATION

Our perception and evaluation of people is influenced not only by what people say, but by the way they say it. By listening to a person talk we can infer his or her social class, and in some cases, the geographic region of the person's growing years. This seems to be especially true in countries such as Great Britain. One American study reported a strong correlation between a listener's judgment of a speaker's social status and the speaker's actual social status (Giles and Powesland, 1975). In the United States the Brooklyn accent would never be con-

speech act theory Theory about the degree of correspondence between what is said and the speaker's meaning or intention.

What are the advantages of using both direct and indirect speech acts?

How does our speech style influence how people judge us?

communication accommodation theory The view that we modify our speech style in an effort to be liked and approved by other people.

standard speech A style of speaking defined socially as desirable or preferable.

Why is Quebec French different from standard French? What misconceptions are associated with this difference?

fused with the upper class Boston accent or the Texas drawl! In Canada, the accents of Montreal francophones and Quebec City francophones can be distinguished. The Ottawa Valley and Newfoundland accents are easily identified. The *Dictionary of Newfoundland English* (Story, Kirwin and Widdowson, 1982) lists many unique words and expressions, such as "figgy tit" which refers to raisins wrapped in a thin cloth and given to older babies to suck.

We often judge an individual's personality, level of education, and intelligence on the basis of language used. It might strike us as odd if we heard a bus driver using big words, or if we heard a highly educated person mispronounce a word. The differences in the complexity of vocabulary have been found to affect the degree to which a person is perceived as competent (Bradac et al., 1977). The speech styles of students have been found to affect teacher's judgments of their intelligence as much or more than actual samples of their school work (Seligman, Tucker and Lambert, 1972). There is also evidence that speech styles can even lead to bias in marks assigned by a teacher to a student (Frender and Lambert, 1972). In Great Britain, the opportunity for socioeconomic advancement can be seriously affected by accent.

Although our judgments of people are influenced by their speech styles, speech styles are not fixed. For instance, people may take elocution lessons to "correct" their speech style. We often deliberately shift our speech style towards that of the person to whom we are talking. We usually speak differently to our physician than to the person who cleans our office or classroom. According to **communication accommodation theory** we modify our speech style in an effort to be liked and approved by other people (Giles, Coupland and Coupland, 1991). Inability to shift our style to that of another person can contribute to communication breakdown. Bourhis, Roth and MacQueen (1989) examined how medical practitioners speak to their patients. They found that the physicians believed that they spoke "medical language" to other health professionals and "everyday language" to their patients. However, their patients and student nurses reported that the physicians did not use "everyday language" when speaking to them.

STANDARD AND NON-STANDARD SPEECH

Not all varieties of a particular language are treated as equal. Some speech styles are viewed as "vulgar" or "low class" by those who speak in a more "refined" manner. Research around the world has demonstrated that from childhood onwards the use of **standard speech** communicates an impression of status and competence to listeners. It also tends to elicit cooperation from the listener (Wiemann and Giles, 1988; Stewart, Ryan and Giles, 1985). How is it that one speech style comes to be the "standard" or prestige form against which others are judged? How is it, for example, that Parisian French is taken to be the model of excellence for French?

Following the French Revolution, language laws were passed in 1794 making the "Ile de France" form of French the "standard" of spoken French and banning other versions of French. Some have argued that the revolutionary leaders adopted this unilingual policy so that everyone in the country would have an equal chance to rise to the top of society (Pagès, 1986). To this day, the "Ile de France" variety of French is considered the "standard" or "international" style of the French language (Bourhis, 1982).

The language policy of the revolutionary leaders in France has had considerable impact on francophones in Canada. The French-speaking population of Quebec

BOX 3-3

MEDICINE, LANGUAGE, AND POWER

Physicians are viewed by most people as successful, intelligent, and high in status and power. When a physician asks someone to undress, the person rarely asks "Why?" If the physician wishes to inject something into the individual's arm, or if the individual is instructed to take two of the little green pills and one of the large red pills each day, few people seek understanding of what the pills really do, what their side effects might be, and so forth. They not only trust, they usually dare not ask. Thus, it should come as no surprise that physicians' speech styles reflect power in their interactions with their patients. In summarizing the research from two different studies (Fisher and Todd, 1983; West, 1984), Wiemann and Giles (1988) found that physicians maintain a very strong position of power in such interactions:

(1) Physician does most of the talking.

(2) Physician initiates 99 percent of the utterances.

(3) Patient poses only nine percent of the questions asked.

(4) Physician asks further questions before patient has been able to answer previous one.

(5) Most interruptions are by physician, except when physician is female.

(6) Physician determines topics of discussion.

(7) Physician determines when interaction ends.

Such an interaction not only reflects the imbalance in social power, it often leaves the patient feeling as though he or she has not obtained all the information that is desired from a visit to the doctor.

---

was not affected by the imposition of the Ile de France variety of French because, for nearly 200 years following the defeat of Montcalm's army on the Plains of Abraham in 1760, Quebec was virtually cut off from France. During that time, Quebec French and Ile de France French developed quite independently. Other francophone groups in Canada, such as the franco-Manitobans, trace their ancestry to post-Revolutionary France. There may be cultural as well as linguistic differences among these francophone groups. Even today, the decision by the French revolutionary leaders still leads some people, both anglophone and francophone, to look down on Quebec French.

This judgment of Quebec French is ill-founded. The preference is based on social norms rather than on qualities of the language. People learning a second language usually learn the prestigious form, and thus tend to view other forms as substandard. This affects not only the evaluation of the language, but also that of the speaker. For example, when undergraduate students at McMaster University were asked to rate tape-recorded speakers speaking with either a standard European French accent, a franco-Ontarian accent, a Québécois accent or an anglophone accent, the standard European French speakers were rated highest in terms of intelligence and linguistic competence, while English-accented speakers were rated least favourably. The Québécois and franco-Ontarian accents were rated midway between the other two (Hume, Lepicq, and Bourhis, 1992). People who are unfamiliar with a language do not show any preferences based on pleasantness or aesthetic appeal for the standard style. Researchers had Welsh students who knew no French listen to tape recordings of the same text spoken by the same person in three different accents: European standard French, educated Canadian French, and working-class Canadian French. Subjects' ratings of the speech in terms of pleasantness and aesthetic appeal, and their ratings of the speaker in terms of status, intelligence, likeability, ambition, and toughness, were not related to the speaker's accent. In a similar study, British undergraduates who knew no Greek showed no preferences for the prestigious Athenian dialect as opposed to the Cretan dialect. These results demonstrate that standard and non-standard dialects are equally pleasing, and that non-standard forms are viewed negatively because of social norms biased against them.

LANGUAGE AND GROUP IDENTITY

How does language serve as a symbol of group identity?

Groups are differentiated by speech style, dialect, and language as well as other characteristics. Language can serve as a symbol of ethnic identity or cultural solidarity (Bourhis, 1979). It can be used to remind the group of its cultural heritage, transmit group feeling, and exclude members of other groups. In times of ethnic threat, it can be used to emphasize in-group feeling. In Canada, language of origin has served as a central force to unite immigrants into ethnic groups. Without a unique language, ethnic survival is extremely difficult.

Carnival in Quebec: A common speech style contributes to a feeling of belonging.

Language can be used to widen or narrow the gap between individuals, depending upon the perceptions and motivations of the people involved. Bourhis and Giles (1977) investigated whether Welsh speakers would emphasize their accent when they were subjected to derogatory remarks about certain attributes of their group by an Englishman speaking with an upper class accent. The Welsh speakers were studying their own language. At one point the Englishman suggested that they were studying a "dying language with a dismal future." The Welsh speakers emphasized their disapproval by significantly broadening their Welsh accent. Bourhis, Giles, Leyens and Tajfel (1979) studied a similar situation occurring in Belgium, a country where linguistic conflicts between the Flemish and francophone communities have toppled many governments. Even though the Flemish and French languages officially have equal status, French enjoys more status in the capital region of Brussels. The study was conducted with Flemish undergraduate students who were trilingual in English, Flemish, and French. They chose to use Flemish rather than English as requested by a francophone interviewer when he gave arguments downgrading the use of Flemish in the capital. Canadians who admire Americans tend to use American spellings when writing to Americans, whereas other Canadians may attempt to accentuate the differences in Canadian and American English by using British/Canadian spellings in writing to Americans. When members of different groups interact, and when group membership or national identity is an important issue, differences in language are likely to be emphasized.

COMMUNICATION BETWEEN BILINGUALS

In 1969 the *Official Languages Act* was passed by Parliament, declaring that both French and English have equal status as official languages in Canada. This policy, which includes the provision of bilingual services and schooling in areas where numbers warrant them, was intended to demonstrate to francophones that they could be at home not only in Quebec but in the whole of Canada (Bourhis, 1990). Efforts were made to attract more francophones into the civil service and to teach French to anglophone government workers.

The official bilingualism policy of the federal government has improved the provision of French-language services to francophones across Canada (Commissioner of Official Languages, 1988). However, in spite of more than two decades of effort, neither the increase in the number of francophones in the public service of Canada nor the large-scale provision of French language courses to anglophone civil servants has succeeded in overcoming the serious imbalance in the use of the two official languages in the federal civil service (Bourhis, 1990). All too often, English tends to be used between bilingual anglophones and francophones. This situation deprives anglophones of the opportunity to practise their French and francophones of the opportunity to work in their own language.

Why should this be so? What determines which language is spoken when bilingual individuals of different mother tongues interact? Of course, linguistic skills play an important role. If one person is fluently bilingual, while the other has some difficulty in the second language, the tendency is to interact in the language that is easier for both. In some cases, norms governing the particular situation determine language choice. For example, when a salesperson is conducting business, the language of the client is used ("the customer is always right").

Another important factor is **ethnolinguistic vitality**. This term refers to the relative status and strength of a language in a particular social structure (Giles, Bourhis and Taylor, 1977). It reflects the proportion of the population that belongs to the particular language group, their socioeconomic status, and the extent of institutional support (such as schools, newspapers, and so on) for the language. Thus, the ethnolinguistic vitality of French is high in Quebec City, but low in Moose Jaw. If two bilingual individuals, one of mother-tongue English and the other of mother-tongue French, were to meet for the first time in Moose Jaw, it is more likely that English would be spoken, whereas if they were to meet in Quebec City they would probably speak French. Studies of language switching carried out in Montreal, a bilingual setting, and Quebec City, a nearly unilingual French setting, have demonstrated how the relative positions of language groups in the societal structure are important in determining which language will be spoken (Genesee and Bourhis, 1982; 1988).

What determines the language in which bilinguals choose to converse?

ethnolinguistic vitality
The relative status and strength of a language in a particular social structure or environment.

SELF-TEST QUESTIONS

11. Indirect speech acts

a) are consistent with the speaker's meaning

b) are more likely to occur when loss of face is possible

c) tend to be threatening

d) refer to the qualities of speech

SELF ? TEST

12. Communication accommodation theory suggests that we modify our speech in order to

a) be understood by other people

b) be liked by other people

c) elicit the attention of other people

d) control other people

13. Speech style to some degree reflects

a) education

b) personality

c) intelligence

d) social class

e) both a and d

14. The term "ethnolinguistic vitality" refers to

a) the assimilation of languages within a country

b) the relative status and strength of a language in a particular social structure

c) the learning of foreign terms by a person

d) the accommodation of new terms in a language

e) the assimilation of dialects within a culture

SECOND LANGUAGE LEARNING

While Canadians continue to wrestle with issues related to bilingualism, it may be surprising to learn that most people in the world are bilingual (Tucker, 1981). Bilingualism is common not only in many European nations, but also in several heavily populated Asian countries, including China, India, and the Philippines. In many countries, most children are given at least part of their education in a language that is not their mother tongue.

Since Canada has not followed the "melting pot" strategy of the United States, many descendants of immigrants have learned their parents' tongue as well as English or French. These individuals are more often bilingual than those whose ancestors came to Canada many generations ago. The languages of the indigenous people of Canada are sadly ignored when linguistic policy is discussed. However, these languages have a long history and are fully adaptable to the complexities of our modern technological society (Darnell, 1971). In recent years an increasing number of native peoples are receiving their formal education in an aboriginal language. These trends in language use contribute to the spread of bilingualism in Canada. And according to the 1991 census, bilingualism is growing widely.

MYTHS ABOUT SECOND LANGUAGE LEARNING

There are several popular beliefs that discourage people from attempting to learn a second language. It is commonly believed that it is very difficult for an adult to learn a second language because ability to acquire language is strongest in childhood and wanes in the pubertal years. The notion that second language learning is easier for children than adults was first given substantial support by the scientific community when the famous Montreal neurosurgeon, Wilder Penfield (Penfield and Roberts, 1959), suggested that neural plasticity gave chil-

BOX 3-4

BILINGUALISM IN CANADA

In 1991, 26 percent of Canadians spoke two languages and 4 percent could speak more than two languages. For most bilingual Canadians, the two languages of fluency were English and French. Of these people, 50 percent lived in Quebec and 25 percent lived in Ontario. Among people reporting French as their mother tongue, the proportion who could speak English was much lower in Quebec (31 percent) than in the rest of the country (83 percent). The reverse was true for bilinguals whose mother tongue was English. Of this group, 59 percent resided in Quebec, and 6 percent lived in other parts of Canada.

In contrast to Canadians who are fluent in both English and French are those who cannot conduct a conversation in either of Canada's official languages. Nationally, 1.4 percent of the population (378 000 people) were in this situation in 1991. Of these people, more than 25 percent reported Chinese as their mother tongue.

Many Canadians (18 percent) reported that they could conduct a conversation in a language other than English or French. The languages most frequently spoken were Italian (702 000 people), German (685 000), Chinese (557 000), Spanish (402 000), and Portuguese (254 000). The most frequently reported Aboriginal languages were Cree (94 000) and Ojibway (30 000).

The rate of bilingualism was highest among youth aged 15–19 (23 percent) and lowest for those aged 65 and over (12 percent). Slightly more males (17 percent) than females (16 percent) reported that they were bilingual. The rate of English-French bilingualism was highest in Quebec (35 percent) and New Brunswick (30 percent). In all the other provinces and territories, bilingualism was considerably lower than the national rate (16 percent). Cities with the highest bilingualism rate were Montreal (48 percent), Ottawa-Hull (43 percent), Sudbury (38 percent), and Sherbrooke (36 percent) (Statistics Canada, 1993).

FIGURE 3-5 **Proportion of the Canadian population able to conduct a conversation in both English and French—1951, 1961, 1971, 1981, and 1991**

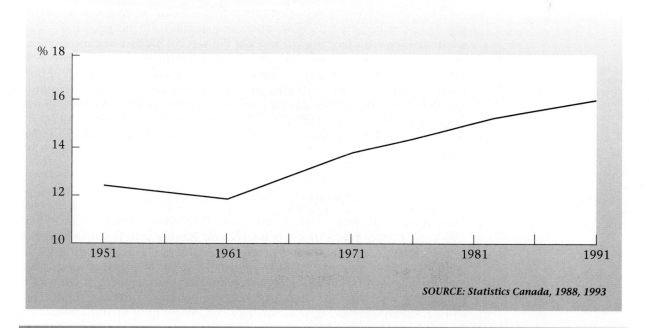

SOURCE: Statistics Canada, 1988, 1993

dren an advantage over adults in second language learning. According to this view, the child's brain is not "fixed" in its organization, and so second language learning is easier. Lenneberg (1967) referred to these early years as the critical period for language learning. However, this view did not remain unchallenged. In 1973, Krashen argued that the critical period lasts only until about five years of age. And other research clearly opposes Penfield's view of second language learning.

The preponderance of research investigating second language acquisition in children and adults argues against the view that children have an advantage over adults. We often underestimate the tremendous difficulty a child has in acquiring language. Research has revealed that adults are almost always better at it than children, except with regard to pronunciation (McNamara, 1973; McLaughlin, 1977). And even older children usually learn more quickly than younger children (Ervin-Tripp, 1974).

The popular view that children learn a second language more easily than adults is commonly based on observations of adult immigrants learning the language of their new country more slowly than their children. People forget to consider the differences in opportunities to learn, especially the differences in exposure to the new language. Suppose you and your child were moved to Beijing, and you spent all your time among the common populace rather than working with people who speak English. Suppose that no one you encountered spoke any English, and furthermore, you had no inhibitions about making errors in Chinese. You learned the language "in the streets" during every moment you interacted with people outside your own family. Given such a situation, it is easier to see how you might be more successful than your child. Consider your adult intelligence and experience, your ability to organize your learning experience, your willingness to resort to a dictionary, and your ability to discern regularities in verbs. You actually have considerable advantage over your child.

Another myth about second language learning is that it is quite a different experience from first language acquisition, and that we must somehow absorb the second language by making it compatible with the structure of the first. This need supposedly results in considerable "interference" in that words that appear to be similar may have quite different meanings. For example, the French word "librairie" means "bookstore," not "library." This sort of confusion can frustrate the anglophone trying to learn French. Yet there is no clear evidence to support the view that acquiring a second language is qualitatively different from learning a first language. A number of studies indicate that a child learning a second language follows the same process of acquisition as a native speaker of that language (McLaughlin, 1987). In fact, very little interference seems to occur between the two languages, particularly when each language is used in a different context.

IMMERSION PROGRAMS IN SCHOOLS

There is increasing interest in Canada in fostering bilingualism among children. This is due to growing social and political recognition of both English and French as official languages, and in some cases, to awareness of job opportunities dependent on bilingualism. Canadian research is at the forefront of second language education. The most widely used approach is some form of immersion program in which the child learns the second language, not as a subject, but through being exposed to it as the language of instruction and interaction. Immersion programs exist across Canada.

There have been fears in the past that immersion schooling might involve some hidden costs, such as slower progress in the student's mother tongue, or poorer attainment in non-language areas. However, research indicates that these fears are groundless (Hakuta and Garcia, 1989; Tucker, 1981). There are no long-term differences in English language proficiency or in academic proficiency in other subjects, e.g. maths and sciences, between students who have been in a regular English-language program and those who have been in French immersion (Genesee, 1984).

WHO SUCCEEDS IN SECOND LANGUAGE LEARNING?

Some children are fortunate enough to live in a bilingual environment, and become proficient in two languages as they grow up. For most people, however, learning a second language requires a good deal of deliberate effort. Why do some people persevere and become proficient in a second language even when their social situation does not demand it? Why do some students from immersion programs go on to become fluently bilingual, whereas others remain essentially unilingual? The most important factors influencing the likelihood of success in learning a second language are intelligence, specific aptitude for language learning, motivation, and anxiety (Gardner, 1985; Lalonde and Gardner, 1984). Each of these factors is addressed below.

(1) **Intelligence.** This is important for the obvious reason that it facilitates any kind of learning. Thus, intellectually superior individuals should normally find language learning an easier task than it might be for someone less capable.

(2) **Specific aptitude for language learning.** Some people are simply better at learning languages than other people. Verbal skills that lead to high ability in one's native language are likely to facilitate learning a second language as well.

(3) **Motivation.** The individual who wants to become bilingual is more likely to succeed than one who does not consider bilingualism to be very important. Motivation has been found repeatedly to be a crucial determinant of second-language success (Gardner and Lambert, 1959; 1972; Gardner, 1979; 1984). Individuals who learn a second language primarily to get ahead in a job do not do as well as those who learn it so that they can participate in the culture (go to movies, talk to friends) of the other language. In addition, attitudes held in the home and in society in general about the importance and difficulty of learning a second language influence motivation to do so (Gardner, 1985).

Motivation is also influenced by how bilingualism is viewed in relation to the ethnolinguistic vitality (see p. 73) of one's own group relative to that of the other language group. There are different views about how ethnolinguistic vitality affects motivation to learn a second language. On the one hand, Clément (1980, 1987) has argued that when there are differences in ethnolinguistic vitality between two groups living side by side, members of the group with low ethnolinguistic vitality will be more motivated to learn the other group's language than members of the group with high ethnolinguistic vitality. In Clément's view this is because attaining proficiency in the language of the majority brings increased psychological and material benefits.

On the other hand, according to Lambert's view of bilingualism as "additive" or "subtractive" (Lambert, 1978; Lambert and Taylor, 1984), members of the group high in ethnolinguistic vitality would be more motivated to learn the language of the other group than members of the group low in ethnolinguistic

Do immersion programs affect academic proficiency in other subjects?

What factors influence the likelihood of a person's success in learning a second language?

vitality. For example, when anglophones in South Africa learn Afrikaans, Israelis learn English, or anglophone Canadians learn French, they are not threatening the continued existence of their sociolinguistic group. In this case, bilingualism is "additive" in that the individuals have acquired another socially useful skill. However, when minority groups with low ethnolinguistic vitality are struggling to maintain their identity, learning the language of the majority can be considered "subtractive" in that it threatens the continued importance of the first language. For example, francophones who never learn English are unlikely to become assimilated into English culture, while bilingualism may make francophones vulnerable to assimilation. Bilingualism is likely to be encouraged, or at worst ignored, when it is additive for a group. It may be actively discouraged when it is subtractive. Accordingly, in Lambert's view groups with high ethnolinguistic vitality are likely to be motivated to learn a second language, whereas those groups with low ethnolinguistic vitality will not.

(4) Anxiety and self-confidence. According to Clément's model, when two linguistic groups both possess high ethnolinguistic vitality, then a personal factor—self-confidence in one's ability to use the second language—becomes an important determinant of who does and does not become bilingual. Self-confident individuals will have less anxiety about learning the new language and more success at mastering it than more anxious individuals (Gardner, 1985; Young and Gardner, 1990). This self-confidence factor predominates in situations where there is neither an advantage to integrating with the other group nor any reason to fear assimilation.

When a person begins to become competent in a second language, there are often some unexpected psychological consequences, not all of them positive. The person may become aware of the stereotypes held by members of each linguistic group about the other group. These new insights can even undermine one's sense of identity as the individual becomes a kind of "marginal person," no longer a typical member of either group. At times he or she may share jokes or criticisms with speakers of the new language about his or her maternal language group. At other times, he or she may try to defend the other group to members of the maternal language group. By becoming bilingual, the person may be required to act in ways that are inconsistent with the maternal language group.

SELF-TEST QUESTIONS

15. Which of the following does not seem to influence success in second language learning?

a) intelligence

b) motivation

c) age

d) specific aptitude for language

e) self-confidence

16. Which of the following motives for learning a second language is likely to result in the least success?

a) to interact in a foreign country

b) to talk to new friends

c) to attend cultural events

d) to enjoy literature in that language

e) to advance one's career

SUMMARY

(1) Non-verbal communication is used to provide information about feelings and intentions, to regulate verbal and other interactions, to express intimacy, to promote social control, and to facilitate goal attainment.

(2) Facial displays of emotion share some universal features, although whatever biological basis there is for this similarity is modified by social conditioning.

(3) Eye contact, "body language," gestures, and facial displays provide powerful non-verbal channels of communication.

(4) Differences in speech style are used as markers of social status, guides for forming impressions of others, and markers of group boundaries.

(5) The prestige or standard form of a language develops from the speech style of those who are in a position of power, rather than from preferences for any more aesthetically pleasing form of a language.

(6) Speech accommodation theory suggests that because people want to be accepted and approved by others, they modify their speech style to make it similar to the speech heard around them.

(7) If group identity is threatened, individuals will accentuate the distinctiveness of their style in the presence of members of the group associated with the threat.

(8) Language often serves as a primary determinant of group boundaries and can be the major focus of ethnic identity.

(9) Factors involved in successful second language learning include general intelligence, specific language learning ability, motivation, self-confidence, and anxiety. Motivation is influenced by the relative status and ethnolinguistic vitality of the second language compared with that of the first.

(10) Learning a second language can lead to unexpected psychological consequences, such as the undermining of one's sense of identity.

FOR REVIEW

Non-verbal behaviour may be used to regulate spoken language, provide information about feelings, express intimacy, help reach goals, and _____(1). Within a culture, _____(2) govern the use of non-verbal communication. The technical term for "body language" is _____(3). _____(4) refers to the perception and use of touch as communication. The interpretation of touch reflects both the _____(5) between the individuals and the _____(6). _____(7) refers to all the non-verbal elements of speech, such as pitch, loudness, sighs, and groans.

Social norms also govern many aspects of spoken language. According to Grice, some of these norms concern the _____(8) we have about conversations. Another set of norms relates to the organization of _____(9) in conversation. On some occasions the speaker's intent is consistent with the meaning of a sentence. Speech acts of this sort are referred to as _____(10) speech acts.

FOR REVIEW

On other occasions the speaker's purpose is to save face. In such situations the meaning the speaker is attempting to convey is not the same as the literal meaning of the sentence. These speech acts are _____(11). Usually listeners infer the speaker's intended meaning.

Listeners also make inferences about the speaker's ethnicity, class, education, and personality based on _____(12). As speakers, we tend to change our speech style in order to be liked and approved by other people, according to _____(13) theory. Research around the world has demonstrated that _____(14) speech style communicates an impression of competence and status to listeners. The "Ile de France" style of speaking is generally used as the standard style in assessing various styles of speaking _____(15).

A widely held but incorrect view of second language learning is that children learn a second language more _____(16) than adults. Another myth about second language learning is that it is a _____(17) from first language acquisition.

A number of important factors influence second language learning. Verbal skills that lead to high ability in one's native language are likely to _____(18) learning a second language. Both the level and the type of motivation are important. People who are motivated to learn a second language primarily to get ahead in a job are _____(19) successful than those who are motivated by a desire to participate in the culture of the second language. _____(20) to use the second language is also important.

ISSUES AND ACTIVITIES

1. Describe some specific gestures that vary in interpretation across cultures. Discuss the implications of these and other cultural differences in non-verbal communication.

2. Discuss the concept of "sexist language." Make a list of gender-specific words that have been replaced by non-gender-specific words (e.g. "chairman" vs "chairperson," "manhole cover" vs "maintenance cover.") Discuss whether we do or do not accomplish something by these changes. Also consider other languages, such as French or Spanish, in which all nouns are classified as "masculine" or "feminine." Does this have any effect on perception of the concepts to which these classifications apply?

3. Working in groups of four, have two people engage in conversation while the other two systematically observe the use of non-verbal communication in regulating the conversation.

4. Work in small groups. Each group will focus on specific situations and speech acts, preparing a brief scenario to be acted out for the class. Discuss the type of speech acts, the nature of the situation, and the relationship between the speakers.

5. View the video segment, *Talking 9 to 5,* and discuss how male and female conversational styles differ. Comment on the implications of these differences for misunderstandings on the job.

• FURTHER READING

BURGOON, J.D., BULLER, D.B. and WOODALL, W.G. (1989). *Nonverbal communication: The unspoken dialogue.* New York: Harper and Row. An excellent treatment of non-verbal communication from simple facial expressions and gestures to the more complicated signals involved in social influence and impression management.

EKMAN, P. (1992). *Telling lies: Clues to deceit in the marketplace, politics and marriage.* New York: W.W. Norton. Lessons on how non-verbal behaviour can signal attempts to deceive.

MORRIS, D. (1994). *Bodytalk: The meaning of human gestures.* New York: Crown Publishers. A guide to human gestures from all around the world.

TANNEN, D. (1990). *You just don't understand: Women and men in conversation.* New York: Morrow. An analysis of how the differences between males and females in the use of language promote misunderstanding and even conflict.

SUGGESTED WEBLINKS

Journal of Personality and Social Psychology (Table of Contents)
http://www.apa.org/journals/psp.html

PSYC SITE A site set up to help psychology students and researchers find information about scientific research in psychology on the World Wide Web. Designed to be a "major jumping-off point" for seeking out psychological information. Maintained by the Psychology Department of the University of Nipissing.
http://www.unipissing.ca/psyc/psycsite.htm

ANSWERS TO SELF-TEST QUESTIONS

1. c; 2. c; 3. d; 4. c; 5. d; 6. a; 7. d; 8. d; 9. a; 10. a; 11. b; 12. b; 13. e; 14. b; 15. c; 16. e.

ANSWERS TO FOR REVIEW

1. establish dominance; 2. social norms; 3. kinesics; 4. Haptics; 5. relationship; 6. social context; 7. Paralanguage; 8. expectations; 9. turn taking; 10. direct; 11. indirect; 12. speech style or accent; 13. communication accommodation; 14. standard; 15. French; 16. easily; 17. different experience; 18. facilitate; 19. less; 20. Confidence in one's ability.

ATTITUDES AND ATTITUDE CHANGE

I have but one love, Canada. One purpose, its greatness…one aim, unity from the Atlantic to the Pacific.

John Diefenbaker

Loyalty to a petrified opinion never yet broke a chain or freed a human soul.

Mark Twain

■ LEARNING OUTCOMES

1. An understanding of the nature of attitudes and values, and the relationship between them.

2. Knowledge about the functions of attitudes and the relationship between attitudes and behaviour.

3. An understanding of how both internal mental processes and external influences lead to attitude change.

4. Knowledge about when and how behaviour which is inconsistent with attitudes can lead to changes in attitudes.

5. Knowledge about when and how persuasion and attitude change occur by thinking about an issue or by other persuasive influences.

6. Knowledge about when and how people resist attempts to be persuaded.

■ FOR REFLECTION

• Do people usually act on the basis of what they believe to be true or right?

• How do people react when they think they are being inconsistent?

• How does advertising persuade us?

• How do we resist persuasion?

■ CHAPTER OUTLINE

Attitudes
    Nature of Attitudes
    Attitudes and Values
    Functions of Attitudes
The Relationship between Attitudes and Behaviour
    Theory of Reasoned Action
    Theory of Planned Behaviour
Cognitive Consistency and Attitude Change
    Basic Principles
    Dissonance in Action
    Reinterpreting Cognitive Dissonance
Persuasion
    Elements of Persuasion
    Two Routes to Persuasion
Resisting Persuasion
    Forewarning
    Inoculation
Summary
For Review
Issues and Activities
Further Reading
Suggested WebLinks
Answers to Self-Test Questions
Answers to For Review

Sue Rodriguez of Vancouver Island was diagnosed as having Lou Gehrig's disease, which is incurable. It gradually destroys muscle function, leaving the afflicted person unable to speak, swallow, breathe, or eat without assistance. Ms. Rodriguez decided that she didn't want to endure the final stages of the disease and went to court to obtain the right to a physician-assisted suicide. In Canada it is not an offence to commit suicide, but it is an offence to counsel or assist someone else to do so. The Court denied her request. Her subsequent appeal to a higher court was dismissed on the basis of a 2–1 split vote. The dissenting judge's opinion was that Ms. Rodriguez had the right under the Canadian Charter of Rights and Freedoms. The other two judges indicated that it would be wrong to grant immunity from liability, in civil or criminal proceedings, to unknown persons for offences not yet committed. In October of 1993, the Supreme Court of Canada upheld the decision by a 5 to 4 majority.

Sue Rodriguez's publicly expressed wishes and the decisions of the courts sparked considerable national debate. Like the question of abortion, the issue of assisted suicide invokes values and attitudes concerning the sanctity of life, religious convictions, and even the role of physicians in the treatment of patients. Do people have the "right to die"? Must every effort be made to prolong life, no matter what the circumstances? The ethical dilemma for physicians and hospitals is fundamental. On the one hand they are dedicated to preserving life, and on the other to alleviating suffering. What is the point, for example, of maintaining a patient with irrevocable brain-damage on a life-support system? Should quality of life not be taken into consideration? Sue Rodriguez believed it was her life to do with what she wanted. Ultimately, she committed suicide. Many people objected—a cure might be just around the corner; the process might be subject to abuse (a handy way to get rid of grandma and grandpa). These are all questions involving attitudes and values. As many Canadians watched Ms. Rodriguez appeal for support for her cause on national television, they examined their attitudes and values about the issues involved. Some eventually changed long-held attitudes. (The CBC video *Sue Rodriguez* portrays the attitudes that make this issue such a contentious one.)

Very few examples of behaviour can be found that are not, in some way, influenced by attitudes and values. The effect of attitudes and values can extend from the mundane, such as food preferences (chow mein or pirogi, hamburgers or sushi), to issues of war and peace and the sublime aspects of religious experience. The form of government we prefer, the candidate we vote for, the type of mate we seek, and even the breed of dog we choose all reflect underlying beliefs and feelings. It is not surprising that the study of attitudes has been at the core of social psychology almost since the beginning. Indeed, during the 1930s social psychology and attitude research were almost synonymous.

This chapter examines the nature and functions of attitudes, the relationship between attitudes and behaviour, and how attitudes change. We will look at the characteristics of attitudes and at the needs they satisfy. Two theories concerned with the attitude-behaviour relationship will be discussed. And we will examine two processes, cognitive consistency and persuasion, that are instrumental in attitude change.

ATTITUDES

NATURE OF ATTITUDES

attitude *A predisposition to act in a certain way towards an object or experience. It includes cognitive, behavioural, and affective components.*

In the 1930s, Gordon Allport (1935), a major contributor to research on attitudes, defined an **attitude** as "a mental and neural state or readiness, organized through experience, exerting a directive or dynamic influence upon the individual's response to all objects and situations with which it is related." This definition emphasizes certain important characteristics of an attitude. First, an attitude implies an internal state which, given the occurrence of certain stimulus events, will result in some sort of response or behaviour. The definition also implies that an attitude is learned and that our actions are consistent with it. This latter characteristic is important because it gives us a basis for deciding whether or not a given attitude exists, that is, whether a label—e.g. "conservative" or "socialist"—can be attached to an individual. It is important to note that we never observe people's attitudes. Even if attitudes are stated, only behaviour is actually observed. We infer or guess at the existence of an attitude on the basis of what people say or do. This, of course, holds true for the measurement of attitudes. We can only measure what we can observe.

Attitudes are probably best thought of as cognitive structures or internal states that reside in long-term memory (Tourangeau and Rasinski, 1988; Eagly, 1992). These states are activated when a person is presented with a relevant stimulus. For example, while watching Sue Rodriguez on TV, we might have been prompted to ask ourselves: "What do you think about assisted suicide?" Depending on our response, we can then be identified as pro-assisted suicide or anti-assisted suicide.

Two other features of attitudes are significant. Not only do we typically describe an attitude a person holds as "pro" or "con," but we also estimate the intensity or strength of an attitude, from "extremely positive" to "extremely negative." For example, it is one thing for an individual to state that "Government policies leave a lot to be desired," and quite another thing to claim that "Government policies make me sick!"

Strong attitudes have a number of characteristics. They are extreme, intense, maintained with considerable certainty, perceived as important, and supported by knowledge (Krosnick and Abelson, 1992). They are also more accessible, that is, more easily remembered, than weak attitudes (Krosnick, 1989).

MODELS OF ATTITUDES

A traditional view holds that attitudes are multidimensional. They consist of a relatively enduring organization of three components—cognitive, affective, and behavioural (Chaiken and Stangor, 1987)—as illustrated in Figure 4-1. For example, consider the attitude of someone who refuses to pick up a college student who is hitchhiking. The cognitive component of this person's attitude towards college students refers to the particular beliefs or ideas held about students. For instance, one may believe that college students are arrogant. The affective component of the attitude refers to the associated emotions. The individual may feel tense in the presence of a college student. The behavioural component refers to an associated action or actions. In this case, the person refuses to pick up a college student who is hitchhiking. It is important to add, however, that attitudes are not always directly expressed in action.

This model of attitude suggests that our thoughts, feelings, and behaviour are integrated in some way. In other words, human nature is characterized by all three components. In contrast, many traditional theories and philosophies have portrayed human nature as being fundamentally rational (thinking) or emotional.

Zanna and Rempel (1988) have attempted to harmonize these divergent views. They define an attitude as a categorization of a stimulus event along an evaluative dimension, taking into account cognitive, affective, and behavioural information. Evaluation can be based on any one type of information, or on any combination of the types of information. An attitude may, for example, be based on only cognitions, or cognitions and affect, or cognitions, affect, and past be-

What are the main features of attitudes?

FIGURE 4-1 **The tripartite model of attitude structure**

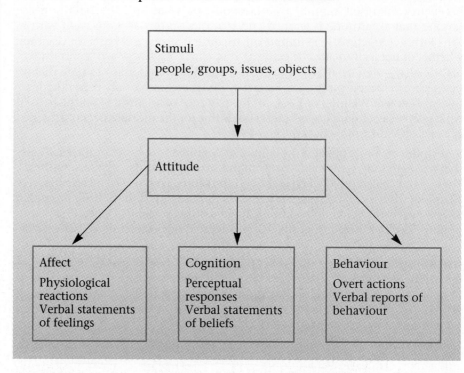

haviour. For example, we may evaluate capital punishment as positive or negative, based on our beliefs about capital punishment as determined by our beliefs and feelings or past experiences with violent crimes.

This conceptualization of attitudes gives rise to a number of intriguing speculations. One important implication of this view is that a person can have more than one attitude towards the same object. For example, a person's attitude about exercise may be negative when based on affect ("Exercise is painful"), but positive when based on cognition ("It will lower my blood pressure"). Depending on the situation, one or the other source of an attitude may be salient or dominate in the formation of the attitude. That is, we are likely to have the negative attitude towards exercise while in the gym, but have the positive attitude while in the doctor's office. Another important implication is that attitudes based on more than one source of information will be better predictors of behaviour.

ATTITUDE COMPLEXITY

Some attitudes are rather simple and straightforward, while others are complex. For instance, a person may be asked, "What do you think of assisted suicide?" and respond, "I think it's very humane," but if pressed be unable to give more details. Another person, in response to the same question, may reply, "I'm generally in favour of it, but we have to worry about possible misuse." Whether an attitude is simple or complex may be determined by the characteristics of the person or by the nature of the particular topic. There are some issues that do not allow for much complexity. For example, attitudes concerning the brushing of teeth after meals would likely be considerably more simple than attitudes towards the economic or political union of Canada and the United States.

Attitudes also have more or less complex associations with other attitudes. For example, a person might believe that agricultural cooperatives are economically beneficial and should be fostered, but this attitude may exist in isolation from attitudes such as those concerning the NDP, or Mennonite communities. In other cases, very complicated networks of interconnected attitudes may occur. Thus an individual's attitude towards immigration may be connected with attitudes concerning unemployment, multiculturalism, prejudice, and the nature of cities.

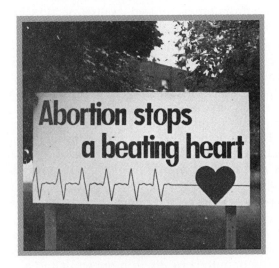

Slogans used by people on both sides of the abortion debate convey how each side defines the issue.

ATTITUDES AND VALUES

In contrast to attitudes, **values** are more fundamental orientations that people have towards such issues as freedom, equality, or comfort and security. While attitudes are associated with specific objects, events, or issues, values are global, abstract principles. They are a person's judgments about what is "desirable," what "ought to be," and what is important in life.

Values guide individuals in choosing situations and appropriate behaviours. Differences in values have been shown to be related to many attitudes and behaviours. These include choice of occupation, cigarette smoking, cheating on exams, political attitudes and voting, as well as choice of friends (Homer and Kahle, 1988). Kristiansen and Matheson (1990) found that values predict attitudes towards nuclear weapons.

Researchers have used values to describe and compare people of different nations. Often the only distinctions that may be observed by an American visitor in Canada are the feeling of being safer on the streets, the colours of money, and the superior quality of the Canadian Broadcasting Corporation. Nevertheless, differences in our "national characters" can be identified and studied. Lipset (1989) described Canadians as being more conservative, less competitive and individualistic, less self-confident and innovative, and more prepared to accept government control, elitism, and inequalities. As Margaret Atwood has noted (1972), we are the only country in the world with a police officer as a national symbol. While Americans are promised "life, liberty, and the pursuit of happiness"

values Central, higher-order set of preferences for goals in life and ways of living that are felt to be ideal and important.

by their Constitution, Canadians are offered "peace, order, and good government" by the British North America Act.

FUNCTIONS OF ATTITUDES

What important needs do attitudes serve?

There is an important reason why people hold their attitudes. Attitudes are functional in the sense that they satisfy important needs. Several functions of attitudes have been identified and studied (Eagly and Chaiken, 1992; Olson and Zanna, 1993). Four of these functions are described below.

(1) Attitudes may serve a utilitarian or instrumental function, leading to greater rewards and fewer costs. In particular, holding certain attitudes may help us gain approval and acceptance from others. Indeed, as discussed in Chapter 7, people tend to be attracted to other people who apparently hold similar attitudes.

(2) Attitudes can serve a knowledge function. They help us to make sense of our world, to cope with everyday decisions, and to feel that we do understand (Fazio, Blascovich and Driscoll, 1992). They assist people to select, from all the objects that enter the visual field, those stimuli that receive attention (Roskos-Ewoldsen and Fazio, 1992a). Attitudes serve as schemata, helping us to avoid the uncomfortable feelings of uncertainty and ambiguity, guiding our reactions and interpretations of events. For example, acts of terrorism seem even more terrifying when they are apparently senseless, inexplicable, beyond understanding. Thus we may more readily accept the explanations of politicians that some people are just evil or are agents of some insane leader.

Sometimes attitudes enable us to avoid thinking. Fazio and his associates have investigated how quickly subjects respond to various objects by pushing buttons labelled "good" or "bad" (Fazio, Sanbonmatsu, Powell and Kardes, 1986). They demonstrated that some attitudes, such as "cockroaches are disgusting," are activated spontaneously or automatically from memory and do not require thinking, while other attitudes require more time and thought to be expressed. Strong, automatically activated attitudes free people from the effort required for information-processing and reflective thought and allow them simply to react.

(3) Attitudes may also serve an ego-defensive function, protecting people from becoming aware of harsh, uncomfortable truths about themselves or their world. People often act in ways that "defend" them from becoming aware of what may be threatening. As discussed in Chapter 6, prejudiced attitudes often serve ego-defensive functions. For instance, the bigot may hate members of some out-group in order to feel important and powerful. If people feel bad about themselves, it is comforting and protective to feel that others are worse.

(4) Attitudes can serve a value-expressive function. Value-expressive attitudes demonstrate our uniqueness, and what is important to us. They may be trivial (opinions about styles in music or cars), or they may be important (salient attitudes that indicate devotion to a religious faith).

SELF-TEST QUESTIONS

SELF ? TEST

1. The tripartite model of attitudes consists of the following three components
a) genetic, environmental, interactive
b) muscular, neural, hormonal

c) *affective, cognitive, behavioural*

d) *developmental, affective, intellectual*

2. Which of the following is not a function of attitudes?

a) *utilitarian*

b) *value justification*

c) *knowledge*

d) *ego-defensive*

e) *value-expressive*

3. Strong attitudes have a number of characteristics. Which of the following is not one of them?

a) *maintained with considerable certainty*

b) *supported by knowledge*

c) *perceived as important*

d) *less accessible than weak attitudes*

e) *intense*

4. The main difference between attitudes and values is

a) *values are held by societies while attitudes are held by individuals*

b) *values are components of attitudes*

c) *attitudes are associated with specific objects while values are abstract principles*

d) *attitudes are complex while values are simple*

THE RELATIONSHIP BETWEEN ATTITUDES AND BEHAVIOUR

THEORY OF REASONED ACTION

Research has shown that attitudes and behaviour are not as strongly related as was once believed. These findings have led to theories that attempt to link attitudes and behaviour. The subject of intentions and the relationship of intentions to behaviour has dominated much research and theorizing about attitudes and the attitude-behaviour relationship. In their **theory of reasoned action**, Ajzen and Fishbein (1980) begin with the premise that people usually consider the implications of their actions, and then act consciously and deliberately. In short, we eventually do what we intend to do. Of course, intentions vary in strength, and we may intend to do a number of different things. A student may intend to study tonight unless he or she is invited to a party. According to Fishbein and Ajzen, the strength of an intention to act in some particular way is determined by attitudes towards that action and subjective norms. That is, our intention to vote for candidate X is determined by our attitudes towards voting that way and our perception that the action is encouraged or approved by other people. Attitudes towards an action are determined by beliefs that the action will lead to certain outcomes and evaluations of those outcomes. Subjective norms are determined by the individual's perceptions of the behavioural expectations of others and by the strength of motivation to comply with these expectations. See Figure 4-2.

theory of reasoned action Our intention to engage in a specific behaviour is influenced by our attitudes towards the behaviour and by social norms.

FIGURE 4-2 **The Ajzen and Fishbein model of reasoned action**

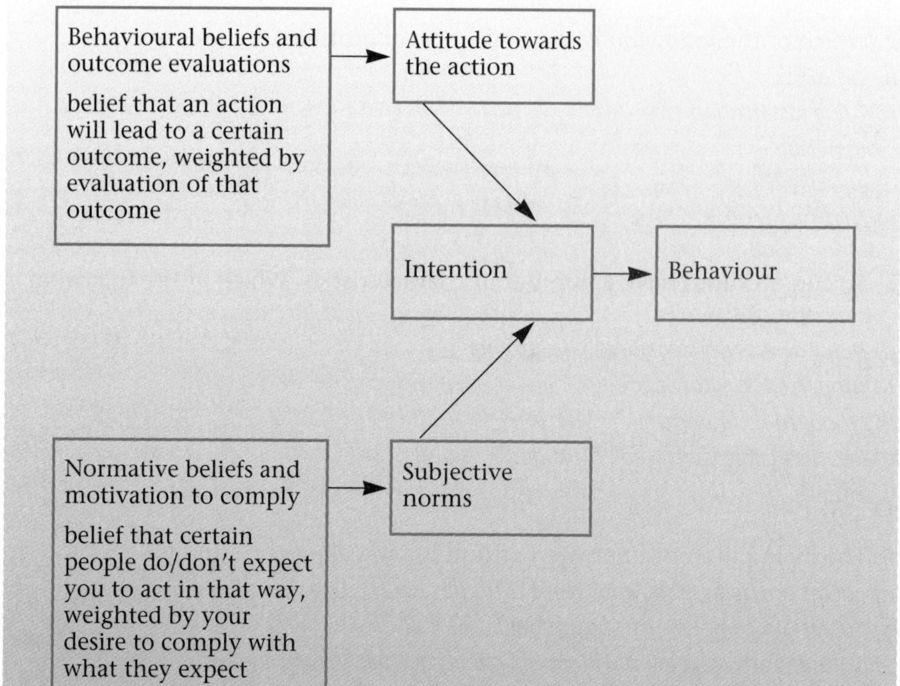

Behavioural beliefs and outcome evaluations

belief that an action will lead to a certain outcome, weighted by evaluation of that outcome

→ Attitude towards the action

→ Intention → Behaviour

Normative beliefs and motivation to comply

belief that certain people do/don't expect you to act in that way, weighted by your desire to comply with what they expect

→ Subjective norms

SOURCE: Ajzen and Fishbein, 1980

What role do intentions play in the attitude-behaviour relationship?

theory of planned behaviour Our intention to engage in a specific behaviour is influenced by our attitudes towards the behaviour and social norms as well as by beliefs about our competency to carry out the behaviour.

The Ajzen and Fishbein model has been supported in a series of studies of socially significant behaviours, such as family planning, consumer behaviour, voting in U.S. and British elections, choice of occupation, changes in smoking and drinking, and losing weight (Ajzen and Fishbein, 1980).

THEORY OF PLANNED BEHAVIOUR

Ajzen (1985, 1987) has pointed out that the theory can sometimes account better for intentions and behaviours if perceived behavioural control is taken into account. Accordingly, in the **theory of planned behaviour**, beliefs concerning the resources and opportunities for performing a given behaviour are added as a determinant of behavioural intentions and behaviour. Madden, Ellen and Ajzen (1992) found that if behaviour is considered to be under high control (e.g. taking vitamins), then intentions will play the dominant role in predicting action. However, as perceived control decreases (e.g. sleep), intentions become less influential.

While these models have an elegant simplicity and have generated much research, they do not fully account for the complexities of the relationship between attitudes and behaviour. Clearly, research will continue and new approaches will emerge that will contribute to a better understanding of this important problem.

BOX 4-1

CAN EXTRANEOUS INFORMATION INFLUENCE OUR ATTITUDES?

Krosnick et al. (1992) were interested in whether attitudes can be influenced by extraneous information or whether they are based on deliberate information processing. They presented subjects with pictures of a target person accompanied by very brief exposures of positive- or negative-affect-arousing photographs. For half the subjects, each presentation was preceded by a subliminal exposure of one of the positive-affect-arousing photos. For the other subjects, each presentation was preceded by a subliminal exposure of one of the negative-affect-arousing photos. For arousing positive affect, the researchers used photos of happy experiences such as a group of people playing cards and laughing, a child with a large Mickey Mouse doll, and a couple in a romantic setting. For arousing negative affect, they used photos of unhappy experiences or scenes such as a face on fire, a bloody shark, an opened chest during open-heart surgery.

After viewing the pictures, subjects reported their attitudes towards the target person by filling out a questionnaire. When the pictures of the target person were paired with positive-affect-arousing photos, the person was liked more and was seen as having more desirable personality traits than when the pictures were paired with the negative-affect-arousing photos. Beliefs about physical attractiveness seemed to be less influenced by the affect-arousing photos, possibly because these beliefs were based on very salient information. The results of this research show that our attitudes can be influenced by extraneous information.

Source: Krosnick, J.A., Betz, A.L., Jussim, L.J., and Lynn, A.R. (1992). Subliminal conditioning of attitudes. Personality and Social Psychology Bulletin, 18, 152–162.

SELF-TEST QUESTIONS

5. Subjective norms in the theory of reasoned action involve

a) beliefs about others' expectations of an action

b) the strength of one's motivations to comply with others' expectations

c) beliefs about the likelihood that an action will produce a particular outcome

d) all of the above

e) a and b

6. Which of the following imply that interactions are the key to the attitude-behaviour problem?

a) theory of reasoned action

b) the mode model

c) theory of planned behaviour

d) both a and c

e) all of the above

7. What criticisms have been directed towards both the theories of reasoned action and of planned behaviour?

a) they underestimate the role of values in determining behaviour

b) behaviour may be a cause as well as an effect

c) they do not fully account for the complexities of the relationship between attitudes and behaviour

d) attitudes may influence behaviour directly

COGNITIVE CONSISTENCY AND ATTITUDE CHANGE

In analyzing how attitudes change, many social psychologists have based their theories on the principle of cognitive consistency. That is, it is theorized that many people want to be consistent in their beliefs and actions. One of the best known and most influential of these theories is that of **cognitive dissonance**, developed by Festinger in 1957 and later modified and expanded (Brehm and Cohen, 1962; Aronson, 1968; Wicklund and Brehm, 1976). In the following paragraphs the basic ideas of the theory are outlined, and some of the research generated by the theory is reviewed. Some criticisms and changes to the theory are also discussed.

BASIC PRINCIPLES

The theory of cognitive dissonance explains how cognitive elements—ideas, beliefs, and preferences regarding behaviour—stand in relation to each other. These elements can have consonant, dissonant, or irrelevant relationships with each other. If the elements seem to fit together, or are consistent, the relationship is consonant. If the elements do not seem to have any relationship or relevance for each other, the relationship is irrelevant. Dissonance is said to exist when one element is logically opposed to another cognitive element. For example, if a person believes that "seals should be protected" and also believes that seals eat many fish in the waters off Newfoundland, thus threatening the recovery of the fish stocks, he or she could be in a state of dissonance. If you know that smoking causes cancer, but you continue to smoke anyway, you will likely experience dissonance.

According to the theory, dissonance is psychologically uncomfortable and will motivate the person to try to reduce the dissonance. For example, if you smoke you will likely avoid information that describes the dangers of smoking because this information would probably increase your dissonance. However, the dissonance will increase in magnitude as the importance or value of the elements increases. For instance, if a family member is diagnosed as having cancer, the importance of the anti-smoking information increases, and your dissonance will increase also. As the magnitude of the dissonance increases, the pressure to reduce the dissonance also increases.

There are a number of ways to reduce dissonance. Depending on the person and the situation, one way may be preferable over others. Five solutions to the problem of dissonance are outlined below and are shown in Figure 4-3.

(1) The person may change behaviour in order to make it consistent with attitudes. For example, a smoker may decide to give up smoking in order to achieve consonance with beliefs about the importance of health.

(2) The person may modify a cognition so that it is now consonant with other cognitions. For example, a smoker may decide that smoking does not pose a health threat: "My grandmother smoked and lived to a ripe old age."

What causes cognitive dissonance? How is dissonance related to changes in behaviour and attitudes?

cognitive dissonance *An unpleasant motivational state caused by awareness of inconsistency among behaviours and cognitive elements.*

FIGURE 4-3 **Reducing dissonance**

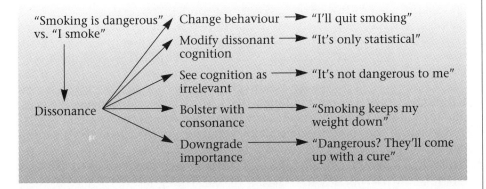

(3) The person may rationalize that the two cognitions are not really relevant to each other. Thus, smokers may conclude that the health risks of smoking really do not apply to their own smoking.

(4) The person may bolster the case for smoking by adding new consonant cognitions, thus increasing the overall strength or importance of these cognitions. For example, smokers may add the idea that smoking is beneficial: "Smoking helps me to avoid overeating."

(5) The person may downgrade the importance of the dissonant cognition. For example, to a sixteen-year-old, the health risks of smoking exist in the future; by that time "medicine will be able to cure anything."

DISSONANCE IN ACTION

We have seen how dissonance is created, what determines its intensity, and how it can be reduced. Research in cognitive dissonance has concentrated on four areas: the discomfort often experienced after a difficult decision; reducing dissonance by avoiding exposure to new, dissonant information; reducing dissonance by seeking support from others; and the dissonance experienced after we act in ways contrary to our beliefs. We will now look at some research in each of these areas.

POST-DECISION DISSONANCE

It is important to understand the distinction between conflict and cognitive dissonance. Before we make a choice among a number of equally desirable alternatives, we are often in a state of conflict, which produces discomfort. Festinger (1957) has argued that while conflict is resolved by making a choice, we may still experience discomfort as a result of **post-decision cognitive dissonance**. In this situation, our evaluations of the chosen and rejected alternatives will differ more immediately after the decision is made than at the time of making the decision. For example, a young woman who has been dating two very interesting men makes a difficult choice between them and announces her engagement to the one chosen. Momentarily she may question her choice, but almost immediately her evaluations of the men will differ more than they did at the actual time of decision making.

What determines the intensity of dissonance? How can dissonance be reduced?

post–decision dissonance
A state of psychological discomfort that occurs after a difficult choice has been made.

What are some of the factors influencing post-decision dissonance? The arousal of post-decision dissonance is influenced by commitment to the decision. Dissonance will not be experienced unless the individual feels committed to or bound by the decision, often by making it in public, and responsible for its consequences (Kiesler, 1968). Whether the person experiences post-decision dissonance is also influenced by volition. That is, if the person made a decision freely, post-decision dissonance may be experienced. If, however, the person was instructed or compelled to make a particular decision, post-decision dissonance is unlikely (Linder, Cooper and Jones, 1967). Three factors influencing the magnitude of post-decision dissonance are: the importance of the decision, the extent to which the choices were equally desirable, and the extent to which the individual perceives that the choice was freely made.

It is also known that we experience a "regret phase" in which we undervalue the choice we have made and exaggerate the value of the rejected alternative. This phase occurs immediately after the decision and is short-lived. It is then followed by the dissonance-reducing over-valuing of our decision. For example, immediately after buying a car, we may have a transitory feeling of panic: "What have I done?!" Then we reduce dissonance: "I bought the best car on the market." In time we judge our decision more objectively.

Knox and Inkster (1968) demonstrated post-decision dissonance at a racetrack in British Columbia. They asked bettors to estimate the chance of their horses winning. Some of the bettors were interviewed before they placed their bets, and others immediately after. Those in the second group showed significantly higher confidence that their horse would win the race. Placing the bet seemed to create post-decision dissonance that the bettors then reduced by increasing their confidence in their choice. Similar results were found by Younger, Walker and Arrowood (1977), who interviewed people right before and after they placed a bet on a game of chance (bingo; wheel of fortune) at the Canadian National Exhibition in Toronto. Frenkel and Doob (1976) found similar effects with respect to people's confidence that their candidate would win in provincial and federal elections.

SELECTIVE EXPOSURE TO INFORMATION

According to dissonance theory, information that decreases dissonance will be sought, while that which increases dissonance will usually be avoided. Festinger (1964) argued that we may seek out dissonant information if it can be easily refuted, in order to increase our confidence and decrease dissonance. More recently, Frey (1986) suggested that seeking out consonant information is important; avoiding dissonant information matters less.

Researchers have studied how people respond to new information which is inconsistent with their previously held beliefs (Silverman, 1971; Macdonald and Majunder, 1973; Bishop, 1975; Sweeney and Gruber, 1984). These studies concerned attitudes towards U.S. political figures involved in highly publicized events: the Chappaquiddick incident in which Senator Ted Kennedy abandoned his female passenger (who drowned) and delayed informing the police; the resignation of Senator Eagleton as a nominee for vice president in 1972 after it became public knowledge that he had been treated for a serious mental disorder; and the resignation of President Nixon when his role in Watergate became evident. In general, dissonance theory was supported in these studies, although a number of individuals were found who appeared tolerant of some degree of inconsistency in public affairs issues.

SOCIAL SUPPORT

Festinger also claimed that dissonance may be aroused by other individuals voicing disagreement with us. This is most likely to happen if the topic is important to us, if it cannot be verified through reference to "facts," and if our opponents are attractive and credible. For example, we may have experienced this type of dissonance in relation to our attitudes about physician-assisted suicide.

Festinger, Riecken and Schachter (1956) studied the role of social support among members of a doomsday cult. The members of this cult believed they would escape a flood by being taken up in a spaceship to a distant planet. Eventually they realized that neither the flood nor the spaceship were coming. They then tried very hard to recruit others to their cause. By winning new recruits they could avoid the conclusion that they had been foolish in their actions. This study demonstrates the importance of social support in reducing dissonance, but attempts to replicate the findings have not been successful.

COUNTER-ATTITUDINAL BEHAVIOUR AND INSUFFICIENT JUSTIFICATION

Cognitive dissonance theory has also been applied to the relationship between attitudes and behaviour. One of the first experiments concerned with dissonance (Festinger and Carlsmith, 1959) showed that if people could be induced to behave in a manner opposite to their attitude, then their attitude would change to be compatible with their behaviour. This outcome is not what we would intuitively expect, since it suggests that we act first and then form an attitude. The experiment is especially important because it generated extensive theory and research.

In the original experiment, subjects were brought individually to a laboratory and seated in front of a board containing a large number of pegs. Their task was to turn each peg a one-quarter turn in sequence and to continue turning for twenty minutes. Imagine how tedious and boring this task was! At the end of the "experimental session" the experimenter informed the subjects that the experiment was designed to test the effect of a "preparatory set on motor performance." Subjects also were told that they were in the "control group" and therefore had not been given any prior instructions. In addition, they were informed that the next subject was waiting and was to be told that the task was interesting and enjoyable; and that, unfortunately, the assistant who was supposed to pass along the information had not yet shown up. Each subject then was asked whether he or she was willing to take the assistant's place. Half of the subjects were offered $1 for their help; the other half were offered $20, a substantial sum in 1958. Most of the subjects agreed to help whether they were in the $1 condition or the $20 condition.

The subjects then proceeded to tell the waiting "subject" (actually a confederate of the experimenter) that the task, which they knew to be boring, was quite interesting. In doing so they expressed a point of view that was quite contrary to their real attitude towards the task. Then, during a post-experimental interview, subjects were asked to rate the extent to which they found the experimental task boring or interesting. The critical question was, would a counter-attitudinal behaviour (lying to the confederate) lead to an attitude change that represented a more positive evaluation of the task?

The key factor in this study was the magnitude of the incentive to lie. Incentive theory predicts that those paid more for their counter-attitudinal sales pitch would experience the situation in general as more rewarding, and would be more likely to adopt a more positive attitude to the boring task. In contrast, dissonance theory predicts that those paid only $1 to lie about the task would have insufficient external justification for their action. They would experience cognitive dissonance, which could be reduced by deciding that the task was "sort of interesting" and that they had not, in fact, lied. Subjects paid $20 could justify their actions by this payment, whereas few people would feel comfortable "selling out" for a dollar.

The results supported dissonance theory. That is, attitude change was greater among those paid $1 than those paid $20.

REINTERPRETING COGNITIVE DISSONANCE

There are problems with the concept of cognitive dissonance. Bem (1970) argued that, for most people, most of the time, inconsistency is "our most enduring cognitive" state. Several investigators argue that inconsistency is uncomfortable only when it threatens our own self-concept (Greenwald and Ronis, 1978; Steele and Liu, 1983). Indeed, Aronson (1984; Thibodeau and Aronson, 1992) now argues that the dissonance effect is really one of **self-justification**. For example, in the "insufficient justification" experiment, those who lied for only $1 had to change their attitude in order to avoid seeing themselves as willing to lie for no good reason.

Cooper and Fazio (1984) have outlined a revised model of cognitive dissonance which accounts for a variety of research findings (see Figure 4-4). They reason that when we act contrary to our beliefs, we assess the consequences of our actions. If our act is perceived as having actual or potential negative consequences, we search for an explanation. If it is clear that we had a free choice to act and that the consequences could have been anticipated, then we attribute responsibility to ourselves. At this point dissonance is aroused. Notice that dissonance arousal depends on the belief that one is personally responsible for negative consequences. If we attribute the feeling of discomfort to our reaction to the act rather than to some external force, then we are motivated to reduce dissonance. As a result of this motivation, our attitude changes.

In summary, four steps are necessary for cognitive dissonance effects:

(1) the attitude-discrepant behaviour produces significant consequences,

(2) individuals feel personally responsible for these consequences,

(3) individuals experience a state of arousal,

(4) individuals attribute this arousal or discomfort to their own behaviour.

Once dissonance is experienced, individuals are motivated to reduce it. Both dissonance arousal and motivation to reduce dissonance involve complex sets of attributions. Dissonance may be reduced by making appropriate changes in behaviour or attitudes.

In attitude change associated with dissonance arousal, internal cognitive processes are of central importance. In some situations, of course, attitude change

self–justification
Expressing attitudes in line with behaviour in order to avoid looking foolishly inconsistent.

Why have some researchers been critical of cognitive dissonance theory? How has the theory been revised?

FIGURE 4-4 "New Look" model of cognitive dissonance

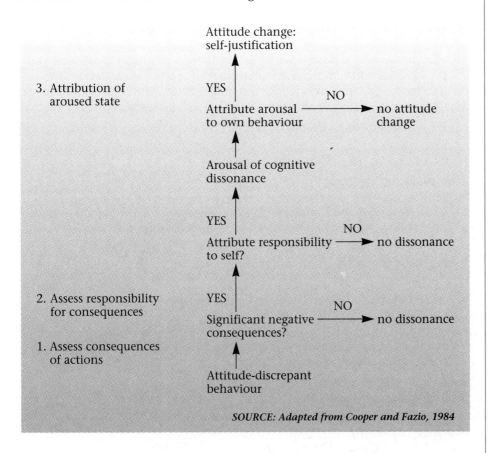

SOURCE: Adapted from Cooper and Fazio, 1984

occurs as a result of external influences. In the following section, we will look at the role of external influences, or persuasion, in attitude change.

SELF-TEST QUESTIONS

8. Under what circumstances is dissonance likely to occur?

a) when behaviour results in negative consequences

b) when behaviour does not correspond to beliefs

c) when someone makes us perform

d) when the behaviour performed is a rare one

e) both a and b

9. What is the difference between conflict and dissonance?

a) conflict deals with emotions and dissonance with attitudes

b) conflict occurs before a decision and dissonance after a decision

c) dissonance occurs before a decision and conflict after a decision

d) dissonance deals with attitude-discrepant behaviour and conflict with emotions

e) conflict is more intense than dissonance

10. In order to reduce dissonance after voting for a particular candidate, you read articles and campaign literature that supports the candidate. This is called

a) discrepant behaviour

b) selective exposure to information

c) social support

d) downgrading the importance of dissonant elements

e) the consistency principle

11. In the Festinger and Carlsmith (1959) experiment on turning knobs and then telling the next subject about it, attitude change was greatest

a) when paid $1 to lie

b) after they told a lie

c) when paid $20 to lie

d) when they had to pay to participate in the experiment

12. According to the theory of cognitive dissonance, how would we expect members of a cult to react when their prophecy that the world will soon end has not come to pass?

a) behave in ways counter to their attitudes

b) quietly disband and go home

c) become active proselytizers, recruiting new members

d) change their beliefs to accord with the failed prophecy

PERSUASION

persuasion *The process of getting others to agree with an advocated position by means of a rational or emotional appeal.*

In the traditional view of persuasion what elements have researchers studied? How have they increased our understanding of how the persuasive process works?

Persuasion is the process of getting others to agree with an advocated position by means of a rational or emotional appeal. The foundations for research on persuasion were established by Carl Hovland and his colleagues at Yale University (Hovland, Janis and Kelley, 1953). They concentrated on the stages people go through in order to be persuaded: attention, comprehension, acceptance or yielding, and retention of the message. The crucial stage is accepting or yielding. For researchers the critical question has been: "Under what conditions will the audience accept the message and yield to the persuasive powers of the persuader?" Thus, traditionally, investigators have organized their research on this question around four elements of persuasion: the source, the message, the channel, and the individual being persuaded. Recently, cognitive psychologists have offered a number of models to account for the process of persuasion (Petty and Cacioppo, 1981, 1986; Eagly and Chaiken, 1992). These models focus on the kinds of processes involved in persuasion. In particular, they focus on how various factors influence whether our responses to persuasive messages are thoughtful and deliberate or comparatively thoughtless and reactive. Our discussion of persuasion is organized around three topics: the elements of persuasion, the elaboration likelihood model of persuasion, and resistance to persuasion.

ELEMENTS OF PERSUASION

THE SOURCE OR COMMUNICATOR

The major characteristic of the source, or communicator, that affects acceptance is **credibility**. Recall the national referendum held on October 26, 1992, when the proposals of the Charlottetown Accord were presented to Canadian voters. The lack of credibility of the political leaders who advocated approval was an important factor in the defeat of the Accord. Credibility has been shown to be mainly a function of perceived **expertness** and **trustworthiness**. Communicators are more effective if the audience assumes they know what they are talking about and are sincere. Trustworthiness is increased if the audience believes the communicator has nothing to gain from his or her efforts. It is no accident that toothpaste is promoted by individuals in lab coats (expertness) and that detergents are recommended by ordinary people who only want to pass on their experience to others. It is also true that the source's credibility will have an impact only if the audience is aware of it before the message is presented rather than after (Mills and Harvey, 1972).

In most cases, the topic or item and the expertise of the source must be compatible. Ordinarily, it would not be very sensible to have a nuclear physicist talk about nutrition. However, "high status" sources may be influential even outside their area of knowledge. For example, Nobel prize winners are often accepted as experts on a wide variety of subjects. Various government departments or agencies who sponsor advertising presumably perceive themselves as "high status" sources, although those viewing the ads may not agree. (See the accompanying photo.)

Source **likeability** will also influence persuasion. This effect is emphasized if subjects are made aware of how likeable the source is. Roskos-Ewoldsen and Fazio (1992) manipulated subjects' awareness of a well-known source, Jacques Cousteau, by having them repeatedly rate his likeability. When this was done, greater attitude change in the direction of Cousteau's message was obtained.

MESSAGE FACTORS

Suppose you have been nominated as a candidate for some elected office and you must now convince the electorate to vote for you. Or suppose that you are a lawyer about to present your summation of a case to the jury. In each case you have to get your message across in a way that increases your chance of winning the election or having your client declared innocent. There is some information available that could help you organize your message in the most effective way.

PLAY IT SMART
WHEN YOU DRIVE DON'T DRINK

Is government perceived as a credible source by young people?

credibility *Believability. A communicator is credible if he or she is perceived as knowledgeable and trustworthy.*

BOX 4-2

PERSUASION SCHEMATA: WHEN WE USE WHAT MESSAGE

What do we do when we want to persuade someone of something?

In fact, we usually begin with some idea of what we are going to do and, if our plan should fail, we often have another plan of attack ready. In other words, we approach the task of changing someone's attitude with a set of persuasion schemata, which are evoked and used almost automatically in a variety of situations.

In one study by Rule, Bisanz and Kohn (1985) subjects were asked whom they persuaded, who persuaded them, and how people tried to persuade their friends, enemies, fathers, and other people in general. Their data showed that most persuasion attempts occur in close relationships, and that attempts tend to be reciprocal, that is, both people attempt to persuade each other. A list of persuasion goals was also derived, the most common being activity (to go somewhere, do something, or acquire some object).

The study also showed that we tend to follow a sequence of methods in our attempts at persuasion. We tend first to ask for what we want, although it is certainly not always advisable to be direct! Then we use "self-oriented methods," citing a personal reason ("I really need it") or personal expertise ("I have one and it's great"). Then, we invoke "dyadic" methods, referring to the ongoing relationship we have with this person ("Be a friend!"), or bargaining ("If you do it for me, I'll take you out for supper"). Finally, we appeal to more abstract principles, such as social norms ("Everybody is doing it"), altruism ("Surely you don't want your child to imitate you and smoke") or morality ("We could accept that bribe but it would be wrong"). Two approaches stand out from the sequence of persuasion strategies observed in the study: we tend to use flattery or "buttering up" quite early, perhaps at the beginning, and we almost always use physical force as a last resort, if at all. If threats, deception, and emotional appeals are to be used (guilt, sulking) they will also be used as last resorts.

A one-sided or two-sided communication strategy. It is important to examine the situation in selecting a one-sided or two-sided communication strategy. Hovland *et al.* (1957) found that, especially with intelligent audiences, it is best to present both the positive and negative sides of an argument, and then to refute the negative evidence. It is also more effective to present both sides when it is probable that the audience will hear the other side from someone else. However, in some situations this strategy is not effective. For example, when delegates at a political convention have a firm position on an issue, it is not effective to present a two-sided argument (Karlins and Abelson, 1970).

Primacy-recency. If both sides of an argument are to be presented, which is likely to have the advantage, the side given first (**primacy**) or the side given last (**recency**)? The critical factor in answering this question is the passage of time. If one set of arguments immediately follows the other, then the set presented first is likely to have the most impact. However, as the time between the sets increases, the one presented last will have more impact (Miller and Campbell, 1959; Insko, 1964; Wilson and Miller, 1968).

Now consider what these results suggest about the impact of lawyers' presentations to a jury. If the two lawyers are to present their cases on the same day, the one who goes first is likely to have the advantage. However, if it is late in the day and the case is adjourned after the presentation of the first lawyer, then the

primacy effect Tendency for information presented early in a sequence to have a greater impact than information presented later.

recency effect Tendency for information presented late in a sequence to have a greater impact than information presented earlier.

lawyer who makes his presentation the next morning is likely to have the advantage. Also consider the implications for the typical practice in our courts, wherein the Crown presents its case and final argument before the defence is heard. Does this practice give the Crown the advantage of primacy or does it give the defence the advantage of recency?

Arousal of fear.   Suppose you are in charge of public relations for a provincial department of highways, and seatbelt legislation has been recently passed. What would be your best advertising strategy to encourage people to obey this law? The Ontario government used a relatively mild approach a few years ago by showing what happens when loose watermelons strike the road, and by comparing loose and taped-down eggs being shaken in a box. In England, on the other hand, television ads have shown the actual fatal aftermaths of automobile accidents.

The research on fear messages began with an experiment by Janis and Feshbach (1953). In this study, students were given one of three messages about dental hygiene. The messages differed in the level of fear they were intended to generate, but not in essential content. The most threatening message used coloured pictures of diseased mouths, gums, and teeth, whereas the least threatening used X-rays and pictures of healthy mouths. They found that the least change in dental habits followed the most threatening message, and the most change followed the mild appeal. The results imply that high fear leads to avoidance. It may be that subjects in the high fear condition did not learn the hygiene techniques presented because high fear interfered with learning. It is also possible that the unpleasantness of the high fear condition led to decreased credibility of the communicator and to discounting the message. In contrast, results of other studies showed that as fear increased, attitude change increased (Higbee, 1969; McGuire, 1969; Leventhal, 1970). In general, researchers have found that low to moderate levels of fear increase attitude change, but high levels do not (McGuire, 1968). See Figure 4-5.

The relationship between the effects of fear and the type of issue is important. Using extreme fear in messages concerning oral hygiene was ineffective because

FIGURE 4-5 **Relationship between fear arousal and persuasion**

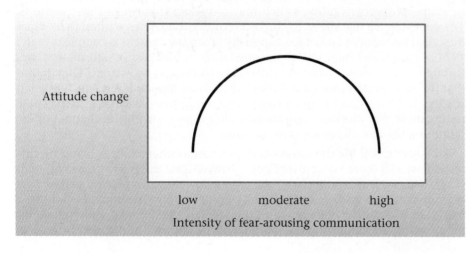

Attitude change

low   moderate   high

Intensity of fear-arousing communication

it led people to avoid the issue altogether, and to neglect cleaning their teeth. Conceivably, avoidance may be desirable if, for example, the issue is AIDS or venereal disease. However, the drawback is that the audience may avoid precautions or hygienic practices, but not sex itself. It is also important to realize that sometimes people who adopt healthier habits such as not smoking are not motivated by messages intended to generate fear, but by other considerations such as saving money or conformity (Health and Welfare Canada, 1987).

AUDIENCE FACTORS

It is often important to obtain some information about characteristics of the audience when developing a persuasive message. For instance, intelligence and socio-economic background are important variables that advertisers must consider. Age is another relevant factor. Older people are less open to attitude change than younger people (Newcomb, Koenig, Flacks and Warwick, 1967). The attitudes people adopt when they are young persist relatively unchanged (Krosnick and Alwin, 1989). Researchers have also been interested in whether certain personality traits make people more or less susceptible to persuasion. McGuire (1968) has argued that it will be difficult to show a direct relationship between a personality trait and persuasion because the same trait can affect both the individual's attention to and comprehension of the message (reception) and changing his or her attitudes in the direction of the message (yielding). He points out that reception may be influenced in one direction, while yielding may be influenced in the opposite direction. Indeed, the literature shows that low self-esteem people have difficulty in receiving the message, high self-esteem people tend not to yield, but those with moderate levels of self-esteem are most readily persuaded (Rhodes and Wood, 1992).

THE CHANNEL

Does it make any difference whether a persuasive message is presented face-to-face, via TV or radio, or in a written document? The data on this question are not consistent. Some studies indicate that messages presented live or via TV are more effective than audio-only messages, which in turn are more effective than written messages (Williams, 1975). Other research has been unable to specify clearly any differences (Worchel, Andreoli and Eason, 1975). Chaiken and Eagly (1976) point out that one factor that may account for these inconsistent findings is message comprehensibility, which may have varied between investigations. There is evidence that messages are better understood when written than when presented by video or audiotape, especially when the content is complex (Eagly, 1974). Chaiken and Eagly (1976) presented subjects with easy or difficult messages through one of three channels: videotape, audiotape, or written. They found that the easy messages were most effective on videotape and least effective when written. In contrast, difficult messages were most effective when written. These results show that message comprehensibility interacts with the channel in determining the effectiveness of the message.

Of course in real life the elements of persuasion interact. In concluding this section, we will discuss a study designed to investigate this interaction. Wiegman (1985) had two Dutch politicians, who represented the main political parties, tape interviews in two distinct styles about whether an airport should be built in a particular location. In one interview, the politician gave a cool, sober, thoughtful presentation supporting the building of the airport. In the other interview,

BOX 4-3
WHAT IS PROPAGANDA?

Think about the following words: persuasion, advertising, selling, education, brainwashing, propaganda. What are their differences? When do education, persuasion, or advertising become "propaganda," a word that evokes the sinister image of people chanting mindless slogans? Can propaganda assume more subtle forms that are accepted in our relatively open and democratic societies? Consider the following examples:

(1) Some of the present-day religious cults indoctrinate their members under conditions of extreme stress, strong group pressure, endless repetition of messages, and deprivation of food or sleep. They may call it "re-education"; we may call it "brainwashing." However, somewhat similar techniques are used to initiate new recruits into some religious orders and into the military.

(2) Education is also concerned with attitude and behavioural changes, usually (or ideally) by providing information and training in intellectual skills and reasoning. Zimbardo, Ebbesen and Maslach (1977) point out that much of the teaching of arithmetic in schools involves problems of buying, renting, selling, and calculating interest. Are these simply practical survival skills, or do they serve a purpose of legitimizing ("propagating") the existing economic system?

(3) A study of the ubiquitous TV crime shows reveals a consistent pattern: the crime is solved by the police and the correct culprit is identified and arrested. Of course, this is far from an accurate picture of crime and punishment today in North America. Does this type of programming represent "wishful thinking" propaganda on behalf of the criminal justice system? (Haney and Manzolatti, 1981)

(4) Propaganda may also be achieved by selective reporting—by omission rather than fabrication. Chomsky (1986) studied reports in the major U.S. dailies of elections held in the mid-1980s in Nicaragua and El Salvador, and found that the vast majority of stories concerning the elections in leftist Nicaragua contained references to irregularities, censorship, and human rights violations. However, violations that were at least equally serious in El Salvador, a country whose government has been strongly supported by the U.S. government, were rarely mentioned, even in the more "liberal" newspapers that purported to include all the news that's fit to print. The result, of course, was a distorted comparative picture of the state of democracy in Central America.

In his terrifying novel *Nineteen Eighty-Four*, George Orwell described a "Ministry of Truth" that dispensed outright lies and propaganda. Truth and propaganda make strange bedfellows, but may often end up together. At times it is difficult to distinguish one from the other and, when propaganda is subtle, it may be even more effective.

---

the politician gave a strongly emotional presentation in a very dynamic manner. One of the four interviews was shown to delegates at meetings of both parties. Therefore, the experimenter varied the source of the message (same versus other political party), the audience (political party), and the message (emotional versus rational presentation). Regardless of the content of the message, attitude change was greater when the source and the audience belonged to the same political party. In addition, Wiegman found that the rational presentation resulted in a higher rating for the speaker, but not in a greater attitude change.

TWO ROUTES TO PERSUASION

While one might say that people are "persuaded" to buy a certain brand of beer, it is unlikely that they have reflected on the merits of the various brands. However,

How do the two routes to persuasion differ?

there are times when we are persuaded because we have been stimulated to think about an issue and are convinced by an argument presented to us. When we are thinking about how to vote in a referendum, we may think about the pros and cons, how the outcome will affect us, whom we trust, and how the proposed changes will affect the country. As we think about these questions, we are engaging in **cognitive elaboration**. Cognitive elaboration can lead to "real persuasion" in which we are "convinced."

cognitive elaboration
Cognitive activity or processing in terms of meaning that involves current information and related information already stored in memory.

THE ELABORATION LIKELIHOOD MODEL

Recent research has investigated the conditions under which the arguments themselves will persuade, and those in which other, peripheral factors will lead to attitude change. A contemporary dual-process theory of persuasion, the elaboration likelihood model (ELM), takes into consideration the fact that people can respond to persuasive messages in either an active, cognitive way, or a more reactive, emotional manner (Petty and Cacioppo, 1981, 1986). Elaboration refers to the extent to which people examine and think about arguments in a message and also perhaps other relevant arguments left out of the message. Thus, elaboration likelihood means the probability that the person will think about a persuasive message.

central route persuasion
Attitude change that follows logical argumentation and thought about the issue.

peripheral route persuasion *Attitude change involving just about any persuasive factors except for careful attention to and analysis of the message.*

The two routes. According to the ELM, there are two different "routes" by which persuasion occurs and attitudes change: central and peripheral. The **central route** involves cognitive activity, that is, making the effort to understand the message and to think about the issue. Basically, the person receiving the message pays attention to the ideas, attempts to understand the arguments, and then evaluates them. In understanding and evaluating, the person may use other relevant information that he or she already knows. This is a very rational and analytical process. The **peripheral route** is very different. It involves factors that are not relevant to the arguments themselves, such as the attractiveness of the source or perceptions about how the majority of the audience is responding to the message. The peripheral route involves just about any persuasive factors, except for careful attention to and analysis of the content of the message.

Differences in attitude changes associated with the two routes. The two routes are associated with differences in attitude change. Central route processes tend to lead to "real" and enduring attitude change and to consistent action, since we have carefully thought about the content of the message. Peripheral processes, on the other hand, require less effort and tend to produce less enduring attitude changes because we haven't really been convinced by the arguments. Attitude change produced by the peripheral route will persist only as long as the relevant cues are present and obvious. For example, we may believe or accept certain policies only as long as the politician whom we associate with them is popular or attractive to us.

When central route persuasion occurs. Most important, the model specifies the conditions that influence the likelihood of cognitive elaboration, and thus of enduring attitude change. Central route persuasion will occur when the person has the motivation, opportunity, and ability to think about the message. Various conditions for such motivation can be identified. For example, people are usually motivated to think about a message that has high personal relevance or importance (Petty and Cacioppo, 1979). However, under high-involvement conditions that reflect people's values or how they define themselves, people are less open to persuasion, perhaps because they are unable to elaborate or think open-mindedly about the message under such conditions (Sherif and Cantril, 1947; Johnson and Eagly, 1989). Another factor that influences motivation to think about a message is the "need for cognition." Individuals differ in their need for such cognitive activities as analyzing situations and solving challenging problems. Note that this need for cognition is not the same as intelligence. While intelligent people are more likely to enjoy using their intelligence, they will not necessarily do so. However, people with a high need for cognition are more likely to be influenced by the quality of arguments than people with a low need for cognition (Haugtvedt and Petty, 1992).

When peripheral route persuasion occurs.   Chaiken (1980, 1987) argues that when people are not motivated to engage in cognitive elaboration they will often use simple schemata or rules to assess arguments, without really tackling their content. For example, people may rely on the "trust the experts" rule in order to accept a persuasive argument presented by someone perceived as an expert. Similarly, they may rely on a schema that "we agree with people whom we like" and accept a message from a likeable source. Of course, if a message seems too difficult to understand, people rely on the peripheral route rather than the central route. Distraction can also influence people to engage in peripheral rather than central processing. Results of a study by Norman (1976) indicated that students engaged in central processing when an unattractive communicator presented them with a message containing several arguments; students presented with a single message did not. However, students presented with the same messages by an attractive communicator engaged in peripheral processing.

A study on the interaction of audience, source, and message factors.   A study by Petty, Cacioppo, and Goldman (1981) demonstrates how variations in the audience, source, and message content influence the type of processing in which people engage. They had university students listen to a message arguing that seniors should have to take comprehensive examinations before graduation. The policy was to take effect the next year (high involvement) or in ten years (low involvement). The expertise of the speaker and the strength of the arguments in the message were also varied. Under high involvement, the strong arguments led to more attitude change than the weak arguments. However, under low involvement, source expertise (a peripheral cue) had a stronger effect on persuasion than did the actual arguments. These subjects simply used a heuristic, "experts know best" to decide on the validity of the arguments.

Important implications of the elaboration likelihood model.   The ELM suggests that "real" attitude change by means of persuasion is difficult and uncommon. Central route persuasion is successful only when the recipient has both the motivation and the ability to process the information. And of course, the arguments must be logical and convincing. As noted in Chapter 2, we often act as "cognitive misers," taking cognitive shortcuts and acting in rather automatic ways. Thus, in our society of the twenty-second commercial and the "newsbite," it is not surprising that peripheral route change is very common.

SELF-TEST QUESTIONS

13. Which of the following is a source characteristic in persuasion?

a) expertise

b) fear arousal

c) persuasibility

d) written versus video

14. When is it advisable to present a two-sided communication?

a) when the message is presented first

b) when the audience is intelligent and not strongly committed to either side of the issue

c) when the audience is committed to your side

d) when your message will be presented last

15. In the experiment involving videotaped Dutch politicians presenting arguments about building an airport, a rational as opposed to an emotional presentation led to

a) more positive ratings of the speaker and a greater degree of attitude change

b) more positive ratings of the speaker but not a greater attitude change

c) more attitude change but lower ratings of the speaker

d) low ratings of the speaker and no attitude change

16. Persuasion by the central route depends on such factors as

a) logical, convincing arguments

b) arousal of cognitive dissonance

c) source attractiveness

d) insufficient external justification

RESISTING PERSUASION

It is easy to be impressed by the great variety of persuasion techniques. Either on a one-to-one basis or as members of a mass audience, we are subjected to an ever-increasing barrage of persuasive messages. Yet it is important to realize the limits of persuasion. Many products fail to win a market, many politicians lose elections, and many used cars are not sold. Most of us remain unconvinced by a great deal of what we see and hear. Even young children react sceptically to the many TV commercials directed at them. In the age of mass communications, people seem to have adapted rather well. It is important to consider how people resist persuasion. In the paragraphs below, we will look at forewarning and inoculation as strategies for resisting persuasion.

FOREWARNING

forewarning Advance knowledge of persuasive intent or message content.

There are two types of forewarning, both of which reduce the likelihood of persuasion. In one type, individuals are warned ahead of time of persuasive intent. That is, they are warned that an attempt to persuade them will occur. In the second type, individuals are warned that an attempt may occur and informed of the message content. In the latter case, individuals are apparently stimulated by the warning to rehearse their own position and to produce their own counter-arguments (McGuire and Papageorgis, 1962). Petty and Cacioppo (1977) provide particularly strong evidence that forewarned subjects review their own arguments. They led students in an introductory psychology class to believe that they were going to have a guest lecturer, a psychologist who worked in the university counselling centre. Half of the students were forewarned, and the other half were not. Those who were forewarned were told that the guest lecturer was going to advocate that all first- and second-year students live in college dorms, and then were given brief activities that encouraged thinking about the issue. Forewarned students were less influenced by the guest speaker than those who were not forewarned. When asked to write down their thoughts on the subject, forewarned students produced more thoughts than unwarned students, indicating more thinking about the issue.

Of course, when only intent and not content is anticipated, rehearsal and counter-argumentation cannot take place. In this situation, "reactance" produces the resistance (Hass and Grady, 1975). The advance knowledge of persuasive intent is perceived as a warning that one's freedom is threatened, thus making one resist the persuasive message when it comes later. In other words, the individual is acting to protect his or her threatened freedom.

INOCULATION

Usually, the more strongly people feel about an issue, the less likely they will be to change their minds about it. Paradoxically, however, certain attitudes are especially vulnerable to persuasion, even when the attitude is held initially with some conviction (McGuire and Papageorgis, 1961). These attitudes are called cultural truisms because a large majority of the population supports them or believes them to be true. Examples include: "We should brush our teeth after every meal if possible," and "Democracy is the best form of government." McGuire used a medical analogy to help explain what he thought accounted for this finding. He pointed out that an individual is susceptible to infection when the body's defences are weak. Inoculations lead the body to build up its defences and resist infection. Similarly, cultural truisms are weak and vulnerable to persuasion. They are so widely accepted that the individual has never thought about any opposing positions. He or she needs to be inoculated by thinking about these opposing arguments and refuting them. That is, in attitude inoculation a person is presented with weak persuasive arguments against his or her beliefs, and has to refute these arguments.

How does forewarning help us to resist persuasion?

***inoculation** Exposure to relatively weak arguments against our own position in order to strengthen our resistance to persuasion.*

How does inoculation help us to resist persuasion?

SELF-TEST QUESTIONS

17. Attitude inoculation seeks to strengthen beliefs
a) by using different channels to communicate the same message
b) by providing social support for the beliefs
c) by giving supporting arguments for the beliefs

SELF ? TEST

d) by presenting persuasive arguments against the beliefs and having the subject refute them

18. Resistance to persuasion is enhanced if a person perceives the intent to persuade. This is called

a) inoculation

b) implosion

c) forewarning

d) hard-sell

SUMMARY

(1) Attitudes serve a number of functions: instrumental or adaptive, knowledge, ego-defensive, and expressive.

(2) The most influential models of the attitude-behaviour relationship are Ajzen and Fishbein's theory of reasoned action and the extension of it, Ajzen's theory of planned behaviour. The most immediate determinant of an action is an intention, which is determined by attitudes towards the action (beliefs that it will lead to valued consequences) and perceived norms (beliefs about what others expect of us and our motives to comply). Under some circumstances behavioural control needs to be taken into consideration.

(3) Attitude change can be viewed in terms of internal processes and external influences.

(4) The theory of cognitive dissonance states that when two related cognitions are not consistent or in harmony, the individual is motivated to reduce discomfort by changing or reducing the importance of a dissonant cognition or adding consonant cognitions (bolstering).

(5) Four important areas of study within cognitive dissonance theory are: post-decision dissonance (after making a difficult choice); social support; selective information seeking; and dissonance after attitude-discrepant behaviour.

(6) Cooper and Fazio have developed a model that explains when cognitive dissonance occurs in response to attitude-discrepant behaviour: significant consequences, personal responsibility, arousal, and attributing the arousal to the action's consequences.

(7) Factors involved in persuasion include the source, audience, message, and the channel. Source credibility is generally determined by judging the source's trustworthiness and expertise.

(8) Message effectiveness is influenced by primacy or recency in presentation. Fear arousal up to a moderate level can increase persuasion.

(9) Whether an audience will be receptive to a message can be determined by certain personality characteristics, such as self-esteem. Complex messages are most effective when written; easy messages are most effective when presented orally.

(10) The elaboration likelihood model of persuasion differentiates between the central route (understanding the arguments, thinking about the issue) and the peripheral route (focusing on characteristics of the source or distraction in

the message, using heuristics). Central route processing is more likely when the person is motivated, has the opportunity to think, and has a strong need for cognition.

(11) While attitude changes are more likely to occur through the peripheral route, they are less likely to persist in the absence of salient cues. Attitude changes due to central route processing tend to be more enduring.

(12) The effect of persuasion is reduced by forewarning the audience of an attempt to persuade, and by inoculation (confronting the audience with mild counter-arguments).

FOR REVIEW

The tripartite model of attitudes involves three components: _____, _____, and _____(1). This model implies that components are _____(2) in some way. Also, a person can have _____(3) attitude towards the same object. In contrast to attitudes, _____(4) are more fundamental orientations that people have about issues.

Attitudes serve a number of important functions. An attitude serving an _____(5) function enables us to gain acceptance or approval from others. One serving a _____(6) function acts as a schema to help determine our reactions to and interpretations of the world. Attitudes serving an _____(7) function protect us from harsh or uncomfortable facts about ourselves or our world. _____(8) attitudes demonstrate our uniqueness, and what is important to us.

The theory of reasoned action deals with the relationship between attitudes and behaviour. According to this theory the best predictor of an action is an _____(9). The difference between the theory of planned behaviour and the theory of reasoned action is that the former includes the additional concept of _____(10).

According to the theory of cognitive dissonance, two cognitions may have a _____, _____, or _____(11) relationship. Bolstering, rationalizing, and changing behaviour are ways of _____(12). Dissonance theory has also been applied to the relationship between attitudes and _____(13). In the spool-winding experiment by Festinger and Carlsmith (1959), subjects who were paid $1 experienced cognitive dissonance because they had _____(14) to lie. According to Cooper and Fazio's revised model of cognitive dissonance (1984), dissonance occurs when one feels _____(15) for serious outcomes of one's behaviour.

In persuasion, the _____(16) of the communicator depends on expertise and trustworthiness. If both sides of an argument are to be presented, the amount of time between the presentations of the two sides determines whether the side given first _____(17) or last _____(18) has more impact. Low to intermediate fear arousal is _____(19) related to attitude change, and high fear arousal tends to be _____(20) related to attitude change. Relatively enduring and "real" attitude change is more likely when accompanied by _____(21). Most television commercials are directed to the _____(22) route of persuasion.

ISSUES AND ACTIVITIES

1. Make a list of five of your attitudes and five of your values. What functions do the attitudes serve? How are the attitudes similar to and different from the values?

2. Make a collection of ads from magazines. Describe the strategies used to sell products (e.g. testimonials, humour, appeal to psychological needs). Discuss features that promote the use of central and peripheral processing. Also consider how effective the ads are in terms of really persuading people to change their attitudes.

3. What are the ethical implications of developing a technology for inducing attitude change?

4. Attitude measurement is very persuasive in contemporary society and big business (consumer, political). What are the implications of this?

5. View the video segment *Sue Rodriguez,* and discuss attitudes portrayed that make assisted suicide a contentious issue.

• FURTHER READING

CIALDINI, R.B. (1993). *Influence: Science and practice,* Third Edition. New York: HarperCollins. An excellent discussion of the variety of means by which people influence people, with many examples from advertising and marketing, public relations, fundraising, and politics.

EAGLY, A.H. and CHAIKEN, S. (1993). *The psychology of attitudes.* New York: Harcourt Brace Jovanovich. An analytical and thorough coverage of attitude theory and research.

PETTY, R.E. and CACIOPPO, J.T. (1981). *Attitudes and persuasion: Classic and contemporary approaches.* Dubuque, Iowa: Wm. C. Brown. A survey of approaches to attitudes and attitude change.

PRATKANIS, A. and ARONSON, E. (1992). *Age of propaganda: The everyday use and abuse of persuasion.* New York: Freeman. An account of the use of persuasion in everyday life: how and why we are persuaded, and how to resist persuasion.

ZIMBARDO, P.G. and LEIPPE, M.R. (1991). *The psychology of attitude change and social influence.* New York: McGraw-Hill. An overview of contemporary thinking and research. Includes good chapters on applications in law and health.

SUGGESTED WEBLINKS

Institute for Propaganda Analysis
http://carmen.artsci.washington.edu/propaganda/ipa.htm

Psychology of Religion
http://www.gasou.edu/psychweb/psyrelig/psyrelig.htm

ANSWERS TO SELF-TEST QUESTIONS

1. c; 2. b; 3. d; 4. c; 5. e; 6. d; 7. c; 8. e; 9. b; 10. b; 11. a; 12. c; 13. a; 14. b; 15. b; 16. a; 17. d; 18. c.

ANSWERS TO FOR REVIEW

1. cognitive, affective, behavioural; 2. integrated; 3. more than one; 4. values; 5. instrumental; 6. knowledge; 7. ego-defensive; 8. Value-expressive;

9. intention; 10. perceived behavioural control; 11. consonant, dissonant, irrelevant; 12. reducing dissonance; 13. behaviour; 14. insufficient external justification; 15. personally responsible; 16. credibility; 17. primacy; 18. recency; 19. positively; 20. negatively; 21. cognitive elaboration; 22. peripheral.

5

SOCIAL INFLUENCE

Only dead fish swim with the stream.

Anonymous

HAMLET: Do you see that cloud, that's almost in shape like a camel?
POLONIUS: By the mass, and 'tis like a camel indeed.
HAMLET: Methinks, it is like a weasel.
POLONIUS: It is backed like a weasel.
HAMLET: Or, like a whale?
POLONIUS: Very like a whale.

William Shakespeare

■ LEARNING OUTCOMES

1. Knowledge about various forms of social influence such as social facilitation, social loafing, conformity, and obedience.

2. An understanding of why people conform and obey.

3. Knowledge about the tactics used to influence others.

4. An understanding of the dangers of conformity, such as groupthink.

5. An understanding of how social influence occurs unintentionally.

■ FOR REFLECTION

- What causes people to yield to the pressure to conform?

- Why do people sometimes do what they are told even when they don't want to?

- What are the dangers and benefits of conformity and obedience?

■ CHAPTER OUTLINE

In 1978, in Guyana, South America, over 900 members of the Peoples Church led by Jim Jones died after drinking Kool-Aid containing cyanide. Why would parents poison their children and then willingly commit suicide in response to the "orders" of a minister? There is a record of the final hours of Jonestown, because it was Jones' policy to tape-record everything that occurred there. The tape reveals that Jones used many of the tactics of social influence discussed in this chapter. He created a view of reality in which death was the only solution, and convinced his followers to accept this view.

Consider the number of times you have changed your opinion or your behaviour so that it became more like that of another person. Why did you do this? Did someone convince you of the "correctness" of another point of view? Or did you change because you became aware that you were thinking or behaving differently than most of your peers? Did anyone pressure you to change, or not? Did you comply with a request or did you obey a direct order without question? Changes caused by all of these factors are examples of social influence.

In this chapter we will explore the conditions under which these various influences lead to changes in behaviour. How do they affect us? And how do they account for such seemingly unreasonable behaviour as that of the people at Jonestown?

THE EFFECTS OF MERE PRESENCE

SOCIAL FACILITATION

How does the presence of others affect our performance?

Let's think about what you do when you're driving and waiting for the traffic light to change from red to green. When the light changes, do you start up more quickly when another motorist is beside you in the next lane, or when you are the only one at the intersection? If you are like most other drivers, you proceed more quickly when there is someone in the next lane. How can we account for this behaviour?

One of the first experiments in social psychology was concerned with this same question. In 1898, Norman Triplett noticed that bicyclists who were paced travelled faster than those who cycled alone. Triplett decided to investigate whether the faster race times were due to the presence of other cyclists. That is, did the presence of others cause improved performance? He used school children as subjects. The task he used was winding fishing reels, a task that children did both alone and in the presence of a classmate. The results of his study showed that in the presence of others as compared to performing alone, twenty children did better, ten did worse, and ten were not affected. Based on these findings, Triplett concluded that with respect to the bicycle racers, "the bodily presence of another contestant participating simultaneously in the race served to liberate latent energy not ordinarily available" (p. 533). In 1939, Crawford used the term **social facilitation** to refer to improvement in individual activity resulting from the presence of others.

social facilitation An increment or decrement in behaviour resulting from the presence of one or more individuals.

Why does the presence of others at some times improve and at other times impair our performance?

EXPLANATIONS FOR SOCIAL FACILITATION

The early research on the effects of the presence of others left many questions unanswered. Why did the presence of others affect performance? Another puzzling question arose as the research accumulated and it became clear that these effects were mixed. That is, why did the presence of others sometimes facilitate performance and at other times hinder it? In the paragraphs that follow we will look at some of the attempts to answer these questions.

AROUSAL

In a review of the research, Zajonc (1965) noticed that responding was improved in the presence of others when the task was simple or well-learned. By contrast, when the task was difficult or called for a new response, responding was impaired. Zajonc (1965, 1980) went on to suggest that a single underlying process —arousal—can either facilitate or impair performance depending on the situation, and that the mere presence of others leads to increased arousal. In his view, when aroused, we usually do whatever first comes to mind. For easy tasks, this dominant response tends to be the correct one. When the light changes at an intersection, we perform the dominant response of stepping on the gas more quickly when another driver is in the adjacent traffic lane than when we are alone. For new or difficult tasks, the dominant response tends to be incorrect, interfering with our making the appropriate response. When we are working on mathematics problems, for example, we make more errors and work more slowly when other people are present than when we are alone.

It's no accident that people of a given segment of society dress in similar clothes.

evaluation apprehension
A concern for how other people are assessing us.

EVALUATION APPREHENSION

Cottrell had a different explanation for social facilitation. He suggested that the nature of the audience, or at least our perception of it, influences our performance. Cottrell and his colleagues (1968) had subjects perform a nonsense syllable task either alone or in the presence of one of two types of audiences. In one of these audience conditions, two people watched the subject from a distance of about six feet ("observer" condition). In the other audience condition, two people were present but they were blindfolded, supposedly in preparation for their participation in a later experiment ("mere presence" condition). The results of the study showed no difference between the "alone" and the "mere presence" conditions. However, responding was considerably facilitated in the "observer" condition. In Cottrell's view, the presence of others is a "learned source of drive" (Cottrell, 1972, p. 227). That is, people learn to associate the presence of others with the anticipation of both rewards and punishments, and both these types of anticipations lead to arousal. In our car at the intersection, we start up quickly when the light changes because this behaviour is rewarded by social approval, whereas starting up slowly is associated with disapproval.

Results of some later research (cf. Geen and Gange, 1977) suggest that only negative evaluations increase arousal. Accordingly, if we perceive observers as critical evaluators rather than passive observers, their presence will facilitate

BOX 5-1

COCKROACHES AND SOCIAL FACILITATION

Zajonc (1965) tested his idea that arousal due to the mere presence of others causes superior performance on a simple task and poorer performance on a complex task on the cockroach, an organism not influenced, of course, by complex factors. He varied a maze to create simple and complex versions of a task. In the simple version, the cockroaches ran in a straight path away from a light to a more desirable dark goal box. In the complex version, the cockroaches ran around a corner on their way to darkness. The cockroaches ran each type of maze both alone and in the company of other cockroaches. Zajonc found that on the simple task the cockroaches took longer to reach their goal when running alone, and on the complex task they took longer when running with other cockroaches.

dominant responses. If we are worried about criticisms we will not do well on complex or new tasks in the presence of critical observers. On the other hand, critical observers will not affect our performance on simple tasks. This issue is not settled.

Bond and Titus (1983) reviewed much of the research on social facilitation, and made the following conclusions:

(1) the presence of others heightens an individual's physiological arousal only if the individual is performing a complex task;

(2) the presence of others increases the speed of simple task performance and decreases the speed of complex task performance;

(3) the presence of others impairs the quality of complex performance and slightly improves the quality of simple performance;

(4) social facilitation effects are unrelated to the performer's evaluation apprehension.

This last conclusion does not mean that evaluation apprehension does not lead to increased arousal and to the facilitation of dominant responses. The critical question is whether evaluation apprehension is necessary for social facilitation to occur.

The answer to this question is not clear. On the one hand, the findings of Cottrell and his colleagues mentioned above suggest that it is. On the other hand, research by Schmitt et al. (1986) suggests that it is not necessary. These researchers recruited subjects who thought they were participating in a sensory deprivation study. When they arrived, they were seated before a computer that asked them, prior to doing the experiment, to type in their name (an easy task), and then to enter a code name by typing their names backward, with ascending digits typed between the letters (a difficult task). The time to complete each task was recorded by the computer. The subjects had been assigned to one of three conditions. In the alone condition, the experimenter left the room before the subject answered the questions. In the mere presence condition, a confederate remained in the room. He was wearing a blindfold and headphones, and was seated facing away from the computer. Subjects were told he was being deprived of sensory stimulation for the sensory deprivation experiment. In the evaluation apprehension condition, the experimenter remained in the room and looked over the subject's shoulder as he typed in the information. Results of the study, shown in Table 5-1, indicate that performance on the simple task was faster and

TABLE 5-1 Mean time in seconds to complete the easy and difficult tasks

	Alone	*Mere presence*	*Evaluation apprehension*
Easy task	14.77	9.83	7.07
Difficult task	52.41	72.57	62.52

SOURCE: Schmitt et al., 1986

performance on the difficult task was slower for both the mere presence condition and the evaluation apprehension condition. These results clearly demonstrate that evaluation apprehension is not necessary for social facilitation to occur.

DISTRACTION-CONFLICT THEORY

Another view of social facilitation, the **distraction-conflict theory**, is offered by Baron and others (e.g. Baron, 1986; Sanders, 1983; Sanders, Baron and Moore, 1978). In the original version of their theory, these researchers argue that the distraction caused by an audience or coactors is the prime source of arousal. In the presence of others, the individual pays attention to the audience or coactors as well as to the demands of the task. Consequently the individual is in a state of "attentional conflict." According to this view, it is the conflict that leads to arousal, which in turn facilitates dominant responses. While waiting for the light to change at the intersection, we experience conflict between watching the light and watching other drivers. The arousal due to this conflict leads to a faster take-off when the light turns green.

distraction-conflict theory When people are in the presence of others, they may experience arousal caused by a conflict over whether to attend to a task or the audience.

NON-AROUSAL THEORIES

Non-arousal explanations for social facilitation are concerned with where attention is focused rather than arousal. Baron (1986), in an information-processing interpretation of arousal-conflict theory, suggested that the presence of others may lead to "information overload." That is, subjects have more sensory input than they can handle efficiently. In order to bring things under control, they concentrate harder on the task itself and try to shut out all competing stimuli. Increased attention leads to better performance on simple tasks, but on complex tasks it restricts thinking, hindering performance.

Bond (1982) believes that the presence of others creates demands on the individual. It may create a need to look good, or to present oneself favourably. Making errors prevents one from looking good. He claims that task impairment is the result of embarrassment that follows errors, and errors are most likely when the task is complex. This view is called the self-presentation explanation. When we proceed quickly when the traffic light turns green, we are trying to present ourselves favourably.

Carver and Scheier (1981) argue that the presence of an audience leads to increased "self-attention." This "self-attention" leads individuals to interrupt their performance, especially on complex tasks, in order to monitor or assess their progress. These interruptions to monitor performance are the source of social facilitation. This view is called the self-awareness explanation.

It is more difficult to demonstrate effects of increased arousal in coaction than in audience situations. Feelings of rivalry or competition are likely present when individuals are responding simultaneously. Carment (1970) demonstrated the effects of both coaction and competition. He had subjects perform a simple motor task either alone or together. Half the coacting subjects were told that two people were performing at the same time to save time. The other coacting subjects, as well as half the subjects performing alone, were told that their performance would be judged against that of other subjects and a prize would be awarded the winner. The results showed that coaction enhanced performance and that competitive instructions enhanced it even further for the coacting subjects. Competitive instructions did not affect individuals performing alone. (See Figure 5-1.) In addition, coaction and competitive motivation may be influenced by cultural factors. Carment and Hodkin (1973) compared performance of Indian and Canadian university students. They found that the students from India were less sensitive than the Canadians to both competition instructions and the presence of coactors.

In summary, the theoretical approaches to social facilitation can be classified as follows (Geen, 1988):

(1) theories that indicate that the presence of others increases drive, such as evaluation apprehension, mere presence, and the older version of distraction-conflict theory;

(2) approaches that suggest that the presence of others creates demands on the person to behave in a particular manner. These approaches include the self-presentation and self-awareness explanations;

(3) Baron's information-processing interpretation of distraction-conflict theory.

FIGURE 5-1 Mean number of responses each minute as a function of competition and coaction

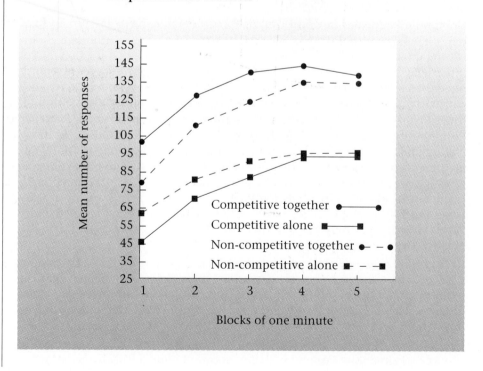

BOX 5-2

BASEBALL AND SOCIAL FACILITATION

Jackson, Buglione and Glenwick (1988) noted that almost all of the research on social facilitation had been conducted in an artificial environment—the laboratory. So with the assistance of professional shortstop Bobby Mercer, they turned their attention to baseball and how a player's performance might be affected by being traded. They argued that batting is a complex task that should be adversely affected by high levels of drive (arousal).

In baseball, one situation that could generate a high level of arousal would be the possibility of being traded to another team, especially in midseason. Since midseason trades usually imply that there is something wrong with the player, an impending trade should create considerable stress—and because complex activities such as batting are adversely affected under conditions of high arousal, performance at bat should decline.

However, once the player is traded the arousal should be reduced. The player will perceive himself as "wanted" by the other team, the likelihood of being traded again will be reduced, and the player will be granted a "honeymoon" period during which expectations of superior performance will be low or moderate. The year after the trade should find the drive level at the point where it was in the seasons prior to the trade.

Jackson et al. (1988) calculated two measures of performance at bat: the batting average and the slugging percentage (the batting average weighted by the number of bases per hit) for 59 major league players (pitchers were not included). The results of their analysis clearly support their predictions (see Figure 5-2). Since players appear to gain an average of 30 points in their batting average, it would seem wise for managers to engage in midseason trades.

Of course, there may be alternative explanations for what happens in this situation. For example, a player may improve because owners choose players who are suited to their ballpark. Thus, if a ballpark has a close right-field fence,

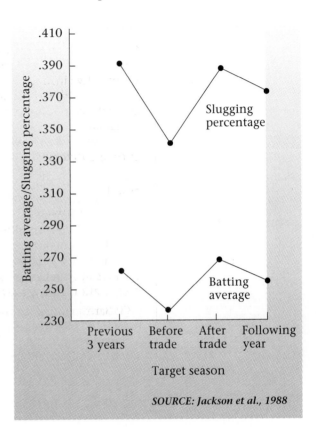

FIGURE 5-2 **Main effect of drive on baseball performance**

SOURCE: Jackson et al., 1988

the owner would look for a left-handed power hitter. It then could be argued that players improve because the field conditions are now in their favour. However, this reasoning could not explain why, in the following year, players' performance declines even though the ballpark conditions remain the same.

Another explanation that has been suggested is that a change in the player's self-esteem, not drive, enhances performance. First, players about to be traded have lowered self-esteem due to poor performance. Then, after the trade, their self-esteem returns, they become confident, and perform better. While this argument does not conflict with the data, it is more likely that self-esteem changes are the result of performance rather than the cause of it.

SOCIAL LOAFING: WHEN MORE IS LESS

social loafing A decrease in our individual effort due to the presence of others who can make up for our slacking off.

How does performance in groups affect individual efforts?

Now let's consider what often happens in a classroom when assignments involve group work. Does the project produced by the group show the combined efforts of all group members? Or does it seem to show less effort? Doing group assignments can be like moving a sofa. If you have ever helped someone move a sofa, you may recall avoiding too much strain by not using all your strength because you thought nobody would notice. When we decrease our individual effort due to the presence of others who can make up for our slacking off, we are engaging in **social loafing** (Latané et al. 1979). In group assignments we may engage in social loafing because we expect other group members to make up for our lack of effort.

Social loafing was first noticed and studied many years ago. While observing French farm workers, Ringelmann (1913) noticed that people exerted less effort while working together pulling ropes than while pulling alone (see Kravitz and Martin, 1986). Many years later, Ingham (1974) had blindfolded subjects engage in a tug-of-war. Subjects pulled harder when they thought they were working alone than when they thought others were pulling behind them. Latané and his colleagues blindfolded people and sat them in a semicircle. Headphones were used to make subjects think they clapped or cheered alone or in the presence of others. People clapped or cheered louder when they thought they were alone than when they thought others were present (see Figure 5-3).

Latané suggests that social loafing has implications for the efficiency of human organizations, such as collective farms in the former U.S.S.R. and kibbutzim in Israel. The collective farms seemed to follow the social loafing principle, while the kibbutzim did not. A possible explanation for this difference is that people usually had a choice about participating in a kibbutz, whereas personal choice was

FIGURE 5-3 Intensity of noise as a function of group size and response mode

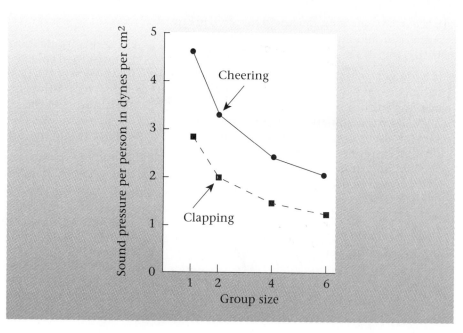

less emphasized in the Soviet Union. People's personal commitment to their goal was strong enough in the kibbutz that individual motivation was not compromised by the presence of other group members.

SELF-TEST QUESTIONS

1. **The first laboratory experiment in social psychology was published in 1898 by N. Triplett. What did Triplett conclude from this study?**
a) that reeling in fishing lines is good therapy for young boys
b) that the presence of another person facilitates behaviour
c) that behaviour is facilitated by male but not female observers
d) that the presence of another person inhibits performance of a task

2. **The distraction-conflict theory states that**
a) an individual is aroused by the presence of others as a result of the conflict between attending to the task at hand while being distracted by the audience or coactors
b) an individual is distracted by the need to outperform other actors in the task
c) an individual's performance on a simple task is a function of environmental distractions and the individual's motivation to perform well
d) an individual is distracted by a noisy and rude audience

3. **Which of the following behaviours is most likely to be enhanced by the presence of others?**
a) a first attempt at diving
b) learning to play tennis
c) trying to fix a broken TV set
d) typing a letter in the office

4. **One of the most likely causes of social loafing as suggested in the text is**
a) inadequate coordination
b) difficulty of identifying individual outputs for evaluation
c) lack of arousal
d) learned helplessness

CONFORMITY

So far we have been concerned with a type of influence that has not involved direct communication between the participants, or obvious cues. In other influence situations, the communication, although subtle, is more evident.

Imagine yourself in a completely darkened room with a pinpoint of light at eye level some distance in front of you. As you look at the light, it seems to move. Your task as an experimental subject is to judge how far the light moves. The task seems very easy, but the room is so dark that there are no reference points to help judge distance, and so you may feel somewhat uncertain. Sherif (1936) placed groups of subjects in this situation. The pinpoint of light in the total

conformity Behaviour that adheres to group norms and yields to perceived group pressures.

darkness did not in fact move at all, but only seemed to move. This phenomenon is called the autokinetic effect. For some people such a light seems to move considerable distances; for others it moves very little. In a number of trials, Sherif asked his subjects to call out estimates of how far the light moved. Although the subjects started out with quite different distance estimates, their estimates gradually became more and more similar until there was very little variability among them. Sherif proposed this as a model of social conformity, in which without any direct pressure subjects gradually arrive at a standard of behaviour. This standard behaviour is called a **social norm.** The participants were merely aware of the judgments of others, and the influence was mutual. Once established the norm shows little, if any, change.

In a similar study, Asch (1951) had subjects match the length of a standard line to one of three comparison lines. (A sample of these lines is shown in Figure 5-4). This study used only one "real" subject at a time along with a number of confederates. The real subject always gave his answer after all the confederates responded. Unknown to the real subject, the confederates had been instructed to make the same wrong choice on twelve out of eighteen trials. What would you do under these circumstances—trust your eyes or go along with the group? The task is not difficult for people judging alone; Asch found that 95 percent of the time they gave the correct answer. However, when there were confederates present, 76 percent of the subjects made at least one error by going along with the group. Asch and other researchers doing similar studies (Crutchfield, 1955; Wiener, Carpenter and Carpenter, 1957) have found that only a few subjects totally succumb to group influence and some resist it completely. However, the effect is so powerful that most people go along with the group at least some of the time.

It is important to realize that the cultural and historical context in which research takes place may influence the results. When Asch carried out his studies in the 1950s, the political and social climate of the United States encouraged

social norm A guide that governs behaviour in a group and applies to everyone in it.

How do social norms develop?

FIGURE 5-4 **Typical comparison lines used in Asch's study of group effects on judgment**

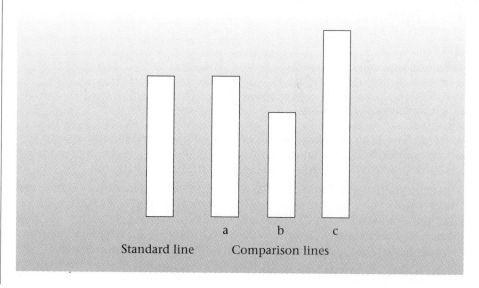

Standard line   Comparison lines
a   b   c

conformity. Twenty-four years later, Larsen (1974) obtained a rate of conformity in the U.S. about one-half of that reported by Asch. There is some question as to whether people in other parts of the world would respond in the same way as American subjects. Perrin and Spencer (1981), for example, noted that the Asch studies had not been replicated outside the U.S. When they placed British students in the same situation, they found that in only one out of 396 critical trials did compliance occur. According to Asch, American students were afraid of "sticking out like a sore thumb." Students in the British study, on the other hand, felt that going along with the group would make them look "weak, ridiculous and stupid."

FACTORS INFLUENCING CONFORMITY

GROUP SIZE

Asch varied the number of confederates in the group to find out whether more confederates caused more conformity. The maximum effect occurred with three confederates, and increasing the group beyond that number did not lead to more conformity. Other researchers have found the maximum effects in slightly larger groups (four to six confederates). However, there is general agreement that the pressure to conform does not simply continue to increase as the size of the group increases. Researchers have offered a number of explanations for these effects. In their Social Influence Model, Tanford and Penrod (1984) suggest that the second and third persons should have more impact on conformity than the first person. After the third person, each new addition to the group has progressively less impact. However, another model, Social Impact Theory, (Latané and Wolfe, 1981) predicts that the first person has greatest impact, and that each additional person has progressively less impact. Campbell and Fairey (1989) suggest that the discrepancies in the number of confederates for the maximum effect may arise from the type of situation in which subjects are placed. When subjects are trying to decide whether their judgment is correct, they rely on information from others. The first person to provide information is most important and has more impact than additional people. However, when subjects go along with the group in order to avoid the social penalties of disagreeing with the majority, normative mechanisms come into play. Larger majorities should lead to more conformity. Wilder (1977) offered another explanation. He argued that the effect of increases in group size is limited. In his view, when the group gets beyond a certain size, the subject does not perceive the group members as separate entities. He demonstrated that four people in two very distinct groups had more impact on conformity than four people in one group. Based on these results, Wilder's advice to candidates for political office is that they should try to get endorsements from individuals with a variety of backgrounds rather than from one type of background. In his view people from distinct backgrounds are perceived individually by voters, whereas people from the same background are treated as a single entity.

THE ADAMANT MINORITY

Asch (1951) discovered that if one person other than the subject responded correctly to the task of judging the length of lines, conformity was reduced or disappeared entirely. Allen and Levine (1971) found that when there was a unanimous majority, subjects conformed 97 percent of the time. With the presence of just one nonconforming supporter (i.e. a person making a correct judg-

*What factors influence
the extent to which
people conform?*

ment), conformity was reduced. When the supporter was competent, conformity dropped to 36 percent. When the supporter was apparently incompetent due to his wearing glasses so thick as to raise serious doubts about his being able to see anything well, conformity dropped to 64 percent.

Morris and Miller (1975) demonstrated that the effect of the supporter varies according to whether he or she speaks before or after the unanimous majority. A supporter who precedes the majority reduces conformity more than one who responds after the majority.

Moscovici and his colleagues (Moscovici, Mugny, and Van Avermaet, 1985) have shown that the impact of a minority on the majority is more influential if it is consistent. In one of their experiments, groups of six women were asked to look at slides and report what colour they saw. In each group of six, two subjects were confederates who gave consistent responses that indicated incorrect colours. When members of the minority consistently said blue slides were "green," 32 percent of the subjects said "green" at least once, and 8 percent of the subjects' responses were "green." When minority members were coached to respond in an inconsistent manner, their influence almost entirely disappeared.

WHY DO PEOPLE CONFORM?

A number of reasons why people conform have been documented by researchers. These reasons are not mutually exclusive and they can operate at the same time and in different combinations.

(1) **Social approval and disapproval.** Groups in general are intolerant, and anyone who chooses to behave in a manner that contradicts or ignores important social norms may experience some unpleasant moments (Schachter, 1951). These pressures encourage conformity. In addition, the group rewards the conformer with liking and social approval. In Asch's study subjects went along with the incorrect answer because everyone else gave that incorrect answer. Conformity in situations like this is based on **normative social influence**.

normative social influence Influence resulting from the desire to gain social approval and avoid disapproval.

It is easy to see why highly cohesive groups exert considerable control over their members. In these groups there is a high degree of interpersonal liking and attachment, and so the desire to maintain approval and acceptance is powerful. In addition, low-status group members are allowed less leeway to deviate than are high-status group members. High-status members have earned idiosyncrasy credits by contributing more to the group than members of lower status (Hollander, 1958; Homans, 1974).

(2) **The need for information.** There are many aspects of our personal worlds that are not clearly defined and are ambiguous in some way. We use what Festinger has termed **informational social influence** to determine whether our answers are correct in such situations. We conform because we expect the answer of the majority to be correct. In Sherif's study, the situation was ambiguous; subjects listened to the answers of others in order to arrive at the correct answer.

informational social influence The matching of our own ideas to those of the group in order to determine if we are "correct."

Consider the drawing in Figure 5-5. What does it appear to be? Some might say "two X's," others may insist on a "W sitting on an M," or a "V superimposed on an inverted V." Or perhaps it is a "diamond with whiskers." Although the design appears to be simple, it can still generate considerable uncertainty. In daily life we are often confronted with such unclearly defined events. In these cases the group serves to structure, label, and identify the situations, thereby reducing both the uncertainty and its accompanying discomfort.

FIGURE 5-5 **What is it?**

"GROUPTHINK"

Few would deny that some conformity is necessary for the well-being of society in general. It is convenient that people line up to buy tickets for a movie. Just think of the chaos if some people in the country chose to drive on the right side of the road and others on the left.

However, there are times when conformity is not productive. For example, would Bethune have gone to China, Riel mounted a rebellion, or Banting and Best have discovered insulin if they had been strict conformists? Progress in many fields occurs because someone is willing to stand up against majority opinion.

There are also times when conformity is not only unproductive, but dangerous. Janis (1972, 1982) and Janis and Mann (1977) have labelled the tendency for people to assume that the group invariably has the correct answer "groupthink." When groupthink prevails, people tend to make risky decisions based on their poorly informed perceptions of the group's view of a situation.

Groupthink occurs when a group seeks a solution to a problem without fully considering all the possible alternatives and their relative merits (McCauley, 1989). The decision makers in the group believe that the group cannot fail. There is excessive optimism and risk taking. Warnings about preferred solutions are discounted and group members set aside any personal doubts. This results in an illusion of unanimity. Finally, self-appointed "mind guards" shield the group from external information that might challenge the group decisions (Tetlock, Peterson, McGuire, Chang and Feld, 1992).

In order for groupthink to occur, a number of situational and structural conditions must be present. The structural conditions include promotional leadership, whereby the leader reveals a favoured policy alternative early in the proceedings. The group members should also have homogeneous social backgrounds and ideologies, and they should be insulated from outside information. The situational conditions include an external threat either of crisis proportions or involving time pressure. The problem under consideration will be complex and difficult and there may have been a recent group failure insofar as a prior decision has had a poor outcome.

Janis (1982) describes several examples of decisions made by American policy-making committees that illustrate groupthink in action. These decisions are: to pursue the defeated North Korean Army beyond the 38th parallel; to launch the Bay of Pigs invasion of Cuba; to escalate involvement in the war in Vietnam; and the Watergate cover-up. More recent examples are: the decision to launch the

Under what circumstances does group interaction characterized by conformity lead to poor decision making?

groupthink *Tendency of a highly cohesive and elitist group to achieve a rapid consensus without dissent or outside influences.*

BOX 5-3

THE SPACE SHUTTLE CHALLENGER DISASTER AND GROUPTHINK

On January 28, 1986, only 73 seconds after blasting off from the ice-encrusted launching pad at Kennedy Space Center, the space shuttle Challenger exploded, killing all seven of its crew. The decision to launch had been made the night before at the Level 1 Flight Readiness Review Meeting. The report of the presidential commission appointed to investigate this tragedy found "flawed" decision making to be at fault. The flaws provide an example of the dangers of groupthink.

Three antecedent conditions of groupthink existed in this fatal decision process: (1) the decision-making group was highly cohesive—its members had worked together for many years and enjoyed a high degree of esprit de corps; (2) the group leaders, two top-level managers, had a clear decision preference which they made well known by actively promoting their pro-launch opinions; (3) the group insulated itself from experts. Indeed, one of the engineers from the engineering company that made the solid-fuel boosters reported to the commission that he would not recommend a launch below 53°F, and that he was not asked for any input for the final decision charts.

A number of symptoms of groupthink are evident in the group's decision making. The extraordinary record of success of the space flight program promoted a feeling of overconfidence, a sense of invulnerability. At the time, NASA had an amazing record of fifty-five successful missions since 1967. NASA officials rationalized warnings about possible problems with the boosters that were put forward early in the Level 1 meeting. The management of Morton Thiokol, the maker of the solid-fuel boosters, objected to making a launch in cold weather. The reliability of the seals at the three joints between the booster rocket's four main segments had been a matter of concern for some time. On a previous mission launched at 30°F, the joint had seriously eroded. They had no data on how the joint would perform at colder temperatures. NASA officials dismissed these concerns because they considered the arguments to be based on insufficient data. The Morton Thiokol managers were regarded as dissenters. Two NASA officials put pressure on the dissenters. NASA officials complained that Thiokol was trying to change the flight criteria at the last minute. Mulloy, chief of NASA's solid rocket booster program, challenged the Thiokol managers to prove their point and asked them, "When do you want me to launch, next April?" Under this pressure, the Thiokol management ignored its engineers (self-censorship), and changed its no-fly stance. NASA officials also dismissed concerns about the icy conditions raised by another contractor, Rockwell International, the maker of the orbiter. Rockwell officials were afraid that ice might break off the gantry and damage the orbiter tiles. NASA experts concluded that the ice did not pose any real danger and chose to ignore Rockwell's warnings.

In the end, an illusion of unanimity prevailed in the Level 1 meeting. This illusion was supported by mindguarding, shielding the group from adverse information. An example of mindguarding is the failure of the Thiokol management to pass along to NASA officials some of the concerns voiced by individual Thiokol engineers. Two of these engineers, Cook and Boisjoly, had each sent internal memos warning that a "catastrophic" failure might occur if the O-rings were not improved. These memos were not forwarded to NASA.

The Level 1 meeting illustrates important decision-making defects. There were few alternatives considered; it was a launch or no-launch decision. Other possibilities were not seriously considered. NASA officials defended their position instead of examining either the Thiokol or the Rockwell positions. Indeed, NASA officials rejected expert opinions and negative information. Furthermore, there was no evidence that they considered the consequences of making a wrong decision. And so the Challenger "blasted into the Florida sky on its brief, one-way flight to oblivion" (Magnuson, 1986).

Sources: Magnuson, E. (1986, March 10). "A serious deficiency": The Rogers Commission faults NASA's "flawed" decision-making process. Time, pp. 38–42.
Moorhead, G., Ference, R., and Neck, C.P. (1991). Group decision fiascoes continue: Space shuttle Challenger and a revised groupthink framework. Human Relations, 44, 539–550.

space shuttle Challenger, and the Iran-Contra affair (Whyte, 1989). In Canada, history will judge whether the Meech Lake Accord and the Charlottetown Accord were reached under similar circumstances.

SELF-TEST QUESTIONS

5. Sherif proposed a model of conformity in which individuals arrive at a common form of behaviour without any direct pressure. This standard of behaviour is called

a) implicit conformity

b) the bandwagon effect

c) a social norm

d) explicit conformity

6. In a classic experiment on conformity, Asch (1951) found that

a) subjects were not influenced by inaccurate judgments made by confederates

b) subjects tended to make inaccurate judgments when in the presence of confederates who also made inaccurate judgments

c) subjects made inaccurate judgments only if eight or more confederates were present

d) subjects were more confident of the accuracy of their judgments when alone than when in a group

7. Researchers have offered a number of reasons to explain why people conform. Which of the following is/are correct?

a) groups tend to be intolerant of non-conformists

b) many situations are ambiguous and individuals allow the group to structure and define these situations for them

c) individuals use the judgment of the majority to answer social questions not amenable to empirical verification

d) conformity may be used as an impression-management technique

e) all of the above

8. Under some circumstances, the opinion of a minority can affect the opinion of the majority. What is crucial for this effect to occur?

a) the minority must be inflexible with regard to its position

b) the minority must be consistent in its opinion

c) the minority must consist of competent individuals

d) the minority must consist of well-liked individuals

COMPLIANCE

compliance Behaviour in which one yields to a direct request.

When we are alone attempts are frequently made to influence our behaviour, to get us to buy some product, to vote for a certain politician, or to donate to a particular charity. Some of the techniques are sophisticated, employed in a deliberate manner, successful, and undetectable by the individual involved. Five of these procedures are reviewed next.

**foot-in-the-door tech-
nique** *A means of securing
agreement to a major
request by first obtaining
agreement to a small
request.*

**What types of strate-
gies are used to per-
suade people to comply
with a direct request?
Why do these strategies
frequently succeed?**

**door-in-the-face tech-
nique** *A means of securing
agreement to a moderate
request by first making an
unreasonable request.*

low-ball technique *A
means of getting someone
to do something by first
securing agreement and
then increasing the cost of
fulfilling the request.*

(1) THE FOOT-IN-THE-DOOR TECHNIQUE

Door-to-door salespeople are very familiar with this technique. They know that an individual who agrees to carry out a small request is more likely to agree to a larger request later. Freedman and Fraser (1966) carried out a study in which the small request was for subjects to either put up a small sign on their lawn or to sign a petition concerning safe driving or keeping California beautiful. The large request was for subjects to allow a large sign that said "Drive carefully" to be placed on their lawn. Subjects who were asked the large request after the small one were much more likely than subjects asked only the large request to agree to have the large sign put on their lawns. Pliner et al. (1974) found that Torontonians asked to wear a small Cancer Society lapel pin the day before they were asked to donate were more likely to give and gave more generously than those who were contacted only to donate. In trying to account for this phenomenon, Freedman and Fraser (1966) and Dejong (1979) have suggested that the people who agreed to the small request experienced a change in their self-perception. In considering their compliance with the small request, they came to the conclusion that they were cooperative and generous people. Then they set out to maintain this image by also agreeing to the second request.

(2) THE DOOR-IN-THE-FACE TECHNIQUE

This is a variation of the foot-in-the-door technique. In this case, the first request made is so extreme that the person is almost certain to refuse. The second request is smaller and by comparison very reasonable. Cialdini and his colleagues (1975) have shown that this strategy is effective in inducing compliance to the second request. They first asked university students if they would be willing to serve as unpaid counsellors for two hours a week for two years. Everyone asked refused. The second request was whether they would accompany a group of juvenile delinquents on a trip to the zoo. Fifty percent of the students were then willing to help. In another group of students who were asked only to go on the zoo trip, less than twenty percent were willing to help.

Two explanations have been offered for the effectiveness of this procedure. One is based on the concept of reciprocal concessions. When the person making the largest request reduces it to a smaller one, the other person then feels obligated to make a matching concession. The other explanation involves self-presentation. Most people like to present themselves to others in a positive light. People think that complying with a moderate request, but refusing to grant a large request, creates a favourable impression (Pendleton and Batson, 1979).

(3) THE LOW-BALL TECHNIQUE

This technique is frequently used by automobile salespeople to encourage people to buy a car at a maximum price. It is based on the idea that once people agree to do something, they will still comply even though the cost is higher than originally anticipated. The salesperson's intention is to get the customer to make an active decision to buy the car. Once this is done, and the necessary forms are filled out, the salesperson says that the price is so low that the supervisor's approval of the deal is necessary. The supervisor rejects the offer, and the purchase price goes up. Anecdotal evidence suggests that the customer will buy the car at the higher price.

BOX 5-4

THE REAL WORLD OF COMPLIANCE

With the exception of a few field experiments, most of the research on compliance has been conducted in the laboratory. This prompted Cialdini (1987) to observe what people who are in the business of influencing people actually do. He got himself hired by a number of sales organizations and at various times took training as a salesman of encyclopedias, photographs, fire alarms, insurance, and advertising. He first found that the tactics such as the door-in-the-face and foot-in-the-door were used, but not very often.

However, it became clear to Cialdini that although his colleagues in sales might not be able to articulate what they were doing, they did rely on six basic principles, much the same as those we have described. These are: (1) people want to appear consistent; (2) they want to reciprocate favours; (3) they want to do what others are doing; (4) they are willing to follow the advice of authorities; (5) the perception of scarcity makes commodities more attractive; and (6) they are more likely to comply with requests of friends than of strangers.

The "four walls technique," often used by encyclopedia salespeople, provides an example of the customer's desire to appear consistent in practice. First, three questions are asked that are likely to elicit agreement from the customer. Then, to remain consistent, the customer is also likely to agree with a fourth question. The technique goes like this:

First wall: "Do you feel that a good general education is important to your children?"

Second wall: "Do you think that a child who does his or her homework well will get a better education?"

Third wall: "Don't you agree that a good set of reference books will help a child do well on homework assignments?"

Fourth wall: "Well, then, it sounds like you'll want to hear about the fine set of encyclopedias I have to offer at an excellent price. May I come in?"

Other methods that also rely on commitment are the foot-in-the-door, low-ball, and bait and switch. Scarcity is implied by time-limited or limited number offers, and the party (e.g. Partylite, Mary Kay) is a prime example of the use of friendship to increase the likelihood of sales.

(4) THE "THAT'S-NOT-ALL" TECHNIQUE

that's-not-all technique
Improving a deal by adding another product or decreasing the price.

This procedure consists of offering a product to a person at a high price, preventing the person from responding for a few seconds, and then enhancing the deal either by adding another product or decreasing the price. For example, Burger (1986) had two experimenters sit at a table in various locations selling cupcakes and cookies. The cupcakes were visible, but the cookies were not. When subjects in the experimental group approached the table they were told that the cupcakes were 75¢ each. Just then the second experimenter tapped the first experimenter on the shoulder. The first experimenter would ask the customer to "wait a second." After a brief exchange, the first experimenter turned to the customer and said that the price included two cookies. In the control group, the subjects were told about the cookies as soon as they asked the price of the cupcakes. In the "that's not all" condition, 73 percent of the subjects bought the cupcakes. In the control condition, 40 percent made a purchase. Burger also showed that lowering the price had the same effect. According to Burger, subjects who are told that the price also includes the two cookies think they have received a favour or gift. Consequently they think that they must reciprocate or return the favour, and so they feel obligated to make the purchase. Subjects who are told that the price has just been lowered are likely to think that they are getting a very good buy. If the first price established is $1, a reduced price of 75¢ looks very good against the anchor point of $1.

(5) GUILT

Feelings of guilt have been shown to have a powerful influence on behaviour. Parents, for example, can be experts at creating feelings of guilt in their children. "After all I've done for you" is a typical remark. Salespeople may also use guilt to encourage customers to make a purchase. When looking for a new pair of shoes, we may try on numerous pairs. Although we may not find any of them really suitable, we are likely to feel obligated to buy a pair because we have taken up so much of the clerk's time.

In laboratory investigations of guilt, subjects are usually led to do something wrong and then a request is made of them. For instance, Freedman, Wallington and Bless (1967) persuaded subjects to lie and then requested their volunteer participation in an additional study. Compared to the non-lie condition, approximately twice as many subjects in the lie condition agreed to participate in the additional study.

Other research has shown that when we feel guilty, we acquiesce—even to those against whom we have done no wrong. Regan, Williams and Sparling (1972) had a male confederate ask female shoppers to take a picture with his camera. When they tried, the camera would not work. Some of the subjects were made to feel it was their fault, while others were assured that they were not to blame. A second confederate then appeared carrying a bag of groceries that was torn so that the contents were falling out. Fifty-five percent of the subjects in the guilt condition and only fifteen percent in the control condition informed the confederate of the problem. These results suggest that subjects who have been made to feel guilty are then motivated to get rid of their guilt by engaging in some positive behaviour.

These procedures, though often applied deliberately and systematically, are rarely detected by the unsuspecting target person. You can probably recall situations when you were the target person, but at the time you were unaware of the strategies being used. On a day-to-day basis, the most frequently encountered procedures for inducing compliance are simple requests such as "Please pick up a case of beer on your way home from work." It is important, however, to distinguish between requests and demands, which are also very direct and undisguised. In the case of demands, the opportunity not to comply is considerably reduced. Parents demand obedience from their children, soldiers must obey their officers, and students are required to obey their teachers. Why do people set aside their independence of action and do what someone else demands even when they find it distasteful? Obedience to authority is considered next.

SELF-TEST QUESTIONS

9. One way to increase the probability of people complying with a target request is to induce them to comply with a small request before asking them to comply with the target request. This technique is known as the

a) door-in-the-face technique

b) low-ball technique

c) foot-in-the-door technique

d) reciprocity technique

10. Inducing compliance by increasing the benefits of the action before a person is allowed to respond is referred to as

a) the low-ball technique

b) the door-in-the-face technique

c) the that's-not-all technique

d) the commitment technique

11. The explanation suggested for the success of the low-ball technique for inducing compliance is

a) commitment

b) self-presentation

c) reciprocal concessions

d) self-perception

12. The door-in-the-face technique assumes that

a) people are more likely to comply with a large request if they have already complied with a smaller one

b) people are more likely to comply with a target request if they have already refused to comply with a larger request

c) people are more likely to comply with a request if they are made to feel guilty

d) people are less likely to comply with a large request if they have already complied with a smaller one

OBEDIENCE

The attention of social psychologists was drawn to the study of obedience by the controversial research of Milgram (1963, 1965, 1974). Milgram's research arose from his reflections on the Holocaust during which, from 1933 to 1945, millions of innocent people, mostly Jews, were slaughtered by the Nazis. He quotes C.P. Snow, who wrote: "The German Officers' Corps were brought up in the most rigorous code of obedience ... in the name of obedience they were party to, and assisted in, the most wicked large scale actions in the history of the world" (1961, p. 24). Was the obedience that led to this horrendous action unique to Germany, Milgram wondered, or given the appropriate circumstances, could it occur elsewhere? Of course, not all obedience has aggressive action as the outcome, but it was this type of "destructive obedience" that Milgram studied. Milgram's basic premise was that "the individual who is commanded by a legitimate authority ordinarily obeys."

MILGRAM'S RESEARCH

Milgram's procedure was to record the amount of electric shock a subject would be willing to administer to another person. He devised a fake apparatus that subjects believed was a "shock machine." Subjects used this "shock machine" to deliver shocks at a range of settings, from "Slight shock" to "Danger: Severe shock" (see Figure 5-6). There were 30 settings in all, each defined in terms of volts that ranged from 15 to 450!

obedience *Behaviour in which one yields in response to a direct order.*

To what extent are ordinary people willing to harm others in order to obey commands issued by an authority figure?

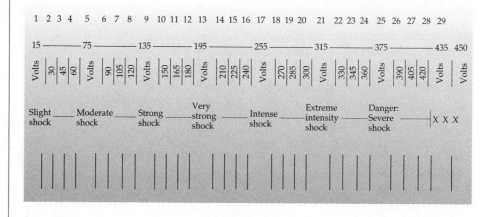

FIGURE 5-6 The panel of Milgram's shock generator

In each session, in addition to the experimenter, there was one subject and an accomplice of the experimenter present. In a rigged selection that appeared to be controlled by chance, the subject and the accomplice were assigned the roles of teacher and learner. The subject was always selected as the teacher, and was informed he was to teach the learner a list of word pairs. In addition, the subject was told to administer a shock whenever the learner was unable to recall a correct word. He was informed that the purpose of the experiment was to study the effects of negative outcomes, such as shock, on the rate of learning. The shock was to be increased one level on each additional trial. The learner had been coached to make many errors. Other verbal responses varied with the shock level, and were presented by means of a tape recorder. For example, at 75 volts the learner would grunt and moan, at 150 he demanded to be released, at 180 he cried that he could no longer stand it and at 300 he refused to provide any more answers. The subject was then told to treat silence as a wrong answer. It should be noted that during the introduction, the learner mentioned that he had a heart condition.

How far would subjects go? Most of them became agitated and tense and frequently tried to break off the experiment. If the subject showed any sort of hesitation, the experimenter told him to proceed and that the experimenter would accept the responsibility if anything happened to the learner. The experimenter was dressed in a white lab coat, and so looked like an important research scientist. His appearance helped make his instructions convincing.

Forty psychiatrists predicted that most subjects would not go beyond the tenth shock level (150 volts), that not more than four percent would reach the twentieth level (300 volts), and that only about one-tenth of one percent would administer the highest shock. However, Figure 5-7 reveals that 62 percent of the subjects completely obeyed the experimenter's commands, delivering the highest shock level!

Remember that in this study the victim was hidden from the subject, although they had been introduced at the beginning of the session. Other experiments by Milgram showed that as the victim and the subject became physically closer, the amount of obedience was reduced. For example, in the closest condition, the subject was required to hold the victim's hand on the shock-plate. In this case,

FIGURE 5-7 Predicted and obtained behaviour in "learning exercise"

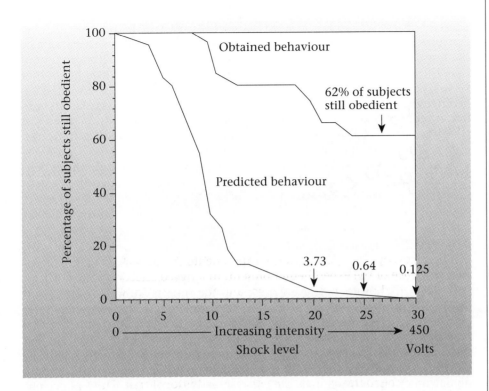

the number of subjects who administered the highest level of shock was reduced to 30 percent, still a substantial and disturbing proportion. Milgram also found that obedience decreased (to 45 percent) when the experimenter was physically absent from the laboratory and gave his orders by phone. These results, and others concerning factors that affected the extent of obedience, are summarized in Table 5-2. In the section below we will consider the question of why obedience occurs.

TABLE 5-2 Shock administered in relation to "social closeness" of learner and teacher

Closeness of learner to teacher	*Percentage of teachers who gave maximum shock*
1. Learner in next room cannot be seen or heard	93%
2. Learner may be heard in next room	62%
3. Learner may be heard and seen in next room	40%
4. Teacher holds learner's hand on shock plate	30%
5. Orders telephoned to teacher	21%

SOURCE: Milgram, 1963, 1974

WHY OBEDIENCE OCCURS

Recall Milgram's premise that, when commanded, individuals usually obey a legitimate authority. The two words in this premise that are particularly relevant to explaining why obedience occurs are "legitimate authority." Also recall that in the research described above Milgram's experimenter wore a white laboratory coat, commonly associated with the authority of a research scientist. In another version of the experiment, an accomplice posing as a subject assumed the experimenter's role and then the experimenter left the room. Subjects in this condition refused to deliver shocks and did not pay attention to the accomplice, who was perceived as lacking in legitimate authority. As Table 5-2 indicates, even distance from the authority was associated with less obedience. A strategy used to make subjects obey when they seemed to be in doubt was the experimenter saying that he took full responsibility for whatever happened. Together these findings show that the presence of a perceived legitimate authority who takes responsibility for the outcomes of behaviour is important in exacting obedience.

In a more recent study, Bushman (1988) also demonstrated that people are more likely to obey someone who has authority. Authority can often be identified by symbols, or the "trappings of office," such as the white coat of a physician, the chain of office of the mayor, or the uniform of the police officer. Bushman had a female confederate dress in a uniform, neat attire, or a sloppy outfit. She then stopped pedestrians near the experimenter, who was searching for change next to an expired parking meter, and ordered: "This fellow is overparked at the meter and doesn't have any change. Give him a nickel!" When the confederate was wearing a uniform, 72 percent of the pedestrians supplied a nickel. In the neat and sloppy conditions about 50 percent obeyed. In addition, no one questioned the confederate when she was in uniform, while 23 percent questioned her when she was neatly dressed, and 29 percent when she was sloppily dressed.

Meeus and Raaijmakers (1986) showed that obedience is commonplace in ordinary, everyday situations. Their study involved a research worker at a university (the experimenter), male and female subjects, and a third person who was applying for a job (an accomplice). The applicant had been invited to the laboratory to take a selection test that, if passed, would guarantee a job. The subjects were instructed to disturb the applicant while he was doing the test by making negative remarks about his test achievement and critical or insulting remarks about his personality. The remarks were to be made in spite of any objections by the applicant and were scripted to become increasingly strenuous as the time passed. If the subject proceeded, the applicant became increasingly unable to cope, failed the test, and did not get the job. Almost all of the subjects (91.7 percent) made all the remarks, thereby ensuring that the applicant failed to get the job. This research shows the power of the symbols of authority in an everyday situation. It also addresses the common charge that Milgram's findings would not occur today or in other settings.

Sometimes people point out that all Milgram's original subjects were males, and they express doubts that females would behave similarly. Hofling et al. (1966) reported that 95 percent of the nurses (all of whom were female) in their experiment were willing to issue an overdose of a certain medicine on the doctor's authority. This figure dropped to 11 percent in another study when the nurses were familiar with the medicine and were given time to consult others (Rank and Jacobson, 1977). Nevertheless, in this setting even an 11 percent rate of obedience could have tragic consequences.

Why do people do what someone else demands even when they find it distasteful?

Milgram's research has been repeated many times in various locations of the United States and in other countries (Jordan, Spain, Germany, Italy, and Australia) with consistent results. Between 50 and 85 percent of subjects in these various locations used the highest shock level. These results clearly reveal that obedience is not restricted to any one social or cultural group. Individuals are willing to assign responsibility for their actions to authority figures and carry out their orders whether refusal is difficult or relatively easy.

SELF-TEST QUESTIONS

13. Milgram's classic experiments, in which subjects administered electric shocks to other individuals, were designed to study the psychological construct of

a) implicit compliance

b) obedience

c) explicit compliance

d) persuasion

14. In the classic Milgram (1963) study mentioned above the real subject was

a) always the learner

b) always the teacher

c) the one who received shocks

d) a confederate

15. What factor(s) decreased the percentage of subjects in Milgram's research who were willing to administer shocks?

a) leading subjects to believe the victim had a heart condition

b) having the experimenter physically absent from the laboratory

c) having the subject hold the victim's hand on the shock plate

d) a and b

e) b and c

16. In the experiment by Hofling et al. (1966) in which nurses were ordered by doctors to give patients an overdose of a certain medicine

a) no nurse was willing to obey the doctor's orders

b) only 5 percent of the nurses were willing to issue an overdose on the doctor's authority

c) 95 percent of the nurses were willing to issue an overdose on the doctor's authority

d) no nurse was willing to issue an overdose

UNINTENTIONAL SOCIAL INFLUENCES

Social influence involves direct or indirect pressure exerted by people to encourage or discourage certain actions by others. In order to get someone to conform, comply, or obey, we may use a wide variety of cues. These cues may range from explicit verbal messages to subtle non-verbal communication. However, there are other social influences that a person or group may not even be aware of exerting. Social modelling is one such process.

SOCIAL MODELLING

From the outset, social psychologists have recognized and been fascinated by imitation. Albert Bandura (1977) has developed a comprehensive analysis of the process of social learning or modelling (social learning theory).

In order for modelling to occur, four conditions must be met.

(1) The observer must attend to the model and what the model is doing. Attention is influenced by such factors as the attractiveness or status of the model, and the novelty and distinctiveness of the behaviour.

(2) The observer must remember what has been observed. Memory may be verbal or visual, and it may be influenced by schemata, as we saw in Chapter 2.

(3) The observer must be able to perform the behaviour. The observer must already have the behaviour in his or her repertoire (the collection of behaviours in the person's memory), or must be able to develop the behaviour out of those he or she already knows. Although Wayne Gretzky may be a favourite model for many young hockey players, few will have his ability to perform.

(4) The observer must have an opportunity and reason for performing the behaviour. That is, he or she must be motivated to remember and engage in the behaviour. The observer will be motivated to a considerable extent by rewards and punishments already experienced and by his or her expectations of the situation. These expectations involve ideas about the outcomes or consequences likely to follow from the behaviour. Sometimes expectations are based on memory of his or her own past experiences. At other times expectations are based on memory of the consequences of the behaviour to the model. The observer may identify with a model on the basis of attractiveness, high status, or similarity to him or herself. If the observer identifies with a model and observes the consequences of the behaviour to the model, then he or she may experience vicarious reinforcement, or feel what the model feels. This experience of vicarious reinforcement may motivate the observer to perform the behaviour. In contrast, if the observer finds the model unattractive or the consequences of the behaviour unpleasant, then the observer is likely to avoid performing the behaviour.

In summary, modelling clearly involves more than imitation. In modelling, we observe what the person does, in what situation, and with what consequences. For example, in the case of television aggression, we see the aggressive act, but we also observe the situation in which it occurs, the characteristics of the victim, and the possible consequences to the aggressor (see Chapter 8). All these observations provide us with information about what is expected or appropriate in a situation, and what is likely to happen.

social modelling *Social influence experienced as a result of observing the behaviour of someone else.*

Under what circumstances does unintentional social influence occur?

SELF-TEST QUESTIONS

17. Social modelling

a) may involve learning a new behaviour

b) is a form of observational learning

c) may have an inhibitory or disinhibitory effect on behaviour

d) all of the above

18. In situations where a model who experiences adverse consequences is observed, modelling would be said to have

a) disinhibiting effects

b) inhibiting effects

c) vicarious reinforcement

d) response facilitation effects

SUMMARY

(1) The most primitive form of social influence arises from the mere presence of others. Mere presence of an audience or coactors facilitates the performance of simple tasks and impedes performance on complex or novel tasks.

(2) Zajonc has argued that the mere presence of others leads to arousal. Cottrell has argued that the presence of others leads to evaluation apprehension, which is learned.

(3) Distraction-conflict theory claims that arousal is due to the conflict that arises from the need to attend to both the others present and the task.

(4) Social loafing occurs in group situations where lack of individual effort cannot readily be detected because resources are pooled.

(5) Most conformity and compliance arise in response to majorities, but consistent and confident minorities can affect majorities.

(6) Tactics employed to enhance compliance include: foot-in-the-door, door-in-the-face, low-balling, "that's-not-all," and guilt inducement.

(7) A negative aspect of conformity is groupthink.

FOR REVIEW

Early research in social psychology by Triplett dealt with how performance is influenced by the mere _____(1).

The phenomenon described above is called _____(2). Behaviour is facilitated by the presence of others when the behaviour is _____(3). Zajonc explains the differing effects of the presence of others on performance in terms of _____(4). Cottrell explains the effects of the presence of others in terms of _____(5) rather than as a biological drive. Social loafing is defined as a decrease in _____(6) in the presence of other coactors.

_____(7) is behaviour that adheres to group norms and yields to perceived group pressure. We use _____(8) when we conform because of a desire to be liked or approved. We use _____(9) to determine whether our answers are correct in situations that are not clearly defined. In an experiment (Moscovici et al., 1974), two confederates in groups of six subjects identified shades of blue as green; this _____(10) influenced responses by subjects. Groups tend to be more accepting of non-conformity from high-status members because of their _____(11) credits.

_____(12) occurs when a group seeks a solution to a problem without fully considering all the possible alternatives and their relative merits. Groups that have _____(13) social backgrounds and ideologies, and which are _____(14) from outside influences, are highly susceptible to groupthink.

When people yield in response to a direct request, _____(15) occurs. If people are more likely to put up a lawn poster after first signing a petition for the same cause, compliance has been elicited through the _____(16) technique. The door-in-the-face technique is effective because of _____ and/or _____(17). _____(18) involves requests to act, and _____(19) involves demands to act. Social modelling is a process of _____(20) social influence.

ISSUES AND ACTIVITIES

1. Interview salespeople about the strategies they use to elicit compliance. How can the consumer be forearmed?

2. It is obviously desirable for governments to attract the best people to advise them, but groupthink may be a danger in this process. How can this danger be minimized?

3. Discuss how conformity, compliance, and obedience have contributed to state-instigated atrocities. What do these events tell us about the nature of human violence?

• FURTHER READING

CIALDINI, R.B. (1993). *Influence: Science and practice,* Third Edition. New York: HarperCollins. A review of the process of social influence that includes practical examples.

MILGRAM, S. (1974). *Obedience to authority.* New York: Harper and Row. The original account of the obedience experiments.

MOSCOVICI, S. (1976) *Social influence and social change.* London: Academic. Social influence from the European perspective.

TUCHMAN, B.W. (1984). *The march of folly: From Troy to Vietnam.* The pursuit of fiascos by governments through the ages, despite the availability of alternatives.

SUGGESTED WEBLINKS

PSYC SITE A site set up to help psychology students and researchers find information about scientific research in psychology on the World Wide Web. Designed to be a "major jumping-off point" for seeking out psychological information. Maintained by the Psychology Department of the University of Nipissing.

   http://www.unipissing.ca/psyc/psycsite.htm

ANSWERS TO SELF-TEST QUESTIONS

1. b; 2. a; 3. d; 4. b; 5. c; 6. b; 7. e; 8. b; 9. c; 10. c; 11. a; 12. b; 13. b; 14. b; 15. e; 16. c; 17. d; 18. b.

ANSWERS TO FOR REVIEW

1. presence of others; 2. social facilitation; 3. simple or well-learned; 4. arousal; 5. evaluation apprehension; 6. individual effort; 7. Conformity; 8. normative social influence; 9. informational social influence; 10. adamant minority; 11. idiosyncrasy; 12. Groupthink; 13. homogeneous; 14. insulated; 15. compliance; 16. foot-in-the-door; 17. reciprocal concessions, self-presentation; 18. Compliance; 19. obedience; 20. unintentional.

PREJUDICE, DISCRIMINATION, AND SEXISM

This has always been a man's world, and none of the reasons hitherto brought forward in explanation of this fact has seemed adequate.

Simone de Beauvoir

To give protection to views that attack and condemn the views, beliefs and practices of others is to undermine the principle that all views deserve equal protection, and muzzles the voice of truth.

The Supreme Court of Canada, April, 1996

■ LEARNING OUTCOMES

1. An understanding of prejudice and an examination of how it develops and is maintained.

2. Knowledge of various theories about the components of prejudice.

3. An understanding of the role of stereotypes.

4. An understanding of discrimination, the behavioural aspect of prejudice.

5. An understanding of the role of the family, education, and the media in the acquisition and maintenance of prejudice.

6. Knowledge of how prejudice may be reduced by intergroup contact and education.

7. An understanding of the process of acculturation.

8. An understanding of the reactions of those who are the victims of prejudice.

9. An understanding of sexism, gender stereotypes, and role assignments.

■ FOR REFLECTION

• What is prejudice? Can anyone be free of it?

• Are stereotypes of people based on prejudice or reality?

• Who is the most prone to prejudice?

• Is contact between groups a solution to prejudice?

• How do people react when they are the victims of prejudice?

■ CHAPTER OUTLINE

The Nature of Prejudice

    The Cognitive Component

    Stereotypes and Prejudice

    The Affective Component

    The Behavioural Component

    Ethnicity

    Reverse Discrimination

Acquisition of Prejudice

    Learning

    Role of Parents

    Role of Teachers and Schools

    Role of the Media

    Role of Peer Groups

The Reduction of Prejudice

    Intergroup Contact

    Acculturation

    Education

The Victims of Prejudice

Sexism

Summary

For Review

The photograph of the cross and the white-robed Klansmen at the beginning of this chapter was taken in the state of Georgia. The Ku Klux Klan, however, has not been confined to the United States. In the 1920s and early '30s the Klan was represented in many Canadian provinces and spread its anti-black, anti-Catholic, and anti-Semitic message. The Klan is no longer as visible as it once was. However, views like those held by its members do linger on.

Over a period of three years in the 1980s, Eckville, a town of about 800 people in central Alberta, captured headlines across Canada and beyond. It was revealed that for more than a decade, high school teacher James Keegstra taught a view of history based on medieval mythology and pure bigotry regarding Judaism and the Jewish people.

Keegstra believed and taught his students that the fundamental fact of past and present history was a powerful Jewish-dominated conspiracy. The aims, he said, were to promote sexual perversion and other sins, to destroy Christianity, and to dominate the world. Not only were the Jews stereotyped as being undesirable, they were considered to be the very enemies of Christianity.

Of course, this led to peculiar interpretations of history. The Jews, according to Keegstra, had somehow caused the French Revolution, the American Civil War, the Bolshevik Revolution in Russia, and World War I. The Nazi Holocaust was said to have been a hoax designed to gain support for Israel, while the Jews secretly cooperated with Hitler! He told his students that the Jewish conspiracy controlled universities, publishing houses, and the media, and had thus "censored" history to suit their purposes. Only the anti-Semitic books and pamphlets provided by Keegstra had escaped this censorship; library sources were not to be believed.

Did Keegstra influence his students to adopt prejudice? Certainly, some rejected his views completely, and many pretended to agree with him in order to pass the course. Others, even years later, continued to express anti-Semitic views.

While parents, principals, and colleagues may be unaware of the views a teacher expresses in a classroom, Keegstra's particular teachings were no secret in this small community. How was he able to continue for so long? When we think of a fanatic, we usually picture a stereotype of a raving, Hitler-type character. In Keegstra's case, this description was not valid. Keegstra was generally well-liked and respected by students, colleagues, and the community. He had even been elected to the town council several times, and to the position of mayor in 1980. He was known as a devout Christian, with values shared by many in his community.

It was two mothers in the community who forced the issue out into the open and onto the school board agenda. Leaders in the Edmonton Jewish community reacted strongly. They were not willing to be passive victims of prejudice. The media, especially the CBC and *The Edmonton Journal,* focused public attention on the issues involved.

In 1984 Keegstra was charged with wilfully promoting hatred and committed for trial. He was convicted, but in 1988 the Alberta Court of Appeal set the conviction aside, saying that anti-hate legislation is unconstitutional. In 1990 the Supreme Court of Canada overturned this ruling and the case was sent back to the Alberta Court of Appeal. In 1991 a new trial was ordered. This trial, held in 1992, resulted in a $3000 fine. The conviction was appealed by both the Crown and Keegstra. What appears to be the final resolution to this case came on February 28, 1996. The Supreme Court of Canada restored the conviction of promoting anti-Semitism. It also affirmed that Canada's anti-hate law is constitutional. This means that people can be charged and convicted under it without the conviction violating their right to freedom of speech.

The fact that Keegstra was brought to trial was due to three significant forces: a minority refusing to be silent, those who were made victims refusing to be passive, and a Canadian public roused from complacency by the media.

Another Canadian teacher, from Moncton, New Brunswick, has been removed from the classroom by the Supreme Court of Canada, in a 9–0 decision handed down in April, 1996. Like Keegstra, Malcolm Ross expressed opinions about what he believed to be an international Jewish conspiracy. This was done in pamphlets and in a television interview. However, unlike Keegstra, his opinions were not taught in the classroom. The Supreme Court found this to be irrelevant because, as Judge La Forest stated, "The conduct of a teacher is evaluated on the basis of his or her position, rather than whether the conduct occurs within the classroom or beyond" (*The Globe and Mail*, April 4, 1996).

Canada with its multiculturalism and regional diversity needs to be especially sensitive to the effects of prejudice. In the discussion to follow we will examine how prejudice and discrimination arise, how they are maintained, and how they may be modified.

Keegstra and his reading material.

THE NATURE OF PREJUDICE

Prejudice is defined as a positive or negative attitude based on information that is either illogical, unrelated to reality, or a distortion of fact. This attitude is then unjustifiably generalized to all members of a group. Although prejudice can be favourable or unfavourable, psychologists use the term most frequently in the negative sense.

Prejudices about individuals or groups are usually developed on the basis of one or more differences. These differences may be physical, sexual, racial, national, or religious. They may be based on language, accent, social status, or age. In other words, any characteristic that sets people apart from others may ultimately be used as the basis for prejudice. Culture plays a role here. For example, Triandis (1967) observed that social class is more important to Japanese and Europeans than to Americans, and skin colour is emphasized more in the United States than in Hong Kong (Morland, 1969). In Wales, Belgium, and Quebec, language is of considerable importance (Giles and Powesland, 1975). Moreover, "normal" behaviour in one culture may be misinterpreted by members of other cultures. Interpersonal distance is a good example. Arabs, for instance, who prefer small interpersonal spaces, may be perceived as "pushy" by North Americans. Arabs may, in turn, view North Americans as cold and aloof.

prejudice A positive or negative attitude that is based on a distorted view of reality.

Upon what differences is prejudice based?

143

intergroup differences
Those that exist between members of different groups.

intragroup differences
Those that exist between members of the same group.

stereotype *The perception of a group based on over-generalized characteristics.*

What is the significance of prejudice as a cognitive filter?

Also important, as Tajfel and Turner (1979) point out, is that once people identify themselves as belonging to one group (the in-group) and others as belonging to another group (the out-group) they will expect to find differences between the groups. People will go as far as to create these **intergroup** differences (Dion, 1973). They may also believe that there is greater similarity within their group (**intragroup**) than really exists.

Although prejudice is an attitude and follows the principles outlined in Chapter 4, it is a significant topic on its own. Prejudice may initiate discrimination (behaviours and actions) that have serious implications for our lives and our society. Much research has been done on this topic. As with other attitudes, prejudice can be thought of as consisting of three components: cognitive, affective, and behavioural.

THE COGNITIVE COMPONENT: WHAT WE BELIEVE

THE USE OF STEREOTYPES

The beliefs that make up the cognitive component of prejudice are called **stereotypes** (see also Chapter 2). The term is usually attributed to the American journalist Walter Lippmann (1922), who described stereotypes as "pictures in the head." Stereotypes organize our cognitions (thoughts) concerning members of a certain group. They are made up of our ideas of the characteristics that best describe this group. These cognitions are usually simple and frequently inaccurate.

Stereotypes may be held by a single person (idiosyncratic stereotypes). They may be held in general by many people (consensual stereotypes). No one can go through life without being aware of stereotypes. In one sense they are useful and help us to deal efficiently with our environment. For example, consider how complicated it would be if single trees had to be considered separately instead of being included in one general category. This process of categorization extends to our classification of people. Just as we might say, "Trees are green" (which is not always true), we might say, "Jocks are not interested in art" (which is not always true).

Stereotypes influence how we relate to people. For example, a series of experiments was carried out by Taylor and Gardner (1969) in which audio or videotape recordings of a French Canadian person were presented to anglophone subjects. The French Canadian, speaking in accented English, described himself in ways consistent or inconsistent with the existing stereotype of that group. When asked later to form an impression of that person, subjects' impressions were influenced by the stereotype they held. Even when the French Canadian indicated that he was neither religious nor emotional, the subjects didn't really believe him. Other information that wasn't relevant to the stereotype was accepted as true. Similarly, Grant (1978) presented anglophone subjects with an Irish target person described as ambitious and scientific, two traits that are not usually part of the Irish stereotype. Subjects later rated the person as scientific and ambitious—as well as stereotypically happy-go-lucky, pleasure-loving, and talkative. Thus, stereotypes are not simply labels. They can act as "cognitive filters" through which we select what information to use, what to ignore, and how to interpret it. Bodenhausen (1988) demonstrated that stereotypes lead to selective processing. He found that people paid more attention to, and were better able to recall, information that was consistent with their stereotypes, and that inconsistent information was neglected or ignored.

In addition to the beliefs about the members of a group, we may also have more abstract, **symbolic beliefs** that affect our attitudes. Symbolic beliefs imply that a group threatens (or upholds) social values and norms (Esses, Haddock and Zanna, 1993). For example, a person may believe that separatists threaten the democratic principles of government and that, in contrast, supporters of the Liberal party in Quebec uphold our concepts of democracy.

symbolic belief The belief that a group threatens or supports certain social values.

THE ORIGINS OF STEREOTYPES

It has been suggested (Crocker,1981; Hamilton and Gifford, 1976; Hamilton, 1979; Hamilton, 1981; Hamilton and Rose, 1980; Hamilton and Sherman, 1989) that many instances of stereotyping arise and are maintained through the operation of **illusory correlation**. Illusory correlations occur when the relationship between two characteristics or events is overestimated. When our attention is caught by the reporting of a different or unusual event, for example, we tend to give it more significance than it actually possesses.

illusory correlation When the significance of a group's behaviour is over-estimated because it is unusual. (See Chapter 2.)

In an experiment by Hamilton and Gifford (1976) subjects were introduced to two groups by simply reading statements about their members. These statements included four undesirable statements for every nine desirable statements. For Group A (majority group) twice as much information was presented as was presented for Group B (minority group). It should be remembered that the ratio of desirable to undesirable statements remained the same for each group. An example of an undesirable statement was "Allan, a member of Group B, dented the fender of a parked car and didn't leave his name." When the results were analyzed it was found that subjects attributed more "undesirable" behaviour to the minority group (Group B). Since there were fewer statements for Group B, the incidence of negative statements stood out and made them seem more significant than they were.

Once such an association has been made, later information will be biased in the same direction. For instance, if the belief has been acquired that francophones are more conservative risk-takers than anglophones, then even if there is no actual difference between the two groups, this expectation will influence subsequent judgments about the extent of risk taking in each group. It has been suggested that this is so because disconfirmations of the stereotype are learned more slowly and/or forgotten more quickly than neutral or confirming information (Hamilton and Rose, 1980).

Why are illusory correlations so powerful?

THE ACCURACY OF STEREOTYPES

It might be argued that because stereotypes are so common they must, at least to some extent, be true (the **kernel of truth hypothesis**). However, there are a number of grounds on which this notion can often be refuted:

the kernel of truth hypothesis The notion that stereotypes must be true if they are commonly believed.

- the simultaneous existence of incompatible stereotypes concerning the same group of people, e.g. "Jews are pushy," "Jews are seclusive";
- the labelling of the same behaviour in positive or negative terms depending on which group exhibits it, e.g. "The Dutch are frugal and careful about their finances," "Scots are miserly and penny-pinching";
- changes in the stereotype not accompanied by any change in the target group, e.g. "Immigrants are energetic, reliable workers," "Immigrants work excessively and take jobs away from Canadians";

• the application of the stereotype to all members of the group without consideration of individual differences. For example, the Welsh are stereotyped as being good singers. Yet, examination of the residents of Wales would reveal a distribution of singing competence and, no doubt, some mediocre singers.

Why then do stereotypes remain so persistent? Perhaps because in some instances it seems possible to verify their accuracy. It is true, for example, that native peoples often score below the national average on standard intelligence tests, that Jews often belong only to their own clubs, and that many blacks excel at sports and music. However, this does not mean that native peoples are innately unintelligent, that Jews are cliquish, and that blacks have a built-in sense of rhythm. What is usually ignored is the situational pressure that makes stereotypes come true.

For instance, if it is believed that native peoples are genetically inferior, then little effort will be directed towards satisfying their educational needs. Even the typical intelligence test, having been standardized on middle-class whites, may yield little relevant information. All these and other types of treatment will guarantee that, at least by the dominant group's standards, native peoples appear intellectually "below normal."

Situational pressure may have also been operating in the past when Jews were refused admission to so many clubs that they formed their own associations. It was then argued that staying together was actually what they preferred. And sports and entertainment have been two occupational fields in which blacks have had a reasonable opportunity for success. It is therefore a logical and rational step for them to enter these professions. (In spite of this inroad, blacks continue to be under-represented as football quarterbacks and coaches and also in the front offices of baseball teams.)

An additional factor that serves to validate stereotypes is the **self-fulfilling prophecy**. Members of minority, or out-groups, are frequently confronted with the stereotypes maintained by the majority, or in-group, about them. Ultimately, they may come to believe that the stereotypes are true, and behave accordingly. For example, females are often stereotyped as inadequate at mathematics. They may therefore avoid academic courses and careers that require some sort of numerical background.

STEREOTYPES AND PREJUDICE

Is it the case that "as long as stereotypes exist, prejudice will inevitably follow"? The answer seems to be, not necessarily. There is no good evidence that knowing a stereotype goes hand-in-hand with prejudice (Devine, 1989, Taylor and Lalonde, 1987). Studies show that while both high- and low-prejudice individuals know the cultural stereotype (e.g. women are not mechanically minded), their personal beliefs (e.g. women should or should not enter engineering) about the target group are different. The beliefs and stereotypes of a prejudiced person will agree, while the beliefs and stereotypes of a tolerant person will conflict. This means that tolerant individuals will bypass the stereotype, and use their personal beliefs to judge others.

THE AFFECTIVE COMPONENT: HOW WE FEEL

Stereotypes do not exist in isolation. They are accompanied by *emotions,* which are usually expressed in terms ranging from the intensely negative, e.g. contempt, disgust, and hate, to the very positive, e.g. admiration and liking.

F·O·C·U·S

How does situational pressure explain why some stereotypes seem accurate?

self-fulfilling prophecy
If individuals or groups believe stereotypes about themselves they might act in ways that make it true.

Feelings such as these may not be verbalized, but there may be some arousal of the sympathetic nervous system. The increased physiological activity can be measured by the galvanic skin response (GSR). Such responses can be used, at least for research purposes, to determine whether there is an emotional reaction, even though the subject may be unable or unwilling to express it overtly. Porier and Lott (1967) used this method to identify individuals who scored high and low on a scale of **ethnocentrism** (the extent to which people believe in the superiority of their own ethnic or cultural group). High ethnocentric subjects showed a greater GSR in the presence of black, compared with white, research assistants, than did those who scored low on the scale.

ethnocentrism *The belief that one's own group is superior to other groups.*

A study conducted by Dijker (1987) in the Netherlands illustrates the relationship between emotions and attitudes, in this case towards three minority groups: immigrants from Surinam (a former Dutch Colony), Turks, and Moroccans. Analyses of the data showed that for all groups the emotions expressed fell into four categories: positive (e.g. admiration), irritation (e.g. annoyance), anxiety (e.g. fear), and concern (e.g. worry). Positive emotions were more predictive of attitudes towards Surinamers, who were generally perceived favourably by the Dutch. Negative emotions (irritation and concern) were more predictive of attitudes towards those from Turkey and Morocco, who were perceived unfavourably.

THE BEHAVIOURAL COMPONENT: HOW WE DISCRIMINATE

Prejudice put into action is **discrimination**. It was not long ago that black members of the Hamilton Tiger Cats (football team) were refused haircuts in a major hotel and blacks in Dresden, Ontario, were refused service in local restaurants. Fortunately, the frequency of overt discrimination has decreased, in part, perhaps, because of safeguards such as the Canadian Charter of Rights and Freedoms. Signs no longer appear in Halifax restaurants stating, as they did during World War II, "Sailors and dogs not admitted." In fact, not long ago, a Nova Scotia Human Rights board ordered that souvenir buttons proclaiming, "I'm a big mouth Cape Bretoner—so kiss me," be destroyed on the grounds that the message was offensive to a group of Maritimers (Hunter, 1987).

discrimination *Overt behaviour that belittles or excludes people of particular groups.*

Discrimination may occur at the level of interaction between individuals, as our previous examples have indicated, or it may be more broadly based. The latter case is known as **systemic discrimination**. It is supported by either implicit or explicit regulations, norms, or laws. For instance, apartheid as practised in South Africa was a case of discrimination required by law. It has been argued that the language, educational, and sign laws enacted in Quebec in the '70s and '80s are also examples of legal support for discrimination. Of course, many of us have forgotten that the Manitoba government passed a law in 1890 that prohibited education in French and abolished it as an official language. This law has only recently been struck down by the Supreme Court of Canada. The term **institutional racism** has a similar meaning, but is often used to refer to organizational policies, in particular employment practices, that put racial minorities at a disadvantage. For example, this may occur when personal recommendations of present employees are used as a basis of hiring, if those recommendations result in the exclusion of certain ethnic or racial groups.

What are some ways that discrimination is practised?

systemic discrimination *This occurs when regulations and laws support racist practices.*

institutional racism *This occurs when organizational policy puts racial minorities at a disadvantage, as with employment.*

Much more discrimination undoubtedly occurs through covert, subtle means. Thus an informal "rule" in a personnel office, although never made explicit, may effectively place a quota on the number of minority group members who are hired or promoted.

Aside from the problems faced by its minorities, Canada faces another, more insidious problem: discrimination against Canadians *by* Canadians who believe that Canada is second-rate. The problems that Canadians encountered in gaining access to jobs in their own universities eventually led the government to insist that applications from Canadians and permanent residents be given first priority. Now, only when it is demonstrated that no qualified Canadian candidates are available can foreign applications be considered. More recently, many provinces have enacted legislation requiring employers to move towards equitable hiring of women, the handicapped, and members of minority groups.

Clearly, discrimination can take many forms and be disguised in many ways. The expulsion of Japanese Canadians from the West Coast during World War II is a case in point. Because they were considered a security risk, these citizens were rounded up on short notice, and their homes and goods, including their fishing boats, were seized. They were relocated in often-secluded areas of British Columbia, Alberta, and Ontario. The comments of one Japanese victim express the resentment that many must have felt:

> *Don't think the authorities weren't waiting for us when Pearl Harbor came. Within two hours things began to happen.... I got a call from Navy Headquarters to report at 9 o'clock next morning. The Commander was very frank. He said, 'Mr. Suzubi, we were caught with our pants down,' and he said that all fishing vessels would have to be turned over to the authorities right then.*
>
> *To this day I don't know what they thought about those fishing boats.... They were small boats, made of wood. We had no radar, no radio, no echo sounder.... But try and convince these people that we were not spies, we were just ordinary fishermen. As far back as the late 1890's they had determined that one day they would kick the damn Japs off the river. There was one common statement you could hear along the river: 'There's only one damn good Jap and that's a dead Jap' (Broadfoot, 1977).*

Yet there was not a single instance of breach of security on which to base this action. There was, however, a history in British Columbia of hostility towards Asians, and it is of interest that the most active agitators for the removal of the Japanese citizens were rival Canadian fishermen to whom the government eventually sold the Japanese boats and equipment at give-away prices. The Japanese Canadians have never been fully compensated for the government's action (for detailed descriptions see Adachi, 1976; Broadfoot, 1977). However, in 1988 the government finally apologized and agreed to a form of redress, the terms of which included: payment of $21 000 to those affected who are still living; granting of citizenship to persons of Japanese ancestry who were expelled from Canada or who had their citizenship revoked; and clearing the names of people of Japanese ancestry who were convicted under the War Measures Act, the National Emergency Transitional Powers Act, or other related legislation. There are 12 000 surviving Japanese in Canada for whom the $21 000 is to be compensation for their enforced isolation, and for the loss of homes, businesses, and fishing boats.

Nor should we forget the experience of those Chinese who helped to build the Canadian Pacific Railway. Fifteen thousand Chinese worked on the transcontinental line and 600 of them died on the job, yet in 1922 the government imposed a head tax of $500 on each Chinese and in 1923 passed the Chinese

Exclusion Act, which was not repealed until 1947 (this act reduced Chinese immigration to fewer than 50 people in the 24-year period). Similar motives may have been behind the expulsion from Uganda of Asians who controlled a large portion of the economy when Idi Amin gained power; and some of the difficulties that Chinese citizens are experiencing in Malaysia.

Discrimination can be based on the belief that certain races are genetically inferior to others—with disturbing consequences. The so-called "medical experiments" conducted by the Nazis were rationalized in this manner. More recently, an experiment has been brought to light in which the United States Public Health Service allowed 200 men to go untreated for syphilis in order to study the disease and its side effects. All the men were black. Similarly, the flawed research of Philippe Rushton (1989), which tries to show that members of certain races are intellectually superior or inferior, could be used to support discriminatory actions. This type of belief was demonstrated in the United States in the early part of the century when intelligence tests were administered to immigrants. Not unexpectedly, many immigrants, coming as they did from other cultures, were shown to be "intellectually deficient." On this basis it was argued that certain ethnic groups were "genetically inferior," and restrictive immigration quotas were applied for many years (Kamin, 1974).

Discrimination based on intelligence was taken to the extreme by Alberta's Sexual Sterilization Act of 1928. This act was responsible for the sterilization of approximately 3000 people labelled "mentally defective" and held in government-run homes. A high proportion of these were youths from poor immigrant families. Although consent was required, it is not clear that the potential patients were aware of what they were agreeing to, and if they were, whether they were coerced into compliance. The plight of these victims was brought to light by Leilani Muir, who was sterilized without her consent at the age of fourteen while having her appendix removed. Classified as a "moron," she was placed in the province's Training School for Mental Defectives. IQ tests administered later in life showed her to have an IQ in the normal range. Ms. Muir brought a lawsuit against the government of Alberta, and in January, 1996 was awarded $740 000. After a six-year battle she received not only the money but also what amounted to an apology when the following judgment was made by the court: "The circumstances of Ms. Muir's sterilization were so highhanded and so contemptuous of the statutory authority to effect sterilization and were undertaken in an atmosphere that so little respected Ms. Muir's human dignity that the community, and the court's sense of decency is offended" (*The Globe and Mail,* March 12, 1996). This and other sterilizations were supported by many as a way of protecting the community from the possibility that people deemed unfit would procreate and pass on their genes to another generation. This act was repealed in 1972. Ms. Muir's story is told in the NFB documentary *The Sterilization of Leilani Muir.*

ETHNICITY

The relationship between ethnicity and discrimination is demonstrated in a survey conducted in Toronto. Henry (1978) observed that not only did the ethnicity of the target relate to the extent of discrimination, but the ethnicity of the source was also important. Among her respondents, individuals from Italy, Greece, and Portugal were least likely to wish close relationships with the members of other groups. As Henry points out, these are people who are strongly committed to their own ethnic origins, suggesting that as in-group identity increases, social distance from other groups also increases.

One factor that may contribute to in-group identity is the number of members of the group in a given location. Kalin and Berry (1979) observe that a very high concentration of a given group may be detrimental to national unity by leading to greater ethnocentrism. If this is so, increased ethnocentrism should challenge the multicultural philosophy of the Canadian social system. The **multicultural hypothesis** states that positive feelings towards members of other groups will be related to how secure and comfortable a person feels with his or her own cultural identity and background. This proposition was tested by Lambert, Mermigis and Taylor (1986), using Greek Canadians in Montreal as subjects. They measured attitudes towards their own group, other ethnic groups, cultural assimilation, and cultural maintenance. Data were also obtained on the degree of ethnocentrism, religiosity, and amount of formal education. It was found that the respondents took a strong stand on the need to maintain Greek culture and language. Compared with a number of other Canadian groups (English, French, Jewish, black, Italian, and Portuguese), the Greeks rated their own group most positively. In addition, social contacts with members of their own group were preferred over contacts with members of the other groups. The other groups were rated most favourably by those Greek Canadians who were the most culturally secure and who were the most ethnocentric. However, these same individuals were less willing to interact with members of those groups. The Greek Canadians who were the least ethnocentric and better educated were the most willing to associate with members of the other groups.

These results do not fully support the multicultural hypothesis. Cultural security and well-being, although correlated with a positive evaluation of the other groups, was not associated with a willingness to socialize with them. Lambert et al. suggest that further research may reveal education as a critical factor in decreasing ethnocentrism while maintaining security and increasing the likelihood of social interaction between groups.

REVERSE DISCRIMINATION

As society becomes more sensitive to racial issues, many people will resist expressing prejudicial attitudes. In fact, some may go as far as to behave in a manner that implies considerable more tolerance than they really possess. This process of **reverse discrimination** has been demonstrated in a number of studies by Dutton and his colleagues (Dutton, 1979; Dutton and Lake, 1973; Dutton and Lennox, 1974). In the first experiment, either black or white couples entered a restaurant in Vancouver or Toronto. In each case the man was wearing a turtleneck sweater in violation of the restaurant's dress code requiring ties for men. Despite the rule only 30 percent of the white couples were seated compared to 75 percent of the black couples. It is evident that the people in charge went out of their way to appear non-discriminatory. It should be noted that this effect appears to be most common among educated middle and upper-middle-class whites who are especially concerned not to appear intolerant.

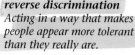

multicultural hypothesis
When groups feel secure they will be more positive towards other groups.

reverse discrimination
Acting in a way that makes people appear more tolerant than they really are.

SELF ? TEST

SELF-TEST QUESTIONS

1. Which of the following statements is *not* true regarding prejudice?

a) it is based on illogical assumptions or distorted facts

b) people in all cultures are equally likely to show prejudices based on race, social status, and language

c) it can be negative or positive, although it is almost always used in the negative sense.

d) it is an attitude

2. The beliefs that comprise the cognitive component of prejudice are called

a) categorizations

b) idiosyncracies

c) stereotypes

d) schemata

3. Which of the following is true regarding stereotypes?

a) they may be held by a single person

b) they help us to distinguish among groups of people

c) they may be based on appearance, attitudes, or aptitudes of people

d) all of the above

4. In a study by Dutton (1971), black and white couples dressed so as to violate the dress codes of the Toronto and Vancouver restaurants to which they attempted to gain entrance. What were the results of this study?

a) the black couple was admitted more often than the white couple in both cities

b) the white couple was admitted more often than the black couple in both cities

c) the black couple was admitted less often in Vancouver but not in Toronto

d) both couples were admitted equally often in both cities

5. Which of the following statements is true of reverse discrimination?

a) it is most widely practised among the less educated

b) it leads to increased and long-term tolerance of the groups towards which it is directed

c) it is an attempt to appear less prejudiced than a person really is

d) all of the above

ACQUISITION OF PREJUDICE

Hebb and Thompson (1968) have described incidents that suggested to them that the higher animals—chimpanzees and human beings—have an inherent fear of the unfamiliar and unusual. If Hebb is correct—though there is not yet any strong empirical support for his belief—it would be reasonable to argue that this tendency could form the basis for the development of prejudice. It is generally agreed that people are anxious or fearful towards people whom they perceive as "different," or in situations that they don't understand.

It has been shown that infants as young as three months of age are able to distinguish between the face of their mother and that of a stranger. At this age their reactions to the unfamiliar stimulus do not show signs of avoidance or fear. By about the age of nine months, aversive reactions often do appear. This can happen even when, much to the embarrassment of young parents, the unfamiliar stimulus is the child's grandmother.

Whether there are in fact inherent predispositions that could form the primitive rudiments of prejudice remains to be confirmed. There is, however, little

How do we acquire prejudice? Is it something we are born with or something we learn?

**How does learning
theory explain
prejudice?**

**instrumental condition-
ing** *Learning from the consequences (reinforcement or
punishment) of behaviour.*

classical conditioning
*Learning to respond to a
stimulus because it is associated with another stimulus that already causes us
to respond in a certain way.*

modelling *Learning by
observing the behaviour of
others.*

doubt concerning the importance of *learning* in the development of prejudice. The
first setting in which this learning takes place is the home.

LEARNING

Learning follows certain basic principles that have been tested over time. These
are best understood by examining three primary types of learning: instrumental
conditioning, classical conditioning, and modelling.

INSTRUMENTAL CONDITIONING

One of the basic principles of instrumental (or operant) learning is that we learn
from the consequences of our behaviour. A behaviour or response that is followed by a reinforcement will be strengthened; that is, it is more likely that the
response will occur again. Conversely, behaviour that is followed by punishment will be weakened. Most of the reinforcements associated with the acquisition
of prejudice are likely to be verbal or non-verbal indications of approval. For
example, if a child says, "Those people are dirty," and the mother smiles and
responds positively, then the child is likely to repeat this remark, make it part of
his or her belief system, and generalize it to other similar-looking people.

CLASSICAL CONDITIONING

Since Pavlov's first experiments with his salivating dogs, the classical conditioning paradigm has become part of almost everyone's psychological repertoire. In the original situation, an unconditioned stimulus (UCS), food, was used
to elicit an unconditioned response (UCR), salivation, in a dog. This UCS was then
paired for a number of trials with the sound of a bell, which had been identified
as neutral. That is, the bell on its own did not cause salivation. After the bell
and food were paired, the dog learned that the bell signalled that food was on the
way. It would then salivate to the bell alone in anticipation of food. At this
point the bell became the conditioned stimulus (CS), and the salivation to the
sound became a conditioned response (CR).

A similar process may account for at least some portion of the emotional or evaluative aspect of prejudice. For example, suppose a white child is playing with a
child of another race (neutral/good relationship at this point) and the white
child's mother, noticing this interaction, rushes out, yells at her child to stop, slaps
her, and drags her into the house. This treatment is the unconditioned stimulus
(UCS) that arouses hostility, fear, and anxiety in the child (UCR). When the interaction is paired with the punishment, the white child will learn to fear (CR)
neutral interaction with children of other racial groups in anticipation of the
mother's anger. Therefore, the interaction that was originally neutral becomes the
stimulus to fear (CS).

MODELLING

Not all learning involves the active intervention of a rewarding or punishing
agent. Often a child will exhibit behaviour or express ideas that haven't been
deliberately taught but that have been observed. Models, usually individuals
with whom the child identifies—e.g. parents, teachers, or peers—have been
shown to be highly effective in teaching attitudes and prejudice (Bandura, 1965).
The process is both subtle and insidious, since the child is not a direct participant
in the event and the model may not be aware of either the information being

transmitted or its effect. It also should be kept in mind that equally important to what the model does may be what the model doesn't do. Thus, a child will observe who is avoided or ignored and may copy this behaviour.

ROLE OF PARENTS

Parents have a powerful influence, not only because they play a role in what the child learns from day to day, but because this learning forms the foundation for all later experience. In order to acquire prejudicial attitudes, children must first become "racially aware." That is, they must be able to distinguish themselves from others who are in some way different. Children are aware of different ethnic groups by the age of four or five (Aboud, 1988), and even as young as three. One study found that 25 percent of the four-year-old children observed were already expressing strong race-related values (Goodman, 1964).

Prejudice can occur before the child's horizons have expanded much beyond the home. In these early years parents or caregivers exert sole control over the child's rewards and punishments. This provides many opportunities for the acquisition of habits of thought and action.

Studies show that parents with authoritarian traits teach their children that status is very important. These parents typically use harsh punishment, don't tolerate any hostility or aggression by the child towards them, act in a cold and impersonal manner, and withdraw love in order to maintain "proper" behaviour. Thus the child is forced to submit without question to his or her superiors and to suppress the hostility that is naturally aroused under these frustrating conditions. At the same time, by defining what is different as inferior the parents give the child an acceptable outlet for pent-up feelings: the denigration of outgroups. They also teach their children that the world is a dangerous place, which sets the stage for fear based on feelings of vulnerability (Altemeyer, 1988).

Authoritarian parents are also likely to be prejudiced and ethnocentric. In this case, prejudice is incorporated in a belief and value system that forms the personality pattern first identified by Adorno, Frenkel-Brunswick, Levinson and Sanford (1950). The concept of the **authoritarian personality** attracted much attention and stimulated numerous subsequent research projects (e.g. Christie and Jahoda, 1954; Cherry and Byrne, 1977). It was found that individuals who can be characterized as authoritarian are likely to be prejudiced, with a rigid outlook that perceives the world in categorical black/white, superior/inferior, us/them terms. Moreover, these individuals are usually highly conventional and cynical.

Much of the recent research on right-wing authoritarianism (RWA) has been carried out by Altemeyer (1981, 1988), who has constructed a scale to measure this characteristic. Some of the items from his RWA scale are:

> *The way things are going in this country, it's going to take a lot of "strong medicine" to straighten out the troublemakers, criminals, and perverts. It would be best for everyone if the proper authorities censored magazines and movies to keep trashy material away from the youths.*
>
> *The real keys to the "good life" are obedience, discipline, and sticking to the straight and narrow.*

An authoritarian would agree with the items above and disagree with items such as:

What are some of the characteristics of the authoritarian personality?

There is nothing wrong with premarital intercourse.

"Free speech" means that people should even be allowed to make speeches and write books urging the overthrow of the government.

There is absolutely nothing wrong with nudist camps.

In addition to confirming that authoritarians are conventional, highly submissive to authority, and aggressive towards those they believe to be inferior or "different," Altemeyer (1988) found that they are also self-righteous and feel themselves to be morally superior. Esses, Haddock and Zanna (1993) report that English Canadians who were identified as high authoritarians by Altemeyer's scale had more negative attitudes towards four minority groups (French Canadians, native peoples, Pakistanis, and homosexuals) than did low authoritarians.

scapegoating *When anger and hostility is displaced onto a group not responsible for the existing problems.*

One other manifestation of authoritarian aggression is **scapegoating**, which may occur when individuals are frustrated by conditions or situations they cannot directly control or change, e.g. "the economic situation" or the "government." When the source of the frustration is vague and difficult to locate, tension and hostility may be aroused and displaced onto a convenient out-group. This out-group is then blamed for the person's discomfort and difficulties. Much of the treatment of the Jews during the Nazi regime in Germany may have been an example of scapegoating. Jews were blamed for all of the economic woes that the Germans experienced after World War I and into the 1930s. A more recent example may be the frequently heard claim that immigrants are taking jobs away from Canadians.

The proportion of individuals that can be described as extreme authoritarians is not large, but it is often vocal. Among them may be found individuals who belong to neo-Nazi and white supremacist movements. Another serious social consequence of the authoritarian personality has been suggested by Bray and Noble (1978). In a mock-jury experiment they discovered that high authoritarians reached guilty verdicts more frequently and imposed more severe punishments than did low authoritarians.

Parents, for better or worse, eventually give up their role as the major influence in children's lives. As children grow older their world gets larger. They interact with peers, enter school, begin to read, and watch TV. All of these experiences may contribute to the formation or reinforcement of prejudice.

ROLE OF TEACHERS AND SCHOOLS

What are some of the ways that teachers and schools might promote prejudice?

While parents are the child's first authority figures, other people—teachers, for instance—also exert considerable influence. Like everyone else, teachers have their prejudices. Although they may try to be as tolerant as possible, there are many opportunities in the classroom for less-than-desirable attitudes to be communicated to the pupils. For example, how does the teacher treat children in multiracial classrooms? How does he or she handle children who are either the butt or the source of racial slurs? Such subjects as geography and history give the teacher the opportunity to impart *correct* information about ethnic, racial, or other groups—but there are dangers here as well. Does the teacher give equal time to both sides of an issue? And, if not all topics can be covered in the time allotted, how is a decision made about what material should be omitted?

Until recently, when some of the worst examples began to be eliminated, many textbooks contained biased and inaccurate information about ethnic and other groups. For example, native peoples were frequently depicted as alcohol-addicted, primitive savages with only a rudimentary social organization (or their depiction was highly sentimental). Texts also typically relegated males and females to traditional roles. (In some cases, modifications of texts and other books designed to correct these biases have been overzealous, creating some backlash. Activist journalist June Callwood (1987) recently criticized the Canadian publishing industry for producing "sanitized" books reflecting a "pious" history that never was.) Bias has also been evident in the *context* in which material is presented to the student. For instance, how is the student affected when his or her arithmetic problems involve only white collar business applications? Why is it that union officials or plumbers never do any calculations? The context within which problems are set can convey to students the attitudes and values of the instructor or author.

ROLE OF THE MEDIA

Textbooks are only a step away from the mass media: magazines, newspapers, radio, television, and films. North American children spend a lot of time watching TV. Some suggest they will watch 5000 hours by the start of grade one and 19 000 hours by the end of high school. This exceeds class hours. (*Time* magazine, October, 1990). There are numerous ways in which attitudes can be influenced by the media, for example through selective or biased reporting in newspapers, or by the repetition of stereotypes in television shows.

Visible minorities rarely appear in television commercials or magazine advertising in Canada. A survey conducted in Canada by Lateef and Bangash (1977) found that television commercials observed over a four-day period involved 2064 people, of whom only 48 were visible minority members. If the commercials of charitable organizations (e.g. CARE) and those from the United States are omitted, the representation of visible minority members drops to .09 percent of the total commercials on television.

Six years later, in 1983, Moore and Cadeau (1985) analyzed the content of 1733 Canadian television commercials. They found that 88 percent of the voice-overs were done by men, and fewer than two percent of the commercials included elderly people as central characters, and that if elderly people were involved they were most likely to be men. Visible minorities appeared in fewer than four percent of all commercials. Moreover, Aranoff (1974) has reported that when the elderly appear in television programs they are portrayed more negatively than other age groups.

ROLE OF PEER GROUPS

Peers exercise more influence over attitudes as the child matures. By adolescence, peers are likely to be more influential in many respects than a child's parents. In the early years, parents exercise considerable control over children's relationships and, since playmates are likely to come from similar socio-economic backgrounds, attitudes encountered in the home are likely to be reinforced and strengthened outside of it. But as children grow older their contacts become more diverse, and they are less apt to be influenced by parental standards. Like parents, the members of peer groups are effective in influencing attitudes and behaviour because they offer information, reward conformity, and punish nonconformity. This pressure to conform, which continues throughout a person's life, is difficult to resist. Expressing ideas and beliefs that the group considers to be correct is just as important as wearing clothes the group considers to be appropriate.

How does the media promote prejudice?

Pettigrew (1961) argues that in the United States most prejudice is based on conformity. One welcome aspect of this theory is that, unlike prejudice associated with deep-seated personality patterns, prejudice based on conformity may be more flexible. If the group norm changes or if individuals join new groups with different views, then their attitudes will likely shift accordingly.

SELF ? TEST

SELF-TEST QUESTIONS

6. Which of the following might produce a classically conditioned prejudice?

a) *each time two-year-old Billy plays at home with a Chinese neighbour his mother goes out with a friend for a couple of hours*

b) *whenever six-year-old Martha telephones her schoolmate Kiran, who is from India, Martha's mother gets upset without saying why—but doesn't do so when Martha telephones non-Indian playmates*

c) *during class, a teacher tells students that members of a particular ethnic group are particularly intelligent*

d) *during a religious service, children are taught that their religion is the one true religion*

7. Which of the following is true of social modelling?

a) *modelling plays an important role in children's acquisition of prejudiced attitudes*

b) *modelling doesn't require direct rewards or punishments in order to influence behaviour*

c) *a model can influence a child's attitudes and/or behaviour without being aware of doing so*

d) *all of the above*

8. People who are highly prejudiced, conventional, and rigid in their views are

a) *likely to encourage prejudiced attitudes in their children*

b) *high in authoritarianism*

c) *low in ethnocentrism*

d) *a and b*

THE REDUCTION OF PREJUDICE

Discrimination is a behaviour and as such can be controlled by laws, but prejudice obviously cannot be addressed in the same way. However, it is possible to lead individuals towards more tolerant attitudes, either directly through education, or indirectly through appropriate intergroup contact, for example. In this section we consider some of the conditions that may lead to the reduction of prejudice.

INTERGROUP CONTACT

It is often assumed that increased interaction between the members of various groups will enhance mutual understanding and good will. However, what is important is not only the frequency but the nature of the contact.

Ideally, intergroup contact should disconfirm the negative stereotypes associated with the out-group. Rothbart and John (1985) propose that this will happen in three ways, as illustrated in Figure 6-1. These are:

(1) The clarity of the potentially disconfirming behaviours. Some traits ascribed to out-groups, such as "messy" or "talkative," are associated with clearly observable behaviours and can therefore be easily confirmed or disconfirmed. However, the behaviours that would confirm or disconfirm such stereotypes as "devious" and "untrustworthy" are more difficult to specify and to observe. These and similar stereotypes would be difficult to modify by interethnic contact. Unfortunately, they are also the stereotypes with the most serious social implications.

(2) The number of relevant observations. Rothbart and John (1985) report that the more *un*favourable a trait, the *fewer* the number of instances required for confirmation and the *greater* the number of instances required for disconfirmation. As they note, favourable stereotypes are difficult to acquire but easy to lose, while unfavourable stereotypes are easy to acquire and difficult to lose. This observation implies that if intergroup contact is infrequent negative stereotypes are not likely to change.

(3) The frequency of intergroup contact. Obviously, there must be an occasion during which confirming or disconfirming actions can occur, but the situation will also determine what *type* of behaviour is likely to be expressed. Talkative or friendly behaviour is likely to be manifested in most social situations, but if the stereotype includes such characteristics as "heroic" or "cowardly" a situation may never arise in which these traits can be confirmed or disconfirmed.

If some modification of a stereotype does occur as a result of intergroup contact, how likely is it that the change will generalize to other members of the same group? Unfortunately, studies (e.g. Cook, 1984) indicate that the generalization may not extend beyond the situation or to other members of the group. This is so, Rothbart and John (1985) argue, because the individuals involved in the contact may be perceived not as "exemplars" of the larger category, but as atypical. For example, a male could express positive views about the ability of a female friend and at the same time reveal stereotypical beliefs about the incompetence of women. If confronted with this apparent contradiction, he would likely respond, "Well, she isn't a typical woman!" Allport (1954) called this phe-

In what ways may intergroup contact disconfirm negative stereotypes?

FIGURE 6-1 Factors influencing the susceptibility of stereotype traits to disconfirmation

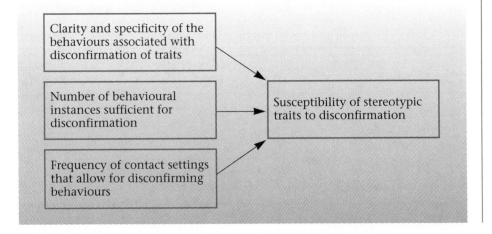

re-fencing *When a person's behaviour does not match the stereotype he or she is treated as an exception.*

intergroup anxiety *This occurs when people assume that there will be negative consequences to interacting with other groups.*

What are some of the fears that might lead to intergroup anxiety?

nomenon **re-fencing**. When a person is unlike the stereotype, they may be treated as an exception while the stereotype itself remains unchallenged.

It is also evident that even when the opportunity for contact exists many people will not take advantage of it. Only five percent of the respondents in a study conducted by Henry (1978) in Toronto who reported that they had black friends had met them in their own neighbourhood. Similarly, Henry cites a survey carried out in Britain, which found that 25 percent of the respondents who had non-white neighbours had never talked to them. On the other hand, it appears that contact is not a necessary condition for tolerance. In Henry's study, almost 44 percent of the very tolerant had experienced no contact with minority group members. Her data, showing the relationship between contact and prejudice, is listed in Table 6-1.

One reason for the lack of contact between members of in- and out-groups is **intergroup anxiety** (Stephan and Stephan, 1985). This anxiety arises from the anticipation that contact could result in one or more of four types of negative consequences. These are:

(1) Negative psychological consequences for the self. People often know very little about the values, norms, non-verbal behaviours, and expectations of the members of other groups. This ignorance about the "subjective culture" (Triandis, 1972) may lead to fear of embarrassment or of being made to appear incompetent in intergroup interactions. These fears can be quite realistic. For example, if an orthodox Hindu is present at a meal, can beef be served to the other guests? Or, should one bow, and if so how low, when introduced to someone from Japan? Such concerns lead to anticipation of discomfort and awkwardness in these types of interactions. One resolution is not to get involved.

(2) Negative behavioural consequences for the self. In-group members may also believe that they will be taken advantage of or exploited, especially when they harbour stereotypes about the out-group as being devious and dishonest. In extreme cases, they may fear that they will be physically abused.

(3) Negative evaluations by in-group members. Members of the in-group may be afraid that if they interact with the out-groups, they will be rejected by their own group.

(4) Negative evaluations by out-group members. Fear of rejection, ridicule, or disapproval by the out-group if contact is attempted is also a possibility. Wilder and Shapiro (1989) point out that the anxiety generated by the antici-

TABLE 6-1 Prejudice and social contact: How subjects described themselves

	None or little contact	Close or very close contact
Very prejudiced	82*	18
Somewhat prejudiced	64.7	35.3
Somewhat tolerant	48.3	51.7
Very tolerant	43.5	56.4
*expressed as percentage of sample		

SOURCE: Henry, 1978

pation of an encounter with an out-group may decrease the impact of any positive behaviour of an out-group member. The anxiety interferes with information-processing and thus reduces the possible effect of any positive actions.

Obviously there must be an opportunity for contact to occur. Such opportunities will be related to the number of members of a particular ethnic group who reside in a given location. This observation is confirmed by Kalin and Berry (1982), who found that attitudes were more negative where the concentration of an ethnic group was low, and more positive where the concentration was high.

We do not know from these data to what extent tolerance results from the contact itself. It may be that individuals who are tolerant are more willing to interact with out-group members. However, since the prejudiced avoid associating with the members of other groups, opportunities for effective contact simply do not occur for them. This is a problem that interferes with any attempt, deliberate or otherwise, to modify people's attitudes. We are often preaching to the converted.

It is likely that if we could somehow, without using force, propel prejudiced individuals into the appropriate social milieu, some positive change might then occur.

Some support for this emerges from a study conducted by Reich and Purbhoo (1975) in Toronto. They measured the attitudes of children attending an ethnically mixed school and a school that was not mixed. They found that children in the mixed school were considerably more tolerant of ethnic diversity. Because they lived in the neighbourhood and had no choice about which school they attended, pre-selection bias is not likely to have seriously influenced this outcome. This observation has been supported experimentally in Toronto by Ziegler (1981), who assigned grade six children to experimental conditions consisting of either cooperative teams or conventional individual teaching methods. The cooperative teams were set up in such a way as to ensure mixed ethnic groups (Anglo, Italian, Chinese, Greek, and West Indian children). The students worked together for eight weeks, three class periods per week. Measures obtained at the end of the procedure showed that in the cooperative teams both casual and close cross-ethnic friendship had increased significantly, as compared to those students who had been treated in the more conventional individual manner.

We should be aware that competition often leads to interpersonal hostility, and that teachers frequently use competition as a means of enhancing the motivation of their students. This might be a dangerous tactic. Sherif and his colleagues (1961) were able to deliberately increase and decrease intergroup hostility and rivalry at a summer camp by manipulating the amount of competitive and cooperative interaction that took place.

ACCULTURATION: HOW DOES YOUR CONTACT WITH OTHER CULTURES AFFECT YOU?

When a country like Canada has many ethnic groups some intergroup contact is very likely. However, some groups may actively avoid contact, while others may seek it out. The amount of contact and the desire to interact should influence the extent of change that may occur in the values, attitudes, and behaviour of each group. This is the process of **acculturation**, which takes place when "two groups come into continuous first-hand contact with subsequent changes in the original culture pattern of either or both groups" (Redfield, 1955, p. 149).

As Berry (1986, 1992) points out, in plural societies there are two important intergroup issues: the strength of the desire to maintain one's cultural distinc-

acculturation When different groups come into contact changes will be experienced by all involved.

159

When different cultures come into contact, what are four potential outcomes?

tiveness, and the strength of the desire for inter-ethnic contact. These two orientations are not really compatible, and Berry (1984) has constructed a framework (see Figure 6-2) that distinguishes the potential outcomes of the four possible combinations of the two motives. These are: assimilation, integration, separation (or segregation), and marginalization. Assimilation occurs when a group surrenders its cultural identity and is absorbed into the larger society (the "melting pot" concept). Integration is the result when the group maintains its culture but also interacts with other groups. In those cases where intergroup contact is unwelcome and cultural integrity is maintained, the outcome will be either segregation (if the group is a weak minority) or separation (if the group is more powerful). The final possibility, marginalization, results when the traditional culture is lost and there is little contact with the larger society. Marginalization is usually accompanied by confusion, anxiety, hostility, and feelings of alienation, a syndrome that has been termed "acculturative stress" (Berry, 1987).

It should be noted that this model can be applied to individuals as well as groups, and that it does not describe an all-or-nothing process. Positions can be taken between the two extremes of cultural distinctiveness and inter-ethnic contact.

EDUCATION

Teachers, instruction, and the classroom milieu are part of the global process of education. Numerous studies have examined the relationship between *level* of education and prejudice. The outcome of this research has been generally consistent in showing that as education increases, prejudice decreases. The data gathered by Henry (1978) in Toronto indicate this quite clearly (see Table 6-2). However, you will recall from our discussion of correlations in Chapter 1 that we cannot conclude from these data that education necessarily produces tolerance. There are many factors associated with school attendance besides education *per se* that might account for this relationship. For example, individuals with more education tend to know more facts, think more flexibly, and come from higher socio-

FIGURE 6-2 Types of in-group and out-group relationships (integration, assimilation, separation, marginalization)

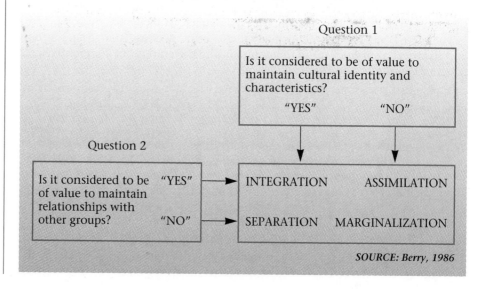

SOURCE: Berry, 1986

TABLE 6-2 **Level of education and prejudice: How subjects described themselves**

	Education attained		
	Primary	Secondary	University
Very prejudiced	17.4*	17.9	3.5
Somewhat prejudiced	53.7	33.6	19.8
Somewhat tolerant	23.6	36.4	37.9
Very tolerant	5.3	12.11	38.8

*expressed as percentage of sample

SOURCE: Henry, 1978

economic levels of society than do people with less education. Or, perhaps the critical factor is the extra-curricular activities—clubs, sports, and discussions—that offer the potential for mixing ethnic groups.

It is difficult to carry out the type of research that would clearly identify what variables in the educational process affect prejudice. Few, if any, experiments dealing with this question are completely satisfactory. For example, it is not sufficient to demonstrate, as have some studies, that first-year university students are more prejudiced than those in their final year. Final-year students are three years older, more highly selected, and have had three more years of extra-curricular experience. As a matter of fact, the effect may simply be due to a higher failure or drop-out rate among the less tolerant. Better investigations take a longitudinal approach and follow the same individuals from one point in their educational career to a later one. These studies also reveal an increase in tolerance over time but, again, are unable to specify the precise variables that may account for the change. It might be due to increased knowledge, improved analytical ability, more heterogeneous social contacts, and so on. Nevertheless, we can state in a general way that education, inside or outside of the classroom, has a positive effect on the development of tolerance.

An extensive project conducted by Six (1989) emphasizes the importance of using more than one educational approach to modify prejudice. The purpose of the study was to reduce prejudice of German students towards Turkish students. To this end, two TV films were produced that showed both the positive and negative aspects of life for a Turkish girl and boy living in Germany. In addition, a teaching program was developed with similar goals to those of the films; that is, to present new information, teach different ways of social categorization, inform students about prejudice in general, and create positive emotional involvement. Students between the ages of ten and fifteen were assigned to five conditions: (1) films only, (2) soundtrack only, (3) teaching program only, (4) a shorter teaching program and the films, or (5) a no-treatment control group. Measures of prejudice were obtained over a ten-week period, beginning one week prior to treatment and then continuing immediately after treatment and three, six, and nine weeks later. All treatments resulted in short-term changes, but long-term change was significant only with the combined teaching and film program. It was also found that the more prejudiced a student had been the less the prejudice was reduced. In fact, the television conditions (video or audio only) had no effect on highly prejudiced students. It appears that pre-existing prej-

What are some of the variables that might explain the correlation between education and tolerance?

How does second-language learning promote more positive attitudes?

integrative motivation
Learning a language because it is part of a culture that is interesting.

instrumental motivation
Learning a language because it will be useful.

udice causes information to be devalued, distorted, and misinterpreted. The teaching program that prepared the students for the films reduced the negative influence of the pre-existing prejudice, and so the films became more effective.

Thus, films or teaching programs by themselves may be ineffective in combating prejudice, especially with high-prejudice individuals. However, a teaching program that reduces the likelihood of distortion or devaluation of a film's contents could make that film more effective.

In Canada, the relationship of second language learning to attitudes has also received attention as an education issue. Much of the research has been carried out by Lambert and his associates at McGill (e.g., Lambert et al.,1963; Gardner and Lambert, 1972). It has been found that individuals who have acquired a second language seem to have more positive attitudes towards other cultural groups than monolinguals *if* their initial orientation was **integrative** rather than **instrumental**. Individuals who learn a language for instrumental reasons do so because they think it will be useful to them, while those with an integrative approach perceive the language as one part of a culture that interests them. It has also been shown that anglophone parents with an integrative orientation have positive attitudes towards francophones, even though they may not know any representatives of that group (Gardner and Lambert, 1959).

The relationship of such attitudes and integrative motivation to competence in another language has been found to hold in locations as diverse as Maine, Louisiana, and Connecticut in the United States, as well as in the Philippines (Gardner, Gliksman and Smythe, 1978).

SELF-TEST QUESTIONS

SELF ? TEST

9. When the behaviour of the members of two different groups is changed because they have interacted with each other, it is called
a) integrative motivation
b) acculturation
c) scapegoating
d) re-fencing

10. Intergroup anxiety arises from
a) fear of negative psychological consequences for the self
b) fear of negative evaluations by in-group members
c) fear of negative evaluations by out-group members
d) all of the above

11. If a person learns a language because she thinks it will be useful, she is demonstrating
a) illusory correlation
b) instrumental motivation
c) integrative motivation
d) ethnocentrism

12. Which of the following is a consistent finding regarding education and prejudice?

a) as education increases, prejudice decreases

b) there is no relationship between level of education and prejudice

c) as education increases, prejudice increases

d) the less education a person has, the less prejudiced he or she will be

THE VICTIMS OF PREJUDICE—HOW WOULD YOU DEAL WITH IT?

Much has been written on how prejudice develops, is maintained, and how the targets of prejudice and discrimination are selected. Less attention has been devoted to the reactions of the victims of prejudice and discrimination. How do minority group members respond and how do they defend themselves? Over thirty years ago Gordon Allport (1954) identified more than fifteen possible consequences of being victimized. Among these are: withdrawal and passivity, clowning, militancy, aggression against own group, and self-hate. Allport also suggested that these reactions could be encompassed within two general categories: **intropunitive** and **extra-punitive.** Intropunitive defences are those that involve self-blame, while extrapunitive defences place the blame on others. Allport argues that minority group members who are intropunitive will be hostile to their own group, whereas those who are extrapunitive will be loyal to their own group and aggressive towards other groups.

Extending Allport's approach, Tajfel and Turner (1979) postulate three types of responses. The victimized can simply accept their situation with passivity and resignation (although not without resentment); they can try as individuals to break free and "make it" in society; or they can attempt collective action and improve the status of the group itself. Building on these alternatives, a five-stage model has been outlined showing how groups deal with prejudice and a disadvantaged position in society (Taylor and McKirnon, 1984). Notice that the model is attributional, and accounts for how the victimized may both interpret and respond to their situation:

(1) **Clearly stratified group relations.** This is a historical situation of deeply entrenched relationships of power and subordination between groups. The power difference is so clear and absolute as to be essentially unchallenged. In some cases, the subordinate group members react with self-hate (Allport, 1954), downgrading themselves as members of the "inferior" group and attributing their own inferior status to the fact of belonging to that group. Thus, in another era, blacks may have attributed their poverty to inherent racial inferiority and French Canadians to their inability to speak English, and women may have attributed restrictions in their lives to their "inability" to compete with men.

(2) **Emergence of an individualistic ideology.** A society that has become an industrialized economy places great value on education, skills, and achievement. In this "meritocracy" it becomes increasingly awkward to discriminate against whole groups as more focus is placed on the individual. How can such societies explain the persistence of status differences between groups? Attributions also shift from group membership in and of itself to the ability, effectiveness, and responsibility of individuals. Thus, if women do not gain their share of high-status jobs, it is not a result of their inherent characteristics as women, but of their lack of ability, motivation, or training. Disadvantaged group members perceive their situation in a similar light.

intropunitive defence
Putting the blame for one's situation on oneself.

extra-punitive defence
Putting the blame for one's situation on others.

What are the ways that victims of prejudice respond and defend themselves?

(3) Individual social mobility. Certain group members try to "pass," to be accepted into the society of the dominant group. Where possible, they may change their names, language, culture, or religion in order to penetrate the dominant group. Or they may accommodate the dominant norms in every way possible, though unable to shed the recognizable characteristics of race or sex. Success or failure has now become almost entirely a matter of personal characteristics, particularly among the exceptional members of the disadvantaged group who have some chance of success. Note that this situation implies an attributional conflict: a disadvantaged position is explained by group membership, yet an individual effort to succeed and "pass" provides an escape from the group.

(4) Consciousness raising. Of course, the dominant group "needs" a few successes from the out-group to support its ideology of individual responsibility and the myth of equal opportunity. Thus, some succeed through tokenism, but many more fail and the disadvantaged status of the group remains unchanged. Over time, attributions within this group shift again, as the majority of those who cannot be accepted and successful in society realize that the fault lies neither in their inherent characteristics as group members nor as individuals. It now becomes apparent that their status in society is an injustice, has been determined collectively, and can change only through collective action. Attribution for failure is attached to a group again, but now the in-group is blamed rather than the out-group.

(5) Competitive intergroup relations. Collective action by the disadvantaged group to improve their position can succeed only at a cost in power and privilege to the dominant group. Thus it will be resisted in some way, and a competitive relationship will endure until some sort of rough equality is obtained or until people in the group revert to individualistic striving. Notice an interesting divergence between attributions about the past and the future: "our" disadvantaged position was due primarily to "them" but "our" future success must depend on "us."

The theorists argue that groups proceed through these stages in sequence, coming ultimately to the point at which self-blame is futile but collective action is necessary. In terms of attributions, the implications of prejudice are particularly crucial. Recall the self-serving bias, in which individuals attribute their own successes to themselves and their failures to external factors. Because our identity as individuals is influenced so powerfully by our identity as members of groups—religious, ethnic, national, sexual—we can also conceive of a group-serving bias, in which we attribute successes to positive group characteristics and failures to such external factors as discrimination.

It is of interest that the members of different ethnic groups report experiencing varying amounts of prejudice and discrimination. Dion (1989) compared the experiences of six ethnic groups in Toronto: Chinese, Indian, Italian, Jewish, Portuguese, and West Indian. He found that the people from India perceived the most prejudice and discrimination, followed by the West Indians. The Chinese reported some but considerably fewer problems. On the other hand, the Portuguese and Italians claimed that they experienced little prejudice and discrimination. Jewish respondents reported prejudice but, unlike the Indians and West Indians, were satisfied with their life in Toronto. As Dion points out, Toronto can be a very different place depending on the ethnic group to which you belong.

SEXISM

Sexism is the term we use to describe prejudice based on gender. Among the many groups experiencing prejudice and discrimination, the largest by far is composed of women. In Canada, women have struggled long and hard to achieve the far from satisfactory status they have today. In many other parts of the world progress has been minimal or non-existent, and women continue to be relegated to the inferior roles they have occupied throughout history (see Table 6-3). Prejudice and discrimination towards women are often subtle and rarely accompanied by the overt hostility that is often directed at other out-groups.

In a majority of the societies of the world, being female means to be perceived as less competent and to have lower status than men. Canada is no exception. As Charlotte Whitton, a former Mayor of Ottawa, commented, "Whatever women do they must do twice as well as men to be thought half as good. Luckily, this is not difficult."

Among the many social stereotypes maintained about women (by both men and women) are those pertaining to *role assignments*. Certain occupations are sex-typed (see Table 6-3). Women make up the overwhelming majority of restaurant servers, telephone operators, secretaries, nurses, babysitters, dental hygienists, librarians, physiotherapists, and elementary and kindergarten teachers, while most of the lawyers, dentists, truck drivers, accountants, secondary school teachers, janitors, and industrial engineers are men (Greenglass, 1982).

In 1994, 70 percent of all employed women were in teaching, nursing, health-related occupations, clerical positions, or sales and service occupations. This compared with 31 percent of employed men. Similarly, levels within occupations are often available to men and women on an unequal basis. We find few women in positions of power in industry or commerce, even though women may be equally or over-represented in the lower ranks (Kanter, 1975). For instance, 73 percent of Canadian bank employees are women. However, these women, as in many other sectors of Canadian business, soon hit the "glass ceiling." They can see the available prospects, but biased attitudes prevent them from achieving their goals. There has been some improvement, however, in several professional fields. In 1994, 43 percent of those employed in management and administration were women (up from 29 percent in 1982). Women made up

"Are you sure it doesn't contravene the Sex Discrimination Act, Harry?"

What does it mean when we say that certain occupations are sex-typed?

FIGURE 6-3 Ethiopian emperor Haile Selassie's edict of 1935, issued during the invasion of the Italians.

> Addis Ababa, Issued by His Highness Haile Salassie in 1935
> Conscription Act.
> All men able to carry a spear go to Addis Ababa.
> Every married man will bring his wife to cook and wash for him.
> Every unmarried man will bring any unmarried woman he can find to cook and wash for him.
> Women with babies, the blind, and those too aged to carry a spear are excused.
> Anyone who qualified for battle and is found at home after receiving this order will be hanged.

SOURCE: Espy, 1975

TABLE 6-3 The occupational segregation of women

Complete list of female-dominated occupations	Partial list of male-dominated occupations
Supervisors (Nursing)	Electrical Engineers
Nurses	Civil Engineers
Nursing Assistants	Mechanical Engineers
Dental Hygienists	Police Officers
Dieticians and Nutritionists	Industrial Mechanics
Supervisors (Secretaries and Typists)	Auto Mechanics
Secretaries	Construction Electricians
Typists, Clerk-Typists	Electrical Equipment Repair
Receptionists	Plumbers and Pipefitters
Telephone Operators	Carpenters
Cashiers and Tellers	Machinists
Sewing Machine Operators	Welders
Babysitters	Farmers
Domestic Servants	Truck Drivers
	Construction Labourers

SOURCE: Statistics Canada, Census 1991, special tabulations

32 percent of all doctors and dentists in 1994 (up from 18 percent in 1982). They also made up 57 percent of the professionals employed in the social services and religion (up from 43 percent in 1982). In areas of natural sciences, engineering, and mathematics, women are very much a minority (19 percent in 1994). Among other things, it has been documented that only one percent of women engineers hold executive positions in Canadian companies. Few women enter engineering at university and few of those who graduate achieve senior positions. (See Figure 6-4 and Table 6-4.)

Broverman and her colleagues (1972) define the sex-role stereotype of women as including the perception that women are less competent, less independent, less objective, and less logical than men. On the other hand, men are perceived as lacking interpersonal sensitivity, warmth, and expressiveness in comparison with women. They also point out that masculine traits are often perceived as more desirable than feminine traits. If these perceptions become incorporated into the self-image of women, it is not surprising that many women have a negative self-concept and low self-esteem, making them more vulnerable to the "self-fulfilling prophecy" syndrome. For instance, they may reduce their aspiration levels and remain satisfied with positions far below their real ability and competence. And even when women do well, they may not receive appropriate credit.

That people are still influenced by traditional sex roles is supported by the work of Simpson, McCarrey and Edwards (1987) who studied supervisors in a large organization and found that those with traditional attitudes towards women judged the women they supervised as less able than men to: (1) autonomously direct their subordinates, (2) assist in the career development of subordinates, and (3) effectively monitor the day-to-day performance of their subordinates. Moreover,

FIGURE 6-4 Equal Opportunity?

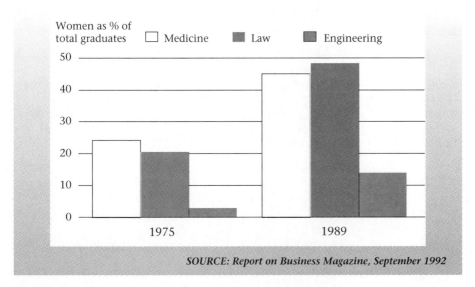

SOURCE: Report on Business Magazine, September 1992

these supervisors were unwilling to assign technical, high-profile projects to women. Along the same lines, Dion (1987) and Dion and Schuller (1991) examined how the titles *Ms., Mrs., Miss,* and *Mr.* were perceived by men and women. He found that women who use the title *Ms.* were stereotyped as being more achievement-oriented, socially assertive, and dynamic, but also less warm. Also the stereotypes associated with the *Ms.* label included those of a successful middle manager, whereas those associated with the traditionally labelled person did not.

There is no doubt that the situation is changing, although more slowly than desirable. Some evidence that attitudes towards women—and out-groups in general—may not have changed as much as expected has been presented by Bechtold, Naccarato and Zanna (1986). They suggest that although overt discrimination has declined in Canada, it has not been accompanied by a parallel decline in underlying prejudice. Current social norms are such that tolerance and goodwill is expected but, under certain conditions, prejudicial attitudes may surface. To test this proposition Bechtold et al. (1986) asked male and female subjects to act as personnel officers and make hiring decisions based on the résumés of either male or female applicants for a marketing position. Some of the subjects were allowed ample time to arrive at a decision, while others were placed under

TABLE 6-4 Women need not apply

Job Responsibility	Number of Women Employed	Women as Percentage of Total
Senior Supervisor	100	3
Senior Manager	66	2
Executive	41	1
Full-time Professor	54	2

SOURCE: Report on Busines Magazine, September 1992

considerable time pressure. It was found that those subjects under time pressure discriminated more against female applicants than did subjects who had no time constraints. In addition, the men discriminated against female applicants more than the women did.

The purpose of personnel selection is to choose the best possible applicant for the job. Therefore, rigid stereotyping on the basis of sex (or age, or ethnic origin, or any other category) is not only an injustice to the job applicant who is victimized, but is even detrimental to the interests of those who may not hire or promote the best available person. Research using the concepts and methods of social perception and cognition has shed light on the problem, which, it is hoped, will lead to better employment decisions.

SELF-TEST QUESTIONS

13. Women are most highly represented in which of the following jobs?
a) librarians
b) lawyers
c) engineers
d) all of the above

14. Intropunitive defences against prejudice involve _____ while extrapunitive defences involve _____.
a) withdrawal; self-hate
b) militancy; aggression against in-group members
c) self-blame; blame of others
d) clowning; withdrawal

15. Dion's (1989) study of six ethnic groups in Toronto had the following results
a) Indians felt the least prejudice
b) Chinese reported few problems
c) all groups felt severe discrimination
d) none of the groups reported any prejudice

SUMMARY

(1) Prejudice is a positive or negative attitude towards perceived differences of characteristics that is unjustly generalized to all the members of a group. Like other attitudes it has three components: cognitive, affective, and behavioural.

(2) Stereotypes are cognitions, or beliefs, about the members of other groups. They are usually overgeneralizations and are often inaccurate.

(3) Stereotypes can change depending on changes in social conditions and changes in the relationships between members of different groups.

(4) Those stereotypes that have some validity may arise from the operation of the "self-fulfilling prophecy" and the situational pressure that prejudice creates to make stereotypes come true.

(5) The behavioural component of prejudice is called discrimination and, in its more extreme form, racism. While laws have been enacted making discrimination illegal, many subtle forms, such as biased hiring practices, still exist.

(6) Innate fear of the unusual or the unfamiliar may be a primitive basis for prejudice. The acquisition of prejudice begins in the home when the child is about three years old. Parents, teachers, peers, and the media all contribute at various times to this process.

(7) Some individuals who have been raised in a certain way are called authoritarian personalities. They are likely to be prejudiced and ethnocentric and may be hostile.

(8) One manifestation of pent-up hostility is called scapegoating, and results in the blaming of out-groups for the frustration experienced by the individual.

(9) Under the appropriate circumstances prejudice can be reduced by intergroup contact. Unfortunately, intergroup anxiety often prevents people from interacting with the members of other groups.

(10) Acculturation refers to the changes in values, attitudes, and behaviours that occur when groups come into direct contact.

(11) A higher level of education is associated with increased tolerance.

(12) The victims of prejudice may react in a number of ways. These include aggression, changes in self-esteem, changes in group allegiance, or modification of the strength of positive or negative stereotypes held about one's own group.

(13) Sexism is usually directed at women and results, among other things, in differential treatment in employment.

FOR REVIEW

In this chapter we examine the issue of _____(1), which is a positive or negative _____(2) based on a distortion of fact. _____(3) make up the cognitive component of prejudice. When these are held by many people we call them _____(4).

Our beliefs can also be abstract or _____(5); that is, we believe that a group threatens the social values of our society.

Stereotypes occur for many reasons; for example when people _____(6) the relationship between a particular group and a behaviour it is known as an illusory correlation. When minority groups believe the stereotypes about them and then act in a way to make them come true, they have demonstrated the power of the _____(7) If a person is prejudiced her beliefs and stereotypes will _____(8).

_____(9) is the belief that one's own culture is superior. This can lead to _____(10), which is prejudice put into action. When this operates at the level of laws, or rules that exclude particular groups, it is known as _____(11). However, studies show that when people feel secure and comfortable they feel more positive towards other groups. This is known as the _____(12). However, not all tolerance is real; people practise _____(13) when they act in a way that is more tolerant than they really are.

For the most part, prejudice is a learned behaviour. _____(14) conditioning means that we learn from the consequences of our behaviour. When children learn by watching what other people do it is called _____(15). When parents identified as having an _____(16) personality (rigid, conventional, and often prejudiced) model behaviour for their children it will likely reinforce prejudice.

Prejudice should be modified when we make contact with other groups, however when a person doesn't conform to the stereotype for her group it is easier to ____(17) than to change the stereotype. Studies show that fear of negative consequences from the interaction with an out-group leads to ____(18). Education seems to hold a part of the answer, for the more educated a person is the less ____(19) she will be. There also seems to be a link between second language learners and tolerance. This is especially true if your motivation is ____(20).

Three of the ways that victims of prejudice cope are: ____(21) the situation; try to break free, perhaps by changing their name; or attempt collective action.

ISSUES AND ACTIVITIES

1. Over a three-day period monitor the ads on TV. Try to watch at different times of the day. Keep a log of the subject matter and who is in the ads. Watch for visible minorities, women, or the elderly. How are they portrayed? Have you noticed any examples of prejudice? In preparation for this project you should read the chapter on racism in the media in Henry et al. (1995), *The Colour of Democracy: Racism in Canadian Society.*

2. Make a clipping file over a period of weeks. Choose magazine or newspaper articles that deal with any kind of prejudice or discrimination. Do you see any pattern to this? Make a mini-presentation to your classmates, sharing your findings and observations.

3. Work with a partner to come up with a program to improve understanding between the different racial or ethnic groups at your college. You might share these ideas with your class. Put together a program with input from all class members, and present it to the school.

4. View the video *The Sterilization of Leilani Muir* (NFB, 1996). Using the information presented on prejudice and discrimination in the text, examine the experience of the young people in the film. To what extent do stereotypes play a role in their treatment?

• FURTHER READING

ABOUD, F. (1988). *Children and prejudice.* Oxford: Basil Blackwell. An account of the developmental aspects of intolerance that culminates in a new social-cognitive theory of prejudice.

ALLPORT, G.W. (1954). *The nature of prejudice.* Reading: Addison-Wesley. This classic account of the development and maintenance of prejudice is still relevant today.

ALTEMEYER, B. (1988). *Enemies of freedom: Understanding right-wing authoritarianism.* San Francisco: Jossey-Bass. This very readable award-winning book outlines the results of a long-term research program and discusses the role of parents, religion, and education in the development of authoritarian attitudes.

BERRY, J.W. and LAPONCE, J. (Eds.) (1993). *Multiculturalism in Canada: A second review.* Toronto: University of Toronto Press. A detailed exposition of the numerous aspects of multiculturalism in Canada.

GARDNER, R.C. and KALIN, R. (Eds.) (1981). *A Canadian social psychology of ethnic relations.* Toronto: Methuen. A review from a variety of perspectives of the cognitions, attitudes, and perceptions of ethnic groups in Canada.

GREENGLASS, E. (1982). *A world of difference: Gender roles in perspective.* Toronto: Wiley. A general discussion concerning women in today's society.

KATZ, P. (Ed.) (1976). *Towards the elimination of racism.* New York: Pergamon. A review of sociological and psychological research and theory concerned with the acquisition and elimination of prejudice.

LEVITT, C. and SHAFFIR, W. (1987). *The riot at Christie Pits.* Toronto: Lester & Orpen Dennys. Fascinating account of an anti-Semitic race riot that took place in Toronto in 1933.

TAYLOR, D.M. and MOGHADDEM, F.M. (1987). *Theories of intergroup relations: International social psychological perspectives.* New York: Praeger. Survey of contributions by social psychologists to our understanding of phenomena such as race riots, labour disputes, sexism, religious intolerance, and social prejudice.

SUGGESTED WEBLINKS

Prejudice

Access to Justice Network. Under "What's New" look for June 14/96, human rights section.

> http://www.acjnet.org/acjeng.html

Culture

Black Cultural Centre for Nova Scotia. The Centre is located in Halifax County and was officially opened in 1983. This site provides a history of Africans in Nova Scotia; a map of black communities in Nova Scotia; documents pertaining to the African community in Nova Scotia; and links to related sites on the World Wide Web.

> http://www.nstn.ca/bccns/index.html

Aboriginal Peoples of Canada

> http://kuhttp.cc.ukans.edu/~marc/geography/northan/canada/canada.html

International Association for Cross-Cultural Psychology
http://www.fit.edu/ft-orgs/iaccp/

ANSWERS TO SELF-TEST QUESTIONS

1. b; 2. c; 3. d; 4. a; 5. c; 6. b; 7. d; 8. d; 9. b; 10. d; 11. b; 12. a; 13. a; 14. c; 15. b.

ANSWERS TO FOR REVIEW

1. prejudice; 2. attitudes; 3. Stereotypes; 4. consensual; 5. symbolic; 6. overestimate; self-fulfilling prophecy; 8. agree; 9. Ethnocentrism; 10. discrimination; 11. systemic; 12. multicultural hypothesis; 13. reverse discrimination; 14. Instrumental; 15. modelling; 16. authoritarian; 17. re-fence; 18. intergroup anxiety; 19. prejudiced; 20. integrative; 21. accept.

INTERPERSONAL ATTRACTION AND INTERPERSONAL RELATIONSHIPS

Marriage is popular because it combines the maximum of temptation with the maximum of opportunity.

George Bernard Shaw

And in the sweetness of friendship, let there be laughter, and sharing of pleasures.
Kahlil Gibran

■ LEARNING OUTCOMES

1. An understanding of how attachment develops in infancy and how our need to be with others is influenced by certain circumstances.

2. Knowledge about the influence of physical proximity and physical attractiveness of an individual on interpersonal attraction.

3. An understanding of how and why attraction develops during interaction as a result of perceived similarity, and of how reinforcing (rewarding) that interaction is to the person.

4. Knowledge about the role of self-disclosure and fairness (equity) in the development of intimacy.

5. Critical evaluation of such commonplace sayings as "opposites attract."

6. An appreciation for the value of social psychological theory and research in understanding relationship problems such as jealousy, loneliness, shyness, and reasons for the break-up of relationships.

■ FOR REFLECTION

• Why do people want and need to be with others?

• How do we know whether we like or dislike someone?

• Do "opposites attract"?

• What is intimacy? Are men and women different in their perception of it?

• Why do such problems as loneliness, jealousy, and divorce occur?

■ CHAPTER OUTLINE

It had been, observed Her Majesty, Queen Elizabeth II, an "annus horribilis." In that horrible year of 1992 the intimate relationships of members of the Queen's immediate family had become the subject of intense public scrutiny and gossip. Prince Andrew had separated from his wife Sarah, the Duchess of York, who was photographed in a less-than-dignified state with her new romantic interest. Princess Anne had divorced her husband and subsequently remarried, something that, fifty years earlier, had led to the downfall of a King. Above all, the heir to the throne, Charles, Prince of Wales, had separated from Princess Diana amid much rumour and speculation.

Why was there so much interest in this, the stuff of soap operas? Clearly, it reflected the importance and glamour of the participants. Perhaps it also reflected the fascination of many with the fact that even the rich and famous are not immune to problems in their lives. It is not surprising that artists, writers, philosophers, and religious leaders have long been interested in the factors responsible for people's attraction to one another. However, only in recent years have scientific methods been applied to the study of relationships.

This chapter begins with a brief discussion of the very human tendency to affiliate with other people. While we are not the only social "animals," our affiliative behaviour is characterized by the most complex patterns of communication and self-consciousness. Therefore, it is important to consider our selectivity—why we choose to affiliate with some people and not others. This leads to the discussion of attraction, a positive evaluation or attitude held by one person about another. Another feature of selectivity is that we choose different people as different types of affiliates. We choose some as colleagues, others as casual friends, and still others as close friends or lovers. Thus it is important to consider attraction in the context of various types of relationships.

While affiliation, attraction, and relationships are important to us all, the course of human relationships does not always run smoothly. In the latter part of this chapter we discuss, from the perspective of social psychology, the individual characteristics of jealousy, shyness, and loneliness, which cause problems in relationships. We will also examine the dissolution of close relationships.

ATTACHMENT AND AFFILIATION

social attachment A state of intense emotional dependence on someone.

What are the main styles of attachment?

Social attachment begins in early infancy and becomes particularly evident when the child learns to distinguish familiar people, especially the mother, and to respond to them in a special way. The infant smiles and vocalizes to the attachment figure, shows distress when she leaves, and is obviously comforted by her. Later, the child forms other attachments to such familiar caregivers as the father, grandparents, regular babysitter, or close family friends.

Early attachment experience may affect one's relationships later in life. Three general types of attachment have been observed in infancy and identified and measured in adulthoood (Hazan and Shaver, 1987). These are avoidant, anxious/ambivalent, and secure. An avoidant attachment style is characterized by the person feeling uncomfortable when too close or intimate with someone. A person with an anxious/ambivalent style feels that others are not as close as one would wish, and may cling to one's partner so much that the partner is driven away. The securely attached person finds interpersonal closeness to be relatively easy and comfortable. This type of person reacts in a more supportive way to his or her partner in an anxiety-provoking situation (Simpson, Rholes and

Nelligan, 1992). Hazan and Shaver and others (e.g. Shaver and Brennan, 1992) find that these styles are related to such personality characteristics as openness to experience, warmth, anxiety, and neuroticism.

Social affiliation is extremely important throughout our lives. Research shows that we spend much of our time interacting with other people. Csikszentmihalyi and Figurski (1982) found that adults spend 71 percent and adolescents 74 percent of their time in situations involving other people. Laboratory research has also identified some of the factors that tend to increase or decrease affiliation behaviour. Not surprisingly, people prefer to be alone when they do embarrassing things (e.g. adult males sucking on rubber nipples or baby bottles). Conversely, people prefer to be with others when they are anxious (Schachter, 1959). When people are uncertain how to react, they turn to others in the same situation as a source of information and to compare their feelings. Sometimes people prefer to be with others who have already gone through a difficult experience similar to one they are approaching. For example, in one study (Kulik and Mahler, 1989), patients about to undergo a coronary bypass expressed a stronger preference for a roommate who was recovering from the surgery than for one who was waiting for it. The recovering patient can provide reassurance to the one awaiting surgery.

Affiliation can be vital to our well-being. Indeed, a lack of satisfying and supportive relationships can be hazardous to our health. (See Chapter 15.)

social affiliation
Association with others.

What types of situations increase and decrease our desire to be with others?

INTERPERSONAL ATTRACTION

There are many kinds of attraction. We may enjoy a casual conversation with the person beside us on an airplane and leave it at that. We may be attracted to a person as a friend but not as a lover, as a tennis partner but not as a close friend, as a colleague at work but not as a companion. Of the thousands and thousands of people who pass through our lives, we become aware of relatively few, have contact with fewer, form relationships with fewer still, and have intimate relationships with even fewer of those. We are often quite content with many of our casual relationships and have no desire to transform them into more intimate ones.

Much of the research on **interpersonal attraction** has emphasized attraction to a stranger. It has been concerned with why one person will like another and evaluate him or her positively. Other research has focused on the qualities that seem desirable at different levels of relationship. The qualities we seek in a casual acquaintance or co-worker are not necessarily the ones we desire in an intimate friend or lover. Social psychologists have studied what these qualities are at various stages in a relationship. They have investigated how long-term relationships begin, develop, and succeed or fail over time.

In this section we will look at what determines the initial attraction between people. We will discuss intimacy in relationships later in the chapter.

interpersonal attraction
Factors that bring people together in the beginning stages of a relationship.

PROXIMITY

While we are more likely to interact with those who are attractive, there must exist the opportunity for the first contact. **Geographic proximity** or **propinquity** substantially increases the likelihood of people meeting and developing relationships.

proximity Physical closeness increases the likelihood of repeated exposures, which facilitates attraction.

A classic study by Festinger, Schachter and Back (1950) provides a good example of the effect of proximity on establishing relationships. The site of this study was the graduate student apartments at Massachusetts Institute of Technology. A diagram of a typical apartment building is shown in Figure 7-1. Notice that the building has two storeys, ten apartments, and a number of stairways. Results showed that friends were most likely to be next-door neighbours, and that the possibility of friendships decreased as apartments became more distant. Also, people living in centrally located apartments (number 8 and number 3) had more friends than the residents of all the other apartments. People living on the first floor near the stairs (number 1 and number 5) had more friends on the second floor than those who lived farther away from the stairs.

Why are we so favourably disposed to those in close physical proximity? First, proximity increases opportunities for interaction, which in turn give people the chance to notice their similarities and the pleasures of the interaction. Proximity also increases the anticipation of interaction, and we generally tend to be pleasant to the people whom we expect to see frequently. Contrary to the old saying, "familiarity breeds contempt," research shows that proximity promotes attraction more often than it leads to animosity (Zajonc, 1970; Moreland and Zajonc, 1982).

PHYSICAL ATTRACTIVENESS

It seems superficial, even undemocratic, to judge a person by his or her physical features. Common sense tells us that "beauty is only skin deep" and that "you can't judge a book by its cover." Yet, in affluent societies, a large amount of time and money is spent on hair, clothing, make-up, personal fitness, and other aspects of physical appearance. Furthermore, research clearly shows that physical attractiveness is an important determinant of liking (Berscheid and Walster,1974a; Curran and Lippold, 1975).

While people might prefer the most attractive friends and lovers, not everyone can engage such partners. Thus, it is not surprising that pairs of friends and lovers tend to be roughly similar in physical attractiveness (Cash and Derlega, 1978; Murstein, 1972; Feingold, 1988). This tendency to choose partners similar to oneself in attractiveness is called the **matching hypothesis**. A review of the literature shows that matching occurs most strongly among romantic partners, less so among male friends, and least among female friends (Feingold, 1988).

It is important to realize that attractiveness is not an absolute. Within any given culture and age group there exists a high level of agreement regarding

How does proximity affect interpersonal attraction?

What part does physical attractiveness play in attraction?

matching hypothesis
People are attracted to others who are similar in physical attractiveness.

FIGURE 7-1 **Design of a typical apartment building**

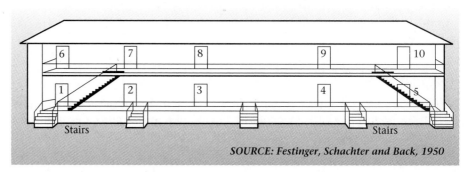

SOURCE: Festinger, Schachter and Back, 1950

what constitutes physical attractiveness (Berscheid and Walster, 1974a). However, there is great variation in opinions as to what constitutes beauty among different cultures and subcultures, as well as within cultures at different times. For instance, the concept of beauty is not the same in Kenya as it is in New Guinea, and both differ from that of Canada. A quick review of famous art in Western civilization shows that the ideal of feminine beauty has been a fully developed figure during some periods in history and a very slim figure during others. The conditions under which the judgment is made also can be important. For instance, Kenrick and Gutierres (1980) found that males who had just watched an episode of a once-popular TV program, *Charlie's Angels,* judged a female of average attractiveness lower than did other males who had not seen the program. Evidently, even an attractive person seems less so in comparison with a glamorous star, putting most of us at an unfair disadvantage. Situational factors can also influence how we evaluate physical attractiveness. For instance, as closing time approaches in bars, patrons' ratings of overall attractiveness of other patrons rises (Pennebaker et al., 1979; Gladue and Delaney, 1990).

Why is physical appearance an important determinant of liking? It seems that in Western societies people believe that physical attractiveness indicates desirable personality characteristics. In one study, Dion, Berscheid and Walster (1972) presented male and female students with photographs of very attractive, average, and unattractive people. The students were asked to rate the individuals in the photographs on a number of personality characteristics. The attractive person was rated as having more desirable personality characteristics and a higher occupational status. Students also said attractive people were more likely to be happily married and content in their social life and occupation. A great deal of research was generated by this study. Eagly et al. (1991) reviewed all these studies and found that we stereotype attractive people as socially competent (popular, likeable, sociable), and to a lesser extent as well-adjusted and intellectually competent. However, physical attractiveness does not affect our judgments of integrity (honesty, faithfulness) or adjustment (e.g. high self-esteem, happiness, maturity).

SIMILARITY

Common sense tells us that "birds of a feather flock together" and that "opposites attract." Which is the case? Although "opposites" may attract in some relationships, research shows that in most situations we tend to like people who are similar to ourselves in attitudes, values, and interests.

In an early study, transfer students to a U.S. university were offered free housing in return for their participation in research (Newcomb, 1961). None of the students knew each other before arriving on campus. On arrival, and at intervals throughout the semester, they were asked to fill out a questionnaire that assessed: (1) their values and attitudes regarding religion, politics, and other matters; (2) their perception of each other's attitudes; and (3) how much they liked each other. The findings showed a strong relationship between friendship and perceived similarity in attitudes and values. Results also showed that perceptions of similarity change as a relationship develops. In the beginning, friends assumed that they were more similar than they really were. Over time the friendships changed, so that by the end of the study actual similarity in attitudes was related to friendship.

In a series of well-controlled experiments, Byrne (1971) investigated the relationship between attraction to a stranger and perceived similarity in attitudes. Subjects filled out attitude questionnaires, and were then given a second ques-

Do "birds of a feather flock together" or do "opposites attract"?

similarity People are attracted to others who have similar attitudes and values.

tionnaire and told that it had been filled out by another subject. The subject was told to look over the responses on this second questionnaire and to indicate the degree of their attraction or liking of this person. In this artificial, controlled situation, other factors relevant to liking such as physical appearance, status, or personality were not present. The results showed that attraction to the stranger increased as the proportion of similar attitudes increased. This has become known as Byrne's law: attraction to a stranger is a function of the proportion of similar attitudes.

LIMITS TO THE SIMILARITY-ATTRACTION LAW

Similarities in attitudes, values, and interests generally promote attraction. But how does achievement influence our feelings towards another person? Research has focused on the situation in which someone performs better than we do on some task, game, or artistic endeavour. How we will react depends upon how important performance is to our own sense of self-worth and how close we are to the other person. If someone "outdoes" us in a task we perceive as important, the closer we are to that person the greater the threat and the worse we will feel. We may find that person less attractive. However, if someone close to us outperforms us on a task that is of little importance to us, we will feel better since we can bask in his or her reflected glory. In this way our attraction is strengthened (Tesser, Millar and Moore, 1988).

Personality differences also influence the extent to which people are attracted to others. For example, friends tend to be more similar to each other in their self-concepts, and this similarity relates to how much the two talk to each other (Deutsch et al. 1991). In another study, Carli, Ganley and Pierce-Otay (1991) found that satisfaction with one's roommate in university was related to similarities in such personal characteristics as leadership, sociability, self-control, tolerance, and physical attractiveness. To some extent, high and low self-monitors appear to be guided by different kinds of information in arriving at an impression of "similarity." High self-monitors (people who are very sensitive to the subtle responses observed in others in evaluating their own behaviour) tend to choose romantic partners on the basis of physical attractiveness, and friends on the basis of similarity in preferences for recreational activities. Low self-monitors, on the other hand, tend to be guided more by similarities in personality traits and attitudes in their relationships (Glick, DeMorest and Hotze, 1988; Jamieson, Lydon and Zanna, 1987).

REINFORCEMENT AND ATTRACTION

We like people who reward us, who say nice things, and do good things for us. Indeed, some theorists believe that reinforcement underlies all attraction. We like someone with similar attitudes because it is rewarding to have someone agree with us. We like someone who is physically attractive because it is rewarding to be with and to be seen with such a desirable person.

Byrne and Clore (1970) argue that we are attracted to people whose presence is rewarding to us, even if we do not consciously attribute the reward to that person. This is known as the **reinforcement-affect model of attraction**. (The model is presented in Figure 7-2.) Direct rewards include the tangible reinforcers we receive as a consequence of being with someone, such as attention, gifts, and opportunities. Indirect rewards involve the reinforcement we receive just by associating with a person. For example, subjects were given false feedback

What kinds of reinforcement influence attraction?

reinforcement-affect model People are attracted to others who are associated with events or stimuli that arouse positive feelings.

FIGURE 7-2 Reinforcement-affect model of attraction

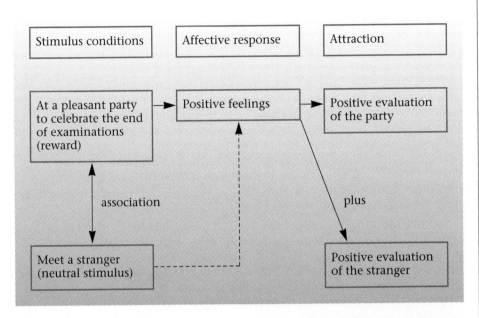

on a personality test they had completed. Half were informed that the test showed many strong, positive characteristics, while the other half were told that the test revealed many personal problems and inadequacies. (Of course subjects were later informed and reassured about the deception.) Then each subject met a stranger in the waiting room. Those who had received the positive feedback indicated greater attraction to this stranger than subjects who had received negative feedback. Those who received the positive feedback associated the positive emotions with the stranger and consequently evaluated him or her more positively.

Of course, we may become attracted to a person in unpleasant circumstances, as indicated in the photograph. People who survived the wartime bombardment of London recall the intense attraction that often developed during that time. Affiliation with others who share stressful circumstances can bring its own rewards.

We may become attracted to a person in the midst of an unpleasant situation.

The mere amount of reinforcement may not be sufficient to account for attraction. Aronson and Linder (1965) show that a gain or loss of positive expression or liking from another is a more potent source of reward or punishment

179

than is constant praise or criticism. In an experiment involving a complicated series of explanations and scenarios, subjects heard themselves being evaluated by a confederate on seven different occasions during the study. In one condition, the confederate was constantly positive about the subject, while in another the confederate was constantly negative. In the third condition, the confederate was initially negative but gradually became more positive about the subject (the "gain" condition). For a fourth group of subjects the confederate began with a positive evaluation and gradually become more negative ("loss" condition). The subjects were then asked to indicate the degree to which they were attracted to the confederate. Needless to say, subjects liked the person who liked them and disliked the person who evaluated them negatively. More importantly, the confederate was liked more in the gain condition than in the constant positive condition and disliked more in the loss condition than in the constant negative condition. Additional research suggests that the gain effect tends to be stronger than the loss effect (Clore, Wiggins and Itkin, 1975).

equity principle *Outcomes received in a relationship are proportional to contributions to it.*

Another limit to the reinforcement effect is represented by the principle of **equity** or fairness in our social relations (Walster, Walster and Berscheid, 1978). While we want rewarding relationships, we also want to feel that we're neither exploited nor taking unfair advantage of others. Thus, situations in which we feel that we are being excessively rewarded by someone can be very uncomfortable. Indeed, people sometimes react quite negatively to generosity from others, particularly if they are unable to reciprocate or if it implies a dependency or incompetence on their part. For example, in one study, subjects from Sweden, Japan, and the United States played a gambling game (Gergen, Ellsworth, Maslach and Seipel, 1975) that was rigged. At a crucial moment another player gave them ten chips, which saved them from bankruptcy and eventually allowed them to win. Regardless of the culture, the other player was better liked if he or she asked for the ten chips back than if he or she wanted no repayment or repayment with exorbitant interest. Findings such as these may explain in part why individuals who receive welfare and nations that receive aid may not always respond with gratitude and good feelings (Chapter 9).

SELF-TEST QUESTIONS

1. In general, when fearful, people seek to be
a) alone
b) with others who are not in the same situation
c) with others who are in the same situation
d) with others who know less than they do

2. The study of friendships within the student apartment buildings showed that those who became friends were most likely to be
a) similar
b) similar in their interests
c) similar in their values
d) similar in their attitudes
e) next-door neighbours

3. Propinquity is a determinant of attraction because it provides

a) more opportunities for interaction

b) increased anticipation of interaction

c) the mere exposure effect

d) all of the above

e) none of the above

4. Newcomb's study of how friendships developed among students in a residence highlights the role of

a) similarity

b) complementarity

c) propinquity

d) physical attractiveness

e) money

INTIMACY AND CLOSE RELATIONSHIPS

According to Levinger and Snoek (1972), an intimate relationship is one in which the two people are to some extent interdependent, and assume some responsibility for the satisfaction and well-being of the other. To a considerable degree, the relationship becomes free of external norms and rules. The individuals have their own understanding of the "rules" of the relationship. They have developed a sense of "us," versus "you" and "I." Self-disclosure is fundamental to this kind of a relationship, and communication is enhanced.

SELF-DISCLOSURE AND COMMUNICATION

The development of a relationship involves "getting to know" the other person, which obviously depends on the willingness of the person to allow this to happen. People will reveal more about themselves to people they like than to those they dislike (Chaiken and Derlega, 1974). Sometimes others will increase their liking for us if we offer them some interesting personal information. However, strangers may be repelled if we are overly intimate. In such cases, intermediate levels of disclosure create a more favourable impression (Cozby, 1973). Within certain limits, personal revelations are likely to be reciprocated (Taylor and Belgrave, 1986). Studies by Rubin (1975, 1976) indicate, however, that if too much is revealed, the other person becomes suspicious and is likely to become less, rather than more, open. The **reciprocity norm** is powerful in human affairs: we try to keep the "books balanced," whether it be Christmas cards or personal information. However, each of us has a limit beyond which it would be too costly, painful, or anxiety-provoking to reciprocate (Altman, 1973; Chaiken and Derlega, 1974).

It is commonly assumed that females disclose more than males. Is this a reality, or a stereotype of the "uncommunicative male"? In a review of 205 published studies, Dindia and Allen (1992) report that females tend to disclose slightly more than males. However, this tendency is moderated by several important factors. In particular, disclosure by both genders occurs more to a female than to a male partner. In addition, when the target person has a relationship with the discloser (friend, parent, spouse), females disclose significantly more than males. However, males disclose as much as females to a stranger. Although research results demonstrate some gender-related differences in communica-

self-disclosure The act of revealing intimate information about oneself to another person.

reciprocity norm People match their partner's intimacy level in self-disclosure.

What part does self-disclosure play in developing intimacy?

BOX 7-1

GENDER DIFFERENCES IN INTIMATE COMMUNICATION

There are gender differences in styles of communication (see Chapter 3), at least in the United States, where most of the studies have been done. In her review of the research, Sharon Brehm (1985) summarizes the important differences in the context of relationships:

(1) Women tend to be more skillful at both sending and receiving non-verbal messages and in communicating warmth or comforting messages.

(2) Men tend to communicate more calmly, to compromise, and to act on feelings of empathy.

(3) Women tend to be more negative and emotional during conflict and to send "double messages" (e.g. smiling warmly while telling him how terrible he is).

(4) Men tend to communicate without appropriate emotional expressiveness.

It is necessary to be cautious about these findings. First, like most gender differences, we are reporting mean differences between two overlapping distributions; there are many calm, even cold, women and many expressive, even occasionally hysterical men; behaviour can also vary considerably across situations. Second, the results may reflect the cultural stereotype of expressive women and practical men in two ways: people may perceive themselves and others as acting in these ways even if they are not; and the self-fulfilling prophecy may cause men and women (and boys and girls) to act in a way that is expected. However, studies of early infant responses suggest the possibility of an inherent, biological basis for these differences (Haviland and Malatesta, 1981). All of these factors probably play a role, and it may never be possible to disentangle them.

Tannen (1990) describes male-female communication as "living with asymmetry." In our relationships, we can try to change our conversational styles, to "speak the same language." Perhaps more realistically, we can accept differences and endeavour to understand them.

---

tion, Dindia and Allen conclude that "It is time to stop perpetuating the myth that there are large sex differences in men's and women's self-disclosure" (Dindia and Allen, 1992, p. 118).

social penetration model
As a relationship develops over time, self-disclosure increases in breadth of topics and intimacy.

Self-disclosing communication is the focus of an interesting model of intimacy, the **social penetration model** developed by Altman and Taylor (1973). According to this model, a relationship typically develops by first talking about a wide variety of topics, and later, gradually becoming more personal or intimate about a few topics. Self-disclosure is important in developing this intimacy. The process of social penetration is described as a wedge, broad at the superficial level and narrow at the more intimate level.

Altman (1975) suggests that people must satisfy two needs: to be close and intimate with someone and to maintain a sense of privacy. These needs for intimacy and privacy constitute an ongoing process of reconciliation through which we seek a balance. Such a balance does not consist simply of a compromise or middle ground between the two states. Rather, it is a dynamic synthesis that is influenced by what is happening to us and our relationships with other people. At times we feel the need for more intimacy; at other times we crave more "space" or emotional distance. Relationships tend to fluctuate rather than to simply move or grow in one direction. Even in a successful marriage the partners feel very close and intense at some times, and relatively more distant and casual at others (Altman, Vinsel and Brown, 1981). This model offers a rich and realistic conception of human relationships.

EQUITY AND SOCIAL EXCHANGE

Of course, equity is an important consideration in any relationship. Even when it entails sacrifice, we are motivated to maintain a sense of fairness between our friends and ourselves. The notion of **social exchange** is most likely to apply to our dealings with strangers and to our relationships with casual acquaintances. In these situations the principle of an interpersonal marketplace prevails as we try to maximize benefits and rewards and to minimize costs.

Foa (1971) proposes that there are six interpersonal resources that can be exchanged: love, status, information, money, goods, and services. These resources can be classified by their particularism and their concreteness. **Particularism** refers to the extent to which a resource's value is influenced by the person who gives it. For example, money is valuable (subject to the rate of exchange), regardless of the person who gives it. Love's value, on the other hand, depends almost entirely on the person who gives it. **Concreteness** refers to the characteristic form of expression of the resources. Goods and services are tangible things that you can see, hear, smell, taste, or touch. Love and money have both symbolic and concrete value. Information (e.g. the shortest route from Nelson, B.C. to Corner Brook, Nfld.) is verbal. Generally speaking we prefer exchanges within the same class. She helps wash his car and he helps hang her drapes, but we rarely exchange money for love. The books are balanced.

In intimate relationships the meaning of equitable exchange is transformed. Exchanges include particularistic and concrete resources: we give and receive affection, support, and praise (status); we take time to do more for each other (services); and to help each other with problems (information). In addition, intimate or "mutual" relationships have the benefit of time and variety of situations. For example, in our casual social lives, we may be very careful to reciprocate a dinner invitation within a reasonable period of time. Among close friends and lovers, however, we may reciprocate immediately with verbal praise and affection and not feel any further obligation. It is true that intimates spend much time "negotiating the terms" of their relationships, coming to know what they expect, hope, like, and dislike about each other. But if they are secure in the sense that the relationship is mutually satisfying (i.e. equitable), they can forego the immediate reciprocation, and won't need to "keep score" of rewards and costs. Indeed, such bookkeeping would violate the concept of mutuality.

COMPLEMENTARITY: DO OPPOSITES ATTRACT?

As mentioned above, in most situations similarities attract. Certainly, there is little evidence that opposite personalities attract (Meyer and Pepper, 1977). However, some differences can complement each other. For example, women have traditionally been more interested in men with financial resources than those who are good looking, whereas men have been more interested in women who are good looking. Even today, when women expect to work, a quick glance at the personal columns in the newspapers suggests that there are still those who express the traditional preferences.

How then can we describe an intimate relationship? Burgess and Huston (1979) suggest the following outline as a consensus of opinions on intimacy.

- The two people interact more often for a longer time and in more situations than do less intimate friends and acquaintances.

- When apart, they attempt to restore proximity.

social exchange theory
The tendency to maximize benefits and minimize costs in our dealings with others.

particularism The extent to which a resource's value is influenced by the person who gives it.

concreteness
Characteristic form of expression of resources.

Why does social exchange apply differently to casual friends than to intimate partners?

complementarity principle People are attracted to each other because they satisfy each other's needs.

What sort of differences complement each other?

- They "open up to each other," revealing secrets, feelings, praise, and criticism.
- They develop their own ways of communicating.
- Each develops the ability to anticipate how the other will behave and feel.
- Their behaviours and goals become "synchronized." Their behaviours and goals are not identical, but they do not get in each other's way.
- Each becomes increasingly "invested" in the relationship.
- The self-interest of each increasingly depends on the well-being of the relationship.
- They see the relationship as virtually irreplaceable and unique.
- They tend to relate to others as a couple.
- They like, love, and trust each other.

Intimacy can be found among family members and close friends as well as married couples and lovers. Since romantic love is a special form of intimacy it has received special attention. Let us review some of this work.

LOVE

Romantic love has always been fascinating. In our culture, we tend to "fall in love" (a revealing expression!) and then marry. But there are many cultures (India, for example) in which the opposite is the rule. Marriages are arranged by the

parents and the couple may not even meet until the wedding. Love is not a motive for marriage, and is expected to develop with the passage of time. In the musical *Fiddler on the Roof*, Tevye, a Jewish peasant living in a ghetto in Russia in the nineteenth century, asks his "arranged bride" of 25 years whether she loves him. After reminding him that she has, for 25 years, lived with him, cooked his meals, shared his bed, and borne his children, he repeats the question, "Do you love me?" Exasperated, she declares, "I'm your wife." Delighted, Tevye realizes she has answered the question: "Then you *do* love me!" In other words, love is an expected outcome of marriage in that culture.

People describe the experience of love in many ways. Romantic love may represent a passionate emotional and physical involvement. It may be an interpersonal "game" of manipulation without deep emotional involvement. Or it may be a relaxed, down-to-earth friendship. Romantic love may involve both passion and game-playing, and be desperately possessive, or it may simply define the process of rationally and deliberately choosing a suitable mate.

Psychologists too seem to have different views of romantic love. Hatfield (1988) distinguishes between two types of romantic love: passionate and companionate. Passionate love is an "intense longing for union with another." Companionate love is the "affection we feel for those with whom our lives are deeply intertwined" (Hatfield and Walster, 1978, p. 9). Passionate love usually exists early in a relationship. As the relationship matures, companionate love in the form of a deep, steady attachment replaces passionate love. Branden (1988) defines romantic love as a "passionate spiritual-emotional-sexual attachment between two people that reflects a high regard for the value of each other's person." For Sternberg (1986), romantic love involves intimacy and passion. He has proposed one of the most interesting theories of love, which captures the nature of romantic love as well as several other varieties. (See Figure 7-3 for an overview of Sternberg's theory.)

What are some of the ways that love has been described?

THE TRIANGULAR THEORY OF LOVE

Sternberg chose the triangular theory of love as the name for his model because he thought that love can be understood in terms of three components that can be viewed as the vertices of a triangle. These components are intimacy, passion, and decision/commitment. Intimacy refers to the closeness or "bondedness" between two people. It includes intimate communication and mutual understanding, sharing one's self and one's possessions with the loved one, the giving and receiving of emotional support, valuing the loved one, and experiencing happiness with him or her. Intimacy alone results in liking or friendship. Passion refers to emotional arousal and physical drives in the relationship. Sexual needs form the main part of passion. Also contributing to feelings of passion are the needs for self-esteem, affiliation with others, self-actualization, and dominance over or submission to others. Passion alone results in infatuation. Decision/commitment represents not only the decision to love someone, but also the commitment to maintain that loving relationship. Decision and commitment do not necessarily go together. Deciding that one is in love does not necessarily imply a commitment extending into the future. Decision and commitment alone result in empty love.

When any two of these components are taken in combination they result in particular types of love. For instance, as mentioned above, intimacy and passion together lead to romantic love, as portrayed in such great works of literature as *Romeo and Juliet*. Intimacy and commitment result in companionate love, the

FIGURE 7-3 **Sternberg's triangular model of love**

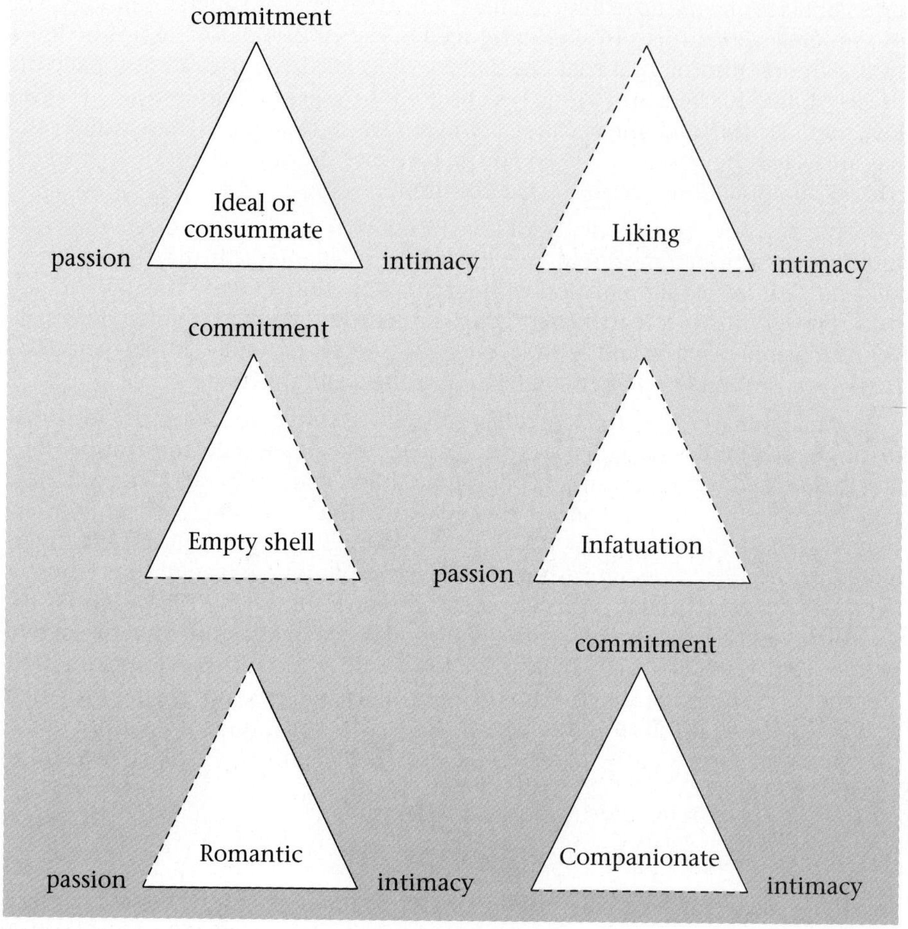

kind found in committed marriage relationships in which the passion has dissipated over the years. Fatuous love results from the combination of the passion and commitment/decision components in the absence of intimacy.

When all three of the components are present in a relationship it is characterized by consummate love. In Sternberg's view, this is the ideal type of love towards which people strive in their most valued relationships. When none of the three components are present in a relationship, it is lacking in love, and is what's commonly called an empty relationship. For Sternberg the components and their combinations constitute all the types of feelings experienced in close relationships.

The types of love just described are extremes. Usually the three components will interact with and affect each other. For example, intimacy in a relationship will often depend considerably on the extent to which passion can be expressed, while passion may often be aroused by feelings of intimacy. For most people, decision and commitment result from feelings of intimacy and the arousal of the passion component. However, in some cases the commitment comes first, such as in arranged marriages or among family members. Since we do not get to choose our parents, brothers, sisters, or cousins, whatever intimacy exists in those relationships results from a cognitive commitment. Thus the interplay among intimacy, passion, and decision/commitment will depend on the nature of the relationship, the characteristics of the people involved, and the time or stage of the relationship.

Sternberg's model offers an interesting new framework that pulls together many previous research findings and concepts in the area. Now it remains for more research to be carried out to determine the usefulness of this model.

GENDER DIFFERENCES

Do males and females differ with respect to romantic love? At least in our culture, there do appear to be differences (Dion and Dion, 1985; Hendrick and Hendrick, 1986; Peplau and Gordon, 1985). Surprisingly, males tend to have a "romantic" view, believing that true romantic love comes once and lasts forever, conquers all barriers and social customs, is essentially strange and incomprehensible, and must be basic to marriage. On the other hand, females tend to be more pragmatic, i.e. they believe they can be in love many times, that it may not last, that it inevitably fades into some disillusionment when the honeymoon ends, and that economic security and friendship are more important as bases for marriage.

BOX 7-2

COHABITATION: AN ALTERNATIVE

For many or most people, a committed romantic relationship is an extremely valued part of their lives and an important source of life satisfaction. Marriage is the most usual form of such relationships, sanctioned by society and religion. Today, however, many people choose to delay entering into marriage. There are many reasons for this trend—the involvement of women in the work force, the emphasis on personal identity and personal development, the desire of both sexes to work hard at careers and advance economically, and a reluctance to get into something that so often fails. Thus, many unmarried couples live together in a social climate that accepts such arrangements as perfectly legitimate.

Newcomb et al. (1986) review evidence that cohabitation offers a way to blend the two opposing needs for independence and relatedness. That is, while many people in this period of life are striving for independence, economic stability, and individual validation, they still want and need an intimate and supportive relationship.

It is interesting that most people who live together now plan to marry in the future. In comparing married couples who had and had not lived together prior to marriage, the investigators found that those who had cohabited perceived themselves as more androgynous, more attractive, more objective about themselves, less religious, and reported greater sexual experimentation. In most other personality and background characteristics, they are not particularly unique (Newcomb and Bentler, 1980).

When and why do they eventually get married? An obvious factor is the desire to have children, although there is no evidence of an unusually high birth rate in their first few years of marriage. Some may marry in response to pressure from the parents, or in the hope that the marriage contract will mend a troubled relationship (which often leads to disaster). For most couples, choosing to marry represents an additional step towards commitment, a stage beyond dating and living together. The research shows that cohabitors are not more or less likely to be satisfied with their marriage. In fact, their marriages are slightly more likely to end in divorce, probably because they are more accepting of divorce as a realistic alternative when the relationship founders. It is probably true that, like any other couple, their success in negotiating solutions to common needs and problems, including the blend of relatedness and independence, will largely determine the outcome of their marriage.

These differences in beliefs may be related to greater emotional dependence by males and/or greater economic dependence by females, although the picture for women is obviously changing dramatically.

However, the actual experiences of women are not especially based on pragmatism. Males report that they tend to fall in love earlier than females in a relationship, and they seem to fall out of love more slowly than females. But females report that they have been in love more frequently and more intensely. Females are also more likely to have had both pleasant and unpleasant (e.g. unrequited love) experiences. They more often report emotional experiences and euphoric "symptoms" such as "floating on air," or having trouble concentrating (Brehm, 1985). Perhaps women are more pragmatic in their selection of a love partner and in defining what love means, and yet more able to experience love as an intense emotional experience. Or perhaps women are simply more willing or able to report intimate, intense experiences and feelings. It is important to note that these differences reflect "average" males and females, and that there is considerable variation within each gender in how romantic love is experienced.

Why have these differences developed in our society? A functionalist interpretation considers how romantic love enables individuals to adapt to society and maintain such social institutions as marriage (Dion and Dion, 1985). Romantic love is seen as a bond keeping a couple together, which is particularly important in the absence of other types of limits such as social pressure, parental duties, or economic interdependence. Since women have traditionally contributed less than men to the family income, they would have to gain by linking love and marriage. Men, on the other hand, are traditionally trained to be economically independent. While the majority of wives now work, it is still considered unacceptable for husbands to be dependent on the income of their wives. Thus they would be less concerned with the uses of romantic love as binding a marriage and would feel free to indulge in idealism or cynicism. It is interesting that men are more likely than women to endorse such sayings as "Marry whom you love, regardless of social position," while women are more likely to agree that "Economic security should be considered carefully before selecting a marriage partner."

CAN PASSIONATE LOVE BE A MISATTRIBUTION?

Berscheid and Walster (1974b) propose that three conditions are necessary for someone to "fall in love." First, the person must be raised in a culture that believes in the idea of romantic love. Second, the person must feel a state of emotional arousal that is interpreted as love. The third condition is the presence of an appropriate love object, most often a physically attractive member of the opposite sex. Crucial to this model is how people interpret symptoms of their own physiological arousal, such as a faltering voice, faintness, erratic eye movements, inability to concentrate, blushing, heart palpitations, and muscle tremors. As an old song advises, "You're not sick, you're just in love."

What is especially interesting is that arousal may be elicited by negative circumstances and then attributed to romantic sentiments. Many intense relationships occur during the tension and terror of wartime. Seriously ill patients often fall in love with their physicians, nurses, or therapists. While we may be quite aware of the initial source of our state of arousal, we may still be vulnerable to romantic involvement because of our intense emotional state.

Both experimental and field studies have supported the model. For one study, unmarried and married couples were asked to report on aspects of their relationship at two different times, six to ten months apart (Driscoll, Davis and

Lipetz, 1972). They found that those who reported more parental interference in their relationship also reported being more in love with their partners at the time. In looking at changes over time, the researchers noted that among the unmarried couples, romantic love increased (or decreased) as parental interference increased (or decreased). For obvious reasons, it was called the "Romeo and Juliet effect." In another study, males were instructed to walk across the shaky Capilano suspension bridge which crosses a deep gorge in Vancouver (Dutton and Aron, 1974). On the other side, they encountered an attractive female experimental assistant. In contrast to those who met the same young woman after crossing a solid, concrete bridge, subjects who met her in their aroused state included more sexual imagery in a projective test and were more likely to telephone her later. Somehow the arousal caused by their fear while wobbling in space was subsequently misattributed to feelings of attraction to the woman.

However, Kenrick and Cialdini (1977) criticize this interpretation of such studies as Dutton and Aron's (1974) "woman on the bridge" experiment. They argue that when subjects were meeting the young woman they were feeling relief at having reached solid ground rather than arousal due to fear. Thus they associated the woman with this feeling of relief, which constituted reinforcement. Other research has linked arousal with attraction, even when the arousal was caused by exercise, a non-threatening source (Allen, Kenrick, Linder and McCall, 1989). Perhaps in situations that involve a highly ambiguous and diffuse state of arousal, and given the presence of the appropriate person, aroused feelings may be attributed to romantic love.

SELF-TEST QUESTIONS

5. Self-disclosure leads to intimacy if it follows the norm of

a) equity

b) social desirability

c) reciprocity

d) social responsibility

e) good manners

6. The social penetration model of self-disclosure is based on the dimensions of

a) equity and equality

b) breadth and depth

c) liking and loving

d) surface contact and mutuality

e) length and width

7. The theory that people who are opposites in certain characteristics attract each other is called

a) cognitive balance

b) the law of proportional similarity

c) attachment

d) complementarity

8. In his triangular model, Sternberg defines romantic love in terms of

a) attachment, attractiveness, caring

b) intimacy, passion, commitment

c) intimacy, attachment, attraction

d) attachment, passion, sexuality

RELATIONSHIP PROBLEMS

Social psychology has turned recently to the study of relationship problems, areas formerly the preserve of other disciplines. Using the theories and methods particularly adaptable to the study of close relationships, progress has been made in understanding problems of jealousy, shyness, loneliness, and the dissolution of relationships. Discussion now turns to these problems.

JEALOUSY

Shakespeare's Othello is but one of many familiar characters destroyed by a tragic susceptibility to "the green-eyed monster." Salovey and Rodin (1984) argue that we can distinguish between two types of jealousy. **Social comparison jealousy** is the desire to feel better than or at least as good as someone else. **Social relations jealousy** is the desire for exclusivity in a relationship.

These investigators conducted a clever study of social comparison jealousy. Subjects working separately in pairs believed they were filling out a test to determine if they had a "suitable personality" for certain career choices. Then they were given bogus feedback in which they were told that their test score was either surprisingly high or surprisingly low on a dimension that was either relevant or irrelevant to their career choice (e.g. medical science aptitude, artistic sensitivity, business insight). At this point they saw the bogus test results of their partner along with an essay apparently written by their partner about themselves (hobbies, interests, career plans, etc.). All subjects received the same essay, but they received different test results indicating success or failure by their partner.

Each subject was then asked to evaluate his or her partner on a questionnaire just before meeting that partner (who was always of the same gender as the subject). The group of interest to the researchers consisted of subjects who had received negative, relevant self-feedback (e.g. those who wanted medicine and who scored poorly on that scale), and who believed that their partners had scored very well on their career-relevant scale. These were the subjects in whom social comparison jealousy had been aroused. They tended to be critical of their partners and rated them lower on a number of socially desirable characteristics. Nevertheless they expressed interest in a possible friendship. They also scored higher in measures of anxious and depressed mood states.

White (1981a) has outlined an interesting model of romantic jealousy. We begin, he says, with **primary appraisal**, perceiving a threat to our relationship that exceeds our tolerance level. For instance, you may react if someone smiles at your partner, dances with your partner, spends the whole evening with your partner, or leaves with your partner. A number of factors will influence this tolerance level. We can tolerate more if we feel secure about the relationship, if we are not completely dependent on it, and if the partner is a casual friend rather than a lover or spouse. On the other hand, we react more strongly to a severe threat, such as a potential rival who is highly attractive, prestigious, wealthy,

social comparison jealousy Desire to feel better than or at least as good as someone else.

social relations jealousy Strong desire for exclusivity in a relationship.

What sort of situations can lead to jealousy?

primary appraisal (in relationship jealousy) Perceiving a threat to a relationship that exceeds our tolerance level.

or socially adept. We react differently to threats to sexual or emotional intimacy (e.g. a partner's close friend may threaten emotional intimacy) than to threats to the time spent with our partner (e.g. the Saturday night "hockey widow" whose husband is obsessed with the game). Notice that the threat to the relationship may be another person, or the partner's other commitments or interests. All can arouse jealousy if threat is perceived.

The individual then proceeds to **secondary appraisal**, trying to understand the situation. The person may review evidence about the threat (was he or she really interested in the other person?), alternative possibilities (he or she was working late that night), and evidence that the relationship really isn't in danger (we're getting along so well together lately). Through secondary appraisal the individual may become convinced either that there is no problem, or that the relationship is seriously threatened. The latter train of thought leads to the intense emotional reactions characteristic of jealousy. The range of feelings is tremendous, from mild twinges to total obsession. Pines and Aronson (1983) found a fascinating mixture of positive and negative feelings: excitement, emotional and physical distress, feeling alive, anxiety, happiness, anger, confusion, victimization, embarrassment, and passion.

White (1981b) found that jealousy in both males and females who were involved romantically at the time is related to expectations of exclusivity in the relationship and to feelings of personal inadequacy as a partner. There do not seem to be any global differences in the level of jealousy reported by males and females, but there are differences in how jealousy is experienced and expressed. Males tend to either deny jealousy or to react in an angry and competitive way. Females tend to acknowledge jealousy, blame themselves, become depressed, and exhibit increasingly dependent behaviour.

How can we best cope with jealousy? Brehm (1992) suggests that it is important to avoid irrational reactions such as thinking that one is worthless without the relationship. Instead, one needs confidence in one's ability to get along in the world. She also suggests that it is important to realize that jealousy reflects self-love rather than love for one's partner.

LONELINESS

Most people have experienced situations in which they feel lonely—visiting a new country, moving to a new location, being temporarily separated from a loved one. We expect to feel lonely on such occasions. And in our society we also expect certain people to be lonely. We have a stereotype of the lonely old person, for example. However, research shows that loneliness sometimes occurs where we do not expect it. For example, Sadava and Matejcic (1987) report surprising evidence of significant levels of loneliness in a group of people who had recently married. Loneliness was higher among husbands who felt less liking and less intimacy towards their wives, and had greater worries about communicating with them. It was higher among wives who felt less liking and less love towards their husbands and manifested less self-disclosure towards them. That is, loneliness reflected the quality of the relationship. In a longitudinal study of students in their first year of university, Cutrona (1982) found that 75 percent experienced some degree of loneliness. By the end of the year 25 percent were still lonely.

What is loneliness? Perlman and Peplau (1981) identify three characteristics of loneliness:

(1) It results from perceived deficiencies in the person's relationships.

secondary appraisal
(in relationship jealousy)
Efforts to understand and evaluate a possible threat to a relationship.

What contributes to chronic loneliness?

(2) It is distressing and unpleasant.

(3) It is subjective rather than objective. It depends on our perception: we can feel intensely lonely in a crowd and not at all lonely when alone.

Loneliness can assume different forms. It may be a temporary feeling that arises from situational factors. Or it may reflect a chronic disposition. People who suffer from **chronic loneliness** typically feel lonely regardless of their situation. Weiss (1973) has distinguished between social loneliness and emotional loneliness. **Social loneliness** is due to a lack of friends, acquaintances, colleagues, or social network. **Emotional loneliness** is due to insufficient intimate relationships.

Since loneliness is not a desirable experience, we might wonder, "What is it about chronically lonely people that keeps them that way?" An examination of the interpersonal communication behaviour of lonely people may help to answer this question. Chronically lonely persons are less effective in both verbal and non-verbal communication. They do not make much of an effort to take part in conversation (Vitkus and Horowitz, 1987). Lonely persons do not express their emotions or judge the emotions of others effectively (Gerson and Perlman, 1979). A study of how lonely students behave in conversation with a stranger revealed that they tend to be more self-focused, asking fewer questions and making fewer statements about the other person. Lonely people also tend to be atypical in their style of self-disclosure (Solano, Batten and Parish, 1982). Either they pour their hearts out to a total stranger or they are unusually closed, revealing little of themselves, even to someone they know well. They are also more anxious about their perceived deficiencies in social skills (Solano and Koester, 1989).

Some researchers have shown that lonely people have distinctive personal characteristics. People who score high on global measures of loneliness tend to manifest introversion, self-consciousness, a lack of assertiveness, low self-esteem, anxiety, and depression (Peplau and Perlman, 1982). There is also some evidence that lonely people, particularly males, are more likely to be hostile or aggressive, especially towards women (Check et al., 1985), and that lonely people who drink are more vulnerable to alcohol problems (Sadava and Thompson, 1986). Of course, any of these personal characteristics may be both a cause and a consequence of loneliness. For example, hostile or depressed people may experience failures in relationships, thereby increasing their loneliness and their anger or depression.

How can people cope with loneliness? Peplau, Russell and Heim (1979) argue that the experience of loneliness depends on how we explain the time or circumstance in which we find ourselves alone or relatively isolated. Our response to loneliness may also depend on our understanding of it. Appraising situations and the people in them in a manner that invites our own participation may be the first step to overcoming loneliness.

SHYNESS

Given our need for satisfying social activities and relationships, and the distress of loneliness, it would seem surprising that so many people deliberately "hang back," withdraw, and are unwilling to take risks. This is the problem of **shyness**, in which people excessively restrain their social interactions. Philip Zimbardo (1977), a social psychologist who has studied it extensively, describes shyness in terms of being afraid of people, particularly those who may be emotionally threatening. Friends who may not like you, members of the opposite sex who may reject you, authorities who may disapprove of you, members of a class who may disagree with you, and strangers who are unpredictable may all be emotionally

chronic loneliness Relatively enduring unpleasant feelings brought about by dissatisfaction with one's social interactions.

social loneliness Loneliness due to a perceived lack of friends, acquaintances, or colleagues.

emotional loneliness Loneliness due to a perceived lack of intimate relationships.

shyness Excessive restraint in social relationships.

threatening. Many people are shy in some situations but not in others. For example, a student may be terrified of speaking in class, but totally comfortable at a party. Some entertainers are at ease on stage but quite shy in one-to-one encounters. Other people are painfully shy in most types of social encounters, and suffer intensely because of it.

Psychologists have developed a number of strategies for helping people to overcome shyness. One technique, developed by Zimbardo and his colleagues, involves **cognitive restructuring** of social situations that arouse anxiety. For example, shy people may enter an interaction with their own agenda, such as getting to know as much as possible about the other person. Concentrating on this goal may distract them from their own anxiety, and give them a sense of control and relative ease in the situation. Another technique involved assigning shy people to a particular social role. The role is sanctioned by the situation and a script is provided. The shy person then simply carries out what is called for by the role and its script. Shyness also can be treated through **social skills training**. Clients observe models who interact comfortably, and then role play using the skills they have observed. Homework includes practising the new skills in everyday life situations.

Finally, it may be important to look at how shy people interpret themselves and others. Since shy people expect rejection and disapproval, they may misinterpret how others view them. Usually shy people experience physiological symptoms, such as increased heart rate or "butterflies in the stomach." They tend to attribute these symptoms to shyness and feel more uncomfortable than ever. In one study (Brodt and Zimbardo, 1981), shy female students were told they were participants in an experiment on the effects of noise. They were informed that they would likely feel effects such as increased heart rate, which would persist for some time after the noise ended. Just after being bombarded with noise the students met an attractive male, a confederate of the experimenter. The shy females behaved in a more than usually outgoing way with this person, and afterwards reported feeling less shy. Because they were able to reattribute the symptoms to the noise rather than to their own shyness, they were able to overcome the problem in that situation.

cognitive restructuring
Changing one's view or perception of a situation in order to interact more effectively.

social skills training
Clients observe models who interact comfortably, and then role play using the skills they have observed.

What can people do to overcome shyness?

DISSOLUTION OF RELATIONSHIPS

It was a storybook romance between the long-time bachelor Prince and the elegant and beautiful Lady Diana. After some years of apparent contentment and an increasingly glamorous presence by the new Princess of Wales, tensions between Charles and Diana began to appear in public, amplified by the incessant scrutiny of the tabloids. The marriage finally ended in 1993, twelve years after the storybook wedding.

Four models may be relevant to an understanding of why relationships fail (Kurdeck, 1993). The principal explanations offered in these models focus on:

(1) Social factors such as class differences or financial difficulties.

(2) Personality traits that may predispose a person to distort the relationship.

(3) An absence of interdependence, perhaps because one or both partners has available alternatives.

(4) Large discrepancies between the partners, such as incompatible personality traits, or conflicts in values, attitudes, or interests.

All of these are relevant to understanding a marriage that is at risk, as discussed below.

THE ANTECEDENTS AND PROCESS OF ENDING A RELATIONSHIP

Can we predict which marriages will survive and which will break up in time? Several longitudinal studies provide information that may help us to do so. Bentler and Newcomb (1978) report that couples who separate are less similar in age, attractiveness, personality, and interest in art. The men among them describe themselves as more extroverted and orderly, and the women describe themselves as less clothes-conscious and less congenial. Gottman and Levenson (1992) report that couples at risk of separation engage in communication characterized by more conflict, withdrawal, and whining, as well as by less affection and interest in their partner. In another study, it was found that both men and women who remain married are more conventional, less over-reactive to stressful events, and less impulsive (Kelly and Conley, 1987).

Why do some people remain in unsatisfying relationships while others do not? In a study involving 103 couples who had broken up and 117 who were still together, Hill, Rubin and Peplau (1976) found that the majority of the breakups were initiated by women. People in relationships where one person was more intensely involved than the other ended these relationships. Kurdek (1993) reports that those who dissolved their marriages were less interdependent, and that there was greater discrepancy between the partners in how interdependent they felt. In a study of dating couples, Simpson (1987) found that the quality of the relationships as well as the perception of available alternatives predicted whether the relationship ended.

Levinger (1979) argues that in deciding whether to remain in a marriage, people weigh the costs and benefits of staying together versus leaving. When people feel they have invested a great deal of time and effort in a relationship, they tend to persist in seeking improvement and are less likely to look for rewarding relationships elsewhere (Rusbult, 1983). Those who remain in relationships tend to be more dependent on them to satisfy various needs (intimacy, sex, emotional involvement, companionship), and to see less opportunity to meet these needs elsewhere, than do those who leave (Drigotas and Rusbult, 1992).

Of course, social changes such as less stigma attached to divorce, or less costly divorce proceedings, influence the durability of relationships. Current divorce rates have stabilized after a period of uninterrupted growth, perhaps because of economic recession.

THE IMPACT OF ENDING A RELATIONSHIP

There is abundant research evidence linking the quality of the marital relationship and marital separation to a wide variety of stress-related disorders (Bloom, Asher and White, 1978; Burman and Margolin, 1992). In comparison to both now-married and never-married people, separated and divorced people are more prone to automobile accidents, psychiatric disorders, alcoholism, suicide, and death from tuberculosis, cirrhosis of the liver, certain forms of cancer, and coronary diseases. People who are unhappily married tend to be less healthy than those who are no longer married. Obviously, stressful factors in divorce such as financial difficulties, sexual problems, feelings of shame, guilt, or failure, problems with children, and sheer loneliness, play a role. Feelings of conflict and ambivalence may add to these burdens. Each partner can have both negative and positive feelings towards the other. Men may suffer more adverse effects of divorce than women. In our culture, men tend to be more dependent on the marital romantic relationship than women. Fischer and Phillips (1982) found that when a man marries he tends to give up friendships but keeps in touch with casual acquaintances, while women do just the opposite. The male who loses the romantic relationship may be emotionally isolated. Divorced women find the time before separation most stressful, while men consider the period after the separation most difficult (Hagestad and Smyer, 1982).

SELF-TEST QUESTIONS

9. Jealousy characterized by the desire for exclusivity in a relationship is called

a) social relations jealousy

b) social comparison jealousy

c) personal comparison jealousy

d) personal relations jealousy

10. In White's model of romantic jealousy, primary appraisal denotes

a) appraising the emotions of one's partner

b) appraising the situation in which one experiences jealousy

c) perceiving a threat in a relationship that exceeds one's tolerance level

d) appraising one's feelings for one's partner

11. Sadava and Matejcic (1987) reported that loneliness was higher among husbands who felt

a) more liking and less intimacy towards their wives

b) less liking and less intimacy towards their wives

c) less liking and more intimacy towards their wives

d) their wives were cold and indifferent

12. Researchers have found that couples at risk of separation engage in communication characterized by

a) more conflict, withdrawal, and whining

b) less affection and interest for their partner

c) both a and b

d) neither a nor b

SUMMARY

(1) The need to affiliate with others begins at infancy and persists throughout life. Certain factors, such as intense fear or stress, increase affiliative needs, while others (e.g. social anxiety) decrease affiliation.

(2) We tend to be attracted to people who are in close physical proximity and who are physically attractive. We are motivated to choose others who are roughly equal to ourselves in attractiveness.

(3) When people are first getting to know each other, attraction is related to the perception that people are similar and that the interaction is rewarding. We are

attracted to people with similar attitudes because it is rewarding to be with them, and because we expect people we like to be similar to us.

(4) Reciprocity in self-disclosure is crucial to intimacy. According to the social penetration model, self-disclosure increases in depth and breadth as intimacy increases, but is limited by a need to preserve privacy.

(5) Equity is important to social relations, including exchange in love, status, information, money, goods, and services. In intimate relationships, exchange becomes more flexible.

(6) Romantic love consists of varying degrees of passion, decision, and intimacy.

(7) Research distinguishes between social comparison jealousy (the need to feel as good as someone else) and social relations jealousy (the need for exclusivity in a relationship).

(8) Loneliness arises from a perception of deficiencies in a person's relationships. It may be situational or chronic. And it may have nothing to do with being alone.

(9) Two techniques used to overcome shyness are cognitive restructuring and social skills training.

(10) The dissolution of a relationship may depend on the anticipated costs and rewards of leaving it, and on the anticipated costs and rewards of staying in it.

FOR REVIEW

In this chapter we discuss how and why we become attracted to others, and how close relationships form over time. Human beings manifest a strong need to be with others, which is called the need for _____(1). This need is rooted in _____(2) which begins in early infancy, when the infant can distinguish familiar faces. The need to be with others is influenced by certain situations, such as those arousing _____(3). However, we are also selective about those with whom we want to relate. Attraction depends on the nature of the relationship. We tend to be initially attracted to people who live and work in close _____(4) to ourselves and who are _____(5). When we begin to interact, attraction is then dependent on such factors as perceived similarity in _____(6) and interests. In addition, according to the reinforcement-affect model of attraction, we are influenced by the _____(7) associated with being with someone we like.

When a relationship can be described as close or _____(8), other factors come into play. Communicating about ourselves _____(9) contributes to intimacy when it occurs _____(10). According to the social penetration model, self-disclosure can be analyzed in terms of _____ and _____(11) of what is disclosed. With casual friends or acquaintances, exchanges of such items as goods, information, and status help to maintain _____(12) or fairness in the relationship. With intimacy, this concept of fairness is transformed. For example, our arrangements become more flexible; we do not need to reciprocate immediately. Love is experienced and defined in various ways. In his _____(13) model of love, Sternberg describes it in terms of three components: intimacy, passion, and decision/commitment.

Relationship problems have also been studied. Jealousy may take different forms. Jealousy characterized by a need for exclusivity in a relationship is called _____(14). The need to feel as good as someone else is called _____(15). When people are troubled by perceptions of deficiencies in their relationships, we say that they are experiencing _____(16). People who typically feel lonely, regardless of the situation, suffer from _____(17) loneliness. Those whose loneliness is due to a lack of satisfying social relationships experience _____(18) loneliness. _____(19) loneliness is due to insufficient intimacy in relationships.

Shyness is related to loneliness and can be treated behaviourally. When relationships become very troubled, partners usually assess the costs and benefits of both staying in the relationship and of leaving it. The impact of ending a relationship is very stressful, especially for men, perhaps because they maintain fewer _____(20) after marriage than women.

ISSUES AND ACTIVITIES

(1) Read a story or see a film or play that portrays an intimate relationship. Discuss the development of this relationship, the expectations of the characters involved, and its success or breakdown in terms of the concepts in this chapter.

(2) Construct a questionnaire about intimate relationships, focusing on the concepts discussed in this chapter. Distribute your questionnaire to twenty people. Present the results in a brief report, using at least one figure and table to illustrate your findings.

(3) Make a collection of song lyrics, poems, and stories that illustrate the types of love depicted in Sternberg's triangular model. Discuss how the items in your collection illustrate the different types of love in the model.

• FURTHER READING

BREHM, S. (1992). *Intimate relationships,* Second Edition. New York: McGraw-Hill. A readable and comprehensive overview of research and thinking on intimate relationships.

HATFIELD, E. and SPRECHER, S. (1986). *Mirror, mirror...the importance of looks in everyday life.* Albany: State University of New York. A paperback that explores research on the effects of physical attractiveness at every stage of life.

STERNBERG, R.J. and BARNES, M. (Eds.) (1988). *The psychology of love.* New York: Yale University Press. A collection of papers about love.

SUGGESTED WEBLINKS

International Society for the Study of Personal Relationships
    http://www.uwinnipeg.ca/~isspr/

Journal of Personality and Social Psychology (table of contents)
    http://www.apa.org/journals/psp.html

Social and Personality Section, Canadian Psychological Association
    http://www.uwinnipeg.ca/~baldwin/14index.html

ANSWERS TO SELF-TEST QUESTIONS

1. c; 2. e; 3. d; 4. a; 5. c; 6. b; 7. d; 8. b; 9. a; 10. c; 11. b; 12. c.

ANSWERS TO FOR REVIEW

1. affiliation; 2. attachment; 3. fear; 4. proximity; 5. physically attractive; 6. attitudes and/or values; 7. rewards; 8. intimate; 9. self-disclosure; 10. reciprocally; 11. depth (and) breadth; 12. equity; 13. triangular; 14. social relations jealousy; 15. social comparison jealousy; 16. loneliness; 17. chronic; 18. social; 19. Emotional; 20. close friendships.

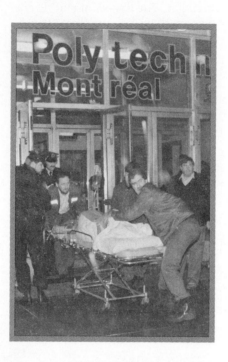

AGGRESSION AND VIOLENCE

In Flanders fields the poppies blow
Between the crosses row on row,
That mark our place ...

Lt. Col. John McCrae
First Canadian Contingent
Killed in Boulogne, France, 1918

It shall be prohibited unnecessarily to torture or brutally to ill treat an animal ... To
ill treat an animal means to cause it pain. Ill treatment is deemed brutal when it is
inspired by lack of feeling.

Animal Protection Act of the Third Reich
Drafted by Goering, signed by Hitler

■ LEARNING OUTCOMES

1. An understanding of the difficulty involved in defining the concept of aggression.

2. Knowledge about the relevance of biological factors in human aggression.

3. Knowledge about the role of social learning in the inhibition or acquisition and display of aggressive behaviours.

4. An understanding of the influence of child-rearing practices on the development of aggressive behaviours.

5. Knowledge about the effects of media violence on violence in real life.

6. An understanding of factors that contribute to violence towards women.

7. An understanding of the role of easily available firearms in violent crime.

8. Knowledge about ways in which violence might be reduced and controlled.

■ FOR REFLECTION

• Is violence a problem of self control or social control?

• Can aggressive tendencies be channelled safely into sports or watching television?

• To what extent do children learn aggression from their families?

• Does pornography lead to violence against women?

■ CHAPTER OUTLINE

What is Aggression?

Causes of Aggression

    Aggression as Instinct or Drive

    Physiological Influences on Aggression

    Social-Developmental Influences

    Aggressiveness as a Personality Trait

    Cultural Influences on Aggression

    Media and Aggression

    Firearms and Homicide

    Hostility and Violence Towards Women

The Reduction and Control of Aggression

Summary

For Review

Issues and Activities

Further Reading

Suggested WebLinks

Answers to Self-Test Questions

Answers to For Review

In August of 1992, an engineering professor armed with three handguns cold-bloodedly murdered four of his colleagues at Concordia University. In 1993, Paul Bernardo was charged with the murders of Leslie Mahaffy and Kristen French. His estranged wife, Karla Homolka, was sentenced to twelve years in prison for her involvement in the killings, and agreed to testify in the sensational trial of her former husband. Bernardo was sentenced to life imprisonment

Wartime sentiments: Mothers issue their own statistics after WW1.

and declared a dangerous offender. In January 1993, a thirteen-year-old boy killed a man and wounded his wife with a pump-action shotgun when the man answered his door at his home near Canso, Nova Scotia. In April of 1994, a twenty-five-year-old McMaster University student was gunned down in her apartment. Also in April of 1994, three men barged into Just Desserts, a restaurant in a trendy Toronto neighbourhood, and fired a sawed-off shotgun, killing twenty-three-year-old Georgina Leimonis. In April of 1995, three boys aged thirteen, fourteen, and fifteen years, intent on stealing items they could sell on the street, broke into the Montreal home of retired Anglican priest Frank Toope and his wife Jocelyn, and beat them to death. In August of 1995, Ottawa broadcaster Brian Smith was fatally shot by a man who had a grudge against the media. In January of 1996, James Huang killed his wife, two daughters, and his mother, and then shot himself in Surrey, B.C. In less than five minutes during one day in April, 1996, Mark Chahal shot and killed his former wife and ten members of her family, and then took his own life in Vernon, B.C.

Every year in Canada, between 600 and 700 people—including 50 to 60 children—are murdered. And every year, in many parts of the world, systematic organized aggression kills large numbers of people, soldier and innocent bystander alike. Over 50 million people died during World War II. Since then, at least another 35 million people have died in military conflicts. And there seems no end: the Gulf War, ethnic battles in the former Yugoslavia, communal violence in India, terrorism in the Middle East, the Oklahoma City bombing. And there is torture currently being carried out in many parts of the world.

Why are human beings so prone to aggression? Is aggressiveness in our genes? Is it something we learn? Social psychologists are interested in why people are aggressive, because aggression is a social behaviour in which the aggressor uses aggressive acts to harm, punish, or control others, or to communicate feelings of anger. Therefore, social learning, social norms, and cultural values should all play a role in aggressive behaviour as they do in any other social behaviour.

WHAT IS AGGRESSION?

aggression *Behaviour that is intended to harm or destroy.*

instrumental aggression *Behaviour intended to harm as a means to some desired end.*

Social psychologists typically define **aggression** as behaviour that is intended to harm or destroy another person. Someone who fires a gun intending to hit another person would be considered to have behaved aggressively even if the shot misses its mark. Aggressive behaviour is often accompanied by aggressive emotions and thoughts (Buss and Perry, 1992). Many psychologists distinguish between instrumental and hostile aggression (Berkowitz, 1984, 1989; Rule and Nesdale, 1974). **Instrumental aggression** is behaviour intended to harm or de-

BOX 8-1

TORTURE AND PAIN

Whether practised by secular or sacred institutions—for punishment, revenge, or the amusement of spectators (as in the days of the Roman Empire)—torture has always been carried out with the secure knowledge that human beings universally fear pain. The deliberate infliction of pain is the torturer's *modus operandi*. For example, during the Inquisition carried out by the Church in the Middle Ages, the ecclesiastical judges insisted even on the torture of suspected witches who had readily confessed their crimes. In other words, victims were not to escape the painful treatment they "deserved" (Masters, 1966).

Centuries of social and technological evolution have replaced the rack with electric shock, and boiling oil with painful or nauseating drugs. Today's methods are more sophisticated, more efficient in provoking suffering, and leave fewer visible traces. But whatever the method, torture is always predicated on the notion that human beings want to avoid pain. In the words of Amnesty International:

> ...[E]ven in an age of violence, torture stands out as a special horror for most people. Pain is a

common human denominator, and while few people know what it is to be shot, to be burned by napalm, or even to starve, all know pain. Within every human being is the knowledge and fear of pain, the fear of helplessness before unrestrained cruelty.... It is significant that torture is the one form of violence that a state will always deny and never justify. The state may justify mass murder and glorify those who kill...but it never justifies torture nor glorifies those who torture.... And yet the use of torture has by all indications increased over the last few years *(excerpted from* Amnesty International Report on Torture, *1975, p. 21).*

We must be careful not to think that it is only bullies and sadists who are capable of cruelty to others. Those who took part in the Nazi butchery "were not sadists or killers by nature; on the contrary, a systematic effort was made to weed out all those who derived physical pleasure from what they did" (Arendt, 1963, p. 93). Similarly, those who became the official torturers for the military junta that ruled Greece from 1967 to 1974 may not have always been sadists, but were systematically conditioned to carry out their work without qualms. The lesson of history is that most people, if subjected to particular training conditions and manipulative techniques, are capable of becoming torturers (Haritos-Fatouros, 1988).

---

stroy as a means to an end. **Hostile aggression** is motivated by anger and its goal is to hurt someone.

hostile aggression
Aggression that is instigated by anger and directed at harming another person.

CAUSES OF AGGRESSION

On December 6, 1989, 25-year-old Marc Lepine took a semi-automatic hunting rifle to the École Polytechnique, an engineering school affiliated with the Université de Montréal, entered a classroom, fired a shot into the air and ordered the men to leave the room. He was heard to say in French, "I want the women" and "you're all a bunch of feminists." A few moments later he opened fire on the group of women, killing six of them. Then for the next twenty minutes he prowled the corridors looking for more victims. In the worst massacre in Canadian history, he killed fourteen women and injured thirteen other people, almost all women, before killing himself.

How can such an outburst of violence be explained? Had we interviewed people at the time, we might have obtained the following explanations:

What are some different views about the causes of aggression?

- Sometimes the pressure builds up inside a person, and you just have to get it out of your system.
- Could be he had a brain tumour or something.
- He must have been brought up that way—to see violence as a way to deal with problems.
- He's just a tough character who lost control of himself.
- It's our society—it encourages violence.
- With all the violence on TV, it's a wonder this sort of thing doesn't happen more often.
- It's too easy; any nut can buy a gun in this country.
- This was an expression of men's deep-seated hostility towards women.

These hypotheses can apply to most violence. They all make pronouncements about factors that promote aggressive behaviour. However, it is extremely difficult to reach any definitive conclusions about what causes a particular act of violence. For example, how could we ever test the hypothesis that Lepine's actions represented an undercurrent of male hostility towards women? In the pages that follow, we will explore each of these hypotheses about violence.

"YOU JUST HAVE TO GET IT OUT OF YOUR SYSTEM": AGGRESSION AS INSTINCT OR DRIVE

It is often tempting to view irrational violence as the product of uncontrollable biological forces. Two prominent theories that have promoted this view are Freud's psychoanalytic theory and Lorenz's ethological theory. In Freud's view, all behaviour is driven by two instincts: the life instinct, Eros, and the death instinct, Thanatos. When blocked by Eros, Thanatos displaces some of its destructive energy outwards onto other people. People behave in a destructive manner towards others in order to avoid their own self-destruction (Freud, 1933). Was Lepine driven by a death wish that he displaced onto others? If so, the displacement was not effective, or he would not have committed suicide immediately. Lorenz (1966) developed his theory of aggression based on his study of aggressive behaviour in birds and animals. In his view, animals and humans possess an aggressive drive that is essential for survival and evolution. Could this explain Lepine's behaviour? Had he built up aggressive energy that was not being regularly discharged in a socially acceptable manner? This explanation is not very convincing because there is no evidence supporting the accumulation of "aggressive energy" in the body or of any spontaneous motive to fight others.

Some theorists who reject the idea of innate aggressive energy have speculated that there may be an inborn tendency to show aggression following frustration of some kind. This view was proposed originally by Dollard, Doob, Miller, Mowrer and Sears (1939). According to their **frustration-aggression hypothesis**, every instance of frustration produces some tendency towards aggression. These theorists defined frustration as any interference in behaviour directed towards a goal. They further argued that every instance of aggression must be preceded by frustration. They assumed that learning and environmental cues determined the form and target of aggressive behaviour. However, research has shown that this view is also untenable, because although frustration can lead to aggression, it also can lead to other types of behaviour.

Berkowitz (1983, 1989, 1990) has rephrased the frustration-aggression hypothesis in a manner that addresses people's tendencies to lash out or be irrita-

---

instinct *Inborn behavioural tendencies that motivate certain behaviours in all members of a species in the presence of appropriate stimuli.*

frustration-aggression hypothesis *Frustration produces a state of unpleasantness, which leads to aggressive behaviour.*

ble when in pain or distress. Berkowitz argues that humans as well as many animals are biologically disposed to react with aggression when faced with pain or unpleasantness. This type of behaviour is called aversively-stimulated aggression. According to this view, frustration produces a state of unpleasantness, which leads to aggressive behaviour. Aversive events that produce frustration may be physical (e.g. pain, excessive heat) or psychological (e.g. frightening information, insults). Such events produce both the motivation to escape and the motivation to attack. Thus, aversively-stimulated aggression involves both a defensive tendency to remove the unpleasant stimulus and an active inclination to harm available targets. Cognitive appraisal of the situation determines the extent and type of negative feelings produced. The negative feelings, such as annoyance, pain, or sadness, lead to anger. Cognitive processes determine whether anger influences behaviour at all, and if it is expressed through aggression.

The instinctual view of aggression has prompted several important controversies. One controversy is concerned with inborn mechanisms of aggression. In contrast to those theorists who hold an instinctual view, social learning theorists argue that aggression can be explained without reference to inborn mechanisms. They believe that aggression is acquired, as is any other social behaviour, and that it is reinforced by its effectiveness.

A second controversy is concerned with the role of **catharsis**. Freud and his followers have argued that built-up aggressive energy has to be discharged through aggressive behaviour or activities related to aggression, such as contact sports or witnessing aggression. According to this view, we feel better after giving vent to our frustrations and anger. Research findings, on the other hand, cast doubt on the idea that catharsis lowers aggression. Some studies have demonstrated that watching or participating in aggression enhances emotional arousal and aggressive behaviour. In one study, subjects who verbalized their hostility towards another person ended up disliking that person even more (Kahn, 1966). In another study, participation in or witnessing of aggressive sports generally produced more aggression (Quanty, 1976). Baron (1983) found that watching television or film violence, and expressing violence verbally or through aggressive behaviour, normally does not reduce aggression but can sometimes lead to increased aggression.

"COULD BE HE HAD A BRAIN TUMOUR, OR SOMETHING": PHYSIOLOGICAL INFLUENCES ON AGGRESSION

Even if aggression is not "instinctive," could it have a physiological basis? Could a brain tumour, or too much of a particular hormone, or a genetic predisposition cause aggressive behaviour? There have been various attempts to demonstrate physiological influences on aggression. A number of researchers have concluded that any effect of neural, hormonal, or genetic factors on human aggressiveness is likely to be indirect (Montague, 1973; Nelson,1974, 1975; Valenstein, 1975). The biological approach to aggression is quite appropriate when dealing with animals. However, the powerful influence of learning upon human behaviour and the complexity of human social interaction compels a shift from a biological to a socio-cultural perspective in accounting for aggression in humans (Tedeschi, 1983). For example, there is no doubt that our reaction to pain and frustration depends on how we have learned to react to similar situations in the past and on how our society encourages us to respond.

Is aggression instinctual? What controversies are associated with the instinctual view of aggression and with frustration-aggression theory?

catharsis Reduction in aggressive drives thought to result from either acting aggressively or watching others do so.

BOX 8-2

THE SEVILLE STATEMENT ON VIOLENCE

The argument that aggression is the result of inborn factors has not died away, but simply taken a slightly different form. Some strongly argue that genetic and biological factors are important contributors to aggression and violent crime (e.g. DiLalla and Gottesman, 1991). Taking issue with this view, scholars meeting at the International Colloquium on Brain and Aggression at the University of Seville in 1986 issued the "Seville Statement on Violence," which has since been adopted by the United Nations Educational, Scientific, and Cultural Organization (UNESCO) and endorsed by the American Psychological Association (*American Psychologist,* 1990). The statement included these five declarations, along with supporting arguments for each:

It is scientifically incorrect to say that we have inherited a tendency to make war from our animal ancestors.

It is scientifically incorrect to say that war and other violent behaviour is genetically programmed into our human nature.

It is scientifically incorrect to say that in the course of human evolution there has been a selection for aggressive behaviour more than for other kinds of behaviour.

It is scientifically incorrect to say that human beings have a "violent brain."

It is scientifically incorrect to say that war is caused by "instinct" or any single motivation.

SELF-TEST QUESTIONS

1. Which of the following would be considered aggression, as the term is defined in the text?

a) a motorist accidentally runs over an unseen child

b) an assertive salesperson manages to sell $250 000 worth of automobiles in one month

c) a boy attempts to hit a classmate with a rock but misses

d) a dentist drills a patient's tooth

2. Whether or not an action is considered to be aggressive depends on

a) the degree of physical harm involved

b) the intentions of the person committing the act

c) the relationship between the people involved

d) the mental stability of the person involved

e) the laws governing aggressive acts

3. The view that aggression is the result of the displacement of the accumulated energy from the death instinct outwards onto others is known as

a) the sociopathic hypothesis

b) the psychoanalytic approach to aggression

c) the learning approach to aggression

d) the modelling hypothesis

e) the frustration-aggression theory

4. According to Lorenz's ethological approach

a) biological influences on human aggression are minimal

b) humans have a basic prosocial instinct and this instinct has enabled the species to survive

c) aggression is a positive force because it promotes the survival of the fittest

d) aggression is a negataive force whose power will eventually destroy the human species

"HE MUST HAVE BEEN BROUGHT UP THAT WAY": SOCIAL-DEVELOPMENTAL INFLUENCES

REINFORCEMENT

Many factors influence whether or not we learn aggression. Often we learn to behave aggressively because it pays off. A schoolyard bully learns to intimidate others to get his own way. Teenage hockey players whose fathers applaud aggressive play are the most aggressive players (Ennis and Zanna, 1991). Adults at bargain sales also find that aggression is rewarded. Football fans reward aggression in their favourite players by attention and applause. Indeed, many **reinforcements** for aggression exist in our society.

MODELLING

Although reinforcement is important in the development and maintenance of aggressive behaviour, people frequently acquire it simply by **modelling**—"watching someone else do it." Through observing both the behaviour of others and the consequences of that behaviour, children learn not only how to aggress, but also when and against whom to aggress (Bandura, 1973). Children more readily imitate the behaviour of models who are rewarded than models who are punished. For example, children watched a film of a boy playing with toys that he refused to share with a second boy. The second boy began to beat the first one and to throw darts at his cars. In one version of the film the second boy managed to take the toys away from the first one. In a second version, the first boy counter-attacked when the second boy tried to take the toys, severely punishing the second boy. Later, those children who saw the unopposed-aggression ending behaved more aggressively in a play situation than those who saw the other ending (Bandura, Ross and Ross, 1963a).

Sometimes models simply facilitate behaviour. For example, a spectator at a football game who watches others throwing beer cans at the referee may be prompted to throw things as well. Moreover, a model's aggressive behaviour can heighten emotional arousal, which in turn can facilitate an aggressive response, given the appropriate situational cues. For instance, watching an individual

Why and how do people learn to be aggressive?

reinforcement *Rewarding consequence that increases the probability of a behaviour occurring again.*

modelling *Learning behaviour as a result of watching others.*

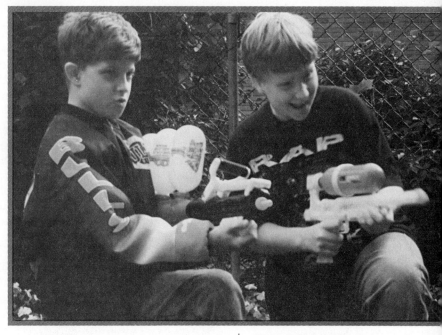

Do water guns ignite aggression or do they just get kids wet?

savagely fight against an opponent may heighten arousal. If one of the protagonists takes a swipe at you, you may react more vigorously as a result of the arousal.

THE CHILD-REARING PROCESS

Parents play at least four different roles in the raising of children (Klama, 1988). First, they are usually the child's first partners in social interaction, and teach the child how to interpret the social environment. Second, they are managers of the child's behaviour, enforcing rules and setting standards of conduct both within and outside the home. Third, they provide models for the child to imitate. Finally, they serve as teachers, directly supplying knowledge, imparting values, and encouraging particular attitudes and manners. Therefore, from a social learning perspective, the behaviour of parents, who largely control the child's world, will play a critical role in determining whether a child grows up to be aggressive.

Research results indicate that parents who frequently use physical punishment or threats tend to have highly aggressive children. First, these parents provide aggressive models for their children to imitate. Their use of punishment and threats indirectly teaches that aggression is effective and acceptable if one is in a position of power. Such physical punishment also produces resentment and frustration in children, which may contribute to subsequent aggression. Second, parents who use physical punishment to control their children often reinforce their children's use of aggressive behaviour in disputes with other children. Third, parents who rely on physical punishment often tend to be emotionally cold and rejecting. Children of cold and restrictive parents typically learn to hide their feelings, developing strong covert aggressive tendencies. Children of cold and permissive parents are often highly aggressive (Becker, 1964).

On the other hand, parents who use such techniques as praise, reasoning, and withdrawal of affection usually have children who rarely behave aggressively. This is true regardless of whether the parents are permissive or overly restrictive. Patterson (1982) found that parents of non-problem boys were more tolerant of undesirable behaviour than parents of problem boys. In addition, the parents of the non-problem boys were more effective in stopping undesirable behaviour when they did react. The parents of problem boys were punitive, but essentially uninvolved. Members of the problem families tended to avoid each other in general, rather than to talk over their problems.

Not only do children learn from their parents to use aggression to control others, but they also learn to use aggression as a problem-solving strategy. If parents use such comments as "If I hear another peep out of you, you're going to get slapped" as a means of solving family problems, the children will learn to use this approach as a means of conflict resolution (Sarles, 1976). In addition, children of these parents do not have the opportunity to learn other, more effective means of solving problems. This deficit may add to the risk that such children will use violence in later life (Moore, Pepler, Mae and Kates, 1989). Children who have experienced neglect as opposed to abuse by parents are also deprived of learning appropriate problem-solving strategies, and also resort to aggression as a means of problem solving. In fact, there is some evidence that children of neglectful parents are more violent in adulthood than children of abusive parents (Widom, 1989).

CHILD ABUSE AND FAMILY VIOLENCE

Marc Lepine's parents separated when Marc was only seven. In her divorce petition, Marc's mother described his father, Rachid Gharbi, as a brutal man who regularly lost control. He beat his wife, Marc, and Marc's sister, for so little provocation as failing to say "good morning" to him. Did such treatment of Marc later lead him to react with such horrific violence towards others?

In recent years considerable attention has been directed to the problem of family violence, including child abuse. Child abuse is different from the physical punitiveness discussed in the previous section. The distinction is based partly on what a given society views as appropriate discipline. It is also based on the severity of the attack and on whether it was intended as punishment or was simply the result of uncontrolled anger.

Abused children are at risk for developing a number of problems and inappropriate behaviours. Studies of children as young as twelve months of age have shown that when children are exposed to anger, even when it is not directed at them, they react in a distressed manner that sometimes includes aggressive behaviours (Emery, 1989). Longitudinal research has shown that aggressiveness tends to perpetuate itself within the family, with each new generation of parents repeating the violence (Sarles, 1976). Children from aggressive families are more likely to marry aggressive individuals, and their children are more likely to be aggressive (Huesmann, Eron, Lefkowitz and Walder, 1984).

Yet we must be careful not to assume that every abused child will become a violent adult and a child abuser. Empirical evidence reveals that the generality of this "cycle of violence" has been somewhat exaggerated (Kaufman and Zigler, 1987; Widom, 1989). Most child abusers were never themselves abused. Most delinquents were not abused as children. Most abused children do not turn into delinquents (Widom, 1989). Abuse produces unwanted behaviours other than violence. Abuse often produces depression, withdrawal, and even self-destruction rather than interpersonal violence. Various psychological characteristics of the child, as well as aspects of family life apart from violence, all play a role in determining how violence affects children (Rutter, 1987).

"HE'S JUST A TOUGH CHARACTER WHO LOST CONTROL": AGGRESSIVENESS AS A PERSONALITY TRAIT

Marc Lepine's personality was no doubt marked by the poor relationship he had with his father. Following the parents' separation his father deserted him, and at age fourteen he insisted on changing his surname to that of his mother. He was described by teachers as a loner, keeping to himself even when at school. Many people who knew him said that he had long appeared troubled. When he applied to join the Canadian Forces, he was rejected as having an unsuitable personality for a military career.

Was there aggressiveness lurking beneath Lepine's quiet exterior? Is it possible that there is a "trait" of aggressiveness—that we can characterize people as being more or less aggressive? Research results show that there is no cluster of traits that describes an "aggressive" person. However, there are a number of individual characteristics that bear on aggressiveness, including intelligence, self-esteem, authoritarianism, self-control, and antisocial personality. Each of these is briefly discussed below.

(1) Intelligence.   Young children become less aggressive as they grow and learn other coping strategies (Eron, Heusmann, Dubow, Romanoff and Yarmel, 1987). Learning these strategies, as well as other skills, may be difficult for children of

How do individual personality characteristics influence aggression?

lower intelligence. Learning difficulties may produce frustration, which may lead to more aggression. Aggressive children may be avoided by peers and teachers. As a consequence, their opportunities for learning and for receiving reinforcement for positive behaviour may be limited.

(2) Self-esteem. Threats to self-esteem, such as criticism or insults, often produce anger and aggression (da Gloria, 1984; Rule and Nesdale, 1974). Individuals whose self-esteem is high but somewhat unstable are most likely to experience anger and aggressiveness. Their self-esteem is more likely to be threatened by insults and criticism than that of people whose self-esteem is high and stable. Individuals with low self-esteem tend to fall between these extremes (Kernis, Grannemann and Barclay, 1989).

(3) Authoritarianism. "Right-wing authoritarianism" may produce a general aggressiveness which is directed at various individuals and which is perceived to be sanctioned by various authority figures (Altmeyer, 1988). (See also Chapter 6.)

(4) Self-control. The appropriately controlled person maintains a balance between assertiveness and inhibition, resorting to aggression only when it might be considered to be socially justified. Megargee (1966) reports that studies of relatively mild aggression show that the overtly aggressive person has fewer controls and a greater need for aggression than does the overtly non-aggressive person. This evidence suggests that the way to discourage mildly aggressive people from acting aggressively is to help them develop internal controls. Extreme aggression cannot be explained by extrapolation from studies of mild aggression. Prison, a setting designed to promote self-control of aggression, does little to help the aggressive but over-controlled individual. Training in how to express hostile feelings non-aggressively might prove to be more beneficial.

(5) Antisocial personality. Individuals who are identified psychiatrically as having anti-social personality disorder typically lack empathy, remorse, or guilt, have little concern for the feelings and well-being of others, exhibit weak self-control, extreme selfishness and impulsiveness, show little fear of punishment, and often fail to learn from the negative consequences of their behaviour. They receive more convictions for violent crimes and behave more violently while in prison than do other prisoners (Hare and McPherson, 1984). Their crimes appear "cold-blooded" and lacking in understandable motivation, although revenge may sometimes be a factor (Williamson, Hare and Wong, 1987).

SELF-TEST QUESTIONS

5. The notion that aggression is learned through the imitation of others is proposed by

a) classical conditioning theory

b) frustration-aggression hypothesis

c) ethological theory

d) psychoanalytic theory

e) social learning theory

6. Which of the following is not a characteristic of parents who are likely to have aggressive children?

a) use physical punishment

b) frequently use power-assertive techniques

c) cold and rejecting

d) teach problem-solving skills

e) neglect

7. Research on child abuse and family violence has shown that

a) all child abusers were themselves abused as children

b) children from aggressive families are more likely to marry aggressive individuals

c) most abused children turn out to be delinquents

d) aggression perpetuates itself within the family

e) both b and d

8. Which of the following is true about research on self-esteem and aggression?

a) individuals who have a high and stable self-esteem are most prone to anger and aggressiveness

b) individuals who have a high but unstable self-esteem are most likely to experience anger and aggressiveness

c) individuals who do not need social approval to maintain their self-esteem are very prone to anger and aggressiveness

d) individuals who need social approval to maintain self-esteem are very prone to despondency and aggressiveness

"IT'S OUR SOCIETY": CULTURAL INFLUENCES ON AGGRESSION

Societies differ greatly in the value they place on aggression. Some encourage it, but there are many in which violence of any kind is actively discouraged. For example, the Pygmies, the Zunis, the Lepchas—and in Canada, the Blackfoot, Saulteaux, and the Inuit—are all traditionally peace-loving groups. The fact that such groups can still be found who prefer and practise a non-aggressive existence illustrates that violence is not an inevitable aspect of social life.

Culture plays a large role in determining how we deal with conflict, whether by negotiation, a flurry of fists, or a knife in the side. In Western culture we encourage aggression, especially in males who are taught that "winning" is important, and that aggression is often a means to that end. By contrast, children in Japan are actively discouraged from quarrelling through learning that yielding is more honourable and more desirable than being assertive in the quest for personal goals. The child who gives in to promote group peace and harmony receives reinforcement from the mother. He or she is told "Makeru ga kachi," which means "To lose is to win."

Canadians like to believe that their history has proven them more peaceful and less aggressive than other nationalities, especially their neighbours to the south, and in many ways this is true. Canada is less militaristic. Three times as many Americans as Canadians are in the armed services, and the U.S. allocates three times as much of its GNP to military expenditures as Canada does. The homicide rate is also much higher in the U.S. than in Canada (see Figure 8-1 and Box 8-3).

How do cultural values influence aggression?

209

FIGURE 8-1 **Comparative homicide rates, Canada and the United States, 1980-1994**

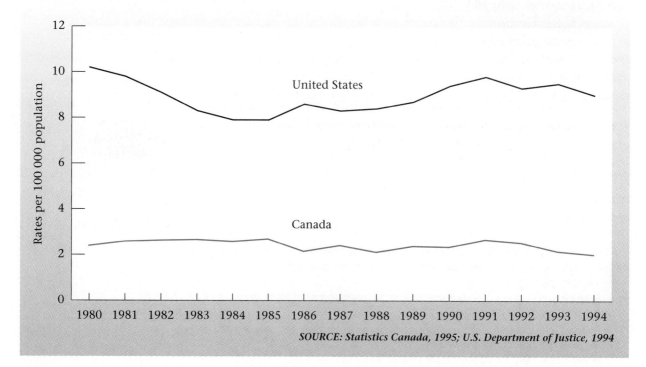

SOURCE: Statistics Canada, 1995; U.S. Department of Justice, 1994

BOX 8-3
A PORTRAIT OF VIOLENT CRIME IN CANADA

Canada is a relatively peaceful country. Historically, the homicide rate in this country has been only a quarter of that of the United States. Canada's 1994 rate—2.04 per 100 000 population—is the lowest rate recorded in Canada in twenty-five years. However, Canada's homicide rate is generally higher than most European countries. For example, in England and Wales the 1994 rate was 1.4 per 100 000, about 30 percent lower than Canada's rate. Statistics Canada (1995a, 1995b) has provided the following picture of violent crime in Canada in 1994:

• Violent crime decreased by 3 percent, the largest annual decrease since 1962. All categories of violent crime decreased. This decrease and the slight decrease in 1993 follow fifteen years of annual increases in violent crime.

• Despite recent decreases in reported crime rates, the 1994 crime rate was 8 percent higher than a decade ago.

• Most violent crime incidents were minor assaults (60 percent).

• Sexual assaults accounted for 10 percent of all violent incidents.

• Homicides and attempted murders accounted for less than one percent of violent crimes.

• About one-third of all homicides were shootings.

• In general, the homicide rate per 100 000 population was highest in the western provinces (British Columbia 3.08) and the Territories (Yukon 9.97), lowest in the Atlantic provinces (Newfoundland 0.69), and in between in central Canada.

"WHAT WITH ALL THE VIOLENCE ON TV...": MEDIA AND AGGRESSION

Traditional members of the Cree community of Norway House on Lake Winnipeg refer to television by the Cree word "koosapachigan," which means "shaking tent," a place where shamans of the past conjured up spirits of the living and spirits of the dead. Some of these spirits were not very friendly.

Indeed, much of what is shown on television is not "friendly." Children, adolescents, and adults spend a considerable proportion of their leisure time watching television. And there is much on TV that is violent. In 1983, the U.S.-based National Coalition on Television Violence reported that CTV was the most violent of 30 television networks, including networks from the U.S., Japan, Germany, Britain, and Australia. Sixty-five percent of CTV's programs were found to be in the "high violence" category, and almost all this violent programming was imported from the U.S. Other research has reported that, on average, there are five to six violent incidents per hour of prime time American television, and 15 to 25 violent incidents for each hour of cartoons (Signorielli, Gross and Morgan, 1982).

Many Canadians are expressing increasing concern about television violence. In November 1992, 21 cartons filled with petitions signed by 1 283 453 Canadians were carried into the office of Communications Minister Perrin Beatty in Ottawa. The petitions called for legislation to control and ultimately eliminate violence from Canadian television. Virginie Larivière, a fourteen-year-old Quebec girl, organized the campaign following the rape and murder of her younger sister. For seven months she and her family gathered signatures from across Canada, in the belief that television violence promotes real-life violence. Keith Spicer, Chairman of the Canadian Radio-television and Telecommunications Commission, met with Virginie and her parents in Montreal. He said he did not think legislative intervention was a realistic solution. Instead he encouraged parents and teachers to screen what children watch and not to subscribe to cable companies whose programs are excessively violent.

There are many sources of violence in the media beyond what is available on television. Films, music, magazines, newspapers, books, and even children's stories and nursery rhymes often have violent themes. The '70s saw the rise of rock groups such as Alice Cooper and Kiss, and "heavy metal" bands such as Iron Maiden, who provided audiences with simulated violence. These and other performers were noted for their emphasis on aggression, sexuality, and sexual aggression. In the '80s rock videos became increasingly popular, and some of these presented violent and sexually aggressive themes, mostly at the expense of women. The '90s have also seen the rise of violent songs and videos directed at women, racial minorities, and unpopular figures such as the police (Armstrong, 1992).

How is media violence related to aggression?

EFFECTS OF TELEVISION AND FILM VIOLENCE

What are the effects of media violence? Does it lead to increased violence on an individual and societal level? What are the consequences for the developing child who is exposed to violent television every day for several years? What are the effects on adult viewers of films that portray typically weak and submissive individuals suddenly using firearms to exact justice from a seemingly unfair world?

Laboratory studies have clearly demonstrated that viewing television or film violence in the laboratory leads to increased aggression, but we must be cautious in applying these results outside the lab (Freedman, 1984). The measures of aggression used in the lab, such as delivering "electric shocks," may not have much to do with "real-life" aggression. However, field studies that are free of the problems associated with laboratory research also demonstrate that watching film violence contributes to aggression (Parke et al., 1977).

A growing body of correlational research provides evidence that viewing violence during childhood contributes to aggressive behaviour. Huesmann (1986) found that males who had watched more TV and who preferred violent programs at age eight were more likely to have been convicted of criminal acts by age thirty. However, it is likely that the relationship between viewing violence and behaving aggressively is not a simple one. Eron (1980) suggests that children are more apt to model violence if they identify with the characters portraying violent behaviour in the media. Heath, Kruttschnitt, and Ward (1986) found that viewing violence and growing up in violent families, but not viewing violence alone, distinguished between male inmates incarcerated for violent crimes and non-incarcerated and non-violent males.

LIFE BEFORE AND AFTER TELEVISION

A study carried out in Notel, a small B.C. logging town, compared the aggressiveness of children before the introduction of TV and two years later when 90 percent of their homes had TV sets (Joy, Kimball and Zabrack, 1977, 1986). After the introduction of television children in Notel were more physically and verbally aggressive. Furthermore, they were more aggressive than children of the same age who had grown up with TV in two nearby towns, Unitel and Multitel, that were similar in size, occupations, and socioeconomic status. Prior to the introduc-

FIGURE 8-2 Television and physical aggressiveness of children in three communities

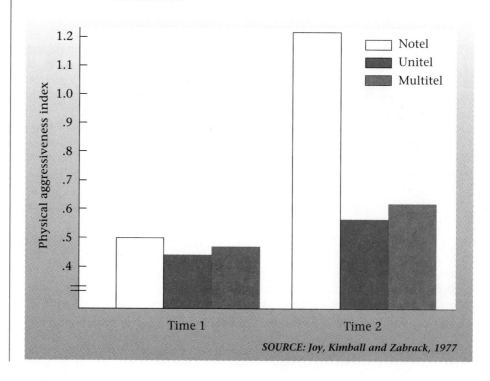

SOURCE: *Joy, Kimball and Zabrack, 1977*

tion of television in Notel, the children in the three towns had not differed in levels of aggressiveness. Since the children were compared to others of the same age, and since the towns in which the children lived were very similar, it seems reasonable to attribute the increase in aggressiveness of the Notel children to the introduction of television.

INDIRECT NEGATIVE CONSEQUENCES OF MEDIA AGGRESSION

There are a number of indirect ways in which television violence can lead to negative social consequences: stimulus pairing, desensitization, imitation and contagion, changes in values, and increased apprehension about real-world violence. Each of these is briefly discussed below.

How can media aggression indirectly lead to negative consequences?

(1) Stimulus pairing. Berkowitz (1971, 1984) proposed that the constant pairing of weapons (e.g. guns) with aggression on television and in films may actually lead to the classical conditioning of aggressive emotional reactions. Berkowitz suggests that people sometimes react aggressively in certain situations because a situational cue (e.g. the presence of a gun) actually elicits an aggressive response because of its past association with violence. Thus, seeing a gun may always evoke aggressive feelings, although normally there is no "reason" to use the gun. However, when an individual is frustrated, angered, or frightened, the presence of a gun may elicit the behaviour it has so often been paired with on TV and film, i.e., shooting another person. However, the effects of cues to violence may depend on the extent to which an individual has characteristically used violence in the past. Josephson (1987) studied stimulus pairing of a cue with violence in third grade Winnipeg schoolboys. Boys in one group saw a walkie-talkie in a violent film segment and then were interviewed by someone using a walkie-talkie just before they played hockey. These boys played more aggressively than boys in a group who had seen a neutral film without any violence-related cue. In addition, the boys exposed to the violent film segment and the violence-related cue played more aggressively than boys exposed to a violent film alone. This study illustrates how powerful the conditioning effects of television and film violence can be: even a previously neutral stimulus, when associated with violence, can lead to increased aggression.

(2) Desensitization. Media violence may lead to increased **desensitization**. In one study, children with histories of high and low exposure to television were shown a moderately violent film. Measures of autonomic arousal (blood volume, pulse amplitude, galvanic skin response) were taken before and after viewing the film. The high-exposure subjects were found to be less autonomically aroused than the low-exposure subjects (Cline, Croft and Courrier, 1973). These results, which have also been found in other studies, suggest that desensitization to violence generalizes. That is, people will experience relatively low arousal not only to the specific forms of violence they have watched repeatedly in particular TV programs or films, but also to other forms of violence in other settings. However, the decrease in arousal appears to occur primarily in those who are less apprehensive about becoming victims of violence (Rule and Ferguson, 1986).

desensitization Reduction in emotional response to violence due to excessive exposure to violence.

(3) Imitation and contagion. Some of the studies reported above demonstrated that children learn to imitate violence. An equally important issue is the imitative repetition by adults of crimes of violence reported in the newspaper. This phenomenon is called **contagion**. History provides numerous examples of such "con-

contagion Imitative repetition by adults of crimes of violence reported in the newspaper or other media.

213

tagion." In nineteenth century England, news of Jack the Ripper's exploits provoked a series of female mutilations in England (Berkowitz, 1971). A flurry of assassination attempts around the world followed U.S. President Kennedy's assassination in 1963 (Weisz and Taylor, 1969). Well-publicized murders have been followed by an unusual increase in violent crimes (Berkowitz and Macaulay, 1971).

(4) Effects on values and attitudes. An analysis of the "message" of violent television programming suggests that in the world of television violence is generally a successful means of obtaining personal goals, that it is not punished, and that law enforcement agencies use violence to resolve conflicts (Gerbner, 1969). The Ontario Royal Commission (1977) reported concern that television's use of violence sets up a system of values which shows a lack of respect for individual rights and which is at odds with traditional Canadian family values.

(5) "School for scandal." Television and cinema may actually teach people how to commit crimes. In their report to the Ontario Royal Commission, Stanley and Riera (1977) cite several instances in which people have used knowledge gained from movies and TV in committing a crime or in eluding police. For example, in June 1976, *La Grande Casse* had a long run in Montreal cinemas. It showed in detail how to steal cars, including how to start them without a key. The car thieves were glorified and the police were portrayed as incompetent. The car theft rate in Montreal jumped almost immediately and a number of youths responsible for at least 45 car thefts were arrested. They admitted getting both the idea and the technique from the film.

SELF-TEST QUESTIONS

SELF TEST

9. Which of the following statements reflects the findings regarding cultural influences on aggression?

a) aggressiveness varies very little from culture to culture

b) aggression cannot be controlled

c) cultural values have little influence on aggressive behaviour

d) cultures differ greatly in the value placed on aggression

e) a and c

10. The pairing of weapons and aggression on television

a) may lead to the classical conditioning of aggression

b) may lead to less violence in the viewer

c) is typically associated with pleasure

d) may lead to intolerance of aggression

e) leads people to fear weapons more

11. The contagion view of aggression suggests that

a) aggressiveness can be transferred from person to person

b) when certain emotions are released, a person becomes frustrated and acts aggressively

c) there is a generalization of desensitization to violence in many forms

d) publicized acts of violence result in an increased incidence of such acts

e) none of the above

12. Which of the following is a major source of social psychological evidence on the effects of viewing violent television?

a) laboratory experiments

b) field studies

c) correlational studies

d) longitudinal research

e) all of the above

"ANY NUT CAN BUY A GUN": FIREARMS AND HOMICIDE

The .223 calibre Sturm Ruger Carbine is a lightweight, accurate, and devastating semi-automatic weapon used by the military, police assault teams, and hunters. Until recently it was sold in Canadian gun stores to any customer with a licence to purchase a gun. This licence could be obtained upon application after taking a firearms safety course, passing a safety test, and paying a nominal fee, as long as the applicant did not have a history of violent behaviour. The Sturm Ruger rifle has been one of the most popular hunting rifles in Canada. It is the rifle that Marc Lepine used to kill his victims.

Recently the federal government passed new gun-control legislation. As of January, 1996, committing a serious crime with a gun will result in a mandatory prison sentence of at least four years instead of one year. Other aspects of the legislation dealing with registration took effect mid-year. Registration is required for unrestricted weapons such as common rifles and shotguns used for hunting and sport as well as for restricted weapons. Some firearms have been reclassified, resulting in a ban on weapons considered unreasonable for hunting and other sports. This ban includes the Sturm Ruger rifle used by Marc Lepine.

However, rifles and shotguns are still readily available, although not so readily as in the U.S. and some other countries. Compared with Canada, controls on guns are lax in the U.S., and the difference is most marked with regard to handguns and automatic weapons. The use of handguns to commit murder is a growing problem in the U.S.; for example, in 1992 guns were used in 68 percent of homicides there (United States Department of Justice, 1993).

Yet opponents of gun control argue that it is criminals who kill, not guns, and that the restriction of guns will only mean that killers have to choose other weapons. There is little doubt that gun controls do reduce the rate of homicide by firearms; the stricter the controls, the smaller the proportion of murders committed with guns (Lester, 1984; Lester and Murrell, 1986).

We should remember that most murderers do not stalk anonymous victims as Marc Lepine did. In 1994, of the homicides where an accused was identified, over 80 percent involved victims who were known to their killers, and about 40 percent were committed by people involved in a close relationship with the victim (Statistics Canada, 1995b). Having a gun in one's home may in itself be a dangerous situation, for when emotions are running high, the use of the gun can be provoked.

What changes in gun control legislation were made in 1996? What are some of the controversies associated with this legislation?

"MEN'S DEEP-SEATED HOSTILITY": VIOLENCE TOWARDS WOMEN

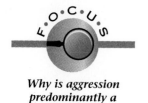

Why is aggression predominantly a male behaviour?

Marc Lepine's violent rampage was a deliberate act against women. According to Marc Lepine's mother, his father regularly expressed the view that women were not men's equals, but their servants. Marc Lepine had wanted to study engineering at the École Polytechnique. He had applied but had been turned down. Is this why he decided to kill women at that institution? When a wounded young woman pleaded with him, he said, "Why should women be engineers and not men?"

Following Lepine's killings, many feminists across the nation saw his actions as symptomatic of a current in Canadian society that teaches, condones, and excuses violence towards women. That such violence, and fear of violence, exists there is no doubt. Only 16 percent of women compared to 48 percent of men feel very safe when walking alone in their own neighbourhoods at night (Statistics Canada, 1995d). In 1994, males accounted for almost 90 percent of all persons charged with violent crimes in Canada (Statistics Canada, 1995c). Although almost 90 percent of murderers are male, one-third of homicide victims are female (Statistics Canada, 1995c). This indicates that proportionately more women are killed by men than vice versa. (See Figure 8-3).

Why is violence such a male behaviour? Through the ages it is men, not women, who have marched off to battle. Men, not women, have duelled to avenge wounded pride. Research shows that male students opt for physical aggression more often than female students as a means of resolving hypothetical interpersonal conflicts (Reinisch and Sanders, 1986). Do these differences reflect differences in physiology or in upbringing?

FIGURE 8-3 **Homicide rates for adult male and female victims, Canada, 1962-1990**

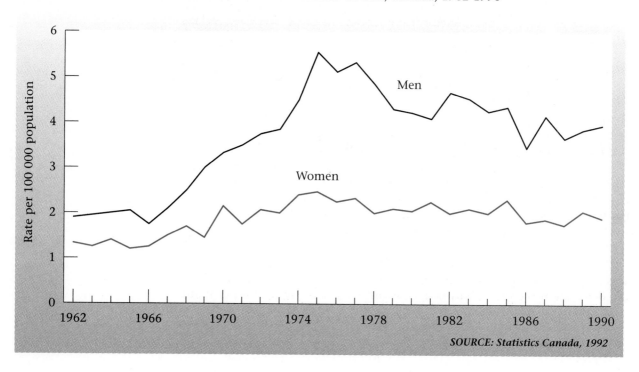

SOURCE: Statistics Canada, 1992

SEX HORMONES

Research has shown that within many species there are substantial gender differences in aggressiveness. Males fight readily while females rarely do except to protect their young (Archer, 1976). These differences have often been attributed to sex hormones. There is evidence that in animals, at least, aggressiveness is related to androgen (male hormone) levels. However, with humans the situation is much more complicated. Androgens enhance musculature and increase available energy. For humans, how that physique and energy are employed depends on socialization. In our society, the male role accepts, even demands, aggressiveness, while the female role discourages it (Eagly and Steffen, 1986; Lubek, 1979).

GENDER ROLES

Our culture has long associated masculinity with aggressiveness: to "back down" in the face of a threat is usually considered sissyish or "effeminate." The *Random House Dictionary of English Language* defines "feminine" as "like a woman; weak; gentle," indicating how ingrained is the association between femininity and non-aggressiveness in our society. The association of aggressiveness with the masculine role is stronger in some cultures than in others.

In our society, women typically experience more guilt and anxiety as a result of aggression, and are more concerned with the harm that comes to victims and with the danger that might come to them if they are aggressive (Eagly, 1987). Yet this is a learned reaction, and the research literature suggests that females could be socialized to be as aggressive as males (White, 1983).

Crime statistics support the view that aggression is predominantly a male behaviour. Males make up by far the larger portion of offenders in the criminal justice system. In 1994, eight in ten people charged with crimes were male. Females were more often charged with property crimes than violent crimes, while the opposite was true for males (Statistics Canada, 1995c). For both youths and adults, there were fewer females than males charged with violent crimes. However, proportionately the picture for violent crime charges differs for youths and adults. In 1993, 24 percent of youths and 12 percent of adults charged were female (Statistics Canada 1995d).

SPOUSAL ABUSE

Women are much more frequently the victims of male violence than vice versa. Twenty-nine percent of all women who have been married or lived in a common-law relationship have been physically or sexually assaulted by their partner at least once (Statistics Canada, 1995d). There is growing evidence that violence occurs frequently in dating relationships as well, even at the teenage level, and such violence is very similar in pattern to spousal abuse (Pedersen and Thomas, 1992, Princz, 1992). Women in Canada are seven to eight times more likely to be assaulted by the man they love than by a stranger (Jaffe, 1990; Statistics Canada, 1995d).

Domestic violence is the most common form of violence in North America (Widom, 1989). In Canada in 1994, approximately one-third of abused women had been victimized more than ten times. One-third of women in violent relationships feared for their lives on at least one occasion (Statistics Canada, 1995d). Forty percent of female homicide victims were killed by a spouse compared to seven percent of male victims (Statistics Canada, 1995b). (See Table 8-1.)

TABLE 8-1 **Solved Homicides by Accused-Victim Relationship[1], 1992-1994**

Relationship Type	1994		1993		1992	
	Number	%	Number	%	Number	%
Accused was						
Family Relationship						
Husband (legal and common-law)	51	10.7	49	9.8	64	10.7
Husband (separated/divorced)	14	2.9	14	2.8	23	3.9
Wife (legal and common-law)	19	4.0	22	4.4	18	3.0
Wife (separated/divorced)	1	0.2	2	0.4	—	0.0
Father	29	6.1	22	4.4	16	2.7
Mother	19	4.0	16	3.2	20	3.4
Child	20	4.2	15	3.0	23	3.9
Sibling	17	3.6	3	0.6	14	2.3
Other family relation	20	4.2	21	4.2	19	3.2
Total family	190	40.0	164	32.9	197	33.0
Acquaintance						
Estranged lover	5	1.1	9	1.8	11	1.8
Intimate relation	13	2.7	22	4.4	23	3.9
Close acquaintance	30	6.3	35	7.0	29	4.9
Business associate (legal)	11	2.3	15	3.0	21	3.5
Business associate (illegal)[2]	48	10.1	41	8.2	39	6.5
Neighbour	14	2.9	27	5.4	31	5.2
Casual acquaintance	98	20.6	105	21.1	145	24.3
Total acquaintance	219	46.1	254	51.0	299	50.1
Stranger	62	13.1	73	14.7	88	14.7
Unknown relationship	4	0.8	7	1.4	13	2.2
Total solved homicides	475	100.0	498	100.0	597	100.0

[1] *Includes only homicide offences in which there are known suspects. If there was more than one suspect, only the closest relationship to the victim was recorded.*
[2] *Includes business relationships such as prostitutes, drug dealers, and their clients.*

Source: Homicide Survey, Policing Services Program, Canadian Centre for Justice Statistics, August 1995.

Although there are occasional reports of women using physical violence against their husbands, it is rare that such violence has not been preceded by the husband's violence towards the woman. Why do men violently abuse the people they presumably love? It is very often the case that the root of men's violence against women is the misuse of power: some men have been socialized to believe that they are justified in controlling the women in their lives, even if they use violence to do so (Walker, 1989).

BOX 8-3
PORNOGRAPHY AND VIOLENCE

WHAT TYPE OF PORNOGRAPHY IS READILY AVAILABLE IN CANADA?

Palys (1986) analyzed 150 sexually oriented home videos from Vancouver video stores (regular video stores and sex shops) in terms of sexual, aggressive, and sexually aggressive content. Palys wanted to test the common belief that triple-X videos would contain more aggressive sexuality and would be more likely to portray women as victims. He found that although triple-X videos contained more explicit depictions of the sex act, adult videos had more aggressive and sexual content and presented this violence with greater severity.

WHO USES PORNOGRAPHY?

A recent survey of English-speaking Canadians found that teenagers under the age of seventeen are the most frequent consumers of sexually explicit movies, whether on television, in cinemas, or on video cassettes. Also people in this age group were found to be more accepting of sexually violent or degrading films than people of other age groups (Check, Heapy and Iwanyshyn, 1994).

WHAT EFFECTS ARE ATTRIBUTED TO PORNOGRAPHY?

(1) Gender schematization. "Gender-schematic" individuals tend generally to view males and females in terms of sex-typed dimensions ("men are strong, women are weak" and so on). A recent study using male introductory psychology students at the University of Waterloo, Ontario, found that gender-schematic males who watched a non-violent pornographic film were subsequently more likely to treat a female research assistant as a sexual object than were those who watched a neutral film (McKenzie-Mohr and Zanna, 1990). Pornographic films most likely do more than prime a schema; they may contribute to the development of that schema. Many males learn about female sexuality from such films.

(2) Desensitization and increased sexual callousness. Studies have shown that male viewers of violent pornography differ from non-viewers in their attitude towards rape (Malamuth, 1984); they view rape as less horrible and the victim as more desirous of being violated. In a Canadian study, Check (1985) found that dehumanizing and violent pornography led to an increase in the self-reported likelihood that subjects would employ force to obtain sexual favours, while erotic films produced no such change.

(3) Habituation. Research has shown that repeated exposure to pornography leads to **excitatory habituation.** That is, as individuals watch more and more pornography, it produces less physiological arousal, less pleasure, and even disappointment and boredom (Zillmann and Bryant, 1984). Such habituation might seem to suggest that people will eventually become bored by pornography. However, other research has shown that habituation to one form of pornography increases interest in more extreme forms (Zillmann and Bryant, 1986).

(4) Increased tendency for violence towards women. Most men find non-coercive sexual scenes more arousing than sexual violence. However, some men are just as aroused or even more aroused by watching violent sex, such as rape. Whether or not this particular group is more likely to carry out such sexually violent acts themselves depends largely on their attitudes about the acceptability of violence towards women (Malamuth, 1986, 1988).

In summary, a variety of undesirable effects are attributed to frequent viewing of pornography. It presents an unrealistic view of sexuality and is associated with sexual callousness and acceptance of violent and degrading behaviour.

Various factors increase the risk for wife abuse. Dutton (1984) presents the following research-based prototype of a male at risk for assaulting his wife. He is a man with a strong need to dominate or control others, and he has poor verbal skills by which to do so. He has witnessed violence as a mode of conflict resolution while growing up, and he is currently experiencing conflict in his marital rela-

habituation *Reduction in physiological response as a result of repeated stimulation.*

tionship. If intimacy or other essential issues are involved in the conflict, he will pressure the woman to comply with his demands, and if this strategy fails, the risk for violence increases. Job stress, and the lack of friends or support groups, also increase the risk for violence. If he lives in a culture that relegates women to subordinate roles and condones both the use of violence for obtaining goal satisfaction and "non-interference" in family matters, the risk for violence increases. If his partner shows more independence from the relationship, through working or the development of new friendships, the risk for violence increases. Thus, many factors increase the risk for violence. Of course, it must be remembered that many abusers do not fit this pattern.

Why does a woman stay with a man who abuses her? A complex process surrounds wife battering. Great displays of contrition and affection between bouts of violent behaviour by the abuser, feelings of powerlessness, belief in their inability to survive economically, and belief that escape from the mate's violence is impossible are some of the most important factors that keep women in abusive relationships (Dutton, 1984).

THE REDUCTION AND CONTROL OF AGGRESSION

What measures can be taken to reduce and control aggression?

It is unlikely that aggression can be eliminated entirely from our society, but steps could be taken to considerably reduce aggression-associated problems.

The deglorification of violence.   Reducing violence in the media would focus less attention on violent events in general. Similarly, the elimination or reduction of violence in sports, especially hockey, would decrease the number of players acting as aggressive role models for children. It is also important to teach children that violent behaviour on television is faked, and rarely occurs in real life (Huesmann et al., 1983).

Gun control.   Stricter gun control laws lead to reduced homicide by firearms, without a corresponding increase in the use of other murder weapons. We must strive to avoid becoming a gun-dominated nation like the U.S. and some other countries.

Parent training.   Most parents are unprepared for the extremely difficult task of training, educating, and socializing their children. It is important to inform parents of the negative effects of watching television violence and to advise them how to control children's viewing rights with a minimum of uproar. Singer and Singer (1981) suggest that teaching parents how to interact with their children, using stimulating games, may be more effective than direct attempts to control the time spent watching television.

As mentioned earlier, certain child-rearing practices are likely to increase aggressive behaviour. Among these are the excessive use of punishment and an emphasis on traditional masculine/feminine role behaviour. Ignoring aggressive behaviour and reinforcing cooperative actions have been shown to increase cooperation and decrease aggression in very young children (Brown and Elliot, 1965).

Another problem that parents, teachers, and eventually employers must face is the management of anger. Singer and Singer (1986) suggest that mediation involving discussion and explanation is more effective than simply telling children to "Stop it!" Another strategy for managing anger involves arousing a response that is incompatible with anger by using empathy or humour (Baron, 1983a, 1983b). Increasing sensitivity to the products of violence, such as suffering and increased hostility, can make aggression less appealing.

Reduction of social inequalities.   Violence is often a symptom of social inequality and injustice. In any society in which some groups are disadvantaged economically and socially relative to others, violence will often appear to be the surest and quickest way to force the majority group to recognize minority needs and to correct injustice. Television, with its display of lifestyles far beyond the reach of the average person, let alone the socially disadvantaged, may raise expectations and increase feelings of powerlessness, possibly leading to violent responses (Lore and Schultz, 1993). Reducing inequities may well reduce violence.

International diplomacy.   Violence is even more complicated at the international level, as will be seen in the chapter on conflict. Terrorism and wars reflect the fact that we have not yet developed social mechanisms for conflict resolution that would make violence unnecessary. The United Nations peacekeeping efforts in Bosnia have been frustrating and discouraging, but it is important to continue to try to find peaceful ways to resolve conflicts.

None of the methods outlined above provides a quick or easy solution to aggression. There is no quick cure. However, we should not be discouraged just because progress is slow.

SELF-TEST QUESTIONS

13. Sex differences in aggression may be the result of

a) differences in physiology

b) differences in attitudes about aggression

c) sex-role differentiation

d) child-rearing techniques

e) all of the above

14. Which of the following is not a factor in the prototype of the male spouse-abuser outlined by Dutton?

a) suffers from job stress

b) strong need for control of others

c) many friends, who are more important than his wife

d) has witnessed violence growing up

e) experiencing marital conflict

15. According to crime statistics, most murders in Canada are committed

a) by people who know their victims

b) by people who are strangers to the victims

c) as a result of domestic violence

d) during random attacks

16. Elicitation of responses that are incompatible with anger, such as humour

a) may increase aggression

b) may reduce aggression

c) have no effect on aggression

d) make aggression seem less serious

SUMMARY

(1) Aggressive behaviour has been explained on the basis of instinct or drive, physiological factors, social learning, and personality.

(2) The instinct or drive theories, psychoanalytic and ethological, have little empirical support. Drive theories assume that aggressive energy held in check must eventually be released (catharsis). However, research evidence does not support catharsis as a means of reducing aggression. Some aggression may be due to frustration. Sometimes aggression is a result of pain or other unpleasant states.

(3) Attempts to isolate specific biological systems directly associated with aggression in humans have not been successful.

(4) Social learning is concerned with the way children learn how to aggress, when to aggress, and against whom to aggress. Learning about aggression can occur by means of reinforcement and punishment or by watching others. Certain child-rearing practices may enhance aggressiveness in children. The socialization factor most strongly related to aggression is the use of physical punishment, especially within a rejecting atmosphere. Children who frequently observe violence in the home may be at risk for becoming violent or abusive adults.

(5) Although personality traits play some role in aggression, their effects are generally outweighed by situational factors.

(6) The prevalence of aggressive behaviour varies considerably between cultures. Some cultures encourage aggression; others frown upon it.

(7) The general consensus is that viewing violence in the media increases the likelihood of aggressive behaviour in children. Media aggression has other potentially harmful consequences.

The pairing of stimuli, e.g. guns and aggression, may increase the likelihood of guns being used when someone is angry. Certain stimuli may prime a series of aggressive, violent thoughts that may lead to aggressive behaviour. Media violence may also desensitize viewers to real-world violence.

(8) Some differences in aggressive behaviour between males and females are related to traditional gender roles that encourage aggression in males and avoidance of physical conflict in females.

(9) Violence by men against their spouses is a continuing problem and usually reflects the need to dominate and control. The portrayal of violence associated with sex may lead to both sexual and aggressive responses in males, posing special dangers to women. One of the most serious problems with pornography is that most of it teaches negative attitudes towards women and may mislead males into believing that women enjoy forced sex.

(10) Stricter gun control has been followed by a decrease in the use of firearms in homicides in Canada, without any corresponding increase in the use of other methods.

(11) Aggressive behaviour could be reduced by teaching parents how to socialize their children towards non-violence. Parents could also learn effective mediation and the proper use of reinforcement to deal with anger in children. Aggression could also be moderated by the deglorification of violence in the media, effective gun control, reduction of social inequities and, at the international level, more effective diplomacy.

FOR REVIEW

Aggression is defined as behaviour that is _____(1) to harm or destroy. It may be used _____(2) to achieve a goal or it may be used deliberately to harm another person.

There are a number of theories about what causes aggression. Freud thought that people behave in an aggressive manner towards others in order to avoid their own _____(3). Lorenz believed that an aggressive drive is essential for survival and _____(4). Other theories postulate that there is a physiological basis to aggression. A number of researchers have concluded that neural, hormonal, and genetic factors have only an _____(5) effect on human aggression. According to frustration-aggression theory, people are predisposed to react with aggression when they confront _____(6). Most research emphasizes the important role of _____(7). Often people are aggressive simply because it pays off. There are many _____(8) for aggression available in our society. Physically punitive parents tend to have aggressive children because such parents act as aggressive _____(9) and may reward aggression in their children. Research results show that there is no cluster of _____(10) that describes an aggressive person, although there are a number of individual characteristics that bear on aggressiveness.

There has been considerable research on the effects of viewing violence. Laboratory studies have clearly demonstrated that viewing violence leads to increased aggression in the _____(11) setting. Longitudinal studies generally find a _____(12) correlation between watching television and aggressiveness. In a study undertaken when television was introduced in a remote British Columbia logging town, children were found to be _____(13) aggressive two years later. With repeated viewing of violence physiological responsiveness to it decreases, a phenomenon known as _____(14). _____(15) occurs when highly publicized acts of violence lead other people to act in similar ways. Repeated exposure to pornography leads to _____(16).

Research shows that male students select _____(17) more often than female students as a means to resolve interpersonal conflicts. Crime statistics show that aggression is predominantly a male behaviour. The most common form of violence in North America is _____(18) violence.

Aggression can be reduced by _____(19) methods that encourage cooperative behaviour, do not reinforce aggressive acts, downplay traditional views of gender roles, and increase the child's sensitivity to the products of violence. Other methods of decreasing violence include such strategies as the deglorification of aggression, _____, and _____(20). At the larger social level it is important to reduce social inequalities and develop more effective diplomatic means of settling disputes.

ISSUES AND ACTIVITIES

(1) Observe the amount and types of aggressive behaviours on some TV programs. Establish a list of the types of behaviours you intend to look for (e.g.

hitting, shooting). Be sure to include a category called "other," since you will probably observe some behaviours that may not seem to fit into your predetermined categories. You should make a few notes describing behaviours in the "other" category. Select one of the following for viewing:

a) prime-time TV programs, one channel from 8 p.m. until 10 p.m. for five evenings

b) news broadcasts, evening and late night broadcasts on one channel for five evenings

c) TV programs aimed at children up to a total of ten hours of viewing time

Write a brief report and share your observations with your classmates.

(2) Save the first three pages of the front section of a newspaper for one week. Note the total number of stories or articles on these pages. Also note the number that include information pertaining to aggressive behaviour. Describe the aggressive behaviours and the other types of themes or behaviours as well. Discuss this news as a reflection of the society or world in which we live.

(3) Work with a group of students who frequently go to movies. Find the pages in the newspaper that advertise films currently being shown. Discuss the themes of these films, identifying aggressive and other themes, and noting the proportions of each type. Also discuss the types of aggressive behaviours portrayed and whether these accurately reflect the real world.

(4) Go into the children's section of a public library or a bookstore. Randomly select ten fiction books for one age group (e.g. preschoolers, young adults). Read each book and identify the theme(s) and types of action. Note whether themes and actions are aggressive, and also note the responses to aggressive behaviours. If you use books for young children be sure to examine illustrations as well as the text. Share your findings with your classmates.

• FURTHER READING

BRICKMAN, J. (1992). Female lives, feminist deaths: The relationship of the Montreal massacre to dissociation, incest and violence against women. *Canadian Psychology, Special Issue: Violence and Its Aftermath, 33,* 128–139. This article is available from the Canadian Psychological Association Web site listed below.

EMERY, R.E. (1989). Family violence. *American Psychologist, 44,* 321–328. A short discussion of the development of abusive relationships within the family.

HUESMANN, L.R. and MALAMUTH, N.M. (Eds.) (1986). Media violence and anti-social behaviour. *Journal of Social Issues, 42* (3). The entire issue of this journal is devoted to the connection between depictions of violence in the media and real-life aggression.

LEYTON, E. (1986). *Hunting humans: The rise of the modern multiple murderer.* Toronto: McClelland and Stewart. An anthropologist's view of the psychological make-up of mass murderers in modern times.

MARANO, H.E. (1995, September/October). Special report: Bullies. *Psychology Today, 28* (5), 50–82. A discussion of why some children become bullies and other children become their victims. Also includes a section on bullying in the workplace.

WALKER, L.E.A. (1989). Psychology and violence against women. *American Psychologist, 44,* 695–702. A discussion of psychology's approach to men's violence against women, and the shortcomings of that approach.

SUGGESTED WEBLINKS

Canadian Psychological Association
    http://www.Phoenix.ca/cpa

Statistics Canada
    http://www.statcan.ca

UCLA Television violence monitoring project
    http://tako.info.ucla.edu/current/hotline/violence/toc.htm

Vis-a-vis A National Newsletter on Family Violence, Canadian Council on
Social Development
    http://www.achilles.net/~council/

ANSWERS TO SELF-TEST QUESTIONS

1. c; 2. b; 3. b; 4. c; 5. e; 6. d; 7. e; 8. b; 9. d; 10. a; 11. d; 12. e; 13. e; 14. c; 15. a; 16. b.

ANSWERS TO FOR REVIEW

1. intended; 2. instrumentally; 3. self-destruction; 4. evolution; 5. indirect; 6. aversive events, frustration; 7. learning; 8. rewards, reinforcements; 9. models; 10. traits; 11. laboratory; 12. positive; 13. more; 14. desensitization; 15. Contagion; 16. excitatory inhibition; 17. physical aggression; 18. domestic; 19. child-rearing; 20. decreasing media violence, effective gun control.

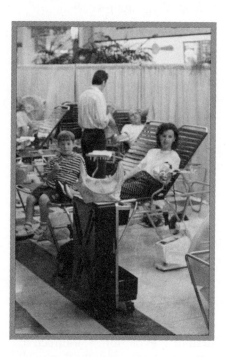

PROSOCIAL BEHAVIOUR

PORTIA: The quality of mercy is not strain'd,
It droppeth as the gentle rain from heaven
Upon the place beneath. It is twice bless'd
It blesseth him that gives and him that takes.

William Shakespeare

The best index to a person's character is (a) how he treats people who can't do him
any good, and (b) how he treats people who can't fight back.

Abigail Van Buren

■ LEARNING OUTCOMES

1. An understanding of the bases of prosocial behaviour.

2. Knowledge of the effects of gender, religion, and other factors on prosocial behaviour.

3. An understanding of the reasons why some people help in an emergency situation while others do not.

4. Knowledge of the nature of heroism and the traits of heroes.

5. An understanding of the measures by which prosocial behaviour might be fostered.

■ FOR REFLECTION

- Is there such a thing as altruism—acting voluntarily to help others without expecting personal gain?
- Is there a "helpful personality" type?
- How can we explain why bystanders fail to help a victim in an emergency?
- What has been learned about heroism?

■ CHAPTER OUTLINE

Suggested WebLinks

Answers to Self-Test Questions

Answers to For Review

Some people devote themselves to selfless service to others. Mother Teresa, a Roman Catholic nun, has chosen to dedicate her life to the orphaned, the sick, and the poor in the slums of Calcutta. Norman Bethune (see Box 9-1) gave up a life of luxury to provide medical support for foreign armies fighting for causes that he believed to be in the best interests of humanity. More recently, in 1992 31-year-old Eric Hoskins was awarded the Pearson Peace Medal in recognition of five years of extraordinary effort to provide humanitarian assistance to children in Iraq, Somalia, and Sudan—countries ravaged by war.

People like Norman Bethune, Mother Teresa, and Eric Hoskins stand as testimony to the human willingness to sacrifice comfort, security, and prestige in order to help less fortunate people. Sadly, the human story has its darker side: not only do most people *not* live up to these models of selflessness, but even worse, they often fail to assist people in urgent need of help, even when doing so might simply involve telephoning an ambulance or the police.

For example, in 1985, a man who tried to stop a group of teenagers who had stolen candy from a counter in the Toronto subway was savagely beaten while more than a hundred people looked on and did nothing; no one even called for help (*The Toronto Star,* January 19, 1985). In 1978, a dozen or more people

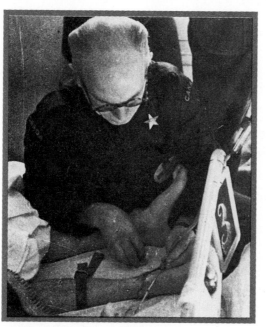

refused to help a father rescue his seven-year-old son who had fallen into the Rivière des Prairies near Montreal. As they watched the boy drown, one person was heard to say "We're not going in there—the water's too dirty," referring to the fact that the boy had fallen in close to a sewage outlet (*The Globe and Mail,* January 6, 1978). In the same year in Edmonton, a 22-year-old woman stepped off a bus on her way home from work one night, unaware that a man from the bus was following her. A short distance from the bus stop, he assaulted her, beating her in the face, stripping off her clothing, and then raping her. Wearing only a coat, with blood flowing from her eyes, she sought help in a nearby apartment where she was told by a tenant to

People like Mother Teresa and Norman Bethune stand as testimony to the human willingness to sacrifice comfort and security in order to help less fortunate people.

get out. She ran out to the street and asked two passersby for help, and was told to go to a nearby pay telephone. Finally, she found help at an all-night grocery where the staff called the police (*The Toronto Star,* November 1, 1978).

This chapter examines the two types of behaviour discussed above. We will explore the factors that influence individuals to donate time, money, and effort to help others, whether on a single occasion or across a lifetime, as well as

BOX 9-1
LIVING ONE'S LIFE IN SERVICE TO OTHERS

Norman Bethune (1890-1939), the son of a Gravenhurst, Ontario evangelical minister, became one of North America's leading thoracic surgeons, inventing some of his own surgical instruments while working in Montreal's Royal Victoria Hospital.

However, he gave up a life of fame and luxury in order to pursue causes that he thought were in the interests of the downtrodden masses. Having witnessed Franco's massacre of defence-less civilians on the streets of Madrid at the out-break of the Spanish Civil War, a war supplied on Franco's side with tanks, planes, and back-up sol-diers—courtesy of Hitler and Mussolini—Bethune went to work as a battlefield physician for the Loyalist forces who opposed Franco.

He founded the Canadian Blood Transfusion Service, the world's first mobile blood bank, which saved the lives of hundreds of Spaniards. After attempting unsuccessfully to rouse Canadian public opinion against the Nazi threat in Spain, his disillusionment with democracy led him to become a Communist. When the Loyalist side was all but beaten in Spain, Bethune went to China to help in the fight against the Japanese invasion. He soon became chief medical officer to Mao Zedong's armies, training uneducated peasants to be field physicians and taking his mobile field hospital to wherever it was most needed. He died on November 12, 1939, after contracting an infection from a wound sustained during emergency surgery. Although recognition was slow to come in his native Canada because of his Communist affiliation, he is revered as a legendary hero—"Comrade Beth"—in China to this day.

the reasons why bystanders often fail to take action to help someone in distress, even in situations of minimal risk.

HELPING BEHAVIOUR: THE TERMS

Prosocial behaviour and **altruism** are terms used to describe actions that are *voluntarily* carried out for the *sole purpose of helping others, without expectation of reward from external sources* (Bar-Tal, 1976). The term "prosocial behaviour" is one invented by social psychologists to avoid some of the connotations histor-ically associated with "altruism." Theologians and philosophers have tradition-ally defined altruism as behaviour that is intended to help others, not only without anticipation of external reward but without anticipation of *self*-reward. Self-reward could be in the form of enhancement of self-esteem, or avoidance of guilt or shame (possible effects of *not* helping). From a philosophical point of view, then, it could be argued that an act that brings pleasure, satisfaction, or re-lief (internal self-rewards) to the actor is no different in principle from one that brings praise or profit, or escape from punishment (external rewards). Debates have continued through the centuries over whether any act can ever be truly altruis-tic in that sense.

However, from the point of view of the social psychologist, it is difficult, if not impossible, to ascertain whether a given behaviour was carried out without any anticipation of self-reward. Moreover, to people who need help, and per-haps even to society as a whole, it makes little difference whether people help self-lessly or because it makes them feel good.

Attributions play a major role in the evaluation of prosocial behaviour, for we must decide what motivates an individual's actions. A politician campaign-

prosocial behaviour Helping behaviour per-formed with no anticipa-tion of an external reward.

altruism Helping others without any expectation of either an external or inter-nal reward.

What motivates helping behaviour?

attributions Our assump-tions about the motivation we attribute to a person's behaviour.

229

ing for office who is seen helping an elderly person across a busy street may not be credited with acting prosocially if observers attribute that behaviour to the desire to "look good" in order to win votes. A policewoman helping a lost child is unlikely to be viewed as acting prosocially, since her action will be interpreted as motivated by duty: she is only doing her job.

HELPING BEHAVIOUR: THE THEORIES

Suppose we stopped people in the street and told them about Norman Bethune's and Mother Teresa's devotion to helping others, and asked them to explain why some people lead their lives in that fashion. Among the answers might be the following:

- Some people just seem to be born saints—always putting other people first.
- Physicians and nuns are supposed to act unselfishly—it's what's expected of them.
- A good upbringing—they were obviously brought up to be helpful to others.
- First you have to feel at peace with yourself—to feel good about yourself—and only then can a person take on other people's problems.
- If you can put yourself in other people's shoes, if you can feel their suffering, then you've just got to help.

Each of these common sense explanations touches on a body of social psychological theory and evidence bearing on the subject of prosocial behaviour. Each will now be explored in turn.

"BORN SAINTS": PROSOCIAL BEHAVIOUR AS AN INBORN TENDENCY

Some theorists argue that natural selection favours the genetic transmission of factors that predispose an organism to be altruistic towards other members of its species. Darwin himself suggested in his *Descent of Man* (1871):

> *As man is a social animal it is almost certain that he would form an inherited tendency to be willing to defend, in concert with others, his fellowmen; and be ready to aid them in any way which did not too greatly interfere with his own welfare or his own strong desires (cited in Latané and Rodin, 1969, p. 189).*

Some research has been interpreted as supporting the position that even animals are genetically programmed to act altruistically (Hebb, 1971; Hebb and Thompson, 1968). For example, it was found that rats would press a bar more often if the action lowered a struggling rat suspended in the air than if it lowered a styrofoam block (Rice and Gainer, 1962). However, such behaviour might be better interpreted in terms of arousal rather than altruism. In another study, it was found that rats would learn to respond in a way that terminated *either* another rat's squeals or loud noise (Lavery and Foley, 1963). It is likely that the "altruistic" rats were motivated to stop the noise made by their distressed brethren rather than by a desire to free them. This example emphasizes that it is very difficult to assess the motivation behind an animal's activity, even if it *appears* to be based on altruism. Reports that dolphins have been known to help other injured dolphins and even human swimmers in distress by lifting them to the surface do not necessarily indicate that the dolphins were trying to "help." After all, we have difficulty trying to decipher the motives of human beings, and we can talk to them!

The contention that prosocial behaviour has a genetic basis still lacks empirical verification. However, it may be that there are more general aspects of personality, such as anxiety-proneness, which might be influenced by heredity and which in turn might make prosocial behaviour more likely. It is not difficult to imagine that people who are more prone to anxiety might grow up to be particularly concerned about the reactions of others to their behaviours. Thus they may strive to do what is socially defined as "the right thing" in any situation. The right thing may often appear to be altruistic—giving blood, helping an elderly person across the street, and so on—but the behaviour may be performed to reduce anxiety rather than to extend help. In a society in which helpfulness is not viewed as socially desirable, such people might act in distinctly unhelpful ways.

How might anxiety-proneness be used to support the notion of a genetic basis for altruism?

"It's what's expected": Prosocial behaviour and norms

As we saw in Chapter 5, social norms exert considerable and often unrecognized control over behaviour. Essentially, they refer to what acts are *not* to be done, and what acts *should* be done. We *should not* blow our noses on our sleeve; we *should* say "thank you" when someone serves us coffee. There are also more specific norms associated with particular roles, although behaviour carried out in the discharge of role responsibilities is not usually considered to be prosocial. The crossing-guard is expected to show more helpfulness to children who wish to cross the street than to other pedestrians. Physicians and nuns are expected to help others, though only in a narrowly defined context.

What are three norms that explain why people help?

Several norms are relevant to prosocial behaviour. The **norm of social responsibility** prescribes that people should help others who need help, whether or not there is a possibility of future reciprocation, and whether or not the people in need had helped the potential benefactor in the past (Berkowitz and Daniels, 1963). The **norm of reciprocity**, which Gouldner (1960) suggests is a universal norm, requires that people help, and not harm, those people who have helped them in the past. If everyone followed the norm, everyone would be helping everyone else and would be receiving help when needed. It is difficult to separate the effects of these two norms in any given situation, that is, to determine whether a person helps because of the obligation to help others in need (social responsibility) or because of anticipated future helping or repayment for past help (reciprocity).

norm of social responsibility *Suggests that in any society there are people, e.g. children, whom we feel deserve our help even if they cannot help us in return.*

norm of reciprocity *Suggests that people return help to those who help them.*

Another norm, the **norm of equity**, specifies that fairness should serve as a criterion for the way that we treat others (Walster, Walster and Berscheid, 1978). If we perceive that another person has tried as hard as we have, whether at some specific task or at life in general, but has not been as fortunate, then this norm would push us to share some of our good fortune with that individual: "It is only fair." If, however, we perceive that the person caused his or her own misfortune, then according to this norm we need not help. Thus, equity considerations motivate us to help someone who has "lost everything" in a fire, but not someone who "lost everything" in a gambling game.

norm of equity *Suggests that we should take what is fair into account when we help. This is especially true if someone is not considered responsible for his or her misfortune.*

We must be careful when trying to explain behaviour in terms of social norms. The research literature indicates generally that people's behaviour often departs from what is prescribed by these norms and that a large number of situational and

The person at the information booth is required to be helpful. Is this prosocial behaviour?

cultural variables influence whether normative behaviour will be performed (Krebs and Miller, 1985). Norms are often both vague and conflicting (Latané and Darley, 1970). They are vague in that they do not generally specify what *specific* behaviour is required (e.g. "We should help those less fortunate than ourselves") and they are often conflicting (e.g. we are taught on the one hand to "keep our nose out of other people's affairs," and on the other to help others when they need help). While social norms may appear useful after the fact for describing behaviour, they may actually mislead or confuse us when we must choose what to do. Thus, while social norms do play some role in prosocial behaviour, it is not a major one.

"A GOOD UPBRINGING": PROSOCIAL BEHAVIOUR AND LEARNING

Norman Bethune was the son of a clergyman, and undoubtedly grew up in an atmosphere that stressed caring for others. The socialization process—perhaps involving reinforcement for prosocial behaviour and the acquisition of parental values that encouraged selflessness—may have played a critical role in shaping his character.

Many studies have demonstrated that, at least in the context of North America and Western Europe, prosocial behaviour increases steadily with age up to about the age of ten (Bar-Tal, 1976). There are two major theoretical approaches regarding how the child acquires such behaviour. The cognitive-developmental or "personal morality" approach views prosocial behaviour as the consequence of attitudes and values shaped by the developing child's experience in the social environment. The social learning view, on the other hand, emphasizes the importance of reinforcement and modelling.

COGNITIVE-DEVELOPMENTAL THEORY

According to this view, people help other people because of a personal set of values and attitudes that oblige them to provide assistance in certain situations. Failure to do so brings about feelings of guilt that are aversive to the individual. This personal morality is said to develop gradually in the growing child. Piaget (1932) believed that the process by which children acquire morality is a universal one. He described different levels of moral thinking acquired at different stages of maturity. Piaget suggested that, in the early stage of the acquisition of morality, children are good or moral in order that the adults in their lives, who set the rules, do not punish them. As children mature and gain more experience with their social environment they understand that other people have needs and rights. So being good or moral at this stage means not abusing those rights.

Building on Piaget's work, Kohlberg (1964) described a six-stage typology of moral development which, he also argued, represented a universal developmental sequence. The stages occur one after the other and always in the same order. In the first stage, the child is concerned with only the physical consequences of his or her actions, and behaves properly only to avoid punishment. Later, in the third and fourth stages, the child's conduct is governed by the desire to appear to be a good person in the eyes of other people through adherence to society's rules. Finally, in the sixth stage, not always attained, the individual's behaviour is guided by reference to self-chosen, abstract, ethical principles that encompass a sense of responsibility towards other people. Therefore a young child may help another child in order to avoid chastisement, and an older child may provide assistance to others in order to "look good," but the "mature" person will do so on the basis of personal principles.

There are many critics of Kohlberg's theory (e.g., Darley and Shultz, 1990), and attempts to demonstrate that moral development is associated with altruistic behaviour have been disappointing (Rushton, 1976). Even if Kohlberg were correct (and this question remains open), his theory still does not explain *how* a person comes to put other people's concerns ahead of personal ones. If the growing child comes to internalize society's values about obligation to others, what is the basis of this internalization? The social learning approach addresses this question.

SOCIAL LEARNING APPROACH

This approach emphasizes the *acquisition* of altruistic behaviour, and takes for granted that prosocial behaviour is learned in the same way that any other behaviour is learned: through reinforcement, self-attributions, and modelling. We now examine the role of these factors, as well as the influence of parental disciplinary techniques, in the acquisition of altruism.

(1) Reinforcement.   Prosocial behaviour is acquired and maintained, at least in part, through consequences deriving from this behaviour. People regulate their actions by self-produced consequences (Bandura, 1974). A child may learn to share toys or to help a sibling because he or she anticipates reward in the form of parental praise that has been bestowed for similar behaviour in the past. Both material and social reinforcement (such as praise) have been found to induce prosocial behaviour in children (Bar-Tal, 1976).

As children develop, so does the capacity for internal self-reward (i.e., feeling good about oneself in some way). In other words, the child learns to help others because he or she anticipates either gain through self-reward or, if no action is taken, punishment through guilt.

(2) Attributions.   Self-reward involves making attributions about ourselves: "I helped that man because I am a good person." Such self-attributions may play an important role in the development of prosocial behaviour because they help define a standard for our behaviour that we strive to maintain in order to avoid negative feelings about ourselves. If you see an elderly person who has just dropped a bag of groceries and is likely to have difficulty picking it up, it is hard to walk by without admitting to yourself that you are unhelpful and even callous. If such a statement contradicts your self-image as a helpful person, you will no doubt experience some discomfort. By fostering the development of positive self-attributions (i.e. helpfulness), prosocial behaviour can itself be encouraged.

Children are more likely to behave well if they attribute their behaviour to internal causes (their own personal morality) than to external causes, such as threats of punishment or hopes of reward (Walters and Grusec, 1977). For example, a child who attributes his acts of charity to a personal concern with the welfare of others may be more likely to repeat such prosocial behaviour than the child who interprets her own generosity as the result of pressure from a parent.

In a study that compared the effects of verbal reinforcement with those of attributions (Grusec and Redler, 1980), children who had won some marbles in a game found themselves in a situation where they could share these marbles with a child who had none. Children in one condition were praised when they

How do Piaget and Kohlberg explain the development of morality?

How do reinforcement attributions and modelling affect the development of altruism?

gave away some of their marbles, while children in another condition were helped to make positive self-attributions by being told that their donations reflected their inherent helpfulness. Children in a third condition were given neither praise nor help with their attributions when they made donations. Reinforcement (i.e., praise) and attribution were both about equally effective in producing donations well above the level of the control group. However, when the children were observed in a different context by different adults either a week or two weeks later, the children who had received the attributional statements were the most generous both in their efforts to be of help and in their willingness to make donations. Those children who had been in the reinforcement condition were the next most generous, while the children in the control condition showed considerably less generosity.

(3) Modelling. While prosocial models do produce *imitative* prosocial behaviour in children (e.g., Grusec, 1972; Grusec and Skubiski, 1970; Staub, 1971; Rushton, 1980), it must be remembered that prosocial behaviour does not necessarily imply prosocial *motivation*. Before we can assume that there is a prosocial motivation, it must be shown that the behavioural disposition endures through time, and can be generalized across situations (Krebs, 1970).

Several studies have demonstrated that children's responses to charitable models are durable and can be generalized. For example, it was found in one study that the observation of an adult donating tokens to a charity positively influenced the children's own donations ten days later, even when the donations were elicited in a different setting by a different experimenter (Midlarsky and Bryan, 1972). In another study (Rushton, 1975) modelled behaviour, whether that of a generous or a selfish model, was still evident two months later despite changes in the situation between test and retest.

If moral development has any effect on altruism, it should be most clearly demonstrated by the extent to which a child is affected by a model's behaviour and preaching (Rushton, 1976), for preaching should remind the child of his or her moral values. Children's *actions* are influenced by the model's *actions*, while children's *words* are influenced by the model's *words* (Bryan and Walbeck, 1970). A model who is actually charitable will have more effect than one who simply preaches charity. This observation has been confirmed empirically (Grusec and Skubiski, 1970): third and fifth grade children were more likely to make a donation after seeing a model donate than after simply hearing the model say that people should donate. Other studies have also found that preaching combined with actually doing what was preached promotes prosocial behaviour (e.g., Radke-Yarrow and Zahn-Waxler, 1984). When models, like many parents, say one thing and do another, the inconsistency of the model is imitated by the child.

Psychologists have naturally been interested in the extent to which children copy altruistic models on TV. In one study that examined this question (Sprafkin, Liebert and Poulos, 1975), thirty first-grade boys and girls watched one of three half-hour programs that were popular with children in the 1970s: an episode from *The Brady Bunch*, a situation comedy, an episode from *Lassie* in which a boy risked his life by hanging over the edge of a mining shaft to rescue a trapped puppy, and an episode from *Lassie* that did not portray altruism. The children were then placed in a game situation arranged so that each child at some point had to choose between continuing to play the game (which led to prizes for points accumulated) and helping a puppy in distress. Those who had seen the *Lassie* program with the helping scene helped significantly more than did the children from the other two groups (Figure 9-1).

FIGURE 9-1 **Duration of children's helping behaviour in Sprafkin, Liebert and Poulos (1975) study**

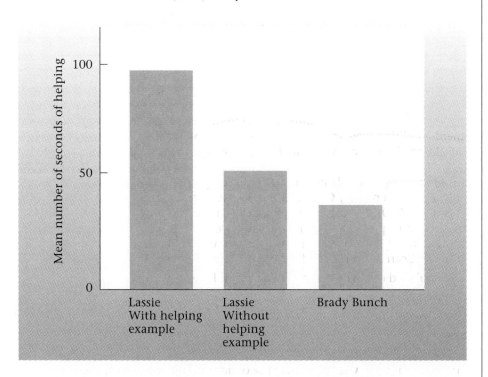

Other studies have resulted in similar findings. Whether a five-minute film clip presented only once is used, or a series of one-hour programs spread over several weeks, the effect on children's free-play behaviour is the same: watching altruistic behaviour on television produces altruistic behaviour in children (Hearold, 1986; Liebert and Sprafkin, 1988). Whether adults are similarly influenced has not yet been established.

(4) Parental discipline. Aside from other factors, one of the most important determinants of the development of prosocial behaviour is the extent to which the parents expressly teach the child about the effects of his or her actions on others (Staub, 1975).

The degree to which the parent displays a nurturing, affectionate attitude towards the child also affects the development of prosocial behaviour. By being guided and controlled through affectionate means, the child is likely to develop an internalized code of conduct involving a positive regard for others and the ability to delay immediate gratification of wants in order to examine other people's needs and feelings.

"FEELING GOOD ABOUT YOURSELF": PROSOCIAL BEHAVIOUR AND MOOD

Do people like Norman Bethune and Mother Teresa help others because they already feel good? There *is* evidence that positive moods facilitate individual acts of charity or helping, while bad moods impede such behaviour (Carlson, Charlin and Miller, 1988; Rosenhan, Moore and Underwood, 1976). For example, when children in one study were asked to reminisce about happy experiences, they gave more to charity than did children asked to reminisce about sad experiences, or children who were not asked to reminisce at all (Rosenhan, 1972). In another study, subjects who had just viewed sad movies donated less money to charity than other subjects who watched neutral movies (Underwood et al., 1977).

Possibly, being in a bad mood limits our ability to turn our attention to other people's difficulties, or even to pay attention to the dictates of our conscience. On the other hand, being in a good mood may increase our *cognitive processing capacity* (Easterbrook, 1959; Rushton, 1980)—that is, increase our ability to notice what is going on around us and to pay attention to our concerns. If this view is correct, then anything that leads to a decrease in cognitive capacity or, at least, a decrease in *available* capacity (for example, being preoccupied by some worry or some important problem), would decrease the tendency towards prosocial behaviour.

THE WARM GLOW OF SUCCESS

If success produces a good mood, then prosocial behaviour should be more evident following success than following failure. This was demonstrated in a study (Isen, 1970) in which subjects were given false feedback about their achievement in a series of tasks. Some subjects were told that they had scored well above the norm, while others were told that they had scored well below the norm. Control subjects were exposed to the same tasks but did not do them. Then, when the experimenter was out of the room, the subjects (who waited one at a time) were observed to see whether or not they would help another person. A confederate, laden down with books, passed in front of the subject and "accidentally" dropped a book. Subjects who had experienced success were more often helpful than subjects in either the failure or the control conditions. In a related study, it was found that "success" led to larger contributions to a charity than did failure. Isen (1970) interpreted these results in terms of a positive mood engendered by success—the "warm glow of success" that predisposes people towards events that will engender more good feelings.

IMAGE REPAIR

image repair hypothesis
People who are embarrassed by some previous behaviour may attempt to repair that damage by being more generous.

Although the "failure" subjects in Isen's study were not especially helpful, other studies have found that making a mistake in public actually influences people to help others. A person who is embarrassed by his or her behaviour may take advantage of a situation in which helping others may improve or repair a damaged self-image. A series of studies (Bégin, 1976) lend support to the **image-repair hypothesis.** In one study, subjects who experienced failure in a motor task subsequently helped the experimenter more than either subjects who had experienced success or subjects who were in a control condition. In a related study, it was found that whether or not the potential beneficiary knew about the subjects' previous success or failure was crucial. Failure subjects helped more when the beneficiary knew of their failure than when the beneficiary did not. In a third study, subjects were assigned to either success or failure conditions on the basis of their *actual* scores obtained on a real exam. As they were leaving the teaching assistant's room after learning their score on the exam, subjects were asked individually to contribute to a worthy cause. The helpfulness of the "success" subjects, who had been informed that their grades were above the class mean, was not influenced by whether or not the canvasser knew their marks. Yet when the canvasser knew the marks of the "failure" subjects, those who had been told their grades were below the class mean contributed considerably more than the "success" subjects. When the canvasser did not know their marks, they contributed significantly less than the "success" subjects.

In summary, when a request for help or charity comes from a person who is unaware of our failure, we will feel no urge to repair our image in his or her presence. However, if that person knows of our failure, we will take steps to mend the damage. Thus, while the warm glow of success leads successful people to act altruistically, those who have failed are likely to help only those who know of their failure.

REPARATIVE ALTRUISM

Experiments have shown that when a person has harmed or hindered another person, he or she often resorts to **reparative altruism**, in which efforts are made to compensate for the harm done, although these efforts are not always directed at the person who was harmed. For example, subjects who administered shocks in a Milgram-type obedience experiment (see Chapter 5) were more likely to volunteer to help in a humanitarian project than were those who did not give shocks (Carlsmith and Gross, 1969). Recall also from Chapter 5 the field experiment carried out in a shopping centre (Regan, Williams, and Sparling, 1972), in which women were asked by a male experimenter to take his picture for a project he was working on. The camera did not work, and he told subjects either that they had broken it (guilt condition) or that it was not their fault (control condition). Shortly afterwards, a female confederate passed the subject, carrying a torn grocery sack trailing various items. While only 15 percent of the subjects in the control condition stopped the woman and told her about the broken bag, 55 percent of the subjects in the guilt condition did so. This phenomenon cannot be explained in terms of image repair, since these subjects were being altruistic towards someone who did not know about their lapse. And unlike the situation in Bégin's studies, failure as such was not involved here. In this case, it can be argued that subjects are trying to lessen guilt by helping others, or at least to bolster their own self-esteem.

Putting the discussion into context, we should be aware that these studies have focused on temporary mood states. More importantly, people who repeatedly have good experiences and find success in life are more likely to develop a greater feeling of well-being than are people who experience repeated failure or rejection (Rushton, 1980). People whose experiences in life are generally positive may well become more happy and optimistic, and possibly more empathic and willing to help others as well.

"OTHER PEOPLE'S SHOES": PROSOCIAL BEHAVIOUR AND EMPATHY

We have learned (Box 9-1) that Norman Bethune was distressed at the sight of helpless civilians being massacred in the streets of Madrid during the Spanish Civil War. Is this why he later returned to Spain to help the Loyalist forces? No one knows for sure, but **empathy** with the suffering of others is a major factor in eliciting prosocial behaviour (Eisenberg and Miller, 1987). Yet the exact nature of empathy is uncertain, and it may well be that more than a single concept is involved when we speak of it. Empathy is not just sympathy. Sympathy refers to a heightened awareness of another person's suffering as something to be allevi-

How important is it that someone knows of our failure in the image repair hypothesis?

reparative altruism
Helping behaviour performed in order to make up for previously harmful behaviour to another person.

How does reparative altruism work?

empathy *A concern for and understanding of the other person.*

How does help differ when it is explained by empathy-altruism versus the negative-state relief hypothesis?

empathy-altruism hypothesis *Suggests that pure altruism comes from empathy.*

negative-state relief hypothesis *Suggests that we give help so that we do not feel sad about another person's situation.*

SELF❓TEST

ated (Wispé, 1986). Empathy is usually defined as an emotional response (a feeling) and a cognitive response (an understanding) of the emotional state of another person (Eisenberg and Miller, 1987; Wispé, 1986; Levenson and Ruef, 1992). It is understood best as seeing things from another's perspective.

Cognitive appraisal likely *precedes* emotional arousal: we must first evaluate the distress produced by another person's plight by putting ourselves in the other person's situation. This leads to an empathic emotional response, which in turn generates the motivation to reduce the person's need (Coke, Batson and McDavis, 1978). For example, if we see a legless man sitting on the sidewalk asking for money we may sidestep him with some annoyance unless we ask ourselves (cognitive evaluation) how the man must feel being reduced to the status of beggar. Then we may feel an empathic response of sadness that will lead us to make a donation.

It was stated at the beginning of the chapter that most social psychologists consider it impossible to determine whether or not an individual ever helps without some anticipation of self-reward. However, research into the role of empathy in prosocial behaviour has rekindled the debate about whether or not "true," selfless altruism exists.

Batson and others (e.g., Batson, 1990; Batson, Batson, Griffitt, Barrientos, Brandt, Sprengelmeyer and Bayly, 1989; Batson, Dyck, Brandt, Batson Powell, McMaster and Griffitt, 1988; Dovidio, Allen and Schroeder, 1990) have presented data in support of the **empathy-altruism hypothesis**, which suggests that pure altruism happens as a result of empathy for a person in distress. Other researchers (e.g., Cialdini, Schaller, Houlihan, Arps and Fultz, 1987; Schaller and Cialdini, 1988) challenge this view and argue that the observer's empathic response to a sufferer's distress produces personal sadness, and that the individual acts to help the sufferer because of the egoistic motivation to relieve his or her own sadness (the **negative-state relief hypothesis**).

It may be that both the empathy-altruism and the negative-state relief hypotheses apply, but to different situations. Batson argues that it is important to distinguish between two different vicarious responses: sympathy and personal distress (Batson, 1987). The former, he suggests, produces altruistic motivation to help, while the latter leads to egoistic help-giving, motivated by a desire to relieve one's own unpleasant internal state. Personal distress is most likely to lead to helping only when an individual cannot easily escape from the situation.

Batson and colleagues support their view that true altruism is involved in prosocial behaviour through research showing that when empathy is high helping occurs at a high level, even when the empathically aroused individual can easily escape the situation.

SELF-TEST QUESTIONS

1. It is difficult to study altruism in animals because

a) their behaviour is programmed genetically

b) they have been influenced by natural selection

c) it is difficult to interpret the motivation behind their behaviour

d) their behaviour is usually motivated by fear in the presence of humans

2. The hypothesis that prosocial behaviour has a genetic basis

a) is accepted as true by most psychologists

b) has not been empirically verified

c) has been verified in animals but not in humans

d) is unrelated to personality

3. According to Kohlberg's six-stage theory of moral development, young children in stage one may help others in order

a) to avoid punishment for not helping

b) to look good to others

c) to uphold moral principles

d) to make new friends

4. Which of the following is described in the textbook as an important parental contributor to the development of prosocial behaviour in children?

a) severe punishment when behaviour is not moral

b) empathy with regard to the child's guilt feelings

c) teaching the child the effects of his or her actions on others

d) being tolerant of all behaviour

OTHER FACTORS THAT INFLUENCE PROSOCIAL BEHAVIOUR

GENDER DIFFERENCES

As we have seen, empathy may play an important role in prosocial behaviour. There are, of course, individual differences in empathy, just as there are differences in the extent to which various situations elicit empathy (Archer et al., 1981). There may also be differences in empathy resulting from gender roles. Since women have been found to experience more vicarious affective responses than men, perhaps because men have been trained traditionally to suppress emotional displays (Hoffman, 1977), we might expect women to be more empathic. Yet, taking the evidence as a whole, it is not clear whether genuine gender differences in empathy exist. Females *do* describe themselves as being more empathic than do males, but this may reflect more the image that is expected of them rather than some predisposition (Eisenberg and Lennon, 1983). Nor is there any clear evidence about gender differences in the willingness to help others, although adult women appear to be more willing to help highly dependent people, while men appear more helpful to those who are not so dependent (Schopler and Bateson, 1965). This could reflect the "caring" role that many females are brought up to assume.

The traditional norms that govern helping are quite different for males and females in our society (Eagly and Crowley, 1986; Eagly, 1987). Males are expected both to rescue others who are in difficulty and to demonstrate courtesy and protectiveness towards subordinates. Such behaviour is expected both in close relationships and among strangers. Women, on the other hand, are expected to help through caring and nurturing other people, especially those within a close relationship. Women are actively discouraged from associating

How does gender affect prosocial behaviour?

239

with strangers, and this prohibition most likely discourages women from giving help to strangers as well.

In general, the research on helping behaviour suggests that men help more often than women, although there is a great deal of inconsistency in this regard from one study to another. It must also be remembered, however, that social psychological research has typically focused on short-term interactions with strangers and has therefore by and large excluded the very behaviours that are prescribed for the female gender role—behaviours that are manifest primarily in close, long-term relationships (Eagly and Crowley, 1986). Furthermore, since men and women still tend to occupy different social and occupational roles, the "masculine" roles and the skills that are acquired in them may better prepare men to assist others in distress. As women begin to assume traditional male roles, the differences in helping between the two genders, even in the short-term interactions of the laboratory, may begin to disappear.

EFFECTS OF RELIGION

We naturally wonder about the effects of religiosity on the propensity to be helpful. After all, Christianity, Judaism, Islam, Hinduism, and Buddhism all promote altruistic behaviour to some degree, and view selflessness as a virtue. Yet various studies suggest that religious orientation does not correlate well with the demonstration of concern and compassion for those needing help; indeed, it may discourage it in some situations (Batson and Gray, 1981).

In one study, the effects of different religious orientations were examined insofar as they influenced the willingness of individuals to provide help to a lonely woman, either in a situation where she expressed a desire for such help or in a situation where she expressly indicated that she did not want help (Batson and Gray, 1981). The data indicated that intrinsically-oriented religious people for whom religion was seen as an end in itself (i.e., who viewed their whole duty as serving God) offered help whether or not the person in need desired it, while those for whom religion was viewed as an open-ended quest to find ultimate values offered help only when it was wanted. Intrinsically-oriented religious people, then, may see providing help to others as a way of helping themselves achieve grace, or a place in heaven. A subsequent study produced similar findings (Batson, Oleson, Weeks, Healy, Reeves, Jennings and Brown, 1989).

RURAL-URBAN DIFFERENCES

Why are people living in cities less helpful than those in rural areas?

Is a person from the country generally more inclined than a person from the city to help others? In a field study directed at rural-urban differences in helping, requests for help (e.g., "I wonder if you could tell me what time it is?") were made in downtown Toronto, in a Toronto suburb, and in a small town just outside Toronto (Rushton, 1978); the response rates, along with comparable data collected in New York City (Latané and Darley, 1970) are shown in Figure 9-2. For every type of request, the percentage of people giving help dropped, moving from the small town to the suburbs to downtown. There was little difference between the results in downtown Toronto and New York City. Further evidence of significant rural-urban differences in helping comes from a review of 67 pertinent empirical studies. Steblay (1987) found that people in rural areas do indeed show significantly more willingness to help others in distress than do city dwellers.

FIGURE 9-2 **Rural-urban differences in helping behaviour**

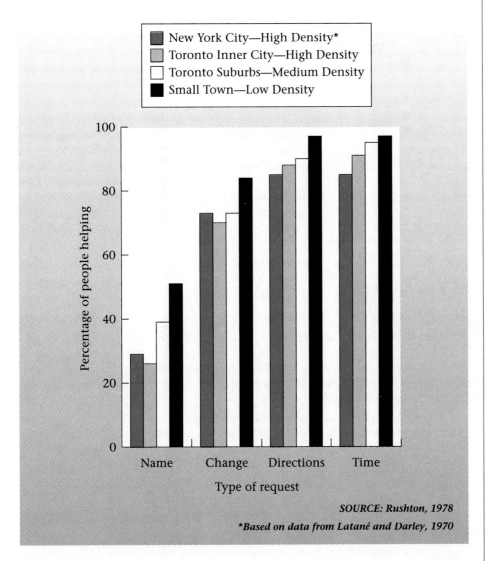

SOURCE: Rushton, 1978
*Based on data from Latané and Darley, 1970

However, even if people's behaviour in the city is less prosocial than in the country, are the people themselves different, or is it the situation? Milgram (1970) argued that it is the latter, that people in the city, surrounded as they are by so many other people, out of necessity limit their social relationships to a minority of the populace. He argued that the urban person cannot afford to help every individual in need and must be selective in order to survive in the urban culture. In addition, while rural people are considerably affected by rare emergency situations such as fires, the city-dweller becomes blasé about them, assuming that there are authorities who will deal with the situation. Furthermore, city dwellers who witness an emergency are more likely to be in (or to think themselves to be in) the company of other witnesses (Latané and Darley, 1969). It has been suggested that the intensity of urban stimuli (noise, pollution) may also lead to less prosocial behaviour. People living in cities have been found to be less trusting than people living in towns (Merrens, 1973; Milgram, 1970). Fischer (1976) suggests another reason why the city environment may discourage prosocial behaviour: since a large city usually provides a great diversity of people individuals may feel insecure among so many "dissimilar others," making social interaction less likely. Thus, in the city, there is a greater chance that the stranger who is in need of assistance will appear to be a member of an unfamiliar group, producing fear in the onlooker and resulting in less willingness to "get involved."

An Australian study (Amato, 1983) found that population size was a strong and consistent predictor of helping rate, with the most help occurring when the population of an area was small. However, the results of that study also suggested that urban lack of helpfulness was primarily limited to situations in which an individual was suddenly faced with the need to provide help to a stranger. This situation may be perceived as potentially more dangerous by the city dweller than by the rural inhabitant. This research points to the importance of the type of helping and the type of situation in any examination of rural-urban differences in prosocial behaviour.

BYSTANDER INTERVENTION

What are the characteristics of emergency situations?

Of all the forms of prosocial behaviour, certainly the most dramatic—by virtue of either its presence or its absence—is intervention behaviour, that is, the behaviour of an individual who voluntarily goes to the aid of someone needing emergency assistance despite the possible risk of personal danger. Emergency situations share several common elements that make them somewhat unique (Darley and Latané, 1970):

(1) They typically involve threat or harm to a victim. The person who intervenes can at best prevent further damage or possibly return the situation to the way it was before the emergency occurred.

(2) Since recipients of such aid are rarely better off following an emergency than before it, the rewards for positive action are often non-existent. Yet the possible costs, including possible legal action or even death or injury, are high.

(3) They are rare events, so that few people have experience in dealing with them.

(4) They are unpredictable, occurring suddenly and without warning, and immediate action is required. Thus people usually cannot plan for emergencies or consult with others about how to respond. The urgency of the situation is in itself stressful.

(5) They vary widely in their form and in terms of what response is appropriate, making it impossible to prepare everyone by teaching people a short list of rules for how to deal with emergencies.

Unfortunately, there are all too many real-life examples of emergency situations in which someone has been in physical danger and other people have stood by and observed the individual being victimized while doing nothing to provide help. This is the **"bystander effect"**: people witness an emergency but stand by passively and do nothing; their willingness to act, as we shall see later, is inhibited by the presence of others. Some examples of the bystander effect were given at the beginning of this chapter. A more important example is the Kitty Genovese murder (Box 9-2). It is important because it was the first well-researched exam-

bystander effect When a number of people all witness the same emergency, people are less likely to help.

ple of bystander inaction in an emergency situation. When asked later why they had not called the police, most of the witnesses to that murder said that they had indeed been afraid to get involved, but they seemed unable to furnish a basis for this fear. Various social scientists proposed a variety of possible explanations for their inaction (Latané and Darley, 1970): alienation and apathy resulting from "depersonalization"; confusion of fantasy and reality brought about by a steady diet of television violence; even the vicarious gratification of sadistic impulses.

However, the witnesses were not apathetic. They did not turn away and ignore what was going on in the street below. Rather—

> *Caught, fascinated, distressed, unwilling to act but unable to turn away, their behaviour was neither helpful nor heroic; but it was not indifferent or apathetic.... (Darley and Latané, 1970, p. 4).*

Almost fifteen years after the Genovese murder, a number of these witnesses were contacted. Again, they reported that they still felt responsible for Genovese's death (Walster, Walster and Berscheid, 1978).

The behaviour of these witnesses was very similar to that of any crowd that gathers around an accident victim, each waiting for someone else to take charge, to indicate what behaviour is appropriate. Sometimes people act; sometimes they do not. Yet, in any case, they are likely to experience distress. Several studies have found that when people witness another person being harmed, they show marked signs of emotional upheaval, such as gasping, running aimlessly around, sweating or trembling hands, chain-smoking, and an increase in galvanic skin response (Walster, Walster and Berscheid, 1978).

BOX 9-2
THE BYSTANDER EFFECT

In March of 1964 in New York City, Catherine Genovese was attacked by a man with a knife as she was walking home at night. Her screams brought her neighbours to their windows, and the sudden glow of their bedroom lights and the sounds of their voices drove the attacker away temporarily. However, when he saw that no one responded to her cries for help, he attacked her again. She managed to get away from her attacker a second time, but again, despite her shouts for help, no one responded. The man returned to attack her yet again—this time killing her. A half hour had elapsed between the first attack and the time the killing took place, and even though at least 38 people watched from the windows of their apartments and houses as he attacked and repeatedly stabbed the young woman, no one even telephoned the police.

Before dismissing this as an example of New York incivility, consider this incident:

In September 1973, a man dragged a struggling, screaming 18-year-old girl 300 yards down a Scarborough, Ontario, street while cars swerved to avoid them but did not stop. She was taken to a grassy area opposite an apartment building, forced at knife-point to undress, and then raped. Despite the fact that several people were sitting on apartment balconies opposite her as she cried for assistance, no one even called the police. No one helped even though an anonymous phone call to the police would have posed no risk to any of them.

(Ironically enough, at some later time the assailant was himself the victim of bystander inaction. He was beaten by three toughs on a busy thoroughfare while pleading in vain with the occupants of a stopped bus and taxi to call the police (Silverman, 1974)).

What are the research findings on the bystander effect?

What accounts for the bystander effect? If people are not apathetic, if their behaviour is not callous, what is it that holds them back from helping a person in distress? There are several possible answers to these questions.

NORMS AND THE BYSTANDER EFFECT

The failure of people to help others is sometimes taken to suggest a breakdown in the power of social norms to regulate social behaviour, a rather alarming prospect. However, we saw earlier that while there are social norms involved in prosocial behaviour, their role is limited. Again, in the case of an emergency, norms are actually not very useful guides, partly because they are too vague to provide any useful information about what to do, and partly because they are conflicting (Darley and Latané, 1970). As an example of such conflict among norms, suppose that you are walking down Lovers' Lane on a wintry night and you see a couple sitting motionless in a parked car with the engine running. One norm tells you to try to help others who need your help: if they are dying of carbon monoxide, you should do something. Yet another norm teaches you to respect people's privacy. After all, they are in Lovers' Lane: if they are just making out or communing with nature, you should not butt in. Thus it is likely that norms have only a small role to play in intervention behaviour. The bystander effect does not reflect a breakdown of social norms, only their inadequacy.

The bystander effect is a social phenomenon; it occurs when a number of people mutually witness an emergency situation. A good way to begin understanding the bystander effect is by examining a series of laboratory experiments that were carried out to establish what happened in the Kitty Genovese situation. These are discussed next.

THE PRESENCE OF OTHERS: THE WOMAN IN DISTRESS

It might seem reasonable to assume that if an individual is the sort of person who is likely to come to someone's assistance in an emergency, that person would be even more likely to do so if there were other people about, for these other people might be expected to lend at least moral support. Yet, before accepting that conclusion, it would be wise to recall the literature on social facilitation discussed in Chapter 5: the presence of others facilitates simple or well-learned tasks, but interferes with complex or novel tasks. Emergency situations probably involve the latter and so there may be some reason to suspect that the presence of others may not always have a positive effect on the readiness of an individual to render assistance.

In one of the earliest experimental studies of the bystander effect (Latané and Rodin, 1969), the influence of the presence of others was clearly evident. In that experiment, subjects who thought they were participating in a market research study heard a woman who had just left them to go into an adjoining room "climb up" on a chair to get something, and then "fall down" and cry for help. (In fact, both the climb and fall were produced by a high-fidelity tape recording.) The experimenters wanted to see whether or not, and how soon, subjects would come to her assistance. Subjects could go directly into her office (the two rooms were separated only by a curtain), could go out into the hallway to seek help, or could call to her to find out what they could do to help.

In one condition, each subject was alone. In a second condition, each subject was with a confederate who had been instructed to be as passive as possible, responding to any queries from the real subject in as natural but neutral a way as possible. At the sound of the crash, the confederate looked up, stared for a moment at the curtain, then shrugged his shoulders and went back to work. In a third condition, two real subjects who were strangers to each other were tested together, while a fourth condition involved two subjects who were friends.

The results showed that when assistance was offered, it was always direct, either going into the room (75 percent of the intervening subjects) or calling out to the woman to see if she wanted help (24 percent). The most notable finding was that while 70 percent of the subjects in the alone condition offered help, the presence of another person strongly reduced the frequency of intervention (the bystander effect): only 7 percent of subjects paired with a passive confederate intervened, while only 40 percent of those in the "two strangers" condition offered help. The bystander effect was reduced when friends were paired together: in 70 percent of the pairs of friends there was at least one person who offered help. (However, it can be shown mathematically that if 70 percent of individuals who are alone are likely to intervene, then pairs of such individuals should contain at least one intervener 91 percent of the time. So, even with friends, the presence of another person is inhibitory.)

It seems strange at first that the presence of others inhibits rather than promotes helping. However, in post-experimental interviews, 59 percent of non-intervening subjects indicated that they were unsure about what had happened, while another 46 percent said they had thought that nothing serious had occurred. Perhaps people hesitate to help because they think that someone else will do it. Diffusion of responsibility merits a closer look; that subject is next.

DIFFUSION OF RESPONSIBILITY: THE EPILEPTIC SEIZURE

Each subject in this study (Darley and Latané, 1968) sat in a separate room and was told that he or she would take part in a discussion of personal problems associated with college life. The discussion was to be conducted by means of an intercom system, ostensibly in order to protect the subjects' identities and spare them any embarrassment. Subjects had been told that the experimenter would not be listening to the initial discussion, and that a mechanical switching device would automatically give each subject in turn about two minutes to talk while all other microphones were switched off.

There was actually only one real subject at any one time. The other subjects were all confederates working for the experimenter, and had prerecorded their comments. From the point of view of the real subject, who believed that all the other speakers were actually present in the discussion, this is what occurred: the first person to speak discussed his adjustment difficulties and the fact that he was prone to epileptic seizures, especially when under stress. The next time it was his turn to speak, he became increasingly loud and incoherent and in a stuttering voice asked for help. Amid choking sounds, he stammered that he was going to die, called once more for help, and then was silent. When the seizure occurred, the real subject believed that all subjects could *hear* the seizure but that only the microphone of the seizure victim was switched on.

The major independent variable in this study was the apparent size of the group of participants, while the dependent variable was the time it took the subject to go and report the emergency to the experimenter. Comments made during the staged seizure and in later self-reports indicated that virtually all subjects believed the emergency was real. Yet the belief that other people were listening had a strong effect on both the rate and the speed of subjects' intervention (Table 9-1). Considerably more of the subjects in two-person (subject plus victim) groups reported the emergency than did people from the three-person groups, and people from the three-person groups responded more often than people from the six-person groups.

It appears that a person is less likely to offer help if others are present or presumed to be present. Subjects in this study who did not report the emergency did not show signs of apathy or indifference. In fact, when the experimenter finally entered the room to end the study, they appeared to be considerably emotionally upset and concerned for the victim. They found themselves in a conflict situation, worried about the victim and about the guilt they would feel if he was not helped, yet concerned about looking foolish, overreacting, or ruining the experiment by leaving the room. When only the subject and the victim were involved, the victim's need could be met only by the subject, while when others seemed to be present (even, in this case, via intercom), the subject had less responsibility in the matter. In other words, a **diffusion of responsibility** occurred: "Other people are listening, and so it's not up to me to take action; someone has probably already done something about it."

Three factors have emerged from the discussion so far. The bystander effect is the result of: (1) misperception of the emergency situation, based on the observation that others are not responding; (2) fear of doing the wrong thing and looking foolish; and (3) diffusion of responsibility. Many other studies and demonstrations have found results similar to those obtained by Latané and Darley. The bystander effect has been demonstrated on the streets of downtown Toronto. In one demonstration, which was filmed by a hidden camera, a confederate collapsed on busy Yonge Street. Many people walked by, stepping around the man, before someone finally stopped to offer help. In another demonstration, a confederate grabbed another confederate's purse in front of City Hall, in full view of a lunchtime crowd. As the victim ran after him she called for people to stop him. No help was forthcoming. It had been expected that for each demonstration, several trials would have to be made before such blatant non-intervention could be observed and filmed. In fact, in each case, only one trial was necessary (Ross, 1978). (The reader is invited to think about the ethical considerations inherent in carrying out such demonstrations.)

The social inhibition of helping is a remarkably consistent phenomenon and, in general, a victim stands a greater chance of being helped when only a single person witnesses the emergency (Latané and Nida, 1981).

diffusion of responsibility When a number of people are present, help may not be given because each may assume that someone else has taken charge.

TABLE 9-1 **Effects of group size on likelihood and speed of response**

Group size	N	*% responding by end of seizure*	*Total % responding within six minutes*	*Average time in seconds*
2 (subject and victim)	13	85	100	52
3 (subject, victim, and one other)	26	62	85	93
6 (subject, victim, and 4 others)	13	31	62	166

SOURCE: Latané and Darley, 1970

THE LATANÉ-DARLEY INTERVENTION MODEL

Latané and Darley (1970) summarize the effects of ambiguity, fear of looking foolish, and diffusion of responsibility in a five-step decision-making model of the intervention process (Table 9-2).

First, we must notice that something is happening and then decide whether or not it is an emergency. If it is, the next step is to select an appropriate action: Do we personally try to do something? Do we call the police? After contemplating the alternatives, particularly if they involve personal risk, we might go back a step to the definition stage and decide that it really is not an emergency after all. The more ambiguous the situation, the greater the likelihood that this backtracking will occur ("If they're really being gassed, I don't know what to do. I'll get them out of the car, I guess, but how do I give them artificial resuscitation? What if they die? Mind you, they're probably OK—just making out quietly. Boy, will I look stupid when I pound on their window and they turn out to be in no danger. Yeah, there's no problem here—after all this is Lovers' Lane.") So we might decide not to do anything, risking some guilt if it turns out there really *was* an emergency. If others are standing around doing nothing, we risk even more embarrassment if we intervene when help is not needed—and the inactivity of others may add to the ambiguity of the situation. (Obviously, however, we are not actually going to go through such a deliberate assessment of a possible emergency situation. These decision-making steps can occur quickly, almost without realization.)

EASE OF ESCAPE AND AMOUNT OF DANGER

A classic experiment carried out in New York City has revealed yet another aspect of the bystander effect. This field experiment, taking place in a city with no outstanding reputation for altruism, found that no bystander effect occurred when a confederate of the experimenter collapsed on a moving subway car. The experiment examined the effects of certain characteristics of a victim (whether he appeared drunk or ill) on the amount of help given. It was expected that the "drunk" confederate (who carried a bottle in a paper bag and who smelled of alcohol) would elicit less aid than an ill one (carrying a cane) since it was assumed people might anticipate the drunk becoming disgusting, embarrassing, or violent. The most surprising outcome was that there was a generally high rate of help-giving in all conditions. In fact, the "ill" person received help on 95 percent of the trials, and even the "drunk" was helped on half the trials. Moreover, when help was given, on 60 percent of those occasions more than one person helped. Since the ill person was not thought to be ill by choice while the drunk was clearly in need of help as a result of his own actions, people may have been less

TABLE 9-2 The Latané-Darley model of bystander intervention

1. The bystander must notice that something is happening.

2. The bystander must interpret the situation as an emergency.

3. The bystander must decide whether or not he or she has a responsibility to intervene.

4. The bystander must decide in what way he or she can best be of assistance.

5. The bystander must choose how best to carry out this course of action.

willing to help the drunk because he "deserved" his suffering (Piliavin, Rodin and Piliavin, 1969).

Why was so much inaction observed in the Darley and Latané laboratory research but not in the Piliavin field experiment? Why was there less diffusion of responsibility on the subway? There were important differences between the two sets of studies. First, the victim was in full view in the Piliavin study; thus the need for help was less ambiguous. Second, the natural groups were considerably larger than the laboratory groups. Thus any diffusion of responsibility that might have occurred may have been *more* than offset by the increased probability of *someone* actually helping in a large group. In other words, the larger number of bystanders in the subway study may have increased the probability of getting a prosocial response from someone (Piliavin et al., 1972). Moreover, it was much more difficult for the subjects in the Piliavin study to leave the area than it was for participants in the Latané and Darley studies to avoid the victim. This difference bears more examination.

Whether or not a person helps another may depend on how easily he or she can avoid the helping situation. In an experiment designed to examine this hypothesis (Staub, 1974), a confederate collapsed, holding either his chest or his knees (to vary the apparent seriousness of his condition) either in the pathway of a pedestrian (difficult escape), or across the street (easy escape). As seen in Table 9-3, many more people helped when escape from the situation was difficult than when it was easy. In fact, the person with the apparent "heart attack" was almost always approached in the difficult escape condition. The results suggest that the perceived degree of need for help also influenced helping. More people approached the apparent coronary victim. Interestingly enough, an obese confederate who clutched his chest was more likely to receive aid than a non-obese confederate. It turned out that subjects more often considered the problem to be a coronary one when the victim was obese. Recall that in the Piliavin study, people could not easily escape; it was several minutes to the next stop.

All that being said, it is sobering to learn that thirty or more passengers, including some hefty men, watched passively as three youths beat up a man in a moving subway car in Toronto in September 1973; no one even stood up or spoke. They watched in silence. While the New York subway riders had relatively little to lose by helping a sick person or a drunk, there is more to risk if we intervene in a fight. Thus, besides the factors already discussed—ambiguity, fear of looking foolish, diffusion of responsibility, difficulty of avoidance—it is clear that the readiness to help will be strongly affected by the potential costs to the helper.

TABLE 9-3 **Number of people helping or refusing to help in the 1974 Staub study**

	Bad knee		Bad heart	
	Help	No help	Help	No help
Easy escape	2	12	5	7
Difficult escape	9	7	14	2

SOURCE: Staub, 1974

ENCOURAGING BYSTANDER INTERVENTION

How might we encourage individuals to render assistance to others in emergencies—even in the presence of others? In other words, how can we prepare people to deal with the bystander effect? Several courses of action are likely to prove beneficial:

(1) **Combatting the bystander effect in the schools.**   We teach children to obey and to conform. We are much more careful to teach them what they are *not* to do than to teach them how to act prosocially. Children in emergency situations often experience a conflict between the wish to help and the desire to act appropriately; the absence of permission to intervene is often as powerful an inhibitor as a direct prohibition (Staub, 1974). This influence may endure into adulthood. It may be beneficial to teach children that it is all right to break rules in certain circumstances.

(2) **Combatting the bystander effect in the home.**   By regularly assigning children the responsibility of caring for or helping others (a responsibility that is often automatic in large families), we may foster the development of a feeling of personal responsibility for the welfare of others. We might teach children that intervention behaviour is desirable—we could even have children rehearse such behaviour and then reward them for it. However, it must not be forgotten that emergencies are difficult to plan for, and that the problem of defining a situation as an emergency is bound to arise.

(3) **Promoting leadership roles.**   Most bystanders in an emergency situation are very willing to help, once someone takes control of the situation and begins to issue orders: "You, go call an ambulance!"; "You, keep the crowd back!"; "You, get some blankets!" One problem in these situations is that often no one will assume leadership.

Research in the laboratory (Baumeister, Chesner, Senders and Tice, 1988) has found that subjects designated as group leaders in an experimental situation (for example, a discussion group) are likely to continue to act as leaders in an unexpected emergency situation, even when intervention involves violating the experimental instructions. While subordinate group members generally fail to intervene, diffusion of responsibility seems *not* to occur to individuals already placed in a role of responsibility and leadership.

Not everyone can be a leader, but by giving children practice at being leaders in different situations and by teaching them the importance of showing leadership when an emergency occurs, we encourage them to consider it appropriate to "take charge" and accept responsibility in emergency situations.

(4) **Increasing public awareness of the bystander effect.**   Dissemination of information about the effects of group size on bystander intervention may help increase intervention as people realize "why" they are hesitating to help and as they pay less attention to the inaction of others around them. In a study of the effects of such knowledge (Rayko, 1977), half the subjects received information about diffusion of responsibility and about the ambiguity created by the inaction of others in emergency situations, while the other half received non-relevant information. Subjects waited either alone or with a confederate and, five minutes

What are the ways that bystander intervention can be encouraged?

later, they heard a loud crash and a cry of pain from a workman they had seen go into the next room. The confederate reacted with a start to the sound of the crash, but then ignored it. The results showed a dual effect. Subjects who waited alone were faster and more likely to help than those who waited with the passive confederate, and subjects who had received information about emergency behaviour responded more rapidly than those who had not. However, the information about emergencies did not lead to a higher *proportion* of people helping since, in fact, all subjects in the alone conditions helped sooner or later, compared with 70 percent of the relevant information group in the presence of a confederate, and 62 percent of the control group (these percentages do not differ significantly from each other).

(5) Removing legal risks. People sometimes believe that the person who provides emergency roadside first aid is liable for damages should he or she unintentionally harm the victim. Some physicians fear being held liable for damages if they give emergency medical care at the scene of an accident and the patient does not recover. This has led to pressure for the passage of Good Samaritan laws, which excuse from liability an individual who has assisted in good faith "unless it is established that the injuries or death were caused by gross negligence ..." (*Emergency Medical Aid Act,* Revised Statutes of Alberta, 1970). In Canada, only three provinces—Alberta, Newfoundland, and Nova Scotia—have passed Good Samaritan laws. It is not known whether the absence of such laws *inhibits* emergency medical intervention, but there has never been a case in North America in which anyone successfully sued a person who offered help in an emergency (Monaghan, 1975; Markus, 1975). There is obviously a need to educate people that their assistance will not result in damage suits.

Most people do not know about the bystander effect and most do not believe that it occurs frequently. It seems to contradict the proper etiquette of "responsible behaviour." By following some of the approaches just discussed, it would be possible to reduce the bystander effect. There is much work to be done towards that end.

SELF-TEST QUESTIONS

SELF TEST

5. According to Milgram (1970), city dwellers exhibit less prosocial behaviour than rural dwellers because

a) of the greater personal risk associated with living in a city

b) of the personality differences between city and rural dwellers

c) city dwellers must limit their social relationships due to the greater number of people living in cities

d) all of the above

6. A person observes an emergency in the presence of several other people, and does not attempt to provide assistance. This is an example of

a) depersonalization

b) the bystander effect

c) frustration-aggression

d) negative empathy

7. What is responsible for the bystander effect?

a) apathy

b) increased galvanic skin response

c) insufficient reinforcement

d) diffusion of responsibility

8. In what way(s) can bystander intervention be encouraged?

a) promote leadership roles

b) raise public awareness of the bystander effect

c) remove legal risk to those who help

d) all of the above

THE BENEFICIARY

WHO GETS HELPED?

Not only are some rather than others likely to help, depending on the situation, but not all people in need are equally likely to be helped. You might be willing to assist a well-dressed senior citizen change a tire, but not if he or she appeared to be drunk. The degree to which a person is dependent on another also generally plays an important part in determining how much help will be given. Several studies have found a positive relationship between the potential beneficiary's level of dependence and the amount of help given, but this relationship may apply only when the cost to the helper is low (Krebs, 1970; Gruder, 1974).

When the cost of helping is great, we may resent the burden that the requester's needs places upon us (Berkowitz, 1973). The greater the person's dependency upon us, the greater our felt obligation to help, and the greater our "reactance," or desire to re-establish our independence and freedom (Brehm, 1966). We may gladly help a person once in a while unless we feel that we are obliged to do so. Perhaps a felt obligation robs us of the "good feelings" we would normally experience if we voluntarily helped the person.

Attributions may play an important role in determining who will or will not be helped. If another person's need appears to be controllable, that is, the person seems responsible for the plight he or she is in, we may be less willing to help than if we perceive the person's need as owing to circumstances beyond his or her control (Weiner, 1980). There has been some limited empirical support for this proposition (Reisenzein, 1986).

Other factors that affect the probability of receiving help are: physical attractiveness (West and Brown, 1975), degree of apparent need (Staub and Baer, 1974), and perceived similarity between the requester and the helper (Sole, Marton and Hornstein, 1975). Thus, you are more likely to help someone who is physically attractive to you, who is in great need of help, and who is part of your in-group (race, social status). Even whether the potential helper and requester both need help can have an important effect. If you are in a very stressful situation and the potential recipient is in the same stressful situation, helping will be facilitated. However, a person will be less likely than usual to help if the requester is in a less stressful situation (Dovidio and Morris, 1975). So, if you want directions to the post office, do not ask someone who is pushing her car to the gas station!

What characteristics are likely to increase a person's chance of receiving help?

251

REACTION OF THE BENEFICIARY

The act of providing help not only clearly distinguishes between helper and beneficiary, it also defines a power hierarchy (Worchel, 1984). If the person who is helped cannot repay the help in any way, then—at least in Western society—accepting help places the person in a position of inferiority. There may even be a perceived loss of face (Fisher, 1983). If you are desperately short of money and someone gives it to you but refuses to accept repayment, you may feel some discomfort—unless, of course, the benefactor is in a role that might justify munificence (e.g., your father or mother). In general, the greater the threat to self-esteem, the more likely it is that the recipient may feel negatively towards the helper (Fisher, Nadler and Whitcher-Alagna, 1982; Fisher et al., 1983).

Experimental studies carried out with subjects from the U.S., Sweden, and Japan have found that subjects give more positive evaluations to "donors" who oblige them to repay the donation than to those who ask nothing in return (Gergen, Ellsworth, Maslach and Seipel, 1975) (see Chapter 8). Negative evaluation of donors who do not want reciprocation may occur at the international level as well. Developing nations may feel less gratitude for aid from developed nations if they have no way of reciprocating, for such aid underlines the beneficiary's position of dependency (Andreas, 1969). If receiving aid leads the recipient to feel inferior to the donor, there may be a strong need on the part of the recipient to repay the aid in order to regain independence. Such a reaction might be more expected when the donor is a close friend rather than a stranger (Nadler and Fisher, 1984), for it is more important to avoid feelings of inferiority with a friend. In fact, most people are mistaken in their worry about "losing face." There is actually little evidence to support the claim that donors perceive beneficiaries as inferior (Rosen, Tomarelli, Kidda and Medvin, 1986).

As we have seen, people do not automatically come to the assistance of others in need. They are often inhibited by feelings of ambiguity and fear. In the next section, a very special kind of intervention behaviour is discussed in which considerations of personal risk seem not to play a role.

HEROISM

- In June 1944, Pilot Officer Andrew Charles Mynarski of Winnipeg was flying an RCAF Lancaster bomber in an attack on German positions when the airplane was hit and set afire. The crew parachuted to safety, except for the tail-gunner, Pat Brophy, who was trapped in his tiny rear compartment by a damaged door, and Mynarski, who lurched back through the flames to attempt to free him. Covered with blazing hydraulic fluid, he worked bare-handed to try to get the door open. Finally, driven back by the fire, he stood and saluted Brophy before bailing out. He had no chance of survival: his parachute was on fire. He was posthumously awarded the Victoria Cross on the evidence of the tail-gunner, who ironically survived the crash of the bomb-laden airplane when he was thrown free upon impact (Franklin, 1977).

- On July 4, 1989, Grace Nolan was at a family resort near Lindsay, Ontario, when she saw a man whom she knew to be mentally ill trying to break down the door of his own cottage, while yelling at his wife to let him in. He finally entered the cottage by jumping through a closed window. She heard screaming and knew that his wife was in peril. Just then, another neighbour yelled through the shattered window, telling him to stop. The man ran out of the cottage and stabbed the neighbour twice in the arm. He grabbed her by the arms and continued to try to jab her with the knife in an apparent attempt to kill her. Nolan saved the woman's life, and probably that of the man's wife as well, by grabbing an aluminum lawn chair, waving it at him menacingly, and screaming at him to stop. He then let the woman go and left, with Nolan in pursuit until he was off the property. The police were alerted and the man was apprehended. She was awarded the Star of Courage, Canada's second highest honour for civilian courage, as well as the Carnegie Hero Medal (*The Toronto Star,* January 24, 1991).

A hero's welcome: Karen Ridd returns to Winnipeg.

- On November 20, 1989, Karen Ridd of Winnipeg, Manitoba, was arrested in El Salvador while working in a church that was providing sanctuary to hundreds of Salvadoreans fleeing from persecution and civil war. She was blindfolded, handcuffed, and occasionally slugged by the police, who led her to believe that she would be taken to an area well-known as a dumping spot for people killed by the "death squads." Following four hours of interrogation, during which she could hear the screams of torture victims, she was finally released into the custody of Canadian diplomatic officials. However, rather than take advantage of her freedom, she refused to leave without her colleague, a Colombian woman who was being even more roughly interrogated in the room next door. She was again blindfolded and taken back inside the prison, where she was berated and threatened by the police. Finally, they capitulated and let both women go (*The Globe and Mail,* November 24, 1989).

These three examples of heroic action demonstrate the finest prosocial behaviour: individuals risking their own lives to try to save others. Such heroism is greatly admired in all societies. In 1972, three decorations were created by the Canadian government to honour those who perform such selfless acts of courage—the Cross of Valour, the Star of Courage, and the Medal of Bravery.

What is the stuff of heroism? While heroism is difficult to define because it is based on perception and attribution, most acts that are considered heroic involve intervention in the face of extraordinary personal risk.

HEROISM AND GENDER

We have seen that the male gender role is more conducive to helping in general. Indeed, despite two of the examples given above, almost all *recognized* acts of heroism have been carried out by men (Eagly and Crowley, 1986), acting alone in most cases. Given what is known about the bystander effect, the fact that they acted alone should not be surprising. For example, consider the Carnegie Heroes. The Carnegie Hero Fund Commission was founded in the U.S. in 1904 to award medals for "outstanding acts of selfless heroism performed in the United States and Canada." An analysis of Carnegie Hero Medal recipients in the United States revealed that 96 of the 101 recipients in 1971 were male and that in the

*Why is a man more
likely to be named a
hero than is a woman?*

vast majority of cases, the hero acted alone (Lay, Allen and Kassirer, 1974). Since the inception of the award, only 8.9 percent of the 6955 medalists have been female (Eagly and Crowley, 1986).

In an analysis of recipients of Metropolitan Toronto Police Civilian Citations, which are awarded to people who have spontaneously come to the aid of the police either directly (e.g. chasing a suspect or helping defend a police officer) or indirectly (e.g. telephoning a police station when a police officer is under attack), it was also found that males were more likely than females to directly intervene (an action that is more likely to constitute heroism), while females were more likely to notify the police rather than take direct action (Lay, Allen and Kassirer, 1974). (However, since most of the aggressors were male, the outcome might be misleading; females may be at greater risk than males in taking direct action against male aggressors.) In about two-thirds of the cases, the recipient acted alone. Only in the pursuit of an offender did it happen more frequently that more than one person was involved.

It is not that women are not given to heroism, but rather that the concept of heroism is defined in stereotypically male terms (Polster, 1992). Indeed, the Carnegie Hero Commission excludes from consideration people who rescue family members, except if the rescuer dies or is severely injured. Thus women (who according to the female gender role should be particularly concerned with the welfare of their children) are not considered heroic if they risk their lives in saving their children. Heroism, therefore, appears to be a "male" concept, and we should not be surprised that women are less often viewed as heroic. As society becomes more egalitarian, and as male and female gender roles become less differentiated and less rigid, this perception will undoubtedly change.

THE SCARLET PIMPERNEL PHENOMENON

The Scarlet Pimpernel is the name of a book and a fictional character created by Baroness Orczy. The book is set during the days of the French Revolution and concerns a British nobleman who could have followed the events of the Revolution in the comfort and safety of his own homeland. Instead, he risked his life to smuggle French aristocrats out of Paris and out of the country, saving them from the certain fate of the guillotine.

Similarly, this type of heroism was replayed again and again during the days of the Third Reich, when an estimated 50 000–500 000 individuals repeatedly risked their lives, and often those of their families, to help Jews escape from the Nazis (Oliner and Oliner, 1988; 1992). Many of them perished as a result of their efforts; the vast majority have never been identified. Only a very few became famous for their courage—for example, Raoul Wallenberg, a wealthy Swedish diplomat, who was able to save tens of thousands of Jews by issuing false Swedish documents to them (Henry, 1985/86). Another example of this courage and determination has recently been brought to public attention through the movie *Schindler's List*.

It was during the trial of Adolph Eichmann in 1960 that interest began to focus on such rescue efforts. Eichmann was charged with crimes against the Jewish people and against humanity arising from his zealous implementation of the Nazi genocidal policy. During the trial, reference was made to Christians who had rescued Jews from concentration camps. Subsequently, social psychologists began to track down as many of these rescuers as possible to determine whether there were any common factors in their personalities or family backgrounds.

An early study, which had to be terminated because of a lack of funds, located 27 rescuers and 42 rescued people (London, 1970). In a subsequent and much more extensive study, known as the Altruistic Personality Project, Oliner and Oliner (1988) interviewed 406 rescuers whose actions had been documented by Yad Vashem (an Israeli institution set up as a memorial to the victims of the Holocaust and which has now identified some 6000 rescuers), as well as 150 rescued survivors. The rescuers were compared with 126 non-rescuers—people who had been in situations where they could have become rescuers but had chosen not to do so.

MOTIVATION OF THE RESCUERS

No single motive for the behaviour of these individuals has been identified. Some had deliberately chosen to rescue Jews. Others got involved by mistake or without thinking about it: one person reluctantly agreed to let his secretary's Jewish husband stay in his office over the weekend to hide from the Nazis. Once involved, however, he was drawn in more deeply and developed considerable compassion for those he helped, eventually rescuing about 200 people at great personal risk and cost. Some of the rescuers were very religious, while others were atheist, and some were even anti-Semitic!

There seem to have been at least three different motivations for the actions of the rescuers (Oliner and Oliner, 1988): (1) Some rescuers were motivated by empathy for the suffering of the Jews. In some cases this empathy was based primarily on emotional attachment to specific victims, which led to a sense of responsibility and care-giving. (2) Others were motivated by the social norms (e.g., "do good unto others") of groups to which they were strongly attached, such as church congregations. (3) For a small minority, it was dedication to a moral code based on justice and social responsibility that motivated them to risk their lives. Morally motivated rescuers rescued people whether they liked them or not, and whether or not they knew them previously (Fogelman and Weiner, 1985).

CHARACTERISTICS OF THE RESCUERS

What personal characteristics did the rescuers share? In his early study, London (1970), while cautioning about the possible non-representativeness of his sample, found three common characteristics. First, rescuers showed a fondness for adventure and excitement, which was crucial to the initiation of the rescue work. Second, the rescuers tended to be socially deviant, and their social marginality provided the impetus and endurance necessary to carry out this rescue work. Third, and most important, the rescuers showed a strong identification with a very moralistic parent who had definite opinions on moral questions and who provided a model for moral conduct.

The importance of parental influence was apparent in the much larger sample studied by Oliner and Oliner (1988). The rescuers they studied were distinguished from non-rescuers by their capacity to feel responsible for the welfare of others, including people outside their circle of family and friends: this sense of moral responsibility was directly attributable to their upbringing. Many rescuers reported that their parents had stressed—both in words and by behaviour—the importance of helping others, and the importance of accepting that differences in group, race, or culture do not make a person superior or inferior. The typical rescuer in their study was raised in a close family relationship in which parents acted in a loving manner towards the children and communicated caring values.

What personal characteristics do rescuers share?

The parents set high standards with respect to caring for other people, and children were encouraged to develop such qualities as dependability, self-reliance, and responsibility—qualities that are associated with caring. Parental discipline experienced by rescuers rarely involved physical punishment, and there was almost never any gratuitous aggression. Discipline involved a great deal of reasoning, with efforts being made to explain to the children why some behaviours are inappropriate and what their consequences are for other people.

These studies recall our earlier discussion of the effects of models and upbringing on prosocial behaviour in general. Identification with an altruistic parent, a parent who both teaches and practises the importance of caring for and helping others, appears to be of outstanding importance in inculcating selflessness in individuals. This strong identification with a moralistic parent was also found to be an important characteristic of "fully committed" American civil rights workers in the late 1950s and early 1960s. These activists had been taught by their parents not only to believe in certain principles but to act upon them (Rosenhan, 1970).

SELF TEST

SELF-TEST QUESTIONS

9. Who is the most likely to receive help?
a) someone physically attractive
b) someone seen to be responsible for their situation
c) someone who is different from the potential helper
d) someone who is angry

10. One of the reasons why there are so few female "heroes" is that
a) the concept of heroism is defined in stereotypically male terms
b) women are less concerned than men with helping others
c) women are rarely strong enough to perform heroic acts
d) women are generally less empathic than men

11. Which of the following was *not* found to be a characteristic of people who rescued Jews from the Nazis?
a) a strong identification with a very moral parent
b) a history of personal suffering
c) a fondness for adventure
d) a capacity to feel responsible for the welfare of others

SUMMARY

(1) Some theorists propose that altruism is genetically transmitted, a position that is not held by most psychologists.

(2) Norms of reciprocity, social responsibility, and equity can influence prosocial behaviour, but their roles are usually minor.

(3) Cognitive development theory proposes that moral thinking matures from a state of concern with pure self-interest, to responsiveness to the reactions of others, to being guided by abstract principles.

(4) Social learning theory emphasizes the acquisition of altruism through processes of reinforcement, self-attribution, modelling, and parental discipline.

(5) Prosocial behaviour may be influenced by various emotional states, and may involve attempts to repair our self-image.

(6) Empathy is not a necessary condition for altruism, but may enhance the probability of such behaviour. There is a renewed debate in psychology about the existence of true altruism.

(7) The manifestation of prosocial behaviour varies from one culture to another, between males and females, and between people in cities and rural areas.

(8) Emergency situations involve threat or harm to the victim, are rare and unpredictable, vary widely in form and appropriate response, and may involve risk or costs to the benefactor.

(9) People are less likely to help in an emergency when other bystanders are present (the "bystander effect").

(10) The bystander effect occurs when each bystander feels that he or she is less responsible for the victim's welfare because there are other people present who could take action ("diffusion of responsibility") and because the inaction of others makes the situation more ambiguous to each bystander with regard to whether help is needed and what response is appropriate.

(11) Bystander behaviour is also influenced by the anticipated rewards and costs of helping.

(12) Bystander intervention could be encouraged by increasing public awareness of the bystander effect, teaching children to "break the rules" of social convention when necessary, training children to take responsibility for helping others, encouraging leadership roles, and removing the risk of legal liability.

(13) People are less likely to receive help if they are perceived as being overly dependent, or if their need for help appears to be controllable or brought on by their own actions.

(14) Recipients of help who cannot reciprocate sometimes react with resentment.

(15) People who repeatedly act heroically to assist others have been typically raised in close-knit, loving families where discipline was not physical in nature, and where parents taught the importance of caring for others.

FOR REVIEW

In this chapter we examine the concept of _____(1), which suggests that we help others without thought of an external reward. _____(2) on the other hand suggests that we help without thought of external or internal rewards. The term _____(3) is used to evaluate what motivates behaviour. There are many explanations about why we help each other. Anxiety-prone personalities lend support to a _____(4) basis for prosocial behaviour. Social norms also play a role in helping. For example, the _____(5) suggests that we take what is fair into account when we help others. When we consider the importance of learning to help others we must take into account both _____(6) and _____(7).

In this process it is important that children learn to view themselves as helpful. In other words, learn to make positive _____(8). With behaviour that

FOR REVIEW

is modelled, what you _____(9) is more important than what you _____(10). People tend to be more helpful when they are happy and may help others simply to avoid feeling sad. This is explained by _____(11). _____(12) suggests that we may try to make up for harming someone by helping them at a later date. Even where you live may play a role in how helpful you are. People who live in _____(13) tend to help more than people who live in _____(14).

The _____(15) is used to explain the fact that when a number of people are witness to an emergency help may not be given. This may be partly due to _____(16), which means that each person expects someone else to take the initiative. People may learn to help in a number of ways. Taking a _____(17) role and increasing _____(18) are two of them. Two characteristics that may increase the chances of help being given are how _____(19) the victim is, and how _____(20) he or she is to the person doing the helping.

Because of the way we define heroism, those most rewarded for these acts are _____(21). When the characteristics of people who act in a heroic manner were studied it was found that as children they were encouraged to develop qualities of _____(22), _____(23), and _____(24).

ISSUES AND ACTIVITIES

1. Using local newspapers over the period of one year, make note of anyone mentioned for helping or for heroic behaviour. Develop a profile of this behaviour based on the accounts. Can you find support for theories discussed in this chapter?

2. Choose two religions and compare what they say about helping behaviour.

3. Using what you now know about helping behaviour, put together a workshop of about two hours that could be delivered to a group of children or adults. What do they need to know about altruism? How could helping behaviour be increased? Try to design at least one exercise that could encourage prosocial behaviour.

• FURTHER READING

DERLEGA, V.J. and GRZELAK, J. (Eds.) (1982). *Cooperation and helping behavior*. New York: Academic Press. A collection of papers on prosocial behaviour written by some of the world's leading scholars in the field.

EISENBERG, N. and MUSSEN, P. (1989). *The roots of prosocial behavior in children*. New York: Cambridge University Press. A review of research into the various factors that influence the development of prosocial behaviour in children.

OLINER, S.P. and OLINER, P.M. (1992). *The altruistic personality: Rescuers of Jews in Nazi Europe*. New York: Free Press. A detailed report of the findings of the Altruistic Personality Project, which studied the psychological make-up of individuals who rescued Jews during the Nazi genocide.

PILIAVIN, J.A., DOVIDIO, J.F., GAERTNER, S.L. and CLARK, R.D. (1981). *Emergency intervention*. New York: Academic Press. This work provides a detailed discussion of factors that influence an individual's likelihood of helping in an emergency situation.

SUGGESTED WEBLINKS

Journal of Personality and Social Psychology (table of contents)
    http:/www.apa.org/journals/psp.html

PSYC SITE A site set up to help psychology students and researchers find information about scientific research in psychology on the World Wide Web. Designed to be a "major jumping off point" for seeking out psychological information. Maintained by the Psychology Department of the University of Nipissing.
    http://www.unipissing.ca/psyc/psycsite.htm

ANSWERS TO SELF-TEST QUESTIONS

1. c; 2. b; 3. a; 4. c; 5. c; 6. b; 7. d; 8. d; 9. a; 10. a; 11. b.

ANSWERS TO FOR REVIEW

1. prosocial behaviour; 2. Altruism; 3. attributions; 4. genetic; 5. norm of equity; 6. reinforcement; 7. modelling; 8. self-attributions; 9. do; 10. say; 11. the negative-state relief hypothesis; 12. Reparative altruism; 13. rural areas; 14. cities; 15. bystander effect; 16. diffusion of responsibility; 17. leadership; 18. public awareness; 19. attractive; 20. similar; 21. men; 22. dependability; 23. self-reliance; 24. responsibility.

SOCIAL CATEGORIES, GROUPS, AND LEADERSHIP

If you are going to lead people, you have to know where they are going.
Camillien Hoode, Former Mayor of Montreal

Who built the seven gates of Thebes?
In the books are listed the names of kings.
Did the kings heave up the building blocks?

Bertolt Brecht

■ LEARNING OUTCOMES

1. An understanding of social categories.

2. An understanding of social identity and social comparison.

3. An understanding of the nature of groups and the effects of group membership.

4. An understanding of different types of power.

5. An understanding of the nature of leadership.

■ FOR REFLECTION

- When does a collection of people become a real group?
- How and why do we classify people as in-groups and out-groups?
- Is effective leadership the result of the leader's personality, the situation, or both?
- What is charisma?

■ CHAPTER OUTLINE

Sir Winston Churchill (1874-1965), Prime Minister of Britain as well as Minister of Defence during the Second World War, was often described as "the greatest living Englishman." He was an inspiring war leader. A great strategist and orator, he welcomed challenge with an inexhaustible energy. His first message to the people was "I have nothing to offer but blood, toil, tears and sweat." Those who heard his speeches drew from them courage, a determination to survive, and the will to win. Churchill had all the characteristics of a great leader, characteristics that are discussed in this chapter. Nevertheless, when the war ended Churchill was rejected. Both he and the Conservative Party were voted out of office; Britons believed that different skills and attributes would be required of a leader in times of peace. Clearly, leaders who wish to maintain their positions must not ignore the needs and concerns of their constituents.

Not only is the group a fundamental aspect of leadership, but of our existence as well. It is hard to think of times when we are not part of a group. We live our lives in groups and spend most of our waking hours in one group context or another—our families, our circle of friends, the people with whom we work or go to school. We define ourselves in terms of groups: "I am a Canadian," "I am a community college student," "I am Québécois." Many of the most important changes in our lives result from changing groups—leaving home, going to college, getting a job—and membership in new groups often leads to changes in our attitudes and values.

It is important to make a distinction between social categories and groups. For example, as you walk along the street you can categorize people into "drivers" and "pedestrians." But you would be unlikely to think of these categories as representing two distinct groups, since there is little or no interaction among the members of either category. There is much more to a group than simply sharing a few similarities.

Each of us belongs to many different social categories: we are male, female, Canadian, American, mother, father, son, daughter, and so on. We each belong to many more categories than we probably even realize, which are based not only on gender, nationality, and relationships, but also on religion, age, ethnicity, or geographical origin. Although such categories may not always mean much to us, under certain circumstances they can become very important. This is the first subject discussed in this chapter. Next we examine small groups, the phenomenon of power within groups, and finally how people achieve and maintain positions of leadership.

SOCIAL CATEGORIES

social category *A means of grouping people based on similar characteristics.*

It would be difficult to interact with other people if we could not view them as part of some organized pattern. We tend to automatically put the people we encounter into categories that we believe we already know something about, e.g. "male-teenager-school drop-out." This quick categorization allows us to act "appropriately" towards that person according to the social norms and stereotypes we have learned. For example, would we act differently towards the category "male-adult-community leader"?

Of course we also interact with people based on their individual characteristics. For example, two people deeply in love may ignore social categories and focus on each other solely as individuals. Most of the time, however, behaviour in a social context depends both on our characteristics as individuals *and* the social categories that describe us and the people with whom we interact.

Of what use are social categories?

Since we each belong to many social categories, our behaviour at any given time will be influenced by whatever category is significant at that moment. Imagine a female general arts student participating in a class discussion in which inappropriate jokes are being made about women. The fact that she is a woman will suddenly become very important both to her and to the men in the class, and will undoubtedly influence both her reaction and their behaviour. Imagine this same student at a women's rights meeting at which her faculty is criticized for not doing more for women students. Then the student category will become very important in determining her reaction. Often without being aware of it, we organize the social world so that the various social categories have a status relationship to one another. Some people are viewed as superior, others as relatively inferior. We might act with deference towards someone we assume to be older and better educated than we are, and with condescension towards someone younger. Another way that we divide people and categories is by thinking in terms of **in-groups** (categories to which we happen to belong) and **out-groups** (categories to which we do not belong), i.e. "us" and "them" (Tajfel, 1970).

There is a great deal of emphasis placed on teams and "team spirit," even in primary school. This is the in-group versus out-group, us against them division in our society. It often produces a competitive relationship between the members of different social categories. We want "our" team, age group, gender, neighbourhood, province, or country to win, whether it is a game of cards or an Olympic medal. If Calgary football fans watch a Western Conference final between Calgary and Vancouver, they will want Calgary to win and will view the Lions as the enemy. Yet, if Vancouver wins and goes on to play in the Grey Cup game, those same Calgary fans will likely cheer for the Lions because as "Westerners" they will want the West to win.

SOCIAL IDENTITY AND SOCIAL COMPARISON: WHO ARE YOU?

If someone were to ask "Who are you?" how would you respond? You might give your name, but if the person continued with "Yes, but who are you?" what would you say? Depending on the circumstances, you might describe yourself as a resident of Victoria or Toronto, a Canadian, a North American, or perhaps a student at a particular college. Our self-esteem, and how we perceive ourselves in relation to other people, is tied up with group identification: "She wouldn't want to go out with me—I'm not in college and she is."

This way of describing ourselves creates a **social identity**. This part of our self-image comes from identifying with the social categories and groups to which we belong (Tajfel and Turner, 1979). We develop this social identity in a three-part process. First is social categorization: we see ourselves and others in terms of membership in distinct categories or groups. Second, we behave according to the typical norms, attitudes, and values of these groups. Third, we conform to what we perceive to be the stereotypes associated with the groups. Tajfel and Turner (1979) predicted that when people's social identities are not satisfactory they will try to improve their own group (in-group), or if this doesn't work they will leave it to

in-group *A group to which we belong and with which we identify.*

out-group *A group to which we do not belong.*

What type of social relationships do in-groups and out-groups lead to?

social identity *A part of our self-image that is created when we identify with specific categories or groups and act in accordance with their norms.*

Our own identity can be involved when we feel that team spirit.

*How do we develop
a social identity?*

group *Two or more people
who influence each other,
share common goals, have
an ongoing relationship,
and who believe they
belong to the group.*

*What are the
characteristics that
define a group?*

join some other group. Members want to feel good about themselves, in other words, they want to have a positive self-identity. One way to achieve this is by believing that their own groups are superior to others. This suggests that the way we develop this identity is basically competitive (Ellemers, Wilke and Von Knippenberg, 1993).

GROUPS

The discussion of social identity helps us to understand why groups are so significant to us. To explore this topic further it is useful to distinguish between social categories, which are loosely defined groups—"males," "females," "drivers," "pedestrians"—and smaller groups who interact with and relate socially to one another in some important and ongoing manner. It is in these smaller groups that the most important social influences occur.

A group, then, is more than just a collection of people or a social category. When does a collection of people become a "group"? If you are part of a crowd milling about the baggage carousel at an airport while waiting for your luggage, it is unlikely that you would think you had just joined a group. What about spectators at a hockey game? Or a classroom of students? Where is the line to be drawn between "groups" of people and simple clusters of people who happen to be sharing the same physical space? A group can be defined as two or more people who:

- exert a mutual influence on each other;
- have an ongoing and relatively stable relationship; that is, roles, rules, and norms remain fairly constant;
- share a sense of purpose, common goals, or interests;
- each believe that they are part of the group.

The definition of a group must include all of the points above. For example, assume that every morning you share a bus shelter with the same set of people. There is likely to be at least some minimal mutual influence, and the relationship, minimal as it is, endures over time in a relatively stable way. All individuals share a common goal—to get on the bus. Yet no one is likely to consider that he or she is part of a "group" because the last and perhaps most crucial characteristic has not been met. That is the belief of the members that they belong to this group.

There are, of course, various kinds of groups. Some are **formal**, with an established structure and clearly defined roles for its members. These include work groups or project teams in an organization, for example. Other types of groups are **informal**, and may develop from

A group is more than just a collection of people sharing the same space.

the attractions and needs of individuals, including social needs. A group of friends who regularly get together for an evening of poker is an example of an informal group. Groups can also be differentiated on the basis of whether or not they are task oriented or social oriented. Task-oriented groups serve to accomplish some specific job, while social groups function to provide pleasure and social interaction.

Using these criteria, consider whether you and your classmates constitute a group. What about your Students' Association, or friends who meet regularly for a game of pool at the pub?

COHESIVENESS

GROUP FORMATION AND PRODUCTIVITY

While children cannot decide what family to join, and while people called for jury duty cannot choose their fellow jurors, most groups involve voluntary membership. Why does an individual become involved in one group and not another? There are several major reasons. Sometimes we join groups because we wish to accomplish some specific goal. For example, someone who wants to learn about photography or about acid rain may join a camera club or an environmental group, respectively.

What are the positive and negative effects of group cohesiveness?

Another major reason for joining groups is for the company they provide. We are attracted both to accomplishing our goals and to the people. Are they like us? Do we wish to be like them?

We may also join groups for reasons of security (e.g. a labour union) and to gain greater control over events (e.g. stopping acid rain). Our chance of meeting our goals is better in the group.

Cohesiveness is the term used to describe all the factors that draw members to a group and keep them there. You may think of it as the glue that holds the group together. In general terms, a cohesive group sticks together and displays feelings of harmony and solidarity. The members are committed to the group and its tasks (Murdock, 1989; Levine and Moreland,1990). Cohesiveness within groups usually increases as the group becomes more important to its members. For instance, when a group competes with other groups, or experiences some kind of external threat, the level of cohesiveness increases.

cohesiveness The elements that draw a group together include participation, cooperation, and communication.

Cohesiveness can have both positive and negative effects on the productivity of task-oriented groups. Members of highly cohesive groups are usually more influenced by group norms, since group membership is very important to them (Berkowitz, 1954; Schacter, Ellertson, McBride and Gregory, 1951). If group norms call for high productivity a cohesive group will produce a high output. If the norms call for low productivity (when members want to work only for a minimum output), cohesiveness will promote low output. Conversely, the productivity of a highly cohesive group can suffer if its members spend too much time socializing. They may even become so absorbed by their social interaction that they lose sight of the group goal.

Finally, cohesiveness leads to greater member satisfaction. This is because it typically leads to greater participation by each member in the group's activities, as well as more cooperation and greater communication (Lott and Lott, 1961).

REGULATION BY THE GROUP: NORMS

Norms are shared beliefs about what behaviours are and are not acceptable for group members. They are formed around issues that are important to the group and that allow it to function effectively. Norms usually involve a certain amount of judgment on the part of group members. For example, if one of the norms of a poker club is that each member be available to play on a specified date once each month, no one may be able to specify how many times a player can miss each year before they are considered to be letting down the group. Sometimes, of course, groups try to formalize their norms into written rules, but it is impossible to anticipate all the situations that group members will encounter.

The group often rewards conformity to its norms. When members deviate from the group's norms, and if the transgression is considered serious, group members will usually take measures to draw the deviant member back into line. The ultimate threat, of course, is rejection by the group. If membership in a particular group is important, such a threat can compel the member to conform.

SELF-TEST QUESTIONS

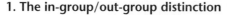

1. The in-group/out-group distinction

a) is an important aspect of the way we categorize our social world

b) separates the categories to which we belong from those to which we do not belong

c) promotes competition between members of different social categories

d) all of the above

2. Suppose Brian, a 20-year-old black student, is participating in a social psychology experiment. The experimenter hands Brian six pictures, three of young black males and three of elderly black males, and asks him to rate these pictures on a number of dimensions. What feature has diagnostic value in this study?

a) age

b) race

c) gender

d) b and c

3. Which of the following is *not* a defining characteristic of a group?

a) six or more people

b) ongoing stable relationship

c) members have common goals and interests

d) members believe they belong

4. Which of the following is true of group cohesiveness?

a) positive effects are possible

b) negative effects are possible

c) leads to member satisfaction

d) all of the above

GROUP DECISION MAKING

THE RISKY SHIFT

Groups are often faced with the need to make decisions, some of which involve taking risks. In the late 1960s, studies of risk-taking in groups became a major research area in North American social psychology. Studies did not examine actual risk-taking, but rather the willingness to take risk. One technique asked subjects to give advice to a fictitious person. Examine Table 10-1 and decide how you would advise Mr. E. When their individual selections had been made, subjects were asked to come to a unanimous decision in groups of usually four people.

Numerous experiments produced the same finding—that people will make a more "risky" decision in a group than they will on their own. The name given to this finding is the **risky shift phenomenon**.

Various explanations have been offered for the risky shift. One of these is the idea of diffusion of responsibility. This suggests that in a group, each member may feel less personally responsible for the decision and therefore be willing to take more risk (Kogan and Wallach, 1967). It has also been suggested that because risk-taking has a positive value in Western society it is likely that a group discussion will produce arguments in its favour.

POLARIZATION

The shift towards risk is only one example of a much more general phenomenon: **group-induced attitude polarization.** Studies have shown that group decisions are more extreme than those made individually. This means that in a group, individuals will alter opinions in the direction of the majority, regardless of whether this is more or less risky. Risky groups shift towards risk and cautious groups towards caution (Turner, Wetherall and Hogg, 1989). Other studies show

How does the risky shift phenomenon work?

risky shift People in a group tend to make decisions that require more risk than decisions they would make on their own.

group-induced attitude polarization Attitudes become more extreme in a group due to a closer comparison and identification with group members and their views.

TABLE 10-1 Sample item from the Choice Dilemmas Questionnaire

Mr. E. is the president of a light metals corporation in the United States. The corporation is quite prosperous, and has strongly considered the possibilities of business expansion by building an additional plant in a new location. The choice is between building another plant in the U.S., where they anticipate a moderate return on initial investment, or building a plant in a foreign country. Lower labour costs and easy access to raw materials in that country would mean a much higher return on the initial investment. On the other hand, there is a history of political instability and revolution in the foreign country under consideration. In fact, the leader of a small minority party is committed to nationalizing, that is, taking over all foreign investments.

Imagine that you are advising Mr. E. Listed below are several probabilities or odds of continued political stability in the foreign country under consideration.

Please check the *lowest* probability that you would consider acceptable for Mr. E.'s corporation to build a plant in that country.

____ The chances are 1 in 10 that the foreign country will remain politically stable.
____ The chances are 3 in 10 that the foreign country will remain politically stable.
____ The chances are 5 in 10 that the foreign country will remain politically stable.
____ The chances are 7 in 10 that the foreign country will remain politically stable.
____ The chances are 9 in 10 that the foreign country will remain politically stable.
____ Place a check here if you think Mr. E.'s corporation should *not* build a plant in the foreign country, no matter what the probabilities.

SOURCE: Kogan and Wallach, 1964

that individual characteristics will affect results. If people perceive themselves as having cautious or risky characteristics, they will not be persuaded by the group to move in the opposite direction. In other words, a "risky" person in a cautious group will not shift to a more cautious position. It was also found that subjects must actively interact with one another for the effect to occur. When subjects were seated in a line there was less polarization than when they were seated in a square, which facilitated interaction (Moscovici and Lecuyer, 1972).

THE SOURCES OF POLARIZATION

What are the reasons why group-induced attitude polarization occurs?

What accounts for group-induced attitude polarization? Why is the group attitude stronger than just the *average* of the attitudes in the group? Recent research has focused on three possible explanations. The first is based on social comparison processes, the second on persuasive argumentation, and the third on social identification.

(1) Social comparison.   This interpretation of the polarization effect (Sanders and Baron, 1977) assumes that individuals try to see and present themselves to others in as favourable a light as possible. This means that group members will observe the behaviour of the other members and try to behave in a way they believe is acceptable to the group. When all the members act this way group judgments shift to a position that is stronger than simply the average of the initial, individual judgments.

(2) Persuasive argumentation.   This explanation (Burnstein and Vinokur, 1977) suggests that group discussion is responsible for the polarization effect.

Individuals are exposed to arguments for and against a certain position. As they hear new information, they add this to what they already know, and feel stronger about the issue. Arguments that are both persuasive and present new information will produce a stronger shift.

(3) Social identification.   In this explanation individuals bear in mind the norms and stereotypes associated with their group, which are usually more extreme than the behaviour of individual members. When members try to conform to this stereotype, polarization (more extreme behaviour) occurs. For example, suppose that the senior class in your college has a reputation for supporting social causes. As a member of that group you may participate in various committees because you believe that's what a senior does, and not because you have a strong personal commitment to these causes. Many members of the senior class doing the same thing would create a shift in behaviour.

It is not possible to say which of these models best explains polarization. Until more studies are done, it is wise to assume that all three processes operate to push a group towards more extreme attitudes, that is, to produce polarization.

SELF-TEST QUESTIONS

SELF ? TEST

5. The phenomenon whereby a group decision is frequently less cautious than the individuals' initial decisions is termed

a) the minimal group effect

b) the risky shift effect

c) the minimal probability effect

d) none of the above

6. An explanation of group-induced attitude polarization based on persuasive arguments states that the strongest shift depends on

a) the presentation of new information

b) the presentation of familiar information

c) long group discussions

d) all of the above

7. According to the social identification explanation of group-induced attitude change, why do individuals shift their decisions in the direction of majority opinion?

a) they have in mind group norms

b) they are conforming to group stereotypes

c) they have forgotten their original position

d) both a and b

POWER

Within any group—and especially within task-oriented groups—there is a distribution of power. Some members have much more power than others. Think of a group to which you belong. You know who has power and who doesn't. In a similar way, some groups have more power than other groups. Power refers to a person's or group's ability to influence another person or group. This means the ability to get another person or group to do what you want them to do.

From the time we are children we know what power is and who has it. You may hear a child on the playground say "my big brother can beat up your big brother." For in its most primitive form, power derives from physical might. Power has always interested and intrigued social scientists and philosophers; some have even argued that power should be the focus of the social sciences (Pollard and Mitchell, 1972). To quote the English philosopher Bertrand Russell (1962): "I shall be concerned to prove that the fundamental concept in social science is Power, in the same sense in which Energy is the fundamental concept in physics" (cited by Pollard et al., 1972, p. 9).

While power has not become the main focus of social psychology, the study of social power has produced many theories. Six major sources or "types" of interpersonal power have been identified (Raven and Kruglanski, 1970; Staheski and Frost, 1989; Hinkin and Shriesham, 1989).

(1) Reward power, through which one person can reward another (with money, approval, love, etc.) for complying. A mother can lead her son to clean up his room by promising him some chocolate cake as a reward. If the boy wants the cake and has no other way of obtaining it, he will likely do what his mother has asked.

(2) Coercive power, through which one person can punish another for noncompliance. The same mother can threaten her child with loss of his allowance if he does not clean up his room. Since she controls the money, she can carry through the threat.

power *All power has at its core the ability to influence other people or groups to do what you want them to do.*

What are the types of interpersonal power and how do they work?

reward power *Influence based on a reward for compliance.*

coercive power *Influence based on a threat to gain compliance.*

legitimate power
Influence based on the acceptance of the right of a given authority figure.

expert power *Influence based on acceptance of the superior knowledge possessed by a person or group.*

informational power *Influence based on our acceptance that a person or a group has information that we do not have.*

referent power *Influence based on the desire to be like the person with the power.*

reciprocal power *Influence based on our desire to return or gain a favour.*

(3) Legitimate power, through which legitimate authorities (teachers, employers, police) exercise their duties. Individuals comply with the demands of such people when they accept their authority. While such power is ultimately backed up by coercive power, if the individual has internalized the respect for designated authorities, no coercion is necessary.

(4) Expert power, through which individuals who have important and special knowledge offer guidance. We follow the orders of a physician, not because of coercion, but because we believe that the physician knows more than we do about how to care for our bodies.

(5) Informational power, through which "people in the know" (newspaper editors, governmental press secretaries, university researchers) provide or withhold information (Pruitt, 1976).

(6) Referent power, through which individuals exact obedience from followers who want to be like them. If you are a member of a political party and you admire and respect the party leader, you will most likely do as the leader says because you will assume it's the appropriate thing to do and because you will want to act in the way the leader would.

A powerful person may use more than one of these types of power to influence others. The list itself does not necessarily cover all aspects of power. For example, Pruitt (1976) adds **reciprocal power** to the above list. Reciprocal power refers to the influence one person has over another as a result of having helped that person in the past. There is a feeling of obligation to return the favour (recall the norm of reciprocity). Various studies have shown that this norm may be used to ensure future help. For example, a politician may provide help to other politicians with the goal of calling in "political IOU's" when he or she needs help.

LEADERSHIP

Power and influence in a group are usually distributed across the membership—sometimes uniformly, especially in social groups. Yet there is often one person who is more influential than others. This person, designated or not, is the leader. Indeed, a group may have more than one leader at the same time. One group member, having the most knowledge about how to achieve the group goal, may serve as the task leader, while another member may be more influential in getting members to cooperate and coordinate their efforts. Another member may play the key role of helping sort out emotional problems that arise among members, thus maintaining group cohesiveness (Hamblin, 1958).

The person designated as the group's formal head may not actually wield the most influence. The designated group leader may have legitimate power, but informal leaders may also emerge who exert more influence based on some special skills or competence. These informal leaders possess referent power. For example, if you were a soldier under the command of a weak sergeant who is laughed at by others in your unit, it may happen that someone else whose competence is more respected, a corporal for example, becomes your real leader. Gradually, the sergeant may come to recognize this and actually yield to the leadership of the corporal.

Rush and Russell (1988) have shown that individuals in varying situations have similar prototypes regarding how a leader should (or should not) act. They asked subjects to describe their ideas of both an effective and ineffective leader, and found that four dimensions of leader behaviour were constantly emphasized. These were: (1) initiating structure (letting followers know what is expected); (2) showing consideration (concern for the comfort and well-being of followers); (3) role assumptions (the active exercise of the leadership role); and (4) production emphasis (pressure for productive output).

Exactly how a person comes to be a leader is a question that social psychologists have been studying for many years, and the question is still without a totally satisfying answer. A related question concerns whether a person who becomes a leader in one set of circumstances is likely to become a leader in another.

CHARACTERISTICS OF THE LEADER

TRAIT THEORY OF LEADERSHIP

It has often been said that history has been shaped by great leaders. Indeed, we think of historical eras in terms of their leading figures—Genghis Khan, Joan of Arc, Napoleon, Churchill, Gandhi, Martin Luther King, and Gorbachev, to name but a few. What is it that made such leaders so remarkable? Was it something in their character that led to their rise to greatness, or was it in their situation? Did they just happen to be in the right place at the right time?

These possibilities, referred to in the literature as the **great person**, or **trait approach**, have been explored in great detail by social psychologists. In the nineteenth century, Francis Galton investigated the hereditary backgrounds of "great men" and attempted to explain leadership on the basis of inherited capability (Stogdill, 1974). Good leaders, he assumed, were born and not made. Many subsequent researchers have focused on trying to distinguish leaders from non-leaders on the basis of such traits as intelligence (Mann, 1959); personality and self-confidence (Gibb, 1969); and physical characteristics such as age, height, and weight (see Box 10-1). One leadership characteristic that has been consistently confirmed is talkativeness. The group member who talks the most is more likely to be chosen as leader (Mullen, Salas and Driskall, 1989), a phenomenon that has been observed in India as well as in the United States (Malloy and Jonowski, 1992; Rubback and Dabbs, 1988). Why should talkativeness be associated with leadership? A number of possible reasons have been suggested. One is that the rate of vocal participation is seen as a measure of how motivated a person is to be a member of the group and to help it achieve its goals. Participation also allows individuals to demonstrate their relevant expertise and leadership characteristics.

The studies on trait theory have identified an almost endless number of potentially significant traits. The research has not consistently established which of these traits best predicts how effective a leader will be. As well, these theories do not take into account that situations differ. For example, leadership traits that are effective in a college setting might not be appropriate in an insurance company.

While the trait theory approach has its problems and may not allow us to predict leadership effectiveness with great accuracy, research in this area continues. Kirkpatrick and Locke (1991) have done an extensive review of the trait literature and they believe that effective leaders are different from the people they lead. Some of these differences include the leader's drive, motivation, ambition, honesty, integrity, and self-confidence.

PERSONAL BEHAVIOUR THEORIES

A second research approach to understanding leadership focused on what the leader actually does. Early studies of leadership effectiveness identified

What traits have been identified as characteristic of leaders?

trait approach The belief that leaders are born with specific characteristics that account for their ability.

BOX 10-1

LEADERSHIP AND THE PERCEPTION OF HEIGHT

People tend to overestimate the height of people who are in high-status positions (Keyes, 1980). During the Trudeau era in Canadian politics, for example, most people believed that Trudeau was rather tall, and certainly taller than then opposition leader Joe Clark. Students at the University of New Brunswick, when asked to estimate the heights of Trudeau and Clark, gave average estimates of 180 centimetres (six feet) for Trudeau and 172.7 centimetres (five feet eight inches) for Clark (Gillis, 1983). In reality, the opposite is the case.

Napoleon, whom the British referred to as the "little corporal," was not so little for the times. In fact, he was the same height as Nelson, five feet eight, which was the average height of a Frenchman in those days. Calling him little was a British putdown.

Most of us consider the height of adults to be fairly stable. Although we may shrink a little as we get older, height certainly shouldn't vary

according to the successes we've experienced. However, a study (Higham and Carment, 1992) has shown that people do, in fact, adjust their estimates of tallness according to changes in the status and prestige of the target.

People were asked to judge how tall Brian Mulroney, John Turner, and Ed Broadbent were before and after the 1988 federal election. Before the election, Turner was judged taller than Mulroney and Broadbent was seen as the shortest. However, after winning the election, Mulroney grew taller while Turner shrank, now giving Mulroney the edge over Turner. Broadbent, the other loser, was judged to be shorter still. It is also the case that the taller the candidate, the more votes he obtained. According to their offices in Ottawa, Mulroney is 185 cm, Turner is 181.7 cm, and Broadbent is 180 cm, the exact order of the election results. Similarly, it has been shown that U.S. presidents from 1905 to 1980 were significantly taller than the runners-up.

Research involving the perception of height of women in high-status positions has never been done, but would undoubtedly yield interesting results.

---

autocratic leadership
When the leader makes all the decisions, there may be greater productivity in situations of high stress.

democratic leadership
When group members are involved in decision making, greater satisfaction is usually the result.

What is the relationship between autocratic and democratic leadership style to satisfaction and productivity?

autocratic and democratic leadership styles. **Democratic** leadership involves group members in the decision making rather than simply passing on direct orders. This approach has been found to produce greater satisfaction among followers (Shaw, 1981), but it does not necessarily lead to greater productivity. Some research has indicated that it does (e.g. Kahn and Katz, 1953); other researchers have recorded that **autocratic** leadership is more effective in this regard (Hare, 1962).

Autocratic leadership, whereby the leader makes all or most of the decisions about the group's activities, leads to greater productivity in stressful situations. Democratic leadership produces greater productivity in non-stressful circumstances (Rosenbaum and Rosenbaum, 1971). Thus, no one leadership style is likely to be effective in all situations. Further research has found that the situation itself is a key factor.

THE SITUATIONAL APPROACH

The **situational approach** to leadership is based on the idea that different situations call for different kinds of leaders. Whoever happens to have those traits and abilities best suited to the leadership needs of the group at a particular time will emerge as leader. For example, Churchill was a great wartime leader, but he lost the election following the war because the voters wanted a different kind of leader to rebuild the country.

The situational approach is superior to the trait and personal behaviour approaches because it does not assume that a person who is a good leader in one situation will be a good leader in all situations. It is limited, however, by its exclusion of such variables as style of leadership (which may be related to personal traits) and the reactions of followers. Leaders influence their followers, but followers also influence their leaders. To be a successful leader, an individual must be in tune with the expectations and needs of the followers (Hollander, 1978; Sims and Manz, 1984). Thus, successful leadership is a combination of "right leader" and "right situation."

CONTINGENCY THEORY

This combination of leader and situation was examined by Fiedler (1967, 1971, 1981), who proposed a **contingency theory** based on the idea that there are two fundamental styles of leadership: the **task-oriented** leader and the **socio-emotional** leader. The leader's effectiveness is contingent upon appropriate matching of the particular leadership style to the group situation. The task-oriented leader, motivated by the need to do the job, will not be overly concerned with the feelings and personal needs of the followers. The socio-emotional leader is more concerned with maintaining good interpersonal relationships than with achieving maximum efficiency or meeting group goals. According to Fiedler, the style of leadership reflects the basic drive of the individual and is very resistant to modification.

In order to determine whether a subject would be a task- or relationship-oriented leader, Fiedler designed a scale called the **LPC** (Least Preferred Co-worker). The LPC is determined by asking a subject (the potential leader) to indicate who, out of all the people that he or she has ever worked with, is the most difficult. This difficult or least preferred co-worker is then rated on a set of eighteen pairs of bipolar adjectives (Table 10-2), such as boring/interesting, using an eight-point rating scale. If the subject rates the LPC in a negative way, it suggests a low LPC leadership style that is more task oriented. The leader who rates the LPC in a positive manner (high LPC leader) is assumed to be more concerned with establishing and maintaining good relationships. Fiedler's model assumes that the effectiveness of either of these leadership styles depends (is contingent) upon the requirements of the given situation.

What is the relationship between leader and situation as discussed by Fiedler?

contingency theory
Leadership style must be matched to a particular group situation in order for leadership to be successful.

task-oriented leader
When the sole concern is for getting the job done, the personal needs of the group's members are often ignored.

socio-emotional leader
The concern is primarily with the relationship in the group rather than with maximum efficiency.

LPC (least preferred co-worker) This scale identifies leadership style based on attitudes expressed about a co-worker.

TABLE 10-2 Sample LPC items

Leaders are asked to select the person whom they least liked as a co-worker across their whole careers, and then to evaluate that person on a series of scales such as the following:

Friendly	8 7 6 5 4 3 2 1	Unfriendly
Agreeable	8 7 6 5 4 3 2 1	Disagreeable
Pleasant	8 7 6 5 4 3 2 1	Unpleasant
Cooperative	8 7 6 5 4 3 2 1	Uncooperative
Helpful	8 7 6 5 4 3 2 1	Frustrating

By adding up the scale values, a total LPC score is derived. Rating the LPC in a negative way yields a low score; an individual producing such a rating is a *low-LPC leader*, while an individual who produces a high score is referred to as a *high-LPC leader*.

What does the LPC scale tell us about leadership?

situational control *The degree of control that a leader can exert depends on the level of trust, how structured is the task, and the amount of power the leader possesses.*

Style of leadership interacts with **situational control**, which refers to the amount of control that the leader can exert over the members of the group. According to Fiedler, situational control depends on a combination of three factors: (1) the leader's relations with group members (reflects the level of trust, respect, and confidence that members have in their leader); (2) task structure (the degree to which tasks and member goals are clearly defined); and (3) the leader's position power (ability to deliver positive outcomes/rewards or punishments).

In Fiedler's theory, leadership situations range from those that are very favourable to the leader to those that are very unfavourable. It is much easier to be an effective leader in groups that feature positive relations with members, highly structured tasks, clearly defined roles, and a leader with high position power.

Task-oriented leadership should be most successful in situations that are either very favourable or very unfavourable to the leader. Under unfavourable leadership conditions (unstructured task, poor leader-follower relations, weak leader power) the group may be more receptive to a leader who can get them moving towards their goal. A person-oriented leader may spend too much time trying to promote greater interpersonal harmony and not enough time on the group's goals. In highly favourable leadership conditions (structured tasks, good leader-follower relations, and strong position power) the task-oriented leader may be able to spend some time on attending to people's concerns, knowing that the group is moving towards its goal.

Relationship-oriented leaders are generally considered to be more effective in situations of moderate/intermediate favourableness. In these situations friction between the group members may become so serious that it will require a person-oriented leader to cope with the group's needs. If the situation is highly favourable and all is going well, the person-oriented leader may start to interfere with the task. This may not be well accepted. If the situation is highly unfavourable, group members may become so desperate that they are willing to put aside personal feelings. If this happens, the person-oriented leader may not be able to exert enough control to get the job done (see Figure 10-1).

The contingency model has received support from a large number of different studies (e.g. Strube and Garcia, 1981). Despite the continuing controversy, it is viewed as a useful approach for determining the effectiveness of leadership (Peters, Hartke and Pohlmann, 1985).

GENDER AND LEADERSHIP

While there has been considerable research into the various aspects of leadership, until recently the issue of gender differences has not been specifically addressed. What may we assume we will find? Are there differences in traits and style?

Leadership has been the traditional prerogative of males. Research indicates that, despite some advances in the elimination of sexual discrimination, males still predominate in leadership roles. Indeed, men and women alike are inclined to look towards males, rather than females, for leadership (Eagly and Karau, 1991).

Women continue to face a number of obstacles to becoming leaders in mixed-gender groups. Above all else, many men and women believe that women are not "suited" to leadership. Gender stereotypes describe men as capable of being tough, assertive, brave, and commanding respect, while women are stereotyped as being not only gentle, but weak, fickle, and submissive. Not only is it more dif-

How does gender affect leadership?

FIGURE 10-1 **Contingency model of leadership and group performance**

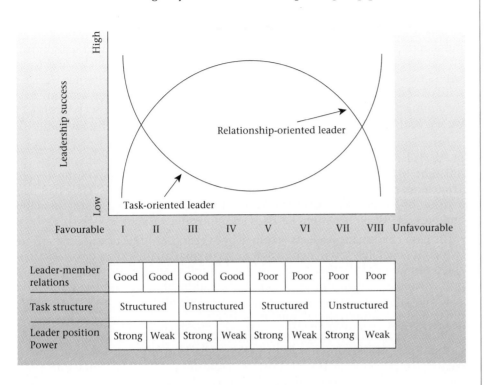

Leader-member relations	Good	Good	Good	Good	Poor	Poor	Poor	Poor
Task structure	Structured		Unstructured		Structured		Unstructured	
Leader position Power	Strong	Weak	Strong	Weak	Strong	Weak	Strong	Weak

ficult for women to assume leadership positions in mixed-gender groups, but when they do they are scrutinized more carefully. Ironically, female subordinates of female leaders in mixed-gender groups have been found to be more negative towards these leaders than male subordinates of the same leaders (Eagly and Karau, 1991). In other words, the successful woman has to struggle against the negative attitudes of both genders.

Women are identified more frequently than men as social rather than as task leaders; they are considered to be less autocratic and more democratic than men (Eagly and Karau, 1991; Eagly, Makhijani and Klonsky, 1992).

As society becomes less discriminatory against women, and as the traditional gender roles become less sharply defined, women will undoubtedly move more steadily into leadership roles. Empirical studies of managers have found that many of the assumptions about differences between male and female managers are unfounded, whether with regard to ability, attitudes, or personality. Women managers do, however, show greater concern for relationships among people (Denmark,1977; Hollander and Yoder, 1980).

In the future we shall no doubt see many more women leaders. It was only in 1957 that Ellen Fairclough became Canada's first cabinet minister; now there are many women in the cabinet. In other areas of government, Rita Johnson became the first woman premier of a province (British Columbia, 1980), Catherine Callbeck the first elected woman premier (P.E.I., 1993), Audrey McLaughlin the first to lead a national party (NDP, 1989) and in 1993, Kim Campbell became the first female prime minister.

THE CHARISMATIC LEADER

In the 1960s, "Trudeaumania" swept a political newcomer—Pierre Elliott Trudeau—into leadership of the Liberal party and eventually into the position of prime minister. For the next sixteen years, Trudeau amazed, amused, astounded, and angered his fellow citizens, depending on their political views and their willingness to accept idiosyncratic aspects of his behaviour. Whether wearing sandals and an open shirt into the House of Commons, "horsing around" in a swimming pool, being adored by the world press, or asking farmers "Why should we sell your wheat?" Trudeau had a powerful effect on everyone he encountered.

charisma Self-confidence, dominance, charm, and a belief in themselves characterize charismatic leaders.

How do charismatic leaders affect their followers?

Pierre Trudeau had **charisma** and his political life was distinguished by charismatic leadership. People admired him or detested him or both, but few were indifferent. Many of those who jumped on the Trudeau bandwagon in the days of Trudeaumania later became disappointed with his performance. They had had a vision of a new leader who would uplift them, who would breathe new life and purpose into our nation, perhaps an impossible task for any person.

The term charismatic leader was coined by Weber (1947). He described charisma (which is Greek for "divine gift") as an exceptional quality in a person that enabled him or her to gather a large number of followers. Charismatic leadership is characterized by an intensely personal relationship between the leader and follower. The follower is inspired to unquestioned obedience, loyalty, commitment, and devotion (Howell and Frost, 1989).

Other examples of charismatic leaders include Churchill, Gandhi, Martin Luther King, Eva Peron, and John F. Kennedy. How do such leaders come to wield such power over their followers? How are they able to appeal to their followers on a raw emotional level? House (1977) argues that the charismatic leader often demonstrates the following characteristics:

(1) An extremely high level of self-confidence.

(2) An extremely high level of dominance. Such leaders seem to have a strong need to influence others, and this need drives them to acquire the necessary persuasive skills to wield such influence.

(3) An apparently strong conviction of the moral righteousness of their beliefs. However, House suggests that it is at least possible that some charismatic leaders believe in neither themselves nor their beliefs, but are capable of acting as though they do in order to influence and control their followers. Certainly, there have been charismatic

Churchill addressing the Canadian parliament: What made him so remarkable?

religious leaders who have been shown to be manipulators, using their charismatic abilities for their own ends (e.g., U.S. cult leaders Jim Jones of the People's Temple and David Koresh of the Branch Davidians, who led their followers to death in 1978 and 1993 respectively; and evangelist Jim Bakker of the PTL Club, who left his TV ministry in 1987 following reports of sexual infidelity and financial exploitation).

To these can be added a fourth point:

(4) Personal characteristics such as charm, originality, or even speech fluency. These are essential attributes of the charismatic leader (Sashkin, 1977).

Charismatic leaders affect their followers in specific ways (Conger and Kanungo, 1992 and House, 1977):

(1) They provide their followers with "transcendent" goals expressed in moral rhetoric. Consider Trudeau's speeches about a "Just Society"; Martin Luther King's civil rights declarations, "I have a dream ..." and "We shall overcome ..."; Churchill's depiction of the British as invincible, "We shall never surrender ..."; and John Kennedy's "Ask not what your country can do for you ...."

(2) Charismatic leaders are innovative and unconventional and they strive to change the status quo.

(3) Because the leader has high expectations of and confidence in the followers, their self-esteem is enhanced and they are motivated towards achieving goals.

(4) The charismatic leader often provides a role model and a value system that continue to influence people even after the leader's death. Even today, Gandhi is respected and admired and his teachings are followed by millions of Indians and non-Indians.

Shils (1965) argued that charisma is, in fact, much more common than we believe, and is distributed fairly widely throughout society. People who have power are often seen as being charismatic as a result of the awe in which we hold the power itself. But there is much more to it than that, since many powerful leaders are not "charismatic." In spite of the research that has been done on charismatic leaders, our knowledge is still very limited.

THE TRANSFORMATIONAL LEADER

Building on the strengths of the charismatic leader, the transformational leader has a strong vision of what the future should hold. This is a leader who can transform an organization based on his or her vision of the future and compel followers or employees to share in this vision.

A transformational leader is innovative and unconventional and works to change things. Followers are encouraged to place the achievement of the organization's goals above personal goals (Conger and Kanungo, 1992, House, 1991). This type of leader motivates people with internal rewards (feeling good about what they do), understands followers' needs, shows them how their needs can be met, encourages creative expression, and allows followers to work without interference if goals are being met.

Research carried out by Bass has identified transformational leadership as the leadership style for the future (Bass, 1985; Avolio and Bass, 1988).

transformational leader
Leadership in the future will combine charisma, innovation, vision, and a commitment to followers to enhance their self-esteem.

How does a transformational leader interact with followers or employees?

SELF-TEST QUESTIONS

8. In the literature on groups, which of the following has not been identified as an important type of power?

a) legitimate

b) coercive

c) derived

d) referent

9. According to the "great-person" theory of leadership, what characteristic seems to bear the strongest relationship to leadership?

a) physical attractiveness

b) health

c) talkativeness

d) age

10. In a task-oriented group, what is the most important measure of successful leadership?

a) group morale

b) output

c) member satisfaction

d) group attendance

11. Which of the following statements is/are true regarding types of leadership?

a) democratic leadership leads to higher levels of member satisfaction

b) autocratic leadership leads to higher levels of satisfaction under stressful conditions

c) autocratic leadership leads to higher levels of member satisfaction

d) a and b

12. According to contingency theory

a) the effectiveness of a leader depends on matching the style of leadership to the group situation

b) there are two basic styles of leadership

c) leadership orientation can be assessed by measuring the leader's attitude towards the "least preferred co-worker"

d) all of the above

SUMMARY

(1) In any society, individuals define themselves largely in terms of groups and social categories.

(2) We construct our social world in terms of social categories, and govern our behaviour according to the most significant category in a particular situation.

(3) One basic construct is the distinction we make between the in-group and the out-group.

(4) Mutual interaction and influence, ongoing and relatively stable relationships, shared goals, and the perception of belonging to a group are the defining characteristics of groups.

(5) People join groups to accomplish goals and to satisfy needs for affiliation. These factors contribute to group cohesiveness.

(6) Within a group, members may assume various roles, and norms regulate their behaviour.

(7) Group decisions tend to be more polarized than individual decisions. Three explanations have been suggested for this: social comparison, persuasive argumentation, and social identification.

(8) Leadership has been explained in terms of the traits of the leader, characteristics of the situation, and the interaction of the leader's and the group's characteristics.

(9) Fiedler's contingency model of leadership effectiveness relates the characteristics of the group to task-oriented and interpersonal relationship-oriented leadership styles.

(10) Leaders described as "charismatic" tend to be self-confident and dominant, hold strong convictions, and provide their followers with transcendent goals.

(11) Leaders who are described as transformational are charismatic and offer a new vision of the future that followers are encouraged to share.

FOR REVIEW

Placing people in _____(1) provides a way of interacting with others based on _____(2) and _____(3) that we have learned to associate with these people. In a similar way, groups provide a means by which we create our _____(4). We call groups to which we belong _____(5), and groups to which we do not belong _____(6). A group is defined by meeting the following criteria: two or more people who exert a _____(7), who have an ongoing and stable _____(8), who share _____(9), and who believe they _____(10) to the group. _____(11) is the term used to describe the factors that keep a group together.

When we are willing to take more risk as part of a group than on our own, it is called a _____(12). Social comparison, persuasive argumentation, and social identification all work to produce _____(13).

There are many types of power. _____(14) suggests we punish to get compliance. _____(15) suggests we accept the legitimate authority of another person or group. _____(16) suggests we believe that others have important information that we do not.

_____(17) suggests that some people have a special knowledge base that we lack. _____(18) refers to the compliance that results from wanting to be like the person. _____(19) suggests that a feeling of obligation exists.

_____(20) theory supports the notion that some people are born leaders. In situations of high stress a _____(21) leader may be more successful than a _____(22) one. The _____(23) scale was designed to identify _____(24) and _____(25) leaders. Relations with group members, task structure, and a leader's power all interact to produce _____(26). In terms of gender, women are less likely than men to be identified as _____(27) leaders.

A leader with a high degree of self-confidence, dominance, charm, originality, and a strong moral belief that they are right are said to have _____(28). The _____(29) leader has all these qualities, and as well provides a vision for the future that followers are encouraged to support.

ISSUES AND ACTIVITIES

1. Choose a group to which you belong. Be sure that it meets the criteria for a group that is outlined in the text. Identify the norms, beliefs, and values of

the group. What stereotypes do you believe are associated with membership in this group? Using the concept of social identity, discuss how this association has contributed to your self-image.

2. Debate the following statement: There is a crisis of leadership in this province/country. Be sure to take into account what you have learned about the leadership role, and draw on other readings and sources as well. Present the debate to your class.

3. Keep a media log (newspapers, magazines, TV) over the semester. Identify as many examples as you can of the seven types of power discussed in the text. Is any one type more common than the others? Be prepared to share your results with classmates. Ask your instructor for the minimum number of examples required.

4. A number of leaders have been mentioned in this chapter. Choose one or another person whom you believe to be a leader. Research this person and produce a biographical sketch discussing their leadership qualities. What type of leader do you think this person is? Why? How wide is this person's influence? What kind(s) of power do they use? Try to find out how this leadership ability evolved. Be sure to cite your sources.

• FURTHER READING

BASS, B.M. (1981). *Stogdill's handbook of leadership*. New York: Free Press. A broad-based review of all aspects of leadership, theoretical and empirical.

CONGER, J.A. AND KANUNGO, R.E. (Eds.) (1988). *Charismatic leadership*. San Francisco: Jossey-Bass. A variety of commentaries on the origin and development of charismatic leaders. Includes case studies.

MUGNY, G. and PEREX, J.A. (1991). *The social psychology of minority influence*. New York: Cambridge University Press. A European perspective on minority influence on social processes.

PAULUS, P.B. (1989). *Psychology of group influence*. Second Edition. Hillsdale, NJ: Erlbaum. A thorough and current analysis of all aspects of group life.

SHAW, M. (1981). *Group dynamics—the psychology of group behaviour*. Third Edition. New York: McGraw-Hill. Research and theory about groups by a leader in the field.

SUGGESTED WEBLINKS

Canadian Journal of Behavioural Science on-line
http://www.cycor.ca/Psych/ac-main.html

Journal of Personality and Social Psychology (table of contents)
http://www.apa.org/journals/psp.html

ANSWERS TO SELF-TEST QUESTIONS

1. d; 2. a; 3. a; 4. d; 5. b; 6. a; 7. d; 8. c; 9. c; 10. b; 11. d; 12. d.

ANSWERS TO FOR REVIEW

1. social categories; 2. norms; 3. stereotypes; 4. social identity; 5. in-group; 6. out-group; 7. mutual influence; 8. relationship; 9. common goals; 10.

belong; 11. Cohesiveness; 12. risky shift; 13. group-induced attitude polarization; 14. Coercive; 15. Legitimate; 16. Informational; 17. Expert; 18. Referent; 19. Reciprocal; 20. Trait theory; 21. autocratic; 22. democratic; 23. LPC; 24. task-oriented; 25. socio-emotional; 26. situational control; 27. task or autocratic; 28. charisma; 29. transformational.

CONFLICT AND ITS RESOLUTION

The grim fact is that we prepare for war like precocious giants and for peace like retarded pygmies.

Lester B. Pearson

Mankind must put an end to war or war will put an end to mankind.

J.F. Kennedy

■ LEARNING OUTCOMES

1. An understanding of the social context within which conflict occurs.

2. Knowledge of different types of conflict.

3. An understanding of zero-sum and non-zero-sum conflict situations.

4. An understanding of collective dilemmas.

5. An understanding of the use of threats, communication, and power in situations of conflict.

6. An understanding of the resolution of conflict.

■ FOR REFLECTION

• Is conflict unavoidable, and is it always undesirable?

• When are people motivated to cooperate with each other? Compete with each other?

• What makes a threat successful?

• Can social psychology help to prevent war?

■ CHAPTER OUTLINE

In March of 1990, the town council of Oka in Quebec decided to expand the local golf course onto land that the Mohawks of the nearby Kanesatake reserve claimed to be theirs. In protest, the Mohawks blocked the main road leading to the golf course. The municipal council then responded by obtaining an injunction from the Superior Court of Quebec ordering the natives to remove the barricade by June 30. The Mohawks ignored the court order and requested that the problem be resolved through discussions with the federal government. In the meantime, the blockade was being joined by armed native "Warriors," some of whom were from outside the reserve. The confrontation remained peaceful until the Mayor of Oka asked the provincial police to enforce the injunction. Two separate assaults by the police, using tear gas and a front-end loader, were unsuccessful. In the process, the Mohawks captured the loader and used it to overturn several police vehicles. After the melee was brought under control, 900 additional police officers were quickly brought in and the whole area was sealed off when a policeman was found dead of a gunshot wound. An autopsy was unable to determine whether the fatal shot had come from a Mohawk rifle or, as the natives claimed, from his own gun.

Attempts by the Quebec government to resolve the situation were sporadic and unsuccessful. Finally, Premier Henri Bourassa broke off negotiations and asked the army to move in. A total of 3033 troops were deployed, supported by artillery, helicopters, CF-5 jets, and a navy vessel on the nearby St. Lawrence River. Then, on August 29, an army officer and a Mohawk chieftain, who had been meeting quietly for a week, reached an informal agreement and both sides jointly began to dismantle the barricades. This incident contained many of the ingredients of **conflict** that we discuss in this chapter, including misunderstanding, confrontation, escalation, and negotiation.

> **conflict** *When two or more parties are in disagreement and believe they cannot achieve their interests at the same time.*

The word "conflict" is often used in common speech as a synonym for warfare or aggression, but there is an important distinction to be made between conflict and aggression. The term "conflict" properly refers to a situation of discord between two or more parties which can sometimes be peacefully resolved or which may, in some circumstances, lead to aggression. Conflict involves a divergence of interest, or the belief that the interests or aspirations of two or more parties cannot be achieved simultaneously (Pruitt and Rubin, 1986).

Unfortunately, far too many conflicts, rather than being regulated through negotiation and compromise, lead either to violence or avoidance. Despite ever-increasing scientific and technological progress, humans have made little advance in their ability to prevent the destructive aspects of conflict. It is usually too appealing to try to force a solution to a conflict rather than to negotiate; forcing the other side to back down often becomes the most important goal. Two devastating world wars and countless smaller wars, thousands of labour disruptions, and spiralling divorce rates demonstrate that we are little better at dealing with conflict in the twentieth century than were our forebears.

CONFLICT: SOME BACKGROUND

SOCIAL PSYCHOLOGY AND CONFLICT RESEARCH

Although the study of conflict was a popular subject for sociologists and political scientists in the latter part of the nineteenth and the early part of the twentieth centuries, by the middle of this century very little development was taking

BOX 11-1

DESTRUCTIVE CONFLICT RESOLUTION

Although it has had neither the quantity nor intensity of the social strife of the United States, Canadian society has not entirely avoided the consequences of destructive conflict resolution. Yet Canadian violence has not generally involved loss of life, certainly not to the extent that is found in the United States. Apart from the terrorism practised by the FLQ and the Sons of Freedom Doukhobors, most of the violence in Canada in this century has been labour-related.

Between 1910 and 1966, 227 strikes were attended by violence, with soldiers and the RCMP often being called in to put them down. The Winnipeg General Strike and the Asbestos Quebec strike are only two examples. And, of course, there was the depression of the 1930s:

The Depression saw some bloody strikes, a violent confrontation during the historical trek of unemployed people to Ottawa in 1935, and suspensions of civil liberties not seen at any time since. Workers protesting unfair management practices, unemployed people demanding work or assistance, people organizing to demand political change—were harassed, often arrested, and sometimes killed by the police ..." (Jackson, Kelly and Mitchell, p. 177, 1977).

place in this area. The discipline of social psychology has not only ignored but often *avoided* the subject of conflict—that is, until the launch of Sputnik, the world's first space satellite, by the Soviets in 1958. The fear that Soviet science and technology had outstripped that of the U.S. suddenly made the need for advancement in the understanding of conflict, at least at the international level, seem much more pressing. New attempts were made to find ways of resolving conflicts on favourable terms, without escalation to a dangerous level. Sputnik was a reminder that Western powers could not count on military superiority to win conflicts.

Not everyone took the same approach to the study of conflict, however. While sociologists and political scientists downplayed the role of individuals in their theorizing, social psychologists tried to reduce groups and nations to the status of individuals in order to make their theorizing less complex. In adopting such a perspective, social psychologists came to view conflict at the international level as amenable to study through the analysis of conflict at the interpersonal level. Consequently, the bulk of social psychological research into conflict has focused on the study of two or more individuals in conflict in the context of controlled laboratory studies.

In this chapter we examine **realistic conflict**, in which there is some actual basis for disagreement, dispute, or hostility. Realistic conflicts between individuals or groups are *rational* in the sense that they reflect either competition for scarce resources, incompatible goals, or incompatible principles (e.g., "The environment must be protected at all costs" versus "Jobs are more important than lakes and rivers"). If a labour union demands higher salaries while management does not want to pay out more money, there is a realistic conflict. If Canada considers the Northwest Passage to be its territory and the United States wants to treat the passage as international waters (as has already occurred), there is a realistic conflict. If the provinces want more power in areas of jurisdiction that the federal government wishes to reserve for itself, there is a realistic conflict.

realistic conflict When there is an actual basis for disagreement due to incompatible needs, goals, or principles.

What are the characteristics of the six conflict types discussed in this section?

veridical conflict *The conflict is real in the sense that each person/group has an objective goal that is in opposition to the other's.*

contingent conflict *When the parties fail to recognize that resources exist to allow each party to satisfy their needs.*

displaced conflict *Directed not at the real problem but at a related issue, often because the real problem is not recognized.*

TYPES OF CONFLICT

As with beauty, conflict may be in the eye of the beholder. Two people involved in a conflict can perceive the issue at stake in very different ways and at very different levels of awareness. They do, however, view their conflict as real. From the point of view of an outside observer, conflicts can be categorized into various types, depending on the relationship between the actual conflict of interest and the manner in which the people involved interpret the conflict. There are at least six different types of conflict, which are distinguished from each other by the relationship between the perceived and the objective state of affairs (Deutsch, 1973):

(1) **Veridical conflict.** An objective conflict exists and is accurately perceived. For example, both husband and wife want to use the spare bedroom, he for an office, she for a darkroom. They have genuinely opposed interests in this case.

(2) **Contingent conflict.** In such conflicts, there are other resources available that would serve to satisfy both parties, but they do not recognize this. The conflict is contingent upon this failure to recognize. For example, in the conflict concerning the spare bedroom, if there is also an attic that can easily be converted to either an office or a darkroom, the conflict could be readily resolved. In contingent conflicts, a third party ("mediator") can often successfully resolve the conflict by pointing to a solution that will readily satisfy both.

(3) **Displaced conflict.** The dispute in this case is not about the real underlying issue. For example, a couple with sexual problems may be embarrassed about admitting their concerns and argue instead over converting the spare bedroom.

Eyeball to eyeball in the Oka crisis.

Since the *actual* issue is not discussed, resolving other issues will not alleviate the basic conflict. A third party may be helpful by directing the couple to identify the real issue.

(4) **Misattributed conflict.** The disputants in this kind of conflict wrongly blame each other for their difficulties. For example, suppose that during a period of financial restraint students criticize professors for not providing enough individual attention, while professors criticize students for demanding too much of their time. Both students and professors actually have *common* cause against the group (e.g., government) that controls the budget.

(5) **Latent conflict.** In this case, there is a conflict in the sense that the two parties have incompatible goals, but they are not yet aware of this incompatibility, or one party may be for the moment unwilling or unable to pursue goal satisfaction. Latent conflicts often involve a dominant-subordinate relationship. Employees and employers may work in relative harmony because of the power of the latter over the former.

BOX 11-2
A CONFLICT OVER FALSE PREMISES

During a smallpox epidemic in Montreal in 1885 (which killed at least 3000 Montrealers that year) physicians successfully persuaded the city to pass a compulsory vaccination law. People who refused vaccinations were imprisoned. Superstition among the less well-educated, faced with a strange new medical procedure, led to strong resistance to the measure, and vaccinating teams were sometimes physically ejected from people's homes. One day, a protest mob rioted, smashing store windows and setting fires as they moved through the streets, and attacking the firemen who tried to extinguish the blazes. The Victoria Rifles were called in to quell the disturbance, and from then on, until the epidemic was over, the vaccination teams moved with armed escorts (Bliss, 1991).

Both the physicians and the protesters had the same goal: the good health of the citizenry. As we have already seen, it is the *perceptions* of the individuals involved that determine whether or not a conflict exists. Yet in a very real sense, it was not a conflict, since there was no *real* conflict of interest. Each side wanted exactly the same thing—the good health of the populace.

However, some employees would undoubtedly like more responsibility and autonomy, while their employers would like to continue to exercise control over them.

(6) Conflict based on false premises. This is a conflict over attributing the causes of a behaviour. There is no objective conflict of interest in this case. A simple example is that of a man and a woman who argue because she forgot to buy him a birthday card. He may attribute this to a lack of love on her part, while she may attribute her oversight to fatigue.

As you can see, conflict can arise from various sources, and often an outsider is better able to see the real basis of conflict than are the disputants themselves. It is also important to understand that these six types of conflict are not mutually exclusive. For example, displaced or misattributed conflict is often associated with a latent conflict.

> **misattributed conflict** *Disputants blame each other when the real source is a common problem outside of both parties.*

> **latent conflict** *Based on the inability of a subordinate to pursue his or her goals. Awareness of this incompatibility may not exist.*

> **conflict based on false premises** *Conflict based on totally different perceptions of what a behaviour means.*

SELF-TEST QUESTIONS

1. Which of the following is a realistic source of conflict?
a) the Canadiens and the Flames compete for the Stanley Cup
b) Bill plays his radio at a high volume to annoy his neighbour
c) Russia and the United States distrust each other
d) social categorization

2. Displaced conflict refers to a situation in which
a) the disputants do not recognize the ability of other resources to satisfy their needs
b) the disputants have incompatible goals but are not aware of this incompatibility
c) the dispute is focused on an issue, but not the real issue
d) none of the above

3. A dominant-subordinate relationship is most often characteristic of

a) the veridical conflict

b) latent conflict

c) biased conflict

d) contingent conflict

4. A third party who may be needed to help resolve a conflict is called a(n)

a) mediator

b) subordinate

c) social psychologist

d) employee

THE STUDY OF CONFLICT

SOCIAL EXCHANGE THEORY

What is the relationship of social exchange theory to our understanding of conflict?

When two parties are in conflict, one simple form of resolution is to end the interaction altogether: sometimes nations break off diplomatic relations; sometimes factories are closed permanently; sometimes people divorce. This does not usually happen, however. For example, a man and a woman living together may endure a considerable level of conflict, even if its consequences are somewhat destructive, if there is no other relationship that can serve the needs this relationship continues to fulfill. In other words, even though there may be considerable bickering, each may bear with the situation in order to have company or share expenses. In such a situation, conflict can be approached from the point of view of social exchange. The two parties are exchanging all sorts of things: affection, finances, housework, babysitting. The exchange may be very good on some levels (e.g., economic) but very poor on others (e.g., affection). Conflict over affection may not be serious enough to break the union because of the importance of other mutual benefits. Similarly, labour and management usually continue to deal with each other, as does nation with nation.

According to **social exchange theory** (Homans, 1958; Thibaut and Kelley, 1959), all social interaction can be viewed as a kind of economic interaction in which an individual or group obtains certain rewards but only at the expense of certain costs. The outcome, or "profit," is the difference between rewards and costs. Presumably an individual will be unhappy with a non-profitable interaction. Social exchange theory suggests that people are very selective in their choice of interactions.

According to Thibaut and Kelley's analysis, an individual assesses the richness of the outcome in a given exchange situation not solely in terms of "rewards minus costs," but also on the basis of two other standards. The first is the **comparison level (CL)**. A wife might compare her "outcome" in her marital situation with what she perceives to be the outcome of other wives, or with what her own outcome was earlier in the relationship, or even with her outcome in prior or other current relationships. Remember that "outcome" is the difference between the perceived rewards and costs of a relationship (good financial situation, but none of the spouse's time or affection). A second standard, called the **comparison level for alternatives (CLalt)**, is used as a basis for deciding whether or not to stay in the relationship (i.e. whether the person can get a better deal anywhere else). If divorce or separation brings great stigma or economic ruin, the per-

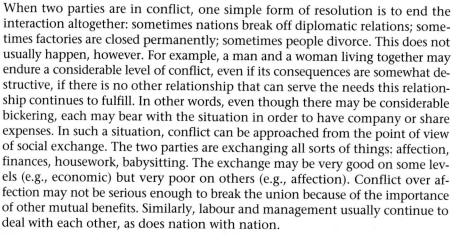

social exchange theory
People choose to interact with each other based on the rewards and costs of the relationship.

CL (comparison level)
People compare their situations with those of others in order to decide if their own relationship is satisfactory.

CLalt (comparison level for alternatives) *By looking at what alternatives are available, people make a decision about whether or not to stay in a relationship.*

son may decide to stay in the relationship, unsatisfying though it is. CLalt, in other words, is the lowest level of outcome the person will accept, given the available alternatives to the relationship. Only if the existing mutual outcomes are above *each* person's CLalt will the relationship continue.

Before most women were in a position to become well-educated and compete professionally with men, many accepted the role of mother/labourer/servant on the basis of such comparisons. When comparing their situation with those of relevant others (CL), they seemed to be doing well enough, and if they chose to leave the relationship, their plight (CLalt) looked even worse. Now, however, women enjoy a variety of options. Consequently, when married women experience severe discontent with their role, the possibility of leaving the relationship is not nearly so horrifying as it once was, for separation and divorce have be-

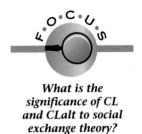

What is the significance of CL and CLalt to social exchange theory?

FIGURE 11-1 Social exchange theory: The CL and the CLalt

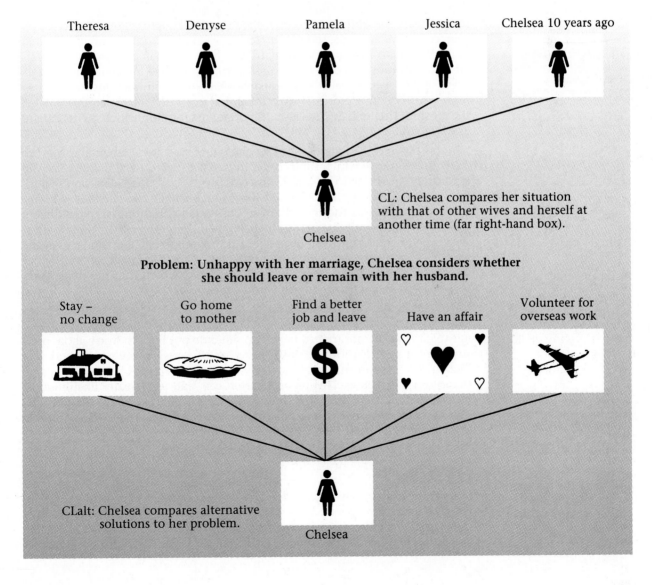

come commonplace and widely accepted. In addition, alternative relationships offering higher rewards, at least in the short term, may be more readily available. Thus, whether or not a conflict leads to rupture of a relationship depends not only upon the disputants themselves and the nature of the conflict, but also upon factors outside the conflict.

Social exchange theory is one model for viewing conflicts between individuals. It is based essentially on the concept of seeking a "fair deal" for both parties. Because social exchange involves tangible or intangible resources such as affection, money, or information, it is referred to as an "economic" theory. Interestingly, one of the major models of conflict which we consider next is also derived from the economic approach.

THE THEORY OF GAMES

In 1944, Von Neumann and Morgenstern published their classic *Theory of Games and Economic Behaviour,* which provided a new model of conflict that influenced not only political science and economic theory but social psychology as well. This model treats all conflicts as though they involve exchanges of a variety of resources—material goods, services, affection. Each party to the conflict is viewed as able to make a **rational choice**, in that each is capable of ordering preferences for various outcomes (e.g., prefers romantic love to friendship; prefers friendship to enmity) and each is capable of acting to minimize losses and maximize gains. In other words, it is assumed that in an exchange, people try to get the most for themselves. This is an important assumption which merits careful examination.

In the '60s and '70s, many social psychologists used "experimental games" to study the degree to which subjects did indeed act in a rational manner, as well as to study the influence of a wide range of psychological variables on the resolution of conflict. By the 1980s, the use of such games had declined substantially because it was thought that they provided situations of questionable external validity (Apfelbaum and Lubek, 1976; Nemeth, 1970). Nonetheless, such experimental games can be used to study conflict resolution and to identify psychological processes, which are fundamental to all conflict, provided that reasonable care is taken to examine the degree to which findings made from such studies are applicable to real-world situations.

This may be difficult because of the complexity of real-world behaviour. For example, if we wish to study international conflict, we must remember that subjects in experiments are not trained negotiators and do not have to worry about pressures from military-industrial sources or the possibility of nuclear war (Etzioni,1969). Unfortunately, however, military strategists have found game theory very attractive. This preoccupation can lead to a greater likelihood of war, as strategists analyze what actions are most likely to produce what effects, or how many citizens their side could "afford" to lose in an international atomic showdown (Rapoport, 1968).

A "game," in its broadest sense, is virtually any kind of situation in which two or more interdependent parties (or "players") make decisions that affect each other according to rules. The outcomes of these decisions depend on the joint actions of the players. There are two major classes of games. **Zero-sum games** are those in which one person's gain is exactly matched by the opponent's loss. Gains and losses always add up to zero and no cooperation is possible. For example, in a two-handed poker game, what you win I lose. Game situations are pre-

rational choice *Acting in such a way as to get the most for oneself.*

zero-sum game *The outcome of a situation whereby one person's loss is exactly matched with another person's gain.*

FIGURE 11-2 Payoff matrix for zero-sum game

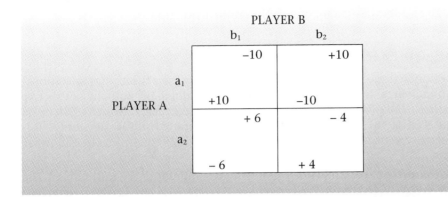

PLAYER B

	b_1	b_2
a_1	−10 / +10	+10 / −10
a_2	+6 / −6	−4 / +4

PLAYER A

sented visually using a payoff matrix, as illustrated in Figure 11-2. In these situations, each player makes a choice. Player A may choose a_1 or a_2. These choices are located in the lower left of each box. Player B may choose b_1 or b_2. These choices are located in the upper right of each box. Now if you, as Player A, choose behaviour a_1 and your opponent chooses b_2, the result will be a 10 loss for you and a 10 gain for her.

In **non-zero-sum (mixed motive) games**, one person's gain does not always match the opponent's loss. The opportunity exists for cooperative action, which may make possible an outcome that is favourable for both players. (An example of a non-zero-sum game follows in the discussion of the Prisoner's Dilemma Game.) While the mathematical analysis of such games treats the players as rational (maximizing gains and minimizing losses), such rationality is not always—or even usually—present in real-life conflicts.

Sometimes it is difficult to assess the magnitude of gains and losses for the parties, since the same amount of money or other resources may have different value or importance for different people. A dollar means much more to a pauper than it does to a millionaire. Game theory requires that **utility**, rather than objective measures of value, be used (Edwards, 1954). Utility refers to the importance, or value, that a given outcome has for an individual. This may change with circumstance. For example, if you are in the desert a glass of water might have much more utility than a new stereo, while if you are sitting comfortably in your living room the opposite would be the case. In the same way, if an adult plays a game of cards with

non-zero-sum game *That which goes beyond pure competition to some form of cooperation so that mutually desirable outcomes are possible.*

utility *The importance or value of an outcome to an individual.*

What would be the maximum utility for grandpa in this game situation?

How do zero-sum games differ from non-zero-sum games?

Prisoner's Dilemma Game *A laboratory game which demonstrates that rational decisions made on an individual level may have mutually destructive consequences for the parties involved.*

a child and wants the child to win, then the maximum utility would be associated with a loss rather than a win for the adult. Rational players act to maximize the utility they can obtain in the conflict situation.

THE DILEMMA GAME

Some conflicts are very difficult to resolve because the actions that are rational on an individual level can lead to collectively irrational or mutually destructive outcomes. The prototype of this problem is the so-called **Prisoner's Dilemma Game** (PDG), which has been used for many laboratory studies of conflict. It is a special type of non-zero-sum game, and takes its name from the following "dilemma":

Two suspects are apprehended following the murder of a wealthy man. The police are quite certain that the two are guilty, but lack the necessary evidence to convict them. A clever Crown Prosecutor decides to suggest a little plea-bargaining, and visits both suspects separately. She tells each suspect that she cannot hope to convict either of them on the murder charge without a confession, but promises that if the suspect confesses, she will agree to ask the court for clemency for him. The murder conviction of the other suspect will carry a sentence of 30 years while the confessor will get off with only a one-year sentence. However, if both confess, they will each get 20 years in prison, and if neither confesses she will see to it that they are charged with breaking and entering, which will lead to a two-year sentence. She then leaves each suspect to think about her offer by himself.

As it turns out, each of the suspects possesses some knowledge of game theory, and scratches out a matrix (Figure 11-3) on the wall of his police cell. A half-hour later, each suspect confesses. The Crown Prosecutor has succeeded.

Why, you might ask, would the two prisoners choose to confess when by keeping silent each would have received only two years in prison? Was each prisoner so eager to get off with only a one-year sentence that friendship ceased to matter?

Before condemning the two as victims of their own selfishness, we must more carefully examine their choices. Since they could not communicate, each had to anticipate what the other would do. A may have said to himself, "Whatever he

FIGURE 11-3 **Prisoner's Dilemma Game**

		SUSPECT B	
		Confess	Don't confess
SUSPECT A	Confess	20 years / 20 years	30 years / 1 year
	Don't confess	1 year / 30 years	2 years / 2 years

does, I am better off confessing. If he confesses, by confessing I'll get 20 years instead of 30. If he doesn't confess, I'll get one year instead of two. So, to confess is my best strategy." But it's also his best strategy for the same reason. "Now even if I put my self-interest aside, and choose not to confess, how can I be sure that he will not confess? After all, for him not to confess, he must not only be prepared to accept two years instead of one, but he must also trust that I won't confess, or he will end up with 30 years." Thus, held *incommunicado,* each prisoner has little choice but to confess. Yet the product of their individually *rational* choices is collectively *ir*rational, since they each receive sentences of 20 years instead of two. That is the nature of the dilemma. Neither person, *regardless of what the other person does,* can improve his or her outcome by remaining silent. Yet, by both being "rational," they each end up with 20 years in prison.

You may find the "normative" (i.e., theoretical) outcome (mutual confession) of the Prisoner's Dilemma Game a little unsatisfying. Surely, you might ask, two people would not act collectively in such an irrational way? This has bothered a great many researchers, even though laboratory studies using the PDG indicate that people do just that. However, one factor that has to be considered is the actual value of the outcomes to the players.

Consider the Prisoner's Dilemma story again, but this time, suppose that the suspects are a pair of lovers, Henry and Maria. For these two, the prospect of one going free after one year while the other languishes in jail for another 29 years is much more unpleasant than it would be for two ordinary criminals. Furthermore, each lover "knows" (i.e., trusts) that the other feels likewise. For these players, the only two outcomes worth thinking about are both confessing or both not confessing. Being free when the other is in prison has little utility for either one.

Since each strongly believes that the other will do the same thing and the only thing to do is *not* confess, neither confesses, and they go free after two years in prison.

One constraint placed on the behaviour observed in the Prisoner's Dilemma Game is the absence of communication. Although communication channels by themselves do not always lead to more cooperation, in a situation as simple as the PDG, the opportunity to communicate would at least allow the parties a chance to inform each other of their real intentions. In fact, when players in a PDG have been allowed to communicate, it has usually had a positive effect on the level of cooperation. However, as in real life, communication is sometimes used only to try to manipulate the other party, rather than to aid in the resolution of a dilemma.

There is no reason why this dilemma should be restricted to only two people. Indeed, in an expanded form involving many participants, it more closely reflects many real-life conflict situations, as is described in the next section.

COLLECTIVE DILEMMAS

A **collective dilemma** occurs whenever the individually rational actions of a number of interacting parties produce an outcome that is collectively undesirable. This is similar to the Prisoner's Dilemma Game, except that more than two players are involved. Collective dilemmas, also referred to as *social* dilemmas (Dawes, 1980), have been receiving more attention from researchers in the last few years (e.g., Brewer and Kramer, 1986; Komorita and Barth, 1985; Samuelson and Messick, 1986; Yamagishi and Sato, 1986; Rapoport, 1989). (The Nature of Things

How does the Prisoner's Dilemma Game explain individually rational choices that are collectively irrational?

collective dilemma A situation that occurs when each person in a group behaves in a way that is best for him or herself—but when everyone does this it can be destructive for the group.

293

documentary *Little Wars* (CBC) features Anatole Rapoport of the University of Toronto discussing collective dilemmas.)

Collective dilemmas occur repeatedly in everyday life. For example, if the installation of pollution control devices on automobiles could lead to considerable improvement in the quality of the air, then everyone should be willing to buy such equipment.

However, closer analysis reveals that the "rational" choice, at least for the short term, is to adopt the selfish alternative; in other words, do nothing. If the majority of people install such devices, the air will be better even if you do nothing. If only a few people install such devices, your investment will be a waste of time, since the air quality will not improve anyway. Population growth and resource depletion represent the same sort of dilemma. Why, even in the face of catastrophic overpopulation, should Indian peasants limit their family to two children? They will receive no old age pension and will need to depend on their children for support. The more children they have, the better off they will be, even though society may ultimately suffer. Even in an overpopulated world, they would be at a disadvantage in old age with fewer children than their neighbours.

Collective dilemmas take two forms, the commons problem (or resource dilemma, as it is also called) and the provision of public goods problem (Brewer and Kramer, 1986). Each will be discussed in turn.

The **commons problem** involves individual decisions as to how much of a public resource one should take for personal use. The problem takes its name from Hardin's (1968) description of the "tragedy of the commons." Historically, in England, public pasture land was set aside for common use by all farmers. However, as individual farmers expanded the size of their cattle herds, the "commons" were overgrazed to such an extent that in the 1800s an enclosure movement led to the fencing off of the commons into individual pastures. The heart of the problem was this: for each herdsman the positive utility associated with enlarging his herd was much greater than the negative utility derived from the overgrazing. The short-term gains were more enticing than the possibility of losses in the long term. So everyone enlarged their herds to the point where everyone suffered.

commons problem *When everyone uses too much of a public resource it may become depleted and lost to all.*

FIGURE 11-4 Public goods problem

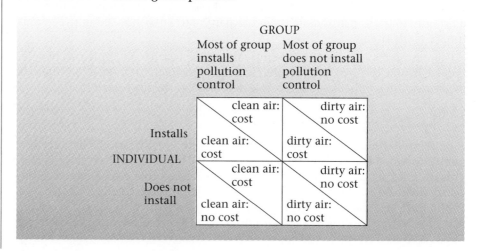

While the commons problem involves people drawing individually from a common resource, the **public goods problem** is related to the contributions of individuals to the collective good, as with our example of pollution control. The truth is that as long as most people act in line with the common good (reduce pollution, donate blood, do not spit on the sidewalk), those who do not contribute benefit as much from the efforts of the majority as if they had contributed—and it has cost them nothing. This has also been referred to as the "free rider" problem (Frohlich and Oppenheimer, 1970). There would be no need to collect tickets on a train if everyone was honest about paying their fare. But such a system would most likely break down because free riders (literally!) would exploit the situation.

The commons problem and the public goods problem are identical in terms of the decision facing the individual. He or she must decide whether to act according to individual self-interest, and risk suffering in the long run if most others do the same, or to act according to the collective interest at some cost to him or herself.

How should people deal with collective dilemmas? The philosopher Immanuel Kant suggested that behaviour should be guided by this precept: "Act only according to that maxim which you can at the same time will to be a universal law" (Joad, 1957, p. 393). Thus you should refrain from installing pollution control only if you would be content to have everyone do likewise. If everyone acted according to the Kantian imperative, collective dilemmas would vanish, although we might continue to damage our environment over disagreement or misunderstanding about the dangers of various actions. For example, governments seem reluctant to do very much about acid rain, which is destroying both American and Canadian lakes. They argue that there is not yet enough evidence to show that industrial pollution is the cause of this destruction. In this case their position may be politically based, but there are many situations in which ignorance of harmful consequences underlies resource depletion or environmental damage. But in any case, people do not follow Kant's dictum. They do not for the simple reason that it is against their individual short-term interests to do so.

DANGEROUS GAMES

In 1963, the Soviets were intent on shipping nuclear missiles to Cuba and the Americans were determined to stop them. The Americans put up a naval blockade around Cuba and threatened to sink any Russian ship carrying missiles to Cuba. Nevertheless, the Soviets sent ships carrying missiles towards Cuba, one of which was eventually spotted and appeared to be heading directly into the blockade. While the world held its breath, the Russian ship eventually stopped and turned back, ending the tense confrontation. American Secretary of State Dean Rusk was quoted as having told a reporter following this incident, "Remember when you report this ... that eyeball to eyeball, they blinked first."

Someone had to back down, or mutual disaster would result. This is known as a **dangerous conflict** (or *dangerous game*, in the language of game theory), in that if neither side backs down, both may suffer catastrophic loss (e.g. nuclear war; see Box 11-3).

There are two important characteristics of the prototypical dangerous game: (1) It is non-negotiable. There can be only one winner; the other must lose, although both can lose disastrously. There is no way that cooperation can help,

public goods problem
If everyone decided not to contribute personally to the public good, nothing would be achieved.

In what way are the commons problem and the public goods problem similar?

dangerous conflict *A conflict so intense that if neither side backs down a catastrophic loss may occur.*

and any conciliatory move by one player will only encourage the other to press on. (2) The dangerous aspect is that the goal-directed behaviour and the threat behaviour are identical: the closer a person gets to the goal, the greater the likelihood of attaining it and the greater the probability of a mutual loss (Swingle, 1970).

Why do people or nations play such games? Insofar as nations are concerned, it is often appealing to force the opponent to back down by appearing to be more ready to accept mutual loss than they actually are (i.e., deceive the other about their utility structure).

BOX 11-3

THE GAME OF "CHICKEN"

The prototypical dangerous game is that of "chicken," which was played by teenagers in the 1950s. In the words of Bertrand Russell (1959):

This sport is called chicken! It is played by choosing a long straight road with a white line down the middle and starting two very fast cars towards each other from opposite ends. As they approach each other mutual destruction becomes more and more imminent. If one of them swerves from the white line before the other, as he passes, he shouts chicken!, and the one who has swerved becomes an object of contempt.

In a later variation, teenagers would stand on airport runways at night, daring each other to remain in the path of an approaching airplane (Swingle, 1970). The game of chicken is not restricted to teenagers. In one way or another, many games of chicken are played out in politics, in labour-management negotiations, and in international disputes.

This game can be translated into a laboratory form by using a matrix such as that shown in Figure 11-5. If one "does not swerve" and the other does, one gains prestige (indicated by +100) while the other loses face (–100). If both decide not to swerve, they lose more than their faces (–1000), while if both swerve, there is a "draw," with a slight loss of prestige (–10). It is obviously a high-risk game, each player being forced to risk substantial loss in order to threaten the other into yielding. It is a "pre-emption" game in that if one player can make it clear that he or she is committed to not swerving, the other must either back down or face almost certain heavy loss.

As long as one person believes that the other will "back down," he or she will continue. Kahn (1962) suggests that getting into the car dead drunk, wearing very dark glasses, and throwing the steering wheel out of the window as soon as the car is travelling at maximum speed will put considerable pressure on your opponent to back down. You have reduced or eliminated *your* freedom to act: the opponent, who *can* act, is now in a weaker position and must back down or face suicide. You have *pre-empted* control of the game.

"Brinksmanship," pushing each other to the "brink" of war, describes the game of chicken as played at the international level. It is the "deliberate creation of a recognizable risk of war, a risk that one does not completely control" (Schelling, 1960, p. 200). The effectiveness of brinksmanship depends on how much the other nation believes you. If one country believes that another is committed to attack it if it invades some third country, it will hesitate. If it does not believe that, but is in fact true, both sides will end up in a mutually destructive war.

FIGURE 11-5 Chicken

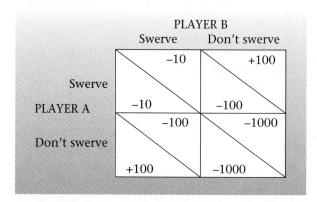

For example, during the Cold War, the leaders of the U.S.S.R. sought to put the U.S. at a disadvantage by claiming that they were quite prepared to accept the loss of 60 percent of their people in all-out nuclear war. If the leaders of a government can appear hardened or demented enough not to care about such losses, they can presumably "pre-empt" the "chicken" confrontation (see Box 11-3 and Figure 11-5), forcing the other side to back down. Rapoport examines both the "chicken" game and the Cuban missile crisis in the CBC video *Little Wars* (The Nature of Things).

Analogues of these two game structures—the dilemma and the dangerous game—appear over and over in real life. However, real-life situations are much more complex than any matrix game, and they involve considerations such as threat and coercion, communication, power, and even group size. These factors are discussed in the next section.

SELF-TEST QUESTIONS

5. In an exchange situation, the attainability of other possible resources is termed

a) *contingent conflict*

b) *comparison level for alternatives*

c) *theory of economic behaviour*

d) *collective dilemma*

6. The view that conflicts involve exchanges of resources is central to

a) *the public resources problem*

b) *the theory of games*

c) *the social exchange model*

d) *the arbitration principle*

7. The use of experimental games to study conflict declined as researchers began to question the _____ of such games.

a) *external validity*

b) *ethics*

c) *social desirability*

d) *demand characteristics*

8. In zero-sum games

a) *some outcomes are mutually preferable to others*

b) *gains and losses of the players add up to zero in a given trial*

c) *cooperation is possible*

d) *b and c*

9. In experimental games, utility refers to the

a) *access to outcomes*

b) *importance of an outcome to a specific individual*

c) *sequencing of outcomes*

d) *reliability of outcomes*

10. Collective dilemmas differ from the Prisoner's Dilemma in that

a) the selfish alternative is usually adopted

b) more than two people are involved

c) communication resolves the dilemma

d) none of the above

11. Which of the following is true of dangerous games?

a) they are non-negotiable

b) there can be only one winner

c) cooperation is possible

d) a and b

THE STRUCTURE OF CONFLICT

THREAT AND CONFLICT SPIRALS

When we promise to buy a toy for a child if he or she cleans up the yard, we are saying that, "If you do action **A** (clean up the yard), I will do action **B** (buy you a toy)." If we have generally carried out our promises in the past, the child is likely to believe that **B** will be done if **A** is done. A *threat* is a kind of promise, except that the outcome, **B**, is undesirable. For example, "If you do action **A** (keep fooling around) then I will do action **B**" (make you go to your room).

For the threat to be successful, it must first be credible. Credibility depends on several factors:

(1) If the party making the threat has in the past failed to carry out such threats, the credibility of the threat will be low. It can be increased if the person making the threat can show that he or she has little choice but to carry it out in the face of non-compliance. Union leaders who threaten illegal walkouts will have more credibility if they have told their followers that they would be failing them if they back down from their threats, and that if they do back down they will resign.

(2) The threatened action must have negative consequences for the person making the threat, in order to assure the threatened party that the threat will not be carried out even if compliance is forthcoming. If a father tells his child who is hiding under the bed that he will spank him if he does not come out right away, the threat will be ineffective if the child believes that he will be spanked in any case.

(3) The threat must not carry too high a cost to either party or it is likely to suffer in terms of credibility (Mogy and Pruitt, 1974). A loving parent who threatens to send his child to an orphanage if the child misbehaves is unlikely to be believed; both parent and child would suffer too much if the threat were carried out.

Threats must be clearly communicated to the target if they are to have any effect. Schelling (1960) pointed out that kidnappers holding a hostage are effectively stymied if all communication with them is cut off. They cannot communicate the threat to harm the hostage or the demand for ransom. (Perhaps, Schelling pondered, a law should be passed that would require the immediate confinement of all relatives and friends of the hostage in order to make the likelihood of a ransom being paid very small!) Even children realize the strategic value of not

What are the conditions that make a threat successful?

"It started with one of their pigeons pecking one of ours."

allowing parents to communicate their threats. If they know their parents will be unlikely to rebuke them verbally in a certain social situation, they will often deliberately avoid their warning glances.

Threats serve the purpose for which they were intended only if they do not have to be carried out. A parent who threatens a child with a spanking does not *want* to give the spanking; otherwise, he or she would just get on with it rather than wasting words.

Why does threat often lead to increased conflict? Once a threat has been made, the preservation of face becomes a primary goal for each player, thus leading to increased determination to "hold one's ground" and to respond with a counter-threat. A couple may have a conflict of interest with regard to some benign issue, such as where to go on an evening out. Once one of them makes a threat, however, the other may respond with a counter-threat. Now the dispute is not over where to spend the evening, but concerns who is going to win and who is going to back down. Often there is a series of escalating threats, a **threat-counter-threat spiral** (or more simply, a *conflict spiral*), wherein each disputant responds to the other's threats by more severe threats.

An arms race involves a threat-counter-threat spiral. One nation interprets another nation's actions as a threat to its security, and expands its armaments. This very action is, however, perceived as a threat by the second nation, which then adds to its arsenal—an act that will appear to the first nation as evidence that the second nation was indeed preparing for war. This is a positive feedback loop, leading each side to interpret the other's reactions as threatening its security.

> *threat-counter-threat spiral* Each threat calls for a more severe threat in response.

COMMUNICATION

In real-life conflict situations, it is only rarely the case that there is no communication between the parties. However, in the typical gaming study of conflict, subjects are not allowed to communicate with each other. After all, if there is any degree of trust between the players, the problem in the Prisoner's Dilemma Game immediately disappears, since each player can assure the other of the intention to choose the collectively beneficial outcome. Various studies have found that cooperative responding is facilitated in the PDG by allowing subjects to communicate (e.g., Swennson, 1967; Terhune, 1968; Voissem and Sistrunk, 1971; Bornstein, Rapoport, Kerpel and Katz, 1989).

The mere existence of channels of communication is no guarantee that communication will indeed take place (see Box 11-4). The greater the competitive orientation of the parties towards each other, the less likely are such channels to be used (Deutsch, 1973).

Of course, even when communication does occur there is no guarantee that it will be understood. This can have serious implications, especially if the conflict is in the sphere of international relations. The "war" between Britain and Argentina in 1982 over the Falkland Islands (Malvinas) is one example. Naturally, the two countries perceived the situation from their own perspective. As far as Argentina was concerned, the Malvinas were a natural part of their territory that had been occupied by a foreign power since 1833. Moreover, recent history had revealed that Britain was quite willing, even eager, to give up its colonies. There seemed little reason to believe that it would not release the Falklands as well. However, the British had quite a different point of view. They did not consider the Falklands to be a colony. It was populated by British citizens who wanted to remain part of Britain. Thus the Argentinian attack was not considered one of liberation but one of pure aggression. Argentina did not believe Britain would defend the Falklands but Britain thought no other course of action was possible, with tragic consequences for both sides (Jervis, Lebow and Stein, 1985).

POWER

Power, the ability to influence what happens to another individual, has been discussed in some detail earlier (see Chapter 10). We now examine how different degrees of power can influence the course of conflict. Of course, power is essential in carrying out a threat. A parent who threatens to spank a 17-year-old high school boxing champion probably lacks the power to carry out the threat.

BOX 11-4
SITTING DOWN TO NEGOTIATE

In real-life situations the physical set-up for negotiations is important, or at least is believed by negotiators to be important. For example, even the seating order is often a matter of dispute, since where people sit may reflect either their status or their perceived relationship to each other (Lott and Sommer, 1967).

In 1848, it took six months of discussion before delegates to the Peace of Westphalia could agree on the order in which they should enter and be seated (Durant and Durant, 1961), and at the 1945 Potsdam conference, Truman, Churchill, and Stalin insisted on entering the room by emerging simultaneously from three separate doors (Kelman, 1965).

In the Paris peace talks dealing with the war in Vietnam, considerable debate raged prior to the talks about the seating plan and the table shape. North Vietnam wanted a seating plan and table shape that would suggest that the National Liberation Front had status as an independent political entity, while the United States and South Vietnam were opposed to this (Kitchens, 1974). Similarly, the participants in the 1993 Middle East peace talks sat at a T-shaped table and none of the Arab delegation directly faced Israel's representatives. Whether or not the seating plan *actually* influences the course of the negotiations is unimportant, as long as the participants *believe* that it has an effect. Prenegotiation may be as important as, if not more important than, negotiation (Rubin, 1989).

There is evidence (Pruitt, 1976) that parties involved in a conflict may be more likely to use coercion when they have moderate, rather than great or small, amounts of power. Little power is often viewed as ineffective, while great power risks mutual destruction. If you are guarding the cookie jar, and if you are *only* allowed to say "bad, bad" when the child takes a cookie without permission, the measure will have no effect on the child if it is not backed up in any way, so why bother to use it? Similarly, if your only source of power is tied to your possession of a pistol, you are unlikely to use that power to protect the cookie jar from marauding toddlers.

What happens when someone thinks he or she has more power than is actually the case? A situation of *illusory power* is created, causing difficulties in many conflict situations. A spouse who assumes that he has power over his wife because she is more committed to the marriage than he is may be able to get his way by threatening a separation if she does not comply with his wishes. However, suppose that his power is illusory, that she indeed is willing to risk separation. If he tries to force her to comply with his demands because he thinks she has little choice, both may ultimately lose (i.e., they separate). His use of illusory power will have led to a destructive, rather than a constructive, approach to the conflict.

Why does a moderate amount of power lead to more coercion than great or small amounts of power?

THE EFFECTS OF GROUP SIZE

Game theory predicts that individualism will predominate when a group is large enough that no individual's contribution makes a significant difference to the group as a whole; individuals will attempt to maximize their own payoffs. It may seem natural that more cooperation would exist in a small group than in a large group—after all, in a small group, an individual receives a larger proportion of the beneficial effects of his or her action, while at the same time, his or her action has a much more significant effect on the group outcome. But what would happen if we compared the behaviour of people in a small group and in a large group when the magnitude of the reward was exactly the same? In other words, if only the size of the group varies and not the actual reward, will people still be more cooperative in smaller groups? This is indeed what has been observed in laboratory experiments. Hamburger, Guyer and Fox (1975) developed a game structure in which the size of the reward for an individual was the same whether a three-person or seven-person group was involved. The three-person groups were found to be more cooperative. In the larger group there was a marked and systematic *decrease* in the probability of a player responding cooperatively.

When a group is large enough so that the actions of a given individual have little effect on the group, and when the immediate outcome is about the same whether one invests time, energy, or resources to cooperate or whether one doesn't, non-cooperation becomes the typical response.

What is the relationship between cooperation and group size?

One way to foster behaviour that is based on the collective good is to make the collective identity of the group more salient. For example, in one set of laboratory studies, individuals were found to be more likely to act in line with the collective good when the collective identity was emphasized than when emphasis was instead put on the identities of various subgroups within the larger group (Kramer and Brewer, 1984).

Berkes, Feeny, McCoy and Acheson (1989) identify a number of cases in which resources have been protected from over-exploitation by the members of the group immediately concerned. These include control over hunting in the James Bay area of Canada, the protection of lobster stocks in Maine, and the safeguarding of forests in Thailand and Nepal. In each case, controls were not imposed by the state, and the right to govern the local resource was assigned to those parties most likely to be affected by misuse.

PREDISPOSITIONAL VARIABLES

What impact do personal characteristics have on conflict situations?

Would the course of World War II have been different had Hitler, Churchill, Stalin, and Roosevelt been replaced by others? Would Quebec's October Crisis of 1970 been handled differently if Brian Mulroney had been prime minister at the time? Would the federal government have acted differently during the 1995 Quebec referendum under a different prime minister? The study of predispositional variables focuses on how the personal characteristics (personality, age, gender, and cultural variables) of the individuals involved affect the course of conflicts.

Cultural differences have been found in studies comparing the behaviour of subjects from various countries. For example, Carment (1973) compared the behaviour of students in Canada and India in a mixed-motive game in which one player (the "benefactor") could, by means of choosing one alternative, allow the other player (the "beneficiary") to choose an outcome that led either to equal point gain or to a large point gain for the benefactor. While Indians were more generous than Canadians at the outset, their response did not last long. More importantly, the Indian subjects, unlike the Canadians, avoided taking advantage of the other player's generosity. When the players later switched roles (something they did not anticipate) the new Indian beneficiary continued to be reluctant to accept the other's generosity, while the Canadians were even more eager to accept it. However, in another study involving a different game, when Indian subjects were led to believe that the opponent had an advantage over them, they became very submissive. When they thought they were at an advantage, they became very competitive—exactly the opposite of what was observed with Canadian males (Alcock, 1975). Many other similar cross-cultural comparisons have been made. Blackfoot children in Canada have been found to be more cooperative in a game situation than urban Canadian children and, in fact, were even more predisposed towards cooperative behaviour than were children from an Israeli kibbutzim, where cooperation and sharing are explicitly encouraged (Miller and Thomas, 1972).

It seems that competitiveness increases with age (McClintock and Nuttin, 1969; Leventhal and Lane, 1970), especially among males. Vinacke and Gullickson (1964) compared subjects of ages seven and eight, twelve to fourteen, and university age, and found that while females were similarly accommodating at all three age levels, males became steadily more exploitative with age. Yet such gender differences are not always found. In some studies males are more cooperative than females, in others the opposite is the case, and in still others there is no difference at all.

It also seems that some people are more predisposed towards cooperation than others, quite apart from gender, cultural, or age considerations, but that such people are still likely to act competitively when dealing with other competitive people (Alcock and Mansell, 1977; Kelley and Stahelski, 1970). A "competitive" person, on the other hand, seems to act competitively regardless of the behaviour of others. For such a person, everyone else will seem to be competitive since even "cooperators" will act competitively against such a person. Cooperators are more likely, as a result of their experience, to develop the view that some people are cooperative while others are not, and to adjust their behaviour according to the behaviour of the other party.

As important as these predispositional effects may be, the evidence from game studies suggests that they are generally overridden by the effects of the structure of the situation. This overriding influence of structural variables may explain why correlations between personality variables and cooperative behaviour are repeatedly found to be very low.

RESOLUTION OF CONFLICT

Although most people are not very adept at solving serious conflicts, there are a number of ways in which conflicts can be lessened and destructiveness avoided. One way that people deal with some conflicts is through appeal to adjudication, that is, by recourse to the legal system. If one neighbour wants to play her CD's at a high volume and the other does not like this, then the offended neighbour might call the police to complain. If there is a municipal ordinance against excessive noise, the neighbour with the CD player may be forced to turn it down. Some disputes ultimately end up in court and thus involve *procedural justice* (see Chapter 13), but generally, the disputants—whether they are individuals, groups, or nations—attempt to resolve the problem by alternative means. For example, one of the protagonists could simply "give in" or, through negotiation, the parties could arrive at a mutually acceptable compromise, such as an agreement to play her CD's only at certain times. Sometimes one of the parties involved may "leave the field," for instance, one of the neighbours may move to another part of town. However, there are many occasions when people cannot resolve their conflict, and reach a stalemate. At this point they may ask for the assistance of another, neutral person (Pruitt, 1981). In fact, it has been shown that a conflict is more likely to be resolved if another person is merely present, even though the person is not actively involved (Meeker and Shure, 1989).

THIRD-PARTY INTERVENTION

Obviously, any efforts that succeed in improving the accuracy of the perceptions of each party will help to reduce the conflict. A husband who thinks that his wife is unhappy because he cannot buy her a larger house will have a difficult time smoothing things out with a wife who is actually unhappy because she thinks her husband values his work more than he values her. A third party, or mediator, may be able to help clear up the misperceptions and identify the basic conflict (Carnevale and Pruitt, 1992, Fisher, 1983, 1989).

Even with perfect perception of each other's motives and goals, conflicts over resources, status, and power still exist. As we have seen, once threats or coercion are employed, a conflict situation is changed to one in which saving face may be more important than the resolution of the original conflict. Obviously, then, if we wish to reduce such a conflict, we must try to find a way to allow the other party to agree to compromise without having him or her lose face in a big way. Such consideration applies as much to a marital fight as to an international "incident," something of which marriage counsellors and international arbitrators are keenly aware.

There are a number of methods that the third party can use. Sometimes the procedure will be selected by mutual agreement of the disputants, while at other

How does third-party intervention (mediation) help resolve conflicts?

mediation *Indirect intervention to identify problems and open a channel of communication.*

arbitration *Direct intervention, or solutions suggested or imposed.*

times the procedure (e.g. labour disputes) might be determined by law. Two third-party procedures that are commonly used are **mediation** and **arbitration**. A major difference between these methods is that arbitration is usually binding, that is, the disputants have agreed to accept the arbitrator's decision. Mediation is more likely than arbitration to involve *process interventions* whereby the mediator helps without actually suggesting any direct resolution of the problem. In other words, the mediator may provide a setting for negotiation and act as a type of chairperson, or as a channel of communication through which the two sides communicate with each other (thus avoiding face-to-face confrontation). Mediators may also teach the disputants proper bargaining techniques or try to change the motivational orientation of the parties, such as redirecting them from competitive concerns to problem-solving. Arbitration, on the other hand, usually involves *content interventions* and is more direct. In other words, solutions are suggested and/or imposed.

It has been found (Carnevale and Henry, 1989) that the particular strategy employed by mediators depends on their evaluation of the probability that the conflict will be resolved and their concern for the disputants' *aspirations*—what each disputant wants to achieve from the mediation process. For example, if there is considerable "common ground" the dispute is likely to be settled without too much difficulty.

According to Carnevale's (1986) strategic choice model of mediation, four strategies are typically used by mediators to facilitate a resolution of conflict. He called these strategies integration, pressing, compensation, and inaction. *Integration* entails finding a solution to the conflict that satisfies both parties. *Pressing* involves attempts to lower the disputants' aspirations or their resistance to yielding. *Compensation* occurs when the mediator gives something to the disputants in exchange for a compromise or agreement. Finally, *inaction* means letting the disputants handle the conflict themselves.

Pressing is most likely to be used when it appears that resolution of the conflict is not probable and there is little concern for the disputants' aspirations. Compensation occurs when resolution appears unlikely and concern for aspirations is high. When agreement seems likely and concern for aspirations is low, inaction occurs, and when concern for aspirations is high, integration is likely to be used. In the latter case it appears that highly concerned mediators will attempt integration regardless of the amount of common ground. A summary of these relationships can be seen in Figure 11-6.

SUPERORDINATE GOALS

superordinate goals *Those which bring together two groups in conflict in order to achieve a common solution.*

Despite being opposed to each other with regard to certain issues, individuals can be brought together when their cooperation is required to achieve some mutually desired **superordinate goal**. This was clearly demonstrated in a classic study by Sherif (1958). He recruited 11-year-old boys, all strangers to one another, to go to a summer camp (at a place called "Robber's Cave") which was set up to serve as the basis for a field experiment. The boys were randomly divided into two groups, and these groups were isolated from each other for the first week. During the second week, the two groups interacted in athletic contests in which prizes could be won by either group. This produced friction between the two groups, and fighting developed as the members of each group began to describe the members of the other group as the "enemy" and to build up stereotypes about

FIGURE 11-6 Strategic choice model of mediator behaviour

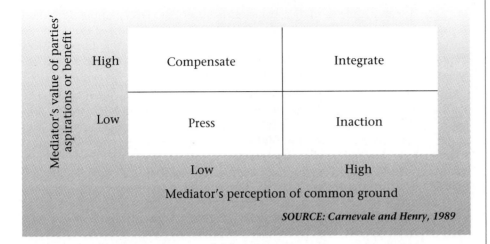

SOURCE: Carnevale and Henry, 1989

them. When asked about their friendships, over 90 percent chose members of their own group as the people with whom they wanted to be friends.

During the third and final week of camp, Sherif and his colleagues attempted to reduce the conflict their manipulation had generated. First, they tried simple intergroup contact: the two groups ate together, watched movies together, and shared common activities. This failed to reduce conflict. Then they set up common goals, in one instance by surreptitiously damaging the camp's water supply so that the boys had to work together to repair it. Other common goals, such as cooperating to raise money to buy a film to be shown at the camp, were also used. Working together towards these common, or "superordinate" goals led to a gradual reduction in hostility, and by the end of the third week, boys from each group were chumming around with each other.

The results of this study indicate that simple contact between hostile groups is not enough to reduce conflict, but that cooperative interaction brought about by the necessity of working together towards common goals can successfully reduce hostility. It must be remembered that the two groups of boys had no basic underlying conflict in the first place. Working together helped reduce incorrect perceptions and artificial differences.

DISPELLING MISPERCEPTIONS

Conflict behaviour is often attended by severe distortion, or misconception, of each party's motives and values, resulting in even greater hostility. We tend to attribute to those we see as our opponents various characteristics that make it much more difficult for us to trust them.

When a mistaken perception can mean war and nuclear annihilation, it is vital for both people and their leaders on two sides of a conflict to view the situation and each other realistically and accurately. However, studies of conflict reveal the extent to which protagonists often misperceive. One common misperception is the belief that the people on the other side are really "pro-us" and that the real enemies are their leaders who mislead and manipulate them

How do superordinate goals work in conflict resolution?

305

(White, 1969). This illusion serves to reinforce one side's "good intentions" towards the other side, and provides hope that the other side will someday see the light. It can also lead to disastrous errors in policy. For example, President Kennedy authorized limited support of the Bay of Pigs invasion of Cuba on the mistaken assumption that it would stimulate the Cuban people to overthrow the revolutionary government of Fidel Castro. Similar illusions have been apparent in U.S. policies in Vietnam and in Central America.

Misperceptions often tend to be shared by both sides of a conflict. Each party attributes the same virtues to itself and the same vices to the other side (a mirror image). A U.S. psychologist who visited the former U.S.S.R. and conversed with Soviet citizens observed that most of them said the same things about the United States that his own compatriots were saying about the U.S.S.R.: that they were militarily aggressive, that they could not be trusted, and that they were deluded by their leaders (Bronfenbrenner, 1961). Other **mirror image perceptions** have been observed in how the Soviets viewed the U.S. military involvement in Vietnam and how the U.S. viewed Soviet actions in Afghanistan (White, 1984). Such impressions only serve to intensify conflict.

Studies of "enemy" images have, for the most part, been conducted in the United States and have focused on the U.S.S.R. There have been three types of studies in this area: those concerned with images obtained from other people and from the media; those concerned with how information is processed; and those concerned with the extremity of these images (Silverstein, 1989). For example, it was found that negative attitudes among Americans towards the Soviet Union were significantly related to nationalism—the view that the United States is superior to all nations and should be Number One. Interestingly, these attitudes were not related to patriotism, that is, feelings of attachment to the United States (Klosterman and Feshbach, 1989). Similarly, Holt (1989) reported that 27 percent of the individuals he interviewed defined an enemy of the United States as any nation with opposing values, especially if these values were non-democratic; however, military strength did not seem to be important in the assessment. Thus both the U.S.S.R. and Cuba were viewed as enemies of the United States. Of course, with the break-up of the Soviet Union, such attitudes may now be less extreme.

Cognitive studies found that American students evaluated Soviet actions more negatively than they evaluated the *same* actions performed by the United States. It is of interest that Canadian students did not typically show the same bias. While American students maintained the moral self-image and the diabolical-enemy image, Canadian students attributed Soviet and American actions to the same motives, with one exception: Canadian students perceived the U.S. but not the U.S.S.R. as engaging in positive actions for self-serving reasons, such as a desire to escalate international tensions, or a desire to dominate other countries (Sande, Goethals, Ferrari and Worth, 1989). It is also evident that, among the U.S. subjects, knowledge of the "enemy" was inadequate. For example, 28 percent of the respondents in one survey believed that the Soviet Union had fought *against* the United States in World War II and another survey discovered that 24 percent of a sample of U.S. college students thought that the Soviets had been the first to develop the atomic bomb. In addition, many did not know the extent to which the U.S.S.R. suffered in World War II. Although approximately 20 million Soviet people died during that war, a common estimate by these subjects was 20 000 (Silverstein and Flamenbaum, 1989). Misinformation and ignorance of this sort may be perpetuated by some media or by what other people

mirror image perception
When two groups are in conflict they view each other in similarly negative ways.

What are some examples of mirror image perception?

say rather than personal experience or accurate evidence. For instance, it has been shown that the *New York Times* reported more stories about Soviet dissidents than about dissidents in other countries (Herman, 1982), and that the same paper allocated more space to negative articles about the U.S.S.R. than to positive articles.

GRIT

One method for reversing the build-up of both armaments and hostility was proposed by Osgood (1962). He argued that unilateral conciliatory action by one of the protagonists is necessary in order to show the other that its perceptions are distorted. He suggested that one nation in a conflict announce its intention to gradually work towards tension reduction and eventual reversal of the arms race. To back up its words, he said, it must take a concrete step, such as stopping certain kinds of weapons testing, a step which, while showing good intent, does not make the nation immediately vulnerable or invite exploitative attack. The action should be accompanied by a call for the other side to reciprocate, but a few more such actions, each announced in advance, should be taken even if the other does not reciprocate, in order to demonstrate the sincerity of the moves. Should the other side reciprocate, then even larger conciliatory moves would be made. On the other hand, if the opponent tries to exploit the moves, the conciliatory approach is temporarily abandoned and retaliation is administered. Osgood called this approach "Graduated Reciprocated Initiative in Tension-reduction," the words being chosen to spell the word **GRIT**, which Osgood thought would be a quality much in demand to carry out the program effectively (Stagner, 1967).

GRIT A strategy whereby each side in a conflict gives up something in turn until the tension is resolved.

A number of studies have used such experimental games as Prisoner's Dilemma in order to compare GRIT to other strategies. For example, it has been shown that GRIT is more effective than a tit-for-tat strategy in enhancing cooperation (Lindskold, Walters and Kotsourais, 1983), and that unlike a competitive strategy, GRIT does not engender animosity or exploitative actions. In addition, it appears that GRIT is most effective when it is announced that it will be used (Lindskold, Han and Betz, 1986).

Although GRIT has been discussed a great deal, it has had little effect on the conduct of world affairs. One major difficulty is that in many inter-nation and intra-nation conflicts (such as those in the former Yugoslavia and in Sri Lanka) the stakes are so high, and the history of suspicion so long, that concessions are unlikely to be seen as anything other than attempts to either deceive the other side, to win points politically, or to seduce the other side into *détente* while the first side secretly builds up its arms.

How does GRIT work as a strategy for resolving conflict?

PREVENTING WAR

Can social psychology contribute to the goal of preventing war? Decisions about war and peace are of course political ones, influenced by public pressure and by historical events and ideologies. In terms of both power and level of knowledge, we have much to be modest about. Yet, some insights derived from psychological studies of conflict have been applied to the resolution of international negotiations.

deterrence schema A situation of increasing levels of aggression being met with concessions, so that when resistance comes it is not taken seriously.

There are two existing and contradictory schemata regarding conflict and how it can lead to war: the **deterrence schema** and the **conflict spiral schema** (Tetlock, 1983, 1987). Deterrence begins with the image of two protagonists, the "aggressor" and the "status quo" power. The aggressor power may doubt the ability of the status quo power to resist encroachment. If this doubt arises, the aggressor makes increasingly ambitious claims, with each concession from the other side leading to a greater demand. Finally, a situation occurs in which the status quo power must resist, but the aggressor cannot believe it and war results. Thus Hitler did not believe that Poland was the end of the line, despite clear and repeated warnings, because of an earlier appeasement policy that conceded the Rhineland, Austria, the Sudetenland, and the remainder of Czechoslovakia. Nor did Saddam Hussein apparently believe that the United States and its allies would take action if he invaded Kuwait.

In a nuclear war, the nation that gets its missiles away first is most likely to come out best (i.e., if it can successfully cripple the opponent's machinery for retaliation). Thus each side strives to protect its counter-strike capability in order to *deter* the other from the temptation of striking first. If each side can assure the other that it will always be able to destroy the other even if the other strikes first, then the other will not be tempted to strike. This is referred to by U.S. military strategists as MAD: Mutually Assured Destruction. The development of anti-missile missiles, nuclear missile-carrying submarines, and the housing of missiles in underground concrete silos are all efforts made to deter the other from giving in to the temptation of "first strike."

Captain William Adcock, a Canadian reserve officer, served with the UN peace-keeping forces in Croatia from September '94 to March '95. He is also a community college curriculum coordinator and professor.

The "conflict spiral" schema begins with the notion of competition between protagonists. In this schema, the defensive and deterrent actions of each side are interpreted as threatening by the other, who must respond with greater levels of counter-threat. Interests and goals are seen as incompatible, and the mutual fear itself causes an escalation (e.g., an arms race) and intensified competition at all levels.

Both schemata have elements of historical and contemporary validity, and it is important to understand that they underlie the decision-making process, particularly at an international level. Both are concerned with the possibility that misunderstanding and misperception can cause a war that is *not* intended. Deterrence types worry that "they" will *underestimate* "our" resolve to defend our interests, while conflict spiralists worry that "they" will *overestimate* "our" hostility (and vice versa). Perhaps by making the two schemata explicit and available for critical examination, an "unfreezing" in the thinking of international politicians and geopolitical strategists is possible.

The issue of nuclear war or peace seems to be massive, even overwhelming. The demise of the Soviet Union may make people feel more comfortable, but it must be remembered that the Soviet nuclear arsenal is now distributed among some of the former Soviet republics. In addition, a number of other nations—China, India, Israel, France, and Great Britain—also have nuclear arms. The overwhelming nature of many of the great social issues of our time causes a state of high arousal that blocks innovative and creative thinking and produces feelings of helplessness, apathy, and avoidance. Weick (1984) argues for the utility of lowering our sights to smaller, explicit, and more manageable issues that we may solve with a much greater probability of success. Thus, rather than thinking in terms of ultimate solutions—"world government" or "complete nuclear disarmament"—we should aim for explicit and achievable goals: a nuclear freeze, a halt on major new technology, a ban or restriction on testing, limitations on weapons production or deployment. Patience in accepting "small wins" may lead to better things and preserve a sense that there is a future.

SELF-TEST QUESTIONS

12. A conflict spiral refers to

a) regulated competition

b) threats and counterthreats

c) misattributed conflicts

d) escalating needs

13. The study by Sherif (1954) of boys at a summer camp indicated that hostility can be reduced through the introduction of

a) rewards

b) coercion

c) superordinate goals

d) process control

14. When two nations interpret the defensive actions of each other as threats, it is referred to as

a) the deterrence schema

b) the conflict spiral

c) a collective dilemma

d) GRIT

15. Subjects choose between _____ in a non-zero-sum game situation

a) trust and suspicion

b) cooperation and competition

c) *threat and coercion*

d) *altruism and selfishness*

SUMMARY

(1) Realistic conflict refers to situations in which there is a real basis for dispute, such as competition for scarce resources, incompatible goals, or incompatible principles.

(2) There are six types of conflict: veridical, contingent, displaced, misattributed, latent, and conflict based on false premises.

(3) Social exchange theory concerns the perception by each person of the relative value of rewards and costs in a relationship, evaluated in terms of the "comparison level" (CL) of others in that situation and the comparison level for alternatives to that relationship (CLalt).

(4) A "game" refers to a situation in which two or more interdependent parties make decisions that affect each other according to rules. The two types of games are zero-sum, in which one party's gains match the opponent's losses, and non-zero-sum (mixed motive), in which some outcomes are mutually preferable to others.

(5) Games such as the Prisoner's Dilemma are based on the assumption that people act rationally to maximize utility. They may be motivated by individualistic, competitive, or cooperative concerns.

(6) A collective dilemma occurs when rational behaviour by individuals produces an outcome that is collectively undesirable, e.g. the commons problem and the provision of public goods problem.

(7) A game that is non-negotiable (only one winner), in which the goal-directed behaviour is threatening, and in which both players can lose disastrously, is called a dangerous game.

(8) A threat is more credible when the threatener has behaved consistently in the past, the threatened action has negative consequences for the threatener as well as for the party threatened, and the threatened consequences are not excessive in the situation.

(9) Threat often intensifies conflict, because people need to "save face," and because of the possibility of a spiralling series of threats and counter-threats.

(10) Communication sometimes reduces conflict by clarifying the intentions of either side, but it is unlikely to be helpful in a "win or lose" situation or when face-saving is important.

(11) The most effective strategy in bargaining combines firm resistance to exploitation with reciprocation of the other party's cooperative behaviour.

(12) Two types of third-party intervention designed to reduce conflict are mediation and arbitration.

(13) Conflict reduction may be accomplished through the graduated reciprocation of tension-reducing acts (GRIT) and the introduction of superordinate goals.

(14) "Deterrence" and "conflict spiral" models are two opposing schemata of conflict at the international level.

FOR REVIEW

FOR REVIEW

Realistic conflict occurs when there exists an actual basis for dispute or hostility. It is _____(1) in the sense that it reflects competition for _____(2), or incompatible goals or principles. Conflict types are identified from the point of view of the _____(3). A conflict that occurs because of the inability of the partners to recognize an available solution is called _____(4). In _____(5) people wrongly blame each other when the problem has an external _____(6) cause. When we wrongly assume that we know the cause of someone's behaviour and this causes conflict, it is called _____(7).

_____(8) theory says that people take into account costs and rewards when making decisions. _____(9) suggests that we compare our situation to that of others. When we examine the alternatives available to us we use a standard called _____(10).

Games can be used to study conflict. In a _____(11) one person's loss is exactly matched by another person's gain.

In _____(12) cooperative action may make it possible for both parties to win. The choice between confessing to a crime or remaining silent is found in the _____(13) game. Two characteristics that might change these choices would be _____ and _____ (14). In the _____(15) individuals take too much of public resources. In the _____(16) individuals choose not to contribute to what is best for society. _____(17) is an example of a dangerous game in which there is a likelihood of serious loss on both sides.

If you do not have the means to carry out a _____(18) it will not be successful. A _____(19) is a situation in which threats and counter-threats lead to increased conflict. Conflict may be increased when people have _____(20) amounts of power, rather than _____(21) or _____(22) amounts of power. Research shows correlations between personality variables and cooperative behaviour to be very _____(23).

Conflict may be resolved in many ways. A _____(24) may be employed who will direct communication and problem solving. _____(25) provide a common goal that may serve to bring groups together. It is important to dispel the negative perceptions that groups in conflict have about each other, which is called _____(26). _____(27) is the term used when each group in a conflict situation gives up something.

ISSUES AND ACTIVITIES

1. In 1984 William Allman set up an experiment to test the commons dilemma. He asked people to write in requesting either 20.00 or 100.00. Everyone would receive what they requested with the exception that if more than 20 percent asked for the 100.00 no one would get anything. Thirty-five percent of those who responded requested the 100.00. So there was no pay-off. This experiment has been repeated many times with similar results. Design an experiment that you could do in class to replicate these findings. Choose two items of different value. Have people write their choices. (You may

also wish to try this with a class not familiar with the research.) How might knowledge, and the ability to communicate about the process, alter the results? Be sure you can pay up if your results are not in line with Allman's!

2. Find real-life examples of the six types of conflict discussed in this chapter. Personal examples are acceptable. How would you resolve these conflict situations?

3. Choose a Canadian conflict issue (e.g. Quebec nationalism, native land claims). Can you identify either the deterrence schema or the conflict spiral schema at work?

4. In the video *Little Wars* (CBC, The Nature of Things), what point is Professor Rapoport making about superstition? How does he suggest that cooperation is possible in conflict situations? You will need to refer to his discussion of his "nice" computer simulation.

• FURTHER READING

FISHER R.J. (1990) *The Social psychology of intergroup and international conflict resolution.* New York: Springer-Verlag. An up-to-date critical appraisal of new and traditional methods of resolving conflicts between groups.

PRUITT, D.G. and RUBIN, J.Z. (1986). *Social conflict: Escalation, stalemate, and settlement.* New York: Random House. Easy-to-read coverage of conflict from sources to solutions with experimental and practical examples.

TEGER, A.I. (1980). *Too much invested to quit.* New York: Pergamon. A discussion of the conditions under which protagonists are unable to disengage from conflict situations.

WHITE, H.C. (Ed.) (1986). *Psychology and the prevention of nuclear war.* New York: New York University Press. A variety of views on the role played by psychological factors in easing tensions surrounding the nuclear arms race.

SUGGESTED WEBLINKS

Contemporary conflicts (clickable map)
  http:/www.cfcsc.dnd.ca/links/wars/index.html

Journal of Personality and Social Psychology (table of contents)
  http://www.apa.org/journals/psp.html

ANSWERS TO SELF-TEST QUESTIONS

1. a; 2. c; 3. b; 4. a; 5. b; 6. c; 7. a; 8. b; 9. b; 10. b; 11. d; 12. b; 13. c; 14. b; 15. b.

ANSWERS TO FOR REVIEW

1. rational; 2. scarce resources; 3. observer; 4. contingent conflict; 5. misattributed conflict; 6. common; 7. conflict based on false premises; 8. Social ex-

change theory; 9. CL; 10. CLalt; 11. zero-sum game; 12. non-zero-sum games; 13. Prisoner's Dilemma; 14. trust and communication; 15. commons problem; 16. public goods problem; 17. Chicken; 18. threat; 19. conflict spiral; 20. moderate; 21. smaller; 22. larger; 23. low; 24. mediator; 25. Superordinate goals; 26. mirror image perception; 27. GRIT.

COLLECTIVE BEHAVIOUR

Only individuals think; gangs merely throb.

Robertson Davies

*The scene during the last few minutes that the Empress remained on the surface
of the water was one of utter, overwhelming despair and helplessness in the
face of death.*

The Globe, 1914

■ LEARNING OUTCOMES

1. An understanding of the nature of crowds.

2. Knowledge of contagion, deindividuation, and emergent norm approaches
   to understanding crowd behaviour.

3. An understanding of the development and functions of rumours.

4. An understanding of the ways in which fads and fashions spread and the
   needs they serve.

5. An understanding of the nature of hysterical contagion.

6. An understanding of the development of social movements.

■ FOR REFLECTION

- Are crowds really "irrational" in their behaviour?
- How are rumours spread and why is the truth often distorted in the telling of a rumour?
- Why are we subject to fads and fashions?
- What causes people to panic?
- How do cults attract and retain their members?

■ CHAPTER OUTLINE

What is "Collective Behaviour"?

Crowds

   Contagion and the Irrationality of Crowds

   Deindividuation

   Emergent Norm Theory

Varieties of Collective Behaviour

   Rumours

   Conspiracy Theories

   Fads and Fashions

   Contagions

   Contagions of Expression

   Contagions of Enthusiasm

   Contagions of Anxiety

   Contagions of Fear: Panic

   Contagions of Hostility

Social Movements

   The Life of a Social Movement

Cults

Summary

For Review

Issues and Activities

Further Reading

Suggested WebLinks

Answers to Self-Test Questions

Answers to For Review

In 1212, Étienne of Cloyes, a French shepherd boy, had a vision of Christ that instructed him to go to the Holy Land and recover the Holy Sepulchre. Thousands of children, some only eight years old, rushed to join him as he paraded through towns and villages on his way to Marseilles. Parents were powerless to keep their children from running away to join him. At Marseilles, the children expected the sea to part at Étienne's command. When it did not, they embarked on ships. Two ships sank and all aboard were lost, while the others sailed to Alexandria where the children were sold into slavery. A subsequent "Children's Crusade" occurred in 1237, and another in 1458.

In 1968, many Canadians found themselves caught up in the excitement surrounding the emergence of a new political superstar, Pierre Elliott Trudeau, a balding, middle-aged man who was destined to become leader of the Liberal Party and prime minister of Canada. While not everyone was impressed, his "magnetism" was such that wherever he went, people crushed around him to shake his hand, to touch him or even to kiss him. Young women shrieked and swooned in a manner usually reserved for rock stars. Even the press was mesmerized by it all: it seemed that Trudeau could do no wrong. Rude gestures or clowning antics were interpreted as being "cute" or "refreshingly non-conformist."

On October 7, 1968, about 30 000 people, some in wheelchairs, and some from as far away as New York and Ontario, waited in vain in the rain and the mud for the Virgin Mary to appear at a location near St. Bruno, Quebec. She had apparently promised six young girls who had seen her two weeks earlier that she would reappear at that time.

Previous chapters have described the effects of the mere presence of others on a person's behaviour (social facilitation), and the pressures that individuals, groups, and organizations can exert (producing conformity, compliance, and obedience). The situations described above, however, cannot be readily understood in terms of these interpersonal or group processes. There were no leaders or systems demanding obedience, nor were there any pre-existing group norms that generated pressures to conform. Each of these examples involved collections of people who, for the most part, were strangers to one another. But in each case, the early actions of a few stimulated the later actions of a great many. Once the story spread that children were flocking in large numbers to join Étienne, once Trudeau was raised to "star" status, and once at least some people were taking seriously the prediction of the Virgin Mary's appearance, the stage was set for those initial reactions to be imitated by many others.

WHAT IS "COLLECTIVE BEHAVIOUR"?

collective behaviour
Spontaneous, unorganized, and unpredictable behaviour.

The foregoing examples illustrate several characteristics that define **collective behaviour**: (1) It emerges spontaneously in a collectivity of people, e.g. a crowd or an entire society or culture; (2) it is relatively unorganized; (3) it is unplanned in its course of development and is therefore fairly unpredictable; and (4) it is the product of interstimulation among the participants, that is, individuals are influenced by the actions of others, and their reactions in turn influence the very people who have affected them (Milgram and Toch, 1969). These features reflect an absence of normal social convention; therefore, such behaviour is most likely to arise in situations where people are strangers, leaving them without the support and the normative framework of their usual groups. The interstimulation of members of the collectivity is reinforcing to some extent, or the behaviour would quickly die out. For example, if one spectator at a football game throws a pop can onto the field and no applause or encouragement is forthcoming, others are unlikely to act similarly. If the crowd cheers, however, perhaps a second person will throw something onto the field, and if this too is met with approval, others may do the same and the behaviour may spread throughout the audience.

Sometimes collective behaviour involves an intensification of reactions that were already anticipated. For example, while teenagers go to see their favourite rock groups expecting to be excited, the interaction that occurs among members of the audience (the "interstimulation" referred to above) can create a collective experience that is more powerful than anticipated and more intense than anything the individual would experience either alone or in a small group. (Indeed, why is it more exciting to watch a football game in a crowded stadium than to watch it with only a small audience or at home on television, even though you might have a better view on TV?)

Even applause and laughter are increased through interstimulation by members of a crowd. In one study, visitors to the Ontario Science Centre watched a film, following which a confederate applauded (Freedman, Birsky and Cavoukian, 1980). They observed the number of people who joined in the applause, and found that when people were all seated closely together, the contagion of the applause was much greater than when the people were more spread out. The actual number of people also had an effect: a large group of people experienced more contagion than a small group.

What are the characteristics of collective behaviour?

Collective behaviour is rather rare. Most groups of strangers, e.g. people queuing for a bus or passengers standing in an elevator, do not exhibit such behaviour, although the potential may be there. Collective behaviour is *never* institutionalized behaviour, so the label must not be applied to large-scale behaviour governed by appropriate social norms, such as the activities of a large group of strangers on New Year's Eve (Brown, 1965). People at a New Year's Eve party may appear to be out of control as they suddenly rush around kissing each other, but this activity is controlled by a norm that allows it to occur at midnight of that particular day and not at other times or on other days.

Riot in Montreal after the Canadiens won the 1993 Stanley Cup.

However, even in this context, collective behaviour can occur: perhaps on one New Year's Eve, all the party participants rush out into the street and begin to dance wildly or smash store windows.

The study of collective behaviour is an important part of social psychology, not only for itself, but because there is hardly any aspect of social behaviour that does not occasionally find extreme expression in some type of collective behaviour episode (Milgram and Toch, 1969). For example, prejudice, aggression, and authoritarianism are readily apparent in the conduct of lynch mobs, and provide the fuel for such extreme public demonstrations as the Nuremberg rallies of the Hitler era.

It is all but impossible to study most kinds of collective behaviour in the laboratory, both for practical and ethical reasons. We would have no idea how to generate something in the laboratory that is equivalent to a rock concert or a lynch mob, even if we wanted to.

It is also difficult to study real-life collective behaviour because, in most instances, the behaviour is underway before we have time to prepare for studying it. Furthermore, it is difficult to isolate and measure the relevant variables; even the participants themselves are unlikely to be aware of all the important influences acting upon them. This no doubt explains why, despite the fact that the earliest social psychology texts gave considerable discussion to collective behaviour, over the intervening years relatively little has been done by psychologists to advance our understanding of the subject.

This chapter begins with a discussion of the nature of crowds and the phenomenon of rumours. Then, a number of different kinds of collective behaviour are explored: fads and fashions, contagions, social movements, and cults.

CROWDS

crowd An unorganized, anonymous, temporary collection of people.

It was the French sociologist Le Bon who stimulated modern interest in the study of collective behaviour through his book *The Crowd* (1895/1960). A **crowd** is a relatively large collection of people who are physically close enough to influence each other's behaviour, although there is no particular relationship among these individuals. A crowd is unorganized, anonymous, casual, and temporary (Milgram and Toch, 1969). Such a collectivity of people is ideal for the development of collective behaviour, given that such behaviour typically depends on a lack of group structure and appropriate norms.

Crowd behaviour can often appear bizarre or irrational, as we shall see when collective phenomena such as panics and riots are discussed. How can such behaviour be explained? Three approaches to understanding such apparent irrationality will be considered: contagion, deindividuation, and emergent norm formation.

CONTAGION AND THE IRRATIONALITY OF CROWDS

contagion theory The notion that emotions, beliefs, and behaviours spread through a crowd in the same way that a disease spreads.

Contagion theory is based on the notion of the rapid spreading of emotionality, beliefs, and behaviour throughout a crowd or population, somewhat in the same way that diseases spread as one individual infects another. Its roots go back to Le Bon, who believed that in some situations a crowd can develop a "collective mind" that is inherently irrational:

> *Under certain given circumstances, and only under those circumstances, an agglomeration of men presents new characteristics very different from those of the individuals composing it. The sentiments and ideas of all the persons in the gathering take one and the same direction, and their conscious personality vanishes. A collective mind is formed, doubtless transitory but*

*presenting clearly defined characteristics. The gathering has become what ...
I will call an organized crowd ... or a psychological crowd (Le Bon
1895/1960, pp. 23-24).*

According to Le Bon, several factors contribute to the development of this "collective mind." First, he argued, the sheer number of people in the collectivity produces a feeling of overwhelming power accompanied by a sense of anonymity and a reduction in individual responsibility (anticipating Darley and Latané's (1968) model of bystander non-intervention). This leads to the liberation of "savage, animalistic instincts" that are normally suppressed, Le Bon said. Members of the crowd imitate the behaviours of others around them, and in turn stimulate others to act similarly. He saw suggestibility as the most important factor because it produces a vulnerability to contagion. He considered this to be a kind of hypnotic process that leads people to set their own judgment aside and act in line with the actions of others.

This early psychology of the crowd put forward by LeBon can be viewed as a reaction to the threat that the "masses" seemed to pose to the social structure of the time. He and his contemporaries devalued crowd behaviour by characterizing it as pathological and focusing on its apparent mindlessness and hysteria, rather than on the relationships of crowd members to each other, or their reasons for acting together as a crowd (Apfelbaum and McGuire, 1986).

However, even though the notion of a hysterical collective mind and hypnotic influence has not held up under careful scrutiny, the metaphor of contagion in a crowd is appealing. Modern contagion theory is similar to Le Bon's conception, except that the basis for the crowd's behaviour is attributed to the observable interstimulation of crowd members rather than some hypnotic influence or the development of a mystical group mind (Wright, 1978).

What factors did LeBon say contributed to the "collective mind"?

DEINDIVIDUATION

Although Le Bon's notion of animalistic instincts and collective mind appears naive and erroneous by contemporary standards, his basic ideas have been honed and repackaged, without the concept of instincts, in the theory of **deindividuation**, a term coined by Festinger, Pepitone and Newcomb (1952). Zimbardo (1970) described deindividuation as a complex process in which a series of antecedent social conditions leads to changes in self-perception (the person comes to see him or herself more as a member of a group than as an individual), leading in turn to a lowered threshold for normally restrained behaviour. When conditions are right, this can produce antisocial behaviour. Thus, this approach views collective behaviour not so much as the spreading of emotionality through a crowd, but as the loss of individuality and the flouting of social norms in a situation of relative anonymity, i.e., a crowd.

deindividuation When people become part of a crowd they may lose their identity.

Deindividuation is the result of several factors (Zimbardo, 1970):

(1) Loss of identifiability. This can occur when a person is standing in a crowd of strangers or wearing a mask.

(2) Loss of responsibility. If many people are engaging in violence, each person's share of the blame may seem to be smaller.

(3) Presence of group physical activity that in itself is arousing and sustaining. For example, when everyone is yelling and screaming at a rock concert, such stimulation may readily lead others to yell and scream.

What are the factors that contribute to deindividuation?

(4) Limited temporal perspective. The person "lives for the moment" and ignores past obligations and future accountings.

(5) A novel or unstructured situation. The absence of the cues that might otherwise restrain behaviour can lead to a lowering of inhibition (see Box 12-1).

Various studies of subjects' behaviour in conditions of anonymity have seemed to lend support to the deindividuation hypothesis. For example, when subjects were asked to discuss their parents in a group discussion, more negative comments were forthcoming when the subjects were dressed in grey laboratory coats and seated in a dimly lit room than when such anonymity was not present (Festinger et al., 1952). In an attempt to demonstrate deindividuation, Zimbardo (1970) compared the "aggressive" behaviour (defined as the number and intensity of shocks given to a simulated victim) of college students in either of two situations. In the first situation, the subjects were dressed in shapeless overcoats, wore hoods over their faces, and sat in a darkened room. No subject could see how much shock the other two subjects were administering to a "victim," in accordance with an experimental deception that permitted subjects to shock the victim as much or as little as they wished. In the second condition, subjects wore no hoods or overcoats, sat in a well-lit room, and even wore name tags. The subjects in the anonymous condition were much more "aggressive" than those in the other condition, in keeping with the deindividuation hypothesis.

In another study, conditions that reduced individual identity in a mock prison (see Box 12-2) led to brutalization of the "prisoners" by the "guards" even though all were, in reality, psychologically healthy college students (Zimbardo, Haney, Banks and Jaffee, 1982). It has even been reported that tribal societies whose warriors disguise themselves with masks or paint are more brutal in warfare than similar societies in which no such anonymity is provided (Watson, 1973). Deindividuation has even been recently accepted as an extenuating factor in several murder trials in South Africa (Colman, 1991). In one case, more than a thousand people, during a night of singing, dancing, and great emotion fol-

---

BOX 12-1

WHEN THE POLICE ARE ABSENT

Police are an important thread in the fabric of restraint against violence. People are afraid of arrest and punishment. What happens when the police are absent? In 1969 in Montreal, the police and fire departments went on strike. Once the formalized social controls the police represented were lifted, groups of people went on a rampage—smashing windows, looting, and setting fires. According to witnesses, while there was extreme tension, a sense of liberation—almost a "country fair" mood—seemed to characterize the demonstrators and those who watched them. The rampage continued until the return

of the police and the deployment of soldiers reinstituted the formal restraints against such activity.

Outbreaks of vandalism also occurred during police walkouts in Sydney, Nova Scotia in 1971 and subsequently in Yarmouth. Even worse, during a massive power failure in New York City in July 1977, which caused the city administration to grind to a halt and greatly reduced the capacity of the police to carry out their duties, tens of thousands of people in ghetto areas all over the city engaged in an orgy of destruction and looting. The final bill for shopkeepers: $150 *million*. What seemed only too obvious was the almost carnival-like atmosphere and the lack of guilt displayed by the participants.

BOX 12-2

BRUTALITY IN THE CELLBLOCK: THE STANFORD PRISON STUDY

At times, the contrived situation of the psychological laboratory can become startlingly real. Researchers in one study (Haney et al., 1973; Zimbardo et al., 1982) set out to simulate the deindividuating conditions of a real social institution by setting up a mock prison in the basement of the Stanford University psychology department. Voluntary subjects were randomly assigned the roles of guards and prisoners. Those designated as "guards" were given identical khaki uniforms, reflecting sunglasses, billy clubs, handcuffs, whistles, and sets of keys. The "prisoners" were picked up on the first day at their homes by police cars, taken to the police station where they were "processed," and then taken blindfolded to the "prison." They were assigned numbers as identification and wore identical hospital-type gowns and stocking caps. The guards were instructed to maintain "law and order," and events were allowed to unfold.

While subjects initially approached their role-playing in a light-hearted fashion, the situation soon began to deteriorate. The guards became increasingly abusive and punitive towards the prisoners, while the prisoners became passive, helpless, and showed symptoms of stress such as crying, agitation, confusion, and depression.

Even Zimbardo, the principal researcher, found himself preoccupied with rumours of a "prison break," forgetting his responsibilities as a scientist. At this point, after six days, an experiment planned to last two weeks was terminated. The roles had become reality to the participants.

The experiment has been criticized on several grounds (Banuazizi and Movahedi, 1975; Thayer and Saarni, 1975). Subjects had signed consent forms in which they agreed to be paid to participate in a study wherein some of their rights would be waived. Thus they might have felt a moral or legal obligation to continue, and might have exaggerated their symptoms of distress in order to get out of their obligation. The "guards" might have been acting as they did, as "good subjects," because it was expected of them in order to make the study more realistic. There were also some individual differences; some of the prisoners did not become apathetic or distressed and some of the guards were not abusive.

Nonetheless, the study shows the power of the situation, particularly in total institutions such as prisons. In a group of normal young people participating in a simulation experiment, loss of personal identity can cause dramatic changes in behaviour over a short period of time. We can readily extrapolate from this to the profound impact of long-term exposure in institutions such as prisons, hospitals, and the military.

lowing the funeral of a popular leader, pursued several vigilantes who had attacked the group. One of the vigilantes was killed, and six people were arrested in connection with the death. After viewing a journalist's videotape of the events, and hearing expert testimony from a psychologist who argued that the defendants were likely "deindividuated" at the time of the killing, the court concluded that deindividuation had been an extenuating factor, and the defendants were given only custodial sentences. It was used successfully in other cases as well. The use of deindividuation as a legal defence raises disturbing questions about the ultimate responsibility of individuals acting in a crowd.

EMERGENT NORM THEORY

An alternative explanation for crowd behaviour is provided by **emergent norm theory** (Turner and Killiam, 1972), which is as capable of describing very som-

emergent norm theory
Suggests that norms of behaviour begin to emerge in a crowd, and that people begin to act according to these norms.

bre crowds as it is highly excited ones (Milgram and Toch, 1969). According to this view, individuals in a crowd act in a given way because they view that action as appropriate or necessary, and not because their personality and motivation are swallowed up into a collective will or because they are succumbing to some normally restrained motivations. From this viewpoint, crowds are considered to be initially heterogeneous with regard to goals, feelings, and behaviour. However, through rumour transmission and non-verbal communication, a shared perception of the situation develops, and individuals begin to perceive a consensus about what behaviour is appropriate (i.e., norms emerge).

A laboratory study (Mann, Newton and Innes, 1982) pitted emergent norm theory against deindividuation theory in a study of aggressive behaviour. Groups of six to eight subjects listened to two people in a debate. In half of the groups there was anonymity among the members (each member sat at a separate table, and curtains among the tables prevented subjects from seeing one another), while the members of the remaining groups were identifiable to one another by name. Subjects believed that the study examined the effects of audience noise on the participants in a debate, and were instructed to indicate their reactions to what the debaters were saying by varying the level of noise heard by the debaters, just as members of a real audience might react with spontaneous applauding or booing. Each subject sat at a separate control panel and could choose a noise level by pressing any one of a series of eleven buttons which they believed corresponded to several levels of noise, from very soft to painfully loud. The subjects were told that the debaters actually heard a noise level that was the average of the choices of all the subjects in the group. The subjects themselves were given false feedback about that average level. Half of the subjects in each of the two conditions—anonymous and identifiable—were led to believe that the group "norm" was a lenient one, in other words, their feedback indicated that the noise being heard by the debaters was not aversive, while the other half was led to believe that the group norm was an aggressive one because the noise level apparently heard by the debaters was very high. The dependent variable was, of course, the noise level chosen by each subject. If deindividuation theory applied, anonymity should have produced the greatest "aggression." If emergent norm theory applied, then the greatest aggression should have been observed in the identifiable condition with the aggressive group norm. It was found, in line with deindividuation theory, that anonymity rather than a group norm of aggressiveness led to greater aggression (defined in terms of higher noise level chosen by the subject). Thus, no support was found for the emergent norm theory.

At this point, then, although emergent norm theory provides a more general explanatory basis for collective behaviour, it still requires much more empirical support. Its appeal lies in the generalizing of a group process (norm formation) to the seemingly unorganized collective situation. However, even if norms do emerge in the collective situation, emergent norm theory does not tell us the basis on which they are formed, or why one norm (e.g., "Run for your lives") emerges in one situation but not in another, similar situation.

Each of the three approaches discussed here—contagion, deindividuation, and emergent norm theory—has a certain "appeal of explanation" in that each can make sense of one collective event or another. Yet all three are problematic as explanations for collective behaviour. They are not well-defined theories to begin with, but this is hardly surprising, given the difficulty of capturing collective behaviour in order to study it.

How does emergent norm theory differ from deindividuation as an explanation for crowd behaviour?

SELF-TEST QUESTIONS

1. Which of the following is not characteristic of collective behaviour?

a) it is relatively unorganized

b) there is mutual stimulation among participants

c) there are strong pre-existing group norms concerning the appropriateness of the behaviour

d) it emerges spontaneously

2. Research on the process of deindividuation has found that

a) there is a relationship between anonymity and antisocial behaviour

b) deindividuation occurs when people are in situations where they are readily identified

c) individuals in crowds invariably show decreases in social inhibition

d) all of the above

VARIETIES OF COLLECTIVE BEHAVIOUR

As we have seen, collective behaviour often occurs in crowds. But crowds are not necessary for the appearance of collective behaviour, which can occur as readily within a collectivity of people who are not in physical proximity. Indeed, some of the most dramatic instances of collective behaviour have occurred in the absence of crowds (e.g. rumour transmission, which creates a collective belief or apprehension).

RUMOURS

A **rumour** is "a specific ... proposition or belief, passed along from person to person, usually by word of mouth, without secure standards of evidence being present" (Allport and Postman, 1947, p. ix). It is an important part of many collective behaviour episodes and, in the view of emergent-norm theorists, is the mechanism by which a collective perception of a situation is formed within a crowd (Wright, 1978).

rumour A specific belief that is passed from person to person and acted upon as though it were true, even without supporting evidence.

We are all familiar with rumours—rumours that the prime minister is going to resign, or that the company we work for or the college we attend may be going broke. Some rumours have a basis in fact, but often they simply reflect uninformed fear or consist of bits of speculation and gossip woven into a coherent story.

To be the subject of a rumour can be an extremely trying experience, for rumours, once begun, are very difficult to stop. Denying the allegations carried in a rumour often makes the rumour even more believable to many, for one expects the guilty to protest. Rumours in the marketplace—if they are nasty ones—can also have a devastating effect, not only on sales, but even on company survival. Would you ignore a rumour that a new candy product has been implicated in the deaths of several children, especially if you are a parent? Could you overlook the rumour that a huge international fast food chain is owned by the Church of Satan? Or that a major brand of bubble gum has been found to contain spider eggs? These are examples of actual rumours that have flourished in recent years, forcing more and more corporations to face the problem of how to stop rumours once they begin (Koenig, 1985). Sometimes rumours in the business

323

world have been deliberately generated in an attempt to put a competitor into serious difficulty. For example, in 1934 the sale of Chesterfield cigarettes in the United States was adversely affected by the rumour that a person suffering from leprosy had been found working in the cigarette factory. The rumour was allegedly started by a rival firm. Two-person teams would enter a crowded commuter train or subway car from opposite ends, move towards each other, and then have a conversation about the leper while other passengers stood between them (Shibutani, 1966). (See Box 12-3 for a more recent example of a rumour planted in an attempt to damage the reputation of a huge corporation.) Rumours—especially during times of war—can be dangerous not only to morale, but—since they may carry information useful to the enemy—can also put ships or personnel at risk (see the Canadian wartime posters on page 325).

BOX 12-3
SATAN ON THE SOAP BOX

Even a large corporation can be the target of rumours. Around the beginning of 1980, malicious (and, it seems, deliberately inspired) rumours began to circulate in the United States and Canada that Procter & Gamble was linked to devil worship, and that it regularly turned over some of its profits to Satanic cults. The basis for the rumour was the company's 135-year-old logo (see illustration), which portrays the Man in the Moon, a popular figure of the 1800s, and 13 stars (representing the original 13 colonies), which was claimed by the rumour-mongers to be a demonic symbol. To some people, the pattern of stars forms two "6's," and these, augmented by another "6" half-hidden in the man's beard, constitute the "mark of the Beast": the number 666 that the Biblical book of Revelation associates with Satan. Derivatory rumours claimed that Procter & Gamble was owned by the Unification Church (the "Moonies"), and that the head of Procter & Gamble had appeared on television and admitted the Satanist connections.

A leaflet campaign in English and in French that called for a boycott of Procter & Gamble products helped spread the rumours far and wide, and despite police investigations, the source of the leaflets was never uncovered. It seemed that many different individuals, alarmed by the charges, made photocopies of the leaflets and distributed them on their own.

Procter & Gamble took many steps to fight the rumours. The company obtained testaments of

The basis for the rumour: Procter & Gamble's company logo

faith from prominent religious leaders, including high-ranking members of the Roman Catholic Church and several evangelical groups, which they disseminated to local clergy wherever the rumours were current. They set up telephone hotlines to deal with consumers' concerns about the subject and, by early 1982, were receiving about 15 000 calls per month from people wanting to find out if the rumours were true. Procter & Gamble's Canadian headquarters in Toronto received thousands of inquiries from concerned individuals and church groups across Canada requesting clarification of the company's position with regard to Satanism. The rumours died off for a while, following an extensive information campaign by the company, but then emerged again in 1985.

On April 24, 1985, the company announced that it would eliminate the Man in the Moon trademark from its packages, although the logo still appears on all corporate communication. In 1991, the logo was redesigned to eliminate the possibility of perceiving a 6 in the curly hairs in the man's beard.

Canadian wartime posters urge citizens to avoid "careless talk."

F·O·C·U·S

What are the four variables that influence rumour development and transmission?

Why do rumours form? Why are they often repeated so uncritically? Four variables influence the development and transmission of rumours (Rosnow (1991): general uncertainty, outcome-relevant involvement, personal anxiety, and credulity.

GENERAL UNCERTAINTY

This term refers to widely-held doubt and apprehension within a collectivity of people: uncertainty about the identity of a stranger who has been "hanging around town"; uncertainty about whether or not the fish plant will be closed and everyone laid off; uncertainty about why the mayor suddenly resigned without explanation. This is an important characteristic of rumour formation.

OUTCOME-RELEVANT INVOLVEMENT

We are likely to be interested in, and repeat to others, information that pertains to something relevant to us. If the possible closing of a fish plant has no particular relevance, we are not likely to pay attention to, or repeat, the stories we hear about the plant's future. However, our involvment does not have to be direct. Whether or not we become involved in rumours about a particular actor's marital problems or Madonna's latest sexual preferences depends on how interested we are in those particular performers or their behaviour.

PERSONAL ANXIETY

In this context, *personal anxiety* refers to the anxiety—acute or chronic—produced by apprehension about an imminent and disapppointing outcome (Rosnow, 1991). If you work for the fish plant and production is down, you may be legitimately worried about your economic future, and this anxiety will heighten your efforts to obtain information about what is going on, making you much more susceptible to participation in rumours. However, while uncertainty about imminent events or about events already underway may well lead to anxiety, anxiety may in turn lead to a lessening of the ability to tolerate uncertainty (Rosnow and Fine, 1976). Cognitive dissonance theory suggests that when people are anxious but without good reason, they will strive to find a reason in order to reduce the dissonance between the two cognitions "I am anxious" and "I have no reason to be anxious." Rumour may reduce this dissonance, e.g. "I am anxious because civil war is imminent." In a similar vein, hostility towards some group can be justified via rumour: "I don't like the neighbours because they may be communist spies."

Only a little research has been carried out to examine the role of anxiety in rumour transmission. In one such study, students were assigned to either high or low chronic anxiety groups on the basis of their scores on a measure of anxiety (Anthony, 1973). A rumour was begun by telling a few students from each group that certain extracurricular activities were going to be reduced for budgetary reasons. Predictably, the results showed considerably more rumour transmission in the groups that scored high in chronic anxiety.

CREDULITY

credulity The level of trust one has in the truth of a rumour.

Credulity refers to the trust one has in the rumour. The more a rumour seems to offer a believable explanation for ambiguous events, the more likely it is to be accepted as true, since it helps to reduce uncertainty. It has been observed, to no one's surprise, that believable rumours tend to be spread more often than unbelievable rumours, and people often repeat a rumour in a way that increases its credibility by omitting the more dubious elements (Rosnow, Yost and Esposito, 1986). Because it seems so exceedingly unlikely, the rumour that Elvis is alive and well is not well-received by most people, despite the many claims that Elvis has been sighted in various parts of the world. While most of us have heard of the rumour, we are not likely to repeat it if we do not consider it credible.

Depending on the particular levels of these four variables, rumour transmission is more or less likely to occur. There seems to be an optimal level of anxiety and uncertainty that will lead to rumour transmission. If there is too much or too little of either, rumour-spreading is less likely to occur (Rosnow, 1980).

Urban legends have much in common with rumours (Cornwell and Hobbs, 1992). Urban legends are accounts of surprising and implausible events that probably never really happened in the way they are described, but are told and retold as though they are true stories, with the source usually being "a friend of a friend." Brunvand (1981, 1986) describes accounts of the alligators that supposedly live in New York sewers (the result of people having flushed down the toilet baby alligators given to children as pets); the cement truck driver who happens to catch his wife in bed with a stranger and fills the stranger's convertible with cement; and the woman who decided to dry her wet dog in the microwave oven. Many such stories endure over time, becoming part of our folklore, and often evolving to reflect societal or technological changes. Some seem to be an expression of underlying, generalized anxiety. For example, the story about the woman who put her dog in the microwave oven to dry began to circulate during a period of concern about the potential dangers of microwave energy leaking from microwave ovens, harming users without their knowledge.

CONSPIRACY THEORIES

Sometimes rumours contribute to and are derived from an interconnected set of beliefs that identify a group of people as conspirators deliberately plotting for the destruction of an individual or society. The attribution of the Black Death in the Middle Ages to the evil plottings of physicians or Jews is but one example. The enduring myth of the "Jewish-Communist conspiracy" to weaken the Western banking system as a step towards world domination is another. Such a phenomenon has been labelled a **conspiracy theory** (Graumann and Moscovici, 1987). A collection of people come to share a common but irrational set of beliefs, or theory, about a group of conspirators who are plotting against them and their society, and then they apply to these beliefs a very rational and very stubborn logic (Groh, 1987). If physicians are spreading the plague, then stone the physicians. (Note the similarity to paranoid thinking.)

conspiracy theory An irrational belief that people or groups are plotting to destroy an individual or society.

A conspiracy theory itself, like an individual rumour, is likely to be believed to the extent that it has some explanatory power for a group distressed by ambiguity and social uncertainty (Kruglanski, 1987). Extreme political movements are often disposed towards the development of a conspiracy theory. The notion of a conspiracy can not only bind the group together emotionally and intellectually, but also explains why the group members seem incapable of obtaining their goals (Inglehart, 1987).

A modern conspiracy theory concerns satanic cults that have supposedly existed for generations in the heart of our society and involve both people in high places as well as professional people in positions of trust. These cults are said to kidnap children and victimize them both sexually and physically as part of a satanic ritual. Children are sometimes even murdered, so the theory goes. This conspiracy theory is widely promoted by some fundamentalist religious groups, and is being disseminated to police departments and social workers across Canada and the United States. However, careful examination of the claims reveals that in all probability there is no such conspiracy (Hicks, 1990a, 1990b; Victor, 1990). Sexual abuse of children is a monstrous societal problem, but the perpetrators are for the most part indistinguishable from the next-door neighbours. It may be anxiety-reducing to target some hypothetical group as the cause of our problems—just as people in medieval times blamed witches for all their woes. If the conspiracy can be broken, if the bad people can be dealt with, then the problem will be solved. This of course distracts from the real problem; that sexual abusers are individuals who are for the most part people who live and work among us.

What are some examples of conspiracy theories?

The collective behaviours to be discussed next include fads and fashions, contagions of expression, contagions of enthusiasm, contagions of anxiety, and contagions of hostility and rebellion.

FADS AND FASHIONS

In England during the 1300s, a passion for twirling a hoop made of wood or metal around the waist swept the country, involving children and adults alike. In 1957, a similar passion, originating in the United States, swept much of the world—this time with hoops made of plastic. Twenty million "hula hoops" were sold in six months. During a three-week period in 1958, over twenty tonnes of hula hoops were brought into Newfoundland alone! (*The Globe and Mail*, January 15, 1991). Before long, the passsion for hula hoops faded, although their use has not died out completely.

fad *A short-lived, extreme, and usually frivolous type of behaviour.*

This is an example of a **fad**, which is one of the most common types of collective behaviour. A fad is a short-lived, extreme, frivolous bit of behaviour that is "fun" because "everybody is doing it" (Klapp, 1972). Typically, fads develop quickly, enjoy widespread popularity for a time, and then vanish, usually never to appear again. Some fads, such as the "streaking" of the mid-'70s which led individuals to run naked through crowds of people, are actually the rebirth of fads that have come and gone decades before. Others, such as flagpole sitting, goldfish swallowing, and telephone-booth stuffing, have come and gone and, so far at least, have never returned.

Fad behaviour involves a great deal of anonymous interpersonal interaction. It is anonymous in that people do not directly communicate about whether or not they should swallow a goldfish or run naked through the crowd, but each "knows" whether or not the behaviour is in keeping with the times. They can anticipate how others will react to them. No one can predict when a fad will appear or what its nature will be.

fashion *Consumer behaviour that may serve to make a person's status known, or to simply relieve boredom.*

A **fashion** is more serious than a fad in that it begins with something perceived as necessary: we all need clothes, and most of us need cars. In 1992, Canadians spent more than 12 billion dollars on clothing, so fashion in clothing is of some considerable consequence! Fashion is more likely than a fad to be cyclical, and bygone fashions may be brought into vogue again. New fashions are often "risky" in that they attack or violate existing social norms. When the brassière first made its appearance, women who wore them were considered to be "risquée" since the undergarment accentuated the bustline. Traditional society reacted somewhat negatively to such "shamelessness." Yet when some women in the 1960s began going without bras as their grandmothers and great-grandmothers had done, they were greeted with similar criticism. As for men, moustaches and vests, definitely "out" in the '50s, were definitely "in" in the '70s and '80s. Long hair, the virtual symbol of counterculture in the '60s and early '70s, became acceptable (and remains widespread among artists and musicians), but then the fashion moved in the direction of shorter hair. In the '90s, earrings have become almost *de rigueur* among teenage males.

Why do fashions continually change? While there is no good research that informs this concern, sociologists have suggested that fashion serves both to mark a person's status in society, or at least his or her status aspiration, and to relieve the banality of modern technological society (Klapp, 1972). Each of these factors merits a brief examination.

How do fad and fashion differ?

STATUS MARKING

Today, designer clothes and automobiles often serve to tell others of the status (real or coveted) of the owner. This is nothing new. Historically, clothing fashions have always distinguished people belonging to different social levels. It was easy to recognize an aristocrat or a peasant because each dressed in a distinctive way. However, for those who could afford it, there was always the temptation to emulate the dress of those a little higher in the hierarchy, which suggests a reason for the ever-changing fashions of the elite: they were constantly seeking to differentiate themselves from those of lower status who imitated them. In fact, there have been occasions when the law itself has been used to prevent people from dressing in attire inappropriate for their social level (Box 12-4).

There seems to be a widely understood "language" of clothes that allows people to "read" other people or to tell others about themselves. For example, research

BOX 12-4
SUMPTUARY LAWS

At various times throughout history there have been so-called "sumptuary laws." The main goal of these laws has been to mark clearly the distinctions among the various classes and to prevent people of lower class from dressing in the manner of a higher class, thereby encroaching on the position of supremacy enjoyed by the nobility:

> Sooner or later the rich, rising man ventures to assume the fine clothes [of those of higher social rank], and consternation, not to say panic, ensues among the upper classes. Hastily a sumptuary law is drafted and hastily passed (Laver, 1964, p. 5).

Such laws were intended to restore respect for the inequality of social ranks (Roach and Eicher, 1965). A secondary goal was to curb the extravagance of people who were risking bankruptcy in order to mimic the attire of the nobility.

Sumptuary laws were in force in ancient Greece and Rome, and existed in Japan until the mid-1800s. In Rome, colour of clothing served to denote rank, and laws were decreed that restricted the peasantry to one colour, officers to two colours, commanders to three colours, and members of royalty to seven colours (Roach and Eicher, 1965).

In Europe, sumptuary laws were common as well. Consider these examples:

- In 1301, the bride of Philip the Fair, who was king of France from 1285 to 1314, made her entry into Bruges, and the whole population turned out in their best attire to greet her. She is said to have announced with annoyance that "I thought I was the Queen, but I see that there are hundreds" (Roach and Eicher, 1965). Subsequently, Philip passed a number of sumptuary decrees, detailing precisely what sort of attire was allowed for people of various social ranks.

- During the reign of Charles IX in sixteenth-century France, silk dresses could be worn only by princesses and duchesses, and only ladies of high rank could carry fur muffs. Hoop skirts, or "farthingales," could be no wider than one-and-a-half yards. These laws were still in effect at the time of the French Revolution, and one of the first acts of the General Assembly was to abolish all laws that concerned distinctions in dress (Roach and Eicher, 1965).

- In England, during the reign of Edward III, pearls and ermine could be worn only by members of royalty, while during the reign of Henry VIII, any woman below the rank of countess was not allowed to wear a train. Elizabeth I sternly enforced her own clothing laws, producing great discontent among her subjects. For example, she decreed that "no great ruff should be worn, nor any white colour, in doublet or hosen, nor any facing of velvet in gowns, but by such as were of the bench.... That no curled or long hair be worn, nor any gown but such as be made of sad colour" (Roach and Eicher, 1965).

On the other hand, some societies have tried to impose uniformity on the way that people dress in order to abolish any class distinctions. For example, when the Communists came to power in China in 1949 they followed the example of the Soviets, and all citizens, men and women alike, were led to wear the "drab, baggy uniform" that we have come to associate with modern China (Horn, 1975).

Today, there are still distinctions of class associated with styles of dress, but there is nothing to stop people of one segment of society from donning the attire more typical of another segment. Bikers can dress in tuxedos if they wish, and magistrates can spend their weekends in blue jeans. Moreover, the recent trend towards producing cheap, copycat versions of designer clothes and accessories—some so authentic in appearance that designers of the original items are truly alarmed—means that class distinctions in dress are even harder to recognize than they ever were.

has found that most people are in agreement about what certain types of clothes indicate. In a British study of teenage girls (Gibbins and Coney, 1981), it was reported that there was substantial agreement among them concerning the characteristics of girls who wore various types of clothes, including whether the girls smoked or drank and how many boyfriends they were likely to have. This "fashion sense" is acquired early: fourth and sixth grade children have been found to make differential personality inferences about others—including inferences about friendliness and popularity—on the basis of the brand of jeans worn (Calvin Klein, Levi Strauss, or Sears) (Solomon, 1986).

Women are faced with a special problem as they compete with men for positions in the world of business: to "dress for success" they must avoid styles that are traditionally feminine. In one study in which business executives were asked to evaluate job applicants on the basis of personnel files which included photographs, it was reported that women who groomed themselves in a somewhat less feminine manner (plainly tailored clothes, little make-up, shorter hairstyles) were chosen over those who portrayed more traditionally feminine grooming styles (Solomon, 1986).

BANALITY

Novelty appears to be a primary reinforcer of human behaviour (Berlyne, 1960); the same is true of many animals ("curiosity killed the cat"). That is, we seem to be predisposed to be curious and curiosity is encouraged by novel stimulation. Thus it should be expected that people living in a world in which there is so much uniformity would seek things that are different; this may lead to creations of new styles. Thus changing fashion, whether in clothing or cars, may be an attempt to alleviate boredom and to assert our individuality.

In summary, fads and fashion do not necessarily involve behaviour that is very serious or consequential for an individual or a society. However, both may serve to provide relief from banality, and fashion likely serves the additional and important function of identifying the individual with regard to actual or aspired status. Fashion also plays an important role in self-definition and in interpersonal relationships, a role that is only now coming to be understood as social psychologists focus more research attention on it.

CONTAGIONS

contagions Strong emotional beliefs and actions that spread throughout a population.

There are several types of collective behaviours in which the development and spread of a strong emotional reaction is a central feature. **Contagions** of expression, enthusiasm, anxiety, fear, and hostility are discussed below. (The term "contagion" is used here to describe the process of beliefs and actions spreading throughout a crowd, and is not meant to suggest a preference for a contagion theory explanation rather than one based on deindividuation or the development of emergent norms.)

While all collective behaviour involves contagion to some degree, sometimes the contagion carries with it such wild ideas and behaviours that the crowd or society almost appears trapped in a collective delusion (Klapp, 1972). For whatever reason, a crowd or a population finds itself at a given point in time *very* susceptible to ideas and rumours. While crowd behaviour involves mutual interpersonal stimulation, contagion is not limited to crowds and, indeed, direct person-to-person interaction is not required.

Unlike typical crowd behaviour, mass contagion often lasts for days or weeks, and sometimes even months and years. Contagions typically begin to build up slowly, and then as more and more people become involved, rise rapidly to a peak and then usually die down quickly, although some persist for much longer periods.

CONTAGIONS OF EXPRESSION

Expressive contagions have no particular goal other than emotional release, whether they be motivated by joy, sorrow, frustration, or guilt (Klapp, 1972). Although such behaviour may infest an entire society, it is often most apparent in crowd settings. An expressive crowd may gather to pay homage to a new Pope or cheer the return of a Stanley Cup champion hockey team. There is no external goal other than to see, touch, or applaud the object of admiration. The crowds that cheered Trudeau in his heyday fell into this category, as do the throngs of gasping teenagers that flock around rock stars wherever they make an appearance.

What are examples of contagions of expression?

CONTAGIONS OF ENTHUSIASM

Tulips were introduced into Western Europe from Turkey in the middle of the sixteenth century. Over the next hundred years they became objects of such admiration, especially in Holland, that any man of substance without a decent collection of bulbs was held in some contempt. In the period 1634–1636, the Great Tulip Mania swept Holland, England, and France. The cost of bulbs soared so much that tracts of land and even small fortunes were sometimes traded for a single bulb. Special arrangements were made for the sale of rare tulip bulbs on the Amsterdam and Rotterdam stock exchanges. So frantic was the pursuit, so greedy were the speculators, so anxious were rich and poor alike to improve their lot by profiting from the rising market in bulbs, that normal industry in Holland fell into serious neglect: the nation had gone tulip-mad. Finally the market for bulbs, held artificially high by speculators, collapsed and many people suddenly realized that they had given up most of what they owned for a collection of tulip bulbs that no one wanted any more.

The Great Tulip Mania is an example of a contagion of enthusiasm. Such contagions embody an extraordinary hope or delusion, usually about becoming wealthy. Thus "Klondike Fever," spiked by rumours of massive deposits of readily obtainable gold, led tens of thousands of people—most of whom had never mined before nor knew anything about survival in the North—to the Yukon gold fields in 1898. While everyone dreamed of making a fortune, few were lucky enough to do so. (See Pierre Berton's *Klondike* (1972) for an excellent description of this contagion.) As with other contagions, "the bubble bursts" sooner or later; in many cases, the costs can be enormous.

What are examples of contagions of enthusiasm?

CONTAGIONS OF ANXIETY

Contagions of anxiety (often referred to as "hysterical" contagions) involve the rapid dissemination of exaggerated fears, and often evoke unrestrained emotionalism. The fears are exaggerated in the sense that the response is hardly warranted by the circumstances.

The great windshield pitting epidemic provides a good example. In the spring of 1954, Canadian newspapers were filled with reports of the American H-bomb

What are examples of contagions of anxiety?

The great "pitting" story hit the Globe and Mail's front page on April 21, 1954.

tests at Eniwetok in the South Pacific. The power of the bomb seemed almost incomprehensible: a whole island disappeared as a result of one blast. One of the blasts was described as a "runaway," an out-of-control explosion that produced effects far beyond what was expected. In addition, the Russians were thought at that time to be very close to the development of their own H-bomb, and many newspaper stories dealt with politicians' and scientists' preoccupation with the imminent danger of nuclear war. Canadian cities were not at all protected against air raids, and concern about building bomb shelters spread.

Radioactivity had been detected in snow in Manitoba and Saskatchewan, presumably a result of the H-bomb tests. As well, paranoia was rampant on the international stage. Western countries feared Communism as much as they feared war, and in the United States, the McCarthy era, during which thousands of Americans were persecuted because of suspected disloyalty, was in full swing.

It was claimed—out of fear—that there were 500 Communist organizations in the Toronto area alone.

It was in the context of this combined fear of atomic war and Communist subversion that the great windshield pitting epidemic began. It started in Seattle, Washington, where it was reported that hundreds of people had found small pockmarks in the windshields of their cars. The windshields also had small blobs of a metallic substance on them which, although not radioactive, were quickly assumed by some members of the public to be due to atomic fallout. While initial reports of damage were attributed to vandals using BB guns, the news emphasis gradually changed to one of mystery. Seattle's mayor finally declared that windshield damage was no longer a police matter, referred to the recent H-bomb test as a possible cause, and made an appeal to the Governor and the President for emergency aid. The stage was set.

While physical scientists from the University of Washington had all emphasized road damage, hysteria, and air pollution as the causes, engineers from Boeing Aircraft suggested physical causes for the pitting, including supercharged particles from the H-bomb explosion, and a shifting in the Earth's magnetic field. By April 19, 1954, the citizens of Vancouver were reporting the same kind of windshield damage, and even those who were initially sceptical changed their tune when they found that their cars too had been affected. A Victoria used-car dealer discovered that the marks suddenly appeared in the windshields of the cars on his lot.

The reports quickly became front-page news, and the incidents spread from B.C. to the prairies to Ontario. During the approximately two weeks that the "epidemic" lasted, the windshield-pitting delusion spread across Canada, although in the United States it was confined to the Seattle area. Newspapers reported that scientists and police officers were desperately searching for the cause. Some car dealers covered the windshields of their cars to protect them. Yet, a short time later, the interest suddenly vanished as quickly as it had materialized. It was noted that although used car dealers were reporting that their cars had been damaged by the mysterious pittings, dealers of new cars could not find any damage to their windshields. The greater the car's mileage, the more likely was it that the windshield would be pitted. Once this began to sink in, it was realized that the pitting was the result of normal damage caused by pebbles thrown up from the roadway. People had not paid much attention to such pitting before. When the publicity struck, however, people would take a good look at their windshields for the first time. Once the real cause was understood, the newspapers dropped their coverage and the epidemic died.

Two researchers (Medalia and Larsen, 1958) interviewed 1000 randomly selected Seattle residents. About 93 percent of the respondents knew of the windshield pitting: about half of those had learned of it from the newspapers, a quarter from radio and TV, about one-fifth from talking to others, and the rest (six percent) from direct experience. Fifty percent of the respondents accepted the "unusual physical agent" explanation while only 21 percent believed the "ordinary road damage" explanation.

The anxiety generated by the fear of after-effects of the H-bomb explosion was apparently relieved by focusing attention on automobile windshields. "Something is bound to happen to *us* as a result of the H-bomb tests—windshields became pitted—it's happened—now that threat is over" (Medalia and Larsen, 1958, p. 25). In other words, the waning of interest was not brought about simply by a more reasonable interpretation of the events and the subsequent lack of media interest, but by diffusion of the anxiety that was responsible for the original reports.

Sometimes more than anxiety is involved; there may be symptoms of physical illness, or a belief that one's body has been damaged or altered in some way. For example, in 1986, two brief power failures affected the operation of visual display terminals in the Manitoba Telephone System. Over the next two weeks, 55 operators complained of numbness and tingling in the limbs, head, or face, as well as lightheadedness and fatigue. Despite the failure of a panel of physicians and engineers to find an objective basis for the symptoms, rumours of "permanent nerve damage" began to circulate, leading to a walkout and eventual shutdown of the workplace. Repeated outbreaks of such symptoms continued for over eighteen months. Only when the union and management combined their efforts in setting up a stress reduction program did the complaints of physical symptoms dwindle away. While the events in Manitoba unfolded, a similar outbreak occurred among telephone operators in St. Catharines, Ontario (Yassi, Weeks, Samson and Raber, 1989).

Note that no mass psychogenic illness occurred following the Chernobyl nuclear disaster in 1986, or the earlier Three Mile Island disaster in the U.S. In these cases, facts about the actual risks were discussed in great detail by the media. People *knew* the risks, and had a reality-based fear. More importantly, however, these disasters did not occur in the context of a pre-existing, generalized, or poorly identified anxiety. Had they done so, this diffuse anxiety could have been transformed into mass psychogenic illness built around the theme of nuclear sickness. (This does not mean to suggest that no anxiety or physical illness occurred, only that the basis was real, not imagined.)

Contagions of fear: Panic

While anxiety refers to a generalized feeling of unease that often cannot be attributed to any specific cause, fear always has some identifiable source and always involves the perception of danger. When a crowd is frightened and in danger, it is not surprising that people in the crowd will try to escape the danger. When **panic** occurs in a building (as in the case of a fire), most people cannot even see the exit but assume that the movement of the crowd is directed towards one. Often, there is a "front-to-rear communications failure" (Janis et al., 1964), with those at the back unaware that people at the front are unable to move more quickly, causing those at the front to be trampled. Consider this example:

On the afternoon of January 9, 1927, children flocked to the Laurier Palace theatre in Montreal's east end to see a comedy called, ironically, "Gets 'Em Young." Most of the children, contrary to the law of the time, were admitted to the theatre unaccompanied by adults. During the film, a child in the balcony dropped a lighted cigarette, starting a small fire. When someone in the balcony cried "Fire!" the theatre ushers were able to hush the resultant anxiety and begin an orderly evacuation. Smoke began to appear in larger and larger quantities. The ground floor spectators were evacuated without incident, while the children in the balcony moved quickly to two exit stairways and clambered downstairs towards the sidewalk:

> *Five steps from the sidewalk, five steps from safety the tragedy was born. Boys and girls in the van of the stampeding mob, pressed suddenly from the rear, stumbled and fell. Instant panic grasped those at the rear ... a minute or two was enough for the stairway to be a solid, suffocating, groaning, shrieking and dying mass (The Globe, January 10, 1927).*

panic *Occurs when people reinforce each other's fear of not being able to escape a dangerous situation.*

Seventy-eight children died, 60 from asphyxiation, 11 from compression, and five from both asphyxiation and burns. No one need have died at all. The fire was a minor one, and there was enough time for an orderly exit. They died, so it was said, because they panicked.

What is the nature of panic? The term is used very loosely in ordinary parlance: "I panicked when I realized I'd lost my wallet"; "When the lights went off, he got very panicky." Yet panic is more than anxiety or fear or terror, even though some earlier conceptualizations emphasized the covert emotional state of the individual (e.g. Cantril, 1940). In the context of collective behaviour, panic involves fear and flight and an avenue of escape (Quarantelli, 1954; Schultz, 1964). Yet, while flight is an essential element of panic, not *all* flight is panic. In a panic, flight is "non-social and non-rational" (Quarantelli, 1954): the individual thinks of his or her own physical survival, and pays no attention to how this action may be detrimental to the collective welfare of the group.

Panic usually occurs in crowds, where individuals mutually reinforce each other's concern about escape in the face of danger. However, sometimes there is only an "implied" crowd—individuals interpret events around them to suggest that others are reacting as they are. Consider this example (Cantril, 1940): In 1939, Orson Welles' Mercury Theatre radio program carried a dramatization of H.G. Wells' *The War of the Worlds*. Of an estimated six million listeners, about one million, many of whom had tuned in after the program had begun, unfortunately ignored cues that pointed to the fictional nature of the broadcast and reacted with panic, "heading for the hills" or looking for a place to hide. Police switchboards were jammed with calls, and traffic snarls occurred in some places as people tried to flee the "invasion." This was the first demonstration that mass panic can be triggered without the involvement of either rumours or crowds (Klapp, 1972). Most of those who were so affected had shown little critical ability and had made no attempt to check by switching to other radio stations or calling friends.

How could so many people react in this way to a radio drama? One reason is that they were faced with what appeared to be a genuine news report. Then, in telephoning the police—as many did—and being unable to get through because other people were making the same call, they were persuaded that the Martians had already knocked out telephone lines. Once begun, the panic reaction was hard to slow down. As people began to flee, it would have been easy to assume that other people who were going about their business in a normal way were just unaware of the emergency, while the sight of anyone else hurrying to get somewhere could easily be interpreted as a reflection of the need to escape.

PANIC AND THE COLLECTIVE DILEMMA

While it is both socially responsible and individually practical for you to await your turn during the orderly exit from a burning building, once there has been a departure from this orderliness, being cooperative is no longer individually profitable and the only "rational" solution is to push your way out as others push you. Once again, we encounter the collective dilemma; however, in this case it is like a collective game of chicken (see Chapter 11). Each individual is faced essentially with two choices of action: remain calm and proceed in turn, or run for the exit. If everyone exits in a calm and orderly manner, then perhaps all will escape. If you remain calm and others run, you may not escape. If everyone runs, then there is likely to be crowding at the door and many may die. Even smelling smoke in a crowded building may be enough to lead people to act non-

How is panic related to the collective dilemma?

cooperatively, since they have been taught the danger of people panicking in a burning building! They expect others to run, so they do so first.

SIMULATING PANIC

The classic simulation of panic is one provided by Mintz (1951), who observed subjects in groups of fifteen to twenty people whose task it was to remove aluminum cones from a narrow-necked bottle by means of a string attached to the cones (Figure 12-2). After the cones were placed in the bottle, each subject was given a piece of fishing line attached to only one of the cones. Then they were told that only one cone could pass through the neck of the bottle at a time. At the signal to start, water began flowing into the bottom of the bottle. Subjects were instructed to try to get their cones out without getting them wet. No "traffic jams" at the bottle's neck occurred when no rewards were given for success. However, in a second condition, subjects were told that 25 cents would be won by getting a cone out completely dry. If a third or less of the cone was wet, there would be no reward, and if more than a third was wet, there would be a fine. In this case, "traffic jams" were experienced by more than half of the groups. This occurred whether or not the subjects were allowed to communicate. Mintz concluded that intense fear is not necessary to cause non-adaptive behaviour similar to panic behaviour.

In panic-producing situations, cooperation is rewarding as long as everyone cooperates. Once the cooperative pattern is disrupted, however, cooperation ceases to be rewarding. Pushing becomes advantageous in exiting a burning theatre if everyone else is pushing and appeals to order and calm are not working.

Organized groups, such as military units, are rarely subject to panic. Because of their training, the individuals are very responsive to the orders of the leader. Only when the leadership structure breaks down is there a danger of panic.

SOCIAL INHIBITION OF ESCAPE BEHAVIOUR

Sometimes a crowd can actually inhibit escape from a dangerous situation by its refusal to become aroused. There have been several instances of fires in night

FIGURE 12-2 **Mintz's apparatus**

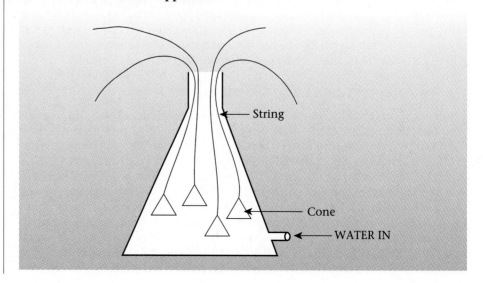

clubs and theatres in which patrons warned of a fire have refused to leave. In 1977, the Beverly Hills nightclub in Kentucky caught fire and, although a busboy ran to the stage and announced that there was a fire, the audience assumed he was part of the act and most people ignored his warning; 165 lives were lost. A fire broke out during a New Year's Eve party in a social club in Chapais, Quebec, in the early hours of January 1, 1980. Most of the 44 people who died could have escaped. As in so many other similar circumstances, the victims apparently underestimated the danger. They carried on dancing or stood in a semi-circle, watching a pile of dry pine branches that had ignited blaze away. The euphoria of the crowd, the loud music, the alcohol, and the wish to avoid looking foolish or cowardly all combined to inhibit escape behaviour.

RATIONAL BEHAVIOUR IN DISASTERS

The popular press, and even some agencies whose job it is to deal with disasters, typically describe people caught up in some disaster as acting in a highly disorganized, irrational, and hysterical way. Authorities sometimes hesitate to announce the possibility of an impending disaster for fear of causing unnecessary panic. (For example, the alarm bells on the *Andrea Doria,* sunk in a collision at sea in 1956, were not rung even though collision with an approaching ship was unavoidable, for fear of causing panic.) Yet careful analysis of actual disasters in several different cultures shows that disorganized flight is seldom the case. Most people manage to maintain a rational approach to situations of great danger. For example, people reacted relatively calmly and rationally following the major earthquake in San Francisco in the fall of 1989. A baseball stadium filled with scared and shaken fans awaiting the start of a World Series game was evacuated without any signs of panic. However, it has also been shown that when people are supposed to evacuate an area because of some oncoming disaster (flood, tornado, etc.), the majority of people may not leave (Quarantelli, 1960).

Researchers who have studied disastrous high-rise hotel fires report that most people do not panic, and that most of those who fail to escape when the opportunity presents itself do so because of errors in judgment rather than irrational behaviour (Keating and Loftus, 1981). However, it must be remembered that panic is a collective behaviour. Only if people are in a group and see other people running about is panic likely to break out. Most people in high-rise fires do not find themselves in circumstances that would promote collective behaviour.

When disaster does strike, another common myth suggests that once the immediate danger has passed, people sit around dazed and unable to cope. Yet in actual observations of disaster victims, this so-called "disaster syndrome" (apathy, shock) has been seen to affect only a minority of people and only for a short time. In general, people react immediately and logically to their situation. Looting in such situations is actually very rare, also contrary to popular myth. The myth of the disaster syndrome may have arisen because people *seem* to run about aimlessly, while in fact they are desperately looking for missing friends and relatives (Killian, 1952). That is precisely what occurred on June 30, 1912, when the worst storm in the history of Western Canada struck Regina, killing 36 people, toppling houses, and moving a grain elevator 50 feet. There was no panic, and once the storm abated the populace rallied to locate survivors and care for the injured and homeless. (The same scene was played out 75 years later in Edmonton, when a tornado killed 25 people and injured at least 250 others.)

Panic can be viewed as the consequence of a process of attributional appraisal. First, something occurs that causes arousal. Then, this arousal must be interpreted in terms of the environmental context. If the context is perceived as dangerous, that arousal is labelled as fear. Whether a person engages in panic behaviour then depends on the behaviour of others in the vicinity whose actions serve as a model to increase or decrease the arousal level.

CONTAGIONS OF HOSTILITY

We have seen how anxiety can sometimes lead to mass psychogenic illness. In other circumstances, people do not seek out a physical cause for a psychophysiological anxiety, but react with irrational hostility and violence towards scapegoats—individuals who provide safe and easy targets. (The word "scapegoat" comes from the Biblical account of the Hebrews ridding themselves of evil by loading their sins onto a goat, which was allowed to escape into the wilderness while a companion goat was sacrificed to God. Today, scapegoats do not escape; they are the objects of hostility and violence—see Chapter 6.) In the Middle Ages, commonplace events—the drying up of crops, the stillbirth of an child or animal, the destruction of crops by hailstorms—were attributed to the actions of witches. Between 500 000 and 700 000 people were convicted of witchcraft and burned at the stake in Europe between the fifteenth and seventeenth centuries (Harris, 1974). In 1692, in Salem, Massachusetts, a witch mania occurred on a much smaller scale. Some young girls who had dabbled in black magic developed a hysterical illness that involved convulsive behaviour. They blamed witches for their problems and readily pointed out the "guilty adults." The mania spread beyond Salem to Boston. Twenty people, including a minister, as well as two dogs, were executed as witches.

Aggressive crowds provide localized and short-lived instances of contagions of hostility. Whether the aggressive crowd takes the form of a mob (whose aggression is directed against a relatively powerless individual or a small group of individuals), or a riot (aggression is expressed against another group having similar or greater power), the behaviour of the participants is still that of individuals for whom normal social restraints have been lifted.

It is impossible to predict with any certainty when an aggressive crowd is likely to form. In June of 1972, 2500 angry fans who could not get into a sold-out Rolling Stones concert in Vancouver rioted and hurled bottles, rocks, and even Molotov cocktails at the more than 200 police who fought to keep them out of the Pacific Coliseum where the concert was being held. In Montreal in 1971, a riot broke out at Blue Bonnets Raceway after angry spectators reacted against what they thought was an exceptionally low quinella payoff. Soccer games have often been marred by rioting and, on a number of occasions in 1985, violence by British soccer fans spilled out into the streets, resulting in pitched battles with police. While some of these incidents appeared to reflect racial tensions, others did not. In 1984, rowdiness by British soccer fans during a game played by a British team against an Italian team in Belgium turned into violence and resulted in the deaths of 38 Italian spectators. When the Montreal Canadiens won the 1993 Stanley Cup at the Forum, the post-game celebrating produced a mob of several thousand people that moved down Ste. Catherine street causing in excess of 10 million dollars damage (see photo on page 317). One hundred and sixty-eight people, including 49 police, were injured, over 100 stores were ransacked, and 15 city buses and 47 police cars were destroyed (see also Box 12-5).

Spectator violence is not new. In Constantinople, fans at the chariot races burned down the Coliseum in 491 AD, and again in 498 and 507. In 532, thirty thousand people died in riots at those chariot races, and once again the Coliseum

Who are the targets for contagions of hostility?

BOX 12-5

THE AUDIENCE STRIKES BACK: VIOLENCE AT THE FORUM

On March 17, 1955, then National Hockey League President Clarence Campbell suspended Maurice "Rocket" Richard from the line-up of the Montreal Canadiens for the remaining three regular season games and all the play-off games. (Richard had twice punched an official in a game a few days earlier.) That night, as the Canadiens played the Detroit Red Wings at the Montreal Forum, the fans expressed their displeasure. When Campbell entered to take his seat after the game had begun, the audience stood up and booed him loudly. By the end of the first period, with Montreal trailing by 4 to 1, the crowd turned nasty. They pelted Campbell with tomatoes and eggs, the game was called off, and then some spectators set off a tear gas bomb that sent thousands coughing and crying to the exits. Outside thousands of other fans were milling about. The building was evacuated and the crowd began to smash windows and set fire to newspaper stands. Even at midnight, 15 000 people were besieging the Forum. Some of the crowd moved uptown, and 30 stores had their windows smashed and were looted along the way. The police were kept busy arresting people and hauling them away. An expressive crowd had become an aggressive crowd.

was burned down. In 59 AD the Roman Senate imposed a ten-year ban on gladiator contests in Pompeii following a rash of violence between fans of differing allegiances (Horn, 1985).

SELF-TEST QUESTIONS

3. Contagion theory is based on

a) hypnotic processes

b) individual personality variables

c) attitudes and behaviour throughout a crowd

d) all of the above

4. Rumours

a) arise as a result of people's need for information in certain situations

b) act to relieve emotional stress

c) are spread through informal communication channels

d) help people to make sense of situations and to decide on what actions to take

5. A short-lived, extreme, frivolous type of collective behaviour is described as

a) a fad

b) a cult

c) a fashion

d) an impulse

6. Compared to a fad, a fashion

a) is more likely to be cyclical

b) involves such things as clothes and hair cuts

c) may be more likely to reflect a person's status in society

d) all of the above

7. What kind of collective behaviour involves the development and spread of strong emotions, does not require direct personal interaction, builds up slowly, rises to a peak, and then dies quickly?

a) a fashion

b) a riot

c) rumour transmission

d) a contagion

8. The great windshield-pitting epidemic is an example of a

a) fear contagion

b) contagion of enthusiasm

c) contagion of anxiety

d) contagion of expression

9. Which of the following statements is true with respect to the phenomenon of panic?

a) panic is a non-rational response to fear

b) panic can be evoked in the absence of rumours or crowds

c) panic is non-social in that the individuals involved show no concern for the effect of their actions on the welfare of other individuals in the collective

d) all of the above

10. Research on behaviour during disasters has shown that

a) in the aftermath of a disaster, many people manifest a disaster syndrome

b) panic tends to occur in situations where escape is impossible

c) most people in disaster situations react in a rational manner

d) all of the above

SOCIAL MOVEMENTS

social movement Large, spontaneous movement that draws people together to solve a social problem.

The contagions described thus far arise relatively quickly in crowds, and are generally short-lived. **Social movements**, on the other hand, are a form of collective behaviour that usually begins very slowly but then spreads and spreads, eventually producing a formal group oriented towards bringing about social change. Such groups can endure for years, decades, or longer.

A social movement is "a spontaneous large group constituted in support of a set of purposes that are shared by the members" (Milgram and Toch, 1969). Although unlike any behaviour examined so far in this chapter, social movements are considered to be a type of collective behaviour because they are spontaneous and because large collections of people are involved. Generally, a social movement is aimed at either promoting or resisting change in society. It attracts people who feel that a problem exists, believe that something can be done about it, and *want* to do something about it (Toch, 1965).

Canada has given birth to many social movements, reflecting the high degree of social fragmentation and lack of consensus in the country (Grayson and Grayson, 1975). Various groups—farmers, women, French-speaking Canadians—have at one time or another felt estranged from the mainstream of society. As a result, movements such as the Farmers' Union, the Cooperation Commonwealth

Federation, Social Credit, the National Action Committee for the Status of Women, and the Parti Québécois have evolved. Sometimes, however, such movements can take on an ugly form and express the dark side of human nature (see Box 12-6).

At its inception, a social movement often reflects no more than a dissatisfaction with contemporary society coupled with a dream about a new kind of society. As a social movement gathers impetus, it gradually takes on organizational form, with formal leaders, division of duties, and an agenda (Blumer, 1951). The suffragette movement, the women's liberation movement, and the gay liberation movement all began when various individuals expressed their dissatisfaction with their treatment and their desire to change society so that they would be admitted to the mainstream.

Social movements vary from being general in nature (e.g. their goal is to obtain equality for women across a wide range of situations—see Box 12-7) to being very specific, such as *reform* movements that accept the basic structure of society but seek to modify part of it (Blumer, 1969). Because they seek to overthrow the existing social order, *revolutionary* movements are often driven underground, while reform movements appear respectable within society and attempt to gain support through discussion and persuasion. Reform movements try to win the support of the middle class, while revolutionary movements typically appeal to those in the oppressed or distressed group. The Front de Libération du Québec (FLQ), which

BOX 12-6
CANADIAN FASCISM

The depression of the '30s, coupled with the prairie drought, was a natural crucible for the birth of social movements. Communists appealed to the hungry unemployed to throw off their capitalist masters and assume control of their nation.

Fascism also made an ugly and not insignificant appearance. In November 1929 Adrien Arcand, a professional journalist in Montreal, started a movement in Quebec based on racial nationalism (Betcherman, 1975). It was called the "Ordre Patriotique des Goglus," and was modelled after Italian fascism. By February 1930 it claimed 50 000 members, although this is probably a gross exaggeration. Even before Hitler came to power, Arcand was a publicist for him. He shared Hitler's anti-Semitism and organized boycotts of stores owned by Jews. Arcand edited a weekly newspaper that he used to promote his idea that the Jews should be expelled. He attacked communism and socialism, a move that won him support among some businessmen.

Once Hitler came to power, Arcand's group became even more virulent in its anti-Semitism.

His followers wore blue shirts, aping the fascists of Europe. Other fascist groups, some competing with Arcand's, sprang up as well. A brown-shirt gang, the Canadian Nationalist Party headed by William Whittaker, an ex-British soldier, was operating in Manitoba. It too published virulent anti-Semitic literature. In Ontario, "Swastika Clubs" sprang up, comprising gangs of youths who wore swastika insignia and who harassed Jews on public beaches or in parks. On July 4, 1939, a National Fascist convention was held in Massey Hall in Toronto, with about 2000 in attendance. Arcand, his group now called bilingually "Le Parti National Social Chrétien/The National Social Christian Party of Canada," wanted to be known as the Canadian *führer*. Eventually, he far outdistanced his closest rivals—the black-shirted Canadian Union of Fascists—in the competition for dominance.

While this movement was continuing to gather momentum, the Nazis invaded Western Europe, Canadian troops were sent overseas, and Arcand and other fascists were arrested and imprisoned for the duration of the war. Following his release after the war, Arcand continued to produce anti-Semitic literature until his death in 1967.

never achieved the status of a social movement, was nevertheless typical of a revolutionary movement in that it tried to alter the social order radically by force. The Parti Québécois, on the other hand, provides a good example of a reform movement which began as an unorganized collectivity and grew into an institution. While the Parti Québécois spoke to the genuine injustices that have been suffered by French Canadians, the FLQ went far beyond that and advocated militant socialism, a stance not very likely to win support from the Québécois middle class. The Reform Party is attempting to become a force in Canada partly by presenting itself as a social movement aimed at reform of the Canadian political scene.

While some social movements are nationalistic in nature, others are of a religious nature (Blumer, 1951). The "Moral Majority" in the United States is an example of a religiously oriented social movement; in this case, there has been a genuine attempt to win political power in order to change the social order. (Religious social movements are discussed in more detail in the section on cults.)

Some social movements evolve into mainstream political forces. The Parti Québécois has already been mentioned in this context. The Social Credit Party and the CCF party, which evolved into the NDP, grew out of social unease on the Prairies and the feeling that existing political parties did not serve Prairie interests and needs. Their aim is to achieve political and social change.

The poverty and hunger of the 1930s formed a natural breeding ground for social movements as people struggled to change a system that seemed to be keeping them down. Communism and socialism had a natural appeal to the unemployed and to the drought-ridden farmers, since the blame for economic depression could be placed on the capitalistic system of ownership in the country. Communists organized workers and many demonstrations were held, demand-

What social movements in Canada have evolved into mainstream political forces?

BOX 12-7
A WOMEN'S SOCIAL MOVEMENT

Dr. Emily Stowe, Canada's first woman physician, had to study medicine in the United States because as a woman she was unable to gain admission into a Canadian medical school. In 1876, she founded the Toronto Women's Literary Club, a reform organization whose name was changed in 1888 to the Toronto Women's Suffrage Association. This group was composed primarily of business and professional women and the wives of wealthy men. In other parts of Canada other women, most notably Thérèse Casgrain in Quebec and Nellie McClung on the Prairies, joined the quest for suffrage. They sought the right to vote not simply to obtain personal equality with men, but also to influence governments to work towards the elimination of serious social problems.

Canadian women working for suffrage preferred to be called "suffragists" rather than "suffra-

gettes," as their British counterparts called themselves. This was because the Canadian women did not want to be seen as sharing the sometimes radical political views associated with the suffragette movement.

The vote for women was first won on the Prairies, where women had received widespread support from various farmers' organizations. Manitoba extended suffrage to women in 1916, followed by Saskatchewan and Alberta in the same year. In 1917, British Columbia and Ontario did the same. Nova Scotia followed in 1918, New Brunswick in 1919, Prince Edward Island in 1922, Newfoundland (then not yet a part of Canada) in 1925, and Quebec in 1940. Women were given the right to vote at the federal level in 1918, but it was only in 1929 that they legally became "people." In that year, the Supreme Court of Canada reversed an earlier ruling that women were not "persons" within the meaning of the British North America Act.

ing more help for the unemployed and changes in the economic order. The federal government tried to intimidate the Communist organizers by arresting them under a provision of the Criminal Code, passed during the Winnipeg General Strike of 1919, which made it unlawful to belong to any party that advocated political change by means of force or violence. Agitators who were not Canadian citizens were deported. Between 1930 and 1934, 22 968 people suffered this fate.

While poverty and hunger in Canada in the 1930s gave rise to many social movements, the same phenomenon has happened and is continuing to happen in many Third World countries today. Some of these actually lead to the overthrow of governments. Castro's 26th of July Movement evolved from a social movement to the controlling political force in Cuba. There are many other examples.

THE LIFE OF A SOCIAL MOVEMENT

A social movement often develops through a series of four stages (Blumer, 1969):

How does a social movement develop?

(1) **Social unrest stage.**   A general discontentment with the status quo coupled with restlessness, but no definite goals, characterizes this stage. At this point, agitators are likely to play an important role as they try to make people aware of the shortcomings of contemporary society for them. The "consciousness raising" undertaken by blacks and by women is typical of this stage.

(2) **Popular excitement stage.**   More definite ideas about the causes of the problems and about the goals emerge.

(3) **Formalization stage.**   At this point a structure begins to develop. Policies are formalized and a leader, likely to be a kind of statesperson, is chosen. An ideology—a collection of beliefs, myths, and doctrines—develops along with it. The ideology defines and defends the goals of the group, condemns the existing social order, outlines the policies and tactics, and contains the myths of the group. The intelligentsia of the group generally provide a highly respectable formal ideology that can be defended to certain of the intelligentsia outside the movement. But the ideology also takes on a popular form for the general masses, composed of emotional symbols, stereotypes, and so on.

(4) **Institutionalization.**   The movement finally evolves into a fixed organization with a formal structure and specific division of duties.

The development of the Parti Québécois and the CCF are good examples of this process. Note, for example, how the rabble-rousing of early spokespeople in the *séparatiste* movement gradually gave way to the statesman-like pronouncements of Réné Levesque, Jacques Parizeau, and Lucien Bouchard.

Social movements are more likely to arise in a society undergoing rapid social change than in a stable one (Lang and Lang, 1961), a society in which changing aspirations and needs cannot be satisfied by the existing social norms. Following changes in the educational system in Quebec during the "Quiet Revolution" brought about by the Lesage administration in the 1960s, the Church's influence was curtailed, and large numbers of French-speaking students pursued studies in areas previously left to the English—business administration, commerce, and marketing. But when these students graduated, they found that proficiency in English was a prerequisite for a good job in the business world. Social change was obviously needed.

As social movements gather momentum, their participants are often led to assume that their continued survival depends on being acceptable to outsiders;

thus they may gradually drop their most radical ideas (Milgram and Toch, 1969) (e.g. the Social Credit dropped its plan for radical changes to the banking system). This leads to an institutionalization of the movement, whereby it becomes a part of regular society and ceases to appeal to those who are most discontented. These individuals are forced to look elsewhere and often to try to start another movement. Again, the Parti Québécois provides an excellent example. "Separatism" became "sovereignty-association," steps were taken to appease large industries which felt threatened by the party's policies and, by increasing its support among the public at large, the party alienated those members who wanted radical social change. Only after the Parti Québécois lost power as a result of an erosion in its popular support did it once again, in the late 1980s, return to a platform of outright separatism.

CULTS

cult A group of people who are drawn to and believe in a particular authoritarian leader. They are persuaded to obey this leader regardless of the cost.

What are the characteristics of cults?

Roch Thériault saw himself as an emissary of God. He and his small cult, including among others his eight wives and twenty-five children, lived on an isolated commune 100 miles northeast of Toronto. In October, 1989, he was convicted of hacking off with a meat cleaver the right arm of one of his followers. Subsequently, he was convicted of an earlier gruesome murder of another follower, and gradually it emerged that he had often been violent and abusive towards those who folllowed him, permanently maiming some of them. Yet, it seems that at least some of them continued to idolize him, even after he was sentenced to life in prison (*Maclean's,* February 8, 1993).

David Koresh, who considered himself to be the Messiah, lived with his cult (the "Branch Davidians") on a commune near Waco, Texas. He was obsessed with power and sex: he hoarded an arsenal of assault rifles, pistols, and even a .50 calibre machine gun. All his male followers were ordered to be celibate, while the females, from teenagers to septuagenarians, became his personal harem. On February 28, 1993, the commune was surrounded by law authorities who attempted to search the compound for illegal weapons. When they tried to enter, they were met with gunfire. In the ensuing gun battle, four federal agents and six cultists were killed. This was followed by a seven-day standoff. Then, on April 19, a tank was used by the authorities to smash a hole through the compound's wall. A fire broke out, and 95 of the 104 people in the compound, including Koresh, died from the fire and smoke.

Many cults are built on authority and strict obedience. Such obedience can create a very dangerous situation. The most chilling modern example of a religious cult becoming a "cult of the leader" is that of a group which was originally part of mainstream fundamentalist religion: the People's Temple, founded by the Reverend Jim Jones in the 1950s. Jones specialized in public faith-healing, as do many of today's television evangelists. In 1977, because of growing criticism in the media, Jones and 1000 of his followers moved his Temple from California to a remote location in the Guyanese jungle, which came to be called Jonestown. Here he exercised even greater control over his followers than he had previously, and began to speak in a more and more violent and revolutionary fashion. He began to hold "white nights," which were rehearsals for mass suicide should the need arise.

In 1978, American congressman Leo Ryan went to Jonestown to investigate charges that some people were being held against their will. Later when Ryan and his party and two defectors from Jonestown tried to board a plane to leave, they were ambushed by Temple members. Ryan and four others were killed. That night, the last "white night" was held. Vats of poisoned fruit drink were brought out, and people lined up to take their final medicine. Those few who refused were forced. Over 900 people died. Jones himself was unable to take the poison and, after almost everyone was dead, pleaded with a camp nurse to shoot him. She did, and then turned the gun on herself.

Osherow (1981) examined the Jonestown phenomenon in terms of three social psychological processes: (1) obedience; (2) persuasion; and (3) self-justification. Each is discussed below:

(1) Obedience.   Jones' power was so pervasive that people did whatever he decreed, even when suicide was ordered. Obedience was deeply instilled in the followers; deviations were met with strict, sometimes sadistic, punishment. Defectors were hounded and threatened. Jones became more and more preoccupied with the "enemies" of his church, and less and less tolerant of any criticism from the faithful. Followers grew to live in fear of brutal punishment for perceived disobedience. He used informers to spy upon his flock. He strove to weaken family bonds by assigning many children to other members' custody, and even forcing parents to sign away their custody rights. He forced spouses into extramarital sexual relationships, often of a degrading nature, and he sometimes decreed that wives should become his sexual partners.

(2) Persuasion.   If people complied with Jones' rules, and if they ultimately stayed because they were afraid to leave, why did they join the Temple in the first place? Jones was an expert at impression management. His charismatic leadership, his careful choice of both the right audience and the most appealing message, and his use of emotional and one-sided messages were all designed to put him and his movement in the most positive light.

Through the use of inculcation techniques, as well as control of information wherever possible, he prepared his followers to reject any information that countered his own pronouncements. By creating an external enemy, he was able to insure the cohesiveness of his own group.

(3) Self-justification.   Once involved at the periphery of the People's Temple group, novices would find themselves being pressured to take on more and more work on behalf of the group, such as letter-writing to the press and to politicians, and going to several meetings each week. The newcomer was first expected to make donations, then subsequently to turn over a quantity of his or her income, and finally to turn over all personal assets (and social security cheques) to the Temple. Hesitation was interpreted as lack of faith. Ultimately, the individuals were persuaded to live in Temple quarters in order to save on living costs.

During the '60s and '70s, while adherence to traditional, mainstream religion dropped, fundamentalist Christian sects and a wide variety of new religions and quasi-religions flourished. Some of these "new religions," most of which have been popularly labelled "cults"—the Church of Scientology, the Unification Church ("Moonies"), the International Society for Krishna Consciousness—have become wealthy and influential, almost mainstream. However, the majority of cults remain relatively small.

Few cults are as violent as those led by Thériault, Koresh, and Jones. It would be unfair to condemn all cults on the basis of a few. Indeed, it is difficult to define just what is and what is not a cult. Cults are generally religious in nature, and "deviant"—that is, not part of the mainstream. Yet, several mainstream religions—and this may well be true of Christianity—could have been considered cults when they began. Most cults are organized around a highly charismatic leader (almost always a man) who is responsible for enunciating the group doctrine, establishing rules and norms, and giving the adherents the promise of something akin to transcendence. Many such groups have been viewed with alarm because of their widespread appeal to teenagers and young adults, and because, once a member, an individual may be constrained to stay through physical or psychological pressure. Many cults employ indoctrination techniques—social isolation, sleep deprivation, personal degradation, discouragement of rationality and individual decision-making, inculcation of total obedience to the leader—that are viewed by critics as constituting "brainwashing." As objectionable as these practices are, however, they may not actually differ very much from those used in certain more acceptable groups—such as the army and even some mainstream religious groups. Because of the way we generally schematize cults, however, their techniques appear in a much more negative light. This was demonstrated empirically by Pfeifer (1992): indoctrination techniques (which actually are used by many cults) were judged to be more offensive if they were described as being used by the Moonies (a large international cult) than if they were described as being employed by the U.S. Marines or the Catholic Church. We must be aware, therefore, that it is not always easy to remain objective in examining the cult phenomenon.

There is even the possibility that some cults provide emotional support to troubled recruits, although what seems helpful in the short term may not necessarily be so in the long term. Levine and Salter (1976) studied 109 members (who were volunteers and not a random selection) of a number of cult groups in southern Ontario. Levine found that the motivation to join such groups was almost exclusively tied to personal dissatisfaction with life and difficulty with coping. This vulnerability was countered by the ability of the group to fulfill needs that were not being met elsewhere, primarily through providing answers to essential questions regarding personal identity and the meaning of life. Stringent rules and regulations give new structure to the lives of people who feel they have been drifting aimlessly through life. The mysticism infusing the belief system of such groups provides a curious comfort. It is soothing to know that there are people who know, people who understand, people who will take care of the novices, and the sense of being part of an (enlightened) community may also contribute to a higher sense of self-worth.

The spreading cult phenomena produced a number of anti-cult groups—often set up by ex-cult members—to fight what they saw as the insidious threat of the cult movement. Often, cult members were considered to have been "programmed," and occasionally, professional "deprogrammers" were hired by distraught parents to kidnap their children who had joined cults and to restore their old belief system so that they would return home and assume their former lifestyle.

SELF-TEST QUESTIONS

11. Which of the following statements is *not* true regarding cults?

a) cults are organized around a charismatic leader

b) cults can be considered a type of social movement

c) individuals who are motivated to join cults are generally well satisfied with life

d) the strict rules and regulations of cults provide security and structure for the members

12. According to Blumer (1969), what is the first stage of a social movement?

a) the social unrest stage

b) the formalization stage

c) the popular excitement stage

d) none of the above

13. Which of the following is *not* one of the stages that Blumer (1969) identifies as important in the development of a social movement?

a) the institutionalization stage

b) the social unrest stage

c) the revolutionary stage

d) the popular excitement stage

14. The institutional stage of social movements is characterized by

a) a general discontent with the status quo

b) the emergence of goals

c) the choice of a leader

d) formal structures and specific divisions of duties

SUMMARY

(1) Collective behaviour emerges spontaneously in a group of people. It is relatively unorganized and unplanned, and is the product of interstimulation among participants.

(2) A crowd is unorganized, anonymous, casual, and temporary.

(3) Contagion refers to the rapid spreading of beliefs, emotionality, and behaviour throughout a crowd by means of suggestion, rumour, and imitation.

(4) Deindividuation, the loss of a sense of personal identity, can lead to a lowering of normal restraints on behaviour. Conditions that contribute to deindividuation include a loss of identifiable characteristics (e.g., wearing a mask), loss of responsibility, an arousing group activity, loss of temporal perspective, and a novel situation without the usual restraining cues.

(5) In a crowd situation, new shared norms may emerge that may lead to apparently uncontrolled behaviour. This theory of emergent norms opposes the deindividuation hypothesis, which interprets crowd behaviour as being exhibited by individuals who are unresponsive to social norms.

(6) In the transmission of rumours, uncertainty, outcome relevance, personal anxiety, and credulity all influence whether or not an individual is likely to be influenced by, and to repeat, the rumour.

(7) Collective behaviours may occur without interpersonal contact. These include fads and fashions, and contagions of expression, enthusiasm, anxiety, fear, and hostility.

(8) Fads and fashions are related to status-marking, the desire of people to identify with certain groups and to differentiate themselves from other groups. They also provide relief from the banality of everyday life.

(9) A hysterical contagion refers to the spread of a strong emotional reaction, sometimes accompanied by apparent physical symptoms that in reality have no physical cause. Uncertainty, the spreading of rumours, and the potentially serious consequences of some event or situation may contribute to these contagions.

(10) A social movement is a large group formed spontaneously in support of shared goals, such as nationalism, revolution, religion, or political change. Social movements often develop through stages of social unrest, popular excitement, formalization, and institutionalization.

(11) Cults tend to attract vulnerable people, providing emotional support along with a strong ideology and a demand for absolute commitment.

FOR REVIEW

FOR REVIEW

Collective behaviour is _____(1), _____(2), and _____(3), and involves _____(4) among the participants. A _____(5) is unorganized, anonymous, casual, and temporary. Crowd behaviour is explained in a number of ways. Emergent norm theory suggests that collective behaviour develops as individuals in a crowd develop a _____(6) and a consensus about appropriate _____(7). LeBon postulated that, in some situations, a _____(8), which is inherently irrational, develops in a crowd.

There are many varieties of collective behaviour. Rumour transmission tends to occur in conditions of _____(9). Rumours tend to be transmitted more when people feel _____(10). _____(11) tend to be more cyclical than fads. Fashions seem to provide some relief from _____(12). The windshield-pitting epidemic was a _____(13). The simulation by Mintz (1951) of panic in a "bottleneck" represents the nature of panic as a _____(14). In the Rocket Richard hockey riot of 1955, an _____(15) crowd became an _____(16) crowd.

A _____(17) is a spontaneous large group constituted in support of shared purposes. Definite ideas about what is the cause of certain problems and what should be done about them emerge during the _____(18) stage of the development of a social movement. Often successful social movements become _____(19) and end up as a part of mainstream society. _____(20) movements seek to modify society, while _____(21) movements seek to overthrow the existing social order. Most cults are organized around a _____(22) leader. Three social psychological processes that Osherow identified as being involved in the Jonestown phenomenon are _____(23), _____(24), and _____(25).

ISSUES AND ACTIVITIES

1. Trace the controversy about mad-cow disease from newspapers and any other available sources. Are there any characteristics of rumour or contagions that you can identify from the reports?

2. Make a "Mintz type" apparatus (see Figure 12-2). Design your own experiment to simulate panic. Be creative in your apparatus design. A note of caution: be sure that what you use for weights (cones) is not too heavy, in order to avoid injury if they are released quickly.

• FURTHER READING

APPEL, W. (1983) *Cults in America.* New York: Holt, Rinehart and Winston. An anthropologist surveys and analyzes the cult phenomenon in the United States.

BURT, S., CODE, L. and DORNEY, L. (1988). *Changing patterns: Women in Canada.* Toronto: McClelland and Stewart. Comprehensive account of past and present transformations in the social and economic roles of Canadian women. Written by feminist scholars.

GALBRAITH, J.K. (1993). *A short history of financial euphoria.* New York: Whittle Books/Viking. A Galbraithian examination of financial follies—from tulipomania to modern-day junk bonds.

GRAUMANN, C.F. and MOSCOVICI, S. (1986). *Changing conceptions of crowd mind and behavior.* New York: Springer-Verlag. A collection of recent articles on the psychology of crowds and crowding.

KAISER, B. (1985). *The social psychology of clothing.* New York: Macmillan. An examination of how choice of clothing influences social behaviour and reflects social norms.

KOENIG, K. (1985). *Rumor in the marketplace.* Dover, MA: Auburn House. A collection and analysis of rumours in the commercial world, how they come about, and how rumour control can be attempted. A fascinating application of the social psychology of collective behaviour to the world of the marketplace.

MACKAY, C. (1841/1932) *Extraordinary popular delusions and the madness of crowds.* New York: Farrar, Straus and Giroux. A classic account of some of the great collective delusions throughout history. Collective behaviour is viewed as irrational and even pathological.

MILES, A.R. and FINN, G. (Eds.) (1982). *Feminism in Canada: From pressure to politics.* Montreal: Black Rose Books. A collection of essays on the development of the women's movement in Canada.

MOSCOVICI, S. (1985). *The age of the crowd.* London: Cambridge University Press. A historical treatise on the psychology of the "masses," with particular consideration given to the approaches of LeBon, Tarde, and Freud.

SOLOMON, M.R. (1985). *The psychology of fashion.* New York: Lexington Books. This book examines the role of psychological factors in the choice of clothing styles.

TOCH, H. (1955). *The social psychology of social movements.* New York: Bobbs-Merrill. A classic introduction to the dynamics of social movements.

SUGGESTED WEBLINKS

PSYC SITE A site set up to help psychology students and researchers find information about scientific research in psychology on the World Wide Web. Designed to be a "major jumping off point" for seeking out psychological information. Maintained by the Psychology Department of the University of Nipissing.

http:/www.unipissing.ca/psyc/psycsite.htm

ANSWERS TO SELF-TEST QUESTIONS

1. c; 2. a; 3. c; 4. c; 5. a; 6. d; 7. d; 8. c; 9. d; 10. c; 11. c; 12. a; 13. c; 14. d.

ANSWERS TO FOR REVIEW

1. spontaneous; 2. unorganized; 3. unplanned; 4. interstimulation; 5. crowd; 6. shared perception; 7. behaviour; 8. "collective mind"; 9. uncertainty; 10. anxious; 11. Fashions; 12. banality; 13. contagion of anxiety; 14. collective dilemma; 15. expressive; 16. aggressive; 17. social movement; 18. popular excitement; 19. institutionalized; 20. Reform; 21. revolutionary; 22. charismatic; 23. obedience; 24. persuasion; 25. self-justification.

SOCIAL PSYCHOLOGY OF JUSTICE AND THE LAW

The jury, passing on the prisoner's life,
May in the sworn twelve have a thief or two
Guiltier than him they try

William Shakespeare (All's Well That Ends Well)

Anyone whose rights or freedoms, as guaranteed by this charter, have been infringed
or denied may apply to a court of competent jurisdiction to obtain such remedy as
the court considers appropriate and just in the circumstances.

Canadian Charter of Rights and Freedoms 24. (1)

■ LEARNING OUTCOMES

1. An understanding of the criminal justice system in Canada, with reference to indictable offences.

2. An understanding of when and how the characteristics of the defendant may affect the results of a trial.

3. Knowledge of what factors contribute to the accuracy of an eyewitness.

4. Knowledge of what factors affect the credibility of a witness in court.

5. An understanding of how the jury process may be studied and how characteristics of jurors may affect the verdict.

6. An understanding of the process of judgment, particularly how people detect whether someone is lying or concealing the truth and how people attribute responsibility.

7. An understanding of how the instructions of the judge may influence the jury, and how decisions about sentencing are made.

■ FOR REFLECTION

• How accurate are people at describing what they witness? Are they reliable witnesses at trials?

• What determines whether someone is believed by someone else?

• How do people arrive at decisions regarding guilt or innocence?

■ CHAPTER OUTLINE

Criminal Justice in Canada

The Defendant

The Witness

   Eyewitness Accuracy

   Testimony: What Makes a Credible Witness?

The Jury

   The Juror

The Verdict: Processes of Judgment

   Detecting Deception

   Attribution of Responsibility

The Judge

   Instructions of the Judge

   Sentencing Practices

Implications and Trends

Summary

For Review

Issues and Activities

Further Reading

Suggested WebLinks

Answers to Self-Test Questions

Answers to For Review

Donald Marshall: a victim of unreliable eyewitness testimony.

In 1971, Donald Marshall, an 18-year-old Micmac, was convicted in a Nova Scotia court of second-degree murder following the stabbing death of Sandy Seale, a 17-year-old acquaintance. After serving 11 years in a penitentiary, Marshall was absolved on appeal and another man was subsequently convicted of manslaughter in the killing. A Royal Commission of Inquiry into this miscarriage of justice was scathing in its denunciation of the process. Its report documented instances of over-reliance on unreliable witnesses, suppression of contrary evidence during and after the trial, and racist attitudes exhibited by the police and other officials. Clearly a system designed to produce "justice" can be distorted by people's attitudes and actions.

It is not surprising that psychology has expressed an interest in the legal system since the early days of the discipline. Consider the questions that arise in a legal case, in which social psychological processes may play a key role:

(1) The police take reports of eyewitnesses. Do the eyewitnesses remember and report accurately?

(2) On the basis of eyewitness and other evidence, the police develop a hypothesis about the crime. How does this influence how they carry out the investigation?

(3) A suspect is apprehended and identified from a police lineup. Could the witness have been subtly pressured by the police to make an identification, or could the lineup itself have biased this identification?

(4) The suspect is charged and given an opportunity to confess. Can people be subtly coerced or tricked into a false confession?

(5) The case goes to trial. How do the persuasive abilities of the Crown and defence lawyers influence the jury? How could biases among the jurors influence the verdict? How might the instructions of the judge influence the verdict?

In 1908 Hugo Munsterberg, an experimental psychologist, published *On the Witness Stand: Essays on Psychology and Crime.* He argued that the principles of psychology could be applied in the courtroom to questions such as whether the "attractiveness" of the accused would affect the verdict. Through the years, social scientific evidence has gained increasing acceptance in courts in demonstrating, for example, racial or sexist discrimination (Tomkins and Pfeifer, 1991). However, it is especially in the past two decades that the study of behaviour in relation to the legal system has proven to be a productive field for research in social psychology. Social psychologists are studying events in the courtroom as a social world in miniature. Every day social psychological processes are magnified because the stakes are so high (Pennington and Hastie, 1990). Here research can help us to evaluate the system and to propose changes that would make it more effective and just. It will be clear to the reader that social psychologists working in this applied area make use of research and theory from a number of basic areas, and employ a variety of the research methods that were discussed in Chapter 1.

CRIMINAL JUSTICE IN CANADA

indictable offence *Crime governed by the criminal code of Canada.*

Criminal law in Canada is governed by the criminal code, which is drafted and amended by the federal government. Criminal code crimes (called **indictable**

offences) are those which carry a maximum penalty "greater than six months in prison and/or a fine of two thousand dollars" (McCormick, 1994). These cover a range of offences, from homicide to possession of stolen goods.

In 1993, a total of 2 736 096 criminal code offences were reported to the police. (See Figure 13-1 for the breakdown of these crimes from 1984 to 1993.) Property crime is the largest category, and covers such activities as theft, fraud, breaking and entering, and possession of stolen goods. Next in size is the "Other" category, which covers such activities as prostitution, arson, offensive weapons incidents, and mischief. The smallest category is the most serious. Violent crime covers homicide, sexual and non-sexual assault, and robbery. Non-sexual assault is the most reported violent crime in Canada, accounting for 77 percent of violent offences and 9 percent of all criminal code offences in 1993. Sexual assault is the second most commonly reported violent crime, while robbery is the third (Statistics Canada, Juristat, June 1995).

Anyone charged with an offence under the criminal code of Canada may be tried in one of three ways: (1) in a "purely provincial" court with a provincial court judge, (2) in a Provincial Superior Trial Court with a provincial superior judge, or (3) in a Provincial Superior Trial Court with a provincial superior judge and a jury. With the exception of murder and a few rare crimes (e.g. piracy), which are always tried in Superior Trial Court, the accused can choose the way he or she is tried (McCormick, 1994).

In this chapter we will focus on the trial itself. While it is neither possible nor desirable for the psychologist to intrude in any way in the courtroom, important

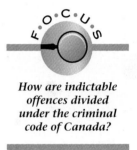

How are indictable offences divided under the criminal code of Canada?

FIGURE 13-1 Police-reported Criminal Code crime rates per 100 000 population, 1984 to 1993

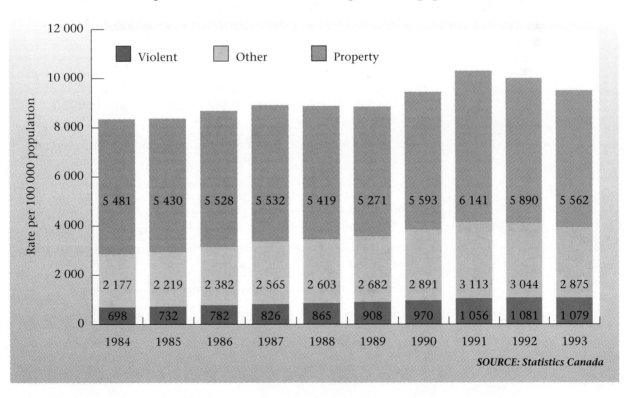

SOURCE: Statistics Canada

353

insights have been provided by research and we examine some of the work in this area. First we will examine the influence of characteristics of the defendant on the process and the outcome of trials. Then we turn to research concerning the vital question of the accuracy of eyewitnesses, and what makes a witness credible. We also discuss the jury in the context of real-life group decision-making. In our discussion of the cognitive processes that underlie judgments in a trial, we will discuss how people can detect whether a person is being deceptive, and how people arrive at an attribution of responsibility. Next we examine the role of the judge in providing instructions to the jury and in imposing a sentence when a guilty verdict is returned. The chapter concludes with a discussion of what the notion of justice itself means to people.

THE DEFENDANT

defendant Person accused and on trial for a crime.

dangerous offender Person who is given an unlimited prison sentence.

What are the characteristics of defendants that might affect the outcome of a trial?

Ideally, justice would be served if the characteristics of the **defendant**, which are not related to the case, were ignored by those who reached a verdict. However, the results of studies of actual court cases and simulations suggest that the opposite is true. Decisions of jurors betray the effect of social psychological processes such as the similarity-attraction rule and the "beautiful is good" stereotype (Chapter 7). When this schema is applied, defendants who are unattractive or who have some physical abnormality such as a facial scar are perceived as more "dangerous looking" (Wormith and Ruhl, 1986; Webster et al., 1985; Esses and Webster, 1988). In Canada, where a defendant can be designated as a **dangerous offender** and given an indeterminate sentence, such a bias can have an important impact on the administration of justice.

Much of the research has been devoted to the influence of extra-evidential factors—e.g. race, ethnicity, or sex of the defendant—on the outcome of a jury trial.

RESEARCH HIGHLIGHT

In a review of the literature, Dane and Wrightsman (1982) have concluded the following:

(1) The gender of the defendant may be of some importance in certain crimes, but the evidence is not clear at present.

(2) No consistent influence of socio-economic status has been found.

(3) A defendant with prior offences (as deduced by the jurors) or who seems to be unrepentant is more likely to be convicted.

(4) Attractive defendants are treated more leniently unless their attractiveness was used to facilitate a crime.

(5) Defendants of the same race as the jurors are less likely to be convicted.

(6) Jurors tend to be more lenient towards defendants who have attitudes similar to their own.

Other research shows clearly that when whites evaluate black defendants, and English Canadians judge French and native Canadian defendants, they perceive them as more guilty and recommend more severe punishments (Pfeifer and Ogloff, 1988; 1989; Pfeifer and Bernstein,1993). In January, 1996 a report on systemic racism (discussed in Chapter 6) in the criminal justice system was released by a provincial commission (Ontario). This commission stated that "systemic racism exists in the Ontario criminal justice system," and that "blacks and other racial minorities experience the system as unfair and...the exercise of discretion has a harsher impact on black people than on white people." Many findings led to this charge. For example, between 1986–87 and 1992–93 prison admissions rose 204 percent for blacks and only 23 percent for whites (*The Spectator*, January 17, 1996).

A new and highly significant ruling from Ontario's Chief Justice has recently been announced (April 1996). Any black person accused of a criminal offence in Ontario has the "automatic right" to question potential jurors on their views about racial minorities. Up until this ruling, questions were permitted only at the discretion of the court. Sometimes they were allowed, and sometimes not. Instrumental in this ruling was the Parks decision in September 1993, which overturned the second-degree murder decision of Carlton Parks, a black man, because the jury had not been questioned on racist attitudes. (The case is discussed in the CBC Prime Time News video *Jury on Trial*). This ruling also says that other visible minorities may have the same rights as blacks if they prove that there is sufficient prejudice against their group that jurors may not be impartial.

In addition to race, physical appearance has an impact on decisions of guilt or innocence. A recent study (Macrae and Shepherd, 1989) used photos of people that had been previously rated as high or low in honesty and aggressiveness. Subjects shown pairs of photos were asked to select which person was responsible for each of a series of crimes. The results indicated that even after accounting for the effects of physical attractiveness, subjects tended to choose photos of those with facial features stereotypically linked to the crimes. That is, jurors tend to be influenced in cases where the defendant apparently "looks like a criminal" (Shoemaker, South and Lowe, 1973). Conversely, adults with "baby faces"—characterized by features such as large eyes, short noses, and low placement of facial features—tend to be convicted of crimes involving negligence but are less likely to be convicted of charges involving intentional criminal behaviour (Berry and Zebrowitz-McArthur, 1988).

THE WITNESS

The evidence, as presented and interpreted by lawyers, is the essence of a case in court. While physical evidence such as a fingerprint, a document, or a weapon may be presented if available, the most convincing evidence is often the testimony of an eyewitness, someone who can identify the perpetrator and describe what happened. Indeed, in cases where a person later shown to be innocent has been convicted, eyewitness testimony was often the most important reason for the conviction, even when that evidence had apparently been discredited in court (Loftus, 1974, 1979; Lindsay, Wells and O'Connor, 1989).

Even if the eyewitness is honestly attempting to be truthful and accurate (see Box 13-1), there are two related issues to consider: (1) Is the testimony of an eyewitness usually accurate, and what factors contribute to error or bias? (2)

BOX 13-1
EYEWITNESS TESTIMONY: WHAT WE KNOW

How would you respond to the following statements?

(1) Eyewitness testimony about an event can be affected by how the questions put to the witness are worded.

(2) Police instructions can affect an eyewitness's willingness to make an identification and/or the likelihood that he or she will identify a particular person.

(3) Eyewitness testimony about an event often reflects not only what was actually seen but information obtained later on.

(4) Eyewitness confidence is not a good predictor of his or her identification accuracy.

(5) An eyewitness's perception and memory of an event may be affected by his or her attitudes and expectations.

(6) The less time an eyewitness has to observe an event, the less well he or she will remember it.

(7) An eyewitness sometimes identifies as a culprit someone previously seen in another situation or context.

(8) The use of a one-person show-up instead of a full lineup increases the risk of misidentification.

(9) The rate of memory for an event is greatest right after an event and then levels off over time.

Kassin, Ellsworth and Smith (1989) submitted these and other items to 63 experts on eyewitness testimony, all of whom had published significant research on this topic. At least 80 percent of them agreed that the data concerning these items are reliable enough to present in court. Interestingly, 54 percent of the group had actually testified in court about eyewitness accounts on at least one occasion, the vast majority of the time for the defence in a criminal case. It appeared that the defence side was most likely to invite such testimony, but the experts indicated that they would be at least equally willing to testify for the prosecution.

What determines whether the testimony will be believed by the jurors? These issues of accuracy and credibility are discussed in turn.

What are the criteria used to judge the reliability of eyewitness testimony?

EYEWITNESS ACCURACY

Eyewitnesses are often not accurate. For example, in a series of experiments in which a "crime" was staged, subjects later showed large variations in their estimates of height (average error of 20 centimetres), hair colour (83 percent in error), and age (average error of eight years) of the perpetrator (Loftus, 1979). In another experiment (Buckhout, 1980), television viewers in New York City were shown a 127-second tape of an incident in which a mugger stole a woman's purse and then ran directly towards the camera. Viewers were then shown a six-person lineup that included the actual criminal, and were invited to identify that person. Of the 2145 viewers who called the station, only 15.3 percent correctly identified the mugger, a figure close to what would be expected by pure chance. In fact, 33 percent identified the white assailant as being black or Hispanic, and a few were even convinced that they had also been victimized by the same actor who appeared in the tape.

The U.S. Supreme Court in 1972 suggested five criteria for judging the reliability of eyewitness testimony:

(1) the opportunity of the witness, as he or she reports it, to view the criminal clearly at the time and place of the crime;

(2) the extent to which the witness was paying attention to the incident;

(3) the accuracy of the witness's description of the criminal *before* seeing the accused;

(4) the extent to which the witness is certain in his or her own mind;

(5) the time elapsed between the crime and the identification.

Many of these criteria are believed to be true by potential jurors as well (Kassin and Barndollar, 1992). In spite of the experience of these eminent jurists, the research does not provide convincing empirical support for any of these apparently reasonable criteria (Wells and Murray, 1983).

One study tested several of the above criteria (Yarmey, 1986a). Subjects were asked to imagine that they were in a park and were bystander witnesses to a crime in which a man assaulted and apparently raped a woman. They were shown a sequence of sixty colour slides depicting the crime, in which the level of light was varied to simulate broad daylight, early or late twilight, or night. Criterion (1) results: Subjects, as expected, recalled more and with greater accuracy in daylight or early twilight conditions. Criterion (3) results: There was no relationship between an accurate description of the criminal and later identification in a lineup. Criterion (4) results: Subjects who expressed a high degree of certainty about their choice were no more accurate than those who were less certain.

The certainty issue has been explored in a number of studies that have suggested that police officers are, somewhat surprisingly, not superior to other people in their capacities to perceive and remember accurately (Yarmey, 1979). Another study has shown that while police officers themselves and prosecuting lawyers agree that police are capable and credible witnesses, defence lawyers and the general public are somewhat more sceptical (Yarmey, 1986b).

A person's ability to remember a criminal incident accurately can be influenced by a number of factors. For example, we are usually better able to identify people of our own race than those of other races (Brigham and Malpass, 1985). In one study, black, white, and Asian students in the U.S. were all most accurate in identifying faces of their own race and differed widely in their capacity to recognize those of the other races (Luce, 1974). Similarly, black Africans and white Europeans were less accurate in identifying photographs of people of the other race (Shepherd, Deregowski and Ellis, 1974). In general, people tend to perceive people of other races as more similar to each other than they really are, hence errors are more likely to occur (Barkowitz and Brigham, 1982).

When people witness an event and are later exposed to new, often misleading information about that event, their recollections often become distorted (Loftus, 1992). In one study, subjects saw a simulated traffic accident. Then they received a written "report" about the accident in which, in some cases, incorrect information was provided; for example, a stop sign was referred to as a yield sign. These subjects tended to report that they had seen a yield sign rather than a stop sign, and those who were not exposed to such inaccurate information were more accurate in recalling the event. In other studies, people have been misled into recalling seeing such nonexistent items as broken glass, tape recorders, a barn (where there were in fact no buildings), and a moustache on a clean-shaven

What are the factors that distort memory?

misinformation effect
Memory becomes distorted when we are exposed to inaccurate information.

man. In the context of an adversarial trial, the implications of the **misinformation effect** are far-reaching indeed.

Stress can often influence and distort memory. For example, witnessing incidents that involve actual or threatened violence can cause stress and distress, even when the violence has not been directed at the witness (Yarmey and Jones, 1983a). Research also shows that people tend to fix their gazes on unusual or highly significant objects, such as a gun or other weapon, or an injured person (see Yarmey and Jones, 1983b; Christianson and Loftus, 1991). Their attention may be thus distracted from the face and other characteristics of the person committing the crime. As witnesses are often not aware of how distracted they were at the time, their testimony may be well-intended but unreliable, especially if the event was traumatic. Considerable research on the relationship between emotional stress and memory shows that eyewitnesses tend to be relatively accurate under these conditions in remembering central details but relatively inaccurate about peripheral details (Christianson, 1992).

Loftus and Burns (1982) compared the recall of subjects who had viewed a movie of a bank robbery in which a boy was shot in the face with the recall of a control group who saw the robbery but not the shooting. Subjects who had viewed the violent episode were much less likely to remember what they had witnessed prior to the shooting, such as the number on the boy's sweater. Other studies suggest that repeated recall trials may assist the person in remembering accurately. In one such experiment by Scrivner and Safer (1988), subjects first viewed a two-minute excerpt from a police training film in which a burglar breaks into a house, shoots several people, and then escapes. Expert viewers had identified 45 important details about the crime and the suspect. Immediately afterwards, subjects were given a few minutes to write down important details from the videotape on an answer sheet containing the numbers 1 through 47. The subjects were instructed to "replay the videotape" as though they had a VCR in their heads. Recall was then retested, and retested again 48 hours later. Subjects recalled increasingly more details on each successive recall trial, and the gain in recall was not a result of guessing.

THE POLICE LINEUP

Consider the police lineup, in which the suspect stands among a group, usually of five to nine persons, and the witness attempts to identify the guilty party. The procedure was devised to overcome the effects of bias that would arise if the witness were asked directly whether a particular person "did it." However, there is some evidence that witnesses are more likely to select someone as the perpetrator if that person is in a lineup than if that person is presented as a single suspect (Gonzalez, Ellsworth and Pembroke, 1993). It is argued that a "show-up" of a single suspect induces in the witness an absolute judgment, "This is the person that I saw," while a lineup leads to a relative judgment as to which of the people most resemble the witness's memory of the perpetrator.

The lineup procedure is subject to its own biases, including police bias, witness bias, situational bias, and response bias (Yarmey, 1979). Indeed, the principles underlying the design of a lineup procedure free of bias are, in some ways, similar to those involved in the design of research itself (Wells and Loftus, 1990) (see Chapter 1). Lineups are conducted by police officers to test their "hypothesis" regarding a suspect, and can be subject to "experimenter biases," such as leading questions to the witness ("How about the guy in the purple shirt on the right?").

The structure of a lineup can seriously bias the outcome (Doob and Kirshen-baum, 1973b). The study was based on an actual case, *Regina vs. Shatford,* in which conviction of the defendant was a direct result of the testimony of an eyewitness. Shatford had allegedly taken part in a holdup in which the cashier could later recall only that the robbers were "very neatly dressed, and rather good looking and they looked enough alike to be brothers." In spite of this vague description, she was able to pick Shatford out of a 12-person lineup nine days later. What she had done was simply select the best looking person in the lineup. If the police had inserted other, more attractive men into the lineup, the probability is that one of them might have been identified instead. The critical feature of a lineup is not the absolute number but the **functional number** of participants from which the witness may identify the culprit. For example, if the suspect is obese, and there is only one other obese person in the lineup, the total number of people in that lineup may be nine but the functional number is only two—and there is a 50 percent probability of one being identified by pure chance.

functional number The number of people in a lineup who share significant characteristics with the culprit.

Like experimental subjects, eyewitnesses generally want to be useful and may react to subtle demand characteristics. For example, they may feel compelled to identify *someone,* although none of the people in the lineup may be guilty. Stereotypes regarding dress, race, age, hair style, and other physical features may reflect response biases, particularly if these stereotypes are shared by the officers conducting the inquiry. Even lighting and noise levels in the room may influence judgments, particularly if these conditions differ from those at the scene of the crime.

How can accuracy be increased in this kind of procedure? In cases of multiple suspects, a mixed lineup might include both the suspects and **foils** who are not suspected of having committed that crime (Wells and Turtle, 1986). Further, a "preceding blank lineup," consisting entirely of non-suspects, may be used to identify eyewitnesses who are particularly prone to making false identifications (Wells, 1984). Yarmey (1979) argues that lineup identification procedures should be standardized more carefully and that the procedure should be conducted by an officer not involved in the case. Even better would be a "double-blind" procedure, in which neither the individual conducting the inquiry nor the others in the lineup would know who is suspected. It is apparent from the research conducted on this issue that social scientists, working with professionals in the law, can develop standards for lineups that would be scientifically defensible and consistent with the goals of justice (Brigham and Pfeifer, 1994).

foils People in the lineup who are not suspects.

How can the accuracy of police lineups be increased?

TESTIMONY: WHAT MAKES A CREDIBLE WITNESS?

In many trials, much hinges on the credibility of **expert testimony**. Expert witnesses can assist juries in evaluating evidence that they might otherwise have difficulty in comprehending, and can provide interpretations of events. As discussed in Chapter 4, the credibility of a source can rest on the perception that the source is expert. This perception is, in turn, based in part on the credentials of the expert and in part on the way he or she presents evidence. In one study, subjects read descriptions of a homicide case in which a battered woman killed her husband (Schuller, 1992). Some subjects were also exposed to expert testimony (by a clinical psychologist) concerning the "battered woman syndrome," a pattern characterized by feelings of fear and anxiety, a cyclical pattern of abuse, and

expert testimony That given by someone who is an authority in some area relevant to the trial.

overwhelming feelings of helplessness. The expert witness also testified about myths concerning abuse, such as the women staying because they "need" the beatings, or that they are "free" to leave at any time (Schuller and Vidmar, 1992). In some cases, the expert went on to identify the defendant as exhibiting this syndrome. Both individual and group decisions were more lenient to the defendant when accompanied by the expert testimony. The world was witness to the full effect of this process during the O.J. Simpson trial. There was a constant parade of expert witnesses, from glove buyers to DNA specialists, produced by one side or the other with the opposing counsel trying to discredit the testimony.

Of course, trials in our country are based upon an adversarial system in which lawyers act as unreserved advocates for one side. Witnesses are called to present evidence supporting one side, and can be cross-examined and challenged by the other side. Indeed, eyewitness testimony can be effectively discredited. A series of experiments shows how testimony can be influenced by the phrasing of questions.

In one study (Loftus, 1979), subjects were shown a film of an automobile accident in which a green car drove past the scene of the accident. Immediately after viewing the film, subjects were questioned about what they had seen. Some were asked: "Did the blue car that drove past the scene of the accident have a ski rack on the roof?" Others were asked the same question without the misleading word "blue." Later, subjects were asked to identify the colour of the car from a set of colour strips of various shades and hues. Most of those subjects who were asked about a "green car" selected a shade of green that closely matched the actual colour of the car. However, those who were asked about a "blue car" selected a shade of blue or blue-green consistent with what was suggested by the **leading question.** The effect occurred after an interval of twenty minutes and persisted over one week.

It must be noted that misleading questions bias the testimony of witnesses only under certain conditions. One study found that if subjects have already reported accurately on the event, e.g. by a free-recall report, then misleading questions are unlikely to cause later inaccuracies (Yuille, 1980). Indeed, memory for items that are central to the witnessed event is less likely to be influenced by misleading questions than is memory for peripheral details (Dritsas and Hamilton, cited in Loftus, 1979). However, the astute lawyer may capitalize on errors in peripheral details to discredit the witness. Any competent lawyer knows that casting doubt on even one minor point in the testimony of a witness can destroy the witness's credibility. Indeed, it seems that the capacity of a witness to recall many details impresses juries, as demonstrated in the following.

In two experiments (Bell and Loftus, 1989), subjects serving as mock jurors read summaries of a case involving robbery and murder. In the first experiment, the apparent ability of the prosecution witness to remember trivial detail was varied in different experimental conditions (e.g. what kinds of candy and pop were purchased by the defendant), while in the second experiment, the ability of the defence witness to recall trivial detail was also varied. In both cases, the condition in which the witness for the prosecution recalled trivial detail resulted in more judgments of guilt, especially when the defence witness was unable to recall such detail. Subsequent questioning of the jurors revealed that they made inferences about the attentiveness, capacity for facial memory, and general credibility of the prosecution witness from this recall of trivial detail.

How do misleading questions affect the recall of witnesses?

leading question One that includes misinformation in order to lead the witness to a desired response.

How does the type of question asked affect accuracy and memory for detail?

Research suggests that the procedures of giving testimony might be improved.

In one study (Marquis, Marshall and Oskamp, 1972), subjects viewed a film in which two young men witnessed a female pedestrian being knocked down by a car. A fight ensues between her male companion and the driver, and the two onlookers subsequently become involved in the argument. Trained observers had previously identified 884 distinct "facts" regarding the people and events in the film. All subjects were first asked to give a report of what happened in as much detail as possible. Then they were questioned in one of four formats: (1) broad, general questions; (2) specific questions equivalent to direct examination; (3) forced-choice "leading" questions equivalent to an aggressive cross-examination; or (4) multiple-choice questions of the type known and loved by most students. The results (Figure 13-2) show that each technique has advantages and disadvantages. Free recall provides great accuracy, but relatively few details. Under more direct questioning, accuracy is somewhat reduced but the testimony becomes more complete. Perhaps witnesses should be allowed to narrate freely with as few interpretations as possible in the early stage of testimony. Then, subsequent questioning could elicit more detail.

FIGURE 13-2 Percentage of facts identified and accuracy under different testimony conditions

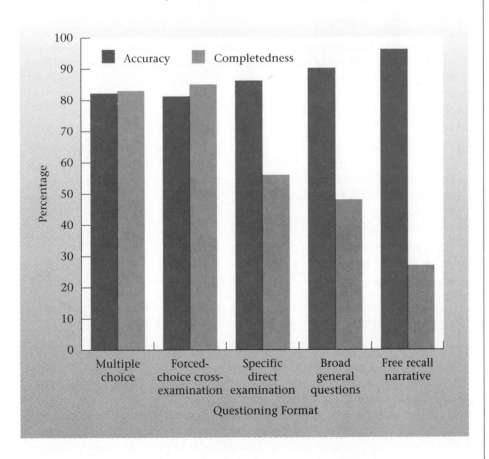

SELF-TEST QUESTIONS

1. Which of the following has *not* been shown by research to be a characteristic of defendants that is relevant to the outcome of trials?

a) gender

b) socioeconomic status

c) prior offences

d) the race of the defendant relative to the race of the jurors

2. Which of the following has been shown to be associated with the accuracy of eyewitness testimony?

a) high level of certainty

b) level of illumination

c) expertise and experience

d) all of the above

3. Eyewitnesses are more able to identify correctly

a) members of their own race

b) members of another race

c) people of any race

d) people in twilight conditions

4. If a suspect is described as being bald, and there are two short bald people and three tall bald people in a lineup of ten, then the functional number in the lineup is

a) 2

b) 3

c) 5

d) 7

5. The study by Loftus in which eyewitnesses saw a film of an automobile accident involving a green car showed the effects of _____ on eyewitness accuracy.

a) demand characteristics

b) leading questions

c) level of illumination

d) colour of the car

THE JURY

Much of the research in the social psychology of law has concerned the deliberations of the jury. Of course, the jury is a natural focus because it is important and visible, and because the deliberations of a jury are so essentially a social psychological process, involving leadership, influence, and conformity. Juries also involve such group dynamics as the fundamentals of social perception, cognition and memory, and prejudice and other relevant attitudes. Of course, it is not possible to intervene directly in a real trial in order to study it, and it is impossible to recapture the environment in the laboratory (see Bray and Kerr, 1982).

Research uses jury simulations, in which summaries of the evidence and arguments are presented briefly to jurors in oral or written form. Many are studies of individual "jurors," in which influences on the decisions of individuals, but not the group decision, are examined. Others use the format of **mock juries**, in which subjects are presented with evidence, perhaps arguments by "lawyers," perhaps instructions by a "judge," and then must deliberate and reach a verdict.

mock juries The study of jury processes using subjects who act as jurors.

One topic that has been successfully studied through simulations is the choice of jury leader. This choice can have a significant effect upon the discussion and final decision of a jury. Research shows that the person most likely to be selected will be:

(1) the person who is sitting at the head of the table at the first meeting,

(2) one who has had previous experience as a juror,

(3) someone of a higher socioeconomic class (Strodtbeck and Lipinski, 1985).

The selection process is generally very straightforward and uncontroversial, apparently influenced by the jurors' prototype of a leader.

But do these simulations really represent the reality of the courtroom? Recall from the discussion in Chapter 1 that the validity of research can be evaluated: (1) in terms of how much we can generalize from our sample and procedures; and (2) in terms of how much the experimental situation represents the real-world environment of the courtroom. On both counts, the simulation studies leave much to be desired.

Who is most likely to be chosen as jury leader?

One problem is that jury studies often use only university students as subjects. A group made up entirely of university students is hardly representative of the typical heterogeneous groups drawn from a pool of eligible jurors. Indeed, there is some evidence that mock juries of students are more likely to acquit than are actual jury pool groups (Simon and Mahan, 1971). Further, some studies simply have people vote on a verdict without allowing them to deliberate to reach a unanimous decision. Such studies eliminate the crucial role of social influence on a group decision.

Real juries sit through an entire trial, while simulated juries read summaries or view videotaped excerpts. Real juries are exposed to a much richer array of information, including important non-verbal cues by lawyers, defendants, and witnesses. In addition, real juries make decisions that can have serious consequences for the defendants and perhaps for society. Real juries are under considerable stress from many different sources.

How do the outcomes of jury simulations compare with those of real trials?

In 1995 there were two very high-profile trials, one in Canada and one in the United States. In both cases the juries were under severe pressure. When football hero O.J. Simpson went on trial in California on the charge of first-degree murder of his wife and her friend, the plight of jury members was one of the many features of the trial that compelled the world's attention. The jurors were locked away (sequestered) for 53 weeks, and allowed only censored newspapers and pre-approved videos, no telephones or radios, and minimal family visits—all for $5 a day. (In contrast, Canadian jurors receive $2.75 for the first 10 days, $40 a day up to day 50, and then $100 per day to trial's end). It is no wonder that by trial's end they were down to the last two alternates (they had begun with twelve). Ten of the original jurors had been dismissed.

While the Simpson trial was filling our homes on a daily basis, Paul Bernardo was on trial in Toronto on a charge of first-degree murder of two Ontario teenagers. Much of the jury's stress in this trial came from viewing the explicit video evidence of the young women's deaths—evidence that reduced many, including members of the court, to tears. Yet as painful and as close to home as the Bernardo trial was, we probably know more about the American justice system than our own.

Of course this is because the laws in the United States and Canada are very different as to the media coverage allowed both before and during a trial. For example, the trial judge in the Bernardo case would not permit the press to talk to, take pictures of, or videotape prospective jurors. TV cameras are not permitted in Canadian courts. Nor is it permitted to report anything that happens out of view of the jurors. In the United States, however, over 40 states allow TV cameras during trials. According to Canadian-born Harvard law school professor Paul Weiler, "the difference between the United States and Canada is the difference between a country that makes freedom of speech a priority and a country that makes due process and a fair trial a priority" (*Maclean's,* May 29, 1995). There are, in fact, many significant differences between the two systems. For example, in Canada criminal law is federal while in the U.S. most criminal law is the responsibility of the state. This makes for a much greater variation in the administration of justice in the U.S.

Because both the process of selection and the pressures on a jury have very significant impacts on the outcome of a trial, we will examine in some detail (Box 13-2) how the Canadian and U.S. systems differ with respect to the jury, using the Bernardo and Simpson trials as illustration.

THE JUROR

The research shows that jurors who are older, less educated, and of lower socio-economic levels are more likely to vote to convict (see Nemeth, 1981). Male and female jurors behave in a similar fashion, except in rape trials. Under these circumstances females are more likely to convict and to favour harsh sentences (Nemeth, 1981). Another predictor is the extent of similarity between jurors and the defendant: for example, a French-speaking female carpenter is more likely to receive a lenient judgment from jurors who also have one or more of these characteristics, an outcome consistent with the similarity-attraction rule (see Chapter 7).

One characteristic that has been studied extensively is **authoritarianism**, behaviour in which individuals display rigid thinking, political conservatism and social conventionality, submissiveness to authority, and a hostile, punitive orientation towards those who deviate in any way from social norms (Adorno, Frenkel-Brunswick, Levinson and Sanford, 1950; see Chapter 6). For example, when mock-jury subjects were contacted one week after an experiment, high authoritarians recalled more about the defendant's character but less about the evidence (Berg and Vidmar, 1975). Authoritarians are more apt to convict and to recommend severe sentences, particularly if the defendant is not similar to themselves (Mitchell and Byrne, 1973). However, authoritarians are *less* likely to convict if the defendant is perceived as representing authority, e.g., a police officer. Apparently, authoritarians and non-authoritarians have different schemata and use different kinds of information in arriving at their decisions.

authoritarianism
Behaviour characterized by rigid thinking, submissiveness to authority, and hostility towards those who are perceived as different.

How does authoritarianism affect a person's decision making?

BOX 13-2

A COMPARISON OF THE JURY SELECTION PROCESS IN THE BERNARDO AND SIMPSON TRIALS

	Bernardo	**Simpson**
Tried under criminal law of	Canada	California
Jury size	12 people chosen in 3 days; no alternates. Dismissed during trial: 0	12 people and 12 alternates. Took 5 weeks. Dismissed during trial: 10
Questioning potential jurors	Minimal questions: 7	Initial questionnaire with 75 pages (294 questions); later extensive oral questions
Rejecting potential jurors	Up to 20 per side without cause (peremptory challenge)	Up to 20 per side without cause (peremptory challenge)
	Unlimited number for cause	Unlimited number for cause
Length of trial	14 weeks	53 weeks
Sequestered	Not until after judge's final instructions because of media ban	Yes, for 38 weeks under strict supervision because of intensive media coverage
Media coverage	Can only report what transpires in presence of jury	Total TV coverage audience estimated at 110 million

Jurors also differ in the important characteristic of prejudice, which may extend to witnesses or even officials of the court as well as the accused. In one study (Pfeifer, 1989), subjects acting in the role of jurors viewed an audiovisual presentation of a trial. The prosecuting lawyer, played by a male or female, was vigorously engaged in questioning a submissive male defendant. Male, but not female subjects rated the defendant as less likely to be guilty when the prosecutor was female. Interestingly, the male jurors also rated the female prosecutor as more effective than did female jurors. Thus, the subjects expressed their sexism in an indirect or "symbolic" manner, not by downgrading the female prosecutor who acted against stereotypical expectations, but by voting "not guilty."

THE VERDICT: PROCESSES OF JUDGMENT

Thus far we have discussed how external factors, such as characteristics of the defendant and the nature of testimony, can influence judgments. Now we turn to a consideration of some of the cognitive processes that contribute to arriving at a verdict. Pennington and Hastie (1992) observe that jurors construct a "story," a narrative of what happened based on information presented at the trial. In this way, causal relationships between events and intentions of the actors are crucial to the decision that is reached. Of course, factors such as the credibility of the witnesses and the input of lawyers on both sides of the case will have a great bearing on how the jurors put together pieces of information to construct a narrative that makes sense to them.

In order to determine that the accused is "guilty," the judge and/or jurors must make judgments regarding who is telling the truth and who is not, and must make an attribution that the person not only acted in a certain way but is responsible for the consequences of that action. The perceived role of Detective Mark Fuhrman in the O. J. Simpson case demonstrates just how important this issue is. Did he find the bloody glove or plant it? The jury had to decide how credible this man was as a witness. We will now consider how people detect deception in others and how they attribute responsibility.

deception clues *Behaviour that suggests an attitude different from what is expressed.*

leakage *Behaviour that mistakenly reveals the truth.*

What are some of the ways we detect deception?

DETECTING DECEPTION

It has been found that, in general, people can distinguish truth from lies at somewhat better than a chance level (Miller and Burgoon, 1982; Zuckerman, DePaulo and Rosenthal, 1981). However, there are several varieties of deception. Ekman and Friesen (1969) have distinguished between **deception clues**, which are present when a person's behaviour suggests that he or she is lying, and **leakage**, in which the truth is mistakenly revealed. For example, patients who wring their hands while assuring the doctor that they feel fine provide a deception clue that they may feel ill, or may be angry at the doctor, or fearful about the future. A slip of the tongue or a non-verbal response to a specific question may provide leakage about the fact that they are feeling ill, angry, or fearful. Research has not indicated that people who are skillful at detecting one of these types of clues are also skillful in detecting the other.

Since deception can sometimes be detected, there must be valid cues that observers use to decide whether or not a person is being deceptive. It appears that there are some verbal and non-verbal indicators that are more likely to occur when a person is lying. In general, when people are lying, their speech has a higher pitch, they are more nervous and less fluent, and they give less plausible and shorter answers with longer hesitations prior to responding. The long pause seems to be particularly powerful in alerting observers to the possibility that deception is taking place (Kraut, 1978). While individuals make some effort to control facial expression when trying to deceive someone, they are less aware of the "language" of the rest of the body (Ekman and Friesen, 1974). It has been reported that judges are more accurate in detecting disguised emotions when viewing the body rather than the face. However, when factual material is involved, judgments based on the face are more accurate (Littlepage and Pineault, 1979). Box 13-3 examines mechanical lie detection with a discussion of the polygraph.

Is the defendant guilty? Some observers would find the gender of the prosecutor important in determining this.

ATTRIBUTION OF RESPONSIBILITY

The concept of responsibility in law is crucial. We can compare two views of responsibility that correspond to two different goals. The older and simpler view is that when laws are broken, the causal agent must be identified in order for justice to be done and to maintain the social order: an eye for an eye, a tooth for a tooth, or amputation of the hand of a thief. Viewed in this manner, motives, intentions, or consequences of the action are not important. What matters is the attribution of responsibility, or who did it. The more modern conception of responsibility is based on the intentions of the actor, not just the act, and on the social desire to reform the actor into a productive citizen and to prevent a recurrence. Therefore, consideration of responsibility must take into account the intentions of the actor.

Convicting someone of a crime such as murder implies not only that an action occurred but that the person intended to cause a consequence; the murderer shot with the purpose of killing the victim rather than in self-defence or accidentally confusing the victim with a nearby moose. As well, a successful lawsuit for medical malpractice implies an attribution of responsibility to the physician in the sense of neglect or incompetence. Of course, the law also accepts the influence of consequences in judging an action. The only difference between murder and attempted murder might be inaccurate shooting, an absence of emergency medical care for the victim, or pure luck.

The law also accepts the attribution of diminished responsibility. In 1843 a young man named Daniel M'Naghten, while attempting to kill British Prime Minister Sir Robert Peel, killed his private secretary instead. M'Naghten's lawyer presented a novel defence, arguing that his client could not be held legally responsible for his actions because he was under the "insane delusion" that he was being hounded by Peel and many other enemies. The historic judgment,

BOX 13-3
LIE DETECTION AND THE POLYGRAPH

It is obvious that we cannot have "justice" in a criminal justice system unless we can determine the truth. In medieval Britain, an accused was required to swallow a "trial slice" of bread and cheese. It was reasoned that an inability to swallow it would indicate a dry mouth, which might indicate lying. Today in our high-tech world we have the polygraph, a controversial technique used not only in the legal system, but by private corporations to screen employees.

The polygraph measures physiological changes, particularly skin conductance (which indicates perspiration), and often blood pressure and respiratory rate. In general, the polygraph can indicate changes in the level of physiological *arousal* as the person responds to various questions. However, we cannot conclude that a person is lying if he or she shows increased arousal to critical questions ("Did you murder your wife?") but not to neutral questions ("Did you eat ice cream in the past week?"). There are many possible reasons for arousal even when one is innocent: one may be upset that the woman was murdered, may fear being falsely accused, may feel shame at being suspected by the police.

Thus, more sophisticated techniques are used. For example, reactions are compared while the person responds to critical, neutral, and control questions. It is reasoned that while the person may show increased arousal to any questions concerning the situation, a heightened level of arousal would be shown if upset is combined with lying. Thus, reactions might be compared while the person responded to a general, control question ("Did *someone* murder your wife?") and then to a specific question ("Did *you* murder your wife?"). Another technique is to ask about details that only the perpetrator and police would know. For example, if the victim was wearing a green sweater, we would ask a series of yes/no questions: Was the victim wearing a green sweater? a white sweater? a blue ski jacket? a grey parka? a brown fur coat? If the accused shows arousal only to the true item while denying knowledge in all of them, then we may be on to something.

The research indicates accuracy from 70 to 90 percent of the time, which is impressive but not foolproof or "beyond a reasonable doubt" (Lykken, 1974; Yarmey, 1979; Horvath, 1977, 1984). There is evidence that certain types of people, or those who have been coached beforehand, can "beat the machine," e.g. by mentally distracting themselves during critical questions or biting their tongues during neutral questions (Honts, Hodes and Raskin, 1985). There are also important ethical and legal issues, such as invasion of privacy and self-incrimination. Perhaps, in the end, there is no substitute for competent and professional police work.

M'Naghten Rule *Used to acquit defendants when they do not know their behaviour is wrong.*

known as the **M'Naghten Rule**, acquitted the defendant because "he did not know the nature and quality of the act he was doing, or if he did know it ... he did not know he was doing wrong." With various modifications, this rule still applies in most jurisdictions. For example, in 1982 a man was not convicted of the attempted murder of President Ronald Reagan because he was acting under the obsession of winning the heart and mind of the movie star, Jodie Foster. The principle is still controversial.

Research has shown that the attribution of responsibility is influenced by the severity of consequences of the act. In an experiment by Walster (1966) subjects were given a report about an accident. The driver, Lennie, left his car parked at the top of the hill. The parking brake cable came loose, and the car rolled down the hill and caused some damage. Subjects were asked to indicate the extent to which they attributed responsibility to Lennie for the accident. Interestingly, Lennie was held more responsible when severe damage happened or when someone was hurt than when the damage was minimal, even though there is no logic in making this distinction. Lennie was no more or less negligent in not having his brake checked, whether the consequences were severe, mild, or non-existent. This effect, although rather small, has been found in many studies (Burger, 1981). In another study that replicated the severity of consequences effect, it was also found that individuals who were described as highly anxious or paranoid were assigned less responsibility for their actions. However, a protagonist described as an alcoholic was assigned more blame, even though the alcoholic was also rated as highest in "mental illness" (Sadava, Angus and Forsyth, 1980).

Why would more responsibility be attributed to someone when the consequences are more severe? Walster (1966) has suggested that we act in a defensive manner. We hold the victim more responsible for the action because to interpret it as an outcome of bad luck or an "act of God" would be to admit to the possibility that it could happen to us. Shaver (1970) has added two conditions that will arouse this defensiveness: (1) the situation described is one similar to our own, and (2) the person involved is similar enough to us that we could imagine ourselves "in that person's shoes."

Many issues surface in rape trials. Certainly a significant one is attribution of responsibility. A discussion of this and other issues can be found in Box 13-4.

What are the factors that influence how we attribute responsibility?

BOX 13-4

PRIOR RECORD OF THE VICTIM: THE CASE OF RAPE

To convict someone of sexual assault we must attribute responsibility to the perpetrator and not to the victim. Indeed, to perceive someone as a victim, one must assume that she or he did not intend or wish for the act or its consequences to occur. While this is reasonable, what is not reasonable is a bias towards blaming the victim, or the strategy of presenting evidence or allegations about the sexual behaviour of the victim in order to cast doubt on her intentions.

In one revealing study (Coates et al., 1979), male and female subjects, believing they were evaluating material for a community crime-awareness program, listened to a tape-recorded interview with a rape "victim." Following a description of the event, the interviewer asked her a number of questions, including "Do you feel in any way responsible for what happened?" In one version the victim attributed the event to pure bad luck, and in another version, the victim claimed that the rape was largely her own fault. In general, subjects were more favourable to the victim when she accepted responsibility and when she seemed to have regained her emotional balance than when she denied personal responsibility and was still suffering consequences. Paradoxically, while

women empathized more with the victim, they also tended to attribute more responsibility to her and expressed more derogatory feelings towards her. We reject the victim precisely when she seems to be most victimized (echoes of the "just world hypothesis" discussed in Chapter 2).

Borgida and White (1978) manipulated two factors in a mock jury study of a rape case: the likelihood that the victim consented and the introduction of evidence on the victim's prior sexual history. Interestingly, jurors were less likely to convict the accused rapist when any evidence about the victim's prior history was introduced, even when it showed the victim in a favourable light. Another study showed that irrelevant characteristics of the victim, including her marital status (especially if divorced), her sexual experience, and her profession, influenced judgments about her responsibility for the rape and how much she was affected psychologically by the assault (Feldman-Summers and Lindner, 1976). It also seems that rape victims who appear to be emotionally restrained, who do not express visible emotional distress, are viewed as less believable (Calhoun, Selby and King, 1976). Finally, if the couple had had sex a number of times previously, people are more reluctant to label a clearly-described act of forced intercourse as rape, and to agree with a statement that the aggrieved partner was obligated to have sex with her partner (Shotland and Goodstein, 1992).

Clearly there are a number of reasons why many crimes, including rape, are not reported to the authorities. Fear of reprisal from the perpetrator, feelings of helplessness, and the conviction that the police are powerless to arrest and/or punish appropriately the perpetrator are important factors (Kidd and Chayet, 1984). A study that examined both court records and the records of a service for sexual assault victims showed that the former consisted of instances of women, some of whom had been drinking, violently assaulted by atypical men, while the latter, those that often did not reach court, recorded larger numbers of women assaulted in the context of pursuing normal heterosexual activities (Yurchesyn, Keith and Renner, 1992). Perhaps most disturbing is the fear of being further victimized by the authorities. Interviews with 140 actual rape victims in the U.S. revealed that the primary reason why the victim often did not press charges was her belief that she would be held up for judgment and that she would be traumatized in court (Holstrom and Burgess, 1978). In response to this problem, recent court practice has been to shift the burden of proof to the defence to demonstrate that any such evidence or examination is relevant to the case.

SELF-TEST QUESTIONS

SELF TEST

6. Studies suggest that jurors are more likely to convict a defendant who
a) has a previous record of criminal conviction
b) is charged with a serious offence
c) gives testimony as a witness
d) is female

7. Mock juries made up of students are more likely to
a) acquit
b) find the defendant guilty
c) ignore the testimony
d) argue with the judge

8. Studies show high authoritarians are less likely to convict
a) women
b) authority figures
c) people unlike themselves
d) well-dressed people

9. Acquiting defendants because they did not know that what they did was wrong is based on
a) legislation
b) testimony
c) The M'Naghten Rule
d) none of the above

10. When the consequences of an act are severe people judge the defendant as being
a) less responsible
b) more responsible

c) unfortunate

d) a and c

THE JUDGE

INSTRUCTIONS OF THE JUDGE

In a jury trial the judge can still exert enormous influence. The judge must interpret the law to the jury, explaining the notions of presumption of innocence, burden of proof, and the phrase "beyond a reasonable doubt." He or she must rule on motions by the lawyers on both sides concerning procedural matters, including the admissibility of evidence. After all evidence has been presented and all arguments made, the judge instructs the jury on the meaning of the charges, the alternative decisions open to them (e.g., first- or second-degree murder) and even on the evidence and the credibility of key witnesses (Cavoukian and Doob, 1980). Indeed, some judges present instructions to the jury that are so lengthy and so technical that the jurors fail to understand them (Elwork, Sales and Alfini, 1982).

This is illustrated by a case in Quebec in 1993. Two jurors voted to convict because they had not understood the judge's discussion of "the right to dissent or disagree" with the rest of the jury. It is possible that up to 60 percent of jury members "do not understand the concepts of dissent, innocence, and reasonable doubt," according to Michael Sabourin of the University of Montreal. He is a psychologist who studies juries. In his view, "judges try to use the simplest words possible, but there are never guarantees—it's a bit worrisome" (*Burlington Spectator*, July 9, 1996).

Judges may instruct juries to disregard a piece of evidence as unreliable or as irrelevant to the case. Research using mock juries suggests that jurors do not always heed these instructions, for example, when information about the prior record of the defendant is presented (Doob and Kirschenbaum, 1972). Indeed, one experiment (Wolf and Montgomery, 1977) found that when judges gave strong instructions—"It must play no role in your consideration of the case. You have no choice but to disregard it"—the testimony had even greater impact on jurors than it did in the absence of any instructions. Even judges may be influenced by the defendant's prior record, perhaps in very subtle ways. A study of actual trials reveals that when judges (but not juries) were aware of the prior record of the defendant, the final instructions tended to lack tolerance or patience, and verdicts were more likely to be guilty (Goleman, 1986).

A realistic experiment was conducted by Tanford and Penrod (1984), in which experienced jurors watched videotaped re-enactments of trials involving a defendant charged with either a single offence or that same offence plus two others. Jurors judging the offence by itself were less likely to vote guilty than those judging the offence in combination with the two other charges (24 percent as opposed to 39 percent). Elaborate and pointed instructions from the judges to ignore the fact that there were three charges failed to have any significant impact on the decisions of jurors. On the basis of evidence from both experimental studies and trial records, Tanford (1990) argues that admonitions to the jury are ineffective and even counter-productive.

However, other studies show that these instructions can have an impact. Jurors in a mock jury study who scored high on a measure of "dogmatism" (a generalized

What effect does the judge's instruction have on jury decisions?

form of authoritarianism) tended to be more influenced by the judges' instructions (Kerwin and Shaffer, 1991). In another experiment (Stephan and Stephan, 1986), subject jurors read summaries of an assault case and then heard the testimony of the defendant who spoke either English or another language (Spanish, Thai) which was translated by an interpreter. Subjects were more likely to find a non-English-speaking defendant guilty. However, the language bias was offset among subjects who had been instructed by the judge to ignore the fact that the testimony had been translated. Perhaps in such multicultural nations as Canada instructions of this nature should be standard procedure.

SENTENCING PRACTICES

The moment finally arrives when the jury is finished with its deliberations, brings in a decision to convict, and the judge must decide on a sentence. The law sets upper and lower limits on sentences, and may also provide latitude in alternatives such as prison, fines, or time spent in public service. In arriving at a sentence the judge must examine the severity of the crime, the prior record of the defendant, and other factors about the defendant that may suggest possibilities of re-offending or rehabilitation. There is great variability in sentences imposed for the same offence. This variability is related to the characteristics of the case and the defendant, the orientation of the judge, and the geographical region in which the trial takes place (Clancy et al., 1981).

There are reasons for this apparent inconsistency in sentencing. Judgments about sentencing, as about guilt, may be influenced by extraneous characteristics of the defendant. One American study recorded the fines or bail amounts set by male and female judges for over two thousand male and female defendants. Attractiveness of each defendant was rated by police officers. Attractive defendants tended to be treated somewhat more leniently in misdemeanor cases but not in the more serious felony cases (termed indictable offences in Canada). In addition, the values or philosophies of judges may differ; some may be biased towards the victim or see crime as a moral problem necessitating retribution, and thus impose harsher sentences. Others may favour rehabilitation rather than harsh treatment of the offender. Still others may be influenced by the deterrent effect of severe sentences, particularly in the case of crimes that are of unusual concern to society at that time. Perhaps declaring Paul Bernardo, convicted murderer and rapist, as a dangerous offender with no opportunity for parole is an example of this. The presiding judge, a man with extensive legal experience and much respected in the legal community, referred to Bernardo as both sadistic and completely untreatable. During sentencing he said: "Mr. Bernardo, your life will be controlled. I hope you spend the rest of your natural life in prison. You have no right to be released...." (*The Globe and Mail*, November 4, 1995).

Attributions of responsibility that support sentencing decisions are also influenced by factors peculiar to each case, such as the apparent remorsefulness of the criminal or the suffering of the victim (Dane and Wrightsman, 1982). Finally, since the system favours individualized sentences—in which the punishment fits the criminal rather than only the crime—judges' decisions are further influenced by such social factors as the employment or marital status of the criminal.

ATTITUDES TOWARDS CRIME AND PUNISHMENT

Clearly, sentencing practices will or should reflect public attitudes. Thus it is a serious matter if many people believe that the punishments handed down do not

In sentencing, what factors do judges take into account?

fit the crimes. In a national opinion poll conducted in 1983, fully 79.5 percent of Canadians believed that the sentences imposed by our courts were generally too lenient (Doob and Roberts, 1984). By 1988 this had dropped to 65 percent. Another interesting finding was that 44 percent believed that criminal courts did a good job protecting the rights of the accused, while only 16 percent saw the courts doing a good job helping the victim (Statistics Canada, 1994).

Several studies show that this impression is not correct (Doob and Roberts, 1984). When subjects were presented with the information about the crime and the criminal that was available to the court, most were then satisfied with the sentence. One particular case had been given extensive newspaper coverage, including an editorial that criticized the "leniency" of the sentence. When presented with only the newspaper accounts, 63 percent rated the sentence as "too lenient," but when given a summary of the information actually presented in court, only 19 percent rated the sentence as "too lenient" and 52 percent as "too harsh." Indeed, a similar pattern is observed with regard to the early release of prisoners. While public attitudes towards parole in general may be negative and punitive, early release is generally accepted when people are informed of the circumstances in specific cases (Cumberland and Zamble, 1992). Evidently we are influenced by the "availability" heuristic, in which we use the few, sensationalized cases that we can remember to arrive at a generalized judgment about the courts.

Perhaps the most controversial and persistent issue is **capital punishment**. Vidmar (1974) points out that proponents of capital punishment support their position for both **retributive justice** and for **utilitarian** reasons. Many argue that for a crime such as murder, the death penalty is the only punishment that "fits," and that justice is retribution in kind. They also argue that capital punishment can fulfill utilitarian functions for society, such as deterring others from committing such crimes, ensuring that the criminal will never do it again, or saving taxpayers' money from being used to support one more prisoner. In one study of 144 adults in Ontario, Vidmar (1974) found that retribution was, indeed, the most important reason cited by proponents, and that the majority of them would still favour the death penalty if provided with information showing that there was no deterrent effect (Sarat and Vidmar, 1976). Proponents of retributive capital punishment tend to be authoritarian and accepting of military "crimes of obedience" (Hamilton, 1976), and are more likely to vote to convict a defendant than are those opposed to the death penalty (Bersoff, 1987).

It may also be true that many jurors would be more reluctant to convict murderers if the death penalty were a possible outcome. Freedman (1990) arranged for special permission to contact Canadian jurors after verdicts had been rendered in murder cases, to ascertain whether their decisions would have been affected if the death penalty had been in effect. Fully 30 percent of them reported that they would have been less likely to convict in those cases, while three percent would have been more likely to convict. It is also interesting to consider that, where the death penalty exists, jurors are generally dismissed if they oppose capital punishment. These individuals also tend to be less authoritarian, and thus the remaining jurors are more likely to convict (Pennington and Hastie, 1990). Therefore, the death penalty introduces bias in jury selection.

The evidence, while never absolutely free of competing interpretations, does not support the hypothesis that capital punishment deters murder. In Canada, while 66.5 percent of Canadians believe that more murders have been committed in the years since the abolition of capital punishment in 1976, the facts show a decrease

How do Canadians view the justice system?

capital punishment *Use of the death penalty.*

retributive justice *Punishment that matches the crime.*

utilitarian *Considered as serving a function in society.*

How would a utilitarian defend using capital punishment?

in that period (Doob and Roberts, 1984). A study conducted in the U.S. also shows that in this century, 343 people are known to have been wrongfully convicted of murder and 25 have actually been executed (*The Globe and Mail,* November 15, 1985). In view of the evidence of bias and error in our judicial procedures, we can assume a similar injustice in Canada. After a study of how the death penalty is applied across the world, Amnesty International has adopted a position that opposes the practice for "all prisoners, without reservation." In 1987, the Canadian Parliament voted to continue abolition of capital punishment, consistent with the practice in most Western democracies except for some states in the U.S.

IMPLICATIONS AND TRENDS

Social psychology has found fertile ground in the study of legal processes. Indeed, research has contributed as much to an understanding of basic psychological processes—how we perceive and remember persons and events, how groups make important decisions, the influence of authority—as it has to an understanding of eyewitness testimony, juries, and the influence of the judge. In this chapter we have only touched upon some of the research and a few of the problems under study. Research is also underway concerning the child as a witness, police investigation, biases in civil law (virtually all of the research conducted up till now has concerned criminal law), as well as the influence of law and the justice system outside the courtroom.

One caveat here pertains to the ethical implications of practising social psychology in this area (see Chapter 1). If social psychologists are to testify in court or to do valid and reliable pre-trial consultation (e.g. jury selection, evaluation of eyewitness testimony), it is imperative that this work be reliable and competent, and that the intent of the process, particularly the goals of justice, not be distorted.

Acceptance of social psychology research is far from universal within the domain of the law; there is still some scepticism and misunderstanding about the scientific method, sampling, and simulation research. As research advances and becomes more sophisticated methodologically, we can expect the effects on the legal process to expand accordingly.

SELF **?** TEST

SELF-TEST QUESTIONS

11. Those who say the death penalty serves a utilitarian function for society use the following argument(s)

a) it deters others from committing murder

b) it ensures the accused will not repeat the crime

c) it saves taxpayers the money required to support the person in jail

d) all of the above

12. In the years since the abolishment of capital punishment in 1976, the murder rate in Canada has

a) decreased

b) increased

c) stayed the same

d) not been recorded

13. Judgments about sentencing vary greatly and are affected by

a) the geographical region in which the trial takes place

b) the values of the judge

c) the apparent remorsefulness of the defendant

d) all of the above

14. When judges' final instructions lack tolerance for the defendant, verdicts are more likely to be

a) guilty

b) not guilty

c) unclear

d) undecided

SUMMARY

(1) Defendants who are attractive or baby-faced tend to be treated better by judges and juries. Jurors tend to be more lenient towards defendants who belong to their own racial group and whose attitudes are similar to their own.

(2) The reliability of eyewitnesses is questionable in a number of circumstances. Important factors include police lineup procedures, stress, time elapsed between incident and recall, and the nature of the protagonist, but not the confidence of the eyewitness.

(3) Testimony can be influenced and biased by the phrasing of questions.

(4) Witness credibility is affected by the capacity of the witness to recall trivial detail, the credibility of the lawyer, and whether the witness identifies or does not identify the defendant.

(5) Findings from simulated jury studies indicate bias in the selection of jurors, and biases among jurors that relate particularly to authoritarianism.

(6) Juries are sometimes not influenced by the instructions of the judges.

(7) Deception may occur by commission (telling a lie) or omission (concealing or omitting something). Individuals vary in their capacity to use verbal and non-verbal cues to detect deception.

(8) Attributions of responsibility are influenced by the severity of consequences of the act.

(9) Inconsistencies in sentencing are related to the characteristics of the defendant and the crime, prior record, the values and legal philosophy of the judge, and the social climate regarding crime.

FOR REVIEW

There are many aspects of the justice system that affect the verdict in a trial. Race and appearance are two factors that might affect how the _____(1) is viewed. Seeing a _____(2) event can cause enough stress to distort the memory of an _____(3). In a _____(4) people may feel pressured to identify someone

FOR REVIEW

even if the guilty person is not present. _____(5) testimony often leads to decisions that are more _____(6).

Juries are often impressed by a witness who has a good memory for _____(7) details. Research suggests that when questioning is more direct _____(8) is somewhat reduced but the testimony is more _____(9).

A problem with decisions made by _____(10) juries is that the role of _____(11) is missing. _____(12) is a characteristic that might lead a juror to convict. Jurors often construct a _____(13) in their minds to help organize their understanding of events. People are able to detect deception by identifying either _____(14) clues or _____(15). When people are lying their speech has a _____(16) pitch and answers become _____(17). Judgments based on the _____(18) rather than on _____(19) tend to be more accurate when the material is factual. The attribution of responsibility takes into account not only that the crime was committed but that there was also _____(20) to commit the crime.

There is some controversy about whether the instructions of the _____(21) to the jury has any real impact on the outcome of the trial. People tend to believe that sentences are too _____(22) when they base their opinion on newspaper accounts. This view is reversed when access to information is available to the _____(23). Research suggests that jurors might be less likely to convict murderers in Canada if we had the _____(24).

ISSUES AND ACTIVITIES

1. Using the Web sites listed at the end of this chapter as a starting point, research some aspect of the Canadian justice system that you find interesting. Examine how your findings relate to the research discussed in this chapter.

2. Visit a provincial court while a trial is in progress. Make notes about your perceptions of the proceedings. Based on what you observed and what you have learned from the studies in this chapter, could you make a prediction about the outcome? Support your "verdict" with these notes. At the end of the trial find out what the real verdict was. If it was guilty, how was the accused sentenced? Based on your observations, what factors do you believe were most influential in reaching this decision?

3. The CBC video *Jury on Trial* (Prime Time News) identifies a controversy about questioning witnesses. What positions do the two lawyers (defence and Crown) take on the subject? What arguments do they use to support their views? Which position takes us closer to the American style? (See Box 13-2.) Discuss which point of view you favour and why.

• FURTHER READING

EKMAN, P. (1985). *Telling lies: Clues to deceit in the marketplace, politics and marriage.* New York: Norton. A fascinating non-technical discussion of the practice and uses of deception in society. Based on solid research and includes an examination of historical and ethical issues.

KAGEHIRO D.K. and LAUFER, W.S. (Eds.) (1992). *Handbook of psychology and the law.* New York: Springer-Verlag. A massive volume of 29 chapters dealing with every aspect of how psychology intersects with the legal system, including eyewitness testimony, expert witnesses, the insanity defence, effects of pretrial publicity, effective jury size, and much more.

KONECNI V.J. and EBBESEN, E.B. (1982). *The criminal justice system: A social psychological analysis.* San Francisco: Freedman. A wide-ranging review of various aspects of the system, including some archival studies.

WRIGHTSMAN, L.S., KASSIN, S.M. and WILLIS, C.E. (Eds.) (1987). *In the jury box: Controversies in the courtroom.* Beverly Hills, CA.: Sage. A useful collection of papers on jury selection, juror biases, the competence of juries, and the jury size and decision rules.

WRIGHTSMAN, L.S., WILLIS C.E. and KASSIN, S.M. (Eds.) (1987). *On the witness stand: Controversies in the courtroom.* Beverly Hills: Sage. A good collection of papers about lie detectors, hypnotic assistance of memory, eyewitness accuracy, the social psychologist as an expert witness, and TV cameras in the courtroom.

YARMEY, A.D. (1979). *The psychology of eyewitness testimony.* New York: Free Press. Dated, but still a good discussion of major issues.

YARMEY, A.D. (1990). *Understanding police and police work: Psychosocial issues.* Irvington, NY: Columbia University Press. An excellent review of such issues as personality characteristics of police officers, leadership and stress in police roles, decision-making process, interrogation and eyewitness testimony, aggression and criminal victimization, and stereotypes.

SUGGESTED WEBLINKS

Access to Justice Network
    http://www.acjnet.org

Department of Justice Home Page
    http://canada.justice.gc.ca

Supreme Court of Canada
    http://www.droit.umontreal.ca/opengov/s-courtf/sc.home.html

ANSWERS TO SELF-TEST QUESTIONS

1. b; 2. b; 3. a; 4. c; 5. b; 6. a; 7. a; 8. b; 9. c; 10. b; 11. d; 12. a; 13. d; 14. a.

ANSWERS TO FOR REVIEW

1. defendant; 2. traumatic; 3. eyewitness; 4. police lineup; 5. Expert; 6. lenient; 7. peripheral; 8. accuracy; 9. complete; 10. mock; 11. social influence; 12. Authoritarianism; 13. story; 14. deception 15. leakage; 16. higher; 17. shorter; 18. face; 19. body language; 20. intention; 21. judge; 22. lenient; 23. court; 24. death penalty.

SOCIAL PSYCHOLOGY AND THE PHYSICAL ENVIRONMENT

Why do Western governments continue to worship at the temple of the Gross National Product? Shouldn't we be replacing our reliance on the GNP with a more revealing figure—a new statistic which might be called Net Human Benefit?
                                                                                    Pierre E. Trudeau

If humanity is to have a sustainable future on this diverse planet with many environmental inequalities, it can only be through a process of international cooperation that transcends anything we see today.
            Martin W. Holdgate, Director General, World Conservation Union

■ LEARNING OUTCOMES

1. An understanding of the relationship between human actions and experience and the physical environment.

2. An understanding of the effects of stress, including noise and air pollution.

3. Knowledge of the effects of crowding, and of the difference between crowding and density.

4. An understanding of the human need for personal space.

5. Knowledge of the determinants of human behaviour in relation to the environment.

6. An understanding of how responsible behaviour towards the environment can be encouraged.

■ FOR REFLECTION

• Why is some noise more tolerable than other noise?

• What is the difference between personal and social distance?

• How are body gestures used as markers of territory?

• How are people affected by crowding?

• How can we encourage people to engage in environment-friendly behaviours?

■ CHAPTER OUTLINE

On the night of December 3, 1984, residents of Bhopal, India, population 800 000, were awakened by noxious fumes from what was first believed to be a massive spray of tear gas. In fact, methyl isocyanate, a highly toxic chemical from the pesticide plant of Union Carbide, a U.S.-based multinational corporation, had been discharged into the air. This was reportedly not the first leakage of toxic gas from this factory, but it was the most catastrophic. More than 2500 people were killed, and another 17 000 seriously injured and permanently disabled; medical facilities subsequently reported increases in various illnesses including tuberculosis, gastroenteritis, and birth defects. In the succeeding years, various lawsuits were launched in India and in the U.S. against Union Carbide.

In 1985, the first scientific reports concerning the depletion of the ozone layer (which protects life below from the ultraviolet radiation of the sun) were published in the journal *Nature*. Subsequent research confirmed this growing problem, and later identified a massive hole in the atmosphere over Antarctica. Agreements in Montreal in 1987, and later in London in 1990, recognized that the damage was caused by chlorofluorocarbons (CFCs), chemicals found in aerosol sprays, air conditioning and refrigerants, and foam containers. Plans were drawn up for their elimination by the turn of the century. Meanwhile, the lack of protection from the harmful rays of the sun has been linked to increases in malignant melanoma (skin cancer), and possibly to a weakening of the immune system. Concern about this problem has caused the government of Australia, where the rate of skin cancer is the highest in the world (Giles et al., 1988), to mount the "slip, slap, slop" advertising campaign: slip on a shirt, slap on a hat, and slop on sunscreen.

In 1990, in the town of Hagarsville, near Hamilton, Ontario, a tire dump containing 15 million used tires began to burn. The fire, later determined to have been deliberately set, lasted for weeks, despite all efforts to extinguish it, and released clouds of thick, black, toxic smoke into the air. More worrisome, however, was the release of chemicals into the ground, which was feared to have contaminated the water table and might affect crops and even the water supply of nearby communities.

Concern about our environment has become an important part of our daily news, and even of the way we think. We have always known that our physical environment can influence how we think, feel, and act. We believe that our moods and behaviour are influenced by the weather and by our particular city or country surroundings. We are also aware that our indoor physical surroundings—the design of classrooms, apartments, and theatres—can affect how we live and experience life.

In the past decade we have become more concerned about our natural environment. Although today, as in the past, we welcome technology, industry, and economic growth, we have become uneasy about what we call "progress." Indeed, human behaviour is changing the natural environment on a global scale, altering the fertility of agricultural land, the viability of our oceans (the decline of Maritime fisheries), and the ecology of interrelated forms of life (Stern, 1992). While we still want economic growth and technology to provide jobs and maintain our standard of living, we are now compelled to consider the quality of the air we breathe and water we drink, the preservation of our agricultural lands, and the quality of life in our cities.

Consider, for example, the "global warming" problem. This has been attributed to depletion of the ozone, which is due to the release of gases that alter the capacity of the atmosphere to transmit or reflect energy, thus changing the heat balance of the Earth. The two most important causes of global warming derive from the use of fossil fuels and CFCs. If we can identify how these causal factors (release of gases) are linked to our individual and collective actions, we can begin to design responses that can make a difference (Stern, 1992).

Our awareness of environmental problems tends to focus on dramatic cases: nuclear accidents at Three Mile Island and Chernobyl; derailment of trains carrying toxic materials through communities such as St.-Basile-le-Grand, Quebec and Mississauga, Ontario; and toxic seepage at sites such as the Love Canal in Niagara Falls, New York. Our vocabulary now includes such terms as toxic contaminants, hazardous waste, PCBs, CFCs, dioxin, and oil spills. The UV (ultraviolet radiation) and pollution indices are now reported as part of the weather forecast. As the examples above show, environmental problems may arise from a single disastrous act or from the collective actions of many people over time.

Concern over the environment has galvanized the efforts of scientists in a number of different disciplines, including social psychology. In this chapter, the relevance of the physical environment to human experience and actions is examined. We will look at how the environment influences our behaviour and how our behaviour influences the environment. In considering the determinants of human behaviour in relation to the environment, we also examine a number of popular concerns: why we litter, why we fail to conserve energy, how to reconcile economic growth with environmental preservation, and how environment-friendly behaviour can be encouraged.

THE IMPACT OF ENVIRONMENTAL STRESSORS

Interestingly, most research on the environment focuses on negative conditions. Very little is known about what environmental conditions make people happy or comfortable. We are aware that our physical environment can generate stressful conditions, such as uncomfortable noise, air pollution, or crowding. It is important to understand the concept of **stress**, a physiological and psychological response to threat or challenge (Lazarus and Cohen, 1977). There are at least three types of stressful conditions: (1) cataclysmic events such as war, or a devastating earthquake or tornado; (2) more limited, powerful events such as illness, loss of a job, a crucial examination, or death of a loved one; and (3) daily hassles such as coping with traffic, smog, noisy neighbours, and other features of normal, contemporary life.

stress Our response to experiences that threaten or challenge us.

It is the daily hassles that intrigue environmental psychologists, because they are so common and because it is possible to control or alter their effects. It is important to understand that environmental stressors are most intense when they are unpredictable and uncontrollable, as the following research demonstrates.

NOISE

Noise is defined as an unwanted intensity or quality of sound. Traffic, construction, and other types of machinery, and crowds of people, not to mention powerful stereo equipment, create constant levels of background noise that are often intense, especially in cities. The effects can be dramatic. For example, Cohen, Glass and Singer (1973) studied residents of an apartment building that was constructed over a freeway. While noise levels inside the entire building were high, they were most intense on the lower floors, which were closer to the freeway. Children who lived on the lower floors performed less well than those on the upper levels on tests of both their ability to discriminate between sounds and of their reading achievement. The noise levels in a neighbourhood near an airport, on the other hand, are of course not only intense, but unpredictable and uncontrollable. Well-controlled studies show that residents in these neigh-

noise The unwanted intensity or quality of sound.

Construction noise is the norm in many large cities and can affect human well-being.

What is the significance of the ability to control noise?

bourhoods have higher rates of admission to mental hospitals, birth defects, and death from strokes (Dellinger, 1979).

The ability to control noise has been shown to reduce stress. In one study, groups of subjects were allowed to start a noise or stop it, or both, or neither. A sense of control reduced the negative effect of noise on performance in a proofreading task. Those given control to both stop and start a noise were least affected by the noise (Sherrod, Hage, Halpern and Moore, 1977). Other research has shown that subjects who experienced noise were more likely to behave aggressively by delivering ostensible electric shocks to another person, particularly after being angered. However, when given a "button" that would stop the noise they rarely used it—but their aggressive behaviour was no longer influenced by the occurrence of the noise (Donnerstein and Wilson, 1976). Thus, awareness that the noise can be controlled reduces the likelihood of aggression, probably by reducing the helpless frustration of being subjected to the noise.

During 1989 in Toronto, residents near the airport protested the construction of a third runway, citing the expected increase in noise as a major concern. The issue in this case was the human capacity to adapt to long-term, continuous noise, as distinct from short-term situations represented in the experiments. Indeed, while people appear able to adapt to immediate, short-term noise, they may not adapt as readily to long-term noise such as that encountered near busy airports.

One important field study demonstrates that this concern is about more than an unpleasant nuisance (Bronzaff, 1981). The study was conducted in a school located under elevated subway tracks in a large U.S. city. About 15 times a day, the classes on the side of the building facing the tracks had to stop while the train went by, producing noise levels measured at an intensely uncomfortable 89 decibels. Students in those classrooms, particularly in the fifth and sixth grades, showed reading levels almost a year behind those of students on the less noisy side of the building. After numerous complaints, including evidence of the underachievement of the students, the city's transit authority installed rubber cushioning on the tracks, and the Board of Education installed sound insulation on the ceilings of the affected classrooms. In the following year the noise levels were reduced to 81 decibels (a significant improvement). The teachers were less dissatisfied, and the differences in reading levels between classes on the noisy and less noisy sides of the building had virtually disappeared.

How we react to noise is determined, to a great extent, by our perception of the control we have over it.

AIR POLLUTION

The adverse effects of air pollution on health, caused mainly by automobile exhaust and industrial emissions, have been recognized for some time. During the summer, residents of large cities are becoming accustomed to warnings on days when the air quality indices exceed government-set limits. The effects on behaviour may be expected to be considerable; our behaviour tends to be affected adversely when we don't feel well, and may affect the amount of time that we spend outdoors, the kinds of work and recreational activities that we engage in,

Social Psychology and the Physical Environment

how well we perform on various tasks, and where we choose to live. However, little research has been conducted on the behavioural effects of air pollution.

One study shows that when non-smokers are in close contact with smokers, the non-smokers feel more irritable and tired (Jones, 1978) and even more aggressive (Jones and Bogat, 1978). In another experiment, subjects who were exposed to moderately unpleasant odours tended to report more negative moods and more dislike of a stranger; however, those exposed to extremely foul odours did not differ from the control subjects in their self-reported moods (Rotton et al., 1979). Perhaps the moderate condition more closely approximates the situation usually encountered in real-life pollution.

Indeed, people seem to adapt to pollution and not notice it after some time, as shown in comparisons between newcomers to Los Angeles, who identify smog as a major problem, and long-time residents, who rank smog low on their lists of problems (Evans, Jacobs and Frager, 1982). And yet, the psychological impact of pollution may be considerable. In an archival study, Rotton and Frey (1985) documented the number of family disturbances reported to the police and the atmospheric ozone levels over a two-year period in a U.S. city. They found a strong relationship between these two situations: when the ozone levels were high (indicating highly polluted conditions), more family disturbances were reported. Apparently, air pollution can lead to lowered thresholds for all sorts of negative behaviours.

The Fifth Estate documentary *All in their Heads* (CBC) demonstrates the real-life cost of chemical sensitivity brought on by prolonged exposure to air pollution.

How does the quality of our air affect our behaviour?

SELF-TEST QUESTIONS

1. _____ is a physiological or psychological response to threat or challenge.

a) stress

b) hassle

c) loss of control

d) arousal

2. According to the text, the negative effects of noise are reduced by

a) positive attitudes towards the noise

b) previous experience in a noisy environment

c) the perception that the noise can be controlled

d) all of the above

3. How does noise affect behaviour?

a) it affects problem-solving skill but not social behaviour

b) uncontrollable noise increases aggression

c) any unpleasant noise increases aggression

d) it reduces aggression by providing a distraction from anger

PERSONAL SPACE AND TERRITORY

Would you feel rather uncomfortable if you were sitting at a table in the library and someone came and sat right beside you, rather than across from you or at the other end of the table? Suppose you are at a party, and someone engages you in conversation: how far from you does he or she stand? When you are on a crowded elevator, have you ever wondered why people all tend to face the front, usually gazing at the lighted panel indicating which floor they are on, avoiding eye contact and conversation? All of these examples suggest that we have distances at which we feel comfortable in social interaction, depending on whom we are with and what we are doing, and that we react to situations in which these distances between us and others are violated. Sommer (1969) describes the physical space around us as our *personal space,* an area with invisible boundaries. The study of how we use space to regulate our social interactions is called proxemics.

Hall (1966), an anthropologist, describes four distances or "zones" at which people interact (at least in the U.S., where the research was conducted): (1) intimate distance (0 to 46 cm), such as that between close friends in conversation, a couple making love, or a mother nursing or comforting her baby; (2) personal distance (46 cm to 1.2 m), such as that between friends in casual conversation; (3) social distance (1.2 to 2.1 m), the distance for rather formal meetings, seminars, or business transactions; and (4) public distance (2.1 to 7.6 m) as typified by a lecture or speech in which the speakers must raise their voices. About 65 percent of our everyday interpersonal contacts while standing occurs between approximately 18 and 24 inches (or 46 to 61 cm) (Altman and Vinsel, 1977). In general, research supports the notion that we use these various distances to signify the type of interaction we are in; for example, friends stand closer than strangers (Ashton, Shaw and Worsham, 1980), and people who are sexually attracted to each other stand closer (Allegeier and Byrne, 1973).

However, we must be cautious about the estimated distances. Women tend to stand closer together than men, particularly in same-sex dyads (Horowitz et al., 1970). There are, however, considerable cultural variations: while North Americans, Britons, and Swedes stand farthest away, Southern Europeans stand closer and Latin Americans and Arabs stand the closest (Hall, 1966; Sussman and Rosenfeld, 1982). This can lead to serious misunderstandings. For example, an English Canadian and a Latin American in conversation at a party have different spatial preferences; the English Canadian feels most comfortable at about 90–120 cm while the Latin American would ordinarily stand much closer. Unaware of the cultural differences, the two unconsciously engage in a dance across the room, the Latin American advancing and the English Canadian retreating. Then they part, the Latin American feeling that the English Canadian was cold and unfriendly, and the Canadian feeling that the Latin American was pushy and excessively intimate.

Personal space preferences can also be determined by personal experience, as illustrated in the following study (Gifford and Sacilotto,1993). Two groups of female employees of a governmental agency (equated for age, job level, and certain personality characteristics) were compared with respect to personal space. One group consisted of employees who worked largely in isolation (data entry on machines that were separated by partitions), while the other consisted of those who did office work in close proximity to others. All subjects were tested using a "stop-distance" technique, in which the subjects were asked to approach the experimenter and stop when they reached "a comfortable distance for conversation."

What is the relationship between personal space and social interaction?

It was found that those who worked in relative isolation indicated a larger personal distance for conversation. Of course, we cannot assume that their work experience conditioned them to different personal space preferences, as there may have been a degree of self-selection into jobs that are relatively isolated or non-isolated.

TERRITORIALITY

While people "carry" their personal space with them from situation to situation, the concept of territory does not imply physical presence; my home and office are mine, whether I am there or not. Altman (1975) identifies three types of territories among humans: (1) **primary territory**, owned and used exclusively by an individual or group, such as a home, office, or automobile; (2) **secondary territory**, used regularly but shared with others, such as a club or neighbourhood pub, a stretch of beach, the sidewalk in front of one's home, or the seat that you always take in social psychology class; and (3) **public territory**, places like parks, libraries, airport waiting lounges, and cafeterias, where everyone presumably has an equal right of access.

We tend to establish territorial rules in order to bring order and predictability to our interactions, and, at times, to establish dominance. Even when we share a territory, we often designate some area of it as ours: my part of the closet, my place at the supper table, my desk in the office, my side of the bed. We may also use markers to indicate territory; for example, we may leave some books or clothing at a library table, in part to discourage others from occupying that space (Becker, 1973). Even body gestures may be used as territorial markers. For example, in an experiment, new players were less likely to approach a video game when a confederate was standing close to it or when he was touching the machine, even though in no case was the confederate actually playing (Werner, Brown and Damron, 1981). Often we seek to personalize a territory, such as with photos, posters, paint or wallpaper, or gardens, perhaps as much to indicate "this is me" as "this is mine."

Being on our own territory can have certain advantages. In one study, male students were assigned the roles of prosecuting and defence lawyers in a mock trial. They were asked to negotiate a sentence for the hypothetical criminal; the debate took place in the room of one of the subjects. The results showed that the occupant of the room won 70 percent of the debates, having spoken more and argued more persuasively (Martindale, 1971). In competitive sports, the "home team" advantage is well recognized and, indeed, most teams actually do win a higher percentage of their games at home than on the road (Hirt and Kimble, 1981). While travel fatigue and familiarity with the surroundings at home play a role, territorial dominance may cause visitors to feel a bit more wary and inhibited (Schwartz and Barsky, 1977). Further, the behaviour of spectators in support of the home team may facilitate the performance of the home team, and may interfere with the concentration and effectiveness of the visitors (Greer, 1983). However, one study provides evidence of an important exception (Baumeister and Steinhilber, 1984). On examining records for World Series baseball games and U.S. national university basketball championships, it was found that teams playing at home tend to win near the beginning of the series but to lose near the end; for example, home teams in the World Series won 60 percent of the first two games, but lost 59 percent of the final two games. Evidently the pressure to win exerted by the fans and the media in the home town may act to the disadvantage of the home town team.

primary territory Space over which we have exclusive use and control.

secondary territory Space that we share with others on a regular basis.

public territory Space to which everyone has equal access.

How does territoriality affect performance?

DENSITY AND CROWDING

Most people know that the population of the world is increasing. Consider that it took much of human history for the world population to reach half a billion, but only about 200 years for the population to double to one billion, 80 years to double again, and 45 years to more than double to the present five and a half billion. It is estimated that the world population will double again in about 41 years, barring war, natural catastrophe, or dramatic success in population control.

Density in such cultures as India's may not be expressed as crowding.

density *The number of people in a given space.*

crowding *The discomfort we experience when we feel there are too many people in a given space.*

The overpopulation issue is not a simple one. While the population of the world is definitely increasing, the area in which these people live remains constant. Moreover, this population is not distributed evenly throughout the land mass of the globe but is concentrated, increasingly, in large urban areas. For example, the eight million people of Tokyo proper live on 580 square kilometres of land, and the 5.7 million inhabitants of Hong Kong live on just 270 square kilometres, equivalent to a 10 km by 27 km sliver of land about the size of an average Canadian suburb. In much of the Third World, people are leaving the rural areas and small towns for urban centres to experience what they hope will be a better life. Thus, cities such as São Paulo, Mexico City, Lagos, Bombay, and Santiago have grown explosively. Even in the developed world, where the birth rate is around or below the replacement level, people are increasingly concentrated in urban areas. For example, the majority of Canadians live in three relatively small areas of an immense nation: the region surrounding the St. Lawrence River from Montreal to Quebec City, the "Golden Horseshoe" around Lake Ontario from Niagara to Oshawa, and the southwest corner of British Columbia. Moreover, the population in affluent Western nations places heavy demands on the food, water, energy, and other resources of the world, using some 30 to 50 times more per capita than the people of the developing world.

It is important to understand that population density is not the same as crowding. **Crowding** is the subjective feeling of discomfort stemming from the perception that there are "too many people." For example, we might enjoy being in a high-density situation at a rock concert or hockey game, but may dislike it intensely in a library or on a bus at rush hour. And, as we all know, there are situations in which "three is a crowd," even though objectively the density is very low.

How do the four theories of crowding discussed here explain behaviour?

THEORIES OF CROWDING

It is not density, but crowding that causes us problems. Four theoretical models have been proposed that relate crowding to stress. Each pertains to somewhat different phenomena:

(1) **Sensory overload.** Milgram (1970) argues that when people are exposed to too much stimulation, sensory inputs are received at rates at which they can-

not be processed. Crowding is one situation that involves too much actual or potential interaction, excessive physical closeness, and too many people doing too much to pay attention to all of it. People react to sensory overload by screening out much of the stimulation, such as by paying attention only to that which seems most important or unusual, and avoiding involvement, social contact, or intimacy. Think of our behaviour on a crowded elevator. To compensate for the unaccustomed physical closeness on elevators, we stand silently with our arms clenched tightly to our sides, facing forward, watching the numbers light up in order to avoid eye contact. On a busy city street, we may not even notice the person who staggers and falls to her knees or we may assume that the person is drunk rather than ill.

Milgram derived most of his analyses from observations made in New York City, which has a very distinctive ambience. Recall that in Chapter 9 we saw evidence that people in downtown Toronto responded in a similar way. But we have no evidence, without further research, that the same symptoms of overload would be equally apparent in other cities in the U.S., in Canada, or in other nations or cultures. The experiences of travellers needing help suggests that we cannot simply consider Edmonton, Quebec City, Buenos Aires, Havana, London, Rome, Beijing, Tel Aviv, Baghdad, and Kinshasa as identical urban environments. Perhaps cultural habits and norms regarding social interaction, trust, and a sense of community are at least as important as stimulation levels in determining how people relate to each other, even in crowded cities.

(2) **Density intensity.** Freedman (1975) has observed that high density situations tend to be either extremely unpleasant or quite pleasant and exciting. It appears that high density magnifies our usual reactions to situations in the same way that turning up the volume of a stereo, within limits, magnifies our reaction to the music. We tend to enjoy a crowded situation more when it is one we like and less if we dislike it to begin with. If we enjoy parties, we enjoy one more with a lot of people. In fact, a few people in a huge room makes for a dull party and the guests will usually congregate in one corner of the room in order to increase density. If we dislike riding a bus, then a crowded bus is even more unpleasant. The notion fits nicely with many of our experiences.

A number of laboratory experiments by Freedman and his colleagues support this hypothesis. In one experiment, subjects worked together to solve complicated problems. The problems involved transforming one word into another by changing one letter at a time so that each change produced an acceptable English word: e.g., transform "gold" to "lead" by the sequence "gold-goad-load-lead." Groups of six to eight subjects worked in either a large room or a small room. Half of the groups in each density condition were given relatively easy problems and succeeded with most of them, while others were confronted with some extremely difficult problems, solving only five or six of the fifteen within the time limit.

After the problem-solving sessions, all subjects were asked to rate their experience on a number of dimensions. Those who had a pleasant, successful experience in a small room rated it as being more interesting, lively, and generally more positive than those who had experienced success in a large room. On the other hand, the groups who failed the task while working in the small room were more negative about their experience than were those in the large room. Thus, increasing the density magnified the effects of both successes and failures. Interestingly, subjects in the crowded room were generally more positive about each other, tending to like each other more and perceiving the others as more friendly (Freedman, 1975).

(3) Loss of control. With many people in a small space, each person is less able to move around freely and to avoid unwanted social or physical contact. In short, we lose a sense of being in control in a high density situation; thus we experience stress and we feel "crowded" (Baron and Rodin, 1978). This loss of control can make us feel helpless and vulnerable and unable to maintain a degree of privacy (Altman, 1976). It can also lead to problems in coordinating activities and sharing resources—anyone who has lived in a small room or apartment with one or more people can testify to problems such as eating, working, studying, and sleeping schedules, use of the bathroom, TV and telephone, invited guests, and so on. One study (Fleming, Baum and Weiss, 1987) has shown that people in high-density neighbourhoods reported feeling more crowded and less able to control their social environment, and showed more psychological and physiological symptoms of stress.

Some high-density situations are pleasant.

We have already reviewed considerable evidence that noise is more stressful when it is experienced as unpredictable or uncontrollable. Similar research evidence shows that the perception of control influences the feeling of being crowded. For example, when subjects working in high density conditions were provided with a button to signal to the experimenter that they "wanted out," high density had considerably less effect on their performance or subjective experience (Sherrod, 1974). Because they were aware that they were free to leave, the effects of high density were less stressful. Thus, we don't feel crowded at a game or party because we expected to find a lot of people, we chose to be there, and we know that we are free to leave. On the other hand, people who must live or travel in high density situations may be there due to poverty, housing shortages, or the need to get to work on time. It is this absence of a sense of control over their environment that causes them to feel *crowded*.

Expectations regarding density may also vary between individuals with different experience in life. For example, people from Asian societies may be quite accustomed to living in situations that would seem crowded to people from Western societies. When suddenly thrust into the typical low-density living arrangements of North Americans, they might feel quite isolated and uncomfortable.

(4) Attributions about crowding. Individuals may react quite differently to the same situation with the same population density. To account for this phenomenon, a model of crowding has been developed based on attribution theory (Worchel and Teddlie, 1976; Schmidt and Keating, 1979). It suggests that people feel crowded when they have been aroused by circumstances such as a violation of personal space or other stressors, and then attribute this arousal to the density of people around them. Thus the feeling of crowding will not result if people do not feel aroused or if they do not attribute their arousal to violations of their personal space. Indeed, many high density situations are experienced as enjoyable because the people involved do not feel that their space is invaded or because they attribute their arousal to the excitement of the occasion. Note that this is an alternative to the density-intensity interpretation of the positive and negative experiences engendered by crowding.

When people are distracted from others, such as when highly interesting pictures are placed on the walls, they feel less crowded (Worchel and Teddlie, 1976). For example, in one experiment (Worchel and Brown, 1984), subjects watched either an arousing movie about boxing, sex, or humour, or a documentary that was not as arousing and attractive. Subjects who watched the movies under conditions of high density felt more crowded when they watched the non-arousing documentary, and enjoyed the arousing movies more. These subjects attributed their arousal to the movie, and so enjoyed the movie more and felt less crowded.

It is easy to see merit in each of these models. Indeed, the overload reaction may be seen as a special case of the need to maintain or regain a sense of control, in this case, over the levels and variety of stimulation to which the person is exposed. A complicating factor is evidence of differences in the way males and females handle overload. In one experiment, all-male and all-female "mock juries" were presented with cases and arrived at decisions in a large or small room. While males in the high density situation recommended more severe sentences and liked each other less, women in the same situation gave more lenient sentences. Other studies have suggested that males tend to react more negatively to high density than do females, perhaps because they prefer greater interpersonal distance when interacting with others (Paulus, 1989).

PRIVACY

As noted in Chapter 7, Altman (1976) argues that in our social lives and relationships we must balance and reconcile two opposing needs: the need for intimacy and the need for privacy. In a more general sense, one important way of controlling our environment is by controlling access to ourselves. In our efforts to maintain privacy, we seek both to manage personal information about ourselves and to control our social interaction with others. That is, we want to control how much others know about us, and how they will interact with us.

privacy Our ability to control the access others have to us.

There are a number of mechanisms by which we can regulate privacy (Altman, 1976). Cultural norms and practices protect us to some extent, for example, by permitting us to drop in on close friends in the early evening but not usually at 3 a.m., and not permitting us to eavesdrop on a conversation (at least not too obviously), or to intrude on an exchange between physician and patient. We can arrange our environment to protect our privacy, such as by using doors, drapes, or blinds, and arranging furniture to create personal zones in shared spaces. Electronically operated locks on the front doors of apartment buildings allow tenants to control the access of others to themselves. We can use various non-verbal devices to maintain privacy even when personal space is invaded inadvertently; for example, on the crowded elevator, we compensate for the close physical proximity by standing side to side rather than face to face and by avoid-

"He's ozone unfriendly."

ing eye contact. Finally, verbal behaviour can certainly indicate our willingness or reluctance to engage in contact, and to regulate the degree of intimacy of that contact.

A FINAL OBSERVATION

Can we derive any practical guidance from what has been described? Clearly, if perceived control is a problem, then informing people in advance of what to expect will lead to less stress in a high density situation. Another approach is to change the environment in order to reduce the effects of overcrowding. For example, designing environments to provide for privacy might reduce stress, even in the event of high density. Above all, it is important to recognize that high density can lead to problems and to anticipate these problems accurately.

SELF-TEST QUESTIONS

4. The actual number of people in a given area is a measure of

a) crowding

b) density

c) social exposure

d) sensory overload

5. If you feel there are too many people in your classroom, you are talking about

a) crowding

b) loss of control

c) population

d) density

6. What does the sensory overload hypothesis predict about social behaviour?

a) people are more involved with each other because they need each other

b) density magnifies the intensity of social experience

c) people are more likely to avoid eye contact and notice less of what is going on

d) people have more acquaintances and friends

7. Freedman's density-intensity hypothesis means that

a) high density magnifies the intensity of an experience

b) the intensity of crowding depends on the density of people in the area

c) highly intense situations are those that are crowded

d) high density situations are more exhausting to most people

8. Which explanation best accounts for the fact that a party of 25 friends is more enjoyable in a relatively small room than in a large hall?

a) sensory overload

b) control

c) density-intensity

d) none of the above

BEHAVIOUR IN RESPONSE TO SPECIFIC ENVIRONMENTAL PROBLEMS

During the past decade we have witnessed some significant environmental changes. Cars have become much more fuel-efficient and anti-pollution devices more effective. More effective insulation of houses conserves energy, and in some cases, utility companies have given incentives for energy conservation. "Blue boxes" have become commonplace, and many cafeterias have bins in which customers can sort their waste. What at first seemed to be dramatic is now taken for granted. Constant updating is required. In fact, community colleges are being encouraged, as are all waste generators, by the government (Regulation 102/94) to reduce the amount of waste going to disposal by at least 50 percent by the year 2000. This regulation outlines a four-step plan: (1) Conducting a waste audit, (2) Developing a waste reduction workplan based on the findings of the audit, (3) Implementing this workplan, (4) Updating the audit and workplan as required. But legislation can only go so far; the public must support these initiatives.

When we consider environmentally beneficial behaviour, we can observe many instances of attitude-behaviour discrepancy (Ajzen and Fishbein, 1977; recall Chapter 3). Virtually everyone agrees that a clean, safe, non-toxic environment is a good thing and that the problems of pollution are increasingly serious. Most people in our society also understand that such individual acts as littering or driving one's car when alternative transportation is available contribute to the problem, and yet few seem willing to change their behaviour to any significant extent (Archer et al., cited in Costanzo et al., 1986). It has been established that environmentally beneficial behaviours such as voluntary recycling is predictable by specific attitudes towards this action, but not by more general attitudes about the environment, such as living in harmony with nature and limits to growth (Vining and Ebreo, 1992).

The commons problem (recall Chapter 13) suggests that actions that are individually insignificant are of great collective significance; if I leave my car at home today the environment will not be improved appreciably and the energy conserved will be insignificant, but if we all leave our cars at home the difference may be significant. The challenge, then, is to instill in everyone a sense of collective responsibility for our common environment. One must note that Hardin (1968), who wrote the original article on the commons dilemma (which he called the "tragedy" of the commons), was not optimistic about changing individual behaviour as a solution to environmental problems. For actions that benefit the environment may involve trade-offs, or sacrifices in our affluent and consumerist lifestyle. Moreover, Costanzo et al. (1986) suggest that when people are given too much information about the environment they suffer from information overload, and are thus unable to understand what they have been told. Hardin argued that environmental problems can be solved only by such social controls as laws with criminal sanctions or taxes on pollution.

Notwithstanding the difficulties in altering a habit that is bad but self-rewarding, some interesting research has been conducted on efforts to change behaviour in several contexts, including littering, energy conservation, recycling, and population control. Littering is a behaviour with an immediate reward (ridding ourselves of a minor nuisance), with consequences that are remote in time and small in magnitude (recall again the "commons problem"). One act of littering by one person has no significant adverse effect, but the same action by many people has a troublesome cumulative effect. Most efforts aimed at the reduction of littering have not attempted to increase the negative consequences but have increased the rewards by delivering more reinforcements, increasing the value of the reinforcement, or directly rewarding the proper disposal of litter.

Several strategies for reducing littering have shown some promise (Geller, Winett and Everett, 1982). One is to bring litter disposal into consciousness, such as by the placement of strategic prompts. In one study, thousands of flyers were distributed to customers of supermarkets and fast food emporiums, announcing special sales or other advertising material. At the bottom of each flyer was the anti-litter prompt. Most effective was the following: "Please help us recycle. Please dispose in the green trash can at the rear of the store." It is interesting that this prompt was four times more successful than one that said "Please don't litter. Please dispose of this properly." Clearly the prompt must give explicit instructions for disposal, and should refer to the positive act of recycling rather than discouraging the negative act of littering. Note also that while the most successful strategy resulted in a 30 percent success rate (in the trash can), it also failed to prevent 27 percent of the customers from littering, with the remainder of the garbage carried from the store to an uncertain fate.

A second strategy is to change behaviour by influencing people to pick up the litter of others. Bickman (1972) placed litter on the ground near a trash can and waited to observe who would pick it up. After a long period of time had elapsed and no one had picked up the litter, the experiment was discontinued. The litter was then placed so that the subjects would have to step over it. Only 1.5 percent picked it up. An anti-littering campaign conducted in a small U.S. city by McDonald's resulted in a 32 percent reduction in litter in the area near the restaurant. However, the expenditure of money on free cookies, ads, and people to conduct the campaign was disproportionate to the results (McNees et al., 1979). At least in the U.S., where these studies have been conducted, appealing to people to pick up the litter around them is not a successful strategy.

What are some ways that research suggests we can increase collective responsibility towards the environment?

A third strategy is to make a clean environment more significant to people, such as by increasing the number and attractiveness of trash cans and by keeping the area as free as possible from litter. In general, these strategies do result in significantly less litter than if the area were to be already littered. In one experiment in a university post office, experimenters placed flyers in student mailboxes. When the area had been "prelittered" with a given number of flyers on the floor, 44 percent of the subjects also littered, but in the tidy condition littering was reduced to only 13 percent, probably indicating a modelling effect (Robinson and Frisch, 1975).

It is important in changing behaviours to note the role of supportive elements in the situation. The findings of one study of the use of recycling in multi-family residential units indicate that the willingness of residents to sort their waste into recycling bins is determined, not only by the individuals' motivation to recycle, but by the support given to the program by the managers of these residences and by the "user friendliness" of the recycling program. That is, a system that is visible, attractive, and clean, and that has clear instructions, is more likely to be used (Katzev et al., 1993).

ENERGY CONSERVATION

Although attempts to conserve energy involve some discomfort and inconvenience, the rewards for environment-friendly behaviour may be more tangible and direct, in particular the monetary savings. Yet behaviour in this area is not easy to change. For example, we tend to drive more than is necessary or desirable, and we waste electricity and other forms of energy in heating our homes. It has been argued that "people do not use energy; they use devices and products" (Crabb, 1992).

A number of studies have experimented with incentive programs for reduced energy consumption; for example, families offered a substantial rebate reduced home energy consumption by a significant 12 percent (Winnett, Kagel, Battalio and Winkler, 1978). In a number of cities in North America, commuters who travel in car pools can use express, toll-free lanes while those who don't pay for the privilege of battling rush-hour traffic. Of course, the incentive must be cost-effective compared to the gains in energy consumption, and it is not at all certain that the behavioural changes produced will endure after the incentives are removed.

Clearly, it is necessary to provide people with accurate and effective information about the economic and other benefits of energy-conservation behaviours (Dennis et al., 1990). One interesting study found that providing consumers with constant feedback about the amount of energy they had conserved (relative to what they would be expected to use during that period), and the money they had saved, produced reductions of 10.6 percent, even without additional incentives (Seligman and Darley, 1977). Indeed, U.S. consumers have been offered home energy audits—a free appraisal of home energy consumption along with recommendations for changes in order to conserve energy and save money. Relatively few householders took advantage of the offer, and even fewer acted on the recommendations. However, in one study (Gonzales, Aronson and Costanzo, 1988), the auditors were trained to apply certain social psychological principles: (1) communicate vividly by describing actual cases of super-conservers, and use vivid language to describe energy problems to the consumer; (2) make the presentation personally relevant to the consumer; (3) induce commitment by en-

What social psychological principles can be applied to increase energy conservation?

gaging the assistance of the homeowner in the audit tasks; (4) frame the recommendations in terms of the possibility of losing money by inaction, rather than gaining money if the suggestions are followed. Significant increases were reported in the number of consumers who acted to conserve energy, even when it involved an investment in a different heating system, weatherstripping, and so forth.

Another approach is to create a state of cognitive dissonance that will lead to behavioural change. In one study (Dickerson, et al., 1992), female subjects were approached as they left a swimming pool on the way to the showers. Some of them were interviewed (briefly, of course) concerning their showering habits, such as turning off the water while soaping up, while others were not subjected to this "mindfulness-inducing" procedure. Some subjects from each group were asked to sign a petition that urged people to conserve water. When the subject then took her shower, another experimental assistant showered nearby in order to observe the total time taken, and how often the water was turned off. It was found that significantly less water was used by subjects who had first been made mindful of water-conservation techniques and then had advocated publicly that people should conserve water. Note that this cannot be considered an attitude-discrepant behaviour: we are all in favour of conservation, at least in principle. This procedure succeeded in having induced a state of dissonance, which led to behavioural changes consistent with their attitudes.

Several conclusions can be drawn from research concerning attitudes and beliefs regarding energy conservation (see Olsen, 1981). First, most people are now convinced that the problem is genuine and serious, regardless of the manipulations of multinational corporations. Secondly, while general attitudes on the issue are poor predictors of behaviour, beliefs about the specific consequences of personal energy consumption patterns, e.g., how it would affect personal comfort, predict behaviour quite well. Finally, increasing awareness of how much energy people actually use, along with its cost, can increase conservation. In one study, an experimental group of homeowners was provided with meters mounted outside their kitchen windows and displaying their daily consumption of electricity. Homeowners who were provided with this immediate daily feedback consumed an average of 10.5 percent less electricity than did a matched control group whose members were simply billed on a monthly basis (Seligman, Darley and Becker, 1978). In other words, constant monitoring seems necessary to alter wasteful habits.

ENVIRONMENTAL HAZARDS

Attitudes are readily galvanized into actions when a hazard is apprehended. We are continually bombarded by claims of hazards in our food, water, and air, which make us feel that we are at risk in our daily lives. It is important to understand that risk can be defined in "objective" terms of the probability of a given outcome and of the severity of that outcome. However, risk can also be defined in subjective or "constructivist" terms, involving judgments about the probability that a certain risk can lead to a certain outcome and about what is valued. Thus, for example, when a tractor-trailer carrying radioactive materials overturned and burned, anti-nuclear groups focused on the risk in transporting dangerous materials while the nuclear industry focused on how the accident was contained without release of radioactivity (Cvetkovich and Earle, 1992).

Because people feel at risk, they often resist having nuclear reactors, garbage dumps, or incinerators located nearby. When avoidance is possible the reaction is often an unyielding rejection, or the NIMBY syndrome ("Not in my back yard!") (Freudenburg and Pastor, 1992). A more extreme form of this has been called the BANANA syndrome ("build absolutely nothing anywhere near anybody").

DESIGN AND HUMAN FACTORS

Our environment includes roads, houses, apartment buildings, universities, stadiums, offices, factories, and shopping centres—that is, the "built environment." In addition to making their designs technically sound and aesthetically pleasing, architects are concerned with making them "work" for the user. Social psychologists have become increasingly concerned with how these designs might be improved. Indeed, architects and interior designers often team up with psychologists, and many schools of architecture include psychologists and psychology courses in their programs.

Let us examine a few research studies that provide scientific foundation for this new collaboration. Baum and colleagues (Baum and Valins, 1977; Baum, Aiello and Calesnick, 1978) investigated the impact of various designs for university residences. Two basic types of dormitory designs were used: (1) single and/or double rooms along a single, long corridor with common social areas

How does design affect human behaviour?

FIGURE 14-1 Two designs of university residences

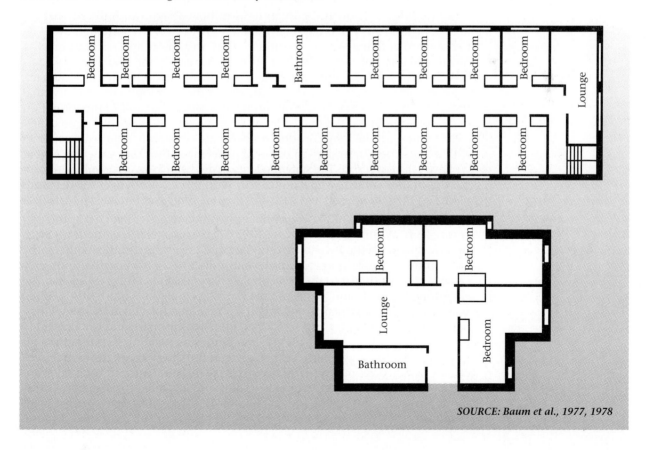

SOURCE: Baum et al., 1977, 1978

395

and bathrooms shared by all on that floor or wing; and (2) suites of several bedrooms located around a smaller common living room and bathroom. While the population density was more or less the same in both designs, the effects on the residents seemed to be quite different.

It was found that students in the suite arrangement tended to be more sociable and friendly. This is not too astonishing, since it is much easier to come to know and interact with nine others in close proximity than with 39 others down a long corridor. However, this pattern of social behaviour was also observable in the psychology laboratory. The students, who had been recruited for another experiment, were taken to a waiting room in which another student, hired by the experimenter, was sitting. Suite residents were more likely to select a chair closer to the other person and were more likely to initiate a conversation than were corridor residents.

However, it is not possible to conclude that the suite design caused these differences in social behaviour. The suites may have been more desirable to many because they were newer units. There may also have been a problem of biased selection of subjects since friendly, sociable people may request suites and less sociable people may prefer corridor arrangements. To overcome these problems, Baum and Davis (1980) obtained permission from the university to institute the proper controls. In the same residence, some floors were converted into suites while others were maintained as long corridors (40 students) or short corridors (20 students). Density was the same in all three settings. Students were randomly assigned to rooms in one of the three living arrangements and were studied repeatedly over the year.

The findings confirmed the hypothesis of how design can influence behaviour. Suite residents perceived their situation as less crowded, although they had the same total living area as the others. They were more successful in making friends and interacted more, both in the residence and in the laboratory. Two factors seem to have been important. First, because of proximity and expectancies, the suite arrangement is more conducive to the development of individual friendship (see Chapter 7 on propinquity and attraction) and to the formation of groups. In addition, the smaller living units increase the residents' sense of personal control. In the long corridor, residents are constantly required to interact with many people, regardless of personal preferences; thus they experience what we have called overload. The suite residents share their living space only with people whom they come to know quite well. With more control over the demands placed on them to interact and socialize, they are more comfortable and satisfied.

An important study of the classroom environment was conducted at the university level (Wollin and Montagne, 1981). These researchers selected two identical classrooms in the Psychology building and then designed them differently. The control or "sterile" classroom had white walls, rows of plastic desks, and a grey carpet—possibly similar to the decor you are experiencing in this very course. The experimental or "friendly" classroom was redecorated with brightly painted walls, art posters, large plants, and bright Chinese kites hanging from the ceilings; part of the room had area rugs, colour-coordinated cushions, and wooden cubes for alternative seating arrangements. Two professors teaching sections of the introductory psychology course participated, and halfway through the term the classes switched rooms so that all subjects spent half a term in each environment. In the experimental "friendly" room, students rated the same professors more positively: more knowledgeable, more interesting, better organized. Moreover, they performed better on course exams in the redecorated room.

Thus, both learning and evaluations of other people are influenced by the physical setting.

In other research, it has been found that subjects are more willing to interact with others when they are in surroundings that they find attractive (Russel and Mehrabian, 1978). But what do we find attractive in physical settings? Of course, individuals differ in terms of past experience, background, and personal taste, but there are some common traits. One study (Lee and Weber, 1984) had 300 subjects rate 200 characteristics of their homes, and the results were analyzed in order to identify factors that people consider when they evaluate a home. Four factors were identified: (1) habitability (how comfortable, convenient, flexible, large, and well-ventilated); (2) appearance (how elegant, fashionable, attractive, the colours used); (3) degree of cleanliness and lack of clutter; and (4) whether it possessed unusual or contemporary features of design.

Finally, it is important to understand that design changes can be simple yet effective. In the 1950s, a new ward for female geriatric patients was constructed in a hospital in Saskatchewan. Although the common room was tastefully decorated, bright and cheerful, the patients seemed listless, depressed, and withdrawn. Psychological consultants noted that the chairs were lined up neatly, side by side, along the walls, facing in the same direction. When the chairs were rearranged in circles around coffee tables, the frequency of conversation doubled within a few short weeks (Sommer and Ross, 1958). In another experiment, subjects were required to converse at a comfortable distance, or at an uncomfortable distance of eleven feet. At the greater distance subjects not only felt ill at ease, but attributed their feelings to their partner rather than to the situation

BOX 14-1
WHAT IS GOOD DESIGN FOR PEOPLE?

In evaluating the merits and drawbacks of the design of buildings, neighbourhoods, rooms, or work areas, questions of aesthetics and engineering have always been paramount. More recently, behavioural scientists have entered this field as consultants and collaborators to architects and planners, in the recognition that the design must "work" for the people in it. One such scientist (Zeisel, 1981) proposes a behavioural approach to design that is based on the necessity of satisfying six human needs:

(1) *Security:* the ability to feel safe in the environment.

(2) *Clarity:* the ability to understand the design or "layout" of the setting in order to find one's way from place to place. For example, some hospitals and other large institutions colour-code different areas.

(3) *Privacy:* the ability to regulate contact with others, to be alone when appropriate, or to have private interactions with clients, patients, students, and so on.

(4) *Social interaction:* the ability to find appropriate areas for contact and conversation with others.

(5) *Convenience:* the ability to accomplish tasks without too much effort caused by the actual design. For example, in a work setting, are the people or departments who must work together most often in close physical proximity?

(6) *Identity:* the ability to feel a sense of belonging to the setting.

Consider buildings such as a local shopping centre, your college, and the federal or provincial parliament or legislature in terms of these needs. Of course, it would be virtually impossible to satisfy all needs fully and simultaneously, and trade-offs are inevitable. Nonetheless, a successful design must take all of them into consideration.

(Aiello and Thompson, 1980). The astute host will take note when trying to arrange a successful social occasion.

This principle has been applied to the design of "open concept" schools and offices in which there are few, if any, walls or physical barriers. While it has been reasoned that students or workers will interact and communicate more frequently and effectively in an open area, the research shows that employees consider "open concept" to be a mixed blessing. Job-related communication and contact is facilitated but privacy is lost (Sundstrom, Herbert and Brown, 1982). Often the lower-level employees work in an open concept area, while executives have private offices. Several years ago, a new building at a Canadian university was designed as "open concept," where faculty would work in a communal area rather than in private offices. After almost unanimous and vociferous objections by the academics, drywall and false ceilings were used to create private offices—perhaps to the detriment of the aesthetic design. However, privacy and boundaries are felt to be essential to certain types of work.

SELF-TEST QUESTIONS

9. The "trade-off" problem involves

a) environmental benefits versus consumerism

b) affluence versus control

c) the notion that high density magnifies positive and negative states

d) none of the above

10. The Baum et al. study of corridor and suite arrangements in student dormitories found that those in the suite arrangement

a) were more friendly

b) were more sociable even outside the dormitory

c) both of the above

d) none of the above

11. The study of a female geriatric ward in a Saskatchewan hospital found that patients became more sociable when

a) chairs were placed side by side along a corridor

b) chairs were arranged in circles around coffee tables

c) chairs were placed around a large rectangular table

d) none of the above

SUMMARY

(1) Research in social psychology has shown the impact on behaviour of environmental stressors, including excessive noise, air pollution, and crowding. All of these can contribute to impaired performance in school and other activities, and increase the risk of aggression and other negative behaviours.

(2) Hall has identified four zones of personal space: intimate, personal, social, and public.

(3) Territoriality refers to a sense of personal possession of space regardless of whether the person is present or not. Primary, secondary, and public territories have been identified, and the impact of territory on performance (the "home team" advantage) has been studied.

(4) Population density is not equivalent to crowding, which is an aversive psychological state. Four models of the effects of crowding have been proposed: sensory overload, density-intensity, loss of control, and an attributional model. In general, the sense of control appears to determine whether a situation of high density will or will not be experienced as crowding.

(5) People have a need for privacy to maintain a sense of control in their environment and in their social interactions. Privacy is sought through solitude, anonymity, reticence, and intimacy.

(6) Actions that may benefit the environment often involve trade-offs, sacrifices that may balance the benefits. Several strategies for changing littering behaviour, increasing energy conservation, and controlling the increase in population have been studied.

(7) Social psychology has studied how the design of buildings and other living spaces affects the behaviour and experience of the inhabitants. For example, while two designs of university residences result in almost identical rates of density, one arrangement is experienced as more crowded than the other. Other designs have been shown to facilitate interpersonal interaction and appropriate activity in school classrooms and hospitals.

FOR REVIEW

Noise is one of the environmental stressors that we deal with daily. Studies have shown that the ability to _____(1) noise lowers stress. Air pollution can affect mood, among other things. _____(2) unpleasant odours have been linked to negative moods.

Personal space preferences are strongly related to culture and can be the basis for serious _____(3). Personal space is linked to territoriality. When we are on our own territory research shows that we have what is called the _____(4) advantage. Social psychologists talk about density and crowding. _____(5) is the term that is used to indicate a feeling of discomfort with the number of people around us. Milgram suggests we suffer from _____(6) when there is too much stimulation from the environment and we may not notice things around us. Freedman's research suggests that high _____(7) magnifies our usual reactions to situations. _____(8) is the term used to indicate our attempt to control access to ourselves.

Environmentally beneficial behaviours are best predicted by _____(9) attitudes towards the issue. People's lack of support may be yet another example of the _____(10) problem. One strategy that has proven successful in encouraging people not to litter is that of _____(11) better behaviour.

Design factors in our environment play a role in our behaviour and well-being. Wollin and Montagne have demonstrated that an attractive classroom setting has a positive effect on both _____(12) and our evaluations of other people.

ISSUES AND ACTIVITIES

1. Taking into account the needs discussed in Box 14-1, examine your college or some other public building to see if these needs are being met and how. You might try to meet with someone who was involved in the design process. What could you suggest if these needs are not being met?

2. Conduct a study of the recycling initiative at your college. Begin with an audit, and design a plan based on your findings. You might design and distribute a questionnaire for students to identify attitudes and levels of support for these initiatives.

3. Using the video *All in their Heads* (CBC, The Fifth Estate) as a starting point, write a paper on the issue of chemical sensitivity. Be sure to take into account the criticism that was raised in the film. You might want to have a clinical ecologist talk to your class.

• FURTHER READING

ALTMAN, I. (1975). *The environment and social behavior: Privacy, personal space, territory and crowding.* Monterey, CA: Brooks/Cole. Somewhat dated, but a major integrative contribution to the field.

BAUM, A. and SINGER, J.E. (Eds.) (1980, 1981, 1982, 1986). *Advances in environmental psychology, Vols. 1–4.* Hillsdale, N.J.: Erlbaum. Professional-level papers on all aspects of environmental psychology, including the impact of environment on health.

FREEDMAN, J.L. (1975). *Crowding and behavior.* New York: Viking. Dated but still a highly relevant and engaging review of research and theory.

GIFFORD, R. (1987). *Environmental psychology.* Newton, MA: Allyn and Bacon. A thoughtful, lively, and thorough review of theories and research on the major topics in this area. Excellent overview of the field.

KRUPAT, E. (1985). *People in cities: The urban environment and its effects.* New York: Cambridge University Press. Interesting review of research and ideas by a social psychologist.

SOMMER, R. (1969). *Personal space: The behavioral basis of design.* Englewood Cliffs, NJ: Prentice-Hall. The ground-breaking book on personal space and how research can be applied to the design of better institutions and other human habitats.

SUGGESTED WEBLINKS

Canadian Psychological Association section on Environmental Psychology
http://www.laurentian.ca/www/psyc/section7/default1.html

Largest on-line environmental information resource
http://enviroLink.org

ANSWERS TO SELF-TEST QUESTIONS

1. a; 2. c; 3. b; 4. b; 5. a; 6. c; 7. a; 8. c; 9. a; 10. c; 11. b.

ANSWERS TO FOR REVIEW

1. control; 2. Moderately; 3. misunderstanding; 4. home team; 5. Crowding; 6. sensory overload; 7. density; 8. Privacy; 9. specific; 10. commons; 11. modelling; 12. learning.

HEALTH AND ILLNESS

It is much more important to know what sort of patient has the disease than what sort of disease the patient has.

Sir William Osler

Health care is not what makes us healthy. The great equation, the idea that somehow health care equals health, is a delusion.

Michael Rachlis and Carol Kushner

■ LEARNING OUTCOMES

1. An understanding of why people sometimes deliberately undermine their health.

2. Ability to identify modelling influences for some health behaviours.

3. An understanding of the relationship between illness and certain personality characteristics.

4. Knowledge about communication in physician-patient relationships.

5. Knowledge about some social psychological issues related to AIDS, including stigmatization and the need to modify some behaviours and attitudes.

■ FOR REFLECTION

- Why do we sometimes ignore common sense advice about our health?
- Are some people more likely than others to develop problems with drugs or alcohol?
- Can stress or depression affect people's health?
- What is a good patient? Is being a good patient good for your health?
- What causes people to adopt a healthy lifestyle?

■ CHAPTER OUTLINE

In the years 1885–1886, an epidemic of smallpox raged through the city of Montreal. Almost 3000 of a population of 167 000 lost their lives to the disease, the majority of whom were children (Bliss, 1991). An absence of public health policy, and public attitudes (including a mistrust of the available vaccine) exacerbated the tragedy. By the mid-twentieth century, the threat of smallpox was virtually eliminated in North America and Europe, and in 1980 the global eradication of the disease was announced by the World Health Organization. However, deadly diseases such as bubonic plague, cholera, typhoid, and malaria still pervade the

Third World. In industrialized nations, advances in medical technology, accessibility of medical care, and effective health measures such as sanitation and immunization have contributed to the control of these deadly infectious diseases. However, inexpensive travel and open borders are currently increasing the mobility of such contagious diseases as diphtheria, cholera, tuberculosis, and malaria. For example, the World Health Organization estimated that 55 000 to 60 000 new cases of diphtheria occurred in 1995 (*The Globe and Mail,* March 30, 1996). Such developments emphasize the importance of continuing to promote the use of effective health measures. At present the most frequent causes of death in industrialized nations are the major chronic diseases (coronary and circulatory, respiratory, and cancers). It is important to note that these life-threatening illnesses are in part caused by voluntary behaviour. Poor diet, smoking, lack of fitness, and excessive alcohol use contribute to heart disease and cancer.

These changing patterns of health and disease are reflected in recent Canadian federal health policy. Since 1989 this policy has been directed towards three important goals (Health and Welfare Canada, 1989): (1) the reduction in inequities, particularly income disparities, which adversely affect health; (2) the prevention of injuries, diseases, and chronic disabilities by means of immunization, lifestyle changes, better prenatal and neonatal care, and the reduction of drunk driving; (3) enhancement of people's abilities to cope with chronic diseases.

Social psychologists interested in the problems of illness and health focus largely on understanding why people choose to act in ways that enhance or undermine their health, and on understanding the patient-practitioner relationship. The insights they acquire can lead to more effective public health measures (Kristiansen, 1986) and to a more effective practice of medicine.

HEALTH-RISK BEHAVIOURS

What are some examples of health-risk behaviours?

Among the mysteries of human nature is the question of why people persist in behaviour that they know to be hazardous to their health, e.g. excessive eating of junk foods, driving recklessly and without seat belts, compulsive overeating, cigarette smoking, alcohol and drug abuse, and not exercising. The relevant problem in behavioural excesses is not necessarily addiction but overindulgence in various pleasures that are not harmful in moderation (Orford, 1985). Indeed, the causes of the excessive use of a drug in specific situations are found primarily not in the drug itself, but in the person who uses it and in the circumstances in which it is used. For example, in the U.K., cancer patients kept on a combination of heroin, cocaine, and alcohol (the Brompton Cocktail) to relieve pain tend to come off these narcotics easily if their cancer goes into remission (Twycross, 1974). By contrast, many addicts withdraw successfully from heroin, alcohol, or nicotine, and then relapse months or years later (Marlatt and Gordon, 1979).

PROBLEM BEHAVIOUR THEORY

problem behaviour theory *Theory that regards adolescent health risk behaviour as part of a syndrome of personal, environmental, and behavioural non-conventionality.*

Much research has been devoted to finding the cause of excessive drug use in certain characteristics of the person or the environment. A more comprehensive and integrated approach is represented in Jessor's **problem behaviour theory** (Jessor and Jessor, 1977; Jessor, 1993). In this approach, excessive alcohol or other drug use by adolescents is viewed as a behaviour consistent with what the adolescent is like as a person, how the adolescent is reacting to his or her home life and peer group (perceived environment), and what the adolescent tends to be involved with apart from drugs. The model is presented in Figure 15-1. Several similar models, all based on the principle of interaction among the person, behaviour, and environment, have generated a great deal of research (see Sadava, 1987).

There are specific characteristics of the person, his or her behaviour, and his or her environment that are associated with problem behaviours. The relevant personality variables include low expectancies for success in school, high values for independence, and an absence of characteristics that constrain deviant behaviour (e.g. low religiosity, tolerant attitudes towards deviant behaviour). Important characteristics of the social environment include the influence of peer groups, opportunities to engage in problem behaviour, and the perception that socially acceptable behaviours are not adequately rewarded. Problem drinking tends to be part of a more general pattern of unconventional behaviour. This pattern also includes the use of marijuana and other drugs, deviant/delinquent acts such as lying and stealing, precocious sexual involvement, and little participation in conventional activities in school and church.

The problem behaviour model has been supported by the results of a longitudinal study of high school and university students who are now being followed in their middle age (Donovan, Jessor and Jessor, 1983; Jessor, Donovan and Costa, 1991). The model has also been supported by results of several other major longitudinal studies that used a national U.S. sample and samples of

What are some examples of personal, environmental, and behavioural factors that contribute to problem behaviour?

FIGURE 15-1 Problem behaviour theory

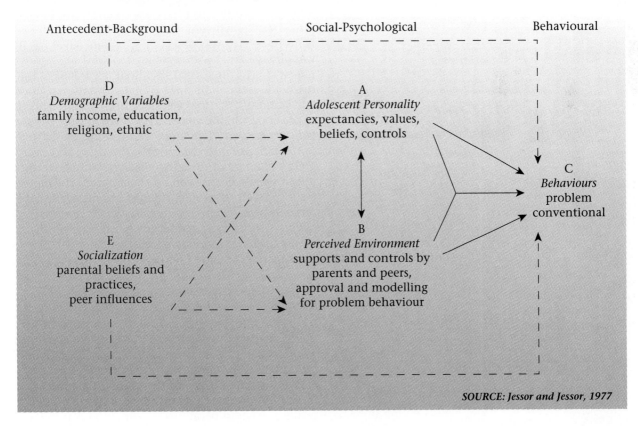

SOURCE: Jessor and Jessor, 1977

Canadian high school and university students (Schlegel, Manske and D'Avernas, 1985; DiTecco and Schlegel, 1982; Sadava and Forsyth, 1977a, 1977b).

It is important to realize that alcohol or drug problems cannot be predicted accurately by knowing only how much alcohol or drugs are consumed (Sadava, 1985). For example, while the rate of alcohol problems is considerably higher among males than females, research also shows that females who drink heavily are more likely to suffer adverse consequences than are heavy-drinking males (Wilsnack, 1982). The fact that heavy drinkers are more likely to engage in other problem behaviours increases their vulnerability. And certain psychological states, such as loneliness, also increase vulnerability to adverse consequences (Sadava and Thompson, 1986).

How do modelling influences contribute to health-risk behaviours?

MODELLING INFLUENCES

In Chapter 5 it was shown that social influence may be unintentional, and that our actions are often modelled after those observed in others (Bandura, 1977). Thus, the peer group may influence the adolescent to begin smoking, may influence where and when smoking occurs, and may facilitate smoking at a given time. Adolescents who are most likely to be influenced by peers tend to be those who lack a sense of self-efficacy in resisting these pressures (Stacy et al., 1992). The behaviour of parents is also an important modelling influence on young people. It has been demonstrated through longitudinal research that when adolescents have parents who drink heavily, they tend to seek out friends who drink heavily, and then begin to drink in the same manner (Huba, Dent and Bentler, 1980).

Modelling influences have also been shown in empirical studies wherein the drinking behaviour of patrons in taverns was observed. In a Vancouver bar it was observed that patrons tended to drink at a steady rate of almost three drinks per hour, regardless of the size of the group or the time spent in the tavern (Cutler and Storm, 1975). However, since larger groups tended to stay longer in the tavern, individuals in large groups consumed more. This study was recently replicated in the U.S. using larger samples (Hennessy and Saltz, 1993). The rate of drinking observed was above the rate at which alcohol can be metabolized. The blood alcohol levels of people in larger groups eventually reached high levels, and intoxication was more frequent, particularly when the group consisted largely of young males (Sykes, Rowley and Schaeffer, 1993).

Modelling influences can also be identified in other health-related behaviours. In a study of binge eating among students in two university sororities (Crandall, 1988), it was found that norms regarding uncontrollable binge eating differed significantly. More frequent binging was reported among members of one sorority than the other. Those who were most popular tended to be those whose eating patterns most closely matched those of the group as a whole. As friendships became closer over time, a young woman's eating behaviour became increasingly similar to that of her closest friends. Thus while binge eating may in part reflect psychological disturbances, it can also be an acquired pattern of behaviour that is learned and altered through social modelling.

So far, we have seen that social psychological variables can influence the extent to which people act to protect or endanger their health. Apart from choices in behaviour, individuals also differ greatly in how vulnerable they are to certain illnesses.

VULNERABILITY TO ILLNESS

Research has shown that people with certain personality characteristics and in certain stressful social circumstances (see Boxes 15-1 and 15-2) are more vulnerable to a range of diseases and disabilities, and are less likely to recover successfully. Let us look briefly at research on three important factors related to vulnerability: social support, perceived control, and the "coronary-prone personality."

SOCIAL SUPPORT

In 1951, Janis conducted a study of how soldiers coped with the conditions of combat. He found that those who were able and willing to endure such severe stress belonged to a cohesive combat unit. Those who did not belong to such a closely-knit group often experienced psychological breakdown. People who lack supportive bonds with others are more likely to suffer illnesses and are less likely to recover quickly (Gottlieb, 1985). Some have not been able to establish intimate relationships, while others have experienced a disruption owing to marital separation or death of a spouse (Bloom, Asher and White, 1978; Stroebe and Stroebe, 1983; Burman and Margolin, 1992). The importance of social support both to maintaining good health and recovering from illness has been demonstrated in numerous research studies.

For example, many clinical and survey studies show relationships between an absence of social supports and heart disease (Lynch, 1977; Shumaker and Czajkowski, 1991). Cardiac patients who receive strong support suffer less from the effects of stress and experience less breathing difficulty and fewer symptoms of angina (Fontana, Kerns, Rosenberg and Colonese, 1989). A longitudinal study that followed patients who had coronary bypass surgery found that esteem support (involving feedback that the person is valued and respected by others) was most consistently related to feelings of well-being and the lessening of uncomfortable physical symptoms (King, Reis, Porter and Norsen, 1993).

Social support has also been found to be important to the health and well-being of mothers and their babies. A longitudinal study followed groups of teenage mothers through their pregnancies and after the birth of their babies (Unger and Wandersman, 1985). Social support from their families, friends, neighbours, and the fathers contributed to the adjustment and life satisfaction of these mothers, and to their effectiveness as parents. Social support was also correlated with the birth weight and subsequent health and development of the child. As a result of these findings, programs were set up in which experienced, older women were able to provide support to the mothers. Research has also shown that the presence of the father in the delivery room, especially for the birth of a first baby, can be a source of social support for the mother (Keiman and Hobfoll, 1989).

It is not entirely clear why social support contributes to health (Cohen, 1988). Perhaps it "buffers" or protects the person against stress, or makes the person

How are social support, perceived control, and personality characteristics related to health?

BOX 15-1

MAJOR STRESS AND MINOR HASSLES: WHAT REALLY AFFECTS US

It is commonly accepted that our state of health and sense of well-being can be adversely affected by stress (Cohen and Williamson, 1988). Since both stress and health problems can lead to negative mood states, we cannot assume that stress in itself is a direct cause of health problems (Watson and Pennebaker, 1989). Indeed, one study measured stress and negative affect, and then exposed subjects to the common cold virus, quarantined them, and monitored them for illness. It was found that those who had recently experienced stressful events in their lives were more likely to become ill, particularly if they had reacted in a negative way to the stress (Cohen, Tyrrell and Smith, 1993). There is also direct evidence that stress tends to elicit the release of stress hormones (e.g. adrenalin) that have negative effects on the immune system and thus leave the person more vulnerable to illness (Johansson, Collins and Collins, 1983; McClelland, Alexander and Marks, 1982).

Holmes and Rahe (1967) proposed that it is the major changes in our lives that create stress and can cause problems. They developed a "social readjustment scale" which, based on research, measures the impact of such changes. The following are examples (the numbers refer to "life change units" or the relative amount of disruption or readjustment caused):

Death of spouse	100
Divorce	73
Jail term	63
Personal illness/injury	53
Marriage	50
Fired at work	47
Retirement	45
Pregnancy	40
Sexual difficulties	39
Mortgage or major loan	31
Trouble with boss	23
Change in social activities	18
Vacation	13

While the notion of life-change stress has been applied in much research, it has also been criticized. For example, the weightings for each event were derived from a particular sample at a particular time and place, and these weightings may differ considerably for other times, places, and types of people. Some obviously stressful events, such as the death of a child, are not even mentioned. In addition, the weightings do not account for the quality of the event. For example, they would predict that a person who divorces (weight of 73) and subsequently remarries (weight of 50) would experience more stress than the person who divorces but remains single, while common sense would suggest otherwise. Indeed, another study in which subjects completed daily diaries over a period of time showed that conflicts in intimate relationships are by far the most important sources of stress in daily life (Bolger, DeLongis, Kessler and Schilling, 1989).

Richard Lazarus and colleagues (Kanner, Coyne, Schaefer and Lazarus, 1981) argue that most of us can cope with most crises quite well, and that it is the minor, daily hassles of life that take their toll. The annoyances of commuting to work on a crowded bus or freeway, the delivery that does not show up, a missing and desperately needed book in the library, the repair job that must be done over, the car that won't start on a January morning, the "mouthy" teenager or whining child, minor arguments with friends—these are examples of daily hassles that infect our lives. Kanner et al. (1981) found the following to be the "top ten" of daily hassles:

Hassle	Percentage of respondents
Concern about weight	52.4
Health of family member	48.1
Increased price of common goods	43.7
Home maintenance	42.8
Too many things to do	38.6
Misplacing or losing things	38.1
Yard or outside home maintenance	38.1
Property investment, taxes	37.6
Crime	37.1
Physical appearance	35.9

They argue that the major life changes have their main effects by increasing the daily levels of hassles. These and several other studies suggest significant linkages with physical and emotional health (Stone and Neale, 1982; DeLongis et al.,

1982). It is also suggested that positive everyday experiences ("daily uplifts") may contribute to our health. Commonly endorsed examples of daily uplifts include relating well to one's spouse or lover (76.3 percent) and to friends (74.4 percent), completing a task (73.3 percent), getting enough sleep (69.7 percent), and eating out (68.4 percent), although surely the last example would depend on the restaurant! Exercise has also been shown to protect people from the negative impact of stressful events on their health (Brown and Siegel, 1988).

---

stronger and more resistant to illness. Conversely, lack of social support may be a stressor. That is, the person who is alienated from others or who loses support through death or separation may be at greater risk for disease. Another possibility is that illness causes a disruption in social support by others who may feel uncomfortable interacting with someone who is seriously ill. Social support may contribute to health indirectly by enhancing the person's self-esteem, which has a beneficial effect on health. Finally, an individual with good support from others is more likely to comply with treatment and to do other things that are beneficial to his or her health.

In spite of the many positive effects of social support, it is not always beneficial. Family and friends may unwittingly reinforce such maladaptive behaviours as overeating, alcohol, drug abuse, or even depression by protecting individuals

---

BOX 15-2

THE LOSS EFFECT: BEREAVEMENT, PSYCHOLOGY, AND IMMUNOLOGY

Inevitably, we must all cope with the death of a family member, spouse or lover, or close friend. Beyond the painful period of mourning, and the permanent sense of loss, there is evidence that such a death can threaten the health of the survivors. Careful analyses of data from Britain, Japan, the U.S., and West Germany show that in the year following the death of a spouse, the survivor is more likely to die than people of the same age group who have not been widowed. When we control statistically for the possibility of suicide and of death from the same illness or accident, we still have a significantly higher mortality rate: the *loss effect* (Stroebe, Stroebe, Gergen and Gergen, 1982).

How can this be explained? Certainly, it is related to stress. The loss of a spouse is rated by most people as the most stressful of all conceivable life changes (Holmes and Rahe, 1967, see Box 15-1). Of course, the surviving spouse has lost the social and emotional support of intimacy (recall evidence of the devastating effects of loneliness presented in Chapter 7). In addition, he or she must now assume sole responsibility for matters that were formerly shared—including finances, running the home, and parenting, to name a few. Interestingly, males seem to be more adversely affected by the loss effect than are females. Perhaps women are more able to seek and obtain social support from family and friends.

While such metaphors as "broken-hearted" and "loss of the will to live" convey the devastating sense of loss, the most likely physical link to the loss effect is through the immune system. Clearly, physiological systems can be measurably affected by psychological factors. Under certain stressful conditions, the manufacture and circulation of white blood cells tends to be somewhat diminished (Maier and Laudenslager, 1985). Reduced immunological defences leave the person more vulnerable to the effects of "foreign" elements such as bacteria, viruses, and cancers. In the current period of intensive research in immunology, spurred in part by the AIDS epidemic, we can expect to learn much more about this process and, perhaps, how to compensate when people are most vulnerable.

from the consequences of their own actions. Overprotection of older people—denying them the normal privileges of caring for themselves and of making their own decisions—can be profoundly debilitating (Langer and Rodin, 1976).

Nevertheless, the research shows that in most cases, social support can protect the person from stress and provide him or her with a sense of self-worth and stability in life (Cohen and McKay, 1984). In societies where people move frequently and divorce almost as often, social support can be difficult to obtain. In these circumstances, community support services such as rape crisis centres, family services, hostels, or services for senior citizens, are essential (Pilisuk and Minkler, 1985).

PERCEIVED CONTROL

internal locus of control
The belief that one's outcomes are determined by one's own efforts.

external locus of control
The belief that one's outcomes are determined by forces outside of oneself.

People differ in the extent to which they believe that events in their lives are caused by their own actions or by external factors such as political institutions, luck, or other people (Rotter, 1966). Those who believe that what happens to them is due primarily to their own actions have an **internal locus of control**. By contrast, people who believe that there is little they can do to influence the course of events in their lives have an **external locus of control**. People with internal orientations tend to know more about their illnesses and are more likely to take care of themselves (Strickland, 1978). When they become ill, internals tend to cope better if they are given appropriate information about their illnesses. They are also more likely to take actions to maintain good health (Seeman, Seeman, and Sayles, 1985).

Feeling that one is not in control of one's life can have an adverse effect on health. Langer and Rodin (1976) investigated the effects of overprotection on the health of seniors in a residential nursing home. Residents of one floor were told that they would be well cared for and that all decisions and responsibilities would be assumed by staff. Another group of residents was told that they would decide on their activities and the arrangement of furniture. They would also select movies and would care for the plants in their rooms. Those for whom personal control was stressed were rated as happier and more active and sociable by nurses, and were reported to be in better health by doctors eighteen months after the study began. In a more recent study, Stirling and Reid (1992) found that geriatric patients who participated actively in their treatment program had better relationships with nurses, a greater sense of involvement in their care, and adjusted more effectively to their circumstances.

PERSONALITY AND HEALTH

An issue of some controversy concerns the relationship between personality and vulnerability to illness (Angell, 1985; Friedman and Booth-Kewley, 1987). A review of the literature has shown personality to be related to risk in the cases of five diseases: asthma, chronic headaches, peptic ulcers, arthritis, and circulatory and heart disease. The three most consistently identified personality variables are anxiety, depression, and anger/hostility. Other research has indicated that those cancer patients who manifest helplessness, hopelessness, and repression tend to have poorer prognoses than do others. This relationship may be due to a linkage between depression and the functioning of the immune system (Levy and Heiden, 1990).

For some time medical researchers have observed that patients who suffer heart attacks are frequently competitive, achievement-oriented, rather impatient, and somewhat hostile. These characteristics make up a personality pattern known as Type A, or coronary-prone personality. (See Box 15-3 for more information about behaviours associated with Type A and Type B personality patterns.) Even after controlling for risk factors—such as cigarette smoking, family history, serum cholesterol levels, and hypertension—some investigators have found a relationship between Type A personality and heart disease (Rosenman, Brand, Jenkins, Friedman, Straus and Wurm, 1975; Nielson and Neufeld, 1986). However, other researchers have failed to confirm this linkage (Ragland and Brand, 1988; Thoreson and Powell, 1992). The inconsistencies in this research may be because only certain kinds of Type A's are at risk, or they may reflect measurement problems. Or it may be that only one or two components of the Type A personality are associated with risk for heart disease (Booth-Kewley and Friedman, 1987). Some studies suggest that an unexpressed "cynical hostility," in which people tend to expect the worst from others, is the specific predictor of coronary illness (Matthews, Glass, Rosenman and Bortner, 1977; Check and Dyck, 1986; Weidner, Istvan and McKnight, 1989).

BOX 15-3

WHAT IS THE TYPE A PERSONALITY?

Rosenman et al.'s (1975) structured interview is a commonly used measure of the Type A pattern. In the interview, both the verbal responses of the subject and his or her observed non-verbal reactions are assessed. Here are some of the observable behaviours exhibited by both personality types.

TYPE A	TYPE B
(1) Vigorous and confident	Relaxed, calm, quiet, attentive
(2) Firm handshake, walks briskly	Gentle handshake, moderate pace
(3) Loud and vigorous voice	Mellow voice
(4) Talks rapidly, especially near end	Talks slowly or moderately
(5) Emphatic one-word response ("Yes!"; "Never!")	No one-word responses
(6) Interrupts other speaker	Rarely interrupts
(7) "Explosive" speech (including expletives)	Explosive speech rare
(8) Hurries other speaker by nodding, saying "Yes," "Uh-huh"	Rarely hurries others
(9) Indicates upset at delay, wasted time	Not upset at delays
(10) Emphasis with clenched fist, pointing	No physical emphasis
(11) Hostility to interviewer or questions	Hostility rare
(12) Tense, abbreviated response	Lengthy, rambling response

Here are a few sample questions from Rosenman et al.'s structured interview:

(5) Would you describe yourself as a hard-driving, ambitious type of man/woman in accomplishing the things you want, getting things done as quickly as possible, or would you describe yourself as a relatively relaxed and easy-going person? (How would your husband/wife describe you?)

(6) When you get angry or upset, do people around you know about it? How do you show it?

(10) When playing games with people your own age, do you play for the fun of it or are you really in there to win?

(19) How do you feel about waiting in lines? Bank lines or supermarket lines? Post office lines?

(21) Do you have the feeling that time is passing too rapidly for you to accomplish all the things you'd like to get done?

Type A's have demonstrated their vulnerability to coronary disease in a number of ways. Cynically hostile people experience more interpersonal conflict and have more difficulty in obtaining social support (Smith, 1992). We have already seen that social support is linked reliably to health. It has also been found that Type A's respond to provocation with much higher levels of aggression (Carver and Glass, 1978). Their anger is associated with higher levels on physiological indices of stress. Angiographic measures taken while subjects are expressing anger show more evidence of stress on the heart in Type A's than in other people (Krantz and Glass, 1984). It is ironic and tragic that the people most at risk are those who are rewarded with success in our competitive society (Thoreson and Powell, 1992).

hardiness *Characteristic of individuals who seem to thrive on challenging events that others find distressing.*

Another personality characteristic that has been found to be related to vulnerability to illness is **hardiness**. Kobasa (1979) studied middle-level executives, whose work involved high levels of stress, in order to understand why some people in such positions enjoy good health while others do not. She found that the healthier executives responded differently to stress, interpreting it as a challenge rather than as a threat. Indeed, these individuals seemed to thrive on challenging events that others found distressing, a characteristic that Kobasa labelled hardiness. In her view, hardiness acts as a buffer against the bad effects of stress. People who score highly on a measure of hardiness show less of an increase in diastolic blood pressure while attempting a difficult task, indicating that they are less responsive physically to stress than other people (Contrada, 1989). The hardy personality style includes a strong sense of self, a belief in an internal locus of control, and a sense of life as being personally meaningful.

SELF-TEST QUESTIONS

1. Which of the following is not a major cause of death in the industrialized world?

a) cancer

b) circulatory diseases

c) typhoid

d) coronary diseases

e) respiratory diseases

2. Problem drinking tends to be part of a more general pattern of behaviour, including the following except for

a) lying and stealing

b) marijuana and other drug use

c) low values for independence

d) precocious sexual involvement

e) less participation in conventional activities in school

3. Janis found _____ to be important in coping with the extreme stress conditions of combat.

a) social support

b) personal characteristics

c) perceived control

d) stressful social circumstances

e) modelling influences

4. In a study of binge eating among students in two university sororities, Crandall (1988) found that

a) those who were least popular tended to be people who binged

b) a person's binge eating could be predicted from the binge eating of her friends

c) the binge eating of friends was not a reliable predictor of a person's eating behaviour

d) those who were most popular tended to be people who binged

e) those who were most popular were those whose eating patterns differed from those of the group as a whole

ILLNESS AND TREATMENT

We now consider what is involved in being ill and seeking treatment. A successful health care interaction follows a sequence of steps:

(1) The patient detects changes and identifies them as symptoms that require medical attention.

(2) The patient presents the problems to the physician.

(3) The physician diagnoses the problem and selects a treatment.

(4) The physician presents the treatment and other recommendations to the patient.

(5) The patient follows the physician's instructions.

Each one of these steps involves knowledge and expectations on the part of the patient and the physician (Ditto and Hilton, 1990; Jones, 1990).

The patient behaves in characteristic ways with respect to communicating with family, friends, and the physician and to responding to the physician's orders. The characteristic actions of the person who is ill, and the reactions of the family, friends, and physician to that person, constitute an interesting and important set of social psychological phenomena.

What are the steps in a successful health care interaction?

SICKNESS AS A SOCIAL ROLE

When people are ill they perceive themselves differently, and others react to them in a different way. There are norms that govern the behaviour of the sick person such as staying in bed, not working, not going out to play ball, and being a "good patient." There are also norms that govern the actions of people responding to the sick person, such as offering sympathy, attention, and chicken soup. Thus, particularly in the case of long-term, disabling, or life-threatening illnesses, sickness can be viewed as a social role and the people involved as behaving in accordance with a role schema for being sick.

Moos (1982) describes seven adaptive tasks faced by people with serious health problems. Some are related to the illness itself, and others concern their social relationships. The individual must:

(1) deal with pain and incapacitation;

(2) deal with stressful medical procedures (including being in the hospital);

What adaptive and coping tasks do sick people face?

(3) communicate with physicians, nurses, and health care personnel about symptoms, diagnosis, and prognosis;

(4) preserve some degree of emotional balance, which may imply hope or acceptance;

(5) maintain a sense of being a person worthy of respect and affection;

(6) preserve relationships with family and friends;

(7) prepare for an uncertain future for him or herself and family.

Being sick has social and physical implications that affect each other. In the health care system, as well as in our own relationships, we are becoming more aware of the social dimension of illness.

Consider the situation of a person who is suffering from a life-threatening condition such as cancer. Dunkel-Schetter, et al. (1992) identify five patterns of coping with cancer. In cognitive escape-avoidance the patient may hope for a miracle, while in behavioural escape-avoidance he or she may try to feel better by eating, drinking, smoking, or drug use. In distancing, the individual tends to make light of the situation, taking the attitude that "you can't let it get to you." Some patients focus on the positive, trying to find what is really important in life, or developing a new faith. Another coping pattern is to seek and use social support, for example by talking to someone about feelings or by trying to get more information about their illness. While social support is an important coping strategy for people in this situation, a person with cancer may be avoided, even stigmatized, by others. The behaviour of others towards the ill person is influenced by feelings and beliefs about the illness itself. The word "cancer" arouses strong feelings of anxiety and personal vulnerability. There may also be reactions of physical aversion if the physical appearance of the person has deteriorated as a result of the disease or treatment (Dunkel-Schetter and Wortman, 1982).

Terminal patients find themselves in a terrible dilemma. Although they are understandably fearful both about their health and their capacity to meet family responsibilities, and need to discuss these matters, they find it difficult to talk and others find it difficult to listen to them. Desperately, patients may try various tactics to gain attention and support. For example, they may become complaining patients, or they may be very positive. A patient recalls, "I got congratulations for being so brave and cheerful. I liked that, so I got more brave and cheerful. And, the more brave and cheerful I was, the more everyone seemed to love me, so I kept it up" (Rollins, 1976, p. 70).

Of course, few people have very much experience coping with serious illness in themselves or in someone close to them. In a situation of intense uncertainty we fall back on stereotyped roles and schematic reactions, or we avoid the issue as much as possible. The result is often isolation and a loss of intimacy at a time when it is most needed.

THE PHYSICIAN-PATIENT RELATIONSHIP

The practice of medicine is becoming increasingly technological and highly specialized. Patients must deal with a number of different specialized physicians, imposing machines, unpleasant procedures, bureaucratic hospitals, and crowded waiting rooms. In this situation, the relationship between the physician and patient is particularly important. The reports of the patient can be a crucial source of information for the physician. Information from the patient may be critical in arriving at a correct diagnosis and in assessing the course of the illness and the effectiveness of treatment. In addition, the cooperation of the patient is often necessary in carrying out a treatment regimen. Considerable research has been devoted to all of these topics.

PAIN

Even with the new medical technologies it is still important for the physician to determine what the patient is experiencing. Patients may interpret what they feel quite differently. They may report the same symptom differently, or not bother to report it at all. Individuals from various ethnic groups have been found to experience and report pain in distinctive ways. For example, contrary to stereotypes, Asian patients do not under-report symptoms, but they are less emotionally expressive while reporting them. As members of this cultural group become more acculturated (adopting the norms and behaviours of the dominant culture) they become less unlike members of that culture in terms of their style of reporting symptoms (Lai and Linden, 1993). It has also been found that ethnic groups are influenced by different factors in their overall experience of pain (Lipton and Marbach, 1984). For example, the responses of Italians were related to how long the pain lasted, whereas the responses of Jewish patients were related to their emotional distress. Irish patients were influenced by the extent to which they felt assimilated into U.S. society. Thus the clinician must be alert to cultural differences in order to interpret the responses of patients.

The experience of pain is related to social psychological factors (Alcock, 1986). We have all learned to identify and label pain, particularly in accidents. The child falls down and cries, and the parent immediately asks, "Where does it hurt?" Although the child may be crying primarily because of fear or surprise, he or she learns to identify pain in this situation. Once we learn how to identify pain, we must learn how to express it appropriately (Craig, 1978). In order that others will take our pain seriously, we must appear to be obviously suffering. Behaving in a disabled manner, showing pain, may become habitual. The disabling effects of pain, for example from rheumatoid arthritis, are increased when people perceive that they lack any personal control over the level of pain they must experience (Tennen et al., 1992). These problems become magnified when the pain is chronic, and may become an issue between patient and physician. The patient may attribute the persisting condition to the inability of the physician to "cure" it. The physician, on the other hand, may attribute it to malingering or exaggeration by the patient. There may be a breakdown in the patient-physician relationship, adding to the patient's stress.

COMMUNICATION AND BEING A "GOOD PATIENT"

Self-disclosure by a patient is dependent to a large degree on the relationship with the physician. Patients may be reluctant to disclose information that seems to be trivial. Most people try to be cooperative, unquestioning of medical authority and rules, and as cheerful as possible under the circumstances (Taylor, 1979). However, the price of being a "good patient" is loss of personal identity (becoming a patient or insurance number), loss of control due to submission to institutional rules and professional decisions, and ignorance of matters about which a normal adult would feel a right to know. One study indicates that physicians like their patients more when they are in better physical and emotional health, and when they are more satisfied with their care (Hall, Epstein, Deciantis and McNeil, 1993).

How does the patient's experience of pain complicate communication between the physician and the patient?

How do being a good patient, non-verbal cues, and gender influence communication between patients and physicians?

Non-verbal communication is particularly important between physicians and patients, for a number of reasons. The physician's non-verbal cues may provide patients with information about their condition, especially about their prognosis for the future. They may also provide the patient with information about the appropriate way to react in an otherwise largely ambiguous situation. Patients may rely on non-verbal cues for information when they are reluctant to ask questions. Certain medical procedures make conversation difficult and awkward, and so the non-verbal channel becomes the only practical means of communication.

As more women have entered medical practice, the question of whether the well-documented gender differences in communication styles (Henley, 1977; Aries, 1987; Eagly and Johnson, 1990) affect communication between physicians and patients has become increasingly relevant. Recent research has shown that female physicians conduct longer visits and ask patients more questions than do male physicians (Roter, Lipkin, and Korsgaard, 1991). However, it is not clear whether female physicians are more empathic (see Wasserman et al. 1984; Hall et al. 1994). Hall and her colleagues found interesting differences between the communication styles of female physicians with female and male patients. Female physician-female patient interactions were "unconflicted, supportive, and egalitarian," but female physician-male patient interactions were "complex and psychologically demanding" (Hall et al., 1994, p. 391). They suggest that female physicians may experience role strains as a result of practising in a traditionally male profession and of being faced with male patients who are generally much older than themselves. Further research will clarify the impact of gender on physician-patient communication and its relation to health care.

WHAT TO TELL THE PATIENT

Perception sometimes may not accord with reality in communication between physicians and patients. Being human, physicians do not like to deliver bad news (Saul and Kass, 1969), and patients who are seriously ill may prefer to cling to illusions and hopes (Miller and Mangan, 1983), even if most say they want to be informed (Blumenfeld, Levy and Kaufman, 1979). In one study it was found that physicians thought they spent more time giving information to their patients than they actually did (Waitzkin, 1984).

How much information physicians should give patients, particularly about a life-threatening or painful procedure, is a troublesome issue. On the one hand, becoming a patient need not imply that one has sacrificed the right to decide about his or her health, or the right to receive the information needed to make such decisions. On the other hand, the physician bears the legal and ethical responsibility for the patient, and may honestly believe that full disclosure would damage his or her health.

PATIENT NON-COMPLIANCE

Typically, a visit to a doctor's office concludes with a recommendation: follow a restricted diet, take a prescribed medication three times a day for two weeks, have your child inoculated for polio or diphtheria, or have some blood tests done. However, research shows that at least one-third of all patients do not comply with the medical regimen prescribed for them (Stone, 1979). For instance, about 20 percent do not have their prescriptions filled (Boyd, Covington, Stanaszek and Coussons, 1974). In some cases, **non-compliance** is much higher, particularly when preventive health measures have been recommended. It is unfortu-

What is involved in the issue of how much information a physician should give a patient?

non-compliance Failure to follow recommendations of a medical professional.

nate that, despite their best efforts, physicians are remarkably ineffectual in influencing their patients to exercise more, smoke less, and eat more moderately.

Non-compliance is a common problem in the later stages of treatment, especially when the original symptoms are no longer evident. However, if a therapeutic measure continues to relieve severe pain or is seen as potentially life-saving (e.g. chemotherapy for cancer), the patient usually will comply. Thousands of patients quit smoking, lose weight, and exercise diligently after their first heart attack. Antibiotic medications are often taken diligently for the first few days of acute illness until the patient begins to feel better. Then compliance starts to wane and the illness often recurs.

It is misleading to attribute non-compliance simply to patients' personality characteristics. Rather, the tactics used by the health professional to elicit compliance and the relationship between physician and patient must be examined. For example, patients do not like assembly-line treatment of their afflicted organs by impersonal specialists, and are more likely to comply when they see the same physician over time. Research shows that patients comply when they perceive their physicians as friendly, caring, and interested in them, as well as having sound knowledge and technical ability (DiNicola and DiMatteo, 1984). Warmth in an interpersonal relationship may be communicated non-verbally by eye contact, physical posture, and movement. Rodin and Janis (1979) also suggest that physicians can enhance the therapeutic relationship by encouraging self-disclosure by the patient, giving positive feedback of acceptance and understanding, asking whether the patient understands and accepts the recommendations, and implying that the patient has the ultimate control and responsibility in the situation. Patients are also more likely to comply with physicians who are satisfied in their profession, who are specialists in the relevant area, who have busier practices, and who make definite follow-up appointments with their patients in order to track progress, regardless of the physician's age, gender, or ethnic group (DiMatteo et al., 1993).

***What contributes to
non-compliance?***

SELF-TEST QUESTIONS

5. Staying in bed, taking medications as directed, and not going to work are part of _____ behaviour.

a) coronary-prone

b) health-risk

c) health-promotion

d) sick role

e) normative

6. According to the text, patients are more likely to comply with their physicians if

a) the patient is given a sense of personal control

b) threatened with the grave consequences of non-compliance

c) the physician conveys a personal concern about the patient

d) a and b

e) a and c

7. According to Alcock (1986), what social psychological process may contribute to chronic pain?

a) social comparison

b) social reinforcement from others

c) cultural differences

d) sick role schemas

8. What is a major social problem faced by people with life-threatening illnesses?

a) cognitive dissonance

b) inability to communicate about the illness

c) social comparison process

d) physician non-compliance

HEALTH PROMOTION

health promotion *Actions taken to enhance and protect health and to prevent illness, particularly through self-responsibility.*

How has legislation been used in an effort to prevent health problems?

We now turn to a discussion of those factors that may assist individuals and society in preventing illness and preserving health. As we have already noted, much of the illness and mortality in our society can be attributed to unhealthy behaviours. In order to save lives, preserve health, and contain the escalating cost of medical care, health promotion and prevention of disease are logical and necessary moves.

In the field of public health, a wide variety of approaches to prevention have been followed with varying degrees of success. One of these is the legislative route. For example, laws that mandate the use of seat belts and lower speed limits have generally reduced fatalities in automobile accidents (Robertson, 1984). While the long-term effect of laws against drunk driving has not been convincingly demonstrated, short-term, highly visible campaigns are relatively effective (Klajner, Sobell and Sobell, 1984). With regard to alcohol use, some researchers have argued that decreasing accessibility to alcohol will decrease the per capita consumption and decrease the incidence of both social and health problems attributable to excessive drinking (Popham, Schmidt and DeLint, 1976). Examples of strategies for limiting access are increasing prices, earlier closing times, and raising the minimum drinking age. Heavy drinkers may well be less affected than others by such measures.

HEALTH-ENHANCING BEHAVIOURS

health-enhancing behaviour *Behaviour that facilitates the maintenance of good health and the prevention of disease and health problems.*

primary prevention *Measures taken to prevent disease and health problems in currently healthy individuals.*

Another approach to health promotion is to persuade people to engage in **health-enhancing behaviours**, which facilitate the maintenance of good health and prevention of disease and health problems. This is the main concern of **primary prevention**, which includes measures taken to prevent disease and health problems in currently healthy individuals. Examples of health-enhancing behaviours whose goal is primary prevention include exercise, moderation in alcohol consumption, not driving after drinking, use of seat belts and child restraints in cars, not smoking, a moderate and balanced diet, inoculation against various infectious diseases, and proper care and precautions during pregnancy. (Secondary prevention, on the other hand, refers to early diagnosis and treatment.)

Health-enhancing behaviours can be an effective means of promoting health and containing the cost of medical care. Thus it is important to understand the

"I don't know if Jack Sprat was on a low cholesterol diet. All it says here is he couldn't eat any fat."

factors that influence whether people engage in these behaviours. A model has been developed that specifically deals with health-related attitudes and behaviours. This is the **Health Beliefs Model** (Becker, 1974), which is outlined in Figure 15-2. We will work through the model using the example of a currently healthy individual whose physician has recommended some form of exercise (jogging, swimming, cycling, or aerobics classes) to promote cardiovascular fitness and reduce the risk of heart attack.

The process begins with the individual's readiness to act, to do something in order to become more physically fit (A). This readiness occurs because the person believes that he or she is susceptible to a serious illness (in this case heart disease, which could be fatal). The readiness to act is experienced as a real and personal threat (E). The sense of threat is influenced by other factors, such as demographic and psychosocial characteristics (C). For example, concern with health risk and

Health Beliefs Model
Focuses on a person's perceived susceptibility to disease or health problems and perceived costs and benefits of actions.

FIGURE 15-2 The Health Beliefs Model

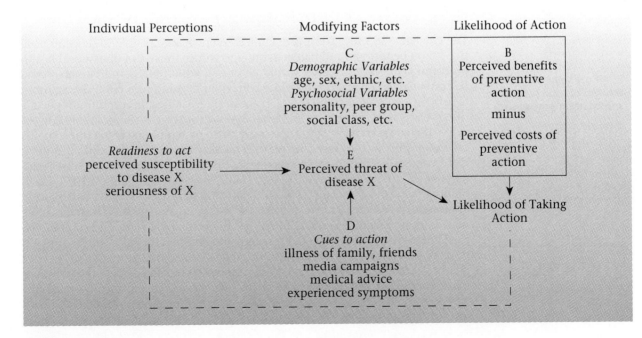

According to the Health Beliefs Model, what factors influence health-enhancing behaviours?

the finite nature of life is more likely to increase the sense of threat in someone who is middle-aged than in a younger person. If the perceived threat of possible illness is accompanied by cues to action (D), then behaviour change is likely to occur. Cues to action may include family members who have heart disease or the repeated urging by a physician. The choice of action will depend upon the relative costs and benefits perceived for various alternatives (B). Aerobic exercise, for example, may be perceived as both a desirable and effective preventive action because of its health benefits and its more immediate benefits of reducing obesity and enhancing physical appearance.

The Health Beliefs Model is based on the premise that people consciously and rationally evaluate the risks and then weigh the benefits and costs of various actions. This may not always be the case. Weinstein (1984) found that students have unrealistically optimistic beliefs about their own health. While they assume, often correctly, that factors such as family history might signify risk for an illness, they ignore the role of their own behaviour. For example, they perceived no relationship between their own risk of a heart attack and their own actions, such as how much they exercised, how much high-cholesterol food they consumed, or how much they smoked. Cohn et al. (1995) found that compared to adults, teenagers minimized the perceived risk of experimental and occasional involvement in health-threatening activities (e.g. driving drunk, smoking cigarettes, using cocaine). In addition, adolescents believed they were more likely than their peers to avoid such risky behaviours as riding with drunk drivers, and more likely to recognize when they drank too much at a party.

A threat to health may be so stressful that people may be more affected by emotional reactions or habitual schematic modes of thinking than by rational deliberation. They may also be influenced by factors other than health. For example, they may be more influenced by concerns for appearance than for health. Describing osteoporosis as disfiguring and highly visible enhances the probability that subjects will exercise and take calcium supplements to reduce this disease (Klohn and Rogers, 1991).

INTERVENTION PROGRAMS

What are some characteristics of a successful intervention program?

The challenge in prevention programs is to encourage people to develop positive health behaviours and habits in order to reduce the risk of disease and health problems. The ideal program would be one in which many individuals would be convinced to change to healthier behaviour at minimum cost. The Stanford Heart Disease Program, which took place in three California communities over a three-year period, was one of the first large-scale intervention programs (Meyer, et al., 1980; Maccoby, 1988). There were three experimental conditions: media campaign plus face-to-face instruction, media campaign only, and a no-treatment condition. Participants in the media-campaign-only condition were recipients of an intensive bilingual (English and Spanish) campaign on TV, radio, billboards, posters, and direct mail. The campaign was designed to heighten awareness of risk factors in heart disease and to encourage specific behaviours such as losing weight, exercising more, and not smoking. In a second community, participants received the media campaign and also became involved in nine sessions of group instruction based on principles of social learning. Subjects were taught specific behavioural skills related to health practices, such as techniques in self-control and how to cope with giving up smoking. The instructors themselves modelled the behaviours, and each week social reinforcement was given by both instructors and the group to those who successfully changed their own behaviour.

The findings were encouraging. People in both towns receiving the media campaign had greater knowledge of the risk factors in heart diseases. Although there was no definitive evidence that heart disease was reduced, the risk factors were reduced. Serum cholesterol levels and blood pressure were reduced in both communities receiving the media campaign. In fact, blood pressure was reduced most dramatically among those whose blood pressure was highest before the study began. In addition, there were some significant behaviour changes. For example, smoking was significantly reduced, particularly in the town where both the media and individualized instruction campaigns were received.

An expanded program added five larger cities, and involved more intensive mass media and community organization strategies. Researchers found that the overall risk of coronary and vascular diseases was reduced by 16 percent over the nine years of the study (Farquhar et al., 1990). These studies clearly indicate that social psychology can be applied successfully to reduce the incidence of demonstrable risk factors for heart disease.

SOCIAL PSYCHOLOGY OF AN EPIDEMIC: AIDS

Acquired immune deficiency syndrome (AIDS) was first identified as such in 1981, although it had probably been around for a lot longer (Hall, 1988). It is brought on by the human immunodeficiency virus (HIV), a retrovirus that damages the immune system by selectively infecting one type of cell, the T-4 "helper-inducer" lymphocyte (or T-cell). This deficiency in the body's normal defences leaves the individual vulnerable to repeated viral, bacterial, and parasitical infection, which would ordinarily be controlled or eliminated. Victims of AIDS typically die from rare forms of pneumonia (pneumocystis carinii) and cancer (Kaposi's sarcoma). Some AIDS victims also suffer from neuropsychiatric disturbances. Although AIDS is found more frequently among males, the survival time after diagnosis for HIV-positive women is shorter (Ickovics and Rodin, 1992). Since the human immunodeficiency virus is fragile, easily killed by bleach, alcohol, detergent or soap, heat, or drying, it is transmitted from person to person only through intimate exchange of body fluids, specifically blood transfusions, open sores, shared intravenous needles, and semen (Batchelor, 1988). While recent advances in research offer hope in the form of drugs which slow the onset and progress of AIDS-related illnesses, no cure is as yet in sight.

Psychology has contributed in several ways to society's response to this epidemic (Morin, 1988). One area of activity concerns the needs of those afflicted with AIDS, in assisting patients in tolerating medical treatment and in coping with a debilitating terminal illness. A second area of activity pertains to the social and political reactions of people and society in general to this epidemic. Finally, social psychology has joined the efforts to break the AIDS transmission chain by changing high-risk behaviour (e.g. promoting "safer sex") and by building community support and awareness of the problem. In this chapter, we discuss the latter two concerns.

How has psychology contributed to society's response to AIDS?

ATTITUDES

Clearly, public awareness of AIDS has been unusually high. Indeed, over a two-year period from 1991–1993, *The Globe and Mail* published over 66 stories on a disease that would kill an estimated 1552 Canadians. In comparison, only 219 articles appeared on all forms of cancer, which would kill over 50 000 Canadians during the same period (Strauss, 1993). As has been historically typical in cases of epidemics, public reactions to AIDS and its victims have not always been characterized by either rationality or empathy (Conrad, 1986). There are many widely held, uninformed beliefs about AIDS and how it is transmitted. As well, many people express a distrust of experts in this area.

People suffering from AIDS often find themselves isolated and deprived of social support because of the fear of the disease (Triplet and Sugarman, 1987). Those identified as AIDS patients have been evicted by landlords, fired from a wide variety of jobs, and refused baptism by church elders. Parents have even tried to bar from public schools children who have contracted AIDS. Pryor, Reeder and Vinacco (1989) conducted a series of studies in which subjects were asked to imagine having their child in a class with a haemophiliac child who was diagnosed as having contracted AIDS through a blood transfusion. They found, as one would expect, that subjects' beliefs about the possibility that AIDS might be contagious were related to their attitudes towards having their child in school with an AIDS victim.

Why are people with AIDS socially stigmatized? There are several reasons why AIDS can be considered a stigma that causes rejection of the infected person (Herek and Glunt, 1988). First, because it is incurable and transmissible, AIDS victims are often erroneously perceived as placing others at risk. Second, people with AIDS are often blamed for having caused their illness through high-risk, avoidable behaviour. Further, people with advanced AIDS may have visible and sometimes disfiguring symptoms, and people may stigmatize and avoid those whom they find "repulsive" in some way. Finally, AIDS victims are associated with intravenous drug users and homosexuals, whether or not they belong to those stigmatized groups. In the study by Pryor, et al. (1989) mentioned above, subjects who were most opposed to allowing the AIDS-infected child in their own child's class also had negative attitudes towards homosexuals. While homosexuals and needle drug abusers are high-risk groups in North America, many people still consider AIDS to be a disease only of stigmatized groups and not a risk to themselves, a misconception that may prove fatal.

PREVENTION

In the absence of a cure or a vaccine, the only way to control the AIDS epidemic involves decreasing the behaviours that put people at risk, and increasing preventive behaviour. Kelly and Kalichman (1995) argue that the success of prevention efforts depends on designing programs that integrate findings from research on human sexuality with cognitive-behavioural and social learning principles. Expressions of sexuality occur within many different relationship, cultural, situational, and role contexts, all of which may influence whether "safer sex" practices are used. For example, the relationship contexts of sexuality (casual relationships, women in power-imbalanced relationships with men who resist "safer sex" practices, gay men, coercive relationships) are associated with different group norms and beliefs about sexual practices. If the "script" for sexual relations calls for spontaneity, then each partner will fear rejection by the other if he or she attempts to bring up the topic of protection at an "inopportune time." If teenagers want to appear willing to take risks, and feel invulnerable, then concern with protective behaviour will be discouraged. Among gay men, condoms are incorporated differently into scripts for short-term as opposed to long-term sexual relationships (Gold, Skinner and Ross, 1994). Similarly, if using condoms is inconsistent with one's religious values, then that kind of protection is unlikely to be used.

What factors are related to AIDS-preventive behaviours?

How to incorporate "safer sex" practices into diverse sexual scripts and group norms presents a challenge to those designing AIDS prevention programs. One possibility is to "sell" preventive behaviour as fashionable, emphasizing the gains in popularity and social acceptance from engaging in "safer sex." If the norms of the group in question favour a fairly free approach to sexual relations, then suggesting abstinence will be useless in preventing AIDS. An emphasis on "safer sex" that does not conflict with the permissibility of sexual relations is more likely to be effective.

One particular problem in AIDS prevention is that it is not based on personal experience, which would lead people to see themselves and others as being at risk (Weinstein, 1989). Thus, high levels of unprotected sex persist among sexually active students. One study (Williams et al., 1992) suggests that many of these students apply a form of **implicit personality theory** in the belief that they "know" who is safe and who is not. For example, individuals whom they have known for some time or are from the same home town, and partners whom they like, are assumed to be safe sexual partners.

implicit personality theory Assumptions a person holds about which traits go together and about human nature.

Fisher, Fisher and Rye (1995) have demonstrated that the theory of reasoned action (see Chapter 4) provides a useful model for understanding and promoting AIDS-preventive behaviour. They found that attitudes towards sexual behaviours were influenced by beliefs about consequences of the behaviours and evaluations of those consequences. For female university and high school students and gay men, intentions to engage in many AIDS-preventive behaviours were a function of norms and of attitudes towards the act. For heterosexual male university students, intentions were sometimes under the control of personal attitudes alone, rather than attitudes and social norms. Departures from the dual attitudinal and normative control of intentions also occurred for some male high school students. Most of the AIDS-preventive behaviours investigated were predicted by behavioural intentions. This relationship was less consistent for the high school subject groups. Taken together, the results suggest that it is important to develop strategies aimed at modifying relevant attitudes and norms in order to change behavioural intentions towards and the practice of AIDS-preventive behaviours.

The voluminous literature on changing AIDS-risk behaviour indicates that change depends on three factors:

(1) people's information about how AIDS is transmitted and how this can be prevented;

(2) people's motivations to reduce AIDS risk, which is influenced by social norms, beliefs, and personal experience with someone who has contracted AIDS;

(3) their behavioural skills in reducing AIDS risk, which includes being able to communicate effectively and assertively with their partners as well as being able to utilize protective strategies and avoid higher-risk practices.

While these components are interrelated, all are necessary if behaviour is to change (Fisher and Fisher, 1992).

SOME FINAL OBSERVATIONS

This chapter began with the assumption that people want to be healthy and can be motivated to act accordingly. However, the research evidence does not show that people act in a consistent manner relevant to their health (Norman,

1985). We cannot assume that people who live very healthy lifestyles will consult a physician when it is appropriate or will comply with his or her recommendations. Clearly, different health behaviours may be influenced by different factors. For example, persons who think of health primarily in terms of medical treatment may be willing to accept medical procedures such as showing up regularly for electrocardiograms, but will not exercise or eat moderately. People may do healthy things for reasons not related to health. For example, people may diet and attend exercise classes solely out of concern for physical attractiveness. Conformity, social acceptance, pleasure, and faith in the physician and in medicine are all powerful determinants of behaviours that influence health.

SELF-TEST QUESTIONS

9. An example of a legislative approach towards prevention would be

a) the mandatory use of seatbelts and lower speed limits

b) increasing prices of cigarettes and alcoholic beverages

c) increasing the minimum drinking age

d) b and c

e) all of the above

10. In the Health Beliefs Model, the perception of rewards and costs determines

a) a readiness to act

b) the perception of threat

c) the cues for action

d) the choice of what action to take

e) whether to remain in a relationship

11. In a large-scale program of intervention in three California communities over a three-year period, it was found that

a) blood pressure was reduced most dramatically among those whose blood pressure was highest before the study began

b) smoking was significantly reduced in both of the towns that received the media campaign

c) the effects were the same for all three communities

d) there was definite evidence that heart disease was reduced

e) a and b

12. According to the text, psychologists have contributed in several ways to society's response to the AIDS epidemic by

a) examining ways of breaking the chain of transmission by changing high-risk behaviour

b) assisting patients in tolerating medical treatment and coping with a debilitating and terminal illness

c) helping to find a permanent cure for AIDS

d) a and b

e) all of the above

SUMMARY

(1) Health is significantly influenced by behaviour.

(2) Problem behaviour theory regards adolescent health-risk behaviour, such as drug abuse, as part of a syndrome of non-conventional personality characteristics, social environment, and behaviours.

(3) Social modelling influences health-risk behaviours by promoting the onset of the behaviour and eliciting it more frequently.

(4) Vulnerability to illness is increased by an absence of social support, a perception that life cannot be controlled, and by characteristics of the Type A personality.

(5) Being ill involves a social role in which we see ourselves differently and others treat us differently.

(6) Patients often fail to comply with medical recommendations. Patient compliance and accurate diagnosis are strongly influenced by the relationship and communication between patients and physicians.

(7) In general, conveying accurate information to patients contributes to their recovery, even when it provokes anxiety.

(8) Primary prevention refers to reducing the probability of the onset of a disease. Secondary prevention refers to early diagnosis and treatment.

(9) Persuasion, including fear arousal with recommended actions, can lead to behaviour change.

(10) According to the Health Beliefs Model, people are ready to do something to promote health if they believe they are personally susceptible to illness and can do something about it.

(11) People suffering from AIDS have been stigmatized, in part through association with other stigmatized groups.

(12) Health behaviours are influenced by many factors, including those not related to health.

FOR REVIEW

In the twentieth century in industrialized nations, the most frequent causes of death are the major _____(1) diseases.

Problem behaviour theory involves a pattern of _____(2), _____(2), and _____(2) characteristics. People who drink with a heavy drinker tend to drink more because of _____(3) influences. In a study of binge eating among students in two university sororities (Crandall, 1988), it was found that _____(4) regarding uncontrollable binge eating differed significantly.

Janis (1951) found that soldiers who were able and willing to endure severe stress belonged to a _____(5) combat unit. The text also discusses the importance of social support to the health of _____(6) and _____(6). Social support may not always be beneficial to health, because others may _____(7) maladaptive behaviours.

The research of Langer and Rodin with elderly residents in a nursing home shows the importance of perceived _____(8) for health. People with an _____(9) locus of control tend to take care of themselves and cope better with illness.

For some time medical researchers have observed that patients who suffer _____(10) are frequently competitive, achievement-oriented, rather impatient, and somewhat hostile. Some studies suggest that a characteristic of ____(11) is the specific predictor of coronary illness.

While speaking to a physician, patients may be reluctant to disclose information that seems ____(12). When they are reluctant to ask questions, they may rely on ____(13) cues for information. When patients perceive that their physician is friendly and interested in them, they are more likely to ____(14) with the physician's recommendations.

The Health Beliefs Model deals with the relationship between health-related ____(15) and ____(15). A major flaw in this model is that it assumes a ____(16) process of decision making.

The challenge to intervention programs is to encourage people to engage in ____(17) behaviours in order to reduce the risk of disease and health problems. Research on the theory of reasoned action in relation to AIDS-preventive behaviours has shown that ____(18) and ____(18) affect behavioural intentions. Also, behavioural intentions predicted ____(19). The literature on changing AIDS-risk behaviour indicates that change depends on three factors: ____(20), ____(20), and ____(20).

ISSUES AND ACTIVITIES

(1) Describe a situation that you found stressful, and make a list of the strategies you used to deal with it. Comment on and account for the success or failure of each strategy.

(2) Consider the information about Mary in the following paragraph and apply the Health Beliefs Model to her situation:

Mary is a 20-year-old college student who is living away from home for the first time. Although she finds most of her college courses reasonably interesting, what she likes to do best is party with her friends. Between classes Mary spends a lot of time in the Merry Duck, the campus pub. Recently Mary has missed many of her History classes. Her academic advisor warned her that she is in danger of failing not only History, but two other courses as well. Lately Mary has been feeling homesick, and so one weekend she suddenly decided to surprise her parents by going home for a visit. As she came up the walk to the front door of her parents' home, she heard her mother angrily accusing her father of spending so much of his salary on alcohol that the family is accumulating a considerable debt.

(3) Debate or discuss whether government medical coverage should be tied to an assessment of the individual's health risk and health enhancing behaviours.

(4) One of the topics discussed in this chapter was sickness as a role, including the role schema for being sick, adaptive tasks faced by people with serious health problems, and patterns of coping with terminal illness. (a) View the *Sue Rodriguez* video segment and discuss the manner in which she dealt with her terminal illness in relation to the material presented in the text. (b) View the video segment *All in their Heads,* and discuss the problems faced by the sick hospital workers at Camp Hill Hospital in relation to Moos' adaptive tasks.

• FURTHER READING

BLANE, H.T. and LEONARD, K.E. (Eds.) (1987). *Psychological theories of drinking and alcoholism.* New York: Guilford. A review of current thinking in this area, including models based on social psychological principles.

TAYLOR, S.E. (1989). *Positive illusions: Creative self-deception and the healthy mind.* New York: Basic Books. A well-supported argument by a social psychologist that unrealistic optimism about one's self, one's health, and the future can enhance physical and mental well-being. Positive illusions can prevent a seriously ill person from giving up, and can act as a buffer against stress.

SUGGESTED WEBLINKS

American Psychological Association journals (selected APA journals, including *Health Psychology*)

> http.www.apa.org/journals/journals.html

European Health Psychology Society

> http://fub46.zedat.fu-berlin.de:8080/~ahahn/ehp/ehps.htm

PSYC SITE A site set up to help psychology students and researchers find information about scientific research in psychology on the World Wide Web. Designed to be a "major jumping off point" for seeking out psychological information. Maintained by the Psychology Department of the University of Nipissing.

> http://www.unipissing.ca/psyc/psycsite.htm

Statistics Canada

> http://www.statcan.ca

ANSWERS TO SELF-TEST QUESTIONS

1. c; 2. c; 3. a; 4. b; 5. d; 6. e; 7. b; 8. b; 9. e; 10. d; 11. e; 12. d.

ANSWERS TO FOR REVIEW

1. chronic; 2. personality, environmental, and behavioural; 3. modelling; 4. norms; 5. cohesive or supportive; 6. cardiac patients and new mothers and their babies; 7. reinforce; 8. control; 9. internal; 10. heart attacks; 11. cynical hostility; 12. trivial; 13. non-verbal; 14. comply; 15. attitudes, behaviours; 16. rational; 17. positive health or health enhancing; 18. attitudes, norms; 19. AIDS-preventive behaviours; 20. knowledge about how AIDS transmission can be prevented, people's motivations to reduce AIDS risk, people's skills in AIDS-preventive behaviours.

GLOSSARY

acculturation *(6)* When different groups come into contact there will be changes to all involved.

actor versus observer bias *(2)* Tendency to attribute the actions of others to personality characteristics while viewing one's own behaviour as being influenced more by the situation.

aggression *(8)* A behaviour intended to harm or destroy.

altruism *(9)* Behaviour whose purpose is to help others, without expectation of an external or internal reward.

arbitration *(11)* Direct intervention, or solutions suggested or imposed.

archival approach *(1)* Research strategy that uses data already collected for other purposes.

attitude *(4)* A predisposition to act in a certain way towards an object or experience. It includes cognitive, behavioural, and affective components.

attributions *(9)* Our assumptions about the motivation we attribute to a person's behaviour.

authoritarian personality *(6)* That which is rigid, conventional, cynical, and prejudiced.

authoritarianism *(13)* Behaviour characterized by rigid thinking, submissiveness to authority, and hostility towards those who are perceived as different.

autocratic leadership *(10)* When the leader makes all the decisions it may result in greater productivity in situations of high stress.

availability heuristic *(2)* Strategy of making judgments in terms of readily accessible and easily remembered information.

base-rate information *(2)* Information about the frequency with which some characteristic or event occurs in a group.

behaviourism *(1)* A theoretical orientation based on the premise that all behaviour is governed by external reinforcement.

blind technique *(1)* Experimental strategy in which subjects are unaware of the group to which they belong.

bystander effect *(9)* When a number of people all witness the same emergency, people are less likely to help.

capital punishment *(13)* Use of the death penalty.

case study *(1)* In-depth analysis and investigation of a single case.

catharsis *(8)* Reduction in aggressive drives, thought to result from either acting aggressively or watching others do so.

causal attributions *(2)* People's explanations for the causes of behaviour or events.

central route persuasion *(4)* Attitude change that follows logical argumentation and thought about an issue.

charisma *(10)* Self-confidence, dominance, charm, and a belief in themselves characterize charismatic leaders.

chronic loneliness *(7)* Relatively enduring, unpleasant feelings brought about by dissatisfaction with one's social interactions.

CL (comparison level) *(11)* People compare their situations with those of others in order to decide if their own relationship is satisfactory.

classical conditioning *(6)* Learning by associating something neutral with something having significant consequences.

CLalt (comparison level for alternatives) *(11)* By looking at what alternatives are available, people make a decision about whether to stay in a relationship.

coercive power *(10)* Influence based on threat in order to gain compliance.

cognitive dissonance *(4)* An unpleasant motivational state caused by awareness of inconsistency among behaviours and cognitive elements.

cognitive elaboration *(4)* Cognitive activity or processing that involves both current and related information already stored in memory.

cognitive perspective *(1)* A psychological perspective that focuses on how we process, store, and retrieve information.

cohesiveness *(10)* The elements that draw a group together include participation, cooperation, and communication.

collective behaviour *(12)* Spontaneous, unorganized, and unpredictable behaviour.

collective dilemma *(11)* A situation that occurs when each person in a group behaves in a way that is best for him or herself—but when everyone does this it can be destructive for the group.

commons problem *(11)* When everyone uses too much of a public resource it may become depleted and lost to all.

communication accommodation theory *(3)* View that we modify our speech style in an effort to be liked and approved by other people.

complementarity principle *(7)* People are attracted because they satisfy each other's needs.

compliance *(5)* Behaviour in which one yields in response to a direct request.

confidentiality *(1)* Protection of the identity of a research subject.

conflict *(11)* When two or more parties are in disagreement and believe they cannot achieve their interests at the same time.

conflict based on false premises *(11)* Conflict based on totally different perceptions of what a behaviour means.

conflict spiral *(11)* A situation of threat and counterthreat with each side in the conflict becoming more defensive.

conformity *(5)* Behaviour that adheres to group norms and yields to perceived group pressures.

conspiracy theory *(12)* An irrational belief that people or groups are plotting to destroy an individual or society.

contagion *(8)* Imitative repetition by adults of crimes of violence reported in the newspaper or other media.

contagion theory *(12)* The notion that emotions, beliefs, and behaviours spread through a crowd in the same way as a disease spreads.

contagions *(12)* Strong emotional beliefs and actions that spread throughout a population.

contingency theory *(10)* Leadership style must be matched to a particular group situation in order for leadership to be successful.

contingent conflict *(11)* When the parties fail to recognize that resources exist to allow each party to satisfy their needs.

control group *(1)* Group in an experiment that does not receive the treatment variable and whose behaviour serves as a basis of comparison.

conversational control *(3)* Use of non-verbal communication to regulate the form and pace of a conversation.

correlation *(1)* Extent to which scores on one measure are predictable by the scores on another measure.

credibility *(4)* Believability. A communicator is credible if he or she is perceived as knowledgeable and trustworthy.

credulity *(12)* The level of trust one has in the truth of a rumour.

cross-cultural research *(1)* Studies in which subjects from more than one society or ethnic group are compared.

crowd *(12)* An unorganized, anonymous, temporary collection of people.

crowding *(14)* The discomfort we experience when we feel there are too many people in a given space.

cult *(12)* A group of people who are drawn to and believe in a particular authoritarian leader. They are persuaded to obey this leader regardless of the cost.

dangerous conflict *(11)* Conflict that is so intense that if neither side backs down a catastrophic loss may occur.

dangerous offender *(13)* Person who receives an unlimited prison sentence.

debriefing *(1)* Explaining to a subject what the experiment was about.

deception clues *(13)* Behaviour that suggests an attitude different from what is expressed.

defendant *(13)* Person accused and on trial for a crime.

dehoaxing *(1)* Explaining, when the experiment is over, what deception was used and why.

deindividuation *(12)* When people become part of a crowd they may lose their identity.

democratic leadership *(10)* When group members are involved in decision making, greater satisfaction is usually the result.

density *(14)* The number of people in a given space.

dependent variable *(1)* A measured outcome in an experiment.

desensitization *(1)* After research, helping the subject to understand and resolve changes in behaviour or attitudes.

desensitization *(8)* Reduction in emotional response to violence due to excessive exposure to violence.

deterrence schema *(11)* A situation of increasing levels of aggression being met with concessions, so that when resistance comes it is not taken seriously.

diffusion of responsibility *(9)* When a number of people are present help may not be given, because each person may assume that someone else has taken charge.

discrimination *(6)* Overt behaviour that belittles or excludes people of particular groups.

displaced conflict *(11)* Conflict directed not at the real problem but at a related issue, often because the real problem is not recognized.

distraction-conflict theory *(5)* When people are in the presence of others, they may experience arousal caused by a conflict over whether to attend to the task or the audience.

door-in-the-face technique *(5)* A means of securing agreement to a moderate request by first making an unreasonable request.

double-blind *(1)* A control in research whereby neither the subject nor the experimenter who interacts with the subject knows to which condition the subject has been assigned.

emergent norm theory *(12)* Suggests that in a crowd norms of behaviour begin to emerge, and that people begin to act according to these norms.

empathy *(9)* A concern for and understanding of the situation of another person.

empathy-altruism hypothesis *(9)* Suggests that pure altruism comes from empathy.

equity principle *(7)* Outcomes received in a relationship are proportional to contributions to it.

ethnocentrism *(6)* The belief that one's own group is superior to other groups.

ethnolinguistic vitality *(3)* The relative status and strength of a language in a particular social structure or environment.

evaluation apprehension *(5)* A concern for how other people are evaluating us.

experimental group *(1)* Group that receives the treatment variable.

experimental realism *(1)* Extent to which the situation encountered in an experiment involves subjects so that they react in a natural way.

expert power *(10)* Influence based on acceptance of the superior knowledge possessed by a person or group.

expert testimony *(13)* That given by someone who is an authority in some area relevant to the trial.

external locus of control *(15)* The belief that one's outcomes are determined by forces outside of oneself.

external validity *(1)* Degree to which findings from a laboratory can be generalized to predict how the subject would act in the real world.

extraneous variable *(1)* A factor not included in the design of the study, and which influences the study's outcome.

extra-punitive defence *(6)* Putting the blame for one's own situation on others.

facial display *(3)* A pattern of expressions that communicates information, particularly about the emotional state of the individual.

fad *(12)* A short-lived, extreme, and usually frivolous type of behaviour.

false consensus effect *(2)* Tendency to overestimate the extent to which others agree with us.

fashion *(12)* Consumer behaviour that may serve to make a person's status known or to simply relieve boredom.

field experiment *(1)* Experiment conducted in a natural setting in which subjects do not know that they are participating in an experiment.

field study *(1)* Direct observation of people in a natural setting.

foils *(13)* People in the lineup who are not suspects.

foot-in-the-door technique *(5)* A means of securing agreement to a major request by first obtaining agreement to a small request.

forewarning *(4)* Imparting advance knowledge of persuasive intent or message content.

frustration-aggression hypothesis *(8)* Frustration produces a state of unpleasantness, which leads to aggressive behaviour.

functional number *(13)* The number of people in a lineup who share significant characteristics with the culprit.

fundamental attribution error *(2)* Tendency to exaggerate the importance of personal factors and to underestimate the influence of the situation.

GRIT *(11)* A strategy whereby each side in a conflict gives up something in turn until the tension is resolved.

group *(10)* Two or more people who influence each other, share common goals, have an ongoing relationship, and who believe they belong to the group.

group-induced attitude polarization *(10)* Attitudes become more extreme in a group due to a closer comparison and identification with group members and their views.

groupthink *(5)* Tendency of a highly cohesive and elitist group to achieve a rapid consensus without dissent or outside influences.

habituation *(8)* Reduction in physiological response as a result of repeated stimulation.

haptics *(3)* Perception and use of touch in communication.

hardiness *(15)* Characteristic of individuals who seem to thrive on challenging events that others find distressing.

Health Beliefs Model *(15)* Focuses on a person's perceived susceptibility to disease or health problems and perceived costs and benefits of actions.

health-enhancing behaviour *(15)* Behaviour that facilitates the maintenance of good health and the prevention of disease and health problems.

health promotion *(15)* Actions taken to enhance and protect health and to prevent illness, particularly through self-responsibility.

heuristics *(2)* Cognitive shortcuts used to simplify judgment or decision making.

hostile aggression *(8)* Aggression that is instigated by anger and directed at harming another person.

hypothesis *(1)* Testable proposition derived from theory.

illusion of control *(2)* Exaggerated belief in our own capacity to determine what happens to us in life.

illusory correlation *(6)* The overestimation of a group's behaviour because it is unusual.

image repair hypothesis *(9)* People who are embarrassed by some previous behaviour may attempt to repair that damage by being more generous.

immersion program *(3)* A form of second-language education in which the second language is used for instruction and interaction rather than being treated as a separate subject.

implicit personality theory *(15)* Assumptions a person holds about which traits go together and about human nature.

independent variable *(1)* A condition in an experiment that is manipulated by the experimenter.

indictable offence *(13)* Crime governed by the criminal code of Canada.

informational power *(10)* Influence based on our acceptance that a person or group has information that we do not have.

informational social influence *(5)* The matching of our own ideas to those of the group in order to determine if we are "correct."

informed consent *(1)* Providing enough information for a subject to make an informed choice about participation in an experiment.

in groups *(10)* Groups to which we belong and with which we identify.

inoculation *(4)* Exposure to relatively weak arguments against our own position in order to strengthen our resistance to persuasion.

instinct *(8)* Inborn behavioural tendencies that motivate certain behaviours in all members of a species in the presence of appropriate stimuli.

institutionalized discrimination *(6)* Occurs when organizational policy puts racial minorities at a disadvantage, e.g. employment practices.

instrumental aggression *(8)* Behaviour intended to harm as a means to some desired end.

instrumental conditioning *(6)* Learning from the consequences (reinforcement or punishment) of behaviour.

instrumental motivation *(6)* Learning a language because it will be useful.

integrative motivation *(6)* Learning a language because it is part of a culture that is interesting.

intergroup anxiety *(6)* Stems from the assumption that negative consequences will result from interacting with other groups.

intergroup differences *(6)* Those that occur between members of different groups.

internal locus of control *(15)* The belief that one's outcomes are determined by one's own efforts.

intragroup differences *(6)* Those that occur between members of the same group.

intropunitive defence *(6)* Putting the blame for one's situation on oneself.

just world phenomenon *(2)* Illusory belief that the world is just and that people get what they deserve.

kernel of truth hypothesis *(6)* The notion that stereotypes must be true if they are commonly believed.

kinesics *(3)* Body language; all the bodily movements that convey information during a conversation except those that involve contact with someone else.

latent conflict *(11)* Conflict based on the inability of a subordinate to pursue his or her goals. Awareness of this incompatibility may not exist.

leading question *(13)* One that includes misinformation in order to lead the witness into a desired response.

leakage *(13)* Behaviour that mistakenly reveals the truth.

legitimate power *(10)* Influence based on the acceptance of the right of a given authority figure.

low-ball technique *(5)* A means of getting someone to do something by first securing agreement and then increasing the cost of fulfilling the request.

LPC (least preferred co-worker) *(10)* This scale identifies leadership style based on attitudes expressed about a co-worker.

matching hypothesis *(7)* People are attracted to others who are similar in physical attractiveness.

mediation *(11)* Indirect intervention to identify problems and open a channel of communication.

mirror image perception *(11)* When two groups are in conflict they view each other in similarly negative ways.

misattributed conflict *(11)* Disputants blame each other, when the real source is a common problem outside of both parties.

misinformation effect *(13)* Memory becomes distorted when we are exposed to inaccurate information.

M'Naghten Rule *(13)* Used to acquit defendants when they do not know their behaviour is wrong.

mock juries *(13)* The study of jury processes using subjects who act as jurors.

model *(1)* A mini-theory or set of propositions and assumptions about a specific phenomenon.

modelling *(6, 8)* Learning by observing the behaviour of others.

morpheme *(3)* Smallest unit of meaning in language.

multicultural hypothesis *(6)* When groups feel secure, they will be more positive towards other groups.

negative-state-relief hypothesis *(9)* Suggests that we give help in order not to feel sad about the situation of another person.

noise *(14)* The unwanted intensity or quality of sound.

non-compliance *(15)* Failure to follow recommendations of a medical professional.

non-zero-sum game *(11)* A game that goes beyond pure competition to some form of cooperation so that mutually desirable outcomes are possible.

norm of equity *(9)* Suggests that we should take what is fair into account when we help. This is especially true if someone is not considered responsible for his or her misfortune.

norm of reciprocity *(9)* Suggests that people return help to those who help them.

norm of social responsibility *(9)* Suggests that in any society there are those people, e.g. children, whom we feel deserve our help even if they cannot help us in return.

normative social influence *(5)* Influence resulting from the desire to gain social approval and avoid disapproval.

obedience *(5)* Behaviour in which one yields in response to a direct order.

out groups *(10)* Groups to which we do not belong.

panic *(12)* Occurs when people reinforce each other's fear of not being able to escape a dangerous situation.

paralanguage *(3)* Non-verbal aspects of speech that convey information.

participant observation *(1)* Study in which observations are made by a researcher who mixes in unobtrusively with the group being studied.

peripheral route persuasion *(4)* Attitude change involving just about any persuasive factors except careful attention to and analysis of the message.

person schemata *(2)* Schemata for specific individuals.

persuasion *(4)* Process of getting others to agree with an advocated position by means of a rational or emotional appeal.

phonemes *(3)* The short, meaningless sounds that are combined into morphemes.

post-decision dissonance *(4)* A state of psychological discomfort that occurs after a difficult choice has been made.

power *(10)* All power has at its core the ability to influence another person or group to do what you want them to do.

prejudice *(6)* A positive or negative attitude based on a distorted view of reality.

primacy effect *(4)* Tendency for information presented early in a sequence to have greater impact than that of information presented later.

primary prevention *(15)* Measures taken to prevent disease and health problems in currently healthy individuals.

primary territory *(14)* Space over which we have exclusive use and control.

Prisoner's Dilemma Game *(11)* A laboratory game which demonstrates that rational decision on an individual level may have mutually destructive consequences for the parties involved.

privacy *(14)* Our ability to control the access others have to us.

problem behaviour theory *(15)* Theory that regards adolescent health risk behaviour as part of a syndrome of personal, environmental, and behavioural non-conventionality.

prosocial behaviour *(9)* Helping behaviour performed with no anticipation of an external reward.

prosodic features of language *(3)* Non-verbal aspects of speech, such as timing, pitch, and loudness.

prototype *(2)* Representation or mental image of the best or most typical example of a category.

public goods problem *(11)* If everyone decided not to contribute personally to the public good, nothing would be achieved.

public territory *(14)* Space to which everyone has equal access.

quasi-experiment *(1)* A field study of the effects of some naturally occurring event or change.

randomization *(1)* Assignment of subjects by chance to various experimental conditions.

rational choice *(11)* Acting in such a way as to get the most for oneself.

realistic conflict *(11)* When an actual basis for disagreement exists due to incompatible needs, goals, or principles.

recency effect *(4)* Tendency for information presented late in a sequence to have greater impact than information presented earlier.

reciprocal power *(10)* Influence based on our desire to return a favour or to gain a favour.

reciprocity norm *(7)* People match their partner's intimacy level in self-disclosure.

re-fencing *(6)* The perception of someone as an exception if his or her behaviour doesn't match the stereotype.

referent power *(10)* Influence based on the desire to be like the person with the power.

reinforcement *(8)* Rewarding consequence that increases the probability of a behaviour occurring again.

reinforcement-affect model *(7)* People are attracted to others who are associated with events or stimuli that arouse positive feelings.

reparative altruism *(9)* Helping behaviour performed to make up for previously harmful behaviour to another person.

replication *(1)* Reproducing the results of a scientific study.

representativeness heuristic *(2)* Shortcut used to judge category membership by comparing the example to typical members of a category.

retributive justice *(13)* Punishment that matches the crime.

reverse discrimination *(6)* Acting in a way that makes a person appear more tolerant than they really are.

reward power *(10)* Influence based on a reward for compliance.

risky shift *(10)* People in a group tend to make decisions that require more risk than they would on their own.

role play *(1)* A research method whereby subjects act out roles as they believe others would.

role schemata *(2)* Cognitive representations that help to define our positions in society.

rumour *(12)* A specific belief that is passed from person to person and acted upon as though it were true, even without supporting evidence.

scapegoating *(6)* When anger and hostility are displaced onto a group not responsible for the problems.

script *(2)* Type of schema that represents routine events.

secondary territory *(14)* Space that we share with others on a regular basis.

self-complexity *(2)* Degree of richness and variety in individuals' images of themselves.

self-disclosure *(7)* Act of revealing intimate information about oneself to another person.

self-enhancement *(2)* Comparison to others that contributes to good feelings about oneself.

self-esteem *(1, 2)* A feeling of self-worth.

self-fulfilling prophecy *(6)* When individuals or groups believe stereotypes about themselves, they might act in ways that make them true.

self-justification *(4)* Expressing attitudes in line with behaviour in order to avoid looking foolishly inconsistent.

self-presentation *(2)* Behaviour intended to create a desirable impression.

self-schemata *(2)* Cognitive representations of information and beliefs about the self.

self-serving bias *(2)* Attributions that are motivated by a desire to protect or enhance one's self-esteem.

similarity *(7)* People are attracted to others with similar attitudes and values.

simulation *(1)* A research method whereby subjects react to situations as they expect others would.

simulation heuristic *(2)* Tendency to use "if only" conditions in responding to near misses and other frustrations.

situational control *(10)* The amount of control that a leader can exert depends on the level of trust, how structured is the task, and the amount of power the leader possesses.

social category *(10)* A means of grouping people based on similar characteristics.

social comparison *(2)* A tendency for people to evaluate themselves in relation to other people, especially when a situation is ambiguous or uncertain.

social exchange theory *(7, 11)* Tendency to maximize benefits and minimize costs in our dealings with others.

social facilitation *(5)* An increment or decrement in behaviour resulting from the presence of one or more other individuals.

social identity *(10)* The part of our self-image created when we identify with specific categories or groups and act in accordance with their norms.

social learning theory *(1)* View that learning can occur as a result of watching other people and the consequences of their behaviours.

social loafing *(5)* A decrease in our individual effort due to the presence of others who can make up for our slacking off.

social modelling *(5)* Social influence experienced as a result of observing the behaviour of someone else.

social movement *(12)* Large, spontaneous movements that draw people together to solve a social problem.

social norms *(3, 5)* Shared beliefs about which behaviours are and are not acceptable for group membership.

social penetration model *(7)* As a relationship develops over time, self-disclosure increases in breadth of topics and in intimacy.

social schemata *(2)* Cognitive representations about people or social categories that help us to organize and remember information.

socio-emotional leader *(10)* His or her concern is primarily with the relationships in the group rather than with maximum efficiency.

speech act theory *(3)* Theory about the degree of correspondence between what is said and the speaker's meaning or intention.

standard speech *(3)* A style of speaking defined socially as desirable or preferable.

status *(1)* The position a person holds to which we attach a high or low ranking.

stereotype *(2, 6)* A kind of prototype that consists of rigid beliefs and for which consensus exists among members of a group.

stress *(14)* Our response to experiences that threaten or challenge us.

superordinate goals *(11)* Those that bring two groups in conflict together to achieve a common solution.

survey *(1)* Technique for collecting data by questioning a representative sample of people.

symbolic belief *(6)* A belief that a group threatens or supports certain social values.

systemic discrimination *(6)* Occurs when regulations and laws support racist practices.

task-oriented leader *(10)* His or her concern is solely for getting the job done, often ignoring the personal needs of the group members.

that's-not-all technique *(5)* Improving a deal by adding another product or decreasing the price.

theory *(1)* A set of statements and assumptions that link concepts and hypotheses to observations.

theory of planned behaviour *(4)* Our intentions to engage in a specific behaviour are influenced by our attitudes towards the behaviour and by social norms, as well as by our beliefs about our competency to carry out the behaviour.

theory of reasoned action *(4)* Our intentions to engage in a specific behaviour are influenced by our attitudes towards the behaviour and by social norms.

threat-counter-threat spiral *(11)* Each threat calls for a more severe threat in response.

trait approach *(10)* The belief that leaders are born with specific characteristics that account for their ability.

transformational leader *(10)* The look of leadership in the future combines charisma, vision, and innovation with a commitment to followers to enhance their self-esteem.

utilitarian *(13)* Considered as serving a function in society.

value *(4)* Central, higher-order set of preferences for goals in life and ways of living that are felt to be ideal and important.

veridical conflict *(11)* The conflict is real in the sense that each person/group has an objective goal that is in opposition to the other's.

zero-sum game *(11)* The outcome of a situation whereby one person's loss is exactly matched with another person's gain.

BIBLIOGRAPHY

ABOUD, F. (1988). *Children and prejudice*. Oxford: Basil Blackwell.

ABRAMSON, L.Y., SELIGMAN, M.E.P. & TEASDALE, J.D. (1978). Learned helplessness in humans: Critique and reformulation. *Journal of Abnormal and Social Psychology, 87*, 49-74.

ADACHI, K. (1976). *The enemy that never was: A history of the Japanese Canadians*. Toronto: McClelland and Stewart.

ADAIR, J.G. (1973). *The human subject*. Boston: Little, Brown.

ADAIR, J. G., DUSHENKO, T.W., & LINDSAY, R.C.L. (1985). Ethical regulations and their impact on research practice. *American Psychologist, 40*, 59-72.

ADORNO, T.W., FRENKEL-BRUNSWICK, E., LEVINSON, D.J., & SANFORD, R.N. (1950). *The authoritarian personality*. New York: Harper.

AIELLO, J.R., & THOMPSON, D.E. (1980). Personal space, crowding and spatial behavior in a cultural context. In I. Altman, J.F. Wohlwill and A. Rapaport (Eds.), *Human behavior and environment: Vol. 4, Environment and culture*. New York: Plenum Press.

AJZEN, I. (1985). From intentions to actions: A theory of planned behavior. In J. Kuhl & J. Beckmann (Eds.), *Action-control: From cognition to behavior* (pp. 11-39). Heidelberg: Springer.

AJZEN, I. (1987). Attitudes, traits and actions: Dispositional prediction of behaviour in personality and social psychology. In L. Berkowitz (Ed.), *Advances in Experimental Social Psychology* (Vol. 20, pp. 1-63). New York: Academic Press.

AJZEN, I., & FISHBEIN, M. (1977). Attitude-behavior relations: A theoretical analysis and review of empirical research. *Psychological Bulletin, 84*, 888-918.

AJZEN, I., & FISHBEIN, M. (1980). *Understanding attitudes and predicting social behavior*. Englewood Cliffs, NJ: Prentice-Hall.

ALCOCK, J.E. (1975). Motivation in an asymmetric bargaining situation: A cross-cultural study. *International Journal of Psychology, 10*, 69-81.

ALCOCK, J.E. (1978). Social psychology and the importation of values. Paper presented at the Annual Conference of the Canadian Psychological Association, Ottawa. June, 1978.

ALCOCK, J.E. (1986). Chronic pain and the injured worker. *Canadian Psychology, 27*, 196-203.

ALCOCK, J.E., & MANSELL, D. (1977). Predisposition and behaviour in a collective dilemma. *Journal of Conflict Resolution, 21*, 443-458.

ALLEGEIER, E.R., & BYRNE, D. (1973). Attraction toward the opposite sex as a determinant of physical proximity. *Journal of Social Psychology, 90*, 213-219.

ALLEN, J.B., KENRICK, D.T., LINDER, D.E., & MCCALL, M.A. (1989). Arousal and attraction: A response-facilitation alternative to misattribution and negative-reinforcement models. *Journal of Personality and Social Psychology, 57*, 261-270.

ALLEN, V.L., & LEVINE, J.M. (1971). Social support and conformity: The role of independent assessment of reality. *Journal of Experimental and Social Psychology, 7*, 48-58.

ALLOY, L.B., & ABRAMSON, L.Y. (1979). Judgements of contingency in depressed and non-depressed students: Sadder but wiser. *Journal of Experimental Psychology: General, 108*, 441-485.

ALLPORT, G.W. (1935). Attitudes. In C.M. Murchison (Ed.), *Handbook of Social Psychology* (798-844). Worchester, MA: Clark University Press.

ALLPORT, G.W. (1954). *The nature of prejudice*. Reading, MA: Addison-Wesley.

ALLPORT, G.W., & POSTMAN, L.J. (1947). *The psychology of rumour*. New York: Holt, Rinehart & Winston.

ALTEMEYER, B. (1981). *Right-wing authoritarianism*. Winnipeg: University of Manitoba Press.

ALTEMEYER, B. (1988). *Enemies of freedom*. San Francisco: Jossey-Bass.

ALTMAN, I. (1973). Reciprocity of interpersonal exchange. *Journal of the Theory of Social Behavior, 3*, 249-261.

ALTMAN, I. (1975). *The environment and social behavior: Privacy, personal space, territory, crowding*. Monterey, CA: Brooks/Cole.

ALTMAN, I. (1976). Privacy: A conceptual analysis. *Environment and Behavior, 8*, 7-29.

ALTMAN, I., & TAYLOR, D.A. (1973). *Social penetration: The development of interpersonal relationships*. New York: Holt, Rinehart & Winston.

ALTMAN, I., & VINSEL, A. M. (1977). Personal space: An analysis of E. T. Hall's proxemics framework. In I. Altman, & J. F. Wohlwill (Eds.), *Human behavior and environment: Advances in theory and research* (pp. 181-259). New York: Plenum.

ALTMAN, I., VINSEL, A., & BROWN, B.A. (1981). Dialectic conceptions in social psychology: An application to social penetration and privacy regulation. In L. Berkowitz (Ed.), *Advances in experimental social psychology* (Vol. 14). New York: Academic Press.

AMATO, P.R. (1983). Helping behavior in urban and rural settings: Field studies based on a taxonomic organization of helping episodes. *Journal of Personality and Social Psychology, 45*, 571-586.

AMERICAN PSYCHOLOGIST (1990). The Seville statement on violence. *American Psychologist, 45*, 1167-1168.

AMERICAN PSYCHOLOGICAL ASSOCIATION (1992). Ethical principles of psychologists and code of conduct. *American Psychologist, 47*, 1597-1611.

ANDERSON, C.A., LEPPER, M.R., & ROSS, L. (1980). Perseverence of social theories: The role of explanation in the persistence of discredited information. *Journal of Personality and Social Psychology, 39*, 1037-1049.

ANDERSON, N.H. (1978). Cognitive algebra: Integration theory applied to social attribution. In L. Berkowitz (Ed.), *Cognitive theories in social psychology*. New York: Academic Press.

ANDREAS, C.R. (1969). "To receive from kings..." An examination of government-to-government aid and its unintended consequences. *Journal of Social Issues, 25*, 167-180.

ANTHONY, S. (1973). Anxiety and rumor. *Journal of Social Psychology, 89*, 91-98.

APFELBAUM, E., & LUBEK, I. (1976). Resolution vs. revolution? The theory of conflicts in question. In L. Strickland, F. Aboud & E. Gergen (Eds.), *Social psychology in transition* (pp. 71-94). New York: Plenum.

APFELBAUM, E., & MCGUIRE, G.R. (1986). Models of suggestive influence and the disqualification of the social crowd. In

C. F. Graumann & S. Moscovici (Eds.), *Changing conceptions of crowd mind and behavior* (pp. 27-50). New York: Springer-Verlag.

ARANOFF, C. (1974). Old age in prime time. *Journal of Communication, 24,* 86-87.

ARCHER, J. (1976). Biological explanations of psychological sex differences. In B. Lloyd & J. Archer (Eds.), *Exploring sex differences* (pp. 241-266). New York: Academic Press.

ARCHER, R.L., DIAZ-LOVING, R., GOLLWITZER, P.M., DAVIS, M.H., & FOUSHEE, H.C. (1981). The role of dispositional empathy and social evaluation in the empathic mediation of helping. *Journal of Personality and Social Psychology, 40,* 786-796.

ARENDT, H. (1963). *Eichmann in Jerusalem: A report on the banality of evil.* New York: Viking.

ARGYLE, M. (1971). *The psychology of interpersonal behaviour.* Harmondsworth: Penguin Books.

ARGYLE, M. (1975). *Bodily communication.* London: Methuen & Co.

ARIES, E. (1987). Gender and communication. *Review of Personality and Social Psychology, 7,* 149-176.

ARMSTRONG. E.G. (1992). The rhetoric of violence in rap and country music. *Sociological Inquiry, 63,* 64-83.

ARONSON, E. (1968). Dissonance theory: Progress and problems. In R.P. Abelson, E. Aronson, W.J. McGuire, T.M. Newcomb, M.J. Rosenberg & P.H. Tannenbaum (Eds.), *Theories of cognitive consistency: A sourcebook* (pp. 5-27). Chicago: Rand-McNally.

ARONSON, E. (1984). *The social animal* (4th ed.). New York: W.H. Freeman.

ARONSON, E., & LINDER, D. (1965). Gain and loss of esteem as determinants of interpersonal attractiveness. *Journal of Experimental Social Psychology, 1,* 156-171.

ASCH, S.E. (1946). Forming impressions of personality. *Journal of Abnormal and Social Psychology, 41,* 258-290.

ASCH, S.E. (1951). Effects of group pressure upon the modification and distortion of judgements. In H. Guetzkow (Ed.), *Groups, leadership and men.* Pittsburgh: Carnegie Press.

ASHTON, N.L., SHAW, M.E., & WORSHAM, A.P. (1980). Affective reactions to interpersonal distances by friends and strangers. *Bulletin of the Psychonomic Society, 15,* 306-308.

ATWOOD, M. (1972). *Survival.* Toronto: House of Anansi.

AVOLIO, B.J., & BASS, B.M. (1988). Transformational leadership. In J.G. Hunt, B.R. Baliga, H.P. Dachler & C.A. Schriesheim (Eds.), *Emerging leadership vistas.* Lexington, Mass: Lexington Books.

BANDURA, A. (1965). Influence of a model's reinforcement contingencies on the acquisition of imitative responses. *Journal of Personality and Social Psychology, 1,* 589-595.

BANDURA, A. (1973). *Aggression: A social learning analysis.* Englewood Cliffs, NJ: Prentice-Hall.

BANDURA, A. (1974). Behavior theories and the models of man. *American Psychologist, 29,* 859-869.

BANDURA, A. (1977). *Social learning theory.* Englewood Cliffs, NJ: Prentice-Hall.

BANDURA, A., ROSS, D., & ROSS, S.A. (1963a). Vicarious reinforcement and imitative learning. *Journal of Abnormal and Social Psychology, 67,* 601-607.

BANDURA, A., ROSS, D., & ROSS, S.A. (1963b). A comparative test of the status envy, social power, and secondary reinforcement theories of identificatory learning. *Journal of Abnormal and Social Psychology, 67,* 527-534.

BANDURA, A., ROSS, D., & ROSS, S.A. (1963c). Imitation of film-mediated aggressive models. *Journal of Abnormal and Social Psychology, 66,* 3-11.

BANUAZIZI, A., & MOVAHEDI, S. (1975). Interpersonal dynamics in a simulated prison: A methodological analysis. *American Psychologist, 30,* 152-160.

BAR-TAL, D. (1976). *Prosocial behavior.* Washington, DC: Hemisphere.

BARKOWITZ, P.B., & BRIGHAM, J.C. (1982). Recognition of faces: Own-race bias, incentive and time delay. *Journal of Applied Social Psychology, 12,* 255-268.

BARON, R.A. (1983a). The control of human aggression: An optimistic perspective. *Journal of Social and Clinical Psychology, 1,* 97-119.

BARON, R.A. (1983b). The control of human aggression: A strategy based on incompatible responses. In R.G. Geen & E.I. Donnerstein (Eds.), *Aggression: Theoretical and empirical reviews* (Vol. 2). New York: Academic Press.

BARON, R.M., & RODIN, J. (1978). Perceived control and crowding stress: Processes mediating the impact of spatial and social density. In A. Baum & Y. Epstein (Eds.), *Human response to crowding.* Hillsdale, NJ: Erlbaum Associates.

BARON, R.S. (1986). Distraction-conflict theory: Progress and problems. In L. Berkowitz (Ed.), *Advances in experimental social psychology,* (Vol. 19). New York: Academic Press.

BASS, B.M. (1985). *Leadership performance beyond expectations.* New York: Academic Press.

BATCHELOR, W.F. (1988). AIDS 1988: The science and the limits of science. *American Psychologist, 43,* 853-858.

BATSON, C.D. (1987). Prosocial behavior: Is it ever truly altruistic? In L. Berkowitz (Ed.), *Advances in experimental social psychology,* (Vol. 20, pp. 65-162). Cambridge, England: Cambridge University Press.

BATSON, C.D. (1990). How social an animal? The human capacity for caring. *American Psychologist, 45,* 336-346.

BATSON, C.D., BATSON, J.G., GRIFFITT, C.A., BARRIENTOS, S., BRANDT, J.R., SPRENGELMEYER, P., & BAYLY, M.J. (1989). Negative-state relief and the empathy-altruism hypothesis. *Journal of Personality and Social Psychology, 56,* 922-933.

BATSON, C.D., DYCK, J.L., BRANDT, J.R., BATSON, J.G., POWELL, A.L., MCMASTER, M.R., & GRIFFITT, C. (1988). Five studies testing two new egoistic alternatives to the empathy-altruism hypothesis. *Journal of Personality and Social Psychology, 55,* 52-77.

BATSON, C.D., & GRAY, R.A. (1981). Religious orientation and helping behavior: Responding to one's own or the victim's needs? *Journal of Personality and Social Psychology, 40,* 511-520.

BATSON, C.D., OLESON, K.C., WEEKS, J.L., HEALY, S.P., REEVES, P.J., JENNINGS, P., & BROWN, T. (1989). Religious prosocial motivation: Is it altruistic or egoistic? *Journal of Personality and Social Psychology, 57,* 873-884.

BAUM, A., AIELLO, J.R., & CALESNICK, L.E. (1978). Crowding and personal control: Social density and the development of learned helplessness. *Journal of Personality and Social Psychology, 36,* 1000-1011.

BAUM, A., & DAVIS, G.E. (1980). Reducing the stress of high-density living: An architectural intervention. *Journal of Personality and Social Psychology, 38,* 471-481.

BAUM, A., & VALINS, S. (1977). *Architecture and social behavior. Psychological studies and social density.* Hillsdale, NJ: Erlbaum.

BAUMEISTER, R.F., CHESNER, S.P., SENDERS, P.S., & TICE, D.M. (1988). Who's in charge here? Group leaders do lend help in emergencies. *Personality and Social Psychology Bulletin, 14,* 17-22.

BAUMEISTER, R.F., & STEINHILBER, A. (1984). Paradoxical effects of supportive audiences on performance under pressure: The home field disadvantage in sports championships. *Journal of Personality and Social Psychology, 47,* 85-93.

BAUMRIND, D. (1964). Some thoughts on ethics of research: After reading Milgram's "Behavioral study of obedience." *American Psychologist, 19,* 421-423.

BECHTOLD, A., NACCARATO, M.E., & ZANNA, M.P. (1986). Need for structure and the prejudice-discrimination link. Paper presented at the Annual Meeting of the Canadian Psychological Association, Toronto, June 19.

BECKER, F.D. (1973). A study of spatial markers. *Journal of Personality and Social Psychology, 26,* 439-445.

BECKER, M.H. (Ed.) (1974). The health belief model and personal health behavior. *Health Education Monographs. 2.* (Whole No. 4).

BECKER, W.C. (1964). Consequences of different kinds of parental discipline. In M.L. Hoffman & L.W. Hoffman (Eds.), *Review of child development research* (Vol. 1). New York: Russell Sage.

BÉGIN, G. (1976). The effects of success and failure on helping behaviour. Unpublished doctoral thesis. McMaster University, Hamilton, Ontario.

BELL, B.E., & LOFTUS, E.F. (1989). Trivial persuasion in the courtroom: The power of (a few) minor details. *Journal of Personality and Social Psychology, 56,* 669-679.

BEM, D.J. (1970). *Beliefs, attitudes and human affairs.* Belmont, CA: Brooks/Cole.

BEM, S.L. (1981). Gender schema theory: A cognitive account of sex typing. *Psychological Review, 88,* 354-364.

BENTLER, P.M., & NEWCOMB, M.D. (1978). Longitudinal study of marital success and failure. *Journal of Consulting and Clinical Psychology, 40,* 1053-1070.

BERG, K.O., & VIDMAR, N. (1975). Authoritarianism and recall of evidence about criminal behavior. *Journal of Research in Personality, 9,* 147-157.

BERKES, F., FEENY, D., MCCAY, B.J., & ACHESON, J.M. (1989). The benefits of the Commons. *Nature, 34,* 91-93.

BERKOWITZ, L. (1954). Group standards, cohesiveness, and productivity. *Human Relations, 7,* 509-519.

BERKOWITZ, L. (1971). The contagion of violence: An S-R mediational analysis of some effects of observed aggression. *Nebraska Symposium on Motivation 1970.* Lincoln: University of Nebraska Press.

BERKOWITZ, L. (1983). Aversively stimulated aggression: Some parallels and differences in research with animals and humans. *American Psychologist, 38,* 1135-1144.

BERKOWITZ, L. (1984). Some effects of thoughts of anti- and prosocial influences of media events: A cognitive-neoassociation analysis. *Psychological Bulletin, 95,* 410-427.

BERKOWITZ, L. (1989). Frustration-aggression hypothesis: Examination and reformulation. *Psychological Bulletin, 106,* 59-73.

BERKOWITZ, L. (1990). On the formation and regulation of anger and aggression. *American Psychologist, 45,* 494-503.

BERKOWITZ, L., & DANIELS, L.R. (1963). Responsibility and dependency. *Journal of Abnormal and Social Psychology, 66,* 664-669.

BERKOWITZ, L., & MACAULAY, J. (1971). The contagion of criminal violence. *Sociometry, 34,* 238-260.

BERNSTEIN, W.M., STEPHAN, W.G., & DAVIS, M.H. (1979). Explaining attributions for achievement: A path analytic approach. *Journal of Personality and Social Psychology, 37,* 1810-1821.

BERRY, D.S., & ZEBROWITZ-MCARTHUR, L.Z. (1988). What's in a face? Facial maturity and attribution of legal responsibility. *Personality and Social Psychology Bulletin, 14,* 23-33.

BERRY, J.W. (1978a). Social psychology: Comparative, societal and universal. *Canadian Psychological Review, 19,* 93-104.

BERRY, J.W. (1978b). Teaching social psychology IN and OF Canada. Paper presented at the Annual Conference of the Canadian Psychological Association. Ottawa, June, 1978.

BERRY, J.W. (1984). Multicultural policy in Canada: A social psychological analysis. *Canadian Journal of Behavioural Science, 16,* 353-370.

BERRY, J.W. (1986). Ethnic minorities and immigrants in a cross-cultural perspective. In L.H. Ekland (Ed.), *Selected papers from the regional IACCP conference: Ethnic minority and immigrant research.* Lisse: Swets and Zeitlinger.

BERRY, J.W. (1987). Finding identity: Separation, integration, assimilation, or marginality. In L. Driedger (Ed.), *Ethnic Canada: Identities and inequalities.* Toronto: Copp Clark Pitman.

BERRY, J.W. (1992). Acculturation and adaptation in a new society. *International Migration, 30,* 69-85.

BERRY, J.W., POORTINGA, Y.P., SEGAL, M.H., & DASEN, P.R. (1992). *Cross-cultural psychology: Research and applications.* New York: Cambridge University Press.

BERRY, J.W., WINTROB, R.M., SINDELL, P.S., & MAWHINNEY, T.A. (1982). Psychological adaptations to cultural change among the James Bay Cree. *Naturaliste Canadien, 109,* 965-975.

BERSCHEID, E., & WALSTER, E. (1974a). Physical attractiveness. In L. Berkowitz (Ed.), *Advances in experimental social psychology* (Vol. 7). New York: Academic Press.

BERSCHEID, E., & WALSTER, E. (1974b). A little bit about love. In T.L. Huston (Ed.), *Foundations of interpersonal attraction.* New York: Academic Press.

BERSOFF, D. (1987). Social science data and the Supreme Court: Lockhart as a case in point. *American Psychologist, 42,* 52-58.

BERTCHERMAN, L.R. (1975). *The swastika and the maple leaf.* Toronto: Fitzhenry & Whiteside.

BERTON, P. (1972). *Klondike: The last great gold rush, 1896-1899.* Toronto: McClelland & Stewart.

BICKMAN, L. (1972). Environmental attitudes and actions. *Journal of Social Psychology, 87,* 323-324.

BISHOP, G.F. (1975). Resolution and tolerance of cognitive inconsistency in a field situation: Change in attitude and beliefs following the Watergate affair. *Psychological Reports, 36,* 747-753.

BLISS, M. (1991). *Plague. A story of smallpox in Montreal.* Toronto: HarperCollins.

BLOOM, B., ASHER, S.J., & WHITE, S.W. (1978). Marital disruption as a stressor: A review and analysis. *Psychological Bulletin, 85*, 867-894.

BLUMENFELD, M., LEVY, N.B., & KAUFMAN, D. (1979). The wish to be informed of a fatal illness. *Omega, 9*, 323-326.

BLUMER, H. (1951). Social movements. In A.M. Lee (Ed.), *New outline of the principles of sociology* (2nd ed., pp. 199-220). New York: Barnes & Noble.

BLUMER, H. (1969). *Symbolic interactionism.* Englewood Cliffs, NJ: Prentice-Hall.

BODENHAUSEN, G.V. (1988). Stereotype biases in social decision making and memory: Testing process models of stereotype use. *Journal of Personality and Social Psychology, 55*, 726-737.

BOLGER, N., DELONGIS, A., KESSLER, R. C., & SCHILLING, E. A. (1989). Effects of daily stress on negative mood. *Journal of Personality and Social Psychology, 57*, 808-818.

BOND, C.F. JR. (1982). Social facilitation: A self-presentational view. *Journal of Personality and Social Psychology, 42*, 1042-1050.

BOND, C.F., JR., & TITUS, L.J. (1983). Social facilitation: A meta-analysis of 241 studies. *Psychological Bulletin, 94*, 265-292.

BOOTH-KEWLEY, S., & FRIEDMAN, H.S. (1987). Psychological predictors of heart disease: A quantitative review. *Psychological Bulletin, 101*, 343-362.

BOOTZIN, R.R., HERMAN, C.P., & NICASSIO, P. (1976). The power of suggestion: Another examination of misattribution and insomnia. *Journal of Personality and Social Psychology, 34*, 673-679.

BORGIDA, E., & WHITE, P. (1978). Social perception of rape victims: The impact of legal reforms. *Law and Human Behavior, 2*, 339-351.

BORNSTEIN, G., RAPPORT, A., KERPEL, L., & KATZ, T. (1989). Within- and between-group communicaion in intergroup competition for public goods. *Journal of Experimental Social Psychology, 25*, 422-436.

BOURHIS, R.Y. (1979). Language in ethnic interaction: A social psychological approach. In H. Giles & B. Saint-Jacques (Eds.), *Language and ethnic relations.* Oxford: Pergamon.

BOURHIS, R.Y. (1990). Organizational communication in bilingual settings: The linguistic work environment survey. In H. Giles, N. Coupland, & J. Coupland (Eds.), *Contexts of accommodation: Developments in applied psycholinguistics.* Cambridge: Cambridge University Press.

BOURHIS, R.Y., & GILES, H. (1977). The language of intergroup distinctiveness. In H. Giles (Ed.), *Language, ethnicity and intergroup relations.* London: Academic Press.

BOURHIS, R.Y., GILES, H., LEYENS, J.P., & TAJFEL, H. (1979). Psycholinguistic distinctiveness: Language divergence in Belgium. In H. Giles & R. St. Clair (Eds.), *Language and social psychology.* Oxford: Blackwell.

BOURHIS, R.Y., ROTH, S., & MACQUEEN, G. (1989). Communication in the hospital setting: A survey of medical and everyday language use amongst patients, nurses and doctors. *Social Science and Medicine, 28*, 339-346.

BOWER, G.H., BLACK, J.B., & TURNER, T.J. (1979). Scripts in memory for text. *Cognitive Psychology, 11*, 177-220.

BOYD, J.R., COVINGTON, T.R., STANASZEK, W.F., & COUSSONS, R.T. (1974). Drug defaulting: II Analysis of noncompliance patterns. *American Journal of Hospital Pharmacy, 31*, 485-491.

BRADAC, J.J., DAVIES, R.A., COURTRIGHT, J.A., DESMOND, R.J., & MURDOCK, J.I. (1977). Richness of vocabulary: An attributional analysis. *Psychological Reports, 41*, 1131-1134.

BRADLEY, G. W. (1978). Self-serving bias in the attribution process: A re-examination of the fact-or-fiction question. *Journal of Personality and Social Psychology, 36*, 56-71.

BRANDEN, N. (1988). A vision of romantic love. In R.J. Sternberg & M.L. Barnes (Eds.), *The psychology of love* (pp. 218-231). New Haven, CT: Yale University Press.

BRAY, R. M., & KERR, N. L. (1982). Methodological considerations in the study of the psychology of the courtroom. In N. L. Kerr, & R. M. Bray (Eds.), *The psychology of the courtroom* (pp. 287-323). Orlando, Fla. Academic Press.

BRAY, R.M., & NOBLE, A.M. (1978). Authoritarianism and decisions of mock juries: Evidence of jury bias and group polarization. *Journal of Personality and Social Psychology, 36*, 1424-1430.

BREHM, J.W. (1966). *A theory of psychological reactance.* New York: Academic Press.

BREHM, J.W., & COHEN A.R. (1962). *Explorations in cognitive dissonance.* New York: Wiley.

BREHM, S.S. (1992). *Intimate relationships.* (2nd ed.) New York: McGraw Hill.

BREWER, M.B., DULL, V., & LUI, L. (1981). Perception of the elderly: Stereotypes as prototypes. *Journal of Personality and Social Psychology, 41*, 656-670.

BREWER, M.B., & KRAMER, R.M. (1986). Choice behavior in social dilemmas: Effects of social identity, group size, and decision framing. *Journal of Personality and Social Psychology, 50*, 543-549.

BRIGHAM, J.C., & PFEIFER, J.E. (1994). Evaluating the fairness of lineups. In D.F. Ross, J.D. Read & M.P. Toglia (Eds.), *Adult eyewitness testimony: Current trends and developments.* New York: Springer-Verlag.

BRIGHAM, J.C., & MALPASS, R.S. (1985). The role of experience and contact in the recognition of faces of own- and other-race persons. *Journal of Social Issues, 41*, 139-156.

BROADFOOT, B. (1977). *Years of sorrow, years of shame.* Toronto: Doubleday Canada.

BRODT, S.E., & ZIMBARDO, P.G. (1981). Modifying shyness-related social behavior through symptom misattribution. *Journal of Personality and Social Psychology, 41*, 437-449.

BRONFENBRENNER, U. (1961). The mirror image in Soviet-American relations: A social psychologist's report. *Journal of Social Issues, 17*, 45-56.

BRONZAFF, A. (1981). Effects of a noise abatement program on reading ability. *Journal of Environmental Psychology, 1*, 215-222.

BROOKS-GUNN, J., BOYER, C.B., & HEIN, K. (1988). Preventing HIV infection and AIDS in children and adolescents. *American Psychologist, 43*, 958-964.

BROVERMAN, I.K., VOGEL, S.R., BROVERMAN, D.M., CLARKSON, F.E., & ROSENKRANTZ, P.S. (1972). Sexual stereotypes: A current appraisal. *Journal of Social Issues, 28*, 59-78.

BROWN, J., & SIEGEL, J.M. (1988). Exercise as a buffer of life stress: A prospective study of adolescent health. *Health Psychology, 7*, 341-353.

BROWN, R. (1965). *Social psychology.* New York: Free Press.

BROWN, R. (1986). *Social Psychology.* (2nd ed.) London: Collier MacMillan.

BRUNVAND, J.H. (1981). *The vanishing hitchhiker: American urban legends and their meanings*. New York: Norton.

BRUNVAND, J.H. (1986). *The choking doberman*. New York: Norton.

BRYAN, J.H., & WALBECK, N. (1970). The impact of words and deeds concerning altruism upon children. *Child Development, 41*, 747-757.

BUCKHOUT, R. (1980). Nearly 2000 witnesses can be wrong. *Bulletin of the Psychonomic Society, 16*, 307-310.

BUGENTAL, D.E., KASWAN, J.E., & LOVE, L.R. (1970). Perception of contradictory meanings conveyed by verbal and nonverbal channels. *Journal of Personality and Social Psychology, 16*, 647-655.

BURGER, J.M. (1986). Increasing compliance by improving the deal: The that's-not-all technique. *Journal of Personality and Social Psychology, 51*, 277-283.

BURGESS, E.W., & HUSTON, T.L. (Eds.) (1979). *Social exchange in developing relationships*. New York: Academic Press.

BURGOON, J.K., BULLER, D.B., & WOODALL, W.G. (1989). *Nonverbal communication: The unspoken dialogue*. New York: Harper & Row.

BURMAN, B., & MARGOLIN, G. (1992). Analysis of the association between marital relationships and health problems: An interactional perspective. *Psychological Bulletin, 112*, 39-63.

BURNSTEIN, E., & VINOKUR, A. (1977). Persuasive argumentation and social comparison as determinants of attitude polarization. *Journal of Experimental Social Psychology, 13*, 315-322.

BUSHMAN, B.J. (1988). The effects of apparel on compliance: A field experiment with a female authority figure. *Personality and Social Psychology Bulletin, 14*, 459-467.

BUSS, A.H., & PERRY, M. (1992). The aggression questionnaire. *Journal of Personality and Social Psychology, 63*, 452-459.

BYRNE, D. (1971). *The attraction paradigm*. New York: Academic Press.

BYRNE, D., & CLORE, G.L. (1970). A reinforcement model of evaluative responses. *Personality: An International Journal, 1*, 103-128.

CALHOUN, L.G., SELBY, J.W., & KING, H.E. (1976). *Dealing with crisis*. Englewood Cliffs, NJ: Prentice-Hall.

CALLWOOD, J. (1987, March 18). Sanitized textbooks reflect a pious paradise that never was. *The Globe and Mail*.

CAMPBELL, D.T. (1969a) Prospective: Artifact and control. In R. Rosenthal and R.L. Rosnow (Eds.), *Artifact in behavioral research* (pp. 351-382). New York: Academic Press.

CAMPBELL, D.T. (1969b). Reforms as experiments. *American Psychologist, 24*, 409-429.

CAMPBELL, J.B., & FAIREY, P.J. (1989). Informational and normative routes to conformity: The effect of faction size as a function of norm extremity and attention to the stimulus. *Journal of Personality and Social Psychology, 57*, 457-468.

CAMPBELL, J.D. (1986). Similarity and uniqueness: The effects of attribute type, relevance, and individual differences in self-esteem and depression. *Journal of Personality and Social Psychology, 50*, 281-293.

CANADA (1985). *Pornography and prostitution in Canada. Report of the Special Committee on Pornography and Prostitution*. Ottawa: Ministry of Supply and Services.

CANTOR, N., & MISCHEL, W. (1979). Prototypes in person perception. In L. Berkowitz (Ed.), *Advances in experimental social psychology* (Vol. 12). New York: Academic Press.

CANTRIL, H. (1940). *The invasion from Mars*. Princeton, NJ: Princeton University Press.

CARLI, L.L. (1990). Gender, language, and influence. *Journal of Personality and Social Psychology, 59*, 941-951.

CARLI, L.L., GANLEY, R., & PIERCE-OTAY, A. (1991). Similarity and satisfaction in roommate relationships. *Personality and Social Psychology Bulletin, 17*, 419-426.

CARLSMITH, J.M., & GROSS, A.E. (1969). Some effects of guilt on compliance. *Journal of Personality and Social Psychology, 11*, 232-239.

CARLSON, M., CHARLIN, V., & MILLER, N. (1988). Positive moods and helping behavior: A test of six hypotheses. *Journal of Personality and Social Psychology, 55*, 211-229.

CARMENT, D.W. (1970). Rate of simple motor responding as a function of coaction, competition, and sex of the participants. *Psychonomic Science, 19*, 342-343.

CARMENT, D.W. (1973). Giving and receiving in Canada and India. McMaster University Technical Report #53.

CARMENT, D.W., & HODKIN, B. (1973). Coaction and competition in India and Canada. *Journal of Cross-Cultural Psychology, 4*, 459-469.

CARNEVALE, P.J. (1986). Strategic choice in negotiation. *Negotiation Journal, 2*, 41-56.

CARNEVALE, P.J., & HENRY, R.A. (1989). Determinants of mediator behavior: A test of the strategic choice. *Journal of Applied Social Psychology, 19*, 481-498.

CARNEVALE, P.J., & PRUITT, D.G. (1992). Negotiation and mediation. *Annual Review of Psychology, 43*, 531-582.

CARROLL, J.S. (1978). The effect of imagining an event on expectations for the event: An interpretation in terms of the availability heuristic. *Journal of Experimental Social Psychology, 14*, 88-96.

CARVER, C.S., & SCHEIER, M.F. (1981). The self-attention-induced feedback loop and social facilitation. *Journal of Experimental Social Psychology, 17*, 545-568.

CARVER, G.S., & GLASS, D.C. (1978). Coronary-prone behavior pattern and interpersonal aggression. *Journal of Personality and Social Psychology, 36*, 361-366.

CASH, T.F., & DERLEGA, V.J. (1978). The matching hypothesis: Physical attractiveness among same-sexed friends. *Personality and Social Psychology Bulletin, 4*, 240-243.

CAVOUKIAN, A., & DOOB, A.N. (1980). The effects of a judge's charge and subsequent recharge on judgements of guilt. *Basic and Applied Social Psychology, 1*, 103-116.

CHAIKEN, A.L., & DERLEGA, V.J. (1974). *Self-disclosure*. Morristown, NJ: General Learning.

CHAIKEN, S. (1980). Heuristic versus systematic information processing and the use of source versus message cues. *Journal of Personality and Social Psychology, 39*, 752-766.

CHAIKEN, S. (1987). The heuristic model of persuasion. In C. P. Herman, M. P. Zanna & E. T. Higgins (Eds.), *Social Influence: The Ontario Symposium* (pp. 3-39). Hillsdale, NJ: Erlbaum.

CHAIKEN, S., & EAGLY, A.H. (1976). Communication modality as a determinant of message persuasiveness and message comprehensibility. *Journal of Personality and Social Psychology, 34*, 605-614.

CHAIKEN, S., & STANGOR, C. (1987). Attitude and attitude change. *Annual Review of Psychology, 38*, 575-630.

CHANDLER, T.A., SHAMA, D.D., WOLF, F.M., & PLANCHARD, S.K. (1981). Misattributional causality: A five cross-national samples study. *Journal of Cross-Cultural Psychology, 12,* 207-221.

CHECK, J.V.P. (1985). *The effects of violent and nonviolent pornography.* Ottawa: Department of Justice.

CHECK, J.V.P., & DYCK, D.G. (1986). Hostile aggression and type A behavior. *Personality and Individual Differences, 7,* 819-827.

CHECK, J.V.P., HEAPY, N.A., & IWANYSHYN, O. (1994). A survey of Canadians' attitudes regarding sexual content in the media. *Canadian Psychology.*

CHECK, J.V.P., & MALAMUTH, N.M. (1984). Can there be positive effects of participation in pornography experiments? *The Journal of Sex Research, 20,* 14-31.

CHECK, J.V.P., & MALAMUTH, N.M. (1986). Pornography and sexual aggression: A social learning theory analysis. *Communication Yearbook, 9,* 187-213.

CHECK, J.V.P., & MALAMUTH, N. (1990). Ethical considerations in sex and aggression research. In D. MacNiven (Ed.), *Moral expertise: Studies in practical and professional ethics.* London: Routledge.

CHECK, J.V.P., PERLMAN, D., & MALAMUTH, N.M. (1985). Loneliness and aggressive behavior. *Journal of Social and Personal Relationships, 2,* 243-252.

CHERRY, F., & BYRNE, D. (1977). Authoritarianism. In T. Blass (Ed.), *Personality variables in social behavior.* Hillsdale, NJ: Erlbaum.

CHOMSKY, N. (1986). *Turning the tide: The U.S. and Latin America.* Montreal: Black Rose Books.

CHRISTENSEN, L. (1988). Deception in psychological research: When is its use justified? *Personality and Social Psychology Bulletin, 14,* 664-675.

CHRISTIANSON, S. (1992). Emotional stress and eyewitness memory: A critical review. *Psychological Bulletin, 112,* 284-309.

CHRISTIANSON, S., & LOFTUS, E.F. (1991). Remembering emotional events: The fate of detailed information. *Cognition and Emotion, 5,* 81-108.

CHRISTIE, R., & JAHODA, M. (Eds.) (1954). *Studies in the scope and method of "The Authoritarian Personality."* New York: Free Press.

CIALDINI, R.B. (1987). Compliance principles of compliance professionals: Psychologists of necessity. In M.P. Zanna, J.M. Olson & C.R. Herman (Eds.), *Social influence. The Ontario Symposium* (Vol. 5, pp. 165-184). Hillsdale, New Jersey. Lawrence Erlbaum Associates.

CIALDINI, R.B., SCHALLER, M., HOULIHAN, D., ARPS, K., & FULTZ, J. (1987). *Journal of Personality and Social Psychology, 52,* 749-758.

CIALDINI, R.B., VINCENT, J.E., LEWIS, S.K., CATALON, J., WHEELER, D., & DARBY, B.L. (1975). Reciprocal concessions procedure for inducing compliance: The door-in-the-face technique. *Journal of Personality and Social Psychology, 31,* 206-215.

CLANCY, K., BARTOLOMEW, J., RICHARDSON, D., & WELLFORD, C. (1981). Sentence decision-making: The logic of sentence decisions and the extent and sources of sentence disparity. *Journal of Criminal Law and Criminology, 72,* 524-554.

CLÉMENT, R. (1980). Ethnicity, contact and communication competence in a second language. In H. Giles, W.P. Robinson & P.M. Smith (Eds.), *Language: Social psychological perspectives* (pp. 147-154). Oxford: Pergamon.

CLÉMENT, R. (1987). Second language proficiency and acculturation: An investigation of the effects of language status and individual characteristics. *Journal of Language and Social Psychology, 5,* 271-290.

CLINE, V.B., CROFT, R.G., & COURRIER, S. (1973). Desensitization of children to television violence. *Journal of Personality and Social Psychology, 27,* 360-365.

CLORE, G.L., WIGGINS, N.H., & ITKIN, G. (1975). Gain and loss in attraction: Attributions from non-verbal behavior. *Journal of Personality and Social Psychology, 31,* 706-712.

COATES, D., WORTMAN, C.B., & ABBEY, A. (1979). Reactions to victims. In I. H. Frieze, D. Bar-Tal & J.S. Carroll (Eds.), *New approaches to social problems* (pp. 21-52). San Francisco: Jossey-Bass.

COHEN, S., TYRRELL, D.A.J., & SMITH, A.P. (1993). Negative life events, perceived stress, negative affect and susceptibility to the common cold. *Journal of Personality and Social Psychology, 64,* 131-140.

COHEN, S. (1988). Psychosocial models of the role of social support in the etiology of physical disease. *Health Psychology, 7,* 269-297.

COHEN, S., & MCKAY, G. (1984). Social support, stress and the buffering hypothesis: A theoretical analysis. In A. Baum, J.E. Singer & S.E. Taylor (Eds.), *Handbook of psychology and health* (Vol. 4, pp. 253-267). Hillsdale, NJ: Erlbaum.

COHEN, S., & WILLIAMSON, G. M. (1988). Perceived stress in a probability sample of the United States. In S. Spacapan & S. Oskamp (Eds.), *The social psychology of health* (pp. 31-67). Beverly Hills, CA: Sage Publications.

COHEN, S., GLASS, D.C., & SINGER, J.E. (1973). Apartment noise, auditory discrimination and reading ability in children. *Journal of Experimental Social Psychology, 9,* 407-422.

COHN, L.D., IMAI, W.K., MACFARLANE, S., & YANEZ, C. (1995). Risk-perception: Differences between adolescents and adults. *Health Psychology, 14,* 217-222.

COKE, J.S., BATSON, C.D., & MCDAVIS, K. (1978). Empathic mediation of helping: A two-stage model. *Journal of Personality and Social Psychology, 36,* 752-766.

COLMAN, A.M. (1991). Crowd psychology in South African murder trials. *American Psychologist, 46,* 1071-1079.

CONGER, J.A., & KANUNGO, R.N. (1992). Perceived behavioural attributes of charismatic leadership. *Canadian Journal of Behavioural Science, 24,* 86-102.

CONRAD, P. (1986). The social meaning of AIDS. *Social Policy, 17,* 51-56.

CONTRADA, R.J. (1989). Type A behavior, personality hardiness and cardiovascular responses to stress. *Journal of Personality and Social Psychology, 57,* 895-903.

COOK, S.W. (1984). Experimenting on social issues: The case of school desegregation. Paper presented at the 92nd Annual Convention of the American Psychological Association, Toronto.

COOPER, J., & FAZIO, R.H. (1984). A new look at dissonance theory. In L. Berkowitz (Ed.), *Advances in experimental social psychology* (Vol. 17, pp. 229-266). New York: Academic Press.

CORNWELL, D., & HOBBS, S. (1992). Rumour and legend: Interactions between social psychology and folkloristics. *Canadian Psychology, 33,* 609-613.

COSTANZO, M., ARCHER, D., ARONSON, E., & PETTIGREW, T. (1986). Energy conservation behavior: The difficult path from information to action. *American Psychologist, 41,* 521-528.

COTTRELL, N.B. (1972). Social facilitation. In C.G. McClintock (Ed.), *Experimental social psychology*. New York: Holt, Rinehart & Winston.

COTTRELL, N.B., WACK, D.L., SEKERAK, G.J., & RITTLE, R.H. (1968). Social facilitation of dominant responses by the presence of an audience and the mere presence of others. *Journal of Personality and Social Psychology, 9*, 245-250.

COZBY, P.C. (1973). Self-disclosure: A literature review. *Psychological Bulletin, 79*, 73-91.

CRABB, P.B. (1992). Effective control of energy-depleting behavior. *American Psychologist, 47*, 815-816.

CRAIG, K.D. (1978). Social modeling influences on pain. In R.A. Sternbach (Ed.), *The psychology of pain* (pp. 73-110). New York: Raven Press.

CRANDALL, C.S. (1988). Social contagion of binge eating. *Journal of Personality and Social Psychology, 55*, 588-598.

CRAWFORD, M.P. (1939). The social psychology of the vertebrates. *Psychological Bulletin, 36*, 407-466.

CROCKER, J. (1981). Judgement of covariation by social perceivers. *Psychological Bulletin, 90*, 272-292.

CRUTCHFIELD, R.A. (1955). Conformity and character. *American Psychologist, 10*, 191-198.

CSIKSZENTMIHALYI, M., & FIGURSKI, T.J. (1982). Self-awareness and overside experience in everyday life. *Journal of Personality, 50*, 15-28.

CUMBERLAND, J., & ZAMBLE, E. (1992). General and specific measures of attitudes towards early release of criminal offenders. *Canadian Journal of Behavioural Science, 24*, 442-455.

CURRAN, J.P., & LIPPOLD, S. (1975). The effects of physical attraction and attitude similarity on attraction in dating dyads. *Journal of Personality, 43*, 528-538.

CUTLER, R.E., & STORM, T. (1975). Observational study of alcohol consumption in natural settings. *Journal of Studies on Alcohol, 36*, 1173-1183.

CUTRONA, C.E. (1982). Transition to college: Loneliness and the process of social adjustment. In L.A. Peplau & D. Perlman (Eds.), *Loneliness: A sourcebook of current theory, research and therapy*. New York: Wiley.

CVETKOVICH, G., &. EARLE, T.C. (1992). Environmental hazards and the public. *Journal of Social Issues, 48*, 1-20.

DA GLORIA, J. (1984). Frustration, aggression and the sense of justice. In A. Mummendey (Ed.), *Social psychology of aggression: From individual behavior to social interaction* (pp. 127-142). New York: Springer-Verlag.

DANE, F., & WRIGHTSMAN, L. (1982). Effects of defendant's and victim's characteristics on jurors' verdicts. In N. L. Kerr & R. M. Bray (Eds.), *The psychology of the courtroom* (pp. 83-115). New York: Academic Press.

DARLEY, J.M., & LATANÉ, B. (1968). Bystander intervention in emergencies: Diffusion of responsibility. *Journal of Personality and Social Psychology, 8*, 377-383.

DARLEY, J.M., & SHULTZ, T.R. (1990) Moral rules: Their content and acquisition. *Annual Review of Psychology, 41*, 525-556.

DARNELL, R. (1971). Sociolinguistic perspectives on linguistic diversity. In R. Darnell (Ed.), *Linguistic diversity in Canadian society*. Edmonton: Linguistic Research.

DARWIN, C. (1872/1965). *The expression of the emotions in man and animals*. Chicago, IL: University of Chicago Press.

DAVIDOWICZ, L.C. (1975). *The war against the Jews, 1933-1945*. Holt, Rinehart & Winston: New York.

DAWES, R.M. (1972). *Fundamentals of attitude measurement*. New York: John Wiley & Sons.

DEJONG, W. (1979). An examination of self-perception mediation of the foot-in-the-door effect. *Journal of Personality and Social Psychology, 37*, 2221-2239.

DELLINGER, R.W. (1979). Jet roar: Health problems take off near airports. *Human Behavior, 8*, 50-51.

DELONGIS, A., COYNE, J.C., KAKOF, G., FOLKMAN, S., & LAZARUS, R.S. (1982). Relationship of daily hassles, uplifts and major life events to health status. *Health Psychology, 1*, 119-136.

DENMARK, F.L. (1977). Styles of leadership. *Psychology of Women Quarterly, 2*, 99-113.

DENNIS, M.L., SODERSTROM, E.J., KONCINSKI, W.S., & CAVANAUGH, B. (1990). Effective dissemination of energy-relevant information: Applying social psychology and evaluation research. *American Psychologist, 45*, 1109-1117.

DEPAULO, B.M., & ROSENTHAL, R. (1979). Telling lies. *Journal of Personality and Social Psychology, 37*, 1713-1722.

DERMER, M.L., & JACOBSEN, E. (1986). Some potential negative social consequences of cigarette smoking: Marketing research in reverse. *Journal of Applied Social Psychology, 16*, 702-725.

DEUTSCH, F.M., SULLIVAN, L., SAGE, C., & BASILE, N. (1991). The relation among talking, liking and similarity between friends. *Personality and Social Psychology Bulletin, 17*, 406-411.

DEUTSCH, M. (1973). *The resolution of conflict: Constructive and destructive processes*. New Haven: Yale University Press.

DEVINE, P.G. (1989). Stereotypes and prejudice: their automatic and controlled components. *Journal of Personality and Social Psychology, 56*, 5-18.

DICKERSON, C.A., THIBODEAU, R., ARONSON, E., & MILLER, D. (1992). Using cognitive dissonance to encourage water conservation. *Journal of Applied Social Psychology, 22*, 841-854.

DIJKER, A.J.M. (1987). Emotional reactions to ethnic minorities. *European Journal of Social Psychology, 17*, 305-325.

DILALLA, L.F., & GOTTESMAN, I.I. (1991). Biological and genetic contributions to violence—Widom's untold tale. *Psychological Bulletin, 109*, 125-129.

DIMATTEO, M.R., SHERBOURNE, C.D., HAYS, R.D., ORDWAY, L., KRAVITZ, R.L., MCGLYNN, E.A., KAPLAN, S., & ROGERS, W.H. (1993). Physicians' characteristics influence patients' adherence to medical treatment: Results from the medical outcomes study. *Health Psychology, 12*, 93-102.

DINDIA, K., & ALLEN, M. (1992). Sex differences in self-disclosure: A meta-analysis. *Psychological Bulletin, 112*, 106-124.

DINICOLA, D.D., & DIMATTEO, M.R. (1984). Practitioners, patients and compliance with medical regimes: A social psychological perspective. In A. Baum, S.E. Taylor & J.E. Singer (Eds.), *Handbook of psychology and health*, (Vol. 4, pp. 55-64). Hillsdale: Erlbaum.

DION, K.K., BERSCHEID, E., & WALSTER, E. (1972). What is beautiful is good. *Journal of Personality and Social Psychology, 24*, 285-290.

DION, K.K., & DION, K.L. (1985). Personality, gender and the phenomenology of romantic love. *Review of Personality and Social Psychology, 6*, 209-220.

DION, K.L. (1973). Cohesiveness as a determinant of ingroup-outgroup bias. *Journal of Personality and Social Psychology, 28*, 163-171.

DION, K.L. (1987). What's in a title? The MS. stereotype and images of women's titles of address. *Psychology of Women Quarterly, 11*, 21-36.

DION, K.L. (1989). Ethnicity and perceived discrimination: A comparative survey of six ethnic groups in Toronto. Paper presented at the 10th Annual Conference of the Canadian Ethnic Studies Association., Calgary.

DION, K.L., & SCHULLER, R.A. (1991). The Ms. stereotype: Its generality and its relation to managerial and marital status stereotypes. *Canadian Journal of Behaviour Science, 23*, 25-40.

DITECCO, D., & SCHLEGEL, R.P. (1982). Alcohol use among young males: An application of problem-behavior theory. In J.R. Eiser (Ed.), *Social psychology and behavioral medicine.* Chichester, UK: J.R. Wiley.

DITTO, P.H., & HILTON, J.L. (1990). Expectancy processes in the health care interaction sequence. *Journal of Social Issues, 46*, 97-124.

DOLLARD, J., DOOB, L.W., MILLER, N.E., MOWRER, O.H., & SEARS, R.R. (1939). *Frustration and aggression.* New Haven: Yale University Press.

DONNERSTEIN, E., & WILSON, D.W. (1976). The effects of noise and perceived control upon ongoing and subsequent aggressive behavior. *Journal of Personality and Social Psychology, 34*, 774-781.

DONOVAN, J.E., JESSOR, R., & JESSOR, L. (1983). Problem drinking in adolescence and young adulthood: A follow-up study. *Journal of Studies on Alcohol, 44*, 109-137.

DOOB, A.N., & GROSS, A.E. (1968). States of frustration as an inhibitor of horn-honking responses. *Journal of Social Psychology, 76*, 213-218.

DOOB, A.N., & KIRSHENBAUM, H.M. (1972). Some empirical evidence on the effect of S. 12 of the Canada Evidence Act on an accused. *Criminal Law Quarterly, 15*, 88-96.

DOOB, A.N., & KIRSHENBAUM, H.M. (1973). Bias in police line-ups—partial remembering. *Journal of Police Science and Administration, 1*, 287-293.

DOVIDIO, J.F., ALLEN, J.L, & SCHROEDER, D.A. (1990). Specificity of empathy-induced helping: Evidence for altruistic motivation. *Journal of Personality and Social Psychology, 59*, 249-260.

DOVIDIO, J.F., ELLYSON, S.L., KEATING, C.J., HELTMAN, K., & BROWN, C.E. (1988). The relationship of social power to visual displays of dominance between men and women. *Journal of Personality and Social Psychology, 54*, 233-242.

DOVIDIO, J.F., & ELLYSON, S.L. (1985). Patterns of visual dominance behavior in humans. In S.L. Ellyson & J.F. Dovidio (Eds.), *Power, dominance, and nonverbal behavior* (pp. 129-149). New York: Springer-Verlag.

DOVIDIO, J.F., & MORRIS, W.N. (1975). Effects of stress and commonality of fate on helping behavior. *Journal of Personality and Social Psychology, 31*, 145-149.

DRIGOTAS, S.M., & RUSBULT, C.E. (1992). Should I stay or should I go? A dependence model of breakups. *Journal of Personality and Social Psychology, 62*, 62-87.

DRISCOLL, R., DAVIS, K.W., & LIPETZ, M.E. (1972). Parental interference and romantic love. *Journal of Personality and Social Psychology, 24*, 1-10.

DROHAN, M. (1996, March 30). Outbreak: Disease goes global. *The Globe and Mail*, pp. D8.

DUNKEL-SCHETTER, C., FEINSTEIN, L.G., TAYLOR, S.E., & FALKE, R.L. (1992). Patterns of coping with cancer. *Health Psychology, 11*, 79-87.

DUNKEL-SCHETTER, C., & WORTMAN, C.B. (1982). The interpersonal dynamics of cancer: Problems in social relationships and their impact on the patient. In H.S. Friedman & M.R. DiMatteo (Eds.), *Interpersonal issues in health care* (pp. 69-100). New York: Academic.

DURANT, W., & DURANT, A. (1961). *The story of civilization: Part VII. The age of reason begins.* New York: Simon and Schuster.

DUTTON, D.G. (1971). Reactions of restauranteurs to blacks and whites violating restaurant dress requirements. *Canadian Journal of Behavioural Science, 3*, 298-331.

DUTTON, D.G. (1984). Interventions into the problem of wife assault: Therapeutic, policy and research implications. *Canadian Journal of Behavioural Science, 16*, 281-297.

DUTTON, D.G., & ARON, A.P. (1974). Some evidence for heightened sexual attraction under conditions of high anxiety. *Journal of Personality and Social Psychology, 30*, 510-517.

DUTTON, D.G., & LAKE, R. (1973). Threat of own prejudice and reverse discrimination in interracial situations. *Journal of Personality and Social Psychology, 28*, 94-100.

DUTTON, D.G., & LENNOX, V.I. (1974). The effect of prior "token" compliance on subsequent interracial behaviour. *Journal of Personality and Social Psychology, 29*, 65-71.

EAGLY, A.H. (1974). Comprehensibility of persuasive arguments as a determinant of opinion change. *Journal of Personality and Social Psychology, 29*, 758-773.

EAGLY, A.H. (1987). *Sex differences in social behavior: A social-role analysis.* Hillsdale, NJ: Erlbaum.

EAGLEY, A.H. (1992). Uneven progress: Social psychology and the study of attitudes. *Journal of Personality and Social Psychology, 63*, 693-710.

EAGLY, A.H., ASHMORE, R.D., MAKHIJANI, M.G., & LONGO, L.C. (1991). What is beautiful is good but...A meta-analytic review of research on the physical attractiveness stereotype. *Psychological Bulletin, 110*, 109-128.

EAGLY, A.H., & CHAIKEN, S. (1992). *The psychology of attitudes.* Fort Worth, TX: Harcourt Brace Jovanovich.

EAGLY, A.H., & CROWLEY, M. (1986). Gender and helping behavior: A meta-analytic review of the social psychological literature. *Psychological Bulletin, 100*, 283-308.

EAGLY, A.H., & JOHNSON, B.T. (1990). Gender and leadership style: A meta-analysis. *Psychological Bulletin, 108*, 233-256.

EAGLY, A.H., & KARAU, S.J. (1991). Gender and the emergence of leaders: A meta-analysis. *Journal of Personality and Social Psychology, 60*, 685-710.

EAGLY, A.H., MAKHIJANI, M.G., & KLONSKY, B.G. (1992). Gender and the evaluation of leaders: A meta-analysis. *Psychological Bulletin, 111*, 3-22.

EAGLY, A.H., & STEFFEN, V.J. (1988). A note on assessing stereotypes. *Personality and Social Psychology Bulletin, 14*, 676-680.

EASTERBROOK, J.A. (1959). The effect of emotion on cue utilization and the organization of behavior. *Psychological Review, 66*, 183-201.

EDWARDS, W. (1954). The theory of decision-making. *Psychological Bulletin, 51*, 380-417.

EISENBERG, N., & LENNON, R. (1983). Sex differences in empathy and related capacities. *Psychological Bulletin, 94*, 100-131.

EISENBERG, N., & MILLER, P.A. (1987). The relation of empathy to prosocial and related behaviors. *Psychological Bulletin, 101*, 91-119.

445

EKMAN, P., & FRIESEN, W.V. (1969). Nonverbal leakage and clues to deception. *Psychiatry, 32,* 88-106.

EKMAN, P., & FRIESEN, W.V. (1971). Constants across cultures in the face and emotion. *Journal of Personality and Social Psychology, 17,* 124-129.

EKMAN, P., & FRIESEN, W. (1974). Detecting deception from the body or face. *Journal of Personality and Social Psychology, 29,* 188-198.

EKMAN, P., FRIESEN, W.V., O'SULLIVAN, M., CHAN, A., DIACOYANNI-TARLAT-ZIS, I., HEIDER, K., KRAUSE, R., LECOMPTE, W.A., PITCAIRN, T., RICCI-BITTI, P.E., SCHERER, K., TOMITA, M., & TZAVARAS, A. (1987). Universals and cultural differences in the judgments of facial expressions of emotion. *Journal of Personality and Social Psychology, 53,* 712-717.

ELLEMERS, N., WILKE, H., & VON KNEPPENBERG, A. (1993). Effects of the legitimacy of low group or individual status on individual and collective self-enhancement strategies. *Journal of Personality and Social Psychology, 64,* 766-778.

ELLYSON, S.L., & DOVIDIO, J.F. (Eds.) (1985). *Power, dominance, and nonverbal behavior.* New York: Springer-Verlag.

ELMS, A.C. (1982). Keeping deception honest: Justifying conditions for social scientific research strategies. In T.L. Beauchamp & R. Faden (Eds.), *Ethical issues in social science research.* Baltimore: Johns Hopkins University Press.

ELWORK, A., SALES, B.D., & ALFINI, J.J. (1982). *Making jury instructions intelligible.* Charlotteville, VA: Michie Press.

EMERY, R.E. (1989). Family abuse. *American Psychologist, 44,* 321-328.

ENNIS, R., & ZANNA, M.P. (1991). Hockey assault: Constitutive versus normal violations. Paper presented at the Canadian Psychological Association convention.

ERON, L.D. (1980). Prescription for reduction of aggression. *American Psychologist, 35,* 244-252.

ERON, L.D., HUESMANN, L.R., DUBOW, E., ROMANOFF, R., & YARMEL, P.W. (1987). Aggression and its correlates over 22 years. In N.H. Crowell, R.J. Blanchard, I. Evans & C.R. O'Donnel (Eds.), *Childhood aggression and violence: Sources of influence, prevention and control.* New York: Academic Press.

ERVIN-TRIPP, S.M. (1974). Is second language learning really like the first? *TESOL Quarterly, 8,* 111-127.

ESPY, W.R., (1975). *An almanac of words at play.* New York: Clarkson N. Potter.

ESSES, V.M., HADDOCK, G., & ZANNA, M.P. (1993). Values, stereotypes, and emotions as determinants of intergroup attitudes. In D.M. Mackie & D.C. Hamilton (Eds.), *Affect, cognition and stereotyping: interactive processes in group perception.* New York: Academic Press.

ESSES, V.M., & WEBSTER, C.D. (1988). Physical attractiveness, dangerousness and the Canadian Criminal Code. *Journal of Applied Social Psychology, 18,* 1017-1031.

ETZIONI, A. (1969). Social-psychological aspects of international relations. In G. Lindzey & E. Aronson (Eds.), *Handbook of social psychology.* (2nd ed.) (Vol. 5, pp. 538-601.) Reading, MA: Addison-Wesley.

EVANS, G.W., JACOBS, S.V., & FRAGER, N.B. (1982). Behavioral responses to air pollution. In A. Baum & J. E. Singer (Eds.), *Advances in environmental psychology* (pp. 322-347). Hillsdale, NJ: Erlbaum.

FARQUHAR, J.W., FORTMANN, S.P., FLORA, J.A., TAYLOR, C.B., HASKELL, W.L., WILLIAMS, P.T., MACCOBY, N., & WOOD, P.D. (1990). Effects of communitywide education on cardiovascular disease risk factors. *Journal of the American Medical Association, 264,* 359-365.

FAZIO, R.H., BLLASCOVICH, J., & DRISCOLL, D.M. (1992). On the functional value of attitudes: the influence of accessible attitudes on the ease and quality of decision making. *Personality and Social Psychology Bulletin, 18,* 388-401.

FAZIO, R.H., SANBONMATSU, D.M., POWELL, M.C., & KARDES, F.R. (1986). On the automatic activation of attitudes. *Journal of Personality and Social Psychology, 50,* 229-238.

FEINGOLD, A. (1988). Matching for attractiveness in romantic partners and same-sex friends: A meta-analysis and theoretical critique. *Psychological Bulletin, 104,* 226-235.

FELDMAN-SUMMERS, S., & LINDNER, K. (1976). Perceptions of victims and defendants in criminal assault cases. *Criminal Justice Behavior, 3,* 135-149.

FERGUSON, G. (1982). Psychology at McGill. In M.J. Wright & C.R. Myers (Eds.), *History of academic psychology in Canada* (pp. 33-67). Toronto: Hogrefe.

FESTINGER, L. (1957). *A theory of cognitive dissonance.* Stanford, CA: Stanford University Press.

FESTINGER, L. (1964). *Conflict, decision and dissonance.* Stanford CA: Stanford University Press.

FESTINGER, L., & CARLSMITH, J.M. (1959). Cognitive consequences of forced compliance. *Journal of Abnormal and Social Psychology, 58,* 203-210.

FESTINGER, L., PEPITONE, A., & NEWCOMB, T. (1952). Some consequences of deindividuation in a group. *Journal of Personality and Social Psychology, 47,* 382-389.

FESTINGER, L., RIECKEN, H.W., & SCHACHTER, S. (1956). *When prophecy fails: A social and psychological study of a modern group that predicted the destruction of the world.* New York: Harper.

FESTINGER, L., SCHACHTER, S., & BACK, K.W. (1950). *Social pressures in informal groups: A study of human factors in housing.* New York: Harper & Brothers.

FIEDLER, F.E. (1967). *A theory of leadership effectiveness.* New York: McGraw-Hill.

FIEDLER, F.E. (1971). *Leadership.* Morristown, NJ: General Learning Press.

FIEDLER, F.E. (1981). Leadership effectiveness. *American Behavioral Scientist, 24,* 619-632.

FIELDS, J.M., & SCHUMAN, H. (1976). Public beliefs about beliefs of the public. *Public Opinion Quarterly, 40,* 427-448.

FISCHER, C.S. (1976). *The urban experience.* New York: Harcourt, Brace, Jovanovich.

FISCHER, C.S., & PHILLIPS, S.L. (1982). Who is alone? Social characteristics of people with small networks. In L.A. Peplau & D. Perlman (Eds.), *Loneliness: A sourcebook of current theory, research and therapy* (pp. 21-39). New York: Wiley Interscience.

FISHER, J.D. (1988). Possible effects of reference-group-based social influence on AIDS-risk behavior and AIDS prevention. *American Psychologist, 43,* 914-920.

FISHER, J.D., & FISHER, W.A. (1992). Changing AIDS-risk behavior. *Psychological Bulletin, 111,* 455-474.

FISHER, J.D., NADLER, A., & WHITCHER-ALAGNA, S. (1982). Recipient reactions to aid. *Psychological Bulletin, 91,* 27-54.

FISHER, R.J. (1983). Third Party Consultation as a method of intergroup conflict resolution. *Journal of Conflict Resolution, 27,* 301-334.

446

FISHER, R.J. (1982). *Social psychology: An applied approach.* New York: St. Martin's.

FISHER, R.J. (1985). The social psychology of intergroup conflict: Toward eclectic theory. Paper presented at the Annual Meeting for the Canadian Psychological Association, Halifax.

FISHER, R.J. (1989). *The social psychology of inter-group conflict resolution.* New York: Springer-Verlag.

FISHER, S., & TODD, A.D. (Eds.) (1983). *The social organization of doctor-patient communication.* Washington: Center for Applied Linguistics.

FISHER, W.A., FISHER, J.D., & RYE, B.J. (1995). Understanding and promoting AIDS-preventive behavior: Insights from the theory of reasoned action. *Health Psychology, 14,* 255-264.

FISKE, S.T., & TAYLOR, S.E. (1984). *Social cognition.* Don Mills, Ontario: Addison-Wesley.

FISKE, S.T., & TAYLOR, S.E. (1991). *Social cognition.* (2nd ed.) Reading, MA: Addison-Wesley.

FLEMING, I., BAUM, A., & WEISS, L. (1987). Social density and perceived control as mediators of crowding stress in a high-density residential neighbourhood. *Journal of Personality and Social Psychology, 52,* 899-906.

FOA, U.G. (1971). Interpersonal and economic resources. *Science, 171,* 345-351.

FOGELMAN, E., & WIENER, V.L. (1985). The few, the brave, the noble. *Psychology Today, 19,* 61-65.

FONTANA, A.F., KERNS, R.D., ROSENBERG, R.L., & COLONESE, K.L. (1989). Support, stress and recovery from coronary heart disease: A longitudinal causal model. *Health Psychology, 8,* 175-193.

FRANKLIN, S. (1977). *A time of heroes 1940/1950.* Toronto: Natural Science of Canada Limited.

FREEDMAN, J.L. (1975). *Crowding and behavior.* New York: Viking Press.

FREEDMAN, J.L. (1982). Theories of contagion as they relate to mass psychogenic illness. In M.J. Colligan, J.W. Pennebaker & L.R. Murphy (Eds.), *Mass psychogenic illness,* (pp. 171-182). Hillsdale, NJ: Erlbaum.

FREEDMAN, J.L. (1984). Effects of television violence on aggressiveness. *Psychological Bulletin, 96,* 227-246.

FREEDMAN, J.L., BIRSKY, J., & CAVOUKIAN, A. (1980). Environmental determinants of behavioral contagion: Density and number. *Basic and Applied Social Psychology, 1,* 155-161.

FREEDMAN, J.L., & FRASER, S.C. (1966). Compliance without pressure: The foot-in-the-door technique. *Journal of Personality and Social Psychology, 4,* 195-202.

FREEDMAN, J.L., WALLINGTON, S.A., & BLESS, E. (1967). Compliance without pressure: The effect of guilt. *Journal of Personality and Social Psychology, 7,* 117-124.

FRENDER, R., & LAMBERT, W.E. (1972). The influence of pupils' speech styles on teacher evaluations. 23rd Annual Round Table Meeting, Georgetown University, Washington, D.C. Cited by Bourhis, Giles & Lambert (1975).

FRENKEL, O.J., & DOOB, A.N. (1976). Post-decision dissonance at the polling booth. *Canadian Journal of Behavioural Science, 8,* 347-350.

FREUD, S. (1933). Why war? In J. Rickman (Ed.) (1968), *Civilization, war and death: Selections from five works by Sigmund Freud* (pp. 82-97). London: Hogarth.

FREUDENBURG, W.R. & PASTOR, S.K. (1992). NIMBYs and LULUs: Stalking the syndromes. *Journal of Social Issues, 48,* 39-61.

FREY, D. (1986). Recent research on selective exposure to information. In L. Berkowitz (Ed.), *Advances in experimental social psychology* (Vol. 19, pp. 41-80). New York: Academic Press.

FRICK, R.W. (1985). Communicating emotion: The role of prosodic features. *Psychological Bulletin, 97,* 412-429.

FRIEDMAN, M., & BOOTH-KEWLEY, S. (1987). The "disease-prone personality": A meta-analytic view of the concept. *American Psychologist, 42,* 539-555.

FRIEDMAN, M., & ROSENMAN, R.H. (1959). Association of a specific behavior pattern with blood and cardiovascular findings: Blood cholesterol levels, blood clotting time, incidence of arcus senilis and clinical coronary artery disease. *Journal of American Medical Association, 169,* 1286-1296.

FROLICH, N., & OPPENHEIMER, J. (1970). I get by with a little help from my friends. *World Politics, 23,* 104-120.

FURNHAM, A. (1985). Just world beliefs in an unjust society: A cross-cultural comparison. *European Journal of Social Psychology, 15,* 363-366.

GARDNER, R.C. (1979). Social psychological aspects of second language acquisition. In H. Giles & R. St. Clair (Eds.), *Language and psychology.* Oxford: Basil Blackwell.

GARDNER, R.C. (1984). *Social psychological aspects of second language learning.* London: Edward Arnold.

GARDNER, R.C. (1985). *Social psychology and second language learning.* London: Edward Arnold.

GARDNER, R.C., & DESROCHERS, A. (1981). Second language acquisition and bilingualism: Research in Canada (1970-1980). *Canadian Psychology, 22,* 146-162.

GARDNER, R.C., GLIKSMAN, L., & SMYTHE, P.C. (1978). Attitude and behaviour in second language acquisition: A social psychological interpretation. *Canadian Psychological Review, 19,* 173-186.

GARDNER, R.C., LALONDE, R.N., NERO, A.M., & YOUNG, M.U. (1988). Ethnic stereotypes and implications of measurement strategy. *Social Cognition, 6,* 40-60.

GARDNER, R.C., & LAMBERT, W.E. (1959). Motivational variables in second language acquisition. *Canadian Journal of Psychology, 13,* 266-272.

GARDNER, R.C., & LAMBERT, W.E. (1972). *Attitudes and motivation in second-language learning.* Rowley, MA: Newbury House.

GARDNER, R.C., & KALIN, R. (Eds.) (1981). *A social psychology of Canadian ethnic relations.* Toronto: Methuen.

GEEN, R. (1988). Alternative conceptions of social facilitation. In P. Paulus (Ed.), *Psychology of group influence.* Hillsdale, NJ: Erlbaum.

GEEN, R.G., & GANGE, J.J. (1977). Drive theory of social facilitation: Twelve years of theory and research. *Psychological Bulletin, 84,* 1267-1288.

GELLER, E.S., WINETT, R.A., & EVERETT, P.B. (1982). *Preserving the environment.* New York: Pergamon Press.

GENESEE, F., & BOURHIS, R.Y. (1982). The social psychological significance of code switching in cross-cultural commuication. *Journal of Language and Social Psychology, 1,* 1-27.

GENESEE, F., & BOURHIS, R.Y. (1988). Evaluative reactions to language choice strategies: The role of sociostructural factors. *Language and Communication, 8,* 229-250.

GERBNER, G. (1969). The television world of violence. In R.K. Baker & S.J. Ball (Eds.), *Mass media and violence: A staff report to the National Commission on the causes and prevention of violence.* Washington, D.C: U.S. Government Printing Office.

GERGEN, K.J., ELLSWORTH, P., MASLACH, P., & SEIPEL, M. (1975). Obligation, donor resources, and the reactions to aid in three nations. *Journal of Personality and Social Psychology, 31,* 390-400.

GERSON, A.C., & PERLMAN, D. (1979). Loneliness and expressive communication. *Journal of Abnormal Psychology, 88,* 258-261.

GIBB, C.A. (1969). Leadership. In G. Lindzey & E. Aronson (Eds.), *Handbook of social psychology* (Vol. 4, 2nd ed.). Reading, MA: Addison-Wesley.

GIBBS, R.W. (1986). What makes some speech acts conventional? *Journal of Memory and Language, 25,* 181-196.

GIBBINS, K., & CONEY, J.R. (1981). Meaning of physical dimensions of women's clothes. *Perceptual and Motor Skills, 53,* 720-722.

GIFFORD, R., & SACILOTTO, P. A. (1993). Social isolation and personal space: A field study. *Canadian Journal of Behavioural Science, 25,* 165-174.

GILES, G. G., MARKS, R., & FOLEY, P. (1988). Incidence of non-melanocytic skin cancer treated in Australia. *British Medical Journal, 296,* 13-17.

GILES, H., BOURHIS, R.Y., & TAYLOR, D.M. (1977). Towards a theory of language in ethnic group relations. In H. Giles (Ed.), *Language, ethnicity and intergroup relations* (pp. 307-348). London: Academic Press.

GILES, H., COUPLAND, J., & COUPLAND, N. (Eds.) (1991). *Contexts of accommodation: Developments in applied sociolinguistics.* New York: Cambridge University Press.

GILES, H., & POWESLAND, P. (1975). *Speech style and social evaluation.* London: Academic Press.

GILLIS, J.S. (1983). *Too tall too small.* Montreal: Book Centre.

GLADUE, B.A., & DELANEY, H.J. (1990). Gender difference in the perception of attractiveness of men and women in bars. *Personality and Social Psychology Bulletin, 16,* 378-391.

GLICK, P., DEMOREST, J.A., & HOTZE, C.A. (1988). Self-monitoring and beliefs about partner compatiblity in romantic relationships. *Personality and Social Psychology Bulletin, 14,* 485-494.

GOFFMAN, E. (1959). *The presentation of self in everyday life.* Garden City, NY: Doubleday.

GOLD, R.S., SKINNER, M.T., & ROSS, M.W. (1994). Unprotected anal intercourse in HIV-infected and non-HIV infected gay men. *Journal of Sex Research, 31,* 59-77.

GOLDBERG, M.E. (1982). TV advertising directed at children: Inherently unfair or simply in need of regulation? In S.J. Shapiro & L. Heslop (Eds.), *Marketplace Canada: Some controversial dimensions.* Toronto: McGraw-Hill Ryerson.

GOLDSTEIN, J.H. (1986). *Aggression and crimes of violence.* (2nd ed.) New York: Oxford University Press.

GOLDSTEIN, J.H., DAVIS, R.W., & HERMON, D. (1975). Escalation of aggression: Experimental studies. *Journal of Personality and Social Psychology, 35,* 162-170.

GOLEMAN, D. (1986). Studies point to power of nonverbal signals. *New York Times,* April 8, pp. C1-C6.

GONZALES, M.H., ARONSON, E., & COSTANZO, M.A. (1988). Using social cognition and persuasion to promote energy conservation: A quasi-experiment. *Journal of Applied Social Psychology, 18,* 1049-1066.

GONZALES, R., ELLSWORTH, P.C., & PEMBROKE, M. (1993). Response biases in lineups and showups. *Journal of Personality and Social Psychology, 64,* 525-537.

GOODMAN, M. (1964). *Race awareness in young children.* (2nd ed.) New York: Crowell-Collier.

GOTTLIEB, B.H. (1985). Social networks and social support: An overview of research, practice and policy implications. *Health Education Quarterly, 12,* 221-238.

GOTTMAN, J.M., & LEVENSON, R.W. (1992). Marital processes predictive of later dissolution: Behavior, physiology and health. *Journal of Personality and Social Psychology, 63,* 221-233.

GOULDNER, A.W. (1960). The norm of reciprocity: A preliminary statement. *American Sociological Review, 25,* 161-179.

GRANT, P.R. (1978). *Attribution of an ethnic stereotype.* Unpublished Masters Thesis, University of Waterloo.

GRAUMANN, C.F., & MOSCOVICI, S. (Eds.) (1987). *Changing conceptions of conspiracy.* New York: Springer-Verlag.

GRAYSON, J.P., & GRAYSON, L. (1975). Social movements and social change in contemporary Canada. *Quarterly of Canadian Studies, 4,* 50-57.

GREENGLASS, E.R. (1982). *A world of difference: Gender roles in perspective.* Toronto: Wiley.

GREENWALD, A.G., & RONIS, D.L. (1978). Twenty years of cognitive dissonance: A case study of the evaluation of a theory. *Psychological Review, 85,* 53-57.

GREER, D.L. (1983). Spectator booing and the home advantage: A study of social influence in the basketball arena. *Social Psychology Quarterly, 46,* 252-261.

GRICE, H.P. (1975). Logic and conversation. In P. Cole and J.L. Morgan (Eds.), *Syntax and semantics: Vol. 3, Speech acts* (pp. 41-58). NY: Seminar Press.

GROH, D. (1987). The temptation of conspiracy theory, or: Why do bad things happen to good people Part I: Preliminary draft of a theory of conspiracy theories. In C.F. Graumann & S. Moscovici (Eds.), *Changing conceptions of conspiracy* (pp. 1-13). New York: Springer-Verlag.

GROSS, A.E., & FLEMING, J. (1982). Twenty years of deception in social psychology. *Personality and Social Psychology Bulletin, 8,* 402-408.

GRUDER, C.L. (1974). Cost and dependency as determinants of helping and exploitation. *Journal of Conflict Resolution, 18,* 473-485.

GRUSEC, J.E. (1972). Demand characteristics of the modelling experiment: Altruism as a function of age and aggression. *Journal of Personality and Social Psychology, 22,* 139-148.

GRUSEC, J.E., & SKUBISKI, S.L. (1970). Model nurturance, demand characteristics of the modelling experiment, and altruism. *Journal of Personality and Social Psychology, 14,* 352-359.

GRUSEC, J.E., & REDLER, E. (1980). Attribution, reinforcement and altruism: A developmental analysis. *Developmental Psychology, 16,* 525-534.

HAAS, A. (1979). Male and female spoken language differences: Stereotypes and evidence. *Psychological Bulletin, 86,* 616-626.

HAGESTAD, G.O., & SMYER, M.A. (1982). Dissolving long-term relationships: Patterns of divorcing in middle-age. In S. Duck (Ed.), *Personal relationships 4: Dissolving relationships* (pp. 211-235). New York: Academic Press.

HAKUTA, K. & GARCIA, E.E. (1989). Bilingualism and education. *American Psychologist, 44*, 374-379.

HALL, J.A., EPSTEIN, A.M., DECIANTIS, M.L., & MCNEIL, B.J. (1993). Physicians' liking for their patients: More evidence for the role of affect in medical care. *Health Psychology, 12*, 140-146.

HALL, J.A., & VECCIA, E.M. (1990). More "touching" observations: New insights on men, women, and interpersonal touch. *Journal of Personality and Social Psychology, 59*, 1159-1162.

HALL, J.A, IRISH, J.T., ROTER, D.L., EHRLICH, C.M., & MILLER, L. (1994). Gender in medical encounters: An analysis of physician and patient communication in a primary care setting. *Health Psychology, 13*, 384-392.

HALL, E.T. (1966). *The hidden dimension.* New York: Doubleday.

HALL, R.S. (1988) The virology of AIDS. *American Psychologist, 43*, 907-913.

HAMBLIN, R.L. (1958). Leadership and crises. *Sociometry, 21*, 322-335.

HAMBURGER, H., GUYER, M., & FOX, J. (1975). Group size and cooperation. *Journal of Conflict Resolution, 19*, 503-531.

HAMILL, R., WILSON, T.D., & NISBETT, R.E. (1980). Insensitivity to sample bias: Generalizing from atypical cases. *Journal of Personality and Social Psychology, 39*, 578-589.

HAMILTON, D.L. (1976). Individual differences in ascriptions of responsibility, guilt and appropriate judgement. In G. Berman, C. Nemeth & N. Vidmar (Eds.), *Psychology and the law* (pp. 239-264). Lexington, MA: Heath.

HAMILTON, D.L. (1979). A cognitive-attributional analysis of stereotyping. In L. Berkowitz (Ed.), *Advances in experimental social psychology* (Vol. 12). New York: Academic press.

HAMILTON, D.L. (1981). Illusory correlation as a basis for stereotyping. In D.L. Hamilton (Ed.), *Cognitive processes in stereotyping and intergroup behavior.* Hillsdale, NJ: Erlbaum.

HAMILTON, D.L., & GIFFORD, R.K. (1976). Illusory correlation in interpersonal perception: A cognitive basis of stereotypic judgements. *Journal of Experimental Social Psychology, 12*, 392-407.

HAMILTON, D.L., & ROSE, T.L. (1980). Illusory correlation and the maintenance of stereotypes. *Journal of Personality and Social Psychology, 39*, 832-845.

HAMILTON, D.L., & SHERMAN, S.J. (1989). Illusory correlations: Implications for stereotype theory and research. In D. Bar-Tal, C.F. Graumann, A.W. Kruglanski & W. Stroebe, W. (Eds.), *Stereotyping and prejudice: Changing conceptions* (pp. 59-82). New York: Springer-Verlag.

HANEY, C., & MANZOLATTI, J. (1981). Television criminology: Network illusions of criminal justice reality. In E. Aronson (Ed.), *Readings about the social animal* (3rd ed., pp. 125-136). San Francisco: W.H. Freeman.

HARDIN, G. (1968). The tragedy of the commons. *Science, 162*, 1243-1248.

HARE, A.P. (1962). *Handbook of small group research.* Glencoe, NY: Free Press.

HARE, R.D. & MCPHERSON, L.M. (1984). Violent and aggressive behavior by criminal psychopaths. *International Journal of Law and Psychiatry, 7*, 35-50.

HARITOS-FATOUROS, M. (1988). The official torturer: A learning model for obedience to the authority of violence. *Journal of Applied Social Psychology, 18*, 1107-1120.

HARRIS, M. (1974). *Cows, pigs, wars and witches: The riddles of cultures.* New York: Random House.

HARRISON, A.A. (1977). Mere exposure. In L. Berkowitz (Ed.), *Advances in experimental social psychology* (Vol. 1, pp. 39-83). New York: Academic Press.

HASS, R.G. & GRADY, K. (1975). Temporal delay, type of forewarning, and resistance to influence. *Journal of Experimental Social Psychology, 11*, 459-469.

HATFIELD, E. (1988). Passionate and companionate love. In R.J. Sternberg and M.L. Barnes (Eds.), *The psychology of love* (pp. 191-217). New Haven, CT: Yale Uiversity Press.

HATFIELD, E., & WALSTER, G.W. (1978). *A new look at love.* Reading, MA: Addison-Wesley.

HAUGTVEDT, C.P., & PETTY, R.E. (1992). Personality and persuasion: Need for cognition moderates the persistence and resistance of attitude changes. *Journal of Personality and Social Psychology, 63*, 308-319.

HAVILAND, J.M., & MALATESTA, C.M. (1981). The development of sex differences in nonverbal signals: Fallacies, facts and fantasies. In C. Mayo & N.M. Henley (Eds.), *Gender and non-verbal behavior.* New York: Springer-Verlag.

HAZAN, C., & SHAVER, P.R. (1987). Romantic love conceptualized as an attachment process. *Journal of Personality and Social Psychology, 59*, 270-280.

HEALTH AND WELFARE CANADA (1987). *The Active Health Report: Perspectives on Canada's Health Promotion Survey, 1985.* Catalogue No. H-39--106/1987E. Ottawa: Supply and Services Canada.

HEALTH SERVICE AND PROMOTION BRANCH, HEALTH AND WELFARE CANADA (1989). *Knowledge development for health promotion: A call for action.* Ottawa: Ministry of Supply and Services.

HEAROLD, S. (1986). A synthesis of 1043 effects of television on social behavior. In G. Comstock (Ed.), *Public communications and behavior: Vol. 1* (pp. 65-133). New York: Academic Press.

HEATH, L., KRUTTSCHNITT, C., & WARD, D. (1986). Television and violent criminal behavior: Beyond the Bobo doll. *Violence and Victims, 1*, 177-190.

HEBB, D.O., & THOMPSON, W.R. (1968). The social significance of animal studies. In G. Lindzey & E. Aronson (Eds.), *The handbook of social psychology.* (2nd ed.) (Vol.1.) Reading, MA: Addison-Wesley.

HEBB, D.O. (1971). Comment on altruism: The comparative evidence. *Psychological Bulletin, 76*, 409-410.

HENDRICK, C., & HENDRICK, S. (1986). A theory and a method of love. *Journal of Personality and Social Psychology, 50*, 392-402.

HENLEY, M. (1973). Status and sex: some touching observations. *Bulletin of the Psychonomic Society, 2*, 21-27.

HENLEY, N. (1977). *Body politics: Power, sex, and nonverbal communication.* Englewood Cliffs, NJ: Prentice Hall.

HENNESSY, M., & SALTZ, R.F. (1993). Modeling social influences on public drinking. *Journal of Studies on Alcohol, 54*, 139-145.

HENRY, F. (1978). The dynamics of racism in Toronto. Unpublished research report. York University.

HENRY, F. (1985/86). Heroes and helpers in Nazi Germany: Who aided Jews? *Humboldt Journal of Social Relations, 13*, 306-319.

HENRY, F., TATOR, C., MATTIS, W., & REES, T. (1995). *The colour of democracy: Racism in Canadian society.* Toronto: Harcourt Brace.

449

HEREK, G.M., & GLUNT, E.K. (1988). An epidemic of stigma: Public reactions to AIDS. *American Psychologist, 43*, 886-891.

HESLIN, R. & ALPER, T. (1983). Touch: A bonding gesture. In J.M. Wiemann & R.P. Harrison (Eds.), *Nonverbal interaction* (pp. 47-75). Beverly Hills, CA: Sage.

HESLIN, R. (1978). Responses to touching as an index of sex-role norms and attitudes. Paper presented at the annual meeting of the American Psychological Association, Toronto. August 1978.

HICKS, R.D. (1990a). Police pursuit of satanic crime. *Skeptical Inquirer, 14*, 276-286.

HICKS, R.D. (1990b). The satanic conspiracy and urban legends. *Skeptical Inquirer, 14*, 378-389.

HIGBEE, K.L. (1969). Fifteen years of fear arousal: Research on threat appeals: 1953-1968. *Psychological Bulletin, 72*, 426-444.

HIGGINS, E.T. (1987). Self-discrepancy: A theory relating self and affect. *Psychological Review, 94*, 319-340.

HIGGINS, E.T. (1989). Continuities and discontinuities in self-regulatory and self-evaluative processes: A developmental theory relating self and affect. *Journal of Personality, 57*, 407-444.

HIGHAM, P.A., & CARMENT, D.W. (1992). The rise and fall of politicians: The judged heights of Broadbent, Mulroney and Turner before and after the 1988 Canadian federal election. *Canadian Journal of Behavioural Science, 24*, 404-409.

HILL, C.T., RUBIN, Z., & PEPLAU, L.A. (1976). Breakups before marriage: The end of 103 affairs. *Journal of Social Issues, 32*, 147-168.

HINKIN, T.R., & SCHRIESHEIM, C.A. (1989). Development and application of new scales to measure the French and Raven (1959) bases of social power. *Journal of Applied Social Psychology, 74*, 561-567.

HIRT, E., & KIMBLE, C.E. (1981). The home-field advantage in sports: Differences and correlates. Presented at the Annual Meeting of the Midwestern Psychological Association, Detroit. May 1981.

HOFFMANN, M.L. (1977). Sex differences in empathy and related behaviors. *Psychological Bulletin, 84*, 712-722.

HOFLING, C.K., BRODZSMAN, E., DALRYMPLE, S., GRAVES, N., & PIERCE, C.M. (1966). An experimental study in nurse physician relationships. *The Journal of Nervous and Mental Disease, 143*, 171-180.

HOLLANDER, E.P. (1958). Conformity, status, and idiosyncrasy credit. *Psychological Review, 65*, 117-127.

HOLLANDER, E.P. (1978). *Leadership dynamics: A practical guide to effective relationships*. New York: Free Press.

HOLLANDER, E.P., & YODER, J. (1980). Some issues in comparing women and men as leaders. *Basic and Applied Social Psychology, 1*, 267-280.

HOLMES, D.S. (1976). Debriefing after psychological experiments: II. Effectiveness of post-experimental desensitizing. *American Psychologist, 31*, 868-876.

HOLMES, T.H., & RAHE, R.H. (1967). The social readjustment rating scale. *Journal of Psychosomatic Research, 11*, 213-218.

HOLSTROM, L., & BURGESS, A. (1978). *The victims of rape: Institutional reactions*. New York: Wiley.

HOLT, R.R. (1989). College students' definitions and images of enemies. *Journal of Social Issues-, 45*, 33-50.

HOLTGRAVES, T. (1986). Language structure in social interaction: Perceptions of direct and indirect speech acts and interactants who use them. *Journal of Personality and Social Psychology, 51*, 305-314.

HOMANS, G.C. (1958). Social behavior and exchange. *American Journal of Sociology, 63*, 597-606.

HOMANS G.C. (1974). *Social behavior: Its elementary forms*. Revised Edition. New York: Harcourt Brace Jovanovich.

HOMER, P.M., & KAHLE, L. (1988). A structural equation test of the value-attitude-behavior hierarchy. *Journal of Personality and Social Psychology, 54*, 638-646.

HONTS, C.R., HODES, R.L., & RASKIN, D.C. (1985). Effects of physical counter measures on the physiological detection of deception. *Journal of Applied Psychology, 70*, 177-187.

HORN, M.J. (1975). *The second skin: An interdisciplinary study of clothing*. Boston: Houghton-Mifflin.

HORN, J.C. (1985). Fan violence: Fighting the injustice of it all. *Psychology Today, 19 (10)*, 30-31.

HOROWITZ, M.J., DUFF, D. F., & STRATTON, C.O. (1970). Personal space and the body buffer zone. In H. Proshansky, W. Ittelson & L. Rivlin (Eds.), *Environmental psychology: Man and his physical setting* (pp. 244-272). New York: Holt, Rinehart & Winston.

HORVATH, F. (1984). Detecting deception in eyewitness cases: Problems and prospects in the use of the polygraph. In G.L. Wells & E.F. Loftus (Eds.), *Eyewitness testimony: Psychological perspectives* (pp. 214-255). Cambridge, UK: Cambridge University Press.

HORVATH, F. (1977). Effect of selected variables on interpretation of polygraph records. *Journal of Applied Psychology, 62*, 127-136.

HOUSE, R. (1977). A 1976 theory of charismatic leadership. In J.G. Hunt and L. Larson (Eds.), *Leadership: The cutting edge* (pp. 189-207). Carbondale: Southern Illinois University Press.

HOVLAND, C.I., HARVEY, O.J., & SHERIF, M. (1957). Assimilation and contrast effects in reactions to communications and attitude change. *Journal of Abnormal and Social Psychology, 55*, 244-252.

HOVLAND, C.I., JANIS, I., & KELLEY, H.H. (1953). *Communication and persuasion*. New Haven: Yale University Press.

HOWELL, J.M., & FROST, P.J. (1989). A laboratory study of charismatic leadership. *Organization Behavior and Human Decision Processes, 43*, 243-269.

HUBA, G.J., DENT, C., & BENTLER, P.M. (1980). Causal models of peer-adult support and youthful alcohol use. Paper presented to the American Psychological Association, Montreal (September).

HUESMANN, L.R., ERON, L.D., KLEIN, R., BRICE, P., & FISCHER, P. (1983). Mitigating the imitation of aggressive behaviors by changing children's attitudes about media violence. *Journal of Personality and Social Psychology, 44*, 899-910.

HUESMANN, L.R. (1986). Psychological processes promoting the relation between exposure to media violence and aggressive behavior by the receiver. *Journal of Social Issues, 42*, 125-139.

HUESMANN, L.R., ERON, L.D., LEFKOWITZ, M.M., & WALDER, L.O. (1984). Stability of aggression over time and generations. *Developmental Psychology, 20*, 1120-1134.

HUME, E., LEPICQ, D., & BOURHIS, R.Y. (1992). Attitudes des étudiants canadiens anglais face aux accents des professeurs de français en Ontario. *La revue canadienne des langues vivantes.*

HUNTER, I. (1987). Human rights: Liberty can't be legislated. In R. Jackson, D. Jackson & N. Baxter-Moore (Eds.), *Contemporary Canadian politics: Readings and notes* (pp. 61-64). Scarborough: Prentice-Hall.

ICKOVICS, J.R., & RODIN, J. (1992). Women and AIDS in the United States: Epidemiology, natural history and mediating mechanisms. *Health Psychology, 11,* 1-16.

INGHAM, A.G., LEVINGER, G., GRAVES, J., & PECKHORN, V. (1974). The Ringelmann effect: Studies of group size and group performance. *Journal of Experimental Social Psychology, 10,* 371-384.

INGLEHART, R. (1987). Extremist political positions and perceptions of conspiracy: Even paranoids have real enemies. In C.F. Graumann & S. Moscovici (Eds.), *Changing conceptions of conspiracy* (pp. 231-244). New York: Springer-Verlag.

INGLIS, J. (1982). Psychology at Queen's. In M.J. Wright and C.R. Myers (Eds.), *History of Academic Psychology in Canada* (pp. 100-115). Toronto: Hogrefe.

INSKO, C.A. (1964). Primacy versus recency in persuasion as a function of the timing of arguments and measures. *Journal of Abnormal and Social Psychology, 69,* 381-391.

ISEN, A.M. (1970). Success, failure, attention and reaction to others. *Journal of Personality and Social Psychology, 15,* 294-301.

JACKSON, J.M., BUGLIONE, S.A., & GLENWICK, D.S. (1988). Major league baseball performance as a function of being traded: A drive and theory analysis. *Personality and Social Psychology Bulletin, 14,* 46-56.

JACKSON, R.J., KELLY, M.J., & MITCHELL, T.H. (1977). Collective conflict, violence and the media. In *Report of the Royal Commission on Violence in the Communications Industry* (Vol. 5, pp. 227-314). Toronto: Publication Centre, Government of Ontario.

JACKSON, J.M., & PADGETT, V.R. (1982). With a little help from my friend: Social loafing and the Lennon-McCartney songs. *Personality and Social Psychology Bulletin, 8,* 672-677.

JAFFE, P. (1990). Hidden victims: The effects of witnessing violence. Paper presented at the Annual Conference of the Canadian Psychological Association, Ottawa.

JAMIESON, D.W., LYDON, J.E., & ZANNA, M.P. (1987). Attitude and activity preference similarity: Differential bases of interpersonal attraction for low and high self-monitors. *Journal of Personality and Social Psychology, 53,* 1052-1060.

JANIS, I.L. (1951). *Air war and emotional stress. Psychological studies of bombing and civilian defense.* New York: McGraw-Hill.

JANIS, I.L. (1972). *Victims of groupthink.* Boston: Houghton Mifflin.

JANIS, I.L. (1982). *Groupthink.* (2nd ed.) Boston: Houghton Mifflin.

JANIS, I.L., CHAPMAN, D.W., GILLIN, J.P., & SPIEGEL, J.P. (1964). The problem of panic. In D.P. Schultz (Ed.), *Panic behavior* (pp. 118-127). New York: Random House.

JANIS, I.L., & FESHBACH, S. (1953). Effects of fear-arousing communications. *Journal of Abnormal and Social Psychology, 48,* 78-92.

JANIS, I.L., & MANN, L. (1977). *Decision making.* New York: Free Press.

JASPARS, J. (1980). The coming of age of social psychology in Europe. *European Journal of Social Psychology, 10,* 421-428.

JERVIS, R., LEBOW, R.N., & STEIN, J.G. (1985). *Psychology of deterrence.* Baltimore: Johns Hopkins University Press.

JESSOR, R. (1993). Successful adolescent development among youth in high-risk settings. *American Psychologist, 48,* 117-126.

JESSOR, R., DONOVAN, J.E., & COSTA, F.M. (1991). *Beyond adolescence: Problem behavior and young adult development.* Cambridge: Cambridge University Press.

JESSOR, R., & JESSOR, S.L. (1977). *Problem behavior and psychosocial development: A longitudinal study of youth.* New York: Academic Press.

JOAD, C.E.M. (1957). *Guide to philosophy.* New York: Dover.

JOHANSSON, G., COLLINS, A., & COLLINS, V.P. (1983). Male and female psychoneuroendocrine response to examination stress: A case report. *Motivation and Emotion, 7,* 1-9.

JOHNSON, B.T., & EAGLY, A.H. (1989). Effects of involvement on persuasion: A meta-analysis. *Psychological Bulletin, 106,* 290-314.

JOHNSTON, I.F., & STRICKLAND, L.H. (1985). Communication mode, affect and recall. *Canadian Journal of Behavioural Science, 17,* 226-231.

JONES, E.E., & HARRIS, V.A. (1976). The attribution of attitude. *Journal of Experimental Psychology, 3,* 1-24.

JONES, J.W. (1978). Adverse emotional reactions of non-smokers to secondary cigarette smoke. *Environmental Psychology and Non-verbal Behavior, 3,* 125-127.

JONES, J.W., & BOGAT, G.A. (1978). Air pollution and human aggression. *Psychological Reports, 43,* 721-723.

JONES, R.A. (1990). Expectations and delay in seeking medical care. *Journal of Social Issues, 46,* 81-95.

JONES, S.E., & YARBROUGH, A.E. (1985). A naturalistic study of the meanings of touch. *Communication Monographs, 52,* 19-56.

JOSEPHS, R.A., MARKUS, H.R., & TAFARODI, R.W. (1992). Gender and self-esteem. *Journal of Personality and Social Psychology, 63,* 391-402.

JOY, L.A., KIMBALL, M.M., & ZABRACK, M.L. (1977). Television exposure and children's aggressive behaviours. Paper presented at the Canadian Psychological Association Annual Conference, Vancouver, B.C.

JUNG, J. (1982). *The experimenter's challenge.* New York: Macmillan.

KAGITÇIBASI, C., & BERRY, J.W. (1989). Cross-cultural psychology: Current research and trends. *Annual Review of Psychology, 40,* 493-531.

KAHN, G.R., & KATZ, D. (1953). Leadership practices in relation to productivity and morale. In D. Cartwright & A. Zander (Eds.), *Group dynamics: Research and theory.* Evanston, IL: Row, Peterson.

KAHN, H. (1962). *Thinking about the unthinkable.* New York: Avon.

KAHN, M. (1966). The physiology of catharsis. *Journal of Personality and Social Psychology, 3,* 278-286.

KAHNEMAN, D., & TVERSKY, A. (1982). The simulation heuristic. In D. Kahneman, P. Slovic & A. Tversky (Eds.), *Judgements under uncertainty: Heuristics and biases.* New York: Cambridge University Press.

KALIN, R., & BERRY, J.W. (1979). *Ethnic attitudes and identity in the context of national unity.* Final report to Multiculturalism Directorate, Secretary of State, Government of Canada.

KALIN, R., & GARDNER R.C. (1981). The cultural context of social psychology. In R.C. Gardner & R. Kalin (Eds.), *A social psychology of Canadian ethnic relations* (pp. 2-17). Toronto: Methuen.

KAMIN, L.J. (1974). *The science and politics of I.Q.* New York: Halsted Press.

KANNER, A.D., COYNE, J.C., SCHAEFER, C., & LAZARUS, R.S. (1981). Comparison of two models of stress measurement: Daily hassles and uplifts versus major life events. *Journal of Behavioral Medicine, 4*, 1-29.

KANTER, R.M. (1975). Women and the structure of organizations: Explorations in theory and behavior. In M. Millman & R.M. Kanter (Eds.), *Another voice: Feminist perspectives on social life and social science.* New York: Doubleday.

KARLINS, M., & ABELSON, H.I. (1970). *How opinions and attitudes are changed.* (2nd ed.) New York: Springer.

KASSIN, S.M., ELLSWORTH, P.C., & SMITH, V.L. (1989). The "general acceptance" of psychological research on eyewitness testimony. *American Psychologist, 44*, 1089-1098.

KATZEV, R., BLAKE, G., & MESSER, B. (1993). Determinants of participation in multi-family recycling programs. *Journal of Applied Psychology, 23*, 374-385.

KAUFMAN, J., & ZIGLER, E. (1987). Do abused children become abusive parents? *American Journal of Orthopsychiatry, 57*, 186-192.

KEATING, J.P., & LOFTUS, E.F. (1981, June). The logic of fire escape. *Psychology Today, 15(6)*, 14-18.

KELLEY, H.H. (1950). The warm-cold variable in first impressions of persons. *Journal of Personality, 18*, 431-439.

KELLEY, H.H. (1971). *Attribution and social interaction.* Morristown, NJ: General Learning.

KELLEY, H.H. (1972a). Attribution in social interaction. In E.E. Jones, D.E. Kanouse, H.H. Kelley, R.E. Nisbett, S. Valins & B. Weiner (Eds.), *Attribution: Perceiving the causes of behavior.* Morristown, NJ: General Learning Press.

KELLEY, H.H. (1972b). Causal schemata and the attribution process. In E.E. Jones, D.E. Kanouse, H.H. Kelley, R.E. Nisbett, S. Valins & B. Weiner (Eds.), *Attribution: Perceiving the causes of behavior.* Morristown, NJ: General Learning Press.

KELLEY, H.H., & STAHELSKI, A.J. (1970). The social interaction basis of cooperators' and competitors' beliefs about others. *Journal of Personality and Social Psychology, 16*, 66-91.

KELLY, J.A., & KALICHMAN, S.C. (1995). Increased attention to human sexuality can improve HIV-AIDS prevention efforts: Key research issues and directions. *Journal of Consulting and Clinical Psychology, 63*, 907-918.

KELLY, L.E., & CONLEY, J.J. (1987). Personality and compatibility: A prospective analysis of marital stability and marital satisfaction. *Journal of Personality and Social Psychology, 52*, 27-40.

KELMAN, H.C. (1965). Social-psychological approaches to the study of international relations: The question of relevance. In H.C. Kelman (Ed.), *International behavior: A social-psychological analysis.* New York: Holt, Rinehart and Winston.

KELMAN, H.C. (1967). Human use of human subjects: The problem of deception in social psychological experiments. *Psychological Bulletin, 67*, 1-11.

KENRICK, D.T., & GUTIERRES, S.E. (1980). Contrast effects and judgements of physical attractiveness: When beauty becomes a social problem. *Journal of Personality and Social Psychology, 38*, 131-140.

KERNIS, M.H., GRANNEMANN, B.D., & BARCLAY, L.C. (1989). Stability and level of self-esteem as predictors of anger arousal and hostility. *Journal of Personality and Social Psychology, 56*, 1013-1022.

KERWIN, J., & SHAFFER, D.R. (1991). The effects of jury dogmatism on reactions to jury nullification instructions. *Personality and Social Psychology Bulletin, 17*, 140-146.

KEYES, R. (1980). *The height of your life.* Boston: Little, Brown.

KIDD, R.F., & CHAYET, E.F. (1984). Why do victims fail to report? The psychology of criminal victimization. *Journal of Social Issues, 40*, 39-50.

KIESLER, C.A. (1968). Commitment. In R.P. Abelson, E. Aronson, W.J. McGuire, T.H. Newcomb, M.J. Rosenberg & P.H. Tannenbaum (Eds.), *Theories of cognitive consistency: A sourcebook.* Skokie, IL: Rand-McNally.

KILLIAM, L.M. (1952). The significance of multiple-group membership in a disaster. *American Journal of Sociology, 57*, 309-314.

KING, K.B., REIS, H.T., PORTER, L.A., & NORSEN, L.H. (1993). Social support and long-term recovery from coronary artery surgery: Effects on patients and spouses. *Health Psychology, 12*, 56-63.

KITCHENS, A. (1974). Shape-of-the-table negotiations at the Paris peace talks on Vietnam. In C.M. Loo (Ed.), *Crowding and behavior* (pp. 224-245). New York: MFS Information Company.

KLAJNER, F., SOBELL, L.C., & SOBELL, M.B. (1984). Prevention of drunk driving. In P.M. Miller & T.D. Nirenberg (Eds.), *Prevention of alcohol abuse* (pp. 441-468). New York: Plenum.

KLAPP, O.E. (1972). *Currents of unrest.* New York: Holt, Rinehart & Winston.

KLEINKE, C.L. (1986). Gaze and eye contact: A research review. *Psychological Bulletin, 100*, 78-100.

KLOHN, L.S., & ROGERS, R.W. (1991). Dimensions of the severity of a health threat: The persuasive effects of visibility, time of onset and rate of onset on young women's intentions to prevent osteoporosis. *Health Psychology, 10*, 323-329.

KLOSTERMAN, R., & FESHBACH, S. (1989). A measure of patriotic and nationalistic attitudes. *Political Psychology, 10*, 257-274.

KNOX, R.E., & INKSTER, J.A. (1968). Post-decision dissonance at post-time. *Journal of Personality and Social Psychology, 8*, 319-323.

KOBASA, S.C. (1979). Stressful life events, personality and health: An inquiry into hardiness. *Journal of Personality and Social Psychology, 37*, 1-11.

KOENIG, K. (1985). *Rumor in the marketplace.* Dover, MA: Auburn House.

KOGAN, N., & WALLACH, M.A. (1967). Risk taking as a function of the situation, the person, and the group. In G. Mandler, P. Mussen, N. Kogan & M.A. Wallach (Eds.), *New directions in psychology III.* New York: Holt, Rinehart and Winston.

KOGAN, N., & WALLACH, M.A. (1964). *Risk taking.* New York: Holt, Rinehart and Winston.

KOHLBERG, L. (1964). Development of moral character and moral ideology. In M. Hoffman & L. Hoffman (Eds.), *Review of child development research.* New York: Russell Sage Foundation.

KOMORITA, S.S., & BARTH, J.M. (1985). Components of reward in social dilemmas. *Journal of Personality and Social Psychology, 48*, 364-373.

KRAMER, R.M., & BREWER, M.B. (1984). Effects of group identity on resource use in a simulated commons dilemma. *Journal of Personality and Social Psychology, 46*, 1044-1057.

KRANTZ, D.S., & GLASS, D.C. (1984). Personality behavior patterns and physical illness: Conceptual and methodological issues. In W.D. Gentry (Ed.), *Handbook of behavioral medicine* (pp. 38-86). New York: Guilford Press.

KRASHEN, S. (1973). Lateralization, language learning, and the critical period: Some new evidence. *Language Learning, 23*, 63-74.

KRAUT, R.E. (1978). Verbal and non-verbal cues in the detection of lying. *Journal of Personality and Social Psychology, 36*, 380-391.

KRAVITZ, D.A., & MARTIN B. (1986). Ringelmann rediscovered: The original article. *Journal of Personality and Social Psychology, 50*, 936-941.

KREBS, D. (1970). Altruism...an examination of the concept and a review of the literature. *Psychological Bulletin, 73*, 258-302.

KREBS, D.L., & MILLER, D.T. (1985). Altruism and aggression. In G. Lindzey & E. Aronson (Eds.), *Handbook of social psychology* (3rd ed.) (Vol. 2, pp. 1-71). New York: Random House.

KRISTIANSEN, C.M. (1986). A two-value model of preventive health behavior. *Basic and Applied Social Psychology, 7*, 173-183.

KRISTIANSEN, C.M. AND MATHESON, K. (1990). Value conflict, value justification, and attitudes toward nuclear weapons. *Journal of Social Psychology, 130*, 665-675.

KROSNICK, J.A. (1989). Attitude importance and attitude accessibility. *Personality and Social Psychology Bulletin, 15*, 297-308.

KROSNICK, J.A., & ABELSON, R.P. (1992). The case for measuring attitude strength in surveys. In J.M. Tanur (Ed.), *Questions about questions: Inquiries into the cognitive bases of surveys.* New York: Russell Sage.

KROSNICK, J.A., & ALWIN, D.F. (1989). Aging and susceptibility to attitude change. *Journal of Personality and Social Psychology, 57*, 416-425.

KRUGLANSKI, A.W. (1987). Blame-placing schemata and attribution research. In C.F. Graumann & S. Moscovici (Eds.), *Changing conceptions of conspiracy* (pp. 191-202). New York: Springer-Verlag.

KULIK, J.A., & MAHLER, H.I.M. (1989). Stress and affiliation in a hospital setting: Preoperative roommate preferences. *Personality and Social Psychology Bulletin, 15*, 183-193.

KURDEK, L.A. (1993). Predicting marital dissolution: A five-year prospective longitudinal study of newlywed couples. *Journal of Personality and Social Psychology, 64*, 221-242.

LACROIX, J.M., & RIOUX, Y. (1978). La communication non-verbale chez les bilingues. *Canadian Journal of Behavioural Science, 10*, 130-140.

LAI, J., & LINDEN, W. (1993). The smile of Asia: Acculturation effects on symptoms reporting. *Canadian Journal of Behavioural Science, 25*, 303-313.

LALONDE, R.N., & GARDNER, R.C. (1984). Investigating a causal model of second language acquisition: Where does personality fit? *Canadian Journal of Behavioural Science, 16*, 224-237.

LAMBERT, W.E. (1978). Some cognitive and sociocultural aspects of being bilingual. In J.P. Alatis (Ed.), *International dimensions of bilingual education.* Washington, DC: Georgetown University Press.

LAMBERT, W.E., GARDNER, R.C., BARIK, H.C., & TUNSTALL, K. (1963). Attitudinal and cognitive aspects of intensive study of a second language. *Journal of Abnormal and Social Psychology, 66*, 358-368.

LAMBERT, W.E., & KLINEBERG, O. (1967). *Children's views of foreign people: A cross-national study.* New York: Appleton.

LAMBERT, W.E., MERMIGIS, L., & TAYLOR, D.M. (1986). Greek Canadians' attitudes toward own group and other Canadian ethnic groups: A test of the multiculturalism hypothesis. *Canadian Journal of Behavioural Science, 18*, 35-51.

LAMBERT, W.E., & TAYLOR, D. (1984). Language and the education of ethnic minority children in Canada. In R.J. Samuda, J.W. Berry & M. Laferriere (Eds.), *Multiculturalism in Canada.* Toronto: Allyn & Bacon.

LANG, K. & LANG, G.L. (1961). *Collective dynamics.* New York: Crowell.

LANGER, E.J. (1975). The illusion of control. *Journal of Personality and Social Psychology, 32*, 311-328.

LANGER, E.J., & RODIN, J. (1976). The effects of choice and enhanced personal responsibility for the aged: A field experiment in an institutional setting. *Journal of Personality and Social Psychology, 34*, 191-198.

LANGER, W.L. (1964). The Black Death. *Scientific American, 210*, 114-121.

LARSEN, K. (1974). Conformity in the Asch experiment. *Journal of Social Psychology, 94*, 303-304.

LARSEN, K.S. (1985). Attitudes toward nuclear disarmament and their correlates. *Journal of Social Psychology, 125*, 17-21.

LATANÉ, B., & DARLEY, J.M. (1969). Bystander "apathy." *American Scientist, 57*, 244-268.

LATANÉ, B., & DARLEY, J.M. (1970). *The unresponsive bystander: Why doesn't he help?* New York: Appleton-Century-Crofts.

LATANÉ, B., & NIDA, S. (1981). Ten years of research on group size and helping. *Psychological Bulletin, 89*, 308-324.

LATANÉ, B., & RODIN, J. (1969). A lady in distress: Inhibiting effects of friends and strangers on bystander intervention. *Journal of Experimental Social Psychology, 5*, 187-202.

LATANÉ, B., WILLIAMS, K., & HARKINS, S. (1979). Many hands make light the work: The causes and consequences of social loafing. *Journal of Personality and Social Psychology, 37*, 822-832.

LATANÉ, B., & WOLF, S. (1981). The social impact of majorities and minorities. *Psychology Review, 88*, 438-453.

LATEEF, O., & BANGASH, Z. (1977). *Visible minorities in mass media advertising.* Ottawa: Canadian Consultative Council on Multiculturalism.

LAU, R.R., & RUSSELL, D. (1980). Attribution in sports pages. *Journal of Personality and Social Psychology, 39*, 28-38.

LAVER, J. (1964, July 13). Laver's law. *Women's Wear Daily.* Cited by Horn (1975).

LAVERY, J.J., & FOLEY, P.J. (1963). Altruism or arousal in the rat? *Science, 140*, 172-173.

LAY, C., ALLEN, M., & KASSIRER, A. (1974). The responsive bystander in emergencies: Some preliminary data. *Canadian Psychologist, 15*, 220-227.

LAZARUS, R., & COHEN, J.B. (1977). Environmental stress. In I. Altman & J.F. Wohlwill (Eds.), *Human behavior and environment* (Vol. 1). New York: Plenum Press.

LEBON, G. (1895/1960). *The crowd: A study of the popular mind.* London: Ernest Benn.

LEE, Y.S., & WEBER, M.J. (1984). Development of an instrument to measure the aesthetic quality of housing environments. *Social Indicators Research, 15*, 255-279.

LENNEBERG, E.H. (1967). *Biological foundatioins of language.* New York: Wiley.

LERNER, M.J. (1977). The justice motive: Some hypotheses as to its origins and forms. *Journal of Personality, 45*, 1-52.

LESTER, D., & MURRELL, M.E. (1986). The influence of gun control on personal violence. *Journal of Community Psychology, 14*, 315-318.

LESTER, D. (1984). The murder of police officers in American cities. *Criminal Justice and Behavior, 11*, 101-113.

LEVENSON, R.W., & RUEF, A.M. (1992). *Journal of Personality and Social Psychology, 63*, 234-246.

LEVENTHAL, G.S., & LANE, D.W. (1970). Sex, age, and equity behavior. *Journal of Personality and Social Psychology, 15*, 312-316.

LEVINE, S., & SALTER, N.E. (1976). Youth and contemporary religious movements: Psychosocial findings. *Canadian Psychiatric Association Journal, 21*, 411-420.

LEVINE, J.M., & MORELAND, R.L. (1990). Progress in small group research. *Annual Review of Psychology, 41*, 585-634.

LEVINGER, G.A. (1979). A social psychological perspective on marital dissolution. In G.A. Levinger & O.C. Moles (Eds.), *Divorce and separation.* New York: Basic Books.

LEVINGER, G.A., & SNOEK, J.D. (1972). *Attraction in relationships: A new look at interpersonal attraction.* Morristown, NJ: General Learning.

LEVY, S.M., & HEIDEN, L.A. (1990). Personality and social factors in cancer outcome. In H.S. Friedman (Ed.), *Personality and disease* (pp. 254-279). New York: Wiley.

LEWIN, K. (1948). *Resolving social conflicts.* New York: Harper & Row.

LIEBERT, R.M., & SPRAFKIN, J. (1988). *The early window.* (3rd ed.). New York: Pergamon Press.

LINDER, D.E., COOPER, J., & JONES, E.E. (1967). Decision freedom as a determinant of the role of incentive magnitude in attitude change. *Journal of Personality and Social Psychology, 6*, 245-254.

LINDSAY, R.C., WELLS, G.L., & O'CONNOR, F.J. (1989). Mock-juror belief of accurate and inaccurate eyewitnesses: A replication. *Law and Human Behavior, 13*, 333-339.

LINDSKOLD, S., HAN, G., & BETZ, B. (1986). The essential elements of communication in the GRIT strategy. *Personality and Social Psychology Bulletin, 12*, 179-186.

LINDSKOLD, S., WALTERS, P.S., & KOUTSOURIS, H. (1983). Cooperators, competitors, and response to GRIT. *Journal of Conflict Resolution, 27*, 521-532.

LINVILLE, P.W. (1985). Self-complexity and affective extremity: Don't put all your eggs in one cognitive basket. *Social Cognition, 3*, 94-120.

LIPPMAN, W. (1922). *Public opinion.* New York: Harcourt, Brace & World.

LIPSET, S.M. (1989). Voluntary activities: More Canadian comparisons—a reply. *Canadian Journal of Sociology, 14*, 377-382.

LIPTON, J.A., & MARBACH, J.J. (1984). Ethnicity and the pain experience. *Social Science & Medicine, 19*, 1279-1288.

LITTLEPAGE, G.E., & PINEAULT, M.A. (1979). Detection of deceptive factual statements from the body and the face. *Personality and Social Psychology Bulletin, 5*, 325-328.

LOFTUS, E.F. (1974). Reconstructing memory: The incredible eyewitness. *Psychology Today, 8*, 116-119.

LOFTUS, E.F. (1979). *Eyewitness testimony.* Cambridge, MA: Harvard University Press.

LOFTUS, E.F. (1992). When a lie becomes memory's truth: Memory distortion after exposure to misinformation. *Current Directions in Psychological Science, 1*, 121-123.

LOFTUS, E. L., & BURNS, T. E. (1982). Mental shock can produce retrograde amnesia. *Memory and Cognition, 1*, 318-323.

LONDON, P. (1970). The rescuers: Motivational hypotheses about Christians who saved Jews from the Nazis. In J. Macaulay & L. Berkowitz (Eds.), *Altruism and helping behavior.* New York: Academic Press.

LORE, R.K., & SCHULTZ, L.A. (1993). Control of human aggression. *American Psychologist, 48*, 16-25.

LORENZ, K. (1966). *On aggression.* London: Methuen.

LOTT, A.J., & LOTT, B.E. (1961). Group cohesiveness, communication level, and conformity. *Journal of Abnormal and Social Psychology, 62*, 408-412.

LOTT, D.F., & SOMMER, R. (1967). Seating arrangements and status. *Journal of Personality and Social Psychology, 7*, 90-94.

LOWERY, C.R., DENNEY, D.R., & STORMS, M.D. (1979). Insomnia: A comparison of the effects of pill attribution and non-pejorative self-attributions. *Cognitive Therapy Research, 3*, 161-164.

LUBEK, I. (1979). A brief social psychological analysis of research on aggression in social psychology. In A.R. Buss (Ed.), *Psychology in social context* (pp. 259-306). New York: Irvington.

LUCE, T.S. (1974). The role of experience in inter-racial recognition. Paper presented at the annual meeting of the American Psychological Association, New Orleans.

LYKKEN, D. (1974). Psychology and the lie detector industry. *American Psychologist, 29*, 725-739.

LYNCH, J. (1977). *The broken heart: The medical consequences of loneliness.* New York: Basic Books.

MACCOBY, N. (1988). The community as a focus for health promotion. In S. Spacapan & S. Oskamp (Eds.), *The social psychology of health* (pp. 175-206). Beverly Hills, CA: Sage Publications.

MACDONALD, D. JR., & MAJUNDER, R.K. (1973). On the resolution and tolerance of cognitive inconsistency in another naturally occurring event: Attitudes and beliefs following the Senator Eagleton incident. *Journal of Applied Social Psychology, 3*, 132-143.

MACNAMARA, J. (1973). Nurseries, streets and classrooms. *Modern Language Journal, 57*, 250-254.

MACRAE, C.N., & SHEPHARD, J.W. (1989). Do criminal stereotypes mediate juridic judgements? *British Journal of Social Psychology, 28*, 189-191.

MADDEN, T.J., ELLEN, P.S., & AJZEN, I. (1992). A comparison of the theory of planned behavior and the theory of reasoned action. *Personality and Social Psychology Bulletin, 18*, 3-9.

MAIER, S., & LAUDENSLAGER, M. (1985). Stress and health: Exploring the links. *Psychology Today, 19,* 44-50.

MALAMUTH, N.M. (1984). Aggression against women: Cultural and individual causes. In N.M. Malamuth & E. Donnerstein (Eds.), *Pornography and sexual aggression.* Orlando, FL: Academic Press.

MALAMUTH, N.M. (1986). Predictors of naturalistic sexual aggression. *Journal of Personality and Social Psychology, 50,* 953-962.

MALAMUTH, N.M. (1988). Predicting laboratory aggression against female and male targets: Implications for sexual aggression. *Journal for Research in Personality, 22,* 474-495.

MALLOY, T.E., & JANOWSKI (1992). Perceptions and metaperceptions of leadership: components, accuracy and dispositional correlates. *Personality and Social Psychology Bulletin, 18,* 700-708.

MANN, R. (1959). A review of the relationship between personality and performance in small groups. *Psychological Bulletin, 56,* 241-270.

MANN, L., NEWTON, J.W., & INNES, J.M. (1982). A test between deindividuation and emergent norm theories of crowd aggression. *Journal of Personality and Social Psychology, 42,* 260-272.

MARKS, M.M., MUTRIE, N., BROOKS, D.R., & HARRIS, D.V. (1984). Causal attributions of winners and losers in individual competitive sports: Toward a reformulation of the self-serving bias. *Journal of Sport Psychology, 6,* 184-196.

MARKUS, R.M. (1975). Good Samaritan laws: An American lawyer's point of view. *La revue juridique themis, 10,* 28-32.

MARKUS, H. (1977). Self-schemata and processing information about the self. *Journal of Personality and Social Psychology, 35,* 63-78.

MARKUS, H., HAMILL, R., & SENTIS, K.P. (1987). Thinking fat: Self-schemas for body weight and the processing of weight relevant information. *Journal of Applied Social Psychology, 17,* 50-71.

MARKUS, H.R., & NURIUS, P. (1986) Possible selves. *American Psychologist, 41,* 954-969.

MARKUS, H.R., & SENTIS, K.P. (1982). The self in social information processing. In J. Suls (Ed.), *Psychological perspectives on the self* (Vol. 1, pp. 41-70). Hillsdale, NJ: Erlbaum.

MARKUS, H., & WURF, E. (1987). The dynamic self-concept: A social psychological perspective. *Annual Review of Psychology, 38,* 299-337.

MARLATT, G.A., & GORDON, J.R. (1979). Determinants of relapse: Implications for the maintenance of behavior change. In P. Davidson (Ed.), *Behavioral medicines: Changing health lifestyles.* New York: Brunner/Mazel.

MARQUIS, K.H., MARSHALL, J., & OSKAMP, S. (1972). Testimony validity as a function of question form, atmosphere and item difficulty. *Journal of Applied Social Psychology, 2,* 167-186.

MARTINDALE, D. (1971). Territorial dominance behavior in dyadic verbal interactions. *Proceedings of the 75th annual meeting of the American Psychological Association, 6,* 305-306.

MASTERS, R.E.L. (1966). *Eros and evil.* New York: Matrix.

MATTHEWS, K.A., GLASS, D.C., ROSENMAN, R.H., & BORTNER, R.W. (1977). Competitive drive, Pattern A and coronary heart disease: A further analysis of some data from the Western Collaborative Study. *Journal of Chronic Disease, 30,* 489-498.

MCCANN, C.D., & LALONDE, R.N. (1993). Dysfunctional communication and depression. *American Behavioral Scientist, 36,* 271-287.

MCCAULEY, C. (1989). The nature of social influence in groupthink: compliance and internalization. *Journal of Personality and Social Psychology, 57,* 250-260.

MCCLELLAND, D.C., ALEXANDER, C., & MARKS, E. (1982). The need for power, stress, immune function and illness among male prisoners. *Journal of Abnormal Psychology, 91,* 61-70.

MCCLINTOCK, C.G., & HUNT, R.G. (1975). Nonverbal indicators of affect and deception in an interview setting. *Journal of Applied Social Psychology, 5,* 54-67.

MCCLINTOCK, C.G., & NUTTIN, J.M., JR. (1969). Development of competitive game behavior in children across two cultures. *Journal of Experimental Social Psychology, 5,* 203-218.

MCCORMICK, P. (1994). *Canada's courts.* Toronto: Lorimer and Company.

MCGUIRE, W.J. (1968). Personality and susceptibility to social influence. In E.F. Borgatta & W.W. Lambert (Eds.), *Handbook of personality: Theory and research.* (pp. 1130-1187). Chicago: Rand-McNally.

MCGUIRE, W.J., & PAPAGEORGIS, D. (1961). The relative efficacy of various types of prior belief-defense in producing immunity against persuasion. *Journal of Abnormal & Social Psychology, 62,* 327-337.

MCGUIRE, W.J., & PAPAGEORGIS, D. (1962). Effectiveness of forewarning in developing resistance to persuasion. *Public Opinion Quarterly, 26,* 24-32.

MCKENZIE-MOHR, D., & ZANNA, M.P. (1990). Treating women as sexual objects: Look to the (gender schematic) male who has viewed pornography. *Personality and Social Psychology Bulletin, 16,* 296-308.

MCLAUGHLIN, B. (1977). Second-language learning in children. *Psychological Bulletin, 84,* 438-459.

MCLAUGHLIN, B. (1987). *Theories of second-language learning.* London: Arnold.

MCMURRAY, G.A. (1982). Psychology at Saskatchewan. In M.J. Wright & C.R. Myers (Eds.), *History of academic psychology in Canada* (pp. 178-191). Toronto: Hogrefe.

MCNEES, M.P., SCHNELLE, J.F., GENDRICH, J., THOMAS, M.M., & BEAGLE, G. (1979). McDonald's litter hunt. *Environment and Behavior, 11,* 131-138.

MEDALIA, N.Z., & LARSEN, D.N. (1958). Diffusion and belief in a collective dilemma: The Seattle windshield pitting epidemic. *American Sociological Review, 23,* 222-232.

MEGARGEE, E.I. (1966). Undercontrolled and overcontrolled personality types in extreme antisocial aggression. *Psychological Monographs, 80,* whole issue.

MEHRABIAN, A. (1971). Nonverbal betrayal of feeling. *Journal of Experimental Research in Personality, 5,* 64-73.

MERRENS, M.R. (1973). Nonemergency helping behavior in various sized communities. *Journal of Social Psychology, 90,* 327-328.

MEYER, A.J., NASH, J.D., MCALISTER, A.L., MACCOBY, N., & FARQUHAR, J.W. (1980). Skills training in a cardiovascular education campaign. *Journal of Consulting and Clinical Psychology, 35,* 331-342.

MEYER, J.P., & PEPPER, S. (1977). Need compatibility and marital adjustment in young married couples. *Journal of Personality and Social Psychology, 35,* 331-342.

MIDLARSKY, E., & BRYAN, J.H. (1972). Affect expressions and children's imitative altruism. *Journal of Experimental Research in Personality, 6,* 195-203.

MILGRAM, S. (1963). Behavioral study of obedience. *Journal of Applied Social Psychology, 67,* 371-378.

MILGRAM, S. (1964). Issues in the study of obedience: A reply to Baumrind. *American Psychologist, 19,* 848-852.

MILGRAM, S. (1965). Some conditions of obedience and disobedience to authority. *Human Relations, 18,* 57-76.

MILGRAM, S. (1970). The experience of living in cities. *Science, 167,* 1461-1468.

MILGRAM, S. (1974). *Obedience to authority.* New York: Harper & Row.

MILGRAM, S., & TOCH, H. (1969). Collective behavior: Crowds and social movements. In G. Lindzey & E. Aronson (Eds.), *The handbook of social psychology.* (2nd ed.) (Vol. 4, pp. 507-610.) Reading, MA: Addison-Wesley.

MILLER, A.G., & THOMAS, R. (1972). Cooperation and competition among Blackfoot Indian and rural Canadian children. *Child Development, 34,* 1104-1110.

MILLER, G.R., & BURGOON, J.K. (1982). Factors affecting assessments of witness credibility. In N. Kerr & R. Bray (Eds.), *The psychology of the courtroom.* New York: Academic Press.

MILLER, N., & CAMPBELL, D.T. (1959). Recency and primacy in persuasion as a function of the timing of speeches and measurement. *Journal of Abnormal and Social Psychology, 59,* 1-9.

MILLER, S.M., & MANGAN, C.E. (1983). Interacting effects of information and coping style in adapting to gynecologic stress. Should the doctor tell all? *Journal of Personality and Social Psychology, 45,* 223-236.

MILLS, J., & HARVEY, J. (1972). Opinion change as a function of when information about the communicator is received and whether he is attractive or expert. *Journal of Personality and Social Psychology, 21,* 52-55.

MINTZ, A. (1951). Non-adaptive group behavior. *Journal of Abnormal and Social Psychology, 46,* 150-159.

MITCHELL, H.E., & BYRNE, D. (1973). The defendant's dilemma: Effects of juror's attitudes and authoritarianism on judicial decisions. *Journal of Personality and Social Psychology, 25,* 123-129.

MOGHADDAM, F.M. (1990). Modulative and generative orientations in psychology: Implications for psychology in three worlds. *Journal of Social Issues, 46,* 21-41.

MOGHADDAM, F.M. (1987). Psychology in the three worlds: As reflected by the crisis in social psychology and the move toward indigenous third-world psychology. *American Psychologist, 42,* 912-920.

MOGY, R.B., & PRUITT, D.G. (1974). Effects of threatener's enforcement costs on threat credibility and compliance. *Journal of Personality and Social Psychology, 29,* 173-180.

MONAGHAN, E.D. (1975). Emergency services and Good Samaritans. *La revue juridique themis, 10,* 20-23.

MONSON, T.C., & HESLEY, J.W. (1982). Causal attributions for behaviors consistent or inconsistent with an actor's personality traits: Differences between those offered by actors and observers. *Journal of Personality and Social Psychology, 18,* 416-432.

MOORE, T.E., & CADEAU, L. (1985). The representation of women, the elderly and minorities in Canadian television commercials. *Canadian Journal of Behavioural Science, 17,* 215-225.

MOORE, T.E., PEPLER, D., MAE, R., & KATES, M. (1989). Child witnesses to family violence: New directions for research and intervention. In B. Pressman, G. Cameron & M. Rothery (Eds.), *Intervening with assaulted women: Current theory, research, and practice.* Hillsdale, N.J.: Lawrence Erlbaum Assoc.

MOOS, R.H. (1982). Coping with acute health crises. In T. Millon, C. Green & R. Meagher (Eds.), *Handbook of clinical health psychology.* New York: Plenum.

MORAY, N. (1959). Attention in dichotic listening: Affective cues and the influence of instructions. *Quarterly Journal of Experimental Psychology, 11,* 56-60.

MORELAND, R.L., & ZAJONC, R.B. (1982). Exposure effects in person perception: Familiarity, similarity and attraction. *Journal of Experimental Social Psychology, 18,* 395-415.

MORIN, S.F. (1988). AIDS: The challenge to psychology. *American Psychologist, 43,* 838-842.

MORLAND, K. (1969). Race awareness among American and Hong Kong Chinese children. *American Journal of Sociology, 75,* 360-374.

MORRIS, W.N., & MILLER, R.S. (1975). The effects of consensus-breaking and consensus preempting partners on reduction of conformity. *Journal of Experimental Social Psychology, 11,* 215-223.

MOSCOVICI, S., & LECUYER, R. (1972). Studies in group decision I: Social space, patterns of communication and group consensus. *European Journal of Social Psychology, 2,* 221-244.

MOSCOVICI, S., MUGNY, G., & VAN AVERMAET, E. (Eds.) (1985). *Perspectives on minority influence.* Cambridge: Cambridge University Press.

MULLEN, B., SALAS, E., & DRISKELL, J.E. (1989). Salience, motivation, and artifact as contributions to the relation between participation rate and leadership. *Journal of Experimental Social Psychology, 25,* 545-559.

MURDOCK, P.E. (1989). Defining group cohesiveness: A legacy of confusion. *Small Group Behavior, 20,* 37-49.

MURSTEIN, B.I. (1972). Physical attractiveness and marital choice. *Journal of Personality and Social Psychology, 22,* 8-12.

MYERS, C.R. (1965). Notes on the history of psychology in Canada. *Canadian Psychologist, 6,* 4-19.

NADLER, A., & FISHER, J.D. (1984). Effects of donor-recipient relationship on recipient's reactions to aid. In E. Staub, D. Bar-Tal, J. Karylowski & J. Reykowski (Eds.), *Development and maintenance of prosocial behavior* (pp. 397-418). New York: Plenum Press.

NELSON, T.M. (1982). Psychology at Alberta. In M.J. Wright & C.R. Myers (Eds.), *History of academic psychology in Canada* (pp. 192-219). Toronto: Hogrefe.

NEMETH, C. (1970). Bargaining and reciprocity. *Psychological Bulletin, 74,* 297-308.

NEMETH, C. (1981). Jury trials: Psychology and law. *Advances in experimental social psychology, 14,* 309-367.

NEWCOMB, M.D., & BENTLER, E.M. (1980). Cohabitation before marriage: A comparison of married couples who did and did not cohabit. *Alternative Life Styles, 3,* 65-85.

NEWCOMB, M.D., HUBA, G.J., & BENTLER, E.M. (1986). Determinants of sexual and dating behavior among adolescents. *Journal of Personality and Social Psychology, 50,* 428-438.

NEWCOMB, T.M. (1961). *The acquaintance process*. New York: Holt, Rinehart & Winston.

NEWCOMB, T.M., KOENIG, L.E., FLACKS, R., & WARWICK, D.P. (1967). *Persistence and change: Bennington College and its students after twenty-five years*. New York: Wiley.

NIELSON, W.R., & NEUFELD, R.W.J. (1986). Utility of the uncontrollability construct in relation to the Type A behaviour pattern: A multidimensional investigation. *Canadian Journal of Behavioural Science, 18*, 224-237.

NISBETT, R.E., CAPUTO, C., LEGANT, P., & MARECEK, J. (1973). Behavior as seen by the actor and as seen by the observer. *Journal of Personality and Social Psychology, 27*, 154-164.

NORMAN, R.N.G. (1985). *The nature and correlates of health behaviour*. Ottawa: Health Promotion Directorate.

NORMAN, R. (1976). When what is said is important: A comparison of expert and attractive sources. *Journal of Experimental Social Psychology, 12*, 294-300.

OLINER, S.P., & OLINER, P.M. (1988). *The altruistic personality: Rescuers of Jews in Nazi Europe*. San Francisco: Free Press.

OLSEN, M.E. (1981). Consumers' attitudes toward energy conservation. *Journal of Social Issues, 37*, 108-131.

OLSON, J.M., & ZANNA, M.P. (1993). Attitude and attitude change. *Annual Review of Psychology, 44*, 117-154.

ONTARIO ROYAL COMMISSION ON VIOLENCE IN THE COMMUNICATIONS INDUSTRY (1977). *Report* (Vols. 1-7). Toronto: Government of Ontario.

ORFORD, J. (1985). *Excessive appetites: A psychological view of addictions*. Toronto: Wiley.

OSGOOD, C.E. (1962). *An alternative to war or surrender*. Urbana: University of Illinois Press.

OSHEROW, N. (1981). Making sense of the nonsensical: An analysis of Jonestown. In E. Aronson (Ed.), *Readings about the social animal* (3rd ed.). San Francisco: W.H. Freeman.

PAGÈS, R. (1986). Personal communication.

PAGE, F.H., & CLARK, J.W. (1982). Psychology at Dalhousie. In M.J. Wright & C.R. Myers (Eds.), *History of academic psychology in Canada* (pp. 20-32). Toronto: Hogrefe.

PALYS, T.S. (1986). Testing the common wisdom: The social content of video pornography. *Canadian Psychology, 27*, 22-35.

PARKE, R.D., BERKOWITZ, L., LEYENS, J.P., WEST, S.G., & SEBASTIAN, R.J. (1977). Some effects of violent and non-violent movies on the behavior of juvenile delinquents. In L. Berkowitz (Ed.), *Advances in experimental social psychology* (Vol. 10, pp. 135-172). New York: Academic Press.

PATTERSON, G.R. (1982). *Coercive family processes*. Eugene, OR: Castilia Press.

PATTERSON, M.L. (1982). A sequential functional model of nonverbal exchange. *Psychological Review, 89*, 231-249.

PAULUS, P.B. (Ed.) (1989). *Psychology of group influence* (2nd ed). Hillsdale NJ: Erlbaum.

PEACOCK, E.E. JR. (1972, September 1). Quoted in *Medical World News*, pp. 45.

PEDERSEN, P., & THOMAS, C.D. (1992). Prevalence and correlates of dating violence in a Canadian university sample. *Canadian Journal of Behavioural Science, 24*, 490-501.

PENDLETON, M.G., & BATSON, C.D. (1979). Self-presentation and the door-in-the-face technique for inducing compliance. *Journal of Personality and Social Psychology, 5*, 77-81.

PENFIELD, W., & ROBERTS, L. (1959). *Speech and brain mechanisms*. Princeton, NJ: Princeton University Press.

PENNEBAKER, J.W., DYER, M.A., CAULKINS, R.S., LITOWITZ, D.L., ACKERMAN, P.L., ANDERSON, D.B., & MCGRAW, K.M. (1979). Don't the girls get prettier at closing time: A country and western application to psychology. *Personality and Social Psychology Bulletin, 5*, 122-125.

PENNINGTON, N., & HASTIE, R. (1990). Practical implications of psychological research on jurors and jury decision-making. *Personality and Social Psychology Bulletin, 16*, 90-105.

PENNINGTON, N., & HASTIE, R. (1992). Explaining the evidence tests of the story model for juror decision making. *Journal of Personality and Social Psychology, 62*, 189-206.

PEPLAU, L.A., RUSSELL, D., & HEIM, M. (1979). The experience of loneliness. In I.H. Frieze, D. Bar-Tal & J.S. Carroll (Eds.), *New approaches to social problems: Applications of attribution theory*. San Francisco: Jossey-Bass.

PEPLAU, L.A., & GORDON, S.L. (1985). Women and men in love: Gender differences in close heterosexual relationships. In V.E. O'Leary, R.K. Unger & B.S. Wallston (Eds.), *Women, gender, and social psychology*. Hillsdale, NJ: Erlbaum.

PEPLAU, L.A., & PERLMAN, D. (1982). Perspectives on loneliness. In L.A. Peplau & D. Perlman (Eds.), *Loneliness: A sourcebook of current theory, research and therapy*. New York: Wiley.

PERLMAN, D., & PEPLAU, L.A. (1981). Toward a social psychology of loneliness. In S. Duck & R. Gilmour (Eds.), *Personal relationships 3: Personal relationships in disorder*. London: Academic Press.

PERRIN, S., & SPENCER, C. (1981). Independence or conformity in the Asch experiment as a reflection of cultural and situational factors. *British Journal of Social Psychology, 20*, 205-209.

PETERS, L.H., HARTKE, D.D., & POHLMAN, J.T. (1985). Fiedler's contingency theory of leadership: An application of the meta-analytic procedure of Schmidt and Hunter. *Psychological Bulletin, 97*, 274-285.

PETTIGREW, T.F. (1961). Social psychology and desegregation research. *American Psychologist, 16*, 105-112.

PETTY, R.E., & CACIOPPO, J.T. (1977). Forewarning, cognitive responding, and resistance to persuasion. *Journal of Personality and Social Psychology, 35*, 645-655.

PETTY, R.E., & CACIOPPO, J.T. (1979). Issue involvement can increase or decrease persuasion by enhancing message-relevant cognitive responses. *Journal of Personality and Social Psychology, 37*, 1915-1926.

PETTY, R.E., & CACIOPPO, J.T. (1981). *Attitude and persuasion: Classic and contemporary approaches*. Dubuque, IO: W.C. Brown.

PETTY, R.E., & CACIOPPO, J.T. (1986). The elaboration likelihood model of persuasion. In L. Berkowitz (Ed.), *Advances in experimental social psychology* (Vol. 19, pp. 123-205). New York: Academic Press.

PETTY, R.E., CACIOPPO, J.T. & GOLDMAN, R. (1981). Personal involvement as a determinant of argument-based persuasion. *Journal of Personality and Social Psychology, 41*, 847-855.

PFEIFER, J.E. (1989). Courtroom prejudice: An application of symbolic sexism. *Contemporary Social Psychology, 13*, 1-8.

PFEIFER, J.E. (1992). The psychological framing of cults: Schematic representations and cult evaluations. *Journal of Applied Social Psychology, 22*, 531-544.

PFEIFER, J.E., & BERNSTEIN, D. (1993). Mock juror decision making and modern racism: Examining the role of task and target specificity on judgmental evaluations. Unpublished manuscript.

PFEIFER, J.E., & OGLOFF, J.R.P. (1988). Prejudicial sentencing trends of simulated jurors in Canada. Presented at the 49th annual meeting of the Canadian Psychological Association, Montreal.

PFEIFER, J.E., & OGLOFF, J.R.P. (1989). Ambiguity and guilt determination: A modern racism interpretation. Presented at the 50th annual meeting of the Canadian Psychological Association, Halifax.

PFUNGST, A. (1911). *Clever Hans (the horse of Mr. von Osten): A contribution to experimental, animal and human psychology* (translated by C. Rahn). New York: Holt.

PIAGET, J. (1932). *The moral development of the child.* London: Routledge & Kagan Paul.

PILIAVIN, I.M., RODIN, J., & PILIAVIN, J.A. (1969). Good Samaritanism: An underground phenomenon? *Journal of Personality and Social Psychology, 13,* 289-299.

PILISUK. M., & MINKLER, M. (1985). Supportive ties: A political economy perspective. *Health Education Quarterly, 12,* 93-106.

PINES, A., & ARONSON, E. (1983). Antecedents, correlates and consequences of romantic jealousy. *Journal of Personality, 51,* 108-136.

PLINER, P., HART, H., KOHL, J., & SAARI, D. (1974). Compliance without pressure: Some further data on the foot-in-the-door technique. *Journal of Experimental Social Psychology, 10,* 17-22.

POLLARD, W.E., & MITCHELL, T.R. (1972). Decision theory analysis of social power. *Psychological Bulletin, 78,* 433-446.

POLSTER, M.F. (1992). *Eve's daughters: The forbidden heroism of women.* New York: Jossey-Bass.

POPHAM, R.E., SCHMIDT, W., & DELINT, J. (1976). The effects of legal restraint on drinking. In B. Kissin & H. Begleiter (Eds.), *The biology of alcoholism* (Vol. 4, pp. 234-278). New York: Plenum.

PORIER, G.W., & LOTT, A.J. (1967). Galvanic skin responses and prejudice. *Journal of Personality and Social Psychology, 5,* 253-259.

PRINCZ, M. (1992). Dating violence: Not an isolated phenomenon. *Vis-à-vis, 9,* 1,4.

PRUITT, D.G. (1976). Power and bargaining. In B. Seidenberg & A. Snadowsky (Eds.), *Social psychology: An introduction* (pp. 343-376). New York: Free Press.

PRUITT, D.G. (1981). *Negotiating behavior.* New York: Academic Press.

PRUITT, D.G., & RUBIN, J.Z. (1986). *Social conflict: Escalation, stalemate, and settlement.* New York: Random House.

PRYOR, J.B., REEDER, G.D., & VINACCO, R. (1989). The instrumental and symbolic functions of attitudes towards persons with AIDS. *Journal of Applied Social Psychology, 19,* 377-404.

QUANTY, M.B. (1976). Aggression catharsis: Experimental investigations and implications. In R.C. Geen & E.C. O'Neal (Eds.), *Perspectives on aggression.* New York: Academic Press.

QUARANTELLI, E. (1954). The behavior of panic participants. *Sociology and Social Research, 41,* 187-194.

QUARANTELLI, E.L. (1960). Images of withdrawal behavior in disasters: Some basic misconceptions. *Social Problems, 8,* 1968-1978.

RADKE-YARROW, M., & ZAHN-WAXLER, C. (1984). Roots, motives, and patterns in children's prosocial behavior. In E. Staub, D. Bar-Tal, J. Karylowski & J. Reykowski (Eds.), *Development and maintenance of prosocial behavior* (pp. 81-99). New York: Plenum Press.

RAGLAND, D.R., & BRAND, R.J. (1988). Type A behavior and mortality from coronary heart disease. *New England Journal of Medicine, 318,* 65-69.

RANK, S.G., & JACOBSON, C.K. (1977). Hospital nurses' compliance with medication overdose orders: A failure to replicate. *Journal of Health and Social Behavior, 18,* 1888-1993.

RAPOPORT, A. (1963). Mathematical models of social interaction. In R.D. Luce, R.R. Bush & E. Galanter (Eds.), *Handbook of mathematical psychology* (pp. 493-579). New York: Wiley.

RAPOPORT, A. (1968). Prospects for experimental games. *Journal of Conflict Resolution, 12,* 461-470.

RAPOPORT, A. (1989). *The origins of violence: approaches to the study of conflict.* New York: Paragon House.

RAVEN, B.H., & KRUGLANSKI, A.W. (1970). Conflict and power. In P.G. Swingle (Ed.), *The structure of conflict* (pp. 69-110). New York: Academic Press.

RAYKO, D.S. (1977). Does knowledge matter? Psychological information and bystander helping. *Canadian Journal of Behavioural Science, 9,* 295-304.

REDFIELD, R. (1955). *The little community.* Chicago: University of Chicago Press.

REGAN, D.T., WILLIAMS, M., & SPARLING, S. (1972). Voluntary expiation of guilt: A field experiment. *Journal of Personality and Social Psychology, 24,* 42-45.

REGAN, D.T., & TOTTEN, J. (1975). Empathy and attribution: Turning observers into actors. *Journal of Personality and Social Psychology, 32,* 850-856.

REICH, C., & PURBHOO, M. (1975). The effect of cross-cultural contact. *Canadian Journal of Behavioural Science, 7,* 313-327.

REINISCH, J.M., & SANDERS, S.A. (1986). A test of sex differences in aggressive response to hypothetical conflict situations. *Journal of Personality and Social Psychology, 50,* 1045-1049.

REISENZEIN, R. (1986). A structural equation analysis of Weiner's attribution-affect model of helping behavior. *Journal of Personality and Social Psychology, 50,* 1123-1133.

RHODES, N., & WOOD, N. (1992). Self-esteem and intelligence affect influencibility: the mediating role of message reception. *Psychological Bulletin, 111,* 156-171.

RICE, G.E., & GAINER, P. (1962). "Altruism" in the albino rat. *Journal of Comparative and Physiological Psychology, 55,* 123-125.

RIMÉ, B. (1983). Nonverbal communication or nonverbal behavior? In W. Doise & S. Moscovici (Eds.), *Current issues in European social psychology, Vol. 1* (pp. 85-141). Cambridge: Cambridge University Press.

RINGELMANN, M. (1913). Recherches sur les moteurs animés: Travail de l'homme. *Annales de l'Institut National Agronomique,* 2e Série-tome *XII,* 1-40.

ROACH, M.E., & EICHER, J.B. (1965). *Dress, adornment, and the social order.* New York: Wiley.

ROBINSON, S.N., & FRISCH, M.H. (1975). *Social and environmental influences on littering behavior.* New York: Pergamon.

RODIN, J., & JANIS, I.L. (1979). The social power of health care practitioners as agents of change. *Journal of Social Issues, 35,* 60-81.

RODIN, J., & LANGER, E.J. (1977). Long-term effects of a control-relevant intervention with the institutionalized aged. *Journal of Personality and Social Psychology, 35,* 897-902.

ROGERS, T.B., KUIPER, N.A., & KIRKER, W.S. (1977). Self-reference and the encoding of personal information. *Journal of Personality and Social Psychology, 35,* 677-688.

ROLLINS, B. (1976). *First you cry.* Philadelphia: Lippincott.

ROSEN, S., TOMARELLI, M.M., KIDDA, M.L. JR., & MEDVIN, N. (1986). Effects of motive for helping recipient's inability to recipro-cate, and sex on devaluation of the recipient's competence. *Journal of Personality and Social Psychology, 50,* 729-736.

ROSENBAUM, L.L., & ROSENBAUM, W.B. (1971). Morale and pro-ductivity consequences of group leadership style, stress and type of task. *Journal of Applied Psychology, 55,* 343-348.

ROSENHAN, D. (1970). The natural socialization of altruistic autonomy. In J. Macaulay & L. Berkowitz (Eds.), *Altruism and helping behavior.* New York: Academic Press.

ROSENHAN, D. (1972). Learning theory and prosocial behavior. *Journal of Social Issues, 28,* 151-164.

ROSENHAN, D.L., MOORE, B.S., & UNDERWOOD, B. (1976). The so-cial psychology of moral behavior. In T. Likona (Ed.), *Moral development and behavior.* New York: Holt, Rinehart and Winston.

ROSENMAN, R.H., BRAND, R.J., JENKINS, C.D., FRIEDMAN, M., STRAUS, R., & WURM, M. (1975). Coronary heart disease in the Western Collaborative Group Study: Final follow-up expe-rience of 8 years. *Journal of the American Medical Association, 233,* 872-877.

ROSKOS-EWOLDSEN, D.R., & FAZIO, R.H. (1992a). On the orienting value of attitudes: Attitude accessibility as a determinant of an object's attraction of visual attention. *Journal of Personality and Social Psychology, 63,* 198-211.

ROSKOS-EWOLDSEN, D.R., & FAZIO, R.H. (1992b). The accessibility of source likeability as a determinant of persuasion. *Personality and Social Psychology Bulletin, 18,* 19-25.

ROSNOW, R.L. (1991). Inside rumor. *American Psychologist, 46,* 484-496.

ROSNOW, R.L. & FINE, G.A. (1976). *Rumor and gossip: The social psychology of hearsay.* New York: Elsevier.

ROSNOW, R.L. (1980). Psychology of rumor reconsidered. *Psychological Bulletin, 87,* 578-591.

ROSNOW, R.L., YOST, J.H., & ESPOSITO, J.L. (1986). Belief in rumor and likelihood of rumor transmission. *Language and Communication, 6,* 189-194.

ROSS, A.S. (1978). *It's shorter in a crowd.* (Film by W. Troyer). Toronto: TAAW Productions.

ROSS, L., GREENE, D., & HOUSE, P. (1977). The "false consensus effect": An egocentric bias in social perception and attribu-tion processes. *Journal of Experimental Social Psychology, 13,* 279-301.

ROSS, M., & CONWAY, M. (1986). Remembering one's own past: The construction of personal histories. In R. Sorrentino & E.T. Higgins (Eds.), *Handbook of motivation and cognition* (pp. 122-144). New York: Guilford.

ROTER, D.L., LIPKIN, M. JR., & KORSGAARD, A. (1991). Gender differences in patients' and physicians' communication during primary care medical visits. *Medical Care, 29,* 1083-1093.

ROTHBART, M., FULERO, S., JENSEN, C., HOWARD, J., & BIRRELL, B. (1978). From individual to group impressions: Availability heuristics in stereotype formation. *Journal of Experimental Social Psychology, 14,* 237-255.

ROTHBART, M., & JOHN, O.P. (1985). Social categorization and behavioral episodes: A cognitive analysis of intergroup contact. *Journal of Social Issues, 41,* 81-104.

ROTTER, J.B. (1966). Generalized expectancies for internal versus external control of reinforcement. *Psychological Monographs, 80,* (1, Whole No., 609).

ROTTON, J., & FREY, J. (1985). Air pollution, weather and violent crimes: Concomitant time-series analysis of archival data. *Journal of Personality and Social Psychology, 49,* 1207-1220.

ROTTON, J., FREY, J., BARRY, T., MILLIGAN, M., & FITZPATRICK, M. (1979). The air pollution experience and physical aggres-sion. *Journal of Applied Social Psychology, 9,* 397-412.

RUBACK, R.B., & DABBS, J.M. (1988). Group vocal patterns and leadership in India: Effects of task, language, and sex of subjects. *Journal of Cross-Cultural Psychology, 19,* 446-464.

RUBIN, J.Z. (1989). Some wise and mistaken assumptions about conflict and negotiation. *Journal of Social Sciences, 45,* 195-209.

RUBIN, Z. (1976). Naturalistic studies of self-disclosure. *Personality and Social Psychology Bulletin, 2,* 260-263.

RULE, B.G., & ADAIR, J. (1984). Contributions of psychology as a social science to Canadian society. *Canadian Psychology, 25,* 52-58.

RULE, B.G., BISANZ, G.L., & KOHN, M. (1985). Anatomy of a per-suasion schema: Targets, goals and strategies. *Journal of Personality and Social Psychology, 48,* 1127-1140.

RULE, B.G., & FERGUSON, T.J. (1986). The effects of media vio-lence on attitudes, emotions and cognitions. *Journal of Social Issues, 2,* 29-50.

RULE, B.G., & NESDALE, A.R. (1974). Differing functions of aggression. *Journal of Personality, 42,* 467-481.

RULE, B.G., & WELLS, G.L. (1981). Experimental social psychology in Canada: A look at the seventies. *Canadian Psychology, 22,* 69-84.

RUSBULT, C.E. (1983). A longitudinal test of the investment model: the development (and deterioration) of satisfaction and commitment in heterosexual involvement. *Journal of Personality and Social Psychology, 45,* 101-117.

RUSH, M.C. & RUSSELL, J.E.A. (1988). Leader prototypes and pro-totype-contingent consensus in leader behavior descrip-tions. *Journal of Experimental Social Psychology, 24,* 88-104.

RUSHTON, J.P. (1975). Generosity in children: Immediate and long-term effects of modeling, preaching, and moral judgement. *Journal of Personality and Social Psychology, 31,* 459-466.

RUSHTON, J.P. (1976). Socialization and the altruistic behavior of children. *Psychological Bulletin, 83,* 898-913.

RUSHTON, J.P. (1978). Urban density: Helping strangers in a Canadian city, suburb, and small town. *Psychological Reports, 43,* 987-990.

RUSHTON, J.P. (1980). *Altruism, socialization, and society.* Englewood Cliffs, NJ: Prentice-Hall.

RUSHTON, J.P. (1989). Evolutionary biology and heritable traits (with reference to Oriental-White-Black differences). Paper presented at the Annual Meeting of the American Association for the Advancement of Science, San Francisco. January 19, 1989.

RUSSEL, J.A, & MEHRABIAN, A. (1978). Approach-avoidance and affiliation as functions of the emotion-eliciting quality of an environment. *Environment and Behavior, 10,* 355-388.

RUSSELL, B. (1959). *Common sense and nuclear warfare.* London: Unwin Brothers.

RUSSELL, B. (1962). *Power.* New York: Barnes & Noble.

RUTTER, M. (1987). Psychological resilience and protective mechanisms. *American Journal of Orthopsychiatry, 57,* 316-331.

SACKS, H., SCHEGLOFF, E.A., & JEFFERSON, G. (1974). A simplest systematics for the organization of turn-taking for conversation. *Language, 50,* 696-735.

SACKS, O. (1986). *The man who mistook his wife for a hat.* New York: Simon and Schuster.

SADAVA, S.W. (1978a). From the outside looking in: The experience of the instructor and student of social psychology in Canada. Paper presented at the Annual Conference of the Canadian Psychological Association.

SADAVA, S.W. (1978b). Teaching social psychology: A Canadian dilemma. *Canadian Psychological Review, 19,* 145-151.

SADAVA, S.W. (1985). Problem behavior theory and consumption and consequences of alcohol use. *Journal of Studies on Alcohol, 46,* 392-397.

SADAVA, S.W. (1987). Interactional theories. In H.T. Blane & K.E. Leonard (Eds.), *Psychological theories of drinking and alcoholism* (pp. 90-130). New York: Guilford.

SADAVA, S.W., ANGUS, L., & FORSYTH, R. (1980). Perceived mental illness and diminished responsibility: A study of attributions. *Social Behavior and Personality, 8,* 129-136.

SADAVA, S.W., & FORSYTH, R. (1977a). Person-environment interaction and college student drug use: A multivariate longitudinal study. *Genetic Psychology Monographs, 96,* 211-245.

SADAVA, S.W., & FORSYTH, R. (1977b). Turning on, turning off and relapse: Social psychological determinants of status change in cannabis use. *International Journal of the Addictions, 12,* 509-528.

SADAVA, S.W., & MATEJCIC, C. (1987). Generalized and specific loneliness in early marriage. *Canadian Journal of Behavioural Science, 19,* 56-66.

SADAVA, S.W., & THOMPSON, M.M. (1986). Loneliness, social drinking and vulnerability to alcohol problems. *Canadian Journal of Behavioural Science, 18,* 133-139.

SALOVEY, P., & RODIN, J. (1984). Some antecedents and consequences of social comparison jealousy. *Journal of Personality and Social Psychology, 47,* 780-792.

SAMUELSON, C.D., & MESSICK, D.M. (1986). Inequities in access to and use of shared resources in social dilemmas. *Journal of Personality and Social Psychology, 51,* 960-967.

SANDE, G.N., GOETHELS, G.R., FERRARI, L., & WORTH, L.T. (1989). Value-guided attributions: Maintaining the moral self-image and the diabolical enemy-image. *Journal of Social Issues, 45,* 91-118.

SANDERS, G.S. (1983). An attentional process model of social facilitation. In A. Hare, H. Blumberg, V. Kent, & M. Davies (Eds.), *Small groups.* London: Wiley.

SANDERS, G.S., & BARON, R.S. (1977). Is social comparison irrelevant for producing choice shifts? *Journal of Experimental Social Psychology, 13,* 303-314.

SANDERS, G.S., BARON, R.S., & MOORE, D.L. (1978). Distraction and social comparison as mediators of social facilitation effects. *Journal of Experimental Social Psychology, 14,* 291-303.

SARAT, A., & VIDMAR, N. (1976). Public opinion, the death penalty and the eighth amendment. Testing the Marshall hypothesis. *Wisconsin Law Review, 27,* 171-206.

SARLES, R.M. (1976). Child abuse. In D.S. Madden & J.R. Lion (Eds.), *Rage, hate, assault and other forms of violence* (pp. 1-16). New York: Spectrum.

SAUL, E.V., & KASS, T.S. (1969). Study of anticipated anxiety in a medical school setting. *Journal of Medical Education, 44,* 526.

SCHACHTER, S. (1951). Deviation, rejection and communication. *Journal of Abnormal Social Psychology, 46,* 190-207.

SCHACHTER, S. (1959). *The psychology of affiliation.* Stanford, CA: Stanford University Press.

SCHACHTER, S., ELLERTSON, N., MCBRIDE, D., & GREGORY, D. (1951). An experimental study of cohesiveness and productivity. *Human Relations, 4,* 229-238.

SCHALLER, M., & CIALDINI, R.B. (1988). The economics of empathic helping: Support for a mood management motive. *Journal of Experimental Social Psychology, 24,* 163-181.

SCHEGLOFF, E.A. (1972). Sequencing in conversational openings. In J.J. Gumperz & D. Hymes (Eds.), *Directions in sociolinguistics* (pp. 346-380). NY: Holt.

SCHELLING, T.C. (1960). *The strategy of conflict.* Cambridge: Harvard University Press.

SCHLEGEL, R.F., MANSKE, S.R., & D'AVERNAS, J.R. (1985). Alcohol and drug use in young adults: Selected findings in a longitudinal study. *Bulletin of the Society of Psychologists in Addictive Behavior, 4,* 213-225.

SCHMIDT, D.E., & KEATING, J.P. (1979). Human crowding and personal control. *Psychological Bulletin, 86,* 680-700.

SCHMITT, B.H., GILOVICH, T., GOORE, N., & JOSEPH, L. (1986). Mere presence and socio-facilitation: One more time. *Journal of Experimental Social Psychology, 22,* 242-248.

SCHOPLER, J., & BATESON, N. (1965). The power of dependence. *Journal of Personality and Social Psychology, 2,* 247-254.

SCHULLER, R.A. (1992). The impact of battered woman syndrome evidence on jury decision processes. *Law and Human Behavior, 16,* 597-620.

SCHULLER, R.A., & VIDMAR, N. (1992). Battered woman syndrome evidence in the courtroom. A review of the literature. *Law and Human Behavior, 16,* 273-291.

SCHULTZ, D.P. (1964). *Panic behavior.* New York: Random House.

SCHWARTZ, B., & BARSKY, S. (1977). The home advantage. *Social Forces, 55,* 641-661.

SCRIVNER, E., & SAFER, M.A. (1988). Eyewitnesses show hyperamnesia for details about a violent event. *Journal of Personality and Social Psychology, 73,* 371-377.

SEARLE, J.R. (1969). *Speech acts.* Cambridge: Cambridge University Press.

SEARLE, J.R. (1975). Indirect speech acts. In P. Cole & J.L. Morgan (Eds.), *Syntax and semantics 3: Speech acts* (pp. 283-298). Hillsdale, NJ: Erlbaum.

SEEMAN, M., SEEMAN, T., & SAYLES, M. (1985). Social networks and health status: A longitudinal analysis. *Social Psychology Quarterly, 48,* 237-248.

SELIGMAN, C., & DARLEY, J.M. (1977). Feedback as a means of reducing residential energy consumption. *Journal of Applied Psychology, 62,* 363-368.

SELIGMAN, C., DARLEY, J.M., & BECKER, L.J. (1978). Behavioral approaches to residential energy conservation. *Energy and Buildings, 1*, 325-337.

SELIGMAN, C.R., TUCKER, G.R., & LAMBERT, W.E. (1972). The effects of speech style and other attributes on teachers' attitudes towards pupils. *Language in Society, 1*, 131-142.

SHAVER, K.G. (1970). Defensive attribution: Effects of severity and relevance on the responsibility assigned for an accident. *Journal of Personality and Social Psychology, 14*, 101-113.

SHAVER, P.R., & BRENNAN, K.A. (1992). Attachment styles and the "big five" personality traits: Their connection with each other and with romantic relationship outcomes. *Personality and Social Psychology Bulletin, 18*, 536-545.

SHAW, M.E. (1981). *Group dynamics: The psychology of small group behavior* (3rd ed.). New York: McGraw-Hill.

SHEPHERD, J.W., DEREGOWSKI, J.B., & ELLIS, H.D. (1974). A cross-cultural study of recognition memory for faces. *International Journal of Psychology, 9*, 205-211.

SHERIF, M. (1936). *The psychology of social norms.* New York: Harper & Row.

SHERIF, M. (1958). Superordinate goals in the reduction of intergroup conflict. *American Journal of Sociology*, 349-356.

SHERIF, M., & CANTRIL, H. (1947). *The psychology of ego involvement: Social attitudes and identification.* New York: Wiley.

SHERIF, M., HARVEY, O.J., WHITE, B.J., HOOD, W.R., & SHERIF, C. (1961). *Intergroup conflict and cooperation: The Robber's Cave experiment.* Norman: University of Oklahoma Press.

SHERMAN, S.J., CHASSIN, L. PRESSON, C.L., & AGOSTINELLI, G. (1984). The role of evaluation and similarity principles in the false consensus effect. *Journal of Personality and Social Psychology, 47*, 1244-1262.

SHERROD, D.R. (1974). Crowding, perceived control and behavioral aftereffects. *Journal of Applied Social Psychology, 4*, 171-186.

SHERROD, D.R., HAGE, J.N., HALPERN, P.L., & MOORE, B.S. (1977). Effects of personal causation and perceived control on responses to an aversive environment. The more control, the better. *Journal of Experimental Social Psychology, 13*, 14-27.

SHIBUTANI, T. (1966). *Improvised news: A sociological study of rumor.* Indianapolis: Bobbs-Merrill.

SHILS, E.A. (1965). Charisma, order and status. *American Sociological Review, 30*, 199-213.

SHOEMAKER, D.J., SOUTH, D.R., & LOWE, J. (1973). Facial stereotypes of deviants and judgements of guilt or innocence. *Social Forces, 51*, 427-433.

SHOTLAND, R.L., & GOODSTEIN, L. (1992). Sexual precedence reduces the perceived legitimacy of sexual refusal: An examination of attributions concerning date rape and consensual sex. *Personality and Social Psychology Bulletin, 18*, 756-764.

SHUMAKER, S.A., & CZAJKOWSKI, S.M. (Eds.) (1991). *Social support and cardiovascular disease.* NY: Plenum.

SIGNORIELLI, N., GROSS, L., & MORGAN, M. (1982). Violence in television programs: Ten years later. In D. Pearl, L. Bouthilet & J. Lazar (Eds.), *Television and behavior: Ten years of scientific progress and implications for the eighties: Vol. 2, Technical reviews* (pp. 158-173). Washington: United States Government Printing Office.

SILVERMAN, I. (1971). On the resolution and tolerance of cognitive consistency in a natural occurring event: Attitudes and beliefs following the Senator Edward M. Kennedy incident. *Journal of Personality and Social Psychology, 17*, 171-178.

SILVERMAN, I. (1974). Some hedonistic considerations regarding altruistic behavior. Paper presented at the Southeastern Psychological Association Annual Meeting, Miami.

SILVERSTEIN, B. (1989). Enemy images: The psychology of U.S. attitudes and cognitions regarding the Soviet Union. *American Psychologist, 44*, 903-913.

SILVERSTEIN, B., & FLAMENBAUM, C. (1989). Biases in the perception and cognitions of the actions of enemies. *Journal of Social Issues, 45*, 51-72.

SIMON, R.J., & MAHAN, L. (1971). Quantifying burdens of proof: A view from the bench, the jury and the classroom. *Law and Society Review, 5*, 319-330.

SIMPSON, J.A. (1987). The dissolution of romantic relationships: Factors involved in relationship stability and emotional distress. *Journal of Personality and Social Psychology, 53*, 683-692.

SIMPSON, J.A., RHOLES, W.S., AND NELLIGAN, J.S. (1992). Support seeking and support giving within couples in an anxiety-provoking situation: The role of attachment styles. *Journal of Personality and Social Psychology, 62*, 434-446.

SIMPSON, S., MCCARRY, M., & EDWARDS, H.P. (1987). Relationship of supervisors' sex role stereotypes to performance evaluation of male and female subordinates in non-traditional jobs. *Canadian Journal of Administrative Science, 4*, 15-30.

SIMS, H.P., & MANZ, C.C. (1984). Observing leader verbal behavior: Toward reciprocal determinism in leadership theory. *Journal of Applied Psychology, 69*, 222-232.

SINCLAIR, C., POIZNER, S., GILMOUR-BARRETT, & RANDALL, D. (1987). The development of a code of ethics for Canadian psychologists. *Canadian Psychology, 28*, 1-8.

SINGER, J.L., & SINGER, D.G. (1986). Family experiences and television viewing as predictors of children's imagination, restlessness and aggression. *Journal of Social Issues, 42*, 107-124.

SIX, U. (1989). The functions of sterotypes and prejudices in the process of cross-cultural understanding: A social psychologial approach. In P. Funckle (Ed.), *Understanding the U.S.A.: A cross-cultural perspective.* Tubingen: Narr.

SMITH, C.P. (1983). Ethical issues: Research on deception, informed consent, and debriefing. In L. Wheeler & P. Shaver (Eds.), *Review of personality and social psychology* (Vol. 4, pp. 297-328). Beverly Hills, CA: Sage.

SMITH, P.M. (1985). *Language, the sexes and society.* Oxford: Basil Blackwell.

SMITH, T.W. (1992). Hostility and health: Current status of a psychosomatic hypothesis. *Health Psychology, 11*, 139-150.

SNYDER, M., & GANGESTAD, S. (1982). Choosing social situations: Two investigations of self-monitoring processes. *Journal of Personality and Social Psychology, 43*, 123-135.

SOLANO, C.H., BATTEN, P.G., & PARISH, E.A. (1982). Loneliness and patterns of self-disclosure. *Journal of Personality and Social Psychology, 43*, 524-531.

SOLANO, C.H., & KOESTER, N.H. (1989). Loneliness and communication problems: Subjective anxiety or objective skills? *Personality and Social Psychology Bulletin, 15*, 126-133.

SOLE, K., MARTON, J., & HORNSTEIN, H.A. (1975). Opinion similarity and helping: Three field experiments investigating the bases of promotive tension. *Journal of Experimental Social Psychology, 11*, 1-13.

SOLOMON, M.R. (1986). Dress for effect. *Psychology Today, 20(4)*, 20-28.

SOMMER, R. (1969). *Personal space. The behavioral basis of design.* Englewood CLiffs, NJ: Prentice-Hall.

SOMMER, R., & ROSS, H. (1958). Social interaction on a geriatric ward. *International Journal of Social Psychiatry, 4*, 128-133.

STACY, A.W., SUSSMAN, S., DENT, C.W., BURTON, D., AND FLAY, B.R. (1992). Moderators of peer social influence in adolescent smoking. *Personality and Social Psychology Bulletin, 18*, 163-172.

STAGNER, R. (1967). *Psychological aspects of international conflict.* Belmont, CA: Brooks/Cole.

STAHELSKI, A.J., & FROST, D.E. (1989). Use of socially dependent bases of power: French and Raven's theory applied to work-group leadership. *Journal of Applied Social Psychology, 19*, 283-297.

STANLEY, P.R. & RIERA, B. (1977). Replications of media violence. In *Report of the Royal Commission on Violence in the Communications Industry* (Vol. 5, pp. 89-170). Toronto: Publication Centre, Government of Ontario.

STATISTICS CANADA (1995a). *Factfinder on crime and the administration of justice in Canada* (Cat. No. 85-002, Vol. 15 No. 10). Ottawa: Canadian Centre for Justice Statistics.

STATISTICS CANADA (1995b). *Homicide in Canada, 1994* (Cat. No. 85-002, Vol. 15 No. 11). Ottawa: Canadian Centre for Justice Statistics.

STATISTICS CANADA (1995c). *Canadian crime statistics, 1994* (Cat. No. 85-002, Vol. 15 No. 12). Ottawa: Canadian Centre for Justice Statistics.

STATISTICS CANADA (1995d). Women and the criminal justice system. In *Women in Canada* (3rd ed.), (Cat. No. 89-503E). Ottawa: Canadian Centre for Justice Statistics.

STATISTICS CANADA (1993). *The nation* (Cat. No. 93-318). Ottawa: Supply and Services Canada.

STATISTICS CANADA (1992a). *Canadian Crime Statistics 1991.* Ottawa: Ministry of Supply and Services Canada.

STATISTICS CANADA (1992b). *Mother tongue.* Ottawa: Ministry of Supply and Services Canada.

STATISTICS CANADA (1985). *Language in Canada.* Ottawa: Ministry of Supply and Services Canada.

STAUB, E. (1971). A child in distress: The influence of nurturance and modeling on children's attempts to help. *Developmental Psychology, 5*, 124-132.

STAUB, E. (1974). Helping a distressed person: Social, personality and stimulus determinants. In L. Berkowitz (Ed.), *Advances in experimental social psychology* (Vol. 7). New York: Academic Press.

STAUB, E. (1975). *The development of prosocial behavior in children.* Morristown, NJ: Silver Burdett/General Learning Press.

STAUB, E., & BAER, R.S. (1974). Stimulus characteristics of a sufferer and difficulty of escape as determinants of helping. *Journal of Personality and Social Psychology, 30*, 279-285.

STEBLAY, N.M. (1987). Helping behavior in rural and urban environments: A meta-analysis. *Psychological Bulletin, 102*, 346-356.

STEELE, C.M., & LIU, T.J. (1983). Dissonance process as self-affirmation. *Journal of Personality and Social Psychology, 45*, 5-19.

STEPHAN, C.W., & STEPHAN, W.G. (1986). Habla ingles? The effects of language translation on simulated juror decisions. *Journal of Applied Social Psychology, 16*, 577-589.

STERN, P.C. (1992). Psychological dimensions of global environmental change. *Annual Review of Psychology, (43)*, 269-302.

STERNBERG, R.J. (1986). A triangular theory of love. *Psychological Review, 93*, 119-135.

STERNBERG, R.J., & BARNES, M.L. (Eds.) (1988). *The psychology of love.* New Haven, CT: Yale University Press.

STEWART, M.A., RYAN, E.B., & GILES, H. (1985). Accent and social class effects on status and solidarity evaluations. *Personality and Social Psychology Bulletin, 11*, 98-105.

STIRLING, G., & REID, D.W. (1992). The application of participatory control to facilitate patient well-being: An experimental study of nursing impact on geriatric patients. *Canadian Journal of Behavioural Science, 24*, 204-219.

STOGDILL, R. (1974). *Handbook of leadership.* New York: Free Press.

STONE, G.C. (1979). Patient compliance and the role of the expert. *Journal of Social Issues, 35*, 34-59.

STONE, A., & NEALE, J.M. (1982). Development of a methodology for assessing daily experiences. In A. Baum & J.E. Singer (Eds.), *Advances in environmental psychology* (Vol. 4). Hillsdale: Erlbaum.

STORMS, M.D. (1973). Videotape and the attribution process: Reversing actor's and observer's points of view. *Journal of Personality and Social Psychology, 27*, 165-175.

STORMS, M.D., & NISBETT, R.E. (1970). Insomnia and the attribution process. *Journal of Personality and Social Psychology, 16*, 319-328.

STORY, G.M., KIRWIN, W.J., & WIDDOWSON, J.D.A. (1982). *Dictionary of Newfoundland English.* Toronto: University of Toronto Press.

STRAUSS, S. (1993, April 10). Mind and matter: Something's wrong when we have 600 stories on AIDS and only six on arthritis. *The Globe and Mail*, pp D8.

STRICKLAND, B.R. (1978). Internal-external expectancies and health-related behaviors. *Journal of Consulting and Clinical Psychology, 46*, 1192-1211.

STRODTBECK, F.L., & LIPINSKI, R.M. (1985). Becoming first among equals: Moral considerations in jury foreman selection. *Journal of Personality and Social Psychology, 49*, 927-936.

STROEBE, M.S., & STROEBE, W. (1983). Who suffers more? Sex differences in health risks of the widowed. *Psychological Bulletin, 93*, 279-301.

STROEBE, W.H., STROEBE, M., GERGEN, K.J., & GERGEN, M.M. (1982). The effects of bereavement on mortality: A social psychological analysis. In J.R. Eisere (Ed.), *Social psychology and behavioral medicine.* London: Wiley.

STRUBE, M.J., & GARCIA, J.E. (1981). A meta-analytic investigation of Fiedler's contingency model of leadership effectiveness. *Psychological Bulletin, 90*, 307-321.

SUNDSTROM, E., HERBERT, R.K., & BROWN, D. (1982). Privacy and communication in an open office plan. *Environment and Behavior, 14*, 379-392.

SUSSMAN, N.M., & ROSENFELD, H.M. (1982). Influence of culture, language and sex on conversational distance. *Journal of Personality and Social Psychology, 42*, 66-74.

SWANN, W.B., & READ, S.J. (1981). Acquiring self-knowledge: The search for feedback that fits. *Journal of Personality and Social Psychology, 41*, 1119-1128.

SWEENEY, P.D., ANDERSON, K., & BAILEY, S. (1986). Attribution style in depression: A meta-analytic review. *Journal of Personality and Social Psychology, 50*, 974-991.

SWEENEY, P.D., & GRUBER, K.L. (1984). Selective exposure: Voter information preferences and the Watergate Affair. *Journal of Personality and Social Psychology, 46*, 1208-1221.

SWENNSON, R.G (1967). Cooperation in the Prisoner's Dilemma game I: the effect of asymmetric payoff information and explicit communication. *Behavioral Science, 12*, 314-322.

SWINGLE, P.G. (1970). Dangerous games. In P.G. Swingle (Ed.), *The structure of conflict* (pp. 235-276). New York: Academic Press.

SYKES, R.E., ROWLEY, R.D., & SCHAEFFER, J.M. (1993). The influence of time, gender and group size on heavy drinking in public bars. *Journal of Studies on Alcohol, 54*, 133-138.

TAJFEL, H. (1970). Experiments in intergroup discrimination. *Scientific American, 223, 5*, 96-102.

TAJFEL, H., & TURNER, J.C., (1979). An integrative theory of intergroup conflict. In W.G. Austin & S. Worchel (Eds.), *The social psychology of intergroup relations* (pp. 33-47). Monterey, CA: Brooks/Cole.

TANFORD, J. A. (1990). The law and psychology of jury instructions. *Nebraska Law Review, 69*(1), 71-111.

TANFORD, J.A., & PENROD, S. (1984). Social influence processes in juror judgements of multiple offence trials. *Journal of Personality and Social Psychology, 95*, 189-225.

TANNEN, D. (1990). *You just don't understand: Women and men in conversation*. New York: Morrow.

TAYLOR, D.A., & BELGRAVE, F.Z. (1986). The effects of perceived intimacy and valence on self-disclosure reciprocity. *Personality and Social Psychology Bulletin, 12*, 247-255.

TAYLOR, D.M. (1981). Stereotypes and intergroup relations. In R.C. Gardner & R. Kalin (Eds.), *A Canadian social psychology of ethnic relations* (pp. 151-171). Toronto: Methuen.

TAYLOR, D.M., & GARDNER, R.C. (1969). Ethnic stereotypes: Their effects on the perception of communicators of varying credibility. *Canadian Journal of Psychology, 23*, 161-173.

TAYLOR, D.M., & LALONDE, R.N. (1987). Ethnic stereotypes: A psychological analysis. In L. Driedger (Ed.), *Ethnic Canada: Identities and inequalities*. Toronto: Copp Clark Puttman.

TAYLOR, D.M., & MCKIRNON, D.J. (1984). A five-stage model of intergroup relations. *British Journal of Social Psychology, 23*, 291-300.

TAYLOR, D.M., & MOGHADDAM, F.M. (1987). *Theories of intergroup relations: International social psychological perspective*. New York: Praeger.

TAYLOR, J., & RIESS, M. (1989). Self-serving attributions to valenced causal factors. *Personality and Social Psychology Bulletin, 15*, 337-348.

TAYLOR, S.E. (1979). Hospital patient behavior: Reactance, helplessness or control? *Journal of Social Issues, 35*, 156-184.

TAYLOR, S.E., & BROWN, J.D. (1988). Illusion and well-being: A social-psychological perspective on mental health. *Psychological Bulletin, 103*, 193-210.

TENNEN, H., AFFLECK, G., URROWS, S., HIGGINS, P., & MENDOLA, R. (1992). Perceiving control, construing benefits and daily processes in rheumatoid arthritis. *Canadian Journal of Behavioural Science, 24*, 186-203.

TERHUNE, K.W. (1968). Motives, situation, and interpersonal conflict within the Prisoner's Dilemma. *Journal of Personality and Social Psychology, 8*, Monograph Supplement, Part 2.

TESSER, A., MILLAR, M., & MOORE, J. (1988). Some affective consequences of social comparison and reflection processes. The pain and pleasure of being close. *Journal of Personality and Social Psychology, 54*, 49-61.

TETLOCK, P.E. (1983). Policymakers' images of international conflict. *Journal of Social Issues, 39*, 67-86.

TETLOCK, P.E. (1987). Testing deterrence theory: Some conceptual and methodological issues. *Journal of Social Issues, 43*, 85-91.

TETLOCK, P.E., PETERSON, R.S., MCGUIRE, C., CHANG, S., & FELD, P. (1992). Assessing political group dynamics: A test of the groupthink model. *Journal of Personality and Social Psychology, 63*, 403-425.

THAYER, S., & SAARNI, C. (1975). Demand characteristics are everywhere (anyway): A comment on the Stanford prison experiment. *American Psychologist, 30*, 1015-1016.

THIBAUT, J.W., & KELLEY, H.H. (1959). *The social psychology of groups*. New York: Wiley.

THIBODEAU, R., & ARONSON, E. (1992). Taking a closer look: Reasserting the role of the self-concept in dissonance theory. *Personality and Social Psychology Bulletin, 18*, 591-602.

THORESON, C.E., & POWELL, L.H. (1992). Type A behavior pattern: New perspectives on theory, assessment and intervention. *Journal of Consulting and Clinical Psychology, 60*, 595-604.

TOCH, H. (1965). *The social psychology of social movements*. Indianapolis: Bobbs-Merrill.

TOURANGEAU, R., & RASINSKI, K.A. (1988). Cognitive processes underlying context effects in attitude measurement. *Psychological Bulletin, 103*, 299-314.

TRIANDIS, H.C. (1967). Toward an analysis of the components of interpersonal attitudes. In C. Sherif and M. Sherif (Eds.), *Attitudes, ego-involvement, and change*. New York: Wiley.

TRIANDIS, H.C., & BRISLIN, R.W. (Eds.) (1980). *Handbook of cross-cultural psychology: Social psychology* (Vol. 5). Boston: Allyn & Bacon.

TRIPLET, R.G. & SUGARMAN, D.B. (1987). Reactions to AIDS victims: Ambiguity breeds contempt. *Personality and Social Psychology Bulletin, 13*, 265-274.

TRIPLETT, N. (1898). The dynamogenic factors in pacemaking and competition. *American Journal of Psychology, 9*, 507-533.

TUCKER, G.R. (1981). Social policy and second language teaching. In R.C. Gardner and R. Kalin (Eds.), *A Canadian social psychology of ethnic relations* (pp. 77-92). Toronto: Methuen.

TURNER, J.C., WETHERELL, M.S., & HOGG, M.A. (1989). Referent informational influence and group polarization. *British Journal of Social Psychology, 18*, 135-147.

TURNER, R.H., & KILLIAM, L.M. (1972). *Collective behavior*. (2nd ed.) Englewood Cliffs, NJ: Prentice-Hall.

TVERSKY, A., & KAHNEMAN, D. (1974). Judgement under uncertainty: Heuristics and biases. *Science, 185*, 1124-1131.

TVERSKY, A., & KAHNEMAN, D. (1982). Judgment under uncertainty: Heuristics and biases. In D. Kahneman, P. Slovic &

A. Tversky (Eds.), *Judgment under uncertainty: Heuristics and biases* (pp. 3-20).

TWYCROSS, R.G. (1974). Clinical experience with diamorphine in advanced malignant disease. *International Journal of Clinical Pharmacology, Therapy and Toxicology, 9*, 184-198.

UNDERWOOD, B., FROMING, W.J., & MOORE, B.S. (1977). Mood, attention, and altruism: A search for mediating variables. *Developmental Psychology, 13*, 541-542.

UNGER, D.G., & WANDERSMAN, L.P. (1985). Social support and adolescent mothers: Action research contributions to theory and applications. *Journal of Social Issues, 41*, 29-46.

UNITED STATES DEPARTMENT OF JUSTICE. (1994). *Uniform crime reports for the United States, 1993.*

VANDERZANDEN, J.W. (1977). *Social psychology*. New York: Random House.

VICTOR, J.S. (1990). The spread of satanic-cult rumors. *Skeptical Inquirer, 14*, 287-291.

VIDMAR, N. (1974). Retributive and utilitarian motives of Canadian attitudes toward the death penalty. *Canadian Psychologist, 15*, 337-356.

VINACKE, W.E., & GULLICKSON, G.R. (1964). Age and sex differences in the formation of coalitions. *Child Development, 35*, 1217-1231.

VINING, J., & EBREO, A. (1992). Predicting recycling behavior from global and specific environment attitudes and changes in recycling opportunities. *Journal of Applied Social Psychology, 22*, 624-633.

VITKUS, J., & HOROWITZ, L.M. (1987). Poor social performance of lonely people: Lacking a skill or adopting a role? *Journal of Personality and Social Psychology, 52*, 1266-1273.

VOISSEM, N.H., & SISTRUNK, F. (1971). Communication schedules and cooperative game behavior. *Journal of Personality and Social Psychology, 19*, 160-167.

WAITZKIN, H. (1984). Doctor-patient communication: Clinical implications of social science research. *Journal of the American Medical Association, 252*, 2441-2446.

WALKER, L.E. (1989). *The battered woman syndrome*. New York: Springer.

WALSTER, E. (1966). Assignment of responsibility for an accident. *Journal of Personality and Social Psychology, 3*, 73-79.

WALSTER, E., WALSTER, G.W., & BERSCHEID, E. (1978). *Equity theory and research*. Boston: Allyn & Bacon.

WALTERS, G.C., & GRUSEC, J.E. (1977). *Punishment*. San Francisco: W.H. Freeman.

WASSERMAN, R.C., INNUI, T.S., BARRIATUA, R.D., CARTER, W.B., & LIPPINCOTT, P. (1984). Pediatric clinicians' support for parents makes a difference: An outcome-based analysis of clinician-parent interaction. *Pediatrics, 74*, 1047-1053.

WATSON, D. (1982). The actor and the observer: How are the perceptions of causality divergent? *Psychological Bulletin, 92*, 682-700.

WATSON, D., & PENNEBAKER, J.W. (1989). Health complaints, stress and distress: Exploring the central role of negative affectivity. *Psychological Review, 96*, 234-254.

WATSON, R.I. (1973). Investigation into deindividuation using a cross-cultural survey technique. *Journal of Personality and Social Psychology, 25*, 342-345.

WEBER, M. (1947). *The theory of social and economic organization*. Glencoe, IL: Free Press.

WEBSTER, C., DICKENS, B., & ADDARIO, S. (1985). *Constructing dangerousness: Scientific, legal and policy implications*. Toronto: Centre of Criminology, University of Toronto.

WEICK, K.E. (1984). Small wins: Refining the scale of social problems. *American Psychologist, 39*, 40-49.

WEIDNER, G., ISTVAN, J., & MCKNIGHT, J.D. (1989). Clusters of behavioral coronary risk factors in employed men and women. *Journal of Applied Social Psychology, 19*, 468-480.

WEINER, B. (1974). *Achievement motivation and attribution theory*. Morristown, NJ: General Learning Press.

WEINER, B. (1979). A theory of motivation for some classroom experiences. *Journal of Educational Psychology, 71*, 3-25.

WEINER, B. (1980). A cognitive (attribution)-emotion-action model of motivated behavior: An analysis of judgements of help giving. *Journal of Personality and Social Psychology, 39*, 186-200.

WEINER, B., FIGUEROA-MUÑOZ, A., & KAKIHARA, C. (1991). The goals of excuses and communication strategies related to causal perceptions. *Personality and Social Psychology Bulletin, 17*, 4-13.

WEINSTEIN, N.D. (1984). Why it won't happen to me: Perceptions of risk factors and susceptibility. *Health Psychology, 3*, 431-457.

WEINSTEIN, N.D. (1989). Effects of personal experience on self-protective behavior. *Psychological Bulletin, 105*, 31-50.

WEISS, R. (1973). Loneliness: *The experiences of emotional and social isolation*. Cambridge, MA: MIT Press.

WEISZ, A.E., & TAYLOR, R.L. (1969). American Presidential assassinations. *Diseases of the Nervous System, 30*, 659-668.

WELLS, G.L. (1984). The psychology of lineup identifications. *Journal of Applied Psychology, 14*, 89-103.

WELLS, G.L., & MURRAY, B.M. (1983). What can psychology say about the Neil vs. Biggers criteria for judging eyewitness accuracy? *Journal of Applied Psychology, 68*, 347-362.

WELLS, G.L., & TURTLE, J.W. (1986). Eye-witness identification: The importance of lineup models. *Psychological Bulletin, 29*, 320-329.

WERNER, C.M., BROWN, B.B., & DAMRON, G. (1981). Territorial marking in a game arcade. *Journal of Personality and Social Psychology, 41*, 1094-1104.

WEST, C. (1984). *Routine complications*. Bloomington, Indiana: University of Indiana Press.

WEST, S.G., & BROWN, T.J. (1975). Physical attractiveness, the severity of the emergency and helping: A field experiment and interpersonal simulation. *Journal of Experimental Social Psychology, 11*, 531-538.

WHITE, G.L. (1981a). A model of romantic jealousy. *Motivation and Emotion, 5*, 295-310.

WHITE, G.L. (1981b). Some correlates of romantic jealousy. *Journal of Personality, 49*, 129-147.

WHITE, J.W. (1983). Sex and gender issues in aggression research. In R.G. Geen & E.I. Donnerstein (Eds.), *Aggression: Theoretical and empirical reviews* (Vol. 2, pp. 1-26). New York: Academic Press.

WHITE, R.K. (1969). Three not-so-obvious contributions of psychology to peace. *Journal of Social Issues, 25*, 23-39.

WHITE, R.K. (1984). *Fearful warriors: A psychological profile of U.S.-Soviet relationships*. New York: Free Press.

WHYTE, G. (1989). Groupthink Reconsidered. *Academy of Management Review, 14*, 40-56.

WICKLUND, R.A., & BREHM, J.W. (1976). *Perspectives on cognitive dissonance.* New York: Wiley.

WIDOM, C.S. (1989). Does violence beget violence? A critical examination of the literature. *Psychological Bulletin, 106*, 3-28.

WIEGMAN, O. (1985). Two politicians in a realistic experiment: Attraction, discrepancy, intensity of delivery, and attitude change. *Journal of Applied Social Psychology, 15*, 673-686.

WIEMANN, J.M., & GILES, H. (1988). Interpersonal communication. In M. Hewstone, W. Stroebe, J-P. Codol & G.M. Stephenson (Eds.), *Introduction to social psychology* (pp. 199-221). Oxford: Basil Blackwell.

WIESENTHAL, D.L. (1974). Reweaving deception's tangled web. *Canadian Psychologist, 15*, 326-336.

WILDER, D.A. (1977). Perception of group size of opposition and social influence. *Journal of Experimental Social Psychology, 13*, 253-268.

WILLIAMS, E. (1975). Medium or message: Communications medium as a determinant of interpersonal evaluations. *Sociometry, 38*, 119-130.

WILLIAMS, S.S., KIMBLE, D.L., COVELL, N.H., WEISS, L.H., NEWTON, K.J., FISHER, J.D., & FISHER, W.A. (1992). College students' use of implicit personality theory instead of safer sex. *Journal of Applied Social Psychology, 22*, 921-933.

WILLIAMS, T.M. (Ed.) (1986). *The impact of television: A natural experiment in three communities.* New York: Academic Press.

WILLS, T.A. (1981). Downward comparison principles in social psychology. *Psychological Bulletin, 90*, 245-271.

WILSNACK, S. (1982). Prevention of alcohol problems in women. In N.I.A.A.A. *Alcohol and health Monograph #4. Special population issues* (pp. 77-110). D.H.H.S. Publication No. (ADM) 82--1193. Washington: US Government Printing Office.

WILSON, G.B.L. (1974). *A dictionary of ballet* (3rd ed.). London: Adam & Charles Black.

WILSON, W., & MILLER, H. (1968). Repetition, order of presentation, and timing of arguments and measures as determinants of opinion change. *Journal of Personality and Social Psychology, 9*, 184-188.

WINETT, R.A., KAGEL, J.H., BATTALIO, R.C., & WINKLER, R.C. (1978). The effects of monetary rebates, feedback and information on residential electricity conservation. *Journal of Applied Psychology, 63*, 73-80.

WISHNER, J. (1960). Reanalysis of "impressions of personality." *Psychological Review, 67*, 96-112.

WISPÉ, L. (1986). The distinction between sympathy and empathy: To call forth a concept, a word is needed. *Journal of Personality and Social Psychology, 50*, 314-321.

WOLF, S., & MONTGOMERY, D.A. (1977) Effects of inadmissible evidence and level of judicial admonishment to disregard on the judgements of mock jurors. *Journal of Applied Social Psychology, 7*, 205-219.

WOLLIN, D.D., & MONTAGNE, M. (1981). The college classroom environment. *Environment and Behavior, 13*, 707-716.

WOOD, J.V. (1989). Theory and research concerning social comparisons of personal attributes. *Psychological Bulletin, 106*, 231-248.

WORCHEL, S., ANDREOLI, V., & EASON, J. (1975). Is the medium the message? A study of the effects of media, communicator and message characteristics on attitude change. *Journal of Applied Social Psychology, 5*, 157-172.

WORCHEL, S., & BROWN, E.H. (1984). The role of plausibility in influencing environmental attributions. *Journal of Experimental Social Psychology, 20*, 86-96.

WORCHEL, S., & TEDDLIE, C. (1976). The experience of crowding: A two-factor theory. *Journal of Personality and Social Psychology, 34*, 36-40.

WORMITH, J.S., & RUHL, M. (1986). *A survey of dangerous sexual offenders in Canada 1948-1877.* (Branch User Report No. 1986-6). Ottawa: Ministry of the Solicitor General of Canada.

WORTMAN, C.B. (1975). Some determinants of perceived control. *Journal of Personality and Social Psychology, 31*, 282-294.

WRIGHT, M.J. (1969). Canadian psychology comes of age. *Canadian Psychologist, 10*, 229-253.

WRIGHT, M.J. (1990). Personal communication.

WRIGHT, M.J., & MYERS, C.R. (Eds.) (1982). *History of academic psychology in Canada.* Toronto: Hogrefe.

WRIGHT, S. (1978). *Crowds and riots.* Beverly Hills, CA: Sage.

YAMAGISHI, T., & SATO, K. (1986). Motivational bases of the public goods problem. *Journal of Personality and Social Psychology, 50*, 67-73.

YARMEY, A.D. (1979). *The psychology of eyewitness testimony.* New York: Free Press.

YARMEY, A.D. (1986a). Verbal, visual and voice identification of a rape suspect under different levels of illumination. *Journal of Applied Social Psychology, 71*, 363-370.

YARMEY, A.D. (1986b). Perceived expertness and credibility of police officers as eyewitnesses. *Canadian Police College Journal, 10*, 31-52.

YARMEY, A.D., & JONES, H.P.T. (1983a). Is the psychology of eyewitness identification a matter of common sense? In S. Lloyd-Bostock & B.R. Clifford (Eds.), *Evaluating eyewitness evidence* (pp. 109-142). London: Wiley.

YARMEY, A.D., & JONES, H.T.P. (1983b). Accuracy of memory of male and female eyewitnesses to a criminal assault and rape. *Bulletin of the Psychonomic Society, 21*, 89-92.

YASSI, A., WEEKS, J.L., SAMSON, K., & RABER, M.B. (1989). Epidemic of "shocks" in telephone operators: Lessons for the medical community. *Canadian Medical Association Journal, 140*, 816-820.

YOUNG, M.Y., & GARDNER, R.C. (1990). Modes of acculturation and second language proficiency. *Canadian Journal of Behavioural Science, 22*, 59-71.

YOUNGER, J.C., WALKER, L., & ARROWOOD, A.J. (1977). Post decision dissonance at the fair. *Personality and Social Psychology Bulletin, 3*, 284-287.

YUILLE, J. (1980). A critical examination of the psychological and practical implications of eyewitness research. *Law and Behavior, 4*, 335-345.

YURCHESYN, K.A., KEITH, A., &. RENNER, K.E. (1992). Contrasting perspectives on the nature of sexual assault provided by a service for sexual assault victims and by the law courts. *Canadian Journal of Behavioural Science, 24*, 71-85.

ZAJONC, R.B. (1965). Social facilitation. *Science, 149*, 269-274.

ZAJONC, R.B. (1968a). Attitudinal effects of mere exposure. *Journal of Personality and Social Psychology*, Monograph Supplement, 9, 1-27.

ZAJONC, R.B. (1968b). Cognitive theories in social psychology. In G. Lindzey & E. Aronson (Eds.), *The handbook of social psychology*. (2nd ed.) (Vol. 1, pp. 320-411.) Reading, MA: Addison-Wesley.

ZAJONC, R.B. (1970, February). Brainwashing: Familiarity breeds comfort. *Psychology Today*. 32-35, 60-62.

ZAJONC, R.B. (1980). Feeling and thinking: Preferences need no inferences. *American Psychologist, 35*, 151-175.

ZANNA, M.P., & REMPLE, J.K. (1988). Attitudes: a new look at an old concept. In D. Bar-Tal & A.W. Kruglanski (Eds.), *Social psychology of knowledge* (pp. 315-334). New York: Cambridge University Press.

ZEISEL, J. (1981). *Inquiry by design: Tools for environment-behavior research*. Monterey, Ca.: Brooks/Cole.

ZIEGLER, S. (1981). The effectiveness of cooperative learning teams for increasing cross-ethnic friendship: additional evidence. *Human Organization, 40*, 264-267.

ZILLMANN, D. (1984). Transfer of excitation in emotional behavior. In J.T. Cacioppo & R.E. Petty (Eds.), *Social psychophysiology: A sourcebook* (pp. 215-240). New York: Guilford Press.

ZILLMANN, D., & BRYANT, J. (1984). Effects of massive exposure to pornography. In N.M. Malamuth & E.M. Donnerstein (Eds.), *Pornography and sexual aggression* (pp. 115-138). New York: Academic Press.

ZILLMANN, D., & BRYANT, J. (1986). Shifting preferences in pornography consumption. *Communication Research, 13*, 560-578.

ZIMBARDO, P.G. (1970). The human choice: Individuation, reason, and order versus deindividuation, impulse, and chaos. In W.J. Arnold & D. Levine (Eds.), *Nebraska symposium on motivation* (Vol. 17). Lincoln: University of Nebraska Press.

ZIMBARDO, P.G. (1977). *Shyness: What it is and what to do about it*. Reading, MA: Addison-Wesley.

ZIMBARDO, P.G., EBBESEN, E.B., & MASLACH, C. (1977). *Influencing attitudes and changing behavior*. (2nd ed.) Reading, MA: Addison-Wesley.

ZIMBARDO, P.G., HANEY, C., BANKS, W.C., & JAFFE, D. (1982). The psychology of imprisonment. In J.C. Brigham & L. Wrightsman (Eds.), *Contemporary issues in social psychology*. (4th ed., pp. 230-35). Monterey, CA: Brooks/Cole.

ZUCKERMAN, M., DEPAULO, B.M., & ROSENTHAL, R. (1981). Verbal and non-verbal communication of deception. In L. Berkowitz (Ed.), *Advances in Experimental Social Psychology* (pp. 1-59). New York: Academic Press.

PROPER NAME INDEX

SUBJECT INDEX